BTEC
NATIONAL
Business

Book 2

Jon Sutherland
Diane Canwell

...hornes

Published in 2007 by:
Nelson Thornes Ltd
Delta Place
27 Bath Road
CHELTENHAM
GL53 7TH
United Kingdom

08 09 10 11 / 10 9 8 7 6 5 4 3 2

A catalogue record for this book is available from the British Library

ISBN 978 0 7487 8124 9

Cover photographs by Rob Melnychuk/Getty Images and SUNNYphotography.com/Alamy
Page make-up by Pantek Arts Ltd, Maidstone, Kent
Printed by Multivista Global Ltd

Contents

Introduction

The business world is a fast-changing environment. Businesses cannot afford to be left behind in this hugely competitive world, they have to either adapt or die. A business has to make its presence known, whether it uses a flier pushed through a letterbox or a flashy television advert. An online presence is also very important to any business.

Each business needs to know what it is about, what it wants to do and how it will do it. They need to strike up lasting relationships with their customers, control and account for their money and continuously communicate. Their most important resource, experienced managers and employees, need to be well rewarded and looked after, their activities need to be supported and the latest business techniques and equipment should be used.

The business world is not as complicated as you might think, it's about ideas, putting them into action, outwitting the competition and getting the right message across to potential customers. Learning about this world is where the BTEC National Business courses come in.

How do you use this book?

Covering nine of the most popular specialist units from the new 2007 specification, this book has everything you need if you are studying BTEC National Certificate or Diploma in Business. Simple to use and understand, it is designed to provide you with the skills and knowledge you need to gain your qualification. We guide you step-by-step towards your qualification, through a range of features that are fully explained over the page.

Which units do you need to complete?

BTEC National Business Book 2 provides coverage of nine specialist units for the BTEC National Certificate or Diploma in Business. To achieve the Certificate, you are required to complete four core units plus eight specialist units that provide for a combined total of 720 guided learning hours (GLH). To achieve the Diploma, you are required to complete four core units plus fourteen specialist units that provide for a combined total of 1080 guided learning hours (GLH). Together *BTEC National Business Book 1* and *BTEC National Business Book 2* provide you with coverage of the following:

BTEC National Business Book 1 Core and Specialist Units	BTEC National Business Book 2 Specialist Units
Unit 1 **Exploring Business Activity***	Unit 6 **Understanding Financial Accounting**
Unit 2 **Investigating Business Resources***	Unit 7 **Introducing Management Accounting**
Unit 3 **Introduction to Marketing***	Unit 8 **Investigating Accounting Systems**
Unit 4 **Effective People, Communication and Marketing***	Unit 10 **An Introduction to Marketing Research**
Unit 5 **Introduction to Accounting**	Unit 12 **Investigating Internet Marketing**
Unit 9 **Exploring Creative Product Promotion**	Unit 13 **Investigating Recruitment and Selection**
Unit 16 **Human Resource Management**	Unit 14 **Understanding Aspects of Employment Law**
Unit 29 **Introduction to the Internet and E-business**	Unit 21 **Aspects of Contract and Business Law**
Unit 37 **Starting a Small Business**	Unit 26 **Managing Business Information**

* Denotes a core unit

Is there anything else you need to do?

1. Start reading a newspaper with a business news section
2. Find out what businesses near you do and what sort of jobs they offer.
3. Visit as many different businesses as possible.
4. Use your work placement to collect useful information.
5. Always look for useful information - it's always easier to understand things if they are happening for real.

We hope you enjoy your BTEC course – Good Luck!

Turn over now for your guide to the features of this book.

Features of this book

Learning Objectives

At the beginning of each Unit there will be a bulleted list letting you know what material is going to be covered. They specifically relate to the learning objectives within the specification.

Grading Criteria

The table of Grading Criteria at the beginning of each unit identifies achievement levels of pass, merit and distinction, as stated in the specification.

To achieve a **pass**, you must be able to match each of the 'P' criteria in turn.

To achieve **merit** or **distinction**, you must increase the level of evidence that you use in your work, using the 'M' and 'D' columns as reference. For example, to achieve a distinction you must fulfil all the criteria in the pass, merit and distinction columns. Each of the criteria provides a specific page number for easy reference.

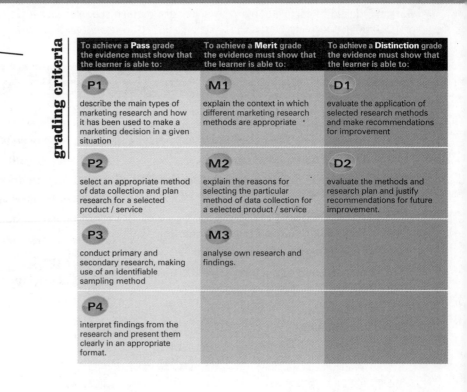

UNIT 10

Marketing Research

This unit covers the following objectives:

- Understand the main types of marketing research and how it is used to make marketing decisions
- Be able to plan simple research
- Be able to carry out simple research
- Be able to interpret research findings.

Marketing research is one of the prime means by which an organisation finds out about its customers and the environment in which it operates. Many carry out continuous investigations into trends, opportunities and threats.

Deciding upon the most appropriate method of research is vital in order to provide answers to the key questions posed by a business. Each market research programme will have its own objectives and set of constraints. This unit will ask you to carry out your own research and interpret the findings as a means by which to answer key questions posed.

grading criteria	To achieve a **Pass** grade the evidence must show that the learner is able to:	To achieve a **Merit** grade the evidence must show that the learner is able to:	To achieve a **Distinction** grade the evidence must show that the learner is able to:
	P1 describe the main types of marketing research and how it has been used to make a marketing decision in a given situation	**M1** explain the context in which different marketing research methods are appropriate	**D1** evaluate the application of selected research methods and make recommendations for improvement
	P2 select an appropriate method of data collection and plan research for a selected product / service	**M2** explain the reasons for selecting the particular method of data collection for a selected product / service	**D2** evaluate the methods and research plan and justify recommendations for future improvement.
	P3 conduct primary and secondary research, making use of an identifiable sampling method	**M3** analyse own research and findings.	
	P4 interpret findings from the research and present them clearly in an appropriate format.		

Case Studies

provide real life examples that relate to what is being discussed within the text. It provides an opportunity to demonstrate theory in practice.

An **Activity** that is linked to a Case Study helps you to apply your knowledge of the subject to real life situations.

case study 1.1

Hampshire County Council Best Value Pestle Analysis

The Government's Best Value initiative provided a catalyst for improving public services and managing local authority performance. Since its introduction in 1999 Hampshire County Council have broadened their approach into their Performance Management Framework. Part of the council's investigation into Best Value means looking at the external influences on the council and assessing their impact.

activity

1. What do you think is meant by Best Value?
2. How might the council deal with the opportunities and threats associated with the Environmental considerations?

Marketing research, on the other hand, is a far broader term used to describe any investigation into any element of the marketing mix, the environment in which the organisation operates or indeed any future impacts on the organisation. Marketing research therefore, is an information gathering exercise, sometimes a continual process that attempts to uncover data, views, concerns and responses to either the organisation itself, its products or services, the market in general or its customers.

Keywords

of specific importance are highlighted within the text, and then defined in a glossary at the end of the book.

i Visit the website of the Marketing Research Society at www.mrs.org.uk

Information bars

point you towards resources for further reading and research (e.g. websites).

activity
GROUP WORK

P1

Describe the main types of marketing research and how it has been used to make a marketing decision in a given situation. You will need to describe the main types of marketing research and how they have been used to make a marketing decision in a situation of your choice. For example, you could look at how marketing research has been used to look at the development of a product or service.

Activities

are designed to help you understand the topics through answering questions or undertaking research, and are either *Group* or *Individual* work. They are linked to the Grading Criteria by application of the D, P, and M categories.

remember

Primary research is the most expensive and time-consuming research. You must be certain that it will provide the information needed and is accurate and valid.

Remember boxes

contain helpful hints, tips or advice.

Progress Check

1. Give three examples of primary research.
2. How might a marketing research project take note of the movement of customers in a supermarket?
3. Give three examples of specialist agencies that provide market research data.
4. What are the six elements of PESTLE?
5. In terms of a professional marketing research project, how many respondents would be involved in a large sample?
6. If a research project got underway and was primarily concerned with the retention of customers, which parts of a retail organisation might be likely to contribute to its budget?
7. Briefly explain the difference between a census and a sample.
8. If a respondent was given a blank space after a question, what type of question would have been used on the questionnaire?
9. Explain the difference between the arithmetic mean, mode and median.
10. Explain the difference between a pictogram and a pie chart.

Progress checks

provide a list of quick questions at the end of each Unit, designed to ensure that you have understood the most important aspects of each subject area.

Acknowledgements

The authors and publishers would like to acknowledge the following people and organizations for permission to reproduce material:

10.03 Ipsos MORI·with kind permission of Ipsos MORI www.ipsos-mori.com; 10.06 Evaluating market ing effectiveness kind permission of Tourism Victoria; 10.12 Pie chart kind permission of NDA Copyright Material http://www.nda.gov.uk; 10.14 Cumulative percentage curve kind permission of The Department for Transport; 10.16 Line graph kind permission of South West Water; 12.01 Amazon ©2007 Amazon.com All rights reserved; 12.06 Dell homepage kind permission of Dell EMEA; 12.08 Priceline kind permission of Priceline.com; Morrisons PLC; 14.11 Unison © UNISON, the Public Services Union; The Independent; The British Computer Society.

Crown copyright material is reproduced with permission of the controller of HMSO and the Queen's Printer for Scotland. Licence number: C2006009492.

Every effort has been made to contact copyright holders and we apologise if any have been overlooked.

Photograph Credits

Andrew Fastow: Corbis/Aaron M Sprecher/ epa, p. 6; Pile of cash: Corel C590 (NT, p. 7; Cows: F Schussler/ Photodisc 17 (NT), p. 13; Looking at documents: Stockpix 6 (NT), p. 21; Counting stock: Alamy/ Ace Stock Ltd, p. 36; Caravan: Alamy/ Alastair Balderstone, p. 44; Car manufacturing: Rex Features/ Jonathan Player, p. 48; Man with calculator: Photodisc 55 (NT), p. 62; Man at computer: Bananastock TE (NT), p. 77; Petty cash: Stockbyte 31 (NT), p. 86; Visa card: Alamy/ Enigma, p. 87; Shop: Alamy/ image100, p. 99; Postman: Alamy/ Image Source, p. 133; Dyson: Alamy/ Adrian Sherratt, p. 147; Questionnaire: Alamy/ Bob Watkins, p. 162; Computer: Cole/ Photodisc 55 (NT), p. 190; Computer game: Alamy/ David J Green- Lifestyle, p. 194; Mobile phone: Nokia, p. 201; IT Worker: Brofsky/ Photodisc 55, p. 227; Yoga: Photodisc 67 (NT), p. 231; Interview: Alamy/ Blend Images, p. 238; Telephone: Alamy/ Rob Wilkinson, p. 241; Interview: Getty Images, p. 251; Policeman: Corel 736 (NT), p. 255; Male model: Corbis/ Patrick Giardino, p. 258; Woman working: Rubberball WW (NT), p. 258; John Hutton: Rex Features, p. 269; Jury: Alamy/ Imagestate, p. 273; Stephen Lawrence: Rex Features, p. 281; Holiday: Photodisc 28 (NT), p. 284; Baby: Stockpix 4 (NT), p. 286; Coaching: Alamy/ Imagesource, p. 296; Retired person: Corel 741 (NT), p. 302; Flag: Stockpix 7 (NT), p. 235; Mechanic: Rex Features/ Alix Phanie, p. 337; Till: Alamy/ David Williams, p. 350; Telephone sales: McVay/ Photodisc 69 (NT), p. 356; Filing: Rubberball WW (NT), p. 367; 26.10 Looking at file: Alamy/ Imageshop, p. 384.

UNIT 6

Understanding Financial Accounting

This unit covers:

- The impact of accounting legislation and concepts on organisations' accounting policies and procedures
- The impact of the regulatory framework on a limited company's accounting policies and procedures
- Making appropriate adjustments to accounting information
- Understanding a cash flow statement for a limited company

Not only must the financial transactions of an organisation be accurate but it is also necessary to prepare financial statements. The same rules must be followed each time that financial statements are completed, so that comparisons can be made.

Accounts are subject to various laws, concepts, conventions and standards. This unit introduces the legislation and regulatory framework that govern accounting practices and looks at why financial statements are prepared as they are. You will also learn how to make adjustments to accounting information, how to understand cash flow statements and what financial statements really tell us.

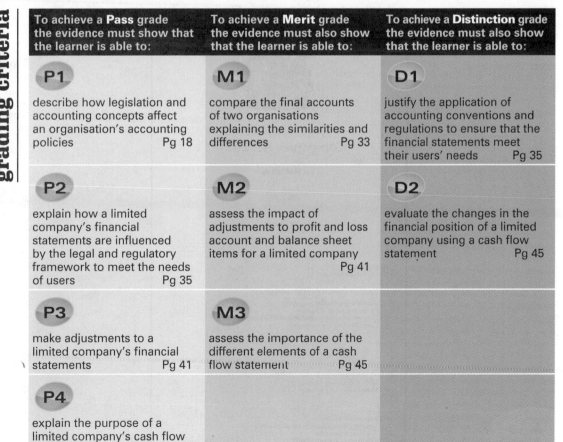

grading criteria

To achieve a **Pass** grade the evidence must show that the learner is able to:	To achieve a **Merit** grade the evidence must also show that the learner is able to:	To achieve a **Distinction** grade the evidence must also show that the learner is able to:
P1 describe how legislation and accounting concepts affect an organisation's accounting policies Pg 18	**M1** compare the final accounts of two organisations explaining the similarities and differences Pg 33	**D1** justify the application of accounting conventions and regulations to ensure that the financial statements meet their users' needs Pg 35
P2 explain how a limited company's financial statements are influenced by the legal and regulatory framework to meet the needs of users Pg 35	**M2** assess the impact of adjustments to profit and loss account and balance sheet items for a limited company Pg 41	**D2** evaluate the changes in the financial position of a limited company using a cash flow statement Pg 45
P3 make adjustments to a limited company's financial statements Pg 41	**M3** assess the importance of the different elements of a cash flow statement Pg 45	
P4 explain the purpose of a limited company's cash flow statement Pg 45		

The impact of accounting legislation and concepts on organisations' accounting policies and procedures

Over the decades accountants, as a profession, and the government, as the legislator, have made great strides in ensuring that all business accounts are created so that they show a true and honest view of the business's performance. Ultimately, the accountant will be held responsible for preparing and checking the accounts of a business. In effect, the accountant signs to indicate that they are confident that the accounts reflect the business's true financial position.

Not only does the government expect businesses to act within the law in all matters, but it must also have a clear and straightforward means by which to assess the tax liability of each business. Like individuals, companies, partnerships and sole traders pay tax. But, unlike individuals, businesses pay tax not according to their earnings but according to their profits.

Legislation

Successive governments often drive legislation. As we will see in this section, some of the legislation is over 100 years old, and there have been amendments and changes over the decades.

Although the Companies Acts 1985 and 1989 are specifically mentioned, it is advisable to refer to the Companies Act 2006, which is in the process of being introduced. It is a useful point of reference as it restates most of the Companies Acts and makes significant changes in places.

Companies Acts 1985, 1989

In November 2006, the Companies Act 2006 received royal assent from Queen Elizabeth II. It is one of the longest acts in history, with 700 pages, 1300 sections and 15 appendices. It amends or restates nearly every law related to companies.

A full one-third of the Act simply repeats the Companies Act 1985; another third modifies that Act, and the remaining one-third is completely new.

Fig 6.1 The Companies Act

(Source: www.opsi.gov.uk)

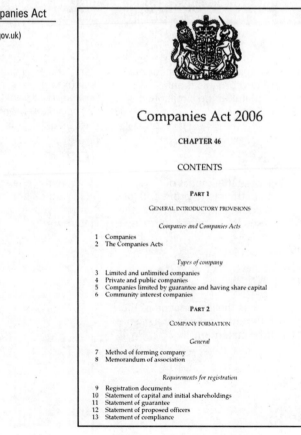

With regard to accounts, the purpose of the Companies Acts over the years has been to ensure that each relevant business performed according to the correct accounting policies and procedures. Foremost amongst these are:

- the duty to keep accounting records
- where and for how long records need to be kept
- determining a business's financial year and accounting reference periods
- ensuring that directors are ultimately responsible for preparing individual company accounts
- ensuring that at the end of a financial year the directors prepare group accounts, if a company owns other companies.

As far as most businesses are concerned, the 2006 Act simply restates what they already know to be their duties and responsibilities. A business's accounting records must be kept so that at any point, with a reasonable degree of accuracy, the business can inform people as to its financial position. It is also important that in doing so a profit and loss account and a balance sheet are created.

The profit and loss account, as we will see later, gives a fully calculated summary of the business's income and expenditure and expresses the balance as either a profit or a loss. The balance sheet measures the business's assets (including buildings, **stock**, machinery and cash), compared with its debts (loans, outstanding payments, etc.).

Businesses have a duty to keep track of all money that they have spent and received. They must also keep a record of any assets (items that they own) and their liabilities (what they owe). The accounting records must also keep a tally of any stock, including statements of all goods sold and purchased.

For the most part, businesses are expected to keep their accounting records for a reasonable period of time in case shareholders or representatives of the government should wish to inspect them at some point in the future.

Not all businesses begin and end their financial year in April to coincide with the normal tax year. A business's financial year will begin the day immediately following the end of a previous financial year. The reason that the business has to identify its financial year is so that a line can be drawn under events and calculations made to coincide with the end of the financial year.

According to legislation, the brunt of the responsibility for accounts falls on directors of companies. It is their responsibility to prepare a balance sheet based on the last day of the business's financial year. At the same time, a profit and loss account must be created. Collectively, these are known as individual accounts. The balance sheet must give a true and fair view of the state of the business at the end of its financial year. The same two criteria apply to the profit and loss account, which obviously will reveal whether the business has made a profit or whether it has made a loss.

Responsibilities are more complex if a business is part of a network of companies. The directors of the groups of companies have the responsibility not only to prepare individual accounts but also to prepare group accounts. As a result, they have to produce two additional items:

- a consolidated balance sheet, incorporating all of the information from the individual balance sheets of each of the companies
- a consolidated profit and loss account, showing both the profit and loss of the parent company and all of the other companies.

As we will see, profit and loss accounts and balance sheets tend to apply only to limited companies rather than to sole traders and partnerships. If a business is incorporated, which means that it is either a private limited company or a public limited company, it will be required to create a balance sheet and a profit and loss account.

For up-to-date specific information on the Companies Act 2006, visit the website of the Department for Business, Enterprise and Regulatory Reform (DBERR, formerly the Department for Trade and Industry)

www.dti.gov.uk

Partnership Act 1890

Under the terms of the Partnership Act 1890, it is the responsibility of partners to complete and present true accounts. They must present this information and anything that might affect the partnership to other partners or their legal representatives.

When a member of a partnership dies or for some reasons ceases to be a partner the surviving or continuing partners will carry on the business. They do not have to close the business or break up the partnership, but the individuals named in a deceased partner's will be entitled to any future profits in line with the share of the partnership that the deceased partner had.

If a partnership is brought to an end the following rules apply:

- Losses should be paid first out of profits then out of **capital**. If this does not cover the costs, the partners have individually to pay out any money owing in the same proportion to their entitlement of the share of profits.

- If there are any assets of the business, each partner will receive their share in proportion to the profits that they were entitled to whilst the partnership was in operation.

It is often the case that individuals are partners, but not equal partners. This is particularly true when two original partners set up a partnership, both receiving 50% of the profits and taking 50% of the risks. New partners who join will probably be given a lesser share. If a new partner's share is 10%, the two original partners are entitled to 45% each and the new partner to 10%.

See page 15 for more on partnerships and information about other types of company.

Division of profits and losses

At its simplest, the division of profits and losses is determined by the amount or proportion an individual owns of a business. In other words, two partners owning 50% each of the partnership are entitled to 50% each of its profits and risk having to cover 50% of its losses.

Obviously, it becomes far more complicated when we talk about limited companies. Sole traders are straightforward enough: to a large extent they will be the only owner of a business and will, therefore, have to shoulder any losses made by it and will benefit from any profits.

All limited companies have a number of shares. If we were to think of these as proportions or fractions of ownership, collectively they would add up to owning the whole of the business. Companies may have hundreds, thousands, tens of thousands or hundreds of thousands of shares. It is therefore possible for many thousands of people to own a proportion of a large business. The shares will have been acquired in a number of different ways. To simplify matters, let us assume that the owners of the shares purchased them. This price paid will be set by the business's current performance or forecasts of its future performance. It will also, to a large extent, be set by just how many people want to buy those shares; the more people chasing the shares the higher the price will go.

Businesses issue shares or make the shares available in order to raise funds. Again, let us assume that the business is actually selling the shares (once an individual owns a share they can sell it to another person, so technically the ownership of the business is continually changing). When the shareholder buys the shares the money can be invested by the business in its operations.

Setting aside the fact that the shares' value may go up or down, the shareholder will actually be looking for payment for having made the investment. They receive the payment in the form of dividends. These dividends are their share of the profits that the business has made. The dividend is worked out per share, so a shareholder will receive the dividend per share multiplied by the number of shares they own.

For private limited companies the sale of shares is a little more difficult. The shares are not available on the open market. In any case, shareholders of limited companies have first to offer other existing shareholders the shares that they wish to sell, before they are allowed to sell them to anyone else. The shares of private limited companies can, of course, go up and down depending on the fortunes of the business. In almost every other respect they work in exactly the same way as public limited company shares. The shareholders' total investment is represented by the shares that they bought. So if a business closes, unless they have sold the shares beforehand, all the shareholders will lose is the money that they paid for the shares. If a business makes a loss, there will not be a dividend to pay the shareholders.

Public limited companies sell their shares on the open market. In fact, the major businesses see their shares being bought and sold in their thousands every day. Some investors purchase shares in the hope that the share price will increase. Once it has, they will resell the shares and make a profit.

Accounting concepts

All accounting statements prepared by accountants are created, kept and presented according to a set of key concepts and conventions. In Great Britain, four of these are to be found in the Statement of Standard Accounting Practice (number 2 SSAP: Disclosure of Accounting Policies). These are:

- going concern
- accruals (or matching)
- consistency
- prudence.

However, for completeness, we will consider all the main concepts applied by accountants.

Business entity

This is also called the 'accounting entity' concept. According to this concept, the financial **transactions** of an individual or a group of individuals must be kept separate from any financial transactions that are unrelated.

Let us take as an example an individual who makes money by working as a sole trader. The business is considered to earn that money and its accounts must therefore be dealt with separately from the individual's personal finances. The sole trader pays him- or herself wages or a salary (called drawings); this is despite only one person being involved. In other words, as an accounting principle, the individual person has two separate entities, first as the sole trader and then as an individual.

Materiality

This concept addresses the fact that accountants need only to concern themselves with matters that could be significant in a business's operations. They should not worry themselves about money matters that are trivial as far as the whole set of accounts is concerned. In other words, if the business cannot account for the loss of a few pounds, this is not an issue. If the business cannot account for the loss of hundreds or thousands of pounds, this needs to be looked at in terms of the whole business.

Going concern

This accounting concept is the underlying assumption that an accountant makes when the sets of accounts are prepared. The assumption is that the business in question will remain in existence for the foreseeable future. In addition to being one of the oldest accounting concepts, the idea of a 'going concern' is part of British law and is referred to in the Companies Act 1985.

Without the 'going concern' concept, the accounts would have to be drawn up on the basis that the business is going to be wound up, and the business would be valued for the accounts as if it were about to be broken up and all of its assets sold off. Clearly, the winding-up value of the business would be very different from the going-concern value of the business. Issues that contribute to the valuation of a business, such as the state of the market and the availability of finance would not be brought into the calculations if the winding-up valuation were adopted.

Accruals (matching)

Accruals are also known as the matching principle. Abiding by this concept ensures that all business revenues and costs are recorded in the appropriate statement at the appropriate time.

When a profit statement is created, all of the costs of goods sold relevant to those sales must be recorded accurately and in full.

Enron

In around 15 years, the American company Enron grew from nowhere to become the seventh largest US business. At its height, Enron employed some 21,000 people and was operating in 40 countries around the world.

The truth was that Enron's success was built on fraud. It had been lying about its profits and concealing massive debts. When the case began to unravel in 2000, Enron's share prices tumbled. When the deception was finally revealed, investors and creditors were stunned.

Fig 6.2 Andrew Fastow, ex Chief Financial Officer at Enron

The motive behind the fraud appears to have been that money was considered more important than honesty. In the four years between 1996 and 1999, Enron had told its shareholders that it had made $2.3bn in profits. At the same time, it told the US tax authorities that it had lost $3bn.

How was this achieved? Mainly through very complicated tax schemes with odd names such as Condor and Apache. They were designed to move money into tax-free areas of operation through a series of increasingly complicated transactions with banks.

The US Joint Committee on Taxation Chief of Staff Lindy Paull said, 'Enron deliberately and aggressively engaged in transactions that had little or no business purpose in order to obtain favourable tax and accounting treatment.'

Enron achieved all of this with the help of its lawyers, accountants and bankers. They were prepared, in return for fees amounting to $87m to claim that the schemes had one purpose as far as the tax authorities were concerned and another for the shareholders.

(Adapted from www.finance.senate.gov)

activity

1   Who should have spotted the problems much earlier?

2   Why did these individuals either not spot the problems or choose not to report them?

3   There were clear materiality issues in this case, what were they?

Costs that relate to a future period have to be carried forward as a prepayment. This means that they are not charged against the current profit statement. An ideal example of this would be the payment of rent for the month when the payment covers the whole month and the profit statement is dated mid-month. Expenses that may be paid in arrears (in other words paid after the period to which they relate) must be shown in the current period's profit statement. This is called accruals adjustment.

Prudence

Prudence, which is also known as conservatism, is perhaps one of the reasons that many people consider that accountants are boring. Whenever there are alternative procedures or values, a prudent accountant always chooses the option that produces the lowest profit. The same is true for asset values and liability values. The key phrase here is 'anticipate no profit and provide for all possible losses'.

The main reason for prudence is to avoid unnecessary payments to shareholders in the form of dividends should the business be more optimistic than the business's true financial state actually demands.

Consistency

The methods employed in dealing with certain items in accounting records can differ over a period of time. This means that the concept of consistency has to be rigidly applied. A prime example is **depreciation**: a business can apply different ways of working out the current value of an asset, gradually reducing its value over a period of years. In fact, a business does have some discretion as to how it treats assets in terms of depreciation. If, for example, a rate of 10% depreciation were applied to an asset worth £100,000, then £10,000 could be charged against the profits of the business. On paper, the asset is now worth £90,000. If the business were to apply 15% depreciation to the asset in the second year, the amount charged against the profit of the business would be £13,500, more than was charged against the profit the year before. The concept of consistency therefore states that the business should always apply the same principles to issues such as this each year. The business would therefore be expected to apply either a 10% or 15% depreciation to the assets year on year. Should the business need to change the methods, an explanation would have to be included in the accounts explaining the effects that the change has on the results of the accounts.

Money measurement

The concept of money measurement is perhaps one of the most straightforward. It suggests that only those transactions that are true financial transactions need to be accounted for in the business's accounts. In other words, only the transactions that are expressed in money terms will be of any interest to the accountant and be included in the accounts records and statements.

Fig 6.3

Historical cost

Historical cost is a concept that suggests that only the actual amount paid for an asset is relevant. This cost is the only one that should be used in the accounts, and the price actually paid for an asset should be the basis of all values allocated to that asset. In other words, when the asset is bought the full price is used; then, as the value of the asset decreases (depreciation), the depreciation is worked out as a percentage of the original (historical) cost.

The application of this concept means that any personal views as to the value of an asset are ignored, and only the historical cost of the asset is used when making any calculations as to its current value. This avoids guessing the value of an asset at a particular time and also avoids disputes as to the value; the value is always a percentage of its historical cost.

Duality (double-entry)

Duality is at the very centre of the universally applied practice of **double-entry bookkeeping**. In this system, every transaction has to be applied twice. The reason for this is that each transaction has a double effect on the business. If a business buys an asset, another asset (cash for example) is decreased. If the asset is bought on **credit**, the liabilities (money owing) are increased.

Consequently, every transaction undertaken by the business has to appear as both an asset and as expenditure or as a lost asset (a sale) and as income (the cash from selling the asset).

If the asset is sold on credit, the debit owing to the business is increased (this is classed as an asset if the business has a reasonable chance of getting the money).

Realisation

Realisation refers to the fact that accounts recognise transactions at the point when the actual sale occurs: in other words, when the legal ownership of something changes from one owner to another. This is distinct from when payment takes place.

When a retail store sells a customer a product on credit, by store card for example, the sale is made on a given day and the store and customer make a contract of sale. Some time later, the customer will pay for the product by making a payment on their store card. As far as realisation is concerned, the transaction took place not when the money changed hands, but when the customer went to the till.

The same is true for credit terms when a business delivers products to a customer and then sends the customer an invoice, stating that payment should be made within 30–60 days. Realisation states that the transaction happened when the business delivered the products to the customer and not 30–60 days later when the customer finally pays the business for the products that they have owned since the delivery was made.

Relevance

The relevance concept relates to the eventual use of the accounting information. Accounts are prepared not just for tax purposes but also for people to make informed decisions regarding the business. The accounts need therefore to be presented in a format such that people can use them to confirm their opinion of the business and perhaps to get an overview of its operations, successes and failures. This usually means helping people to make a decision as to whether or not to invest in the business, lend it money or, in the case of potential employees, whether or not to work for the business.

Reliability

According to the concept of reliability, the accountant involved in the preparation of the accounts should present them in:

- a truthful manner
- an accurate condition
- a complete format without omissions.

In addition, the accountant needs to be clear that an investor or a potential investor could independently verify the data included in the accounts.

Comparability

Comparability refers to the fact that users of the accounts may need to be able to compare the information included in the accounts with information in the accounts of a similar business. Comparisons are usually made with a business in the same industrial group (e.g. comparing a sheet metal business with a minicab business would be of little use).

By comparing like with like, a person can look at the performance of both of the businesses and make a judgement as to how well they are performing over a period of time.

Understandability

This simple principle is very important. It means that the accounts information has to be presented in such as way as to allow people to comprehend the data that has been included. In other words, a reasonably well-informed individual should be able to grasp the main points and key figures in the data.

Framework for the Preparation and Presentation of Financial Statements

The International Accounting Standards Board has created a Framework for the Preparation and Presentation of Financial Statements, which describes the basic concepts behind the preparation of all financial statements.

The Framework is designed to work as a guide to the Board in developing accounting standards. It is also used as a guide to resolving accounting issues that are not directly covered in an International Accounting Standard or International Financial Reporting Standard or Interpretation.

The Framework:

- defines the objective of financial statements

- identifies the qualitative characteristics that make information in financial statements useful

- defines the basic elements of financial statements and the concepts for recognising and measuring them in financial statements.

The key aspects of the Framework are detailed in Table 6.1.

Table 6.1 Key aspects of the Framework

Aspect	Explanation
General purpose financial statements	The Framework addresses general-purpose financial statements that a business prepares and presents at least annually to meet the common information needs of a wide range of users.
Users and their information needs	The main users are defined as present and potential investors, employees, lenders, suppliers and other trade creditors, customers, governments and their agencies and the general public. All of these categories of users rely on financial statements to help them in decision making. Because investors are providers of risk capital to the business, financial statements that meet their needs will also meet most of the general financial information needs of other users. Common to all of these user groups is their interest in the ability of the business to generate cash and cash equivalents and in the timing and certainty of those future cash flows. Although financial statements cannot provide all the information that users may need to make economic decisions, the effects of past events and transactions, are useful.
Responsibility for financial statements	The management of a business has the primary responsibility for preparing and presenting the financial statements.
Elements of the financial statements	Financial statements portray the financial effects of transactions and other events by grouping them into broad classes according to their economic characteristics. These broad classes are termed the elements of financial statements.
Financial position	The elements directly related to financial position (balance sheet) are: ■ assets ■ liabilities ■ equity.
Performance	The elements directly related to performance (income statement) are: ■ income ■ expenses.
Notes	The financial statements also contain notes and supplementary schedules and other information that (a) explain items in the balance sheet and income statement, (b) disclose the risks and uncertainties affecting the enterprise, and (c) explain any resources and obligations not recognised in the balance sheet.

The Framework also recognises and defines the entire key accounting concepts and the key terms used by accountants.

Accounting policies and procedures

The basis of accounting policies and procedures is to ensure that the directors or the business carry out their financial duties. For the most part, the accounting concept of internal control is used. This means that the operations of any business need to be carried out in an orderly fashion and that the business's assets are safeguarded. It also means that the resources available to the business are used to their best effect.

Principles and conventions

At a very basic level a business must apply both financial and non-financial controls, as well as establishing an internal control system. Typically, the financial controls are:

- controlling the business's cash receipts
- controlling payments
- controlling the financing operations or the raising of finance
- managing incoming funds and outgoing funds.

As far as the non-financial controls are concerned, the business should:

- establish control over the use of its fixed assets
- establish policies that must be followed by all employees.

The internal control system needs to ensure:

- that the organisation is run in an orderly manner
- that its assets are not misused
- that its records are kept
- that individuals comply with the organisation's policies.

Over and above this, the business must ensure that it is in a position to apply any legislation or regulations. It will find this impossible if it has not set control mechanisms in place. The organisation will therefore need to define the duties and responsibilities of those in the organisation who have a role to play in ensuring that the financial statements are a true record of the organisation's activities.

Rules and practices applied to financial statements

Assuming that the sets of figures prepared by an accountant are a true reflection of the business's performance over a period of time, it is common practice for the accountant to handle the financial data in a number of generally accepted ways. Many of these standard approaches and conventions are outlined in the regulatory framework that we will look at later in this unit.

See page 19 for more information on the regulatory framework.

Other requirements are derived from government legislation, related to the type of business in question. Before we move on to look at specific ways in which calculations can be made, we need to consider two underpinning rules and practices, specifically the valuation of assets and the matching of income and expenditure.

Valuation of assets

Asset valuation is simply the calculation of the current monetary value of an asset. As we will see shortly, most assets that are used by a business will tend to fall in value over a period of years. Not all assets act in this manner: for example, a building may increase in value over a period of time due to the general rise in property prices and the value of land or the perceived usefulness of the site. It may also accrue in value as a result of additions, modifications or improvements made by the business.

Most assets, including machinery, vehicles, computers, office furniture and even stock tend to drop in value over time, simply because they are outdated, worn or become obsolete as better makes or models are made available.

The current value of a business's assets will appear on its balance sheet. It is therefore important for the business to regularly update the valuation of its assets, so that the current value, rather than the value at the time of purchase, is included in its balance sheet. Valuations tend to be based on the replacement cost, as a business that owns machinery worth far less than its original purchase price would have to replace the machinery at the current cost. Businesses keep an asset register so that the current values of the assets can be updated on a regular basis, prior to the creation of a balance sheet.

Matching of income and expenditure

As the term implies, a balance sheet is just that: matching the income and the expenditure of a business. In other words, the business has to show exactly where all income has been spent or saved, whilst at the same time showing how expenditure was funded.

The basic principles come from double-entry bookkeeping, where a sale means a corresponding drop in the value of assets, in this case stock. Equally, a corresponding drop in the cash held by a business matches the purchase of assets.

Fig 6.4

A business needs to maintain a focus on matching its income and expenditure. In fact this is something of an obsession for accountants, and they insist that it begins with double-entry bookkeeping. They will then transfer the double-entry transactions into what is known as a nominal ledger. This shows opening and closing balances and will form the basis of the balance sheet and profit and loss account, as accountants will make a trial balance from this data and, after some recalculation, will be able to produce a balance sheet and profit and loss account.

Depreciation

As we have already seen, assets purchased by a business tend to lose their value over time. Accountants call this 'depreciation'. Assets are any items, other than an expense, purchased by a business. In effect, depreciation is used to wipe out or write off the cost of the asset over its useful lifetime.

It is important to note that in gradually reducing the value of the asset by depreciation the business is not actually showing the cost to it of the asset's use. It is gradually recognising that the value of the asset is reduced to nil or a negligible value by the time that it needs to be replaced.

When valuing assets, an accountant uses the useful term 'net book value', which means the cost of the asset less its depreciation. The important distinction here is that it is the asset's value to the company, rather than the asset's market value if it were sold.

An ideal example would be a computer that a business decides to depreciate over a four-year period. It may show that the computer is worth half its value after two years. In actual fact the market value of the machine would probably be considerably less than that after two years, as technology would have moved on.

A business may use what is known as a straight-line depreciation method. With this method, if it was writing off the computer over a four-year period it would knock 25% of the cost price off the asset valuation each year.

It is important to note just how depreciation is handled in accounts. If a business purchased a computer for £1,000 it could not set against its profits the entire cost of the computer in the year that it was purchased. Instead it would have to decide over how many years the computer would be written off. Again, let's say four years. In the first year in which the computer was purchased the business would be able to offset £250 against its profits. It would then do the same for the next three years, until the asset was written off.

Bad debts

A bad debt is money owed to a business where there is a strong likelihood that the money will never be paid to the business. Some businesses set aside money to cover bad debts; this money is known as a bad debt reserve. The businesses attempt to calculate the likelihood of bad debts occurring and will hold that money in reserve in case payment is not made. Bad debt always occurs when products or services have been sold on credit.

Provision for doubtful debts

The provision for doubtful debts reflects any money that, the business feels, will be unlikely to be recovered. The percentage amount varies from business to business.

There are three ways in which the provision for bad or doubtful debts can be calculated; these are estimates or calculations based on:

- the debtors' accounts, focusing on how long outstanding money has been owed
- the total outstanding debt
- the total value of sales on credit.

Usually, a business that has to make provision for bad or doubtful debts has already experienced problems collecting money from its debtors. It may even have had to write off some of the money owed and will be basing its provision on the likelihood that a similar amount will be equally difficult to recover.

remember

Most businesses make their provision on an annual basis, but larger businesses may do this on a monthly or six-monthly basis.

Accruals

Accruals are expenses incurred by the business for which invoices have not yet been received by the end of the accounting period. Strictly speaking, this money is not owed and the business or individuals providing the products or services are not creditors. The reason is that the invoices have not yet been received by the purchasing business.

However, following the accrual concept, they do need to be included. In order for the accounts to be consistent, the money involved has to be included in the profit and loss account for the period.

A closely associated concept is deferred income. This is very similar to accruals. When including accrued expenses and excluding deferred income on the profit and loss account, it is important to show the total amounts accrued on the balance sheet otherwise the accounts will not balance. In the next financial year:

remember

Businesses need to match costs and income, or costs and assets.

- When accruals have been invoiced, they are switched from accruals to creditors.
- When products or services related to deferred income or prepayment are supplied, revenue is recognised and the deferred income on the balance sheet is reduced.

Prepayments

We have seen that deferred income is money received during an accounting period for products or services that the business has not supplied by the end of the accounting period. Closely linked to the concept of deferred income is prepayment. If one business makes a prepayment the supplier will have deferred income.

Accruals and deferred income are sometimes shown as a single balance sheet item. Some businesses choose to separate them in order to make it more straightforward to see future revenues.

When a business pays for products or services before it receives them, it has made a prepayment. The amounts paid are shown in the balance sheet as a prepayment, but they are not shown as costs in a profit and loss account. Once the products or services have been received, the amounts are added to the profit and loss account and also deducted from prepayments on the balance sheet.

Stock valuation

Stock is considered a current asset, which can be resold. Stock can consist of any of the following:

- products that can be sold as they now appear or as finished goods for a manufacturer
- work in progress or unfinished goods
- **raw materials** (items that will need to be processed before they can be sold).

Fig 6.5 A farmer's stock

Stock is valued at the lowest of:

- cost (the price the business paid for the stock plus the cost of processing)
- the net realisable value (which is the amount for which an asset can be sold less the cost of selling it).

Clearly, the cost of stock, even of the same type, will change over time as suppliers' prices change. It is therefore difficult, if not impossible, to track the value of each individual item. For example, over the course of the year a business may purchase 100,000 bricks from a supplier. The price for each brick will be dependent upon the supplier's price, so the business may pay somewhere between 20p and 40p per brick. It is impossible to identify which of the 100,000 bricks cost the business 20p and which cost 40p.

The accounting convention is therefore to assign a cost to that stock when it is used or sold. This will obviously have an impact on the balance sheet and on the profit and loss account.

Businesses adopt one of two approaches to the costing of stock:

- Even if they have not physically sold the oldest stock, they assume that they have by adopting a first-in, first-out (FIFO) method of valuing stock. The cost of the stock takes the oldest price first, assuming that the oldest available stock is actually being sold.

- The alternative is to use last-in, first-out (LIFO). Stock sold is assumed to be the most recent purchase. The advantage of using LIFO is that the prices used to calculate cost of sales and gross profit reflect more closely the current value of that stock.

A further complication in stock valuation is assigning costs to stock that has been processed. If raw materials come into a business and go through a series of processes, the business will incur costs in the processing. It is difficult to decide which costs are allocated to what stock.

Organisations

The first major consideration is that, regardless of the type of business, HM Revenue and Customs requires information. Table 6.2 outlines the main requirements.

Table 6.2　HM Revenue and Customs requirements

Trading status	Profit/loss reporting method	Sent to	Date/deadline	How the information is used
Self-employed	Self-assessment tax return, self-employment pages SA103	HM Revenue and Customs	30 September or 31 January	To check that you are paying the right amount of tax
Limited company	Corporation tax return form CT600 and annual accounts	HM Revenue and Customs	12 months after the end of the company's financial year	To check that the company is paying the right amount of tax
Limited liability partnership where one or more partner is a limited company	Annual accounts	Companies House	10 months after the end of the firm's financial year	To make the information available to the general public
Partnership Limited partnership	Partnership tax return form SA800	HM Revenue and Customs	30 September or 31 January	To check that the partnership is paying the right amount of tax
Limited liability partnership	Annual accounts	Companies House	10 months after the end of the firm's financial year	To make the information available to the general public

Whatever the type of business, the law states that there is a requirement to keep accurate records of income and expenditure. Sole traders are required to keep records for five years. For limited companies and partnerships, the period is six years.

The main advantages in ensuring that records are accurately kept are that:

- It gives the business the information necessary to manage it and help it grow.
- It enables the business to quickly work out its profit or loss.
- It improves the business's chances of obtaining a loan.
- It ensures that the business does not have to pay too much tax.
- Any claims for certain allowances can be backed up with evidence.
- The business can plan more easily and budget for tax payments.
- The business pays less for accounting services as the accountant does not have to work out the tax liabilities from scratch.

At the most basic level, the business should keep the following information:

- all sales and income
- all expenditure including any day-to-day expenses
- a separate list of **petty cash** items
- a record of any goods taken for personal use and any payments made to the business for these items
- a record of any money taken out for personal use or any money paid in from personal funds (this only applies to limited companies)
- back-up copies of all of the above in case of fire or theft.

Sole trader requirements

Sole traders need to keep a track of all financial transactions that affect their business, and the key to managing sole trader finances is bookkeeping. Sole traders can claim tax relief for some expenses that are incurred before they start trading.

The self-employed or sole traders are responsible for reporting all of their income and expenditure as accurately and honestly as possible. Sole trader accounts are easier and quicker to prepare than those for other types of business. The following should be recorded:

- each sale
- bank transactions
- cash payments and receipts for each purchase
- credit card payments.

Sole traders must keep their records and supporting receipts for five years and nine months after the return has been submitted to HM Revenue and Customs.

Businesses that operate as sole traders pay tax and national insurance on the profits of the business, regardless of how much income the sole trader takes as a salary (known as drawings). The tax is payable in two instalments: in January and July each year.

Partnership requirements

Remember that two or more individuals own a partnership.

The requirements for partnership accounts depend upon the nature of the partnership. For the most part, the accounting requirements relate solely to each individual in that partnership. Their accounts must take into consideration any profits or payments that they have received from the partnership. Each partner takes a share in proportion to their investment in the business. Therefore a partnership that simply allocates the profits to each partner does not have to complete accounts in its own right.

Each of the partners can be classed as a sole trader as far as tax and accounts are concerned. Alternatively, they can be classed as a private limited company, for which they will have to produce a profit and loss account and a balance sheet.

In other cases, a partnership will need to prepare and have audited accounts, in exactly the same way as if it were a company created under the Companies Act. The accounts can cover up to 18 months but are usually drawn up for a 12-month period, ending on 31 March each year. The partnership accounts must be prepared within 10 months of the end of the financial year.

When partnership accounts are prepared the accounts of any partner that is trading as a limited company have to be delivered to Companies House. The partnership needs to make sure that the latest accounts are available for inspection, and each member of the partnership has to supply a copy of the latest accounts of the partnership if requested.

There is another version of a partnership, known as a limited liability partnership. Most partnership accounts can be compiled without **auditing**, but limited liability partnerships' accounts have to be prepared and audited under much tighter guidelines. The limited liability partnership itself and each individual member must make annual self-assessment returns. It is usually the case that each member takes an equal share of the profits, unless there is another agreement.

Limited company requirements

There are two different types of limited company. The first is a private limited company that has one or more shareholders and does not offer its shares for sale to the public. This type must be registered at Companies House and, at present, it must have at least one director and a company secretary. However, from October 2008, it will no longer be necessary for a private limited company to have a company secretary.

To find out more about Companies House, the official British government register of British companies, visit

www.companieshouse.gov.uk

Public limited companies must have at least two shareholders and can offer their shares for sale to the public. The company must have issued shares to a value of at least £50,000 before it can trade. Like a private limited company, it must be registered or incorporated with Companies House. A public limited company has to have two directors and a professionally qualified company secretary.

Fig 6.6 Companies House
home page

(Source: www.companieshouse.
gov.uk)

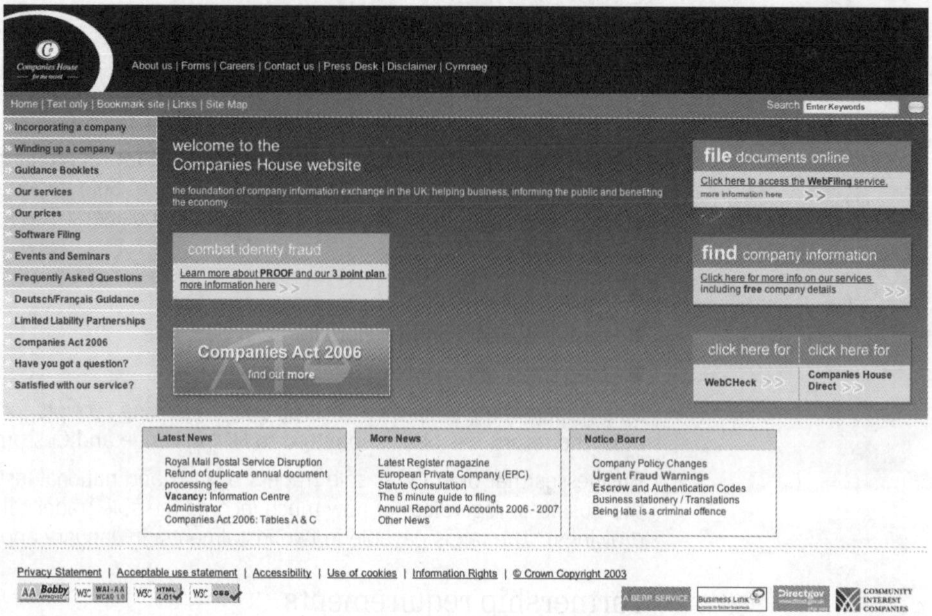

> A limited company
> pays its tax nine
> months after
> the end of the
> accounting period.

remember

Both types of limited company have to file their records and accounts with Companies House. An annual return is sent before the anniversary of incorporation each year and needs to be checked, amended and returned to Companies House. The directors and the company secretary are responsible for liaising and informing Companies House about any significant changes.

Profits are usually distributed to shareholders in the form of a dividend. Some profits may be retained by the business as working capital (money needed to fund day-to-day activities). Companies pay **corporation tax** and make an annual return to HM Revenue and Customs.

Charity and club requirements

Charities

Each charity must comply with the legal requirements for the preparation of its accounts and reports. Most of the requirements are covered under the Charities Act 2006. Charities are effectively companies registered under the Companies Act, but which have been established exclusively for charitable purposes. They may prepare their accounts on one of two bases (receipts and payments or accruals):

■ If the accounts are prepared on a receipts and payments basis, the charity must summarise all the money received and paid out. It must also provide a statement giving details of its assets and its liabilities. This basis is usually used by non-company charities that have an income of less than £100,000 per year.

■ When its accounts are based on accruals, the charity is required to produce a balance sheet showing its financial position. The charity is also required to provide a statement of financial activities, usually an income and expenditure account and additional notes.

There are in fact four different types of charity: registered, non-company charities; registered charitable companies; excepted charities; and exempt charities.

Regardless of the type of charity all of them must:

■ prepare and maintain accounts records, retaining them for at least six years

■ prepare accounts

■ make the accounts available to the public on request.

For registered charities that are not companies the following applies if neither their gross income nor expenditure exceeds £5,000:

■ Accounts can be prepared either using receipts and payments or accruals.

■ The accounts do not have to be independently examined or audited.

■ The exception to this is if the charity has an income of less than £5,000 but expenditure of more than £250,000 in the same year, in which case it must prepare an **annual report**.

If a registered charity is not a company and has an income or total expenditure of over £5,000, it must either prepare its accounts on a receipts and payments or an accruals basis. The charity must allow its accounts to be audited, prepare an annual report and send a copy of the annual report to the Charity Commission.

There are different requirements if the income of the charity is over £100,000 per year. In this case, the charity must use the accruals system, prepare an annual report and submit it to the Charity Commission. Its accounts must be audited.

For more information on the Charities Act 2006 and the role of the Charities Commission, visit

www.charity-commission.gov.uk

Under the Companies Acts, charitable companies must prepare directors' reports and accounts and must submit these to Companies House. Their accounts must be prepared using the accruals basis; they must produce an annual report and send this, along with the accounts and annual return to the Charities Commission.

There are two other types of charity: an excepted charity uses the same accounting and reporting systems as other registered charities if it is registered. Even if it is not registered, it must still produce annual accounts. Exempt charities are required to keep proper records and accounts, usually audited and have copies available for members of the public should the request be made.

Clubs

Clubs are required to keep records of all income and expenditure. It is usual for the club treasurer to make a report at each committee meeting, so that the executive committee is aware of the financial position. It is also usual for committee members to be able to see copies of bank books so that they can check that the funds are as stated by the treasurer.

Table 6.3 Example of simple income and expenditure accounts

Date	Income			Date	Expenditure	
01/06/2008	Subscriptions	£40.00		02/06/2008	Footballs	£54.00
01/06/2008	Sweeper money	£64.00		03/06/2008	First aid kit	£12.00
10/06/2008	Subscriptions	£60.00		10/06/2008	Pitch	£8.65
10/06/2008	Sweeper money	£42.00		10/06/2008	Referee	£15.00
10/06/2008	Donation	£10.00		10/06/2008	Juice	£2.50
15/06/2008	Subscriptions	£20.00		12/06/2008	Laundry	£12.50
30/06/2008	Subscriptions	£100.00		15/06/2008	Pitch	£8.65
				15/06/2008	Referee	£15.00
				15/06/2008	Juice	£2.50
				17/06/2008	Laundry	£12.50
B	**Total Income**	£336.00		A	**Total Expenditure**	£143.30
	Less Expenditure	£143.30				
C	**Balance**	£192.70	B–A			
	Carried Forward					
D	From May	£320.00				
F	Total Funds	£512.70	C+D			
	Represented by				Total of F should equal G	
	Bank Account	£412.70				
	Cash In Hand	£100.00				
G	Total	£512.70				

Sole trader and partnerships

Laura Buchan runs her own small business, Buchan Soft Furnishings, as a sole trader. She owns and runs the business herself and buys in stock from a number of suppliers. As she is a relatively new customer, most of the suppliers require her to pay for the goods with the order, so she does not have any debts to suppliers.

Her bank manager is a little concerned about this; she feels that Laura should push the suppliers to give her credit that would help her cash flow. Laura takes £20,000 out of the business as wages and has a loan with the bank.

Her first set of accounts were a mess, and she had to pay an accountant nearly £400 to sort them out. She now wants to create her own proper accounts without involving an accountant. At present, she is confused as to what to do. Last financial year, she showed a £12,400 profit overall and she is quite pleased with the progress.

Two partners, Mr Smith and Mr Jones purchased a care home. Mr Smith managed the home and he also lent Mr Jones over half of the funds his partner needed to buy his share of the home. Mr Smith was paid a salary out of the profits of the partnership and the two partners equally shared the balance of the profits. It had been agreed by the partners that all of the assets of the partnership would be equally owned.

After a short while, the business began to run at a loss and, in April 2007, the partnership was dissolved. Mr Jones applied to have the partnership wound up, and Mr Smith continued to run the care home after the dissolution and began to make a profit.

Mr Smith claimed that the profits he had earned after the dissolution of the partnership and the winding up belonged to him. Mr Jones disagreed. He believed that he was still entitled to half of the profits as he had always been. In any case, Mr Smith argued that any money supposedly owed to Mr Jones was offset by the fact that he had lent money to him to set up the partnership in the first place and this had not been paid back. Mr Jones still owed him £96,000.

In court, the judge considered Section 42 of the Partnership Act 1890; this deals with the dissolution of partnerships. The judge concluded that the share of the partnership assets meant the share of the assets on the dissolution of the partnership and not some point later before winding up. Therefore the post-dissolution profits belonged to Mr Smith. Accordingly, the division of the assets would be based on the values at the time of dissolution.

When a partnership itself ceases trading and until the partnership is wound up, any partner continuing to use the assets of the partnership does so at their own risk. To protect themselves they need to make sure that a full valuation of the assets at the time of the dissolution is made so that, when the division of assets is made on winding up the partnership, the division reflects the value of the assets then and not now.

Mr Smith and Mr Jones did not have a written partnership agreement. It was therefore the court's role to judge the dispute according to the law. Unsurprisingly, Mr Jones disagreed with the judgment.

1   What is the legislation that underpins the accounting and reporting requirements of these two businesses?

2   What are the key accounting concepts that must be used by the two businesses?

3   What lessons can be learned in terms of legal requirements and the use of accounting concepts in these two cases?

The impact of the regulatory framework on a limited company's accounting policies and procedures

All limited companies need to carry out certain administrative tasks in order to keep the information held by Companies House up to date. Individuals in the business are legally responsible for getting the jobs done. There may be penalties or legal sanctions if things are not done in the correct manner.

Companies must keep official records of the following:

- shareholders and the shares they own
- the business's directors and secretaries
- the other commercial interests of any directors
- loans or other obligations that may affect the financial status of the business
- any others that have an interest in the shares of the business, other than the registered owners.

Normally, the responsibility for compiling this information falls ultimately on the company secretary. It is also important that company records are made available to those who are entitled to see them. This means that:

- The business must send its accounts to company members and others at least 21 days before the meeting in which they are due to be approved.
- Any individual has the right to inspect the company's register of members.
- All members have the right to inspect and have copies of minutes of General Meetings.
- Whilst only directors have a right to see the minutes of directors' meetings, others may wish to see them.

Directors are legally responsible for submitting yearly accounts. In addition, the company's annual return has to be submitted to the Registrar of Companies. This is normally in the format of Form 363, the Annual Return, which is a record of general information about the business, including the registered office, directors' details, shareholders and **share capital**.

The business's annual accounts must also be filed within time limits. Filing a paper submission costs £30; an online annual return costs £15.

In addition to the specific legal requirements, a range of regulations have become common practice in an attempt to standardise the way in which accounts and other financial data are processed, audited and presented.

Regulatory framework

The Financial Reporting Council (FRC) is an independent, British regulator for **corporate reporting and governance**. The Department of Trade and Industry and the Bank of England are responsible for appointing the FRC's chairperson. As a regulator, the FRC uses operating bodies to supervise corporate reporting and governance. These include the Accounting Standards Board (ASB) and the Auditing Practices Board.

In 1990, the Accounting Standards Board took over responsibility from the Accounting Standards Committee. Its first task was to develop principles to guide standards, under the terms of the Companies Act 1985. In addition, the ASB was to provide a framework to regulate financial accounting and corporate reporting. It was also charged with responsibility for creating new accounting standards or amending the existing ones.

The ASB was given the power to issue its own standards, which its predecessor was not allowed to do. The purpose was to create quality accounting standards and to respond quickly to any problems encountered in accounting. Through the ASB, the FRC is able to concentrate on improving standards of financial accounting and corporate reporting.

The ASB has up to ten board members and three observers. In order to adopt, revise or cancel an accounting standard, seven of the board members must agree. The ASB is also involved with accounting standard organisations in other countries, as well as with the International Accounting Standards Board. The aim is to harmonise accounting standards across the world.

Statements of Standard Accounting Practice and Financial Reporting Standards

The ASB has issued its own accounting standards called the Financial Reporting Standards (FRSs). The Statements of Standard Accounting Practice (SSAPs) were the original standards designed by the ASC. Gradually over a period of years, the ASB is amending the SSAPs and replacing them with FRSs. However, some SSAPs are still in use because, as far as the ASB is concerned, they are adequate and match the legal definition of accounting standards. As the Financial Reporting Council said in 2004:

> 'Accounting standards are authoritative statements of how particular types of transactions and other events should be reflected in financial statements and accordingly compliance with accounting standards will normally be necessary for financial statements to give a true and fair view.'
>
> (Source: www.iasb.org.uk)

This statement by the FRC is at the heart of any attempts to create an authoritative set of accounting standards. The accounting standards are designed to lay down the guidelines of how transactions should be reported in financial statements. Above all the financial statements need to give a true and fair view.

Initially, the creation of accounting standards was designed to define good practice in accounting within a legal framework. It has gone further than this and has resulted in the creation of a common understanding about accounting practice between users of the information and the individuals who prepare that information.

Accounting standards apply directly to all companies and other types of businesses that are required to prepare accounts showing a true and fair view. Without having to defer to any other organisation or government, the ASB can issue accounting standards; it also develops the principles behind the standards.

For a full version of the SSAP and its replacement, the FRS, visit the website of the Financial Reporting Council

www.frc.org.uk.

It is the responsibility of the ASB to research and identify any accounting topics that will eventually become FRSs. The board carries out significant research and consultation, extending not just to Great Britain but also to the Republic of Ireland and other countries. This is to ensure that any new accounting standard does not conflict with legal, economic or practical circumstances in other countries.

International Accounting Standards

The International Accounting Standards (IASs) were derived from the International Accounting Standards Board (IASB). This independent organisation was formed in 2001 and is based in London. Rather like the ASB, the IASB has an International Accounting Standards Committee, which until 2001 was involved in setting International Accounting Standards. Since then the IASB has had the Standards Advisory Council and the International Financial Reporting Interpretations Committee.

There are 41 International Accounting Standards covering:

- the presentation of financial statements
- depreciation
- cash flow
- balance sheets
- tax
- investments
- shares
- assets.

Obviously, the standards cover a wide range of different aspects, some of which may not be relevant to all businesses. Some of the standards have been withdrawn and the standards included within other, more wide-ranging standards. This is true of Standards 3 to 6, 9, 13, 15, 22, 25, 30, 32 and 35.

Perhaps the most important is Standard 1, which covers the presentation of financial statements. It sets out clearly and precisely the objectives of financial statements, which are to provide information about:

- the financial position of a business
- its financial performance
- its cash flow.

In order to achieve these aims, the standard suggests that a complete set of financial statements should include:

- a balance sheet
- an income statement
- a statement of changes in **equity**
- a cash flow statement
- notes, including explanatory ones and a summary of accounting policies.

Fig 6.7

In addition, the standard recommends that:

- Financial statements must be presented in a fair manner.
- All of the statements assume that the business is a going concern.
- The accrual basis of accounting is used.
- The presentation of the financial statements should remain the same from one year to the next.
- The financial statements should be prepared at least annually.
- A classified balance sheet should be created, showing assets and liabilities, separating **current assets** and non-current assets and liabilities.

As far as the balance sheet is concerned, the standard recommends that the following items be included as a minimum:

- property, plant and equipment
- investment property
- intangible assets
- financial assets
- investments accounted for using the equity method

- **biological assets**
- inventories (stock)
- trade and other receivables
- cash and cash equivalents
- trade and other payables
- provisions
- financial liabilities
- liabilities and assets for current tax
- deferred tax, liabilities and assets
- **minority interests**
- issued capital and reserves.

There is also a requirement to create an income statement. Importantly, the standard requires this to state profit or loss, rather than net profit or loss. As a minimum, the income statement should include:

- revenue
- financial costs
- share of the profit or loss of associated businesses or **joint ventures**
- post-tax profit or loss/post-tax gain or loss
- tax expense
- profit or loss.

There are also requirements for the cash flow statement; this should show:

- profit or loss for the period
- each item of income or expense
- total income and expense for the period
- any changes in accounting policies or correction of errors.

For more information and a full set of the standards, visit IASPlus

www.iasplus.com

International Financial Reporting Standards

The International Financial Reporting Standards (IFRSs) are currently issued by the IASB. In effect, these are seeking to replace the International Accounting Standards. The original IASs were issued between 1973 and 2000 by the International Accounting Standards Committee. In 2001 new IFRSs were required. The current IASs are no longer produced but remain in effect until they are replaced by an IFRS.

IFRSs are used throughout the European Union, Commonwealth countries and Russia.

From 2005, all public limited companies in the European Union had to adopt IFRS for their accounts. Before that time only a handful of companies used them. The accounting standards are a framework covering the following:

- setting out the objectives of financial statements
- identifying the characteristics of financial statements, in terms of their usefulness
- defining, recognising and measuring parts of financial statements
- dealing with concepts of capital and **capital maintenance**.

For further information about International Financial Reporting Standards, visit

www.iasplus.com

Financial statements

The term 'financial statement' is a general one; it can refer to the profit and loss account or to the balance sheet or the cash flow statement. For our purposes, the term will refer to all three.

Financial statements are therefore any written documents that contain details concerning the financial performance of a business. In addition to their use for tax purposes, the statements are helpful for the following reasons:

- If the business wishes to raise finance, investors or lenders will want to see three years' worth of accounts.
- Customers offering large contracts want to see audited accounts.
- By producing formal accounts, such as a balance sheet, the business can monitor its own performance.

Profit and loss account (income statement)

A profit and loss account, sometimes called an income statement, is a summary of a business's financial transactions over a period of time. It is usually designed to look at the transactions over a period of 12 months.

A profit and loss account will show the business owners, shareholders and potential investors just how well the business is performing. Most of the information shown on the profit and loss account is used by HM Revenue and Customs to work out the tax liability of the business.

See pages 67–75 of Unit 7 for information on reviewing business performance and pages 94–105 of Unit 8 for information on preparing financial statements.

Above all, the profit and loss account is used to show the 'bottom line', in other words whether the business is actually making a profit or a loss.

If a business is a limited company or a partnership whose members are limited companies, it must produce a profit and loss account for every financial year that it operates.

Sole traders and most partnerships have no need to produce a profit and loss account for the financial year. When they complete a tax return form, they are supplying HM Revenue and Customs with a version of the profit and loss account.

It is advisable to produce a profit and loss account in any case, as it will be useful when seeking additional sources of finance. For the most part, lenders will want to see at least three years' accounts before making a decision on borrowing.

The profit and loss account is one of the two most important financial statements for a business, as it shows the profit and loss of the business over a given time. As we have seen, companies are expected to present their profit and loss accounts in certain formats. Typically a profit and loss account shows the revenues received by the business and the costs involved in generating that revenue. Put simply, costs are deducted from revenues to reveal the profit (or loss).

Several different types of profit appear in a profit and loss account:

- Gross profit is shown as income less cost of sales.
- Operating profit takes the gross profit and deducts any expenses.
- Net profit includes any interest paid on loans or interest received.

Table 6.4 Consolidated profit and loss account for the year ended 31 March 2006

	Notes	31 March 2006 £m	31 March 2005 £m
Continuing operations			
Revenue	3, 4	401.2	509.7
Cost of sales		(334.6)	(491.5)
Gross profit		66.6	18.2
Administration expenses		(55.5)	(93.5)
Operating profit/(loss) before non-recurring costs	5	11.1	(75.3)
Non-recurring costs	6	(1.8)	(288.2)
Operating profit/(loss)		9.3	(363.5)
Finance income		1.9	2.2
Finance expense		(69.7)	(29.9)
Net finance costs	7	(67.8)	(27.7)
Share of post-tax profits from joint ventures	8.1	0.3	0.2
Loss before taxation		(58.2)	(391.0)
Tax on loss	11.1	0.1	2.6
Loss for the year from continuing operations		(58.1)	(388.4)
Discontinued operations			
Post-tax profit from discontinued operations	13.1	1.5	56.3
Loss for the year		(56.6)	(332.1)
Attributable to:			
Equity holders of the Company		(56.6)	(331.8)
Minority interests		–	(0.3)
		(56.6)	(332.1)
(Loss)/earnings per ordinary share	.		
Basic and diluted			
– Continuing		(40.4)p	(270.4)p
– Discontinued		1.0p	39.2p
Total	14	(39.4)p	(231.2)p

The trading profit and loss account is derived from the day-to-day accounts kept by the business.

This profit and loss account contains figures for the years ending 31 March 2005 and 31 March 2006, enabling shareholders and potential investors to compare the performance of the business in the two years. As we can see, the business is making a loss, although it is not as significant as the loss made in the previous year. Note that negative figures are shown in brackets. Also each of the items has notes attached to it to explain the details behind the figures. It is common practice, as shown in the example, for the top half of the profit and loss account to deal with gross profit. Then the net profit is calculated.

Link   See Units 7 and 8 where a number of calculations that can be made from or applied to a profit and loss account are covered in detail.

Balance sheet

It is important to note that a balance sheet only gives a snapshot of what the business owns or is owed at a particular point in time. Balance sheets tend to have a date, which states exactly when all the calculations were made. The balance sheet shows how the business is being funded and how those funds are being used. Of particular importance is the listing of assets, which are owned by the business, and the liabilities, which is what the business owes to other organisations.

A business uses its balance sheet for three different purposes:

■ for simple reporting purposes, as an integral part of the annual accounts

■ to help the business and its investors, creditors and shareholders to assess the business's worth

■ as a tool that the business can use to analyse and improve its operations.

Limited companies and limited liability partnerships must produce a balance sheet as part of their annual accounts, which are submitted to Companies House, HM Revenue and Customs and shareholders.

As the absolute minimum, the balance sheet should show:

■ fixed assets that the business owns

■ current assets (what the business is owed)

■ **current liabilities** (what the business owes in the short term)

■ long-term liabilities (what the business owes over a longer period).

Let's look in more detail at the specific parts of the balance sheet. First, fixed assets; these comprise:

■ tangible assets – land, office equipment, machinery, buildings and other items, the value of which is shown as their resale value or their depreciated value

■ intangible assets – for example trademarks, long-term investments, patents, goodwill and even website domain names.

Current assets are, of course, short term and change from day to day; the balance sheet shows the value of the current assets on the day that the balance sheet was prepared. They include:

■ current stock

■ work in progress

■ cash in safes or at the bank

■ money owed to the business by customers

■ prepayments

■ short-term investments.

The same sets of circumstances can be applied to current liabilities. Strictly speaking, these are liabilities that fall due within the next year, including:

■ tax payable within the year

■ **VAT** payable within the year

■ National Insurance payable within the year

■ overdrafts

■ short-term loans

■ money owed to suppliers.

Long-term liabilities shown on the balance sheet include:

■ amounts due after a year for repayment of loans or financing

■ capital and reserves (share capital and retained profits after dividends).

remember There are strict deadlines for submitting accounts to Companies House and HM Revenue and Customs.

remember The balance sheet is so called because the total value of all the assets must always be equal to the total value of all of the liabilities.

 Link
See pages 38–39 for more information on assets and liabilities.

Table 6.5 Consolidated balance sheet as at 31 March 2006

	Notes	31 March 2006 £m	31 March 2005 £m
Non-current assets			
Goodwill	15	0.7	0.8
Property, plant and equipment	16	28.0	26.8
Interests in associates	8.2	2.3	2.3
Interests in joint ventures	8.2	1.0	1.2
Deferred tax assets	12.1	0.7	0.7
Retirement benefit asset	22.4	22.0	5.0
		54.7	36.8
Current assets			
Inventories	17	7.4	8.2
Debtor related to PFI/PPP non-recourse financing agreement	18	–	11.0
Trade and other receivables	19	104.8	139.2
Cash and cash equivalents	23.2	9.5	10.8
		121.7	169.2
Assets held for sale	13.3		33.3
Total assets		176.4	239.3
Current liabilities			
Borrowings			
– Bank loans and overdrafts	23.2	27.4	303.7
– Obligations under finance leases	23.3	0.9	1.1
PFI/PPP non-recourse term loan	18	–	0.9
Trade and other payables	20	139.3	235.0
Tax liabilities		0.5	0.1
Provisions	22	6.4	25.1
		174.5	565.9
Non-current liabilities			
Borrowings			
– Bank loans	23.2	1.7	5.3
– Obligations under finance leases	23.3	1.9	2.9
PFI/PPP non-recourse term loan	18	–	9.9
Retirement benefit obligation	22.4	17.9	20.8
Provisions	21	8.3	32.7
		29.8	71.6
Liabilities associated with assets held for sale	13.3	0.3	16.1
Total liabilities		204.6	653.6
Net liabilities		(28.2)	(414.3)
Equity			
Capital and reserves			
Share capital	24	7.6	7.2
Share premium	24	556.6	142.3
Revaluation reserve	25	–	3.0
Capital redemption reserve	25	7.2	–
Other reserve	25	89.7	89.7
Translation reserve	25	–	0.4
Accumulated losses	25	(689.3)	(656.9)
Equity shareholders' deficit		(28.2)	(414.3)

For legal reasons, the balance sheet must have those elements shown in bold. In our example, which is for the same company as the one for which the profit and loss account was shown earlier, there are some differences. In fact, the accountant will usually decide how the information is presented.

The balance sheet will show the following:

- how the business is financed
- how its money is being used
- how much of its assets is cash or can be easily converted into cash
- how easy the business is finding paying its current liabilities (this is known as being solvent).

Figures can change over a period of time, but a business's net assets do not tend to change in a dramatic manner. On the balance sheet the current liabilities will reveal any money owed by the business for goods and services that it has received but not yet paid for. The debtors section works on the assumption that debtors will pay on time, but many businesses make a provision if they are doubtful that the debtors will pay.

See page 37 for information concerning provision for doubtful debts.

Intangible assets are difficult to deal with because items such as goodwill can change from day to day. Fixed assets are rather more straightforward; these are shown at their depreciated rates and it is therefore easy to see what these assets might be worth in the near future.

There is a strong relationship between the profit and loss account and the balance sheet. On the one hand, as we have seen, the profit and loss account is a summary of the business's transactions. The net result of these transactions shows as a profit or a loss. The balance sheet does not show any day-to-day transactions, nor does it show current profitability. Its figures do, however, relate to the current state of the business. It will show any profits that have not been paid out as dividends and note them as retained profits. Under current assets, it will show, as cash or at the bank, available money determined by the income and spending that has been shown on the profit and loss account.

A short-term loan will not appear on a profit and loss account, but the profit and loss account will show the interest payments made on that loan. The loan itself will be on the balance sheet, under current liabilities.

It is possible to use a balance sheet rather than a profit and loss account to assess just how well a business is performing. Several measures could be used: one is the level of stock. A rise in the level of stock from one period to another could indicate problems. Looking at the profit and loss account can identify these. If sales have not increased, stock could be sitting, unused and unsold, which may affect the business's cash flow.

The success or otherwise of **credit control** can be examined by looking at the amount that debtors owe the business. If the amount owed is growing faster than sales, there could be a severe problem with cash flow in the near future.

The same can be said for suppliers. It is important for businesses to have a good payment record if they might wish in the future to extend their credit with their suppliers. Making early payments to suppliers may attract a **discount**, but on the down side the money paid out will have an effect on the cash flow.

It is also possible to see how much a business is borrowing to finance its operations. New businesses tend to have a high level of borrowing. The more a business relies on loans to exist, the more difficult the situation becomes if it wants to borrow further money.

There are several accounting ratios that can be used to identify the performance of the business. These ratios use the figures included on the balance sheet. Briefly, the four key ratios are:

- liquidity ratios (which show how well the business can cover its current liabilities with its current assets)
- solvency ratios (which look at the amount of money owed by a business, in terms of loans and overdrafts, compared with the money that it is actually making)
- efficiency ratios (which look at the business's ability to recoup money from debtors, how much credit is being taken from suppliers and how long the business is holding stock before selling it)

■ profitability ratios (which look at the net profit before income tax and at the amount of capital used by the business compared with how much capital it is creating).

See pages 71–72 in Unit 7, where the four key sets of ratios are looked at in more detail, and pages 86–94 in Unit 8 for preparation of financial statements.

Cash flow statement

A cash flow statement is useful when trying to predict the amount of cash that a business may require in the future. This is particularly helpful when the business has to weather a tough period with low sales.

The statement is also used to show how much money a business has generated in the past and where the funds were used. The net result shows the balance of money at the end of a given period of time. Using a cash flow, it is possible to identify the main areas of costs related to the business. These are known as the business's capital requirements. By calculating the capital costs, the business will be able to identify how much money it will need to fund itself.

See pages 94–105 in Unit 8 for monitoring and recording financial information.

Table 6.6 Cash flow forecast

	START-UP		1		2		3	
	F/CAST	ACTUAL	F/CAST	ACTUAL	F/CAST	ACTUAL	F/CAST	ACTUAL
Opening Balance	0	0	1,170	535	1,750	1,170	2,360	1,295
CASH/CHEQUES RECEIVED								
Received from Cash Sales	800	900	1,000	1,200	1,000	900	1,000	1,200
Received from Debtors	100	50	300	300	300	400	400	400
Other Income								
Capital and/or loans introduced	3500	3500						
TOTAL £	4,400	4,450	1,300	1,500	1,300	1,300	1,400	1,600
EXPENDITURE								
Materials/Stock/Subcontractors		120		160		120		
Wages	25	25	25	25	25	25	25	25
Directors remuneration (Ltd Co)								
Salaries – Administration								
Rent and rates		180						
Heating and lighting						100		
Insurances	20	20	20	20	20	20	20	20
Postage and stationery								
Repairs and renewals	15		15		15	90	15	
Travelling & motor expenses								
Telephone	40	40	30	30		115		
Professional fees								
Advertising		200				75		
Miscellaneous expenses								
Finance charges – Bank								

	START-UP		1		2		3	
	F/CAST	ACTUAL	F/CAST	ACTUAL	F/CAST	ACTUAL	F/CAST	ACTUAL
Finance charges – HP								
Interest								
Other payments								
VAT								
Taxation								
Personal drawings	600	600	600	600	600	600	600	600
Class 2 National Insurance	30	30	30	30	30	30	30	30
Capital expenditure	2,500	2,700						
TOTAL £	3,230	3,915	720	865	690	1,175	690	675
Income less expenditure (A–B)	1,170	535	580	635	610	125	710	925
i.e. monthly working capital								
Cumulative working capital	1,170	535	1,750	1,170	2,360	1,295	3,070	2,220
i.e. closing balance								

As you can see, the top half of the cash flow statement is either existing cash held by the business or income from trading for the period. This is totalled before turning to the expenses of the business. Each of the specific costs is detailed for each period and then these are totalled. The figure is deducted from the income or cash held by the business to produce a balance. In our case, the balance is always positive, but it is possible during the start-up period of a business for the balance to be negative (in other words, for the expenditure to be greater than the income). The business would then have to rely on other funds to pay its expenses (typically a bank loan or an overdraft).

When the calculation has been made for each period, the balance is carried forward as the opening balance for the next period. The process is continued until the whole period in question has been looked at.

Ultimately, a cash flow shows the business cycle. Income and expenditure are rarely timed to match one another. Often inflows of cash will lag behind outflows of cash. Ideally, at some point, there should be an occasion when there is more money coming in than going out. By creating a cash flow the business can begin to try to address these imbalances.

Although we will look at cash flows in considerable detail at the end of this chapter, it is important to note the different types of cash inflows and outflows. Typical cash inflows include:

- customer payments for products and services
- the receipt of a bank loan
- interest from any investments or savings
- incoming investments from shareholders
- an increased overdraft or loan.

Typical cash outflows include:

- payment for stock, raw materials or tools
- daily **operating costs**
- wages and rent
- the purchase of fixed assets
- dividend payments to shareholders
- loan repayments to lenders
- VAT
- corporation tax
- income tax
- a reduced overdraft.

Fig 6.8 Cash flow

There are several different ways in which a business can improve its cash flow, such as:

- encouraging customers to pay earlier
- chasing debtors
- selling invoices to debt factoring companies (The debt factor buys the debt owed to the business by a customer and pays around 80–90% of the outstanding debt; it then owns the debt and chases the customer for payment.)
- **extended credit** with suppliers
- ordering stock less often and only ordering what is needed
- **leasing** equipment rather than buying it.

For more information on debt factoring, look under 'debt recovery' in 'finance and grants' on the Business Link website

www.businesslink.gov.uk.

Users

Most people assume that the only groups interested in a business's accounting information would be its shareholders or owners. In fact, there are many other different users of accounts information.

Shareholders and potential investors

Whether individuals are already shareholders or are interested in investing in a business, their main concerns are the risks that they may be taking in investing and the possibility of a financial return on the investment. Both groups need information so that they can decide whether the business is a good investment. They will be looking to see whether the business will pay out dividends. Furthermore, they will also be looking to see how efficiently the business is managed; key figures on the profit and loss account and balance sheet will be useful here.

The two groups will want to know about:

- the business's growth, as shown by sales
- the business's profitability, in terms of its overall level of profit and profit margins
- its current investments, in terms of the cash value of investments and the assets that the business owns
- the market value of the business, as reflected in its share price
- how all these measures compare with those of similar competitors or other investment opportunities.

Directors, managers and employees

The business's directors will have an operational use for financial statements. From the profit and loss account and balance sheet, they will be able to see in clear detail precisely how well the business is performing as a result of their decision making and problem solving. They should be able to identify areas that are performing well and key areas of concern and apply relevant support where necessary.

For many employees below director level, the financial statements will be the only way that they can judge how the organisation is performing, particularly in relation to their contribution to the performance.

At a very basic level, anyone employed directly by the business is interested in its stability and its continuing profitability. This extends even beyond employment, because when employees retire they will want to know that their pension funds are safe and that they will receive their retirement benefits.

Individuals at any level of an organisation look to receive at least the competitive rates for their pay and benefits. In this respect, all employees are likely to be interested in:

- the business's revenue and profit growth
- how much the business is investing
- the numbers of individuals employed, their wages and salary costs
- the valuation of the business pension scheme and how much the company is putting into the pension.

Suppliers

Suppliers are likely to be trade creditors. Their primary concern is whether the business is able to pay its short-term debts to them. In other words, they will be looking at the short-term liquidity of their customer business. As far as financial statements are concerned, they will look for information regarding:

- cash flow – showing the key income and expenditure of the business and its relevant balances
- how much working capital (current assets to pay current liabilities) the business has and how it is managed
- what the business's payment policies are in relation to prioritising the payment of invoices.

Customers

Some customers are direct consumers, who purchase from the business; others are themselves businesses. The latter are known as trade debtors, as when they purchase products or services they expect to pay for them at a later date.

Both types of customer will have a longer-term interest in the business's ability to continue to trade, as they are used to buying, using or reselling its products and services. Therefore, they will be looking for information on:

- the development of new products
- sales figures and growth
- whether the business is investing in itself and increasing its capacity.

Lenders

Any individual or organisation that lends money to a business wants to know that the business is able to keep up the interest payments and pay back the loan when it is due. In this respect, lenders will focus on the following:

- the business's cash flow
- the security of any assets, against which lending has been secured
- the short-, medium- and long-term investment requirements of the business.

Government

Several government agencies and departments take an active interest in the financial information of a business. Local government requires businesses to pay local taxes and rates; HM Revenue and Customs handles VAT and collects corporation tax.

The business may also attract the interests of the Environment Agency, which looks at the impact that the business is having on the environment and makes a judgement as to whether its production and processes justify the contribution that the business is making to the country.

case study 6.3 — Sole trader and partnership final accounts

Table 6.7 Laura Buchan, Buchan Soft Furnishings

Trading and profit and loss account for the year ended 31 December 2008	£	£
Sales		112,000
Opening stock	12,500	
Purchases	70,500	
	83,000	
Less closing stock	10,500	
Cost of sales		72,500
Gross profit		39,500
Less overheads:		
Administration expenses	5,000	
Wages	20,000	
Rent paid	500	
Telephone	200	
Interest paid	1,100	
Travel expenses	300	
	27,100	
Net profit	12,400	

Table 6.8 Mr Smith and Mr Jones

Trading and profit and loss account for the year ended 31 December 2008	£	£	£
Sales			320,000
Opening stock (1 January 2006)		5,000	
Purchases	190,000		
Less goods for own use	900	189,100	
		194,100	
Less closing stock (31 Dec 2006)		10,000	
Cost of sales			184,100
Gross profit			135,900
Less overheads:			
Office expenses		8,000	
Wages to Mr Smith		33,000	
Vehicle expenses		5,000	
Provision for depreciation:			
Vehicles		4,000	

Trading and profit and loss account for the year ended 31 December 2008			
	£	£	£
Office equipment		1,000	
Net profit			51,000
			84,900
Share of profits:			
Mr Smith (50%)			42,450
Mr Jones (50%)			42,450
			84,900

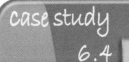

activity

INDIVIDUAL WORK
6.2

M1

Compare the final accounts of two organisations, explaining the similarities and differences. Using the two sets of accounts, answer the following questions:

1 What are the key similarities between the sole trader and the partnership accounts?

2 What are the main differences between the sole trader and the partnership accounts?

3 Identify the main legislations that determine how both the sole trader and the partnership accounts are presented and submitted.

4 Identify the main accounting concepts that are required in both sets of accounts.

case study
6.4

Limited company final accounts

Table 6.9 Name of company limited

Trading and profit and loss account for the year/period ended *** date ***			
	£	£	
Sales	x	(1)	
Opening stock	x		
Purchases or production costs	x		
	x		
Less closing stock	x		
Cost of goods sold		x	(2)
Gross profit (1) – (2)		x	(3)
Less expenses:			
e.g. Selling and distribution costs	x		
Administration costs	x		
Finance costs	x		
		x	(4)

Trading and profit and loss account for the year/period ended *** date ***			
	£	£	
Net profit for year before taxation (3) – (4)		x	(5)
Less corporation tax		x	(6)
Profit for year after taxation (5) – (6)		x	(7)
Less interim dividends paid			
Ordinary shares	x		
Preference shares	x		
Final dividends proposed			
Ordinary shares	x		
Preference shares	x		
		x	(8)
Retained profit for year (7) – (8)		x	(9)
Add balance of retained profit at beginning of year		x	(10)
Balance of retained profits at end of year (9) – (10)		x	(11)

Production costs will replace purchases in the case of a manufacturing organisation. Depreciation of fixed assets is included where appropriate (e.g. costs of production). Expenses also include debenture interest and directors' remuneration.

Table 6.10 Name of company limited

Balance sheet as at *** date ***				
	Cost (1) £	Dep'n (2) £	Net (1)–(2) £	
Fixed assets				
Intangible				
Goodwill	x	x	x	
Tangible				
Freehold land & buildings	x	x		
Machinery	x	x	x	
Fixtures & fittings etc.	x	x	x	
	X	x	x	(3)
Current assets				
Stock (closing)		x		
Debtors		x		
Bank		x		
Cash		x		
		x		(4)
Less current liabilities				
Creditors	x			
Bank overdraft	x			
Proposed dividends	x			
Corporation tax	x			
	x			(4)
Working capital (4) – (5)	x			(5)
			x	(6)

Balance sheet as at *** date ***				
	Cost (1) £	Dep'n (2) £	Net (1)–(2) £	
Debentures	x̱			(7)
Net assets (6) – (7)	x̱			
			Financed by **Authorised share capital**	
X (number) preference shares of £x (nominal value) each	x			
X (number) ordinary shares of £x (nominal value) each	x̱			
	x̱			
			Issued share capital	
X (number) preference shares of £x (nominal value)				
Each, fully/partly paid			x	
X (number) ordinary shares of £x (nominal value)				
Each, fully/partly paid			x̱	
			x	
Capital reserves				
Share premium account	x			
Revaluation reserve	x̱		x	
			Revenue reserves	
Profit and loss account		x		
General reserve		x̱	x̱	
Shareholders' funds			x̱	(9)

activity

INDIVIDUAL WORK 6.3

P2

Explain how a limited company's financial statements are influenced by the legal and regulatory framework to meet the needs of users. You should:

1. In respect of the trading and profit and loss account, explain the accounting concept behind the calculation, the legal requirements and the relevance to users of all of the calculations marked on the case study from (1) to (11).

2. In respect of the balance sheet, explain the accounting concept behind the calculation, the legal requirements and the relevance to users of all of the calculations marked on the case study from (1) to (9).

Note:

You should specifically look at the British Standards of SSAP 5, SSAP 9, SSAP 13, FRS 1, FRS 15 and FRS 18. Be aware of the fact that British Standards are gradually being replaced by International Accounting Standards. Check to see that they have not already been replaced. If so, you should look at IAS 1, IAS 2, IAS 7, IAS 16, IAS 18, IAS 38.

activity

INDIVIDUAL WORK 6.4

D1

Using the conventional formats for the trading and profit and loss account and the balance sheet, answer the following questions to help you justify the application of accounting conventions and regulations to ensure that the financial statements meet their users' needs:

1. Who are the main users of accounting?

2. What are their interests in the information and their requirements?

3. What are the relevant accounting concepts and regulations?

4. How have these had an impact on the creation and format of the financial statements?

Making appropriate adjustments to accounting information

At the end of a financial year, prior to the final accounts being prepared, it is common practice for businesses to create a trial balance; this is a list of all balances remaining on the ledger accounts, including the cash and bank balances.

In this section we will look at adjustments to trading and profit and loss accounts and balance sheets. The effect may appear on either the profit and loss account or the balance sheet.

Adjustments

A number of different adjustments can be made. For example, a prepayment for stationery would appear on a profit and loss account as sundry expenses, less prepaid amounts. In effect, this is stock that can be used for the next financial year. Because of this it is classed as a current asset and has to be included on the balance sheet under current assets. In this example, both financial statements have been affected.

Valuation of stock

It is important for the business to count the stock remaining at the end of a financial year. This means counting every single item in stock and then arriving at a total valuation.

Fig 6.9 Everything has to be counted

For the most part, accountants use the value at cost: in other words, the amount of money that the business paid for that stock. This may not, however, be a precise figure, as the valuation of the stock may not take into account changes in general market value. If, for example, a business purchased several items at the beginning of a financial year for £100, it could now find that it would only cost £75 to purchase that stock a year on. The question is whether the stock is worth £75 or the £100 that the business paid for it. A similar problem arises when stock has increased in value, perhaps due to rarity, fashion and trends. It is now more common for accountants to assign a market value to existing stock by valuing items at the price paid for the latest purchase of that stock item.

Depreciation on fixed assets (non-current)

We have already seen that fixed assets may decrease in value. The amount of depreciation is charged to the profit and loss account as an expense. On the balance sheet, however, the value of the fixed asset is shown at its original cost, minus the amount of depreciation to date.

The amount charged for depreciation is an expense and is therefore set against the profits of a business and found on the profit and loss account. As a fixed asset, taking depreciation into account, it is reduced in value, so it is included on the balance sheet under fixed assets, less depreciation.

Bad debts

A debtor is a customer, either an individual or another business, owing money to the business. A debtor becomes a bad debtor when they cannot pay their debt. In effect, a bad debt is a loss to the business. It is therefore treated in exactly the same way as any other losses or expenses and is charged against the profits of the business.

On a balance sheet, under current assets, there is an item detailing the amount of money owed by debtors. It is included under current assets to show a true and fair view of the likelihood of receiving this money; the amount of bad debt is subtracted from the debtor total. This gives a truer reflection of the current assets as far as debtors are concerned.

On a profit and loss account, bad debts are classed as a debit entry and therefore deducted from the profit of the business.

Provision for doubtful debts

As we have seen, making provision for doubtful debts means setting aside a certain amount of money to cover the likelihood of future bad debts. How this affects financial statements depends on whether the business feels that it is necessary to increase or decrease the provision. The normal course of action is for a provision to be set aside and then reviewed on an annual basis, to see whether any adjustments are required. Normally, a business sets a provision as a percentage of its average amount of debt at a given point over the year.

If, for example, a business is on average owed £5,000, it may choose to set a provision of 5%, which would be £250. It may choose to increase its provision to 10%, making the provision £500. On the balance sheet, under current assets, the debtors would be shown as £5,000. But the provision would then be deducted, making the actual current asset worth £4,500. On the profit and loss account it would be a debit entry, charged against the profits and shown as the difference between the existing provisions compared with the new provision, in this case £250.

Alternatively, the business may choose to decrease its provision for doubtful debt. Again under a balance sheet entry, the new provision would be subtracted from the debtor total in the current assets section. On the profit and loss account the figure by which the doubtful debt provision has been reduced is included as a credit entry, rather than as a debit entry, as less money is being set aside.

Accruals and prepayments

There are two key types of accrual. The first is the expenditure accrual when products or services have been received by the business but the related purchase invoice will not be included in the accounts until the next financial year. The rule is that it is not the date on the purchase invoice that determines which year the expenditure belongs to. It is actually determined by the date of supply of products or services. Where goods or services have been received by the end of the financial year, but the purchase invoice will not be processed until the next financial year, the cost needs to be accrued.

Alternatively, an income accrual is required when the business supplies products or services to a customer, but the sales income is not expected before the end of the financial year. In this case, the date of the sales invoice that has been raised does not determine which year the income belongs to. It is determined by the actual date the products or services were supplied. Consequently, where products or services have been supplied before the end of the financial year, but the sales invoice and payment will not be processed until the next financial year then the income should be accrued.

Prepayments also fall into two categories: expenditure and income. Prepaid expenditure is expenditure by the business that has been incurred and the purchase invoice is included in the accounts, but the products or services have not been received and will not be until the next financial year. The actual date on the purchase invoice does not determine which year the expenditure belongs to. This is determined by the date of the supply of the goods or services. If the purchase invoice has been processed but the products and services are not to be received until the next financial year, this is a prepayment and therefore an expenditure prepayment.

Prepaid income is money that the business receives where the sales invoice has been included in the accounts, but the products or services have not been supplied to the customer and will not be until the next financial year. Again the date of the sales invoice does not determine the year in which the income belongs. It is determined by the supply date. This means that, if the products or services are supplied after the end of the financial year but the sales invoice has been processed, that income should be prepaid.

Accounting information

A number of key accounting terms, which are associated directly with either the profit and loss account or the balance sheet, are described in this section. Note that adjustments made to accounting information will have a direct impact on them.

Assets

An asset is anything of value owned by the business. This includes cash. Assets appear on the balance sheet in terms of their cash value. Even if a business has used credit to purchase an asset, it still counts as an asset owned by the business. An asset's full cash value is recorded on one side of the balance sheet as an asset, but the amount that the business owes is recorded on the other side of the balance sheet as a liability.

There are, however, several different types of assets, some of which we have already encountered. We can identify four key types of asset:

- Current assets – these are assets with a cash value that will continually change. Prime examples are cash, money owed, stock or raw materials. They are sometimes listed on the balance sheet in order of their liquidity, which means the rate at which they can be converted into cash.
- Investments – companies can own shares in other companies or have made loans to individuals or other businesses. Just like cash and property, investments are considered to be assets.
- Capital assets – in the USA they call capital assets 'plant assets', as they are permanent things that the business owns. Land, equipment, vehicles and buildings are typical examples. The term is extended to include computers, furniture and appliances, as long as these are used by the business and are not items that the business sells.
- Intangible assets – a wide variety of non-material assets fits into this category; typical examples are copyrights, patents and goodwill. It is important to remember that, although intangible assets cannot be sold as physical items, they have a monetary value. Patents and copyrights could be sold to another business or individual. If the business were to be sold it would not just be worth the sum total of its physical assets and money that is owed to it. It would be worth more as it has established itself as a going concern and will have an existing bank of customers. This is shown as goodwill on the balance sheet.

Liabilities

Liabilities are amounts of money that a business may owe to individuals, businesses, banks or lenders. In effect there are two different types of liabilities, which are distinguished by the period over which they must be paid back. The two key liabilities are:

- Current liabilities – these are any cash liabilities that are required to be paid back within a year. These will include utility bills, unpaid invoices to suppliers, wages and salaries to employees, and any short-term loans.
- Long-term liabilities – these are business debts whose payment extends beyond the financial year. Typically, these would include longer-term loans, mortgages and extended credit from suppliers.

Income and expenditure

As we have seen, it is rare for income and expenditure to match one another so there will always be imbalances between the two. Obviously, a business's income primarily relies on its ability to sell and receive payment for products and services. There is a distinction between sales figures achieved and cash coming into the business. This is because there is often a difference between the actual sales figures and the business's ability to bring cash in as a result of issuing invoices. There will always be late payments, rescheduled payments and bad debts.

The balance between the actual incoming cash and the expenditure of a business determines its liquidity. The pressure points over a period of time are plain to see on a cash flow statement. A business can only fund itself to the extent at which it is able to bring in cash or secure additional funding. Expenditure has to be organised in such a way as to take into account the funds available from actual income.

It is normally the case that a new business will have a significantly higher level of expenditure than income. At some point, however, in order to be profitable and to survive, the business has to reverse this trend and ensure that income exceeds expenditure. At the very least the two need to be equal.

> **remember**
>
> A business may be investing the vast proportion of its surplus cash, either to consolidate or grow the business.

Balances in the trial balance

A trial balance is prepared towards the end of a financial period. It is important that the totals of the debit and the credit columns are equal. The trial balance should be zero.

The trial balance is derived from double-entry bookkeeping. However, trial balances do not always guarantee an error-free series of calculations. Transactions could have been put in the wrong account; for example debit and credit entries may have been transposed.

In effect, a trial balance is a worksheet and is used as a tool to identify errors in the bookkeeping.

Many businesses prepare three trial balances, these are:

> **remember**
>
> If the two sides do not balance one another out, there is an error and this needs to be found.

- The preliminary trial balance – this is prepared, using the double-entry bookkeeping records and before any adjustments are made.

- An adjusted trial balance – this is created after adjusting entries have been included. Ultimately, this will be the basis upon which the financial statements will be created.

- A post-closing trial balance is then created. This will normally contain only balance sheet accounts, making sure that the debits and credits are in balance for the beginning of the new financial period.

case study 6.5 | Limited company financial accounts

Table 6.11 Alun and Stuart Limited

Profit and loss account for year ended 31.3.07			
	£	£	£
Sales			387,000
Less sales returns			12,000
Net sales (turnover)			375,000
Less cost of goods sold			
Opening stock		42,000	
Purchases	212,000		
Less purchase returns	6,000		
Net purchases		206,000	
		248,000	
Less closing stock		27,000	
Cost of goods sold			221,000

Profit and loss account for year ended 31.3.07	£	£	£
Gross profit			154,000
Rent received			19,000
			173,000
Less expenses			
Administration			
Rent & rates	35,000		
Wages and salaries	81,000		
Insurance	4,100		
Motor expenses	4,400		
Debenture interest	6,200		
Depreciation			
Buildings			
Equipment	6,000		
Motor vehicles	3,500	140,200	
Net profit before tax		32,800	
Less corporation tax		16,200	
Profit for year after tax		16,600	

Table 6.12 Alun and Stuart Limited

Balance sheet as at 31.03.07	Cost £	Accumulated Depreciation £	Net Book Value £
			Fixed assets
Buildings	88,000	0	88,000
Equipment	42,000	8,000	34,000
Motor vehicles	18,000	12,000	6,000
	148,000	20,000	128,000
			Current assets
Stock		42,000	
Debtors	29,000		
		71,000	
Bank		19,000	
Cash		4,000	
		94,000	
		Less current liabilities	
Creditors	26,000		
Overdraft	0		
Proposed dividends			
Preference shares	0		
Ordinary shares	12,000		

Balance sheet as at 31.03.07	Cost £	Accumulated Depreciation £	Net Book Value £
Corporation tax	16,000		
		54,000	
Working capital			40,000
			168,000
Less long-term liabilities			
10% debentures			40,000
Net assets			128,000
Financed by:			
Authorised share capital			
100,000 ordinary shares at £1 each			100,000
			100,000
			Issued share capital
5,000 ordinary shares at £1 each			5,000
			5,000
			Revenue reserves
General reserve		6,400	
Profit and loss account		16,600	23,000
			128,000

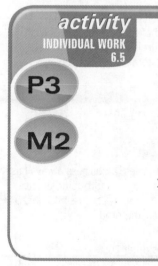

activity

Transfer the accounting information given in the case study to a spreadsheet.

activity

INDIVIDUAL WORK 6.5

P3

M2

1 For P3, use the spreadsheet that you devised for Case study 6.5 and make the following adjustments, commenting on the required changes and their implications:

    (a) Sales increase to £402,000

    (b) Purchases increase by £14,000

    (c) Rent received reduced by £2,500

    (d) Wages and salaries decrease by £1,500

    (e) Depreciation on buildings 20% more than predicted

    (f) Motor expenses up by 25%.

2 For M2, write a brief report assessing the impact of each of the adjustments that you have made. The following two questions should be focused on in particular:

    (a) What is the effect on profit and loss?

    (b) What are the effects on assets and liabilities?

Cash flow statement for a limited company

There are two different types of cash flow documents or worksheets. Both are usually created to show monthly figures. The first type of document is known as the **cash flow forecast**. It is a forecast because the business is estimating its future income and expenditure. The period of time covered is usually 12 months; many businesses amend the forecast on a quarterly basis.

The cash flow document of particular interest for this unit is the cash flow statement. This records the actual cash income and expenditure of the business. It can be compared with the cash flow forecast to see how accurate the business was in its estimates. It also helps the business understand and control its operations.

It is important to remember that in both a cash flow forecast and a cash flow statement only cash is involved. Sales that are made on credit are not included until the money has actually been paid or is due.

Purpose

The cash flow statement backs up the information included on a balance sheet and on the profit and loss account. It records the amounts of cash or equivalents entering and leaving the business. The primary purpose of the cash flow statement is to help the business, shareholders and potential investors understand the business's operations. It also illustrates to them where cash is coming from and where it is being spent.

Financial position

On a cash flow statement, it is relatively easy to see where cash is being generated from the business's operations, investment and financing. As a key measure the cash flow statement shows whether there is an increase or decrease in cash. If there is a sudden or even gradual decrease in available cash then the business could have problems. At a glance it is easy to see the relationship between the inflows and outflows of cash. In this way, it is possible to analyse what needs to be done in order to make quick corrections to the situation.

Liquidity

Liquidity is a measure of a business's immediate ability to pay its current liabilities from its current assets. Since the cash flow statement focuses on cash in and out of the business, this is a far quicker but more brutal way of judging whether a business can pay its own bills.

The cash flow statement ignores the fact that the business could borrow additional money to see its way out of a short-term cash flow problem. The business's owners or potential investors will be concerned as to whether the business can generate cash to pay for its current liabilities.

Businesses look to improve their liquidity. The primary way is to ensure that income is always in excess of expenditure and that gradually, over a period of time, a surplus of cash is generated. Businesses may choose to set aside some of this surplus to cover them over periods when, according to forecasts, there are likely to be short-term liquidity problems.

Use of funds

Broadly speaking, the use of funds can be allocated to one of two key areas:

- direct cost of sales
- running costs.

It is important to note that, regardless of the level of operations or sales, a business always has certain fixed costs that have to be paid, including rent, mortgages, wages and **business rates**. A business normally sets these costs against different parts of its operation and assigns what is known as a contribution to each product or service sold. In effect, the products and services finance the fixed costs by contributing a small proportion towards the total.

Fixed costs can also be referred to as running costs. But there are other costs directly associated with the actual level of operation. These are known as direct cost of sales or variable costs. As these costs are directly associated with the volume of sales, they will fluctuate. If, for example, a business normally sells 10 products a day and suddenly begins selling 100 products a day, it might appear that direct costs have increased 10-fold. This is not usually the case. The business may have to buy 90 more products from its suppliers, but it does not need to employ 10 times as many staff or spend 10 times as much on electricity bills.

It will be clear from a cash flow statement that the business is spending certain amounts on fixed costs every month. It will also be easy to see where there have been changes in the direct costs associated with selling or supplying products and services. Investors look for a business to limit its fixed costs but understand increases in direct costs if these are associated with increases in sales.

Relationship between profit and cash

In business studies there is often confusion between the terms profit and cash. There is a major difference between the two. Profit is the difference between income and costs. A business cannot spend its profits; it can only spend cash. Cash is notes and coins, whether in the bank or in the business's safe or tills.

There is, however, a strong relationship between the two. Cash is the most immediate sign on a cash flow statement of how well the business is doing. A business may be profitable, but it can run out of cash. A business needs money to cover its day-to-day running costs. This is known as working capital.

If a business's profits look good but it needs more cash, it may be able to find a lender. Cash can have a direct affect on profit, as in the long term the purchasing of machines, for example, could enable the business to make more products.

We will look at working capital in more detail shortly, as it is important to understand the crucial part that it plays in the short- and long-term fortunes of a business.

Sources of finance

In effect, there are three different sources of finance, these are:

- Loans obtained from lenders, in the form of short- or long-term loans or overdrafts – whilst these are classed as liabilities, in terms of a cash flow statement they are injections or sources of cash.

- Retained profit – businesses choose to set aside some of the profits that they make in order to reinvest that cash either to improve or replace machinery, processes or materials. Businesses may choose to hold on to some of their cash to deal with possible liquidity problems in the future, to set against possible bad debts or as a contingency fund should an immediate investment be required.

- Cash from investors – the owners or shareholders of the business will have made an investment when they purchased their share of the business. Every time a business issues shares, these are sold (in the case of public limited companies) on the open market at the current market value. The purchase of these shares brings vital new money to the business. It must, however, be careful in the amount of shares that it issues, as this may adversely affect the value of all investors' shares. Obviously, the business will have to pay dividends to the shareholders in return for their cash investment.

Costs of finance

The costs of finance can depend upon the source of the finance and the way in which it has been acquired. Typically, costs related to finance include:

- loan or current account interest
- overdraft payments
- other financial charges
- consultancy fees for filling in applications
- management fees or commission
- time taken by employees to fill in loan applications
- financing related to the purchase of equipment or buildings (such as mortgages)
- the cost of finance leases.

It is important for a business always to try to achieve the best deal when it attempts to obtain finance. **Interest rates** are often lower if better security for the loan is offered by the business. It is true to say that most finance tends to be risk related. This means that the more risk the lender attaches to the business, the higher the rate of interest that will be required to convince the lender to make the loan.

> **remember**
>
> Accounts only show a snapshot of a business's financial position.

Analysis of working capital

Traditionally, analysis of working capital looks at whether the business is in a position to pay its short-term liabilities. Working capital also shows potential investors, as well as the business's directors, just how well or efficiently the business is functioning.

There is what is known as a cash flow cycle, or cash conversion cycle, which is a measure of the efficiency of working capital. The cycle shows the average number of days that working capital is invested in operations. It measures just how long it takes for the investment of working capital to be converted into cash received by the business from its customers.

Comparison with previous periods

The first major comparison is between the cash flow statement and the cash flow forecast for the same period. Remember that the cash flow forecast is merely an estimation based on existing data of what the cash inflows and outflows are expected to be over a future period.

Whilst existing companies use trends and data from previous years to create cash flow forecasts, a new business does not have this advantage. A new business will find it very difficult to create a cash flow forecast and may well find that the actual cash flow statement for the same period is very different.

A business using previous periods looks to see if similar trends have occurred. The business also looks to see if any changes that were intended to improve cash flow have had the desired effect. By comparing cash flow statements from different periods it is possible to see the following:

- how the financial position of the business has changed
- if the business has a greater or lesser degree of liquidity
- the rate at which cash is actually being generated and brought into the business, compared with investments made
- the changing sources of finance and whether loans taken out in previous periods have been paid off or extended
- the comparative costs of finance compared with previous periods, certainly in terms of looking for better deals
- how the business is using its working capital and how the levels of working capital have changed.

See pages 94–104 in Unit 8 for more on recording and monitoring financial information.

case study 6.6

Cash flow

Fig 6.10

Heathfield Motor Caravans is a newly established motor caravan hire business. The owners, Jake and Jocelyn Heathfield, have four motor caravans that they house in a garage near to the market town of Beccles in Suffolk. They also have a small booking and administration office on the market square of the town.

The price of a week's hire per motor caravan is £850. In January and February, they have no customers. In March and December, they have one. In April and November, they have five; in May, they have nine. In June, July and August they have 12. In September, they have four and in October they have six. Income from travel insurance per booking is £65 and from cancellation insurance it is £25.50.

The business also has a modest income from servicing other people's motor caravans, but this only brought in £300 in March, £500 in May, £700 in July and £890 in October.

Salaries are £2,000 per month and payroll taxes are £800 per month. Office expenses run at £25 per month, and office rental is £230 per month. Garage rental is £800 per month, but the business receives £200 per month sub-renting it to four people who house their own motor caravans there. Utilities average at £120 per month; maintenance on the motor caravans is £60 each time one is hired out. Cleaning and laundry per hire is £12.50. Business insurance is £132 per month; brochure costs per month are £50, advertising is £240 per month and business rates are £3,600 payable in 12 instalments.

activity
INDIVIDUAL WORK 6.6

P4

M3

1   For P4, use the cash flow devised for Case study 6.6 and answer the following questions, which will help you to explain the purpose of a limited company's cash flow statement:

    (a)   What is the role of a cash flow statement?

    (b)   How does profit link with changes in assets and liabilities?

    (c)   What is the relationship between profit and cash?

2   For M3, assess the importance of the different elements of a cash flow statement by answering the following questions:

    (a)   What are the importance and contents of operating cash flows?

    (b)   What are the importance and contents of investing cash flows?

    (c)   What are the importance and contents of financial cash flows?

    (d)   What is the importance of a cash flow in terms of being able to measure the liquidity of a business?

    (e)   What are links between liquidity and survival?

activity
INDIVIDUAL WORK 6.7

D2

In this follow-up task to P4 and M3 you are required to evaluate the changes in the financial position of a limited company using a cash flow statement. You should:

1   Write a report reviewing the financial performance and position of the business.

2   Make a presentation answering the following questions:

    (a)   Where are the negative cash flows and what is their importance?

    (b)   Is the business making appropriate use of available funds?

    (c)   Is the business generating sufficient reserves of cash to fund further expansion and spending?

    (d)   What would an accountant be particularly interested in on the cash flow?

    (e)   Why would these be of interest to an accountant and what possible advice might be given or comments made?

Progress Check

1.   How might a partnership divide profit and loss?

2.   What do you understand by the term 'going concern'?

3.   Explain the term 'depreciation'.

4.   Which organisation created the framework for the preparation and presentation of financial statements?

5.   What are the key accounting principles?

6.   Briefly explain how assets are valued.

7.   List the official records that must be kept by a limited company.

8.   Which set of standards is gradually replacing the SSAPs?

9.   How might a business make an accounting preparation for unpaid invoices?

10.   Distinguish between cash and profit.

UNIT 7

Introducing Management Accounting

This unit covers:

- How production costs are determined and used to calculate prices
- Using break-even analysis
- Using statistical information to review and predict business performance
- Using budgetary techniques

Costs and pricing are closely linked and determine an organisation's profitability. It is important to know the point at which income covers costs and a business breaks even. This unit begins by looking at issues relating to costs and prices before explaining how break-even analysis is used.

The unit then goes on to examine how a business uses statistical information not only to review its current performance but also to predict how well it will perform over the longer term. The final section covers the budgetary techniques that a business uses when controlling its expenditure.

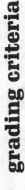

grading criteria

To achieve a **Pass** grade the evidence must show that the learner is able to:	To achieve a **Merit** grade the evidence must also show that the learner is able to:	To achieve a **Distinction** grade the evidence must also show that the learner is able to:
P1 describe how an organisation can cost a product and determine its price at any activity level　Pg 57	**M1** suggest activity levels using the results of break-even analysis for a selected organisation　Pg 66	**D1** evaluate the reliability of break-even analysis in estimating budgeted activity levels for a selected organisation　Pg 66
P2 carry out break-even analysis for a selected organisation　Pg 66	**M2** analyse the importance of accounting data and statistical information to assess and predict business performance　Pg 74	**D2** evaluate the implications of budget variances for a selected organisation　Pg 83
P3 describe how to use accounting data and statistical information to measure business performance　Pg 74	**M3** analyse the impact on a budget of changes in costs and selling prices for a selected organisation　Pg 82	
P4 use budgetary techniques to prepare budgets for a selected organisation　Pg 82		
P5 describe how budgets can be used to set targets, monitor and control an organisation　Pg 82		

How production costs are determined and used to calculate prices

It is essential that a business works out its production costs so that it can see what it can produce to make a profit and if anything that is being produced is making a loss. It also allows a business to identify parts of any production process that are unnecessary and needlessly increasing costs.

Essentially, costing can show a business the following:

- how much it costs to produce a product or carry out an activity, so that the business can then price the item accordingly
- how much of the total costs of the business can be directly related to a particular process or product
- which costs are currently too high
- which costs could be eliminated
- comparisons between the costs of different activities.

As we will see, there are two main types of costs involved in production:

- Direct costs include all the materials or **components** that go into making a product and also the direct labour costs or number of hours worked by employees and their cost.
- Indirect costs, which are known as overheads, are unavoidable costs; they include the rent on a factory, the wages of people not directly involved in production, lighting and a host of other costs.

Fig 7.1 Car manufacturing plants have direct costs, both in components and in labour

Once a business has established both its direct and indirect costs, it can then:

- work out the price that it should be charging its customers
- make a judgement as to which of its products is most profitable
- identify how it can save on its production costs.

Costs

Working out the costs related to production is not simple, particularly if the business has no real grasp of the costs involved in purchasing raw materials or components, or of how long it takes its employees to make products. It is also difficult to allocate portions of the business's overheads to particular products or areas of production.

Businesses take their costs in turn, calculating both the direct and the indirect costs, as well as what is known as semi-variable costs. Only by doing this can they hope to see precisely what production costs and if they are charging the right price for their products or activities.

Direct and variable costs

Direct costs, as we have seen, are costs that can be directly associated with production. It is important to remember that these direct costs are not fixed. In other words, the direct costs will vary according to the business's activity level.

The direct costs for producing 100 products may be £1,000, but if 200 products are manufactured over the same period the direct costs will increase. This is what is meant by variable costs. These costs represent payments made for raw materials, labour and fuel. If production or output rises, these costs also rise, as extra costs will be incurred to purchase the raw materials, run the machinery, and either more employees would have to be taken on or existing employees paid more through overtime.

Direct or variable costs rise proportionately with the level of output. Under normal circumstances, it is reasonable to assume that if the output increases by 50% then the direct or variable costs will increase by a similar amount. This does not of course take into account the fact that if the business is purchasing half as much more raw materials it could negotiate a lower price with its suppliers.

It is, however, reasonable to assume that as output increases so variable costs increase. As we will see, when direct variable costs are shown on a graph, the line depicting them rises gradually as output increases.

Typical direct variable costs are outlined below.

Raw materials
Many businesses use raw materials (e.g. crops, meat, metals, wood or paper) in their production. The price of raw materials varies according to the overall demand for them in the market place, and businesses seek to obtain their raw materials at the most competitive price. Businesses would certainly seek additional discounts if they consume more than was originally anticipated.

Unfinished goods
These are essentially components or part-processed materials that a business has purchased from another manufacturer or even from a primary producer. Unfinished goods could be flour in a bakery or rivets that will be used to hold the panels of a car together. As components have been already processed, they attract a higher price than raw materials.

Direct labour costs
The actual number of employees and the skills required depend on the production process. Some production processes require a few extremely well-trained staff to manage a largely automated line; others use semi-skilled labour to carry out repetitive tasks on basic production lines. Car manufacturing and food processing are examples of the two extremes.

Direct expenses
These are all the other costs directly associated with the production of products, including the fuel or energy required to run a production line and the lighting that enables employees to see what they are doing. Any ongoing maintenance on the machinery in the production line also counts as a direct expense. Direct expenses need to be factored into the overall costs of producing the products.

Depreciation
Depreciation measures the current value of machinery and any raw materials, unfinished goods or finished goods. After purchase, the value of machinery is bound to decline as it has been used. For example, once a car is bought from a car showroom and driven just a mile or so it is worth considerably less, as it is now second hand. A business needs to factor in the loss in the value of its assets that comes from using them. Materials that are unused and those that are part-processed may also fluctuate in value. Prices may fall in the market, but the business still has materials that it purchased at a higher price. Largely, however, depreciation is associated with the loss in the value of major assets directly associated with production.

Semi-variable costs

Direct variable costs are straightforward enough to classify, as they are directly associated with the output level of a business. Some costs, however, which are also associated with output levels, fluctuate in a different way.

The same business that has been producing 100 products may use a single delivery truck to take the **finished products** to its customers. The costs of operating the vehicle may appear to be fixed but are not. If output increases, the delivery truck will have to make more journeys more often. The vehicle will need to be serviced on a more regular basis; more fuel will be consumed, and the vehicle will almost certainly wear out far quicker with the higher demand for deliveries.

The costs associated with the vehicle are partly fixed because the vehicle has to be purchased and a driver has to be paid. The business also has to insure the vehicle and pay road tax for it. These are relatively fixed in terms of cost. But when the vehicle is used more frequently, additional variable costs have to be taken into account. The vehicle is therefore a semi-variable cost, linked directly to the output of the business.

Stepped costs

Suppose that we use the same example as we used for semi-variable costs. There may come a point when the output of the business increases to such an extent that the current driver and the vehicle cannot cope with the number of deliveries required. A second vehicle and driver have to be paid for.

This is an example of a stepped cost. The level of activity of the business has reached a threshold at which current systems are under serious strain; once the threshold has passed current systems cannot cope, and additional expenses have to be incurred in order to continue working at the higher level.

Indirect costs

Indirect costs are also known as overheads. Although incurred by a business to maintain its overall activities, these costs are not directly related to the production of the products. Indirect costs are general management costs. Typical examples are the costs of administration and of the employees and activities that support the production system: sales, marketing, accounts and other areas.

Indirect costs are, however, directly related to the running of the business and the manufacture and sale of the products. They are the costs of the support services necessary for acquiring raw materials and components, paying the employees on the production line, and selling the finished products to a range of different customers. As we will see, production has to shoulder the costs of all of the rest of the business because it is the only part that actually produces something that can be sold.

Fixed costs

Fixed costs are any type of cost that does not vary with the level of output. Fixed costs exist whether the business is producing one product or a million. Fixed costs include:

- rent
- business insurance
- payment to salaried employees
- interest paid on loans
- business rates paid to local authorities
- depreciation.

No matter what a business does in terms of its production, the fixed costs will rarely change. The rent on an empty factory would be exactly the same as the rent on the factory if it were full of machinery and busy employees. This means that fixed costs remain high even if the business is not very busy.

For our purposes, we are considering fixed costs over the short term, so they do not change. But it is important to be aware that they might in the long term. For example, a business that is doing particularly well and has gradually increased its output may need additional loans, a larger factory space and more machinery. Interest payments would rise and so would the rent.

We now have all of the basic components that are needed to work out the cost of production. We can say that adding the total fixed costs to the total variable costs will give us the total costs of production. However, this is only the beginning because, in order to work out the actual selling price of a product, we need to take into account the number of products being produced. Once this is done, we can decide how much of the total costs should be allocated to each product, add a desired level of profit and then arrive at our selling price.

Cost centres and profit centres

Not all parts of an organisation are directly involved in bringing in revenue. Large businesses are often split into departments, each of which may be a cost centre. In schools or colleges, departments are cost centres. Each department spends money on teachers' salaries, stationery and books; it also consumes energy in the form of lighting and heating. A fixed amount is allocated to the departments to cover all of their costs, and departments would be expected to spend only within the budget that they have been allocated.

Some parts of an organisation bring revenue directly into the business. Broadly speaking, a production department is a profit centre, and all of the support services, including sales, are cost centres. What then would you class as a profit centre or a cost centre in a college? It is the teachers who produce revenue, as indirectly their expertise has attracted students to the college.

Identifiable profit and cost centres are set up for:

- accounting purposes – so that the business can monitor the activities and performance of each part of the organisation
- organisational reasons – so that the business can see which parts of the organisation are doing well
- motivational reasons – so that departmental managers can control their own budgets and spending. They will attempt to make their area more profitable than others.

In order to identify a cost centre a business may choose one of the following options:

- by product – so that each different product is a different cost centre
- by machines – so that particular areas of work can be assessed by their costs and their revenue
- by department – so that specific areas of activity in the business are classed as separate centres
- by location – so that each separate geographical location is a separate cost centre
- by individual – so that managers within the organisation are held responsible for their own spending and income.

Businesses choose cost and profit centres according to their type. For example, a business with several different products may opt for product-based division, whereas a business with several different locations might opt for division by location.

Non-production (service) department overheads

As we have seen, overheads are costs that are used to support the business as a whole. It is difficult to directly allocate these costs because the services are used by several different internal departments or cost centres. It is therefore necessary to allocate these overheads across a range of cost centres.

The costs of any service provider include employee and other costs. The main point is to allocate costs on a reasonable basis, according to the level of work that each service provides to each cost or profit centre.

Overheads allocation

The performance of a business's profit or cost centres depends very much on how the business has decided to allocate the indirect costs. As an example, let us consider a business that produces two different products; we'll call the first product A and the second product B. The business makes 500 of product A and 1000 of product B.

Product A sells for £10, bringing in total revenue of £5,000; product B also sells for £10, bringing in total revenue of £10,000. The cost of producing all the units of product A is £5, so the total cost is £2,500. The cost of producing all the units of product B is £4, so the total cost is £4,000.

The business decides to spend £1,000 on advertising both products. The way in which the costs of the advertising, which is a non-production or service overhead, are allocated will have a drastic impact on the profitability of the two products. Table 7.1 shows what would happen if the allocation were to be split evenly between the two products.

Table 7.1 Allocation of costs between Products A and B

Product A		Product B	
Sales revenue	£5,000	Sales revenue	£10,000
Direct costs	(£2,500)	Direct costs	(£4,000)
Marketing spend	(£500)	Marketing spend	(£500)
Profit	£2,000	Profit	£5,500

Note that the cost figures have been presented in brackets. This is a common convention.

Although the marketing costs have been apportioned on a 50:50 basis, the impact on product A is more drastic than the impact on product B: the £500 being 20% of the potential profit for product A. On the other hand, the £500 represents just 8.33% of the potential £6,000 profit for product B.

An alternative would be to split the overheads on the basis of the quantities produced, which would mean allocating approximately 66p to each product sold. Product A's contribution would then be £330, and product B's would be £660. This would leave £10 unallocated, but for our purposes this allocation seems to be an acceptable split. The effects on profits are shown in Table 7.2.

Table 7.2 Effects on profits

Product A		Product B	
Sales revenue	£5,000	Sales revenue	£10,000
Direct costs	(£2,500)	Direct costs	(£4,000)
Marketing spend	(£330)	Marketing spend	(£660)
Profit	£2,170	Profit	£5,340

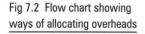

remember

When looking at the performance figures for each centre it is important to remember how the costs have been allocated, because not taking these into account could mean fewer resources being allocated to a cost centre in the future.

As we can see from the two examples, the allocation of indirect costs or overheads can have an effect on how each cost centre's performance appears.

We will shortly be looking at other ways in which costing can help to allocate overheads.

Apportionment

Apportionment means sharing out. A business should fairly and reasonably split its costs between the cost centres, so that none is adversely affected.

It is sometimes difficult to apportion costs, but a business will usually resort to looking at each cost centre's use of support services and try to apportion according to the level of use.

As not all costs can be apportioned to business activities that produce revenue, part of the costs has to be applied to other cost centres. A business categorises its costs and then apportions on a fair basis.

Fig 7.2 Flow chart showing ways of allocating overheads

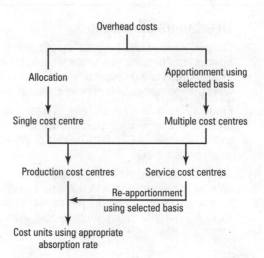

Overhead absorption rate

Overhead absorption rate is a means by which overheads can be attributed to particular products or services. This could be on direct employee hours or machine hours. As we will see, overhead absorption rates are required when using the full-cost method of pricing products and services. A business's overhead absorption rate can be calculated using the following formula.

Fixed production overheads/levels of activity = overhead absorption rate

Absorption costing

This is, as we will see, a version or improvement on full-costing methods. Rather than allocating total overheads proportionately to each cost centre, each overhead is absorbed by cost centres on an appropriate basis, meaning that the allocation depends on the type of cost.

Typical examples include:

■ allocation of rent and rates overhead – based on the physical area taken up by the cost centre (this would also be true of heating and lighting costs)

■ canteen overhead costs – by the number of employees in the cost centre (this would also be the case for health and safety costs and personnel costs)

■ depreciation overhead costs – based on the value of any **capital equipment** used by the cost centre (this would also be the case for insurance).

In practice, this means that the business needs to collect rather more information on its cost centres than is usual. It will have to know the total number of employees and the square metres taken up by each cost centre and will have to carry out an evaluation of any capital equipment. The key advantages of absorption costing are that:

■ To a large extent it is considered to be fair, as cost centres that use more or are bigger pay more.

■ The business can try to make an accurate judgement as to the cost of each unit of output. This will be of particular use when establishing the pricing policy.

The main disadvantages are that:

■ It is sometimes difficult to divide costs, for example some parts of the business or its employees may be used by more than one cost centre.

■ It is more expensive to set up and run, as things need to be measured and assets valued.

Activity-based costing

This type of costing is used to determine the actual costs associated with each product or service that is made or offered by the business. In order to carry out activity-based costing a business will need to:

■ analyse its activities

■ gather the costs

■ trace the costs to activities

■ establish output measures then analyse costs.

Direct labour costs, as well as materials, are fairly easy to trace directly to products. Indirect costs are rather more difficult to pin down; some overheads, such as senior management salaries, are very difficult to assign.

Activity-based costing, or ABC, was developed as a more accurate way of dealing with the traditional problems experienced when older cost management systems are used to determine actual production and service costs. Without using ABC businesses cannot really make good decisions, as they are working from inaccurate data.

remember

ABC does not change the costs. It shows where the costs were incurred.

Table 7.3 shows a traditional way of breaking down costs compared with an ABC version:

Table 7.3 Breaking down costs

Traditional		ABC	
Wages and salaries	£2,000	Clean main drain	£750
Equipment	£1,000	Construct new manholes	£1,500
Supplies	£2,000	Inspect sewer system	£1,500
Overheads	£1,000	Fit new main sewer	£2,250
Total costs	£6,000	Total cost	£6,000

The ABC system directly associates costs with products and services. It assigns costs to activities based on the latter's use of resources. It is then possible to assign the cost to objects, such as products or customers. The ABC approach allows for:

- activities and processes (by comparing before and after)
- the frequency and cost of the activity or process (again comparing before and after)
- not doing anything (to see what would happen if the business did not do the project)
- identifying which processes provide value (both to attract and retain customers and to result in savings for the business).

Marginal costing

When marginal costing is used, valuations of a cost centre's costs are based on direct costs. Overheads tend to be excluded from the total costs for the centre; they are only applied when the business prepares its profit and loss account.

Marginal costing is also known as contribution costing, as financial decisions in the business are based on contribution (the amount of money from the sale of a product that can be made available for the business to pay off its fixed costs). The following formula is used.

Contribution per unit = selling price – marginal or direct costs

If a business produces a product that has direct costs of £100 per unit and then sells that product for £150, the £50 made on the product can be put to paying off part of the business's overheads. In other words the single sale has contributed £50 to fixed costs.

The primary concern is that the products are always sold for more than the direct costs; otherwise the business would never be able to pay off its fixed costs. Once all fixed costs have been covered any further sales are profit.

Marginal costing allows a business to compare different cost or profit centres. But it does not necessarily allocate any of the costs on a fair basis.

Standard costing

Manufacturers that want to measure the exact cost of processing and delivering a single unit of production often use standard costing. The way in which the standard cost is calculated differs from business to business, but the underlying principle is that the standard cost is the ideal cost. In other words, it is what the product should cost to produce, rather than what it does cost to produce.

Actual costs will of course differ over time: raw materials, parts and components may fluctuate in price. Similarly, there may be a change in the number of defective products made.

Prices

Whether it sells products or services, a business has to decide how flexible its pricing policy will be. When its pricing policy is very inflexible, a business expects a certain amount of profit from every product or service. A more flexible policy takes into account features such as discounts for multiple purchases. Ultimately, the choice is between:

- ensuring a standard level of return per unit sold with the prospect of not selling as many units as the business would wish
- a more practical approach that considers the total amount of turnover, or income, to be more important than the amount made per unit.

Cost plus

Cost plus pricing is also known as full cost plus pricing. It aims to arrive at a price that takes into account all of the costs of production. Typically, the following formula would be used.

$$\frac{\textit{Budgeted factory cost + selling and distribution costs + other overheads + mark-up on costs}}{\textit{Budgeted sales volumes}}$$

In order to appreciate exactly how it works, we will look at an example of a business that only makes one type of product.

Table 7.4 Cost plus pricing 1

Fixed costs	
Factory production costs	£75,000
Research and development	£25,000
Fixed selling costs	£55,000
Administration and other overheads	£32,500
Total fixed costs	£187,500
Variable costs	
Variable cost per unit	£0.80
Mark-up	
Mark-up % required	35%
Budgeted sale volumes (units)	500,000

The business now has to work out the total costs of production in order to calculate the selling price of the units on a full cost plus basis.

Table 7.5 Cost plus pricing 2

Total fixed costs	£187,500
Total variable costs (£0.80 x 500,000 units)	£400,000
Total costs	£587,500
Mark up required on cost (£587,500 x 35%)	£205,625
Total costs (including mark up)	£793,125
Divided by budgeted production (500,000 units)	
= Selling price per unit	£1.586 (or £1.59)

The main advantages of cost plus pricing are:

- They are straightforward to work out.
- Prices can be increased (with justification) if the costs increase.
- Assuming that competitors have similar costs, the prices across the industry will be fairly stable.

There are, however, disadvantages:

- Cost plus pricing ignores **price elasticity of demand**, as it does not take into account that a business could charge a different price (either higher or lower). It is important to remember that the potential demand is reliant on the customer's response to the price changes.

Link
See page 61–62 for more on price elasticity of demand.

- Under the cost plus system the business has less of an incentive to control its costs. If the costs increase, the selling price increases, and the price rise could make the business less competitive.

- The allocation of contributions to the overheads is not sufficiently precise. The total overheads need to be assigned to each product made by the business; sometimes this assignment is not clear or fair.

- If budgeted costs are overestimated, the business will try to sell its products at a price that is higher than needed. This could lead to a fall in the demand for the products. The business will be left with expensive unsold stock and lower profits.

Settling on the percentage mark-up is difficult; it is often dependent on a number of different factors, including:

- Whether the business should adopt the same kind of mark-up used by its competitors

- Whether the business should abandon its mark-up percentage if it is selling bulk orders to particular customers

- If the business should abandon the mark-up and sell its products at a lower price so that it can take a larger share of the market.

- Also, if the business's products are already established in the market, there may be an argument for having a higher percentage mark-up because customers would still buy the products at a higher price.

- A product goes through a series of stages in its life: initial launch (when traditionally the price is low to establish the product in the market); level sales as the product gains and retains its share of the market; and finally the product's decline as it falls out of favour with customers. It could be argued that the mark-up should be different at each stage in order to match the needs of the product at that particular time.

Discounting

Once a business has worked out all of its costs and allocated overheads to each product, it will have a total cost for each product. At the very least, the business needs to achieve this figure in order just to break even on producing and selling the product. Breaking even, however, is not something that a business can be prepared to do for the long term. It does not allow for profit to be made and makes it difficult for the business to make any investment.

Discounting, therefore, has to be carefully considered and the decision will usually be based on the following considerations:

- If the customer is purchasing multiple products, a discount from the usual selling price is often expected. But this must not be below the actual cost for the product (except in exceptional circumstances).

- The business should consider the fact that sales may be lost if discounts are not offered; therefore it must accept less profit per unit in order to achieve overall a higher income from the bulk sale.

- If a product is performing badly, discounting could possibly stimulate sales. The reduction in the selling price, coupled with some advertising or promotion, may attract customers who were reluctant to purchase the product at the previous price. This discounting situation can be temporary, and the business may be able in the future to return to the original sales price.

- If a product is reaching the end of its effective life and has been superseded by newer and better ones, there may be no other alternative but to make a serious cut in price by discounting, in the hope that excess stock can be cleared. At this point, the products would have probably been in stock for a considerable period of time. The cash tied up in this stock is not available to the business; discounting and achieving whatever price is possible will release this cash for other activities.

Pricing policies, production and costs

In an ideal world an organisation would set its production levels, know its costs and be able to set its pricing policies accordingly. However, it is not always possible to synchronise sales and production. Neither is it possible wholly to control costs.

The net effect of changing a pricing policy will undoubtedly impact on production and costs. Production is based on forecast sales; therefore, costs of raw materials and other direct costs are known. If, as a result of the pricing policy, there is a mismatch between sales and production, there will be problems.

- If the pricing policy encourages greater sales, production will be out of step with demand. Costs will rise as direct variable costs increase. The pricing policy needs to be able to absorb these additional costs, particularly if they are in excess of the costs that were directly attributable to each production unit before the production increased.

- If the pricing policy does not stimulate demand then production will exceed demand. In other words, supply will exceed demand, and the business will be making products that it has no immediate and realistic chance of selling. All costs related to the production of the excess products will be tied up until those products are sold. This can mean that either the pricing policy is incorrect or the production levels are too high.

Fig 7.3 It is never wholly possible to control costs

Income

Businesses can choose to receive a set income, based on a forecast number of sales at a known price that generates known revenue. The business's expectation is that its costs, both direct and indirect, will be covered. This approach requires production levels to be set in advance and the problem is that demand will inevitably fluctuate.

The alternative is to seek a higher level of income by having a more flexible pricing policy.

In the first example, a business may have been rigidly sticking to a cost-plus pricing system. The more flexible approach would encompass discounting. The business will seek a sale at a reasonable price, provided that it has covered the costs assigned to that product. In other words, turnover or revenue is more important than achieving standardised revenue that covers costs.

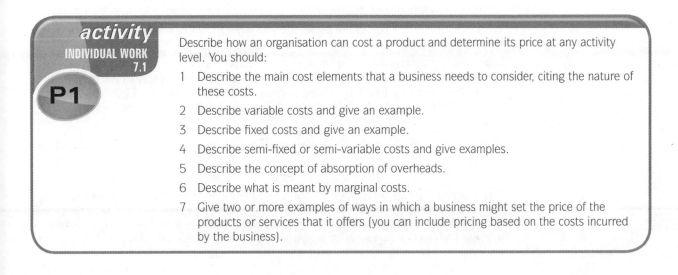

activity

INDIVIDUAL WORK
7.1

P1

Describe how an organisation can cost a product and determine its price at any activity level. You should:

1   Describe the main cost elements that a business needs to consider, citing the nature of these costs.

2   Describe variable costs and give an example.

3   Describe fixed costs and give an example.

4   Describe semi-fixed or semi-variable costs and give examples.

5   Describe the concept of absorption of overheads.

6   Describe what is meant by marginal costs.

7   Give two or more examples of ways in which a business might set the price of the products or services that it offers (you can include pricing based on the costs incurred by the business).

Using break-even analysis

Break-even analysis is an extremely important tool for examining the relationship between a business's income and expenditure. As the name implies, break even applies to the point at which a business's levels of sales are neither high enough to make a profit nor low enough to make a loss. In other words, the earnings of the business are just sufficient for the business to cover its total costs. Obviously, this is the point at which the total revenue from sales exactly equals the total costs of production and all overheads.

In reality, of course, a business would never actually be able to determine a precise time or day when break even occurred. So, break-even analysis looks at the point when (hopefully) the business has covered all of its costs by generating sufficient sales.

Break-even analysis

As we will see, there are two key ways in which break even can be calculated. Neither is particularly complicated, but it is important that all the key elements and figures that are required for the calculation of the formula and the drawing of the graph are used.

When a business's total revenue exceeds its total costs, it has made a profit. But break-even analysis takes this even further by identifying the relationship between costs and revenue, as well as identifying levels of activity that would generate a profit and levels of activity that would create a loss.

Contribution and break-even formula

When the break-even point is calculated, the following information is required:

- the selling price of the product
- the business's fixed costs
- the variable costs per unit of production.

Fixed costs do not change even when demand or output changes (Figure 7.5). Fixed costs have to be paid no matter what, so they must be included in the calculation.

Variable costs, on the other hand, do change in line with demand and output (Figure 7.6). As we have seen, when output increases more raw materials, components and labour are needed.

To work out the break-even output level, the following formula is used.

Fixed costs/selling price per unit – variable costs per unit

The following example shows how this works.

Laura runs a ghostly pub tour of Norwich. She runs her trips twice a day. The maximum number of people on each tour is 20 and the cost of the tour includes a drink in each of the five pubs that she visits. The cost for the five drinks per person is £5 each, so the total cost to her of each tour is £100. Laura, however, has decided to charge £12 per person per trip. She has already arranged the drinks in each pub, so that they are ready when the party arrives. So this is her fixed cost per trip.

We now know the first part of our break-even output level formula. We need now to work out the rest of it.

Laura also gives each customer a small, printed booklet explaining each of the haunted sites. These are £2 each at cost to her. We can now begin to work out the break-even output. Laura's fixed costs are £100; the selling price per unit is £12 minus the £2 for the booklet. In other words, if we take the £2 from the £12 the amount that is left is the contribution made by each customer to Laura's fixed costs.

Putting these costs into the formula, we have the following.

$$£100/£12 - £2 = \frac{£100}{£10}$$

This means that Laura would need 10 customers per trip in order to cover her fixed costs. Since she is averaging 20 per trip and she is doing two trips per day, she is in fact more than covering her fixed and variable costs. She is attracting 20 more customers than she needs to break even and taking her variable costs into account, this means she is in profit by £200 per night.

Break-even graph

A break-even graph can produce almost exactly the same information, but it can reveal rather more than using the simple formula seen on page 58. In fact, it can show a business's revenues and costs at all levels of demand and output.

The three elements required are the costs, revenues and output levels. First a suitably scaled graph is created, and the first piece of information required is the total amount of fixed costs of a business. This will always appear as a horizontal line, parallel to the X-axis. Note that these fixed costs remain the same, regardless of the level of output.

The second item to add is the variable costs. These, as seen, are in direct relation to the level of output. The variable costs, when no units of production are being created, will be zero and then they will continue upwards, again in a straight line, reflecting additional costs as the output of the business increases.

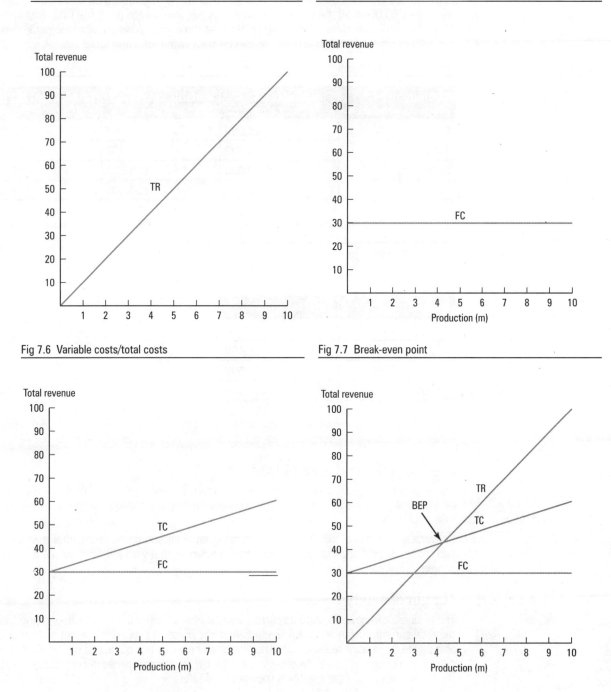

Fig 7.4 Total revenue

Fig 7.5 Total fixed costs

Fig 7.6 Variable costs/total costs

Fig 7.7 Break-even point

The third element to add is the total costs. Note that the total costs will include both the fixed and the variable costs, so it will be a diagonal line, just like the variable costs. The major difference is that the total costs will begin at the zero point on the units of production, but rise from the fixed cost line on the cost side of the graph. It should run parallel to the variable cost line.

The final line to add is the total revenue. This line will begin at zero on both axes of the graph. The total revenue line will rise as the units of production increase. If we know the sale price of each unit then we can calculate the total revenue generated by selling 100, 1000 or 10,000 units. This will produce another straight line.

Where the total revenue line crosses the total cost line, this is the break-even point.

Break-even point

Let's work through an example to illustrate how the break-even point is identified:

A business has fixed costs of £5,000. The business has worked out that its total variable costs per unit produced are £5. This means that if the business did not produce any units at all its total variable costs would be 0. If it produced 10,000 units then its variable costs would be £50,000. On the break-even chart it is possible now to place the fixed cost line at £5,000. A little calculation is required to arrive at the correct position for the variable costs and help us work out the total costs, as can be seen in the following table:

Table 7.6 Break-even point

Quantity of products produced	Fixed costs (FC)	Variable costs (VC) @ £5 per unit	Total costs (TC) (FC + VC)
0	£5,000	0	£5,000
1000	£5,000	£5,000	£10,000
5000	£5,000	£25,000	£30,000
10,000	£5,000	£50,000	£55,000

In order to complete our calculations we now need to know how much the business sells its products for. We will set the price at £6.50. Using the same range of output figures we then have the following:

Table 7.7 Output/total revenue

Output	Total revenue
0	0
1000	£6,500
5000	£32,500
10,000	£65,000

It is now possible to plot all of the figures onto the graph. As we have seen, where the total revenue line crosses the total cost line the break-even point has been achieved.

Area of profit and area of loss

The area of profit is any level of output beyond the break-even point and between the total revenue line and the total cost line. The business can see what level of output achieves the best total revenue.

Conversely, the area of loss is below the break-even point and between the total revenue line and the total cost line. This will illustrate to the business that with a limited output it will not achieve break even.

Margin of safety

The business can now calculate its current margin of safety. The margin of safety represents the total current output and total revenue. In other words, it shows the current level of output at a point on the total revenue line. The difference between this point and the break-even point is the margin of safety. In other words, the bigger the gap between current sales and the break-even point, the greater is the margin of safety.

A business needs to be aware of its margin of safety as this indicates the amount by which demand for its products or services can fall before it starts making a loss.

Fig 7.8 Profit/loss and margin of safety

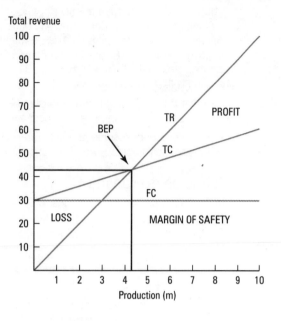

Budgeted activity and sales levels

A budget, as we will see later in this unit, is a plan that sets out the business's future financial targets: in this case, level of production or activity and sales levels.

Budgets are for a defined period of time and are designed to provide a focus for the business so that it can improve its control; they are always prepared in advance. Note that a budget:

■ is a financial plan

■ helps the business quantify financial targets

■ is often expressed in terms of cash

■ is an agreed plan of action.

Forecasts, however, are not budgets. Forecasts are predictions of the future, and budgets are agreed levels of activity or sales.

Budgeted activity levels seek to place the actual output and the consequent sales further away from the break-even point, giving the business a greater margin of safety.

As you can imagine, an actual change in the unit price charged by the business would have a marked effect on the total revenue. It would, therefore, also have a marked effect on the break-even point. The total revenue line would be steeper, as more revenue is being generated per unit. This means that the total revenue line will cross the total costs line at a lower level of output.

Conversely, a drop in the price per unit would make the total revenue line shallower and it would cross the total cost line further along in terms of output.

What a budget seeks to do is to identify the best course of action in terms of production and sales where, for similar effort, the business can cover its total costs more easily, either by increasing the sale price or by dropping the price and selling significantly more units.

Numerical calculations

Unfortunately just making the decision to drop (or raise) prices is not the answer. The outcome will depend on the demand for the product at the lower (or higher) price.

Some products are what are known as 'elastic'. Price elasticity of demand measures the responsiveness of customers' demand to a change in the price. It is not about whether or not demand changes: it is the degree of change that is important. A business needs to know whether, if it were to cut its prices, demand would rise by, say, 5%, 10% or 100%. Some products are very sensitive to price changes, others less so.

Price elasticity can be calculated using the following formula.

Price elasticity = the percentage change in quantity demanded/the percentage change in price

A business could see the net effect of price changes by experimentation. It could also try to judge the changes in demand if one of its competitors changes prices. If, for example, a business increased its prices by 10%, it might see a 20% fall in sales. Using the formula we simply divide 20 by 10 to give us a figure of 2. This is actually –2, expressed as a percentage and indicates to the business that for every 1% change in the price of the product the demand is likely to change by 2%.

Note that there is a negative relationship between price and quantity demanded. It suggests, therefore, that a drop in price will boost sales, and a price rise will reduce sales.

There are exceptions: some products rarely change in terms of their demand, as they are either extremely luxurious goods or absolute basics.

Changing overheads

A change in the costs of overheads will affect several aspects of the break-even chart:

■ The fixed cost line will move, as either the overheads have increased, in which case the line will move up, or they have fallen, in which case the fixed cost line will drop.

■ There will be a consequent change in the total cost line. If the overheads have increased this line will be steeper, and if the overheads have dropped then this line will run at a gentler angle.

■ The net result is that the total revenue line will cross the total cost line at a different point, changing the break-even point.

■ The area of profit and the area of loss will change, as will the margin of safety.

Direct costs

A similar effect will take place if direct costs change. Changes in the direct costs will not affect the fixed cost line but they will affect the variable cost line and therefore the total cost line. Once again the total revenue line will cross the total cost line at a different point, with the same net effects as mentioned above for changing overheads.

Fig 7.9 Working out the impact of a change in demand, by adjusting prices, needs calculation

Target profit levels of activity

Having created a break-even chart and calculated the break-even point, the business now knows precisely how many units and at what price products need to be made and sold, in order to cover its total costs. The area beyond the break-even point, where the total revenue line begins to move away from the total cost line is, as we have seen, the area of profit. A business will not be content with merely being in that area beyond the break-even point but will want to extend the total revenue so that it exceeds the total costs by the greatest margin. Of course, in order to do this, one or more of the following need to take place:

- The fixed costs need to be reduced, so that the total costs can be brought down.

- The variable costs associated with each level of output need to be brought down per unit of production, again bringing the total cost line down.

- The final option is to increase the price of each product sold, which will mean that fewer units have to be sold before the total cost line is crossed at the break-even point.

Use of computerised spreadsheets (tabulation, charts and goal-seeking)

The use of computer software, such as Excel, allows a business to create a break-even chart and to present the figures both in chart or graphical form and as a table. It is a relatively simple task to change basic or fundamental parts of the calculation in an attempt to see the best balance between costs, output and prices charged for each product.

See pages 374–379 in Unit 26 for information on how to use Excel.

Limitations and assumptions

For businesses the ideal state of affairs in terms of total revenue compared with total cost is to achieve as much profit as possible. In reality, however, there are limitations that restrict a business's ability to achieve an output beyond a certain level or reduce its costs below a certain amount. Also, as we have already seen, customers are sensitive about price increases and will not accept certain increases in product price.

A business will therefore seek to work within the limitations that it has. It knows its optimum or even maximum possible output levels; this is a severe block on the business's ability to produce an excess number of products, whether or not it can afford the additional variable costs. It will also have looked at all the fixed costs and have brought these down wherever possible. Eventually, the business will reach a point where nothing more can be trimmed from its fixed costs.

With regard to pricing, a business knows that its costs of production limit its ability to drop prices below a certain level. It will also be aware that a product may be price sensitive in terms of demand and that the price can only be increased so far without an adverse effect on demand.

The limitations discussed above are imposed by the business itself, in terms of its level of activity and its ability to change costs and price. Break-even analysis has its own set of limitations and assumptions.

Sales levels being identical to production levels

There are rare situations when sales levels are equal to production levels. There is always a mismatch between the two figures: either sales will exceed production capability, in which case the products will be in short supply but still highly in demand, or production levels will exceed actual sales, in which case the business will have to store the additional products until they can be sold, even though it has already incurred the costs of their production.

Break-even analysis is a crude tool for looking at the relationship between sales and production levels. It makes the assumption that everything that can be made by a business will be sold by the business. Any manager will tell you that this is rarely the case. Conversely, when production levels cannot be stepped up to the point of demand, the business loses some of its potential total revenue whilst still shouldering its fixed costs. For these reasons, the break-even point is an artificial creation and the break-even analysis presents an ideal, but unreal situation.

> **remember**
>
> Break-even analysis is a basic measure of the relationship between output, revenue and costs. It cannot be the entire answer to controlling costs, setting prices or determining output levels.

Consistency of selling price

The selling price that can be achieved for a product will fluctuate throughout its life. Products are often considered to be rather like living creatures: they are born; they are shown to the world; they mature; they age; and, eventually, they die. Many products, in fact the vast majority, follow this pattern. This suggests that pricing may have to take into account the different stages of a product's life. If a product is being introduced to a crowded market with plenty of competitors, the business may have only one choice: to offer its products at a low price. This should stimulate demand and sales. The business recognises that it cannot make the margin that it would have liked per product whilst the product is being established.

As the product's popularity gradually increases, along with consequent increases in demand, the price can be raised. This will bring a larger profit per unit, until the point when the price reaches a level that is unacceptable and demand is adversely affected.

For a time the price of the product may be stable, with a fairly regular demand and a fairly loyal set of customers. There will come a point, however, when the product is no longer as popular as it was previously. Newer, better products will have come onto the market. The business now has two choices. Either it can retain the price, and see demand fall, or it can drop the price in the hope that demand will once again be stimulated.

Eventually, the product will come to the end of its useful sales life, and the business will discount the selling price in order to rid itself of leftover stock.

None of this can be incorporated into a single break-even chart. The break-even chart makes the assumption that the selling price remains consistent.

Contribution and overheads behaviour

The contribution required from particular products may fluctuate over a period of time. If the product becomes easier or quicker to process, there may be fewer associated costs. More of the product may be made within the same timeframe so the contribution per unit falls.

Say, for example, that a business in the first year of producing a particular product manages to process 500 units in a year and the necessary contribution is £2 a unit to net £1,000 of contribution. If the business managed to double production then, assuming that all other costs remain equal, the contribution per unit would be down to £1. This would have a marked effect on the profitability of every unit sold.

As far as overheads are concerned, we know that they are classed as fixed costs, payable regardless of output. Overheads, however, can change: an increase in factory floor space would probably attract more rent and a higher business rate. If a business were to move to smaller premises, the rent might be lower and so might the business rate. A business will keep a close eye on its overheads, making sure that they remain at an acceptable level compared with the total cost of running the operation. By allowing overheads to run out of control a business is placing an enormous strain, in terms of contribution, on each product made.

External factors

So far we have looked at the largely internal factors that can have an impact on the break-even analysis of a business. Businesses, however, do not operate in isolation: they are affected by external factors well beyond their control. These are no less important when we consider a business's total costs and its ability to raise revenue.

Inflation

Inflation is much misunderstood. Some people believe that inflation actually leads to lower customer spending because prices have increased. We have already said that price increases tend to affect demand in an adverse manner. But price rise, as a measure of inflation, is only one side of the argument.

When inflation is happening, prices may rise by, say, 2%, but wages will also rise by 2%. This means that customers can afford to buy the 2%-higher-priced products with their 2%-higher wages. So demand is not necessarily changed.

What inflation does mean, however, is that working out future total sales revenue is notoriously difficult. There will be price changes caused by suppliers passing on inflationary increases to the business. (The business cannot usually absorb these increases to its costs and has to pass them on to its own customers.) Consequently, inflation is rampant throughout each level of business, whether it is in raw materials, components, processing or retail. Ultimately, as the products pass down the production chain, they will become more expensive due to inflation, as well as becoming more expensive because value has been added by each link in the chain.

Inflation will affect the costs of the business first. Fixed costs may be higher because wages and salaries may have to be increased so that they are not adversely affected by the inflation. Variable costs will also increase because suppliers are passing on their additional costs, making raw materials and components more expensive. The net result is that the total cost line is pushed up, moving the break-even point. Assuming that the extra costs have not been passed on, the business will have to sell far more products in order to reach its new break-even point.

The inflation can be offset if the business passes on its extra costs. This can be achieved by increasing the prices that it charges its customers. In theory, this should stabilise the break-even point, but what we cannot tell is whether the price increase will adversely affect demand.

Interest rates

Interest rates affect the cost of borrowing. The Bank of England sets interest rates, independently from the government. The Bank of England is concerned with inflation and uses interest rates to manipulate inflation. When inflation increases, the natural assumption is that the Bank of England will increase interest rates on the basis that an increase in interest rates will push down demand because it makes it more expensive to borrow money.

In normal circumstances, the level of demand would be a key factor in setting the price for a product. By artificially dampening down demand by increasing interest rates, the Bank of England would hope to lower prices, because businesses would have to attract sales at a lower price.

Therefore, interest rates can have one of two impacts on a business:

- A drop in interest rates will make it easier for the business to cope with its own debts and it should encourage customers to purchase more products, because borrowing money is cheaper.

- A rise in interest rates will make it more expensive for a business to service its own debts, adding to the costs of the business. At the same time, the business's total revenue may be driven down because demand will have been affected by the interest rate rise.

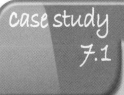

remember

There is a close relationship between demand and price levels.

case study 7.1 — Break-even

Alexander Glass Ltd makes just one product, a windscreen for a major car manufacturer. It is called the Windscreen One. The company has prepared a budget for the forthcoming year.

Table 7.8 Alexander Glass Ltd: budget

	£
Direct material costs per unit of production	30
Direct labour costs per unit of production	20
Rent on factory	4m
Business rates	1m
Depreciation of machinery per year	3m
Insurance of premises	750,000

The current sales price of the Windscreen One is £60. At present, the factory is producing 300,000 products each year. The factory has the capacity to make 400,000 products each year.

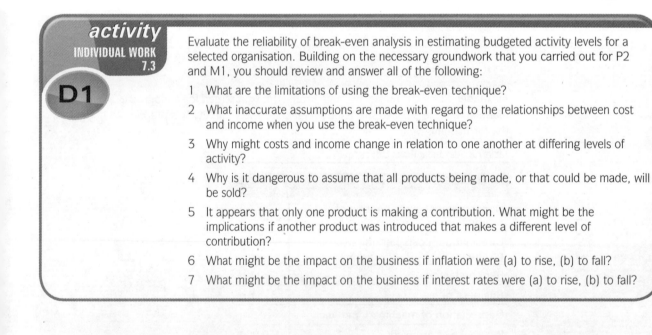

1   For P2, using the information given in Case study 7.1:

(a)   Explain what is meant by break-even analysis.

(b)   Describe how you would use the break-even technique to explain the relationships between costs and income.

(c)   Calculate the break-even point from the information in the case study.

(d)   Calculate the margin of safety.

(e)   Calculate the target profit levels of activity.

(f)   Using the same information, create a break-even chart.

  (i)   Label the break-even chart.

  (ii)   Label the break-even point on the chart.
  (iii)   Label the budgeted activity level.
  (iv)   Label the margin of safety.
  (v)   Label the area of profit.
  (vi)   Label the area of loss.

2   For M1, suggest activity levels using the results of break-even analysis for a selected organisation. Building on the work that you carried out for P2:

(a)   Work out the appropriate selling price for the product.

(b)   Suggest an activity or production level.

Make sure that your suggestions take into account the appropriate mark-up on cost, that you take account of the current market prices, and that you take the break-even point and the required margin of safety into account.

Evaluate the reliability of break-even analysis in estimating budgeted activity levels for a selected organisation. Building on the necessary groundwork that you carried out for P2 and M1, you should review and answer all of the following:

1   What are the limitations of using the break-even technique?

2   What inaccurate assumptions are made with regard to the relationships between cost and income when you use the break-even technique?

3   Why might costs and income change in relation to one another at differing levels of activity?

4   Why is it dangerous to assume that all products being made, or that could be made, will be sold?

5   It appears that only one product is making a contribution. What might be the implications if another product was introduced that makes a different level of contribution?

6   What might be the impact on the business if inflation were (a) to rise, (b) to fall?

7   What might be the impact on the business if interest rates were (a) to rise, (b) to fall?

Using appropriate statistical information to review and predict business performance

One of the major functions of accounting is to compile and provide information to stakeholders, including managers, creditors and shareholders. The purpose of this information is to show the business's performance over a given period of time. As limited companies are required to complete their accounts and present them on a yearly basis to Companies House, a year is usually the period in question.

Particular information can be found on both the balance sheet and the profit and loss account.

Link

See pages 19–36 in Unit 6 and pages 85–131 in Unit 8 for information on the creation of final accounts.

Accounting data

The profit and loss account can be used for a number of different purposes:

■ It can show a business's performance compared with its performance in previous years.

■ The level of profit can be compared with the business's budgeted profit levels.

■ It can assist in obtaining loans because it can show that the business has been capable in the past and will be capable in the future of paying back the loan.

■ It provides information that enables the owners of the business and managers to make operational plans for the future.

The balance sheet is what is known as a 'snapshot'; it shows the business's position at a given point in time. It is designed merely to show what the business owns (its assets) and what it owes (its liabilities) on the particular date when the balance sheet was prepared.

Previous period (sales, production, costs and profits)

The profit and loss account is used to calculate the level of profit that has been made by a business. Table 7.9 shows the calculations and information that are included.

Table 7.9 Profit and loss

Calculation	Profit and loss account item
	Revenue (total sales)
Minus	Cost of sales
Equals	Gross profit
Minus	Overheads
Equals	Operating or trading profit
Plus	One-off items
Equals	Pre-tax profits
Minus	Tax
Equals	Profit after tax
Minus	Dividend payments
Equals	Retained profit

The data for the current year is usually presented alongside that for the previous year, so that straightforward comparisons between performances can be made. The example of a simple profit and loss account in Table 7.10 shows how this works.

Table 7.10 Profit and loss account

	2006	2005
Turnover	23,982	20,461
Cost of sales	(11,124)	(9,623)
Gross profit	12,858	10,838
Administrative expenses	7,864	6,257
Distribution costs	1,578	1,461
Interest	283	341
Net profit before tax	3,133	2,779

A quick comparison can be made between the two sets of sales figures for the period. Note that in our example sales (turnover) are up, by around £3,500.

The business's cost of sales are consequently higher, as these are variable costs associated with production. Gross profit is up, but additional fixed overheads are also up, making the actual net profit before tax only slightly higher than it was the year before.

Information from published financial reports

The key information provided by published financial reports can be used directly to see how successful the business was, both in this year and in comparison with the previous year. Shareholders, for example, will be looking to see whether the business is more profitable than it was the year before.

Government agencies, such as HM Revenue and Customs, will look at the profit and the losses so that they can calculate the tax liability of the business. Suppliers will also look at the profit and loss account; it will reveal whether the business is stable and if they can rely on the business paying back any outstanding invoices for products bought on credit. Potential investors can look at the business's financial position, before deciding whether or not to invest.

Statistical information

Statistical information is collected by industry trade associations and, more commonly, by the government. Unfortunately, statistical data collected by other organisations may not reveal anything of particular relevance to the business. Certain overall trends and seasonal variations, for example, may not be applicable: for example, a business that sells bread would not necessarily be affected by changes in demand due to weather conditions or holidays.

What this data often reveals, however, is a general trend, which could be reflected in the sales figures of a business. There are various ways of dealing with statistical information and applying it to assess any impacts that may have occurred for the business.

Changes over time

Changes over time make use of aged data. The idea is to see a general trend over a period of years. Fig 7.10 shows a set of data that has been created from information from the **Scottish Executive** and the **Economic Statistics Division**. The Office for National Statistics, a government agency, collects a vast range of data. In this case, the data compares unemployment changes over time in Scotland with unemployment changes in a part of the country, North Lanarkshire.

Note that the gradual drop in unemployment in North Lanarkshire mirrors a national trend. The unemployment levels in North Lanarkshire are slightly higher, but they still follow the general downward trend. For businesses in North Lanarkshire, this could be of particular interest as it suggests that with more people in work in that area there should be more money in the local economy and greater opportunities to sell products and services.

Fig 7.10 Changes in unemployment over time in Scotland and North Lanarkshire

(Scottish Executive, www.scotland.gov.uk)

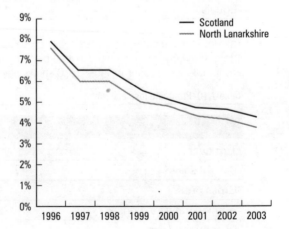

Businesses can look for changes over time in their own statistical data. They may, for example, look at their profit levels over the last five to ten years, their cost of sales or their turnover. However, when looking at these figures, it is important to remember that other factors may be relevant. Take, for example, a business that experienced a marked change in output costs and sales five years ago; it would be relevant to know that until five years ago the business was operating from relatively small premises and that it had subsequently moved to larger premises. Looking at statistical figures in isolation is never a good basis for making decisions; they must be placed into context.

Moving averages

Moving averages is a common way of identifying trends. The business does, however, need to have access to aged statistical data on, for example, its sales. Each year is split into quarters, and the sales revenue from each quarter is calculated. In order to work out the moving average for each quarter a series of calculations have to be made. First, the data for the first four quarters are added, giving a four-quarter moving total. Once this calculation has been made, adding each successive pair of four-quarter moving totals can create an eight-quarter moving total. From these figures it is possible to work out the moving average, based on four-quarter totals, and the moving average based on eight-quarter moving totals. An example is shown in Table 7.11.

Table 7.11 Moving averages

Year	Quarter	Sales revenue £000	Four-quarter moving total £000	Four-quarter moving average £000	Eight-quarter moving total £000	Eight-quarter moving average £000
2004	1	20				
	2	22				
	3	22				
	4	23	87	21.75		
2005	1	24	91	22.75	178	22.25
	2	24	93	23.25	184	23
	3	25	96	24	189	23.63
	4	27	100	25	196	24.5
2006	1	26	102	25.5	202	25.25
	2	25	103	25.75	205	25.63
	3	25	103	25.75	206	25.75
	4	24	100	25	203	25.38
2007	1	28	102	25.5	202	25.25
	2	30	107	26.75	209	26.13
	3	31	113	28.25	220	27.5
	4	30	113	29.75	232	29

As we can see from the data, the similarities between the four-quarter moving averages and the eight-quarter moving averages are quite marked. Generally, the eight-quarter moving averages are lower, as a poor performance in any of the years would adversely affect the average.

Nonetheless, it is possible for a business to extrapolate or extend the moving average to predict what may happen in the short to medium term. We can see from both sets of moving averages that the general trend is upwards. There are modest increases of somewhere between 0.25 and 1.5 from each set of figures. A business may consider that the next four-quarter moving average would be 32.25 and the next eight-quarter moving average 30.

 Link   See page 364 in Unit 26 for more on extrapolation.

Seasonal variations

Seasonal variations can affect the sales in a given quarter. For example, businesses offering products or services that have seasonal appeal may see a surge in sales during a particular part of the year. So businesses that sell products that are more likely to be consumed in hot weather will usually see increased sales in the summer and a slump in sales in the winter months. This helps explain why moving averages are used: they smooth out seasonal variations.

Seasonal variations in sales are blips. They are important and must be planned for, but they do not impact on the overall trend.

Price indices

The Office for National Statistics produces extensive consumer price index figures, charting the prices of products purchased by consumers and comparing them with the **Retail Price Index** (RPI). The **Consumer Price Index** is the main domestic measure of UK inflation. The figures date back to 1996. Like the Retail Price Index, which dates back to 1987, it maps trends in prices to consumers.

Both the Consumer Price Index and the Retail Price Index are calculated by collecting samples of prices from representative products and services in a range of UK retail outlets. Around 650 representative consumer products and services are selected from 150 different areas of Great Britain. This gives 120,000 separate price quotations. They are designed to reflect the cost of buying a representative basket of products and services.

The Consumer Price Index focuses on the normal basket of products purchased by people on a weekly or monthly basis, whilst the Retail Price Index looks at a broader range of prices and costs. For example, the Consumer Price Index collects the prices of frozen pizzas, pork sausages, yoghurt, and kiwi fruit. The Retail Price Index looks at a similar basket of products from fruit pies to frozen prawns, as well as looking at prices on restaurant menus, in takeaways, off-licences and staff canteens. The Retail Price Index also takes housing costs into account, as well as lighting and fuel, household goods, household services (such as childminder fees), clothing and footwear, motoring expenditure, travel costs and leisure services.

Office for National Statistics

www.statistics.gov.uk

Trends to assess and predict business performance

Where there are recognisable trends, either in price indices or in the industry overall, the expectation is that a business in an associated area of work would experience similar trends in its sales. It is always difficult to compare similar businesses, as they have different operating standards, priorities and ownership of assets. Nonetheless, businesses in similar industries should see similar trends and variations in their costs, profits and sales revenue. It should therefore be a relatively simple task to see how these trends have affected a particular business and then, by extrapolation, to predict its future performance.

Performance

Many different groups (or stakeholders) are interested in the performance of a business. Typically, the following groups would be concerned:

- the management of the business – who will want to judge whether initiatives and decisions that they have made have had a positive impact on the performance of the business

- the business's owners (or shareholders) – who will be looking at the performance of the business in terms of its ability to provide them with a good financial return in the shape of dividends

- potential investors – who will be looking for a business that has a good all-round performance, as shown in profit figures, good dividends to the shareholders, low borrowing, good use of the assets, and the potential to achieve a higher share price in the future

- finance providers – who will be looking at the performance of the business in terms of its ability to pay its short and long term debts.

Ratio analysis

Ratio analysis is an accounting procedure used to compare one set of figures with another. As a simple example, let's take Company A, which has sales revenue of £120,000, and Company B, which has sales revenue of £60,000. Ratio analysis shows us that Company A has twice as much sales revenue as Company B; therefore, the ratio is 2:1.

When the requirement is to look at the performance of an individual business, ratio analysis can help us see how well the business has performed in different time periods. For example, we could look at the current situation compared with the situation a year ago. Ratios tend to be of particular use when:

- we want to look at the trends in a business's results over a period of years
- we need to compare the results of one business with those of another similar business
- we want to compare the performance of one business with the industry average performance.

There are a number of different ratios, each revealing a different aspect of a business's performance.

Liquidity ratios (current ratio and liquid capital ratio)

These are designed to look at the short-term financial health of a business. They look at the working capital and see whether it is sufficient and is being managed in the correct manner. If a business has too little working capital it may not be able to pay off its short-term debts. On the other hand, if it has too much then it may not be making the best use of this financial resource. There are two ways of calculating the liquidity of the business.

Current ratio

The first is the current ratio. It is sometimes called the working capital ratio as it focuses on current assets and current liabilities. The current ratio is shown as a ratio of the business's current assets compared with its current liabilities. For example, if a business had current assets of £100,000 and current liabilities of £20,000 this could be expressed as 5:1, as the current assets outweigh the current liabilities by five.

Ideally a business should have around £1.50's worth of assets for every £1 of debt. So the ideal ratio is 1.5:1. If a business has less than 1:1, it does not have sufficient assets to pay its current liabilities.

Liquid capital ratio

The liquid capital ratio is also known as the quick ratio or the acid test. It, too, looks at current assets and liabilities, but unlike the current ratio it does not include stock. The reason for this is that, although a current asset, stock is the hardest asset to turn into ready cash. It may simply take too long to sell the stock. It may also be valued at a particular price but be worth less because it is old. The acid test compares cash and close to cash, such as debtors, to the short-term debt of the business. The formula is:

Current assets – stock:current liabilities

The ideal result is 1:1; anything less shows that the business will have problems in paying off its short-term debt.

Profitability ratios

Whether businesses in the private sector are private or public limited companies, their primary objective is to produce a profit. It is therefore important to examine exactly how the profit has been made. Profitability ratios allow comparisons to be made between businesses. They tend to provide a percentage figure, rather than a ratio as such.

Gross profit mark-up

Gross profit mark-up compares the gross profit with the cost of sales. If a business has a gross profit of £6,000 and sales cost £2,000 we can use the following formula to calculate the gross profit mark-up:

Gross profit/cost of sales × 100

In our example, £6,000 divided by £2,000 multiplied by 100 equals 300%.

Gross profit margin

This examines the relationship between profits before allowing for overhead costs. Remember that this is gross profit, so the formula is as follows.

Gross profit margin = gross profit/turnover × 100

If a business had a gross profit of £6,000 from sales of £10,000 then dividing the £6,000 by £10,000 and then multiplying it by 100 calculates the gross profit margin. This gives a percentage of 60%. Whilst this may appear to be a particularly good profit margin, none of the overheads has yet been taken into account.

A business could increase its gross profit margin by increasing its sales revenue whilst keeping its cost of sales down, or by reducing its cost of sales whilst trying to maintain the same sales revenue.

Net profit margin

The net profit margin ratio differs from the gross profit margin ratio because it looks at profits after overhead expenses have been taken out. The formula for net profit margin is:

Net profit/sales × 100

Using the same example, the business has £10,000 of sales and a gross profit of £6,000. However its overheads are £5,000. In order to work out the net profit we must take the £5,000 from the £6,000, leaving us with £1,000. We now divide the £1,000 by the £10,000 and multiply this by 100 to give us our net profit margin. In this example it is just 10%.

This goes to show that expenses need to be kept down or reduced, whilst sales revenue has to remain static or increased.

Overheads to sales margin

Overheads to sales margin is another straightforward measure. It compares overheads to sales turnover. The formula is:

Overheads/sales turnover × 100

Using the same example we know that the overheads of the business are £5,000 and that the sales turnover is £10,000. Once again we multiply the total by 100. This will give us a figure of 50%. This reveals that the overheads are currently half of the sales turnover.

A business would be interested to see whether this is an industry standard or whether it has excessive overheads.

Return on capital employed

The return on capital employed (ROCE) looks at the efficiency of the business to generate profit from the money that has been invested in it. It asks the basic question: 'What kind of return will be received by an investor?' The return on capital employed looks at net profit and compares this with the capital employed to create that profit. The formula is:

Net profit/capital employed × 100

As far as most businesses are concerned, a 20% return on capital employed would be acceptable.

Efficiency

Ratios that measure efficiency are often referred to as activity ratios, as they show how good a business is in using its resources. These ratios are all directly or indirectly involved in assessing the generation of working capital, as they look at turning stock into cash, collecting debts, the payment of creditors and how fixed and current assets are used.

Stock turnover days

Stock turnover is a measurement of the number of times a business sells and replaces items of stock. There are two formulae involved. The first is the stock turnover ratio:

Cost of sales/average stock held

If a business's cost of sales is £2.5m and the average stock held is £300,000, we divide the £2.5m by the £300,000 to give us 8.3. This shows that the stock has turned over 8.3 times to achieve sales of £2.5m. We can express this as number of days by using another formula:

Average stock/cost of sales × 365

Using the same figures, we divide £300,000 by £2.5m and then multiply it by 365. This gives us 43.8 days, which means that stock is turned over approximately every 44 days.

Some businesses, such as greengrocers, may have stock turnovers of 300 per year, whereas a second-hand car dealer may only have a stock turnover of 10 or 12 per year.

Debtors' collection days

This ratio is used to assess how long it takes the business on average to collect debts owed to it by its customers. This is expressed in number of debtor days, using the formula:

Debtors/sales turnover × 365

Lower figures show that the business is efficient in collecting debts, but bear in mind that many businesses do not expect invoices to be paid before 30, 45, 60 or 90 days after delivery of the products or services.

Creditors' payment days

The creditors' payment ratio works in exactly the same way, calculating on average how promptly the business pays its bills to suppliers. The formula is:

Trade creditors/credit purchases × 365

There may be more than one way to interpret the outcome of the calculation. For example, if the figure shows that the business is paying its trade creditors promptly this could, on the one hand, be seen as a good sign: it is able to pay. On the other hand, paying too quickly could place an unnecessary strain on the business's working capital; the debts could be paid later, when they are due.

Fixed assets turnover ratio

The fixed assets turnover ratio looks at the relationship between sales turnover and the use of fixed assets. The ratio is:

Sales turnover/fixed assets

If a business generates £3.2m of sales with fixed assets of £1.9m then using the formula we divide £3.2m by the £1.9m, giving 1.68. This shows that the business is able to generate £1.68 worth of sales for every £1 that it has invested in fixed assets.

Net current asset turnover ratio

This ratio compares sales turnover with net current assets. The formula is:

Sales turnover/net current assets

This formula reveals how much of a business's sales turnover can actually be classed as working capital. It is a prime measure of a business's ability to generate a profit, rather than having to use profits from sales turnover to pay off debt or purchase new stock.

Capital gearing

Gearing ratios are used to measure the level of debt and can reveal the level of financial risk that an investor might face. The first is the debt to equity gearing ratio, which looks at long-term loans compared with capital employed. The formula is:

Long-term loans/capital employed × 100%

If using the formula reveals that the loans represent more than half of the capital employed then the business is highly geared. It will have to pay off interest before it can either retain profit for investment or make dividends to shareholders. The higher the gearing, the higher is the risk; and the lower the gearing is, the lower the risk investment. Long-term loans are bank loans and debentures, whereas capital employed is loans, share capital and reserves.

Previous periods

Obviously, when measuring a business's performance, it is a useful to compare its profitability, efficiency and capital gearing from year to year. This will give the owners, shareholders or potential investors an indication as to the business's progress, or lack of it. They will be looking for gradual improvements, as a general upward trend shows stability, and may be suspicious of huge changes, whether negative or positive. They will also be looking for evidence of sensible management and decision making.

case study 7.2 — Accounting data

Lector Associates plc is a business consultancy company. It has prepared a table that shows potential investors and new consultants wishing to join the company how the business has performed over the past three years. The company hopes to be able to show that the business is successful.

Table 7.12 Performance data

	2006 £	2007 £	2008 £
Sales	200,000	300,000	450,000
Cost of sales	120,000	180,000	235,000
Gross profit	80,000	120,000	215,000
Expenses	42,000	55,000	87,000
	38,000	65,000	128,000
Debenture interest	5,000	5,000	5,000
	33,000	60,000	123,000
Taxation	6,000	12,000	25,000
	27,000	48,000	98,000
Other information			
Ordinary share capital	100,000	100,000	100,000
Retained profits	22,000	34,000	42,000
5% debentures	50,000	50,000	50,000
Inflation rate	3.4%	4.2%	5.1%
Interest rate	4.5%	5.2%	6.0%
Average competitor growth	2%	3%	5%

activity
INDIVIDUAL WORK 7.4

P3

M2

1   For P3, use the information in Case study 7.2 and describe how to use accounting data and statistical information to measure business performance. You should:

(a)   Describe the value of the business's previous year's data.

(b)   From the sales income and costs, make an initial assessment of the business's performance.

(c)   Compare the available data to make a further assessment of performance and relative success.

(d)   Detect any trends (particularly using moving averages and indices).

(e)   Explain the use of statistical information, particularly how it could be useful in forecasting future trends and performance.

2   For M2, continue the work for P3 and analyse the importance of accounting data and statistical information to assess and predict business performance. You should:

(a)   Identify the various factors that can influence the figures used in a budget.

(b)   Explain the importance of costs, profits, production and sales during the previous accounting period.

(c)   Explain the significance of changes over time, moving averages, seasonal variations, price indices, performance and trends. (Some of these will be immediately obvious when you look at previous accounting periods.)

Using budgetary techniques

The purpose of budgeting is to:

- define the business's goals and objectives
- encourage analysis
- focus on the future
- communicate plans and instructions
- coordinate business activities
- provide a basis for evaluating performance against either past or expected results
- act as a motivating tool to exceed expectations.

Budgets

Budgeting is simply a planning process undertaken so that the business has access to the most appropriate and accurate information. There are no fixed time periods for a budget, but budgets usually coincide with a business's financial year. It is common for businesses to split their budgets into monthly statements. Some budget on a one-to-four-week cycle.

Fig 7.11 shows that there is a budget hierarchy in which information from various areas is brought together to create what is known as a master budget.

Fig 7.11 Master budget hierarchy

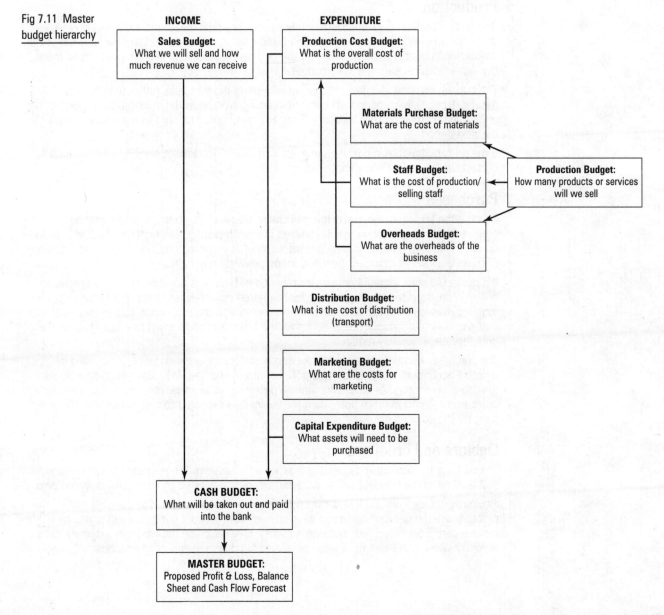

Master

Only the smallest of businesses will be able to put all of its financial data into one single document. It is therefore common for businesses to split their budgets into more manageable areas, typically: sales, production, purchases, debtors, creditors and cash. Once all these budgets have been worked out the data produced can be brought together to compile a master budget.

Sales

The sales budget is usually the first to be created because some of the other budgets are dependent on the creation of the sales budget. A business usually calculates its probable sales figures by multiplying the expected number of sales by the selling price of the product. If the business has been looking at accounting data from the previous period, it will have a stronger grasp of precisely what the sales budget should be. It is important to remember that, for a sales budget, the business must only count sales in the month that it receives the money and not when it made the sale. For example, a business that sells products to a customer in January and gives them 60 days' credit will not count the revenue until it arrives in the March.

Usually a business breaks down expected sales on a monthly or even a weekly basis, by product, product line or product type.

Production

'Production budget' is an appropriate title when a business makes products, but businesses that offer services refer to the production budget as an operating budget. The purpose of the production budget is to make sure that the business is producing enough products to meet the expected sales from the sales budget.

The budget will show the flow of stock, usually using product units rather than financial figures. Typically, each period will note the opening stock, add the units produced, deduct the units sold and then present a closing stock, which is carried forward as the opening stock for the next period.

If the sales budget has predicted a marked increase or decrease in demand, the production budget can be altered accordingly.

Purchases

This is often known as the **materials purchase budget**. Obviously, it would only be prepared by an organisation that is involved in manufacturing. The materials budget is based on the production budget. It identifies the costs of any raw materials or components required to make the level of stock, as identified in the production budget.

If a business knows its requirements for a period of time, it is possible for it to negotiate a bulk-purchasing discount and arrange for staggered deliveries, so that these arrive only when required. It is important to remember that, even though the production budget has indicated that particular purchases need to be made, the business should avoid having to pay for these until they are absolutely required.

The purchases budget may have to take into account capital expenditure. Purchasing or hiring of equipment needs to be incorporated into the budget. Whereas the budget would have to allow for regular, probably monthly, payments to be made for hired equipment, for purchases it is important to note when the business is expected to pay, either in whole or in part, for the equipment.

Debtors and creditors

The budgets for debtors and creditors indicate an assessment of, respectively, when money that is owed to the business will be paid and when money owed by the business will be paid.

Obviously, the debtors' budget is closely linked to the sales budget. The business will probably use the debtors' collection days ratio in order to work out its current ability to retrieve cash from customers that owe it money. It will also use the creditors' payment days ratio to make an assessment of when payments fall due to suppliers or providers of finance.

Cash

The cash budget is the link between the individual budgets and the master budget. The cash budget gives an overview of how the business's money will move into and out of its bank accounts. It can form the basis of a cash flow forecast covering the budgeted period.

Fig 7.12 Bringing together financial information is vital in the creation of projected balance sheets, which can be done on computerised spreadsheets

The information that is presented in the cash budget can be used to create a projected profit and loss account. The data can also provide the base information for a projected balance sheet. The most practical way of bringing each of the budgets together is to use a computer spreadsheet such as Excel. Typically, the cash budget includes:

- income – sales, other income and total income for the month
- payments – creditors, other payments, the purchase or hire of fixed assets and total payments for the month
- bank account – opening balance at period start, a total of income made during the period to add to the balance, a total of all payments made during the period taken from the balance and leaving a bank balance at the end of the period.

Link See pages 19–36 in Unit 6 and pages 85–131 in Unit 8 for information on the creation of final accounts. See also pages 374–379 in Unit 26 for more on Excel.

Departmental (consolidation)

Consolidation is designed to bring together all the budgets from the different departments of a business, to check to see whether they match their appropriate partner budget. For example:

- sales will be matched to all other budgets
- production should match sales
- purchases should match production
- debtors and creditors should match sales and purchases respectively
- cash should match all other budgets.

Standard costing

We have already seen that standard costing is a way to estimate the overall costs of production, assuming normal operations. Having established the potential demand by creating a sales budget, the business uses the production budget to identify the necessary raw materials and components, and purchasing is left with the task of estimating actual future costs.

There are always fluctuations in the prices of raw materials, parts and components. It is also to be expected that a number of products will be defective and will have to be remade. Standard costing – which looks into the future – is, in this respect, less than an exact science.

See page 49 for standard costing.

Analysis of variances

Once the budgets have been brought together into a master budget, this can be compared with the actual figures that the business achieves. Some of the differences, which are known as variances, may be due to calculation errors or perhaps to changes in plans. Some may be due to external factors, including fluctuations in demand and changes in the interest rate.

When variances are noticed, it is important for the business to act upon them in a timely manner, even if the variances are favourable. If the actual figure is more favourable than the budgeted figure, the letters FAV are noted. Conversely, if the actual figure is worse than the budgeted figure, the letters ADV, meaning adverse, are noted.

A business's sales budget may, for example, show the following:

■ a budgeted sales figure of £500,000

■ an actual figure of £400,000

■ a variance of £100,000 (since the actual sales are less than the budgeted figure this is an adverse variance).

Obviously some variances are going to be very small and will not even affect the cash flow in any great way. Businesses expect to see variances. The most significant ones need to be investigated. This will help prevent the problem occurring again.

Use of accounting and statistical information

Budgetary control and investigations into budget variances are important when making financial decisions. Budget variances should be monitored throughout the year in conjunction with the performance ratios and available statistical information. From these, the business can see the underlying reasons behind the budget variances.

Although there should be flexibility in the management of budgets, the following criteria are usually applied:

■ Managers responsible for budgets should be clear about what they are responsible for.

■ Budget holders need to be accountable and must negotiate and inform when price increases are affecting areas for which they have financial responsibility.

■ If the business has made any changes in the accountability arrangements this needs to be passed on.

■ All budget holders are responsible for contributing to the budget-setting process.

■ Timetables for budget monitoring need to be set and met.

■ The business needs to set budget-reporting timescales, either weekly or monthly.

■ The monitoring of the information needs to be a top-down process, so management at all levels should be actively involved.

■ Any budgetary reports should include statements of actual expenditure and forecasts of expenditure.

Budgetary techniques

A number of budgetary techniques can be applied, both to prepare and revise the budgets. Budgetary techniques incorporate control measures, which need to be taken if the budgets are at variance with actual figures. Reliability is very important: budgets should be checked for accuracy and should be as error-free as possible; and no incorrect assumptions should be made about future sales and costs.

Preparing and revising budgets

If it appears that the budgets are in extreme variance with the actual figures, the business will have no other choice but to prepare new ones or amend the existing budgets. Obviously, the further into the future it is that budgets are created, the less chance there is for them to be accurate, because there will be changes to costs and to selling prices.

Changes to costs will have an impact on:

■ a cash budget (as more money will be spent)

■ the creditors' budget (as more raw materials and components are purchased)

■ the purchasing budget (as this will absorb the additional costs).

If there is a favourable variance, the reverse will be true.

If there is a change to the selling price, the following budgets will be affected:

■ the debtors budget (as more customers, perhaps not as a percentage but as a whole, will owe more money to the business)

■ the cash budget (as more money will be moving into the business's bank accounts)

■ the purchases budget (as more products, raw materials and components will need to be purchased)

■ the creditors' budget (as more items bought by purchasing will be on credit)

■ the production budget (production levels will need to increase thereby placing more strain on purchasing)

■ the sales budget (as this will increase assuming demand has increased).

If the sales price has come down, the business will actually be making less money from each sale. This will place greater strain on the cash budget.

Use of budgets for short-term target setting

The natural inclination for a business is to grow and become more profitable. The creation of budgets can be used as a key tool in this endeavour. Budgets can identify important areas of cost and of income thereby helping to control spending (costs) and achieve future profit targets.

Budgets are more likely to be accurate in the short term rather than in the longer term. By careful manipulation of key costs and income a business can set realistic targets, which it has a better chance of achieving.

Monitoring

We have already mentioned that budgets should be constantly monitored in order to compare budgeted costs with actual costs, as well as to identify and explain the root cause of variances.

Although it is perhaps seen as an onerous task, many businesses insist that monitoring is done either on a weekly or a monthly basis, in line with the periods set out within the budget plan. If changes in costs are quickly identified, the business can take remedial action to offset any negative impacts.

As we have seen, variances can have an impact on all budgets and force the business to revise its budgets and exert more control to offset the impact of negative variances, or to take advantage of advantageous ones.

Control measures

Budgets are used to help a business to exercise control over its operations. When individual managers have created the budgets for which they are responsible, the budgets are brought together to form the master budget. Remember that the numbers in budgets represent what are expected to be real costs and real income. Checking sales against budget expectations enables the business to spot variances and decide quickly what action should be taken to control the situation. Possible actions include:

■ cutting down on waste

■ looking for sources of unnecessary cost

■ increasing advertising and promotions (particularly when sales are lower than were expected).

As budgets are exercises in calculation, budgetary control means applying pressure to independent budget holders. By analysing what has happened, the source of the variance can be identified and actions can be taken to limit any adverse affects.

Reliability

Every business should understand the importance of accurate, error-free budgets and appreciate that basing budgets on inaccurate assumptions about future costs and income could drastically affect their value. When budgets are correct, they are invaluable as a planning tool. However, although it is reasonably simple to identify short-term targets, it is far more difficult to make accurate predictions when budgets cover periods further into the future.

Any final budget should not just include a profit and loss account; it should also incorporate a balance sheet and a cash flow. These will show any expectations about working capital or debt requirements and indicate where there are likely to be cash flow problems. It is one way of avoiding dangerous situations.

 Link

See pages 23–30 in Unit 6 for more information on financial statements.

If the budgets are inaccurate, breaking down the master budget to its constituent parts enables the source of the inaccuracy to be identified. Whilst it is unlikely that there will be simple mathematical errors, incomplete or inaccurate figures may have been entered into one of the constituent budgets. These errors will have had a knock-on effect on the other budgets. As we saw, some budgets cannot be fully constructed until other budgets have been completed.

A business should be able to use accounting data from its own financial reports in conjunction with relevant statistical information to identify trends and predict business performance. The projected figures in the budget should have mirrored these trends and historical data.

Relationship between costs and incomes at different activity levels

When we examined many of the performance ratios, it was clear that there is a strong relationship between a business's costs and a business's income. We have also seen that costs fall into different categories: some are directly related to the production of products or the provision of services; whilst others are fixed and must be paid, no matter what the level of activity.

It is clear that income relies on a business's level of activity. To some extent, costs do too.

- Income is sales revenue; in order to attract additional sales revenue, it is necessary to produce products or provide services at increased levels.

- Additional activities mean that there are additional direct costs and semi-variable costs. These are associated precisely with the activity levels that generate sales revenue or income.

- The other area of costs is fixed, such as overheads. These cost figures remain static regardless of the level of activity, the direct costs or the sales revenue.

As we can see in the following example, the relationship between costs and income and therefore profit is linked, regardless of the level of activity involved.

Table 7.13 Costs/profit

Year	Fixed costs (£)	Direct costs (including semi-variable costs) (£)	Sales revenue (£)	Gross profit (£)
2006	100,000	125,000	285,000	60,000
2007	100,000	120,000	280,000	60,000
2008	110,000	140,000	310,000	60,000

In this example, we have three different sales revenue totals, but all have produced the same profit level. As we can see, fixed costs have increased over the period by £10,000, whilst direct costs have fluctuated between £120,000 and £140,000. It is, therefore, apparent that the close relationship between incomes at different activity levels is directly influenced by associated and non-associated costs.

Strengths and weaknesses of budgetary techniques

Budgets can be almost entirely prepared by the accounts or finance department of a business, provided that the people concerned are given the correct data. As a result, as the data comes in, it can be checked and cross-referenced for accuracy.

Unfortunately, it takes a considerable amount of time to collect the data, which comes from perhaps dozens or hundreds of budget holders. The budget holders may well be using different data sources, and there may be gaps in the information that they provide. Most accounts departments find themselves struggling to complete the budgets on time; there may be little time left to carry out data analysis.

Budgetary data can quickly lose its significance, mainly due to the problems of compiling accurate and timely data. Budgets tend to be somewhat detached from normal operational activities, and as a result budget holders may ignore them and the process just becomes a formality: a form filling exercise that can be forgotten until the next memo comes around requesting the information. If budget holders pay little attention to the budgets, the budgets will have little bearing on the business's performance. In any case, budgets have to be radically revised when new business conditions arise and existing data becomes obsolete.

Comparing real figures with budget figures to highlight variances is a time-consuming exercise and may be perceived as a burden. Nevertheless, it is crucial to effective business planning.

case study 7.3 — Budgets

Lector Associates plc is a business consultancy company. It has added in some additional figures and is working on the figures for 2009.

Table 7.14 Additional information

	2006 £	2007 £	2008 £
Sales	200,000	300,000	450,000
Cost of sales	120,000	180,000	235,000
Gross profit	80,000	120,000	215,000
Expenses	42,000	55,000	87,000
	38,000	65,000	128,000
Debenture interest	5,000	5,000	5,000
	33,000	60,000	123,000
Taxation	6,000	12,000	25,000
	27,000	48,000	98,000
Sales breakdown	**2006 £**	**2007 £**	**2008 £**
Total sales	200,000	300,000	450,000
Small businesses	50,000	75,000	110,000
Medium businesses	120,000	150,000	200,000
Large businesses	30,000	75,000	140,000
Number of customers per category	**2006**	**2007**	**2008**
Small businesses	40	55	70
Medium businesses	2	4	7
Large businesses	1	3	5

▶

Cost breakdown	2006 £	2007 £	2008 £
Cost of sales	120,000	180,000	235,000
Small businesses	22,000	25,000	35,000
Medium businesses	38,000	95,000	120,000
Large businesses	60,000	60,000	80,000
Other information			
Ordinary share capital	100,000	100,000	100,000
Retained profits	22,000	34,000	42,000
5% debentures	50,000	50,000	50,000
Inflation rate	3.4%	4.2%	5.1%
Interest rate	4.5%	5.2%	6.0%
Average competitor growth	2%	3%	5%

activity

INDIVIDUAL WORK 7.5

P4

M3

1   For P4, use the information in Case study 7.3 to help you prepare a budget and deal with the following tasks.

   (a)   Applying the trends that you calculated, calculate the budgeted figures for the next accounting period.

   (b)   Prepare your budget in table format.

   (c)   Calculate the moving average.

   (d)   Apply the trend to your forecast figures.

2   For M3, base your information on the budget that you prepared for P4 and analyse the impact on the budget of changes in costs and selling prices. In particular:

   (a)   Identify any cost increases that cause increases in overall costs and reductions in profit.

   (b)   Identify any increase in costs that will probably mean that the selling price will have to change.

   (c)   Why might these changes be necessary if the business relies on a cost plus system to work out its selling price?

   (d)   How will changes in cost have an impact on the break-even point of the business?

   (e)   Why might an increase in the business's activity levels compared with its budgeted activity levels offset the impact on the break-even point?

activity

INDIVIDUAL WORK 7.6

P5

Describe how budgets can be used to set targets, monitor and control an organisation. Specifically, you should:

1   Explain why target setting is of vital importance in preparing budgets.

2   Explain the purpose of the monitoring process when you compare budgeted figures with actual figures.

3   Say why it is important to calculate and analyse variances.

4   Say why it might also be important to explain the underlying reasons behind a variance.

5   Using the example business from Case study 7.3, explain how the business could take action or make decisions in order to control its budgets.

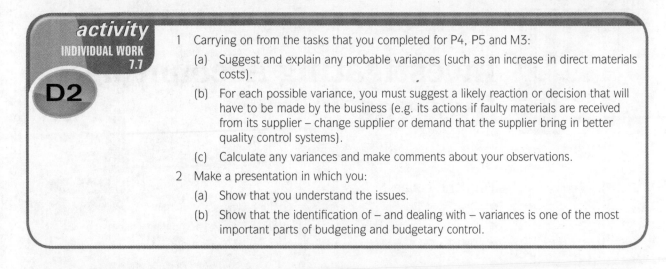

activity

**INDIVIDUAL WORK
7.7**

D2

1 Carrying on from the tasks that you completed for P4, P5 and M3:

  (a) Suggest and explain any probable variances (such as an increase in direct materials costs).

  (b) For each possible variance, you must suggest a likely reaction or decision that will have to be made by the business (e.g. its actions if faulty materials are received from its supplier – change supplier or demand that the supplier bring in better quality control systems).

  (c) Calculate any variances and make comments about your observations.

2 Make a presentation in which you:

  (a) Show that you understand the issues.

  (b) Show that the identification of – and dealing with – variances is one of the most important parts of budgeting and budgetary control.

Progress Check

1. Distinguish between direct and indirect costs.

2. Give three possible examples of semi-variable costs that might have to be paid by a vehicle manufacturer.

3. Briefly explain absorption costing.

4. Distinguish between marginal and standard costing.

5. What is the margin of safety?

6. How might an increase in interest rates affect a business that relies on borrowing to maintain its operations?

7. What might the liquid capital ratio tell you about a business?

8. What is ROCE and what does it measure?

9. Where might you find the letters FAV and what do they mean?

10. If a business increases its level of activity, which two types of cost are most likely to increase?

UNIT 8

Investigating Accounting Systems

This unit covers:

- The use of financial documents in recording business transactions
- How to record and monitor financial information in the accounting systems
- The purpose of extracting a trial balance from the accounting records
- How to prepare a trading and profit and loss account and balance sheet

Accurate accounting information is required to provide a well-founded view of the business's financial performance and position. When information about transactions is transferred into a business's accounting system, a trial balance can be calculated and subsequently a trading and profit and loss account and balance sheet can be constructed, providing not only a snapshot of the business's performance but also a reliable record of its financial transactions.

This unit begins by introducing the financial documents that are required to record all business transactions. It then explains how financial information is monitored and recorded. The final sections of the unit examine the reasons for extracting a trial balance and show how a trading and profit and loss account and balance sheet are constructed.

grading criteria

To achieve a **Pass** grade the evidence must show that the learner is able to:	To achieve a **Merit** grade the evidence must also show that the learner is able to:	To achieve a **Distinction** grade the evidence must also show that the learner is able to:
P1 identify the documents used to record business transactions Pg 93	**M1** compare the benefits of using manual and computerised accounting systems to record business transactions Pg 104	**D1** analyse the circumstances under which a business would adopt a computerised accounting system instead of a manual one Pg 104
P2 describe the manual accounting procedures used to record business transactions Pg 101	**M2** explain the purpose of a trial balance Pg 118	**D2** evaluate the value of a set of final accounts to a business Pg 129
P3 explain the benefits of using a computerised accounting system Pg 103	**M3** explain why the extended trial balance is used to make adjustments to the accounts Pg 129	
P4 describe how a trial balance is extracted from a set of accounting records Pg 117		

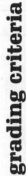

To achieve a **Pass** grade the evidence must show that the learner is able to:	To achieve a **Merit** grade the evidence must also show that the learner is able to:	To achieve a **Distinction** grade the evidence must also show that the learner is able to:
P5 prepare a trading and profit and loss account and a balance sheet from a trial balance or list of ledger balances Pg 129		

Using financial documents in recording business transactions

Recording business transactions is an essential operational and legal function of a business. The financial documents are used to provide proof of transactions, detailing precisely what was involved. It is essential for the information to be accessible and kept up to date in order to:

- assist with the planning and control of the business's activities
- keep shareholders informed of the business's performance
- ensure that creditors are aware of the business's performance
- ensure that legal requirements are met
- show prospective investors the current status of the business.

Eventually, all of the business's transactions will be used to create a series of ledgers from which a set of accounts is prepared as a summary of all transactions.

Documents

Whatever a business's size, it will set a budget and have objectives that it will wish to meet. It would be impossible for the management to monitor the business's performance if documents relating to the amount of money coming into the organisation and the amount spent were not readily available and accurate. Obviously, the larger the organisation, the more documentation it will generate.

When organisations purchase goods on a credit basis, they order and receive goods as the need arises and pay for them later. They may also sell their products and services on a credit basis, receiving payment later. A business may deal with a huge number of transactions at any one time, and another good reason for creating documents is to help the business check the details of each transaction. Many organisations use computer software packages to generate documents; others use manual methods of handling transactions.

Having the correct documentation in place can help a business avoid or deal quickly with day-to-day problems that might lose it business, for example:

- sending products to the wrong customer
- sending incorrect products to a customer
- a delay in the payment for goods
- complaints from customers
- confusion about orders.

Although businesses' activities vary, they use similar documents when planning and controlling the way in which the business performs. Documents have to be checked and the lynchpin of this process is the accounts department, which has to be fully aware of all financial transactions taking place. The accounts department must have copies of each document received or sent out so that it can generate the business's accounts. To record the business's financial transactions, the accounts department creates a series of ledgers, using a method known as double-entry bookkeeping which requires each transaction to appear in two places.

Link | See page 8 in Unit 6 for information about double-entry bookkeeping.

In addition to recording information on purchases and sales, businesses have to keep records of the following:

- bank transactions
- employees' **timesheets** and **clock cards**
- wages and salaries
- tax and insurance
- petty cash transactions.

Fig 8.1 A petty cash box. The cash is used for small, incidental business expenses, but purchases must be accounted for

Cash receipts

Cash sales are always recorded on a receipt or a till roll. A cash receipt shows the following details:

- date and probably the time of the transaction
- products/services purchased and price
- discounts received if relevant
- name of customer
- total amount received, including value added tax (**VAT**)
- amount tendered (for example £10 to pay for a £7.99 product)
- change given
- name of the person carrying out the transaction on behalf of the business.

Till receipts are printed in duplicate: one copy, the till roll, provides the business with a printed record of the transaction; the second copy is given to the customer as a receipt.

Handwritten receipts containing similar information can also be given, but the receipt may have to be either a copy or created on a duplicate pad.

Cheques

Cheques are still a common payment method and are issued to customers with current accounts at a bank. The cheque is, in effect, an order to the bank to pay a specified sum of money to the person named on the cheque.

Most cheques are personalised, as the name of the account holder is printed close to where the account holder will sign their name. It is important for a business to check all the details; otherwise the issuing bank may not necessarily accept the cheque. The three parties named on a cheque are:

- the drawee – the name of the bank that is holding the money on behalf of the customer
- the payee – the person or business to whom the cheque has been made payable
- the drawer – the account holder (the person who has signed the cheque).

The drawer has to write four things on a cheque. These are:

- the date
- the payee's name
- the amount of money in both words and figures
- their own signature.

The drawer will also write a copy of the details on the counterfoil of the chequebook. This is the part of the cheque that remains in the chequebook after the cheque has been torn out and given to the payee. The counterfoil is, in effect, the drawer's receipt.

Drawing two parallel lines down the cheque makes it into a crossed cheque, and it cannot be exchanged for cash but has to be paid into a bank account. Most cheques have a general crossing printed on them as a safeguard against fraud. Cheques can have special crossings, which state 'account payee only', which means that the cheque can only be paid into the account of a named payee and not into another account.

When a business accepts a cheque it will have to be paid into a bank account. When paying cheques in at a bank, it is no longer strictly necessary to complete an old-fashioned paying-in slip; this is a document the size of a cheque, detailing each cheque and any cash that was going to be paid into the account. The slip stated the amount to be paid in and the form the payment would take, so a business could pay in cash, cheques, money orders and postal orders at the same time. It is now common practice for a business to present a cheque to the bank without completing a paying-in slip. However, there is an advantage to using a paying-in slip. The slip has what is known as a counterfoil, which acts as a receipt to the business to prove that the cheques were paid into a named account on a particular day. Once the bank has checked the amounts being paid in, it stamps the counterfoil in recognition that the cheques have been deposited and that all of the cheques were in order.

Debit and credit cards

Debit and credit cards have largely replaced cheques and are often used by customers instead of cash. There are key differences between the two types of card.

Debit card

To all intents and purposes, debit cards work in exactly the same way as cash. When a customer presents a debit card, it is inserted into a machine that communicates with the issuing bank. The customer is prompted to insert their PIN number to confirm their identity. To see if sufficient funds are in the current account, the issuing bank then checks the transaction. If there are sufficient funds, the appropriate amount is automatically transferred from the customer's account to the business's account. The receipt provided confirms the transaction, just as a cash receipt would do. Debit cards can be used without the customer being present, for example on websites and over the telephone. Normally, in both these types of transaction the last three digits of a security code which appears on the strip on the back of the debit card, where the customer's signature is, are given to confirm the identity of the person wishing to carry out the transaction.

Fig 8.2 A VISA card

Credit card

This type of card is issued by a bank or a credit card company that has extended a line of credit to the customer. The customer can then use the credit card up to the credit limit. The checking procedures in place for when the customer is present or carrying out a remote transaction are exactly the same as for a debit card. Credit card companies, however, charge a percentage of the transaction to the business, making these cards a slightly less attractive means of accepting payment. Just as with cheques, cash and debit cards, receipts are generated to confirm the transaction.

Purchase orders

Purchase orders are also known as order forms. They are usually numbered and dated so that they can easily be traced and checked.

Typically, an order form includes:

- the name of the supplier
- the order number
- the order date
- the delivery address
- special instructions
- the supplier's product reference number
- the quantity required
- a description of the product(s)
- the **unit price of product**
- the total amount of each product required
- the signature of an authorised purchaser.

A number of copies of the same order form are generated:

- The top copy goes to the supplier.
- One copy is kept by the purchasing department that is buying the goods.

Fig 8.3 An example of an order form

ORDER FORM				
To: _____ _____ _____		Order no. _____ Date: _____		
Delivery address: _____ _____ _____		Special instructions: _____ _____ _____		
Ref. no.	Quantity	Description	Unit price £	Amount £
Authorised by: _____				

- Another copy is sent to the warehouse or to whoever handles deliveries so that when the goods arrive they can be checked against the order.
- Another copy is sent to the accounts department so that it can marry up the original order with the copy checked by whoever has accepted the delivery. The accounts department also checks the order against any invoice sent to the business by the supplier.

Delivery notes

The supplier sends a delivery note to the customer. The note details precisely what has been included in the delivery, identifying the products using a reference number and giving the quantity and a description. The note may not necessarily include the price or the total amount of the order, but it will explain whether the accompanying goods complete the delivery of the order or represent a part delivery.

The delivery note has two purposes:

- It is the supplier's confirmation that particular products are now en route to one of its customers. It also provides the supplier's warehouse with what is known as a 'picking list'. This is a list of products to include in a particular delivery and is given to warehouse staff; they take the products from stock, pack them and usually tick each entry on the note as the corresponding item is packed. The delivery note is then put into the box and sent to the customer.
- When the delivery arrives at the customer's premises, boxes are opened and the delivery note is extracted. As the delivery is unpacked, the items in the delivery can be checked against the delivery note. The delivery note can then be compared with the order form, to check that the delivery is complete and that the correct quantities have been sent. If the delivery is satisfactory, the delivery note is forwarded to the customer's accounts department, where it is checked against the order form ready for the arrival of the invoice from the supplier.

Goods received notes

The goods received note is an internal document, used to inform the department or section of the business that has ordered the goods that they have arrived. The goods received note is usually generated by the customers' goods inwards section, which creates two copies of the goods received note: one is sent to the department that ordered the goods in the first place, and the second goes to the accounts department.

Problems could occur during the purchasing process. For example, there could be:

- Missing goods – the goods received do not tally with the original order.
- Additional goods – the delivery contains goods that weren't ordered or too many of what was ordered.
- Incorrect goods – the goods received are different from those that were ordered.
- Replacement goods – the supplier has chosen to send an alternative, as the product that was ordered is unavailable.
- Damaged or faulty goods – these may have either been faulty before they were despatched or have been damaged in transit.

Regardless of who is receiving the goods on behalf of the customer, checks must be made to ensure that the delivery is correct. The goods received note will confirm precisely what was in the delivery and whether or not the delivered goods tally with the original order and the delivery note.

Sales and purchase invoices

The main objective of any sales department is to generate sales for the business. It must have a way in which it can record transactions in a reliable and accurate manner.

Orders can originate in a number of ways: for example, the customer who wishes to make a purchase may contact the supplier directly, or the supplier's sales department may have contacted the customer and persuaded them to make an order.

When the customer completes an order form they are entering into a contract, which is legally binding, to purchase products from the business. The sales department will issue a sales invoice to the purchasing business once the products have been ordered. The sales invoice will contain the following information:

- a sales invoice number
- the order number, given to the supplier by the customer
- the supplier's VAT registration number
- the name and address of the customer
- the quantity of goods sent
- a description of the goods sent, including any reference or code numbers used by the supplier to identify stock
- the price of the goods
- the discounts allowed to the customer, if applicable
- the VAT calculation
- the amount owed by the customer on the particular invoice.

It is worth looking at some of the specific parts of a sales and purchase invoice in order to understand why some of the calculations on invoices may differ.

Fig 8.4 An example of an invoice

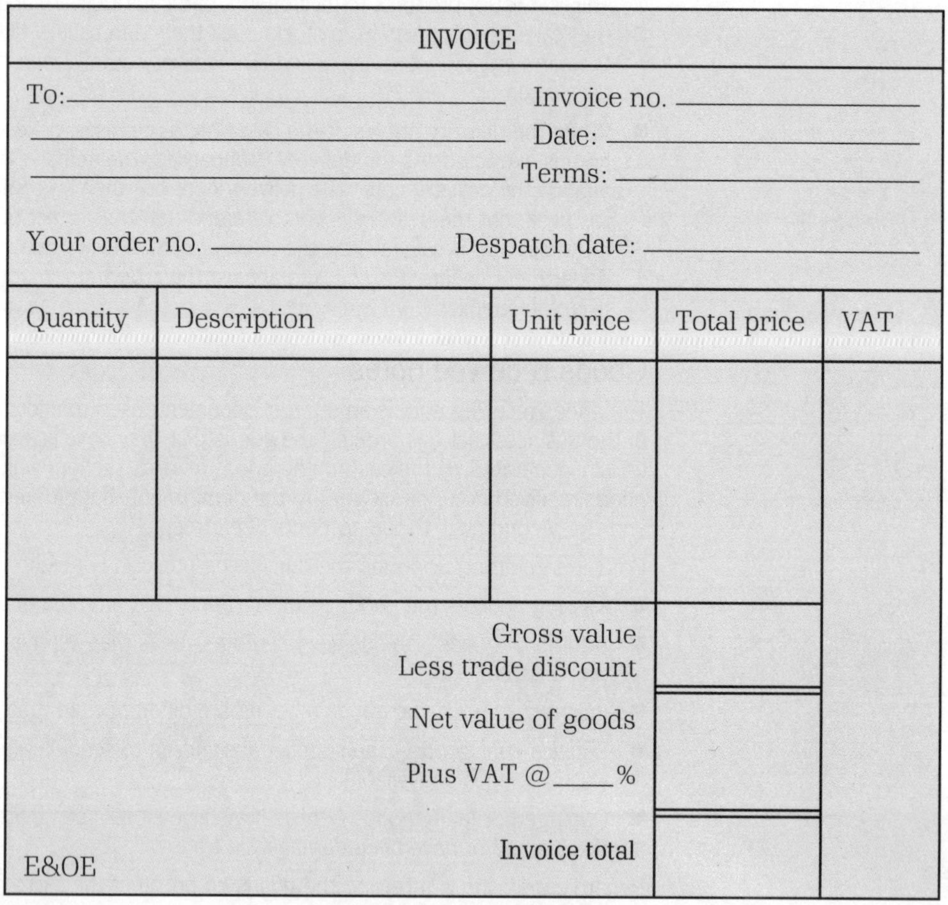

INVOICE					
To: _____			Invoice no. _____		
_____			Date: _____		
_____			Terms: _____		
Your order no. _____			Despatch date: _____		
Quantity	Description		Unit price	Total price	VAT
			Gross value		
			Less trade discount		
			Net value of goods		
			Plus VAT @ ____%		
E&OE			Invoice total		

Trade discount

The supplier may have issued a price list for its products based on the assumption that an ordinary customer, rather than another business, will purchase them. Trade discount applies when businesses purchase from businesses, making the price charged to businesses less than the price charged to ordinary customers. When products are sold to other businesses, a supplier may apply a blanket discount percentage on all prices, such as 20%. The total of the ordinary price of all of the products ordered will be calculated, and the trade discount will be applied before VAT is added.

Cash discount

It is obviously in the interests of any supplier to receive payment for products and services at the earliest possible point. It is also advantageous to the supplier if the payment does not take time to process or lose some of its value, as is the case with payment by credit card. An invoice may state that there will be an additional discount if the customer pays in cash. This reflects the fact that cash can immediately become part of the supplier's working capital.

Value added tax

Businesses with total sales revenue in excess of £61,000 (the threshold at the time of writing) must add the current rate of VAT to the total value of the invoice. Note that some products are not eligible for VAT and the use of VAT will depend on the nature of the business.

See page 44 in Unit 6 for more information on working capital.

For more information about VAT, visit the website of HM Revenue and Customs and see the annual reports and performance reports

www.customs.hmrc.gov.uk

Credit notes

Credit notes are issued by a supplying organisation when:

- The customer has been charged too much on an invoice.
- The goods received were faulty or damaged.
- The goods were despatched but not received.

By issuing a credit note the supplier is accepting an error. A credit note is issued after the invoice has been raised. When the customer pays the invoice, they pay its total minus the value of the credit note. This balances the money expected by the supplier against the money actually paid by the customer.

If the invoice is paid before the error is noticed, either a credit note will be issued against future purchases or the customer will receive a payment back from the supplier to the value of those products already paid for but in dispute.

Statements of account

Each month the customer receives a statement of account from the supplier; this summarises all of the transactions that have been carried out between the supplier and the customer during the month. There will usually be two columns:

- the debit column – which shows all of the purchases that have been made by the customer during the month
- the credit column – showing all of the payments made by the customer over the month.

The document also contains the following information:

- the VAT registration number of the supplier (if relevant)
- the name, address and contact details of the supplier
- the name and address of the customer
- an itemised list of each date on which goods were sent, along with the goods' descriptions; this will also include any customer reference numbers
- the total invoice price of each set of products despatched by the supplier
- the date of any payments that have been made
- the details of any credit notes that have been issued
- the balance owing by the customer, or the amount that will be refunded by the supplier.

At the top of the statement of account the supplier will give the balance for the previous period and then add any additional purchases and subtract any payments made. Not all customers will begin each month with a zero balance. The balance at the start of the month depends on the credit arrangements between the customer and the supplier and on payments made. There may be money owing from previous months but not yet due.

Statements of account are particularly useful because business customers tend not to settle each invoice on an individual basis. They may settle their accounts once a month or pay a proportion of the month's invoices at various points during the month.

Remittance advice

When the customer receives a statement of account, they need to check the supplier's figures against their own records. If the figures tally and the customer is happy that everything is correct and in order, payment will be made either to settle the statement of account in full or to make a part payment on it. Depending on the credit arrangements already in place, the payment can be made by cheque, cash or credit card payment or by transfer of money from one bank account to another.

Whichever method of payment is used to settle the statement of account, the customer is likely to send a document known as a remittance advice to inform the supplier that a certain amount of money has been sent.

A remittance advice includes:

- the name and address of the customer
- the date
- the supplier's number or name
- the supplier's name and address
- the supplier's invoice date
- the supplier's invoice reference number
- the invoice or invoice numbers that are being paid
- the payment total
- the payment method.

Transactions

Accounts may be settled in person or by sending payment with a remittance advice. The type of transaction tends to depend on the type of business. Retail businesses are more likely to make what are effectively cash sales, with payment made at the point of sale. When businesses are involved in supplying other businesses, the arrangements are usually far more complicated, requiring paperwork to confirm an order, its fulfilment, billing and eventual payment.

Cash, bank and credit

The payments that a business receives and the money that it is owed by debtors contribute towards the availability of its working capital. A business looks at working capital as a way of measuring the funds that it has immediately available to pay its own bills.

A business will therefore consider different payments in terms of their liquid nature. This is an odd phrase to use with regard to money; what it means is that some of the payments made to the business are more accessible and usable than others. Also, at any one time, the business will be owed money that will be more or less difficult to obtain.

A business would consider cash payments to be the most liquid of transactions, as the cash can be used immediately to pay any invoices that are due. Money paid into the business's bank account is also relatively liquid, as the funds can be drawn from the bank once the issuing bank (that of the customer) has approved their payment.

Credit card payments take slightly longer to be processed. But it is money owed by debtors on credit that is the least liquid of any of the transactions. The supplier has to wait longer for its money when it has credit arrangements with its customers. Even though the products or services have already been supplied, the credit arrangements state that payment need not be made until the end of the credit period, which may be between 30 and 120 days.

As we have seen, a business which supplies goods to customers and to other businesses would routinely deal with cash transactions, bank transactions, including those using debit and credit cards, and will extend credit to its business customers.

It is important that the business's documents refer specifically to the amounts and type of payments that have been received, as well as stating any conditions, such as eligibility for discounts and the payment of VAT.

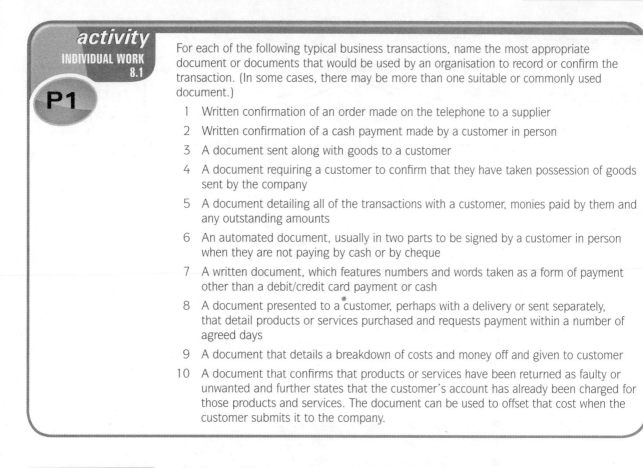

For each of the following typical business transactions, name the most appropriate document or documents that would be used by an organisation to record or confirm the transaction. (In some cases, there may be more than one suitable or commonly used document.)

1   Written confirmation of an order made on the telephone to a supplier

2   Written confirmation of a cash payment made by a customer in person

3   A document sent along with goods to a customer

4   A document requiring a customer to confirm that they have taken possession of goods sent by the company

5   A document detailing all of the transactions with a customer, monies paid by them and any outstanding amounts

6   An automated document, usually in two parts to be signed by a customer in person when they are not paying by cash or by cheque

7   A written document, which features numbers and words taken as a form of payment other than a debit/credit card payment or cash

8   A document presented to a customer, perhaps with a delivery or sent separately, that detail products or services purchased and requests payment within a number of agreed days

9   A document that details a breakdown of costs and money off and given to customer

10   A document that confirms that products or services have been returned as faulty or unwanted and further states that the customer's account has already been charged for those products and services. The document can be used to offset that cost when the customer submits it to the company.

Recording and monitoring financial information in the accounting systems

It is impossible to overemphasise the importance of keeping proper and accurate records of financial transactions. Having the correct financial information is vital to the success of any business. In order to do this many businesses maintain a set of books of account, which are designed to record various transactions. Although the word 'book' is used, it does in fact refer to computerised accounting systems as well as to manual accounting systems.

Typically, a business records all of its transactions under three main headings:

■   the ledger – which is the principle book of accounts

■   the cashbook – which is used to record cash transactions only

■   books of original entry – which will depend on the type of business and the sorts of transactions in which it is normally involved.

Manual accounting systems

As we will see shortly, the main book of accounts is the ledger. It is maintained using the principles of double-entry bookkeeping. Many businesses carry out hundreds or thousands of transactions a day, a week, a month or a year, and these need to be sorted into convenient groups before being recorded in the ledger. This is achieved by creating a number of books of original entry, sometimes called books of primary entry, subsidiary books or daybooks. For our purposes we will call them daybooks.

We also need to consider the petty cashbook before we can turn to the general ledger itself.

Daybooks

The five main ones are:

■   the sales daybook

■   the purchases daybook

■   the returns inwards book

Fig 8.5 Manual accounting
systems flow chart

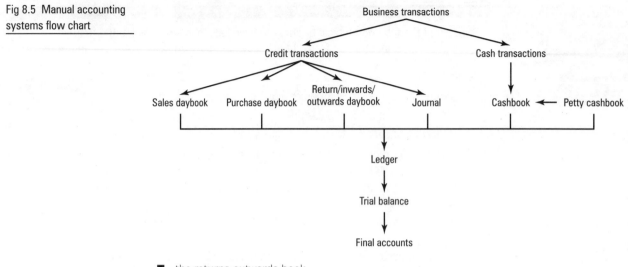

- the returns outwards book
- the journal.

Sales daybook

The sales daybook is also known as the sales journal. It is used to record all credit sales.
These are put into the daybook in strict chronological order, using information from sales
invoices. Not all of the details on an invoice need to be recorded in a sales daybook. It is
sufficient to record the following:

- the date of the sale
- the name of the customer
- the invoice number
- the total net sales value.

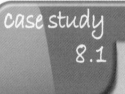

case study 8.1

Writing up a sales daybook

Yarmouth Supplies Limited has issued six invoices during January. On 7 January, the
company sold £200 to B Travis (invoice number 0120). On 13 January, there was an
invoice to S Springer (invoice number 0121) for £400. B Travis had another invoice
(0122) for £620 on 17 January. Two invoices were issued on 22 January for £500
and for £410. The first was to L Smith (invoice 0123) and the second to M Meakins
(0124). The final transaction of the month took place on the 29 January when P Smith
was invoiced for £350 (invoice 0125).

activity

1 Record the above transactions in a sales daybook, using the headings 'date',
   'customer account', 'invoice number' and 'amount'.
2 Give a total of transactions to sales account.

Purchases daybook

The purchases daybook is also known as the purchases journal. All credit purchases, in
chronological order, are recorded. The source of the information is purchase invoices. Like the
sales daybook the purchases daybook is totalled at the end of the day.

Returns inwards book

The returns inwards book is also sometimes known as a sales returns journal or the returns
inwards journal. It is designed to record goods that have been returned by customers. Goods
may have been returned because they were faulty or because the wrong goods were sent.
The supplier sends a credit note to the customer showing the amount of credit given to
them for the goods returned. The returns inwards book is totalled at the end of the day or at
another convenient point.

Returns outwards book

The returns outwards book is also known as the purchases returns book or the returns outwards journal. When goods are returned by the business to a seller a debit note is created. From these debit notes the returns outwards book is created.

Cashbook

For the majority of businesses some transactions will involve cash or cheques, so these are put into a separate book. The cashbook is a combination of cash and bank accounts. It is a book of original entry and a part of the ledger.

Every business receives bank statements from its bank. The balance shown on a particular bank statement may not always agree with the balance in the bank column of the cashbook, so the two balances have to be reconciled by creating a **bank reconciliation statement**.

Cashbooks can be set up in two different ways: with two columns or with three columns. The two-column cashbook brings together the cash account and the bank account. Instead of having two columns on each side recording the value of transaction there are two pairs of columns. The first is headed 'cash' for recording cash transactions and the second is headed 'bank' for cheque transactions.

Table 8.1 Cash account

Dr.								Cr.	
			£	p				£	p
June	1	Balance b/d	20		June	2	Rent	15	
June	5	Sales	25		June	10	Wages	17	50
June	15	Sales	17	50	June	28	Gas	10	
June	28	Sales	30		June	28	Balance c/d	50	
			92	50				92	50
June	1	Balance b/d	50						

Table 8.2 Bank account

Dr.								Cr.	
			£	p				£	p
June	1	Balance b/d	100		June	3	Rates	8	
June	7	G Smith	51		June	12	M Poole	53	50
June	20	P Lewis	27	50	June	19	K Nichols	10	
June	25	R Blyth	10	50	June	26	Insurance	9	
			189		June	27	N Baker	20	50
					June	28	Balance c/d	88	
June	1	Balance b/d	88					189	

Table 8.3 shows the two accounts brought together, as they would appear in a two-column cashbook.

The three-column cashbook is an extension of the two-column version. It contains three pairs of columns each side; the third shows the cash discount. Here, the word discount refers to the allowance given to the customer, and we mean either trade discount or cash discount. In the cashbook, the following applies:

■ Discount received – this refers to the allowance for fast payments made by the business to its suppliers.

■ Discount allowed – this refers to allowances given by the business to customers who have paid their credit invoices early or on time (i.e. they have been sold products or services on credit).

Table 8.3 Cashbook

			Cash		Bank					Cash		Bank	
			£	p	£	p				£	p	£	p
June	1	Balance b/d	20		100		June	2	Rent	15			
June	5	Sales	25				June	3	Rates			8	
June	7	G Smith			51		June	10	Wages	17	50		
June	15	Sales	17	50			June	12	M Poole			53	50
June	20	P Lewis			27	50	June	19	K Nichols			10	
June	25	R Blyth			10	50	June	26	Insurance			9	
June	26	Sales	30				June	27	N Baker			20	50
							June	28	Gas	10			
							June	28	Balance				
									c/d	50		88	
			92	50	189	00				92	50	189	00
July	1	Balance											
		b/d	50	00	88	00							

Petty cash book

Usually, when a business becomes larger it creates a petty cash book in which to record the many small expenses that occur over a given period of time.

Reasons for creating a petty cash book are that:

■ One individual, usually a junior member of staff, can manage and record these small expenses whilst other members of the accounts section get on with other work.

■ It avoids having to put a large number of small or insignificant amounts of money into the main cashbook, thereby reducing the chance of error creeping into the cashbook.

The petty cash book usually has a number of columns so that each monthly period can be worked out independently. The petty cash book is usually maintained using something called the imprest system. The petty cashier begins each period, perhaps a week or a month, with a sum of money in petty cash, known as the imprest or the float. At the end of the period the petty cashier will receive back the amount that has actually been spent during the period, so the petty cash begins each period with the same level of float or imprest. However, this does not necessarily mean that the float never changes in size, as it can be changed according to demand.

A voucher has to be completed for each payment that is made by the petty cashier. The vouchers are needed to reclaim VAT and for internal auditing.

When a petty cash book is written up, the first two columns represent the debit side. On receipt of a float the petty cash book will be debited with the amount of the float and a corresponding credit entry will be made into the cashbook. All payments are recorded twice on the credit side of the cashbook. They are entered first in the total column and secondly in the appropriate analysis column. When the petty cash period ends, the columns on the credit side are totalled. The total from the total column should be exactly the same as the totals from the analysis columns.

Once this is done, the debit column and the total column are balanced. The balance is brought down on the debit side. The petty cashier is then given an amount of money equal to the total expenses made over the period to bring the float back up to its normal level. As we will see, to complete the double-entry side the total of each expense column is entered into the debit side of the appropriate expense account in the general ledger.

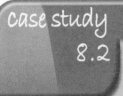

Mark's first petty cash book

During March the following transactions took place.

Table 8.4 Transactions

March 1	Cash in hand	£25.00
March 1	Cash received to make up Imprest	
March 1	Postage	£5.90
March 2	Photocopy paper	£10.60
March 4	Cleaning products	£3.75
March 9	Bus fares	£6.30
March 12	Postage	£5.95
March 19	Postage	£4.90
March 21	Window cleaner	£5.25
March 23	Bus fares	£3.80
March 25	Postage	£8.05
March 26	Envelopes	£4.50
March 31	Bus fares	£5.30

The imprest is £80.

activity

1 Write up the cashbook and balance it to 31 March.
2 Make an analysis column for each of the following:
   (a) postage
   (b) stationery
   (c) sundry expenses.

General ledger

All of a business's accounts are kept in a ledger. Each ledger page is divided into two halves. The left is the debit side; the right is the credit side. Each account kept in the ledger appears on a different page. As the double-entry system of bookkeeping states that each transaction has two parts, all transactions have two entries in the ledger.

The general ledger is the collective term for the accounts that represent the transactions undertaken by the business. The general ledger is sometimes called the nominal ledger, but within that there are nominal accounts, such as the sales and purchase accounts, which are revenue and expense accounts, and there are asset accounts, such as bank, office equipment, etc.

Purchases and sales

It is important to remember that a business does not sell products at the same price as it buys them because it hopes to make a profit from the transaction. This is why purchases and sales have different meanings in accounting and why the account for purchases has to be separate from the account for sales.

When a business buys products for resale, these are known as purchases. Any products sold by a business are called sales. They must be kept separate.

Products that a business buys for resale are bought in the hope that they can be resold at a profit. The purchases account keeps a track of every transaction. One account will be debited because it receives value, whilst the other will be credited because it has given value.

When some products are bought, payment is made straight away; these are known as cash purchases. In this case the business will receive the products, so a debit entry has to be made in the purchases account. This is where the record of all the purchases is kept. When payment is given immediately the value is entered into the cash account or the bank account (cash account if the payment was in cash and bank account if the payment was by cheque).

Sales of goods on credit need to be entered twice: one entry is in the personal account of the customer, because they have received the value of the goods; and the other is in the sales account because the goods have been sold.

For cash sales (regardless of whether payment was in cash or by cheque), the business receives the money, so that amount is put into the cash account if it was in cash or in the bank account if payment was by cheque. Again the sale will be noted in the sales account.

Key points are that:

- When entering transactions, you should never write the word 'goods'. If goods are bought they are 'purchases', so purchases need to be put into the personal account of the supplier and in either the cash account or the bank account, as cash purchases. When goods are sold on credit, 'sales' is written into the personal account of the customer and 'sales' appears either in the cash account or the bank account when a cash sale has been made.

Returns

All businesses find sometimes that they have either sold or bought goods that need to be returned. As we have seen, goods can be returned for many reasons, including damage, faults or simply being the wrong size or colour. Goods that are returned to the business by its customers are called 'returns inwards'. Goods returned by the business to its suppliers are called 'returns outwards'.

When we look at returns inwards, it is clear that once a sale has been made any goods returned by customers need to be recorded using double-entry bookkeeping. The transaction has to be recorded in two accounts: one account will be debited because it has received value and the other account will be credited because it has given value. In this case, the debit entry will be on the returns inwards account and the credit entry will be on the personal account of the customer.

Businesses often refer to goods that are returned as 'sales returns'. In effect, it is a reverse sale. Although the sale was made, the product that was sold has come back. In this case, the debit entry is made on the sales returns account but the credit remains on the customer's account.

In the reverse situation, when the business itself returns goods to its suppliers, it uses the returns outwards account. The supplier will receive the goods, so the debit entry goes onto the supplier's account. The credit entry is put in the returns outwards account, where the business keeps a record of all goods that have been returned to suppliers. Some businesses call the goods that they return to suppliers 'purchase returns'. This makes perfect sense as purchases that the business has made have been returned to the supplier. In this case the credit entry goes into the purchase returns account whilst the debit entry remains in the supplier's account.

Components of the general ledger

In many respects, the general ledger could appear to be a single book. However, as we have seen, ledgers are split up into smaller units, so that the task of recording transactions can be shared. The names of the new ledgers are very straightforward and self-explanatory; they are:

- The purchase ledger – this contains all of the suppliers' personal accounts. Any goods purchased on credit are purchased from suppliers that are classed as creditors.

- The sales ledger – this contains all of the customers' personal accounts. Any sales made on credit to customers make the customers become debtors.

- The cashbook – as we have seen, the cashbook is usually split into a cash account and a bank account. For our purposes the cashbook is purely concerned with the paying out of money and the receiving of money, either in cash or by cheque.

- The private ledger – this is a ledger that is kept secret, such as the capital account or the drawings account. Sometimes the loan account may also be kept confidential. These contain information that the business does not want to be in general circulation. Drawings would include wages and salaries paid to staff.

All of the above accounts are kept in the general ledger, which also includes the returns inwards account and the returns outwards account.

Double-entry bookkeeping

We have already mentioned on several occasions that each transaction needs to be entered into the accounts twice because each transaction affects two items on the business's balance sheet. The way in which the bookkeeping is carried out is known as 'double entry'. Learning how to operate it is not as difficult as many people believe, but it must be done systematically and with precision.

If the business were not carrying out very many transactions, a balance sheet could be created at the end of every day. Most businesses, however, carry out so many transactions that this would be an impossible task.

As we have seen, businesses call any sale or purchase a transaction. Every single transaction has to be recorded. The business needs to know precisely what it has spent and how much it has received. Provided that transactions are recorded accurately, any information needed from the accounts can be found with ease.

Fig 8.6 Every transaction means the transfer of either property or services in return for payment

Buying a newspaper in the morning on your way to school or college is a transaction. You exchange money for one of the newsagent's stock of newspapers. Two things have occurred: the shopkeeper has received money and you have received goods. On his side, he has received the money, but he has given away an item of his stock. In every business transaction, there is always a giver and a receiver and it is on this basis that the double-entry bookkeeping system hinges.

As already said, a transaction affects a single business in two ways, so it will affect two accounts. To make sure that the transaction is properly recorded the business must ensure that one account is debited because it has received value, whilst another account is credited because it has given value.

The words debit and credit are confusing because debit comes from the Latin, meaning value received; and credit derives from the Latin, meaning value given.

Remember that double-entry bookkeeping does not mean that one party has given something and another has received it. What it does mean is that in the transaction one party has received value and the other party has given value at the same time.

Importantly, when we turn to the balance sheet and consider three other variables (assets, liabilities and capital), we need to remember the following points:

■ Assets – when we record an increase in an asset, we debit the asset account. When we record a decrease in an asset, we credit the asset account.

■ Liabilities – when we record an increase in a liability, we credit the liability account. When we record a decrease in a liability, we debit the liability account.

■ Capital – when we record an increase in capital, we credit the capital account. When we record a decrease in capital, we debit the capital account.

Link   See page 24 in Unit 6 for more information on assets and liabilities.

Balancing ledger accounts

The term 'balance' is used in accounting to describe the difference between both sides of an account. The balance is one of the most important figures in any account, as it tells us the value of that account.

Accounts can be balanced at any time, but most businesses balance their accounts at the end of each month. A balance is achieved in the following way:

1. The side of the account that has the greatest value is added up.
2. The other side of the account is added up.
3. The smaller total is deducted from the larger total and the difference between the two sides is called the balance.
4. The balance on the side that is the smallest in value is now entered. This is called the balance c/d. This means that the balance is to be carried down.
5. The totals on both sides of the account are now entered. It is important to make sure that the two totals are level as the differences between the two sides has been added to the smaller side so that both sides now appear equal.
6. The balance is then brought down to the opposite side of the account and called balance b/d, which means balance brought down.

Table 8.5 shows how it works.

Table 8.5 Cash account 1

			£				£
June	1	Sales	35.00	June	2	Car	3.50
				June	4	Rent	5.00
				June	9	Paper	1.50
				June	15	Drawings	10.00

Note that the cash received is placed on the debit side of the account and the cash paid out is on the credit side of the account. The debit side is the greatest and totals £35. The credit side adds up to £20. There is a difference between the two sides of £15, which is the balance. It is now possible to see how the cash account would look after it has been balanced:

Table 8.6 Cash account 2

			£				£
June	1	Sales	35.00	June	2	Car	3.50
				June	4	Rent	5.00
				June	9	Paper	1.50
				June	15	Drawings	10.00
				June	30	Balance c/d	15.00
			35.00				**35.00**
July	1	Balance b/d	15.00				

The balance is carried down and abbreviated as c/d. Assuming that the business balances its accounts at the end of each month, the balance is written onto the account on the last day of the current month. The balance is then brought down on the first day of the next month. This makes the two balancing entries double entry.

When the balance is brought down to the debit side it is called a debit balance. When it is brought down on the credit side it is called a credit balance.

activity

INDIVIDUAL WORK
8.2

P2

For each of the following financial transactions, identify the book of prime entry and the ledger accounts that would be used to record the transaction.

1 A customer buys a product on credit.

2 A customer brings back a faulty item.

3 A supplier fulfils an order and the items are now in the warehouse.

4 The supplier picks up three faulty items.

5 A member of staff buys teabags, milk and sugar for the office.

6 A member of staff is given £20 to pay for stamps to post off some invoices.

7 A customer settles the balance of a statement of account by cheque.

8 A customer settles an invoice in person, paying in cash.

9 A customer calls to order 12 items, pays for them and they are despatched the same day.

10 A customer calls and sets up a credit account and then makes an order.

11 A confirmation is sent out to a supplier following a telephone order for some components.

12 The company pays an outstanding invoice for items ordered on credit terms.

13 A customer exchanges an unsuitable item for another one.

14 A distributor of the company's products doubles an outstanding order to be despatched.

15 A member of staff processes mail orders from customers for items and the accompanying cheques.

Computerised accounting systems

Businesses may choose to purchase an accounts package to deal with all of their financial transactions. It is important for the business to match its requirements against the features of the available packages in order to make the right choice. A business that deals primarily in cash may not need a system that works in the same way as one that would suit a business dealing mainly with credit. Other key considerations include:

- The type of business – if the business is a sole trader a personal accounts package may be better; whereas if it is a limited company it may be advantageous to have an accounts package that is designed for a larger business and includes payroll.

- The number of transactions carried out – if fewer than 10 transactions take place per month, a manual system is probably better. The higher the number of transactions, the more likely it is that a computerised system would be the ideal choice.

- The number of individuals using the accounts package at the same time – the system may need to be far more sophisticated if several people will be inputting data concurrently.

- The computer system currently used by the business – this will determine the choice on offer. The range of accounts software available is wider for systems using Windows than for those using Mackintosh or Linux.

Specialist accounting packages

In many respects, a business has to choose a software package that most closely matches its immediate requirements. It needs to look for the type of accounts package that could take the strain off manual systems and would help with any problems particular to the business. The business should therefore define its requirements and see if it needs a specialist accounting package.

Typically, specialist accounting packages include:

- basic bookkeeping – dealing with sales and purchase ledgers, nominal ledgers and invoicing

- VAT calculations – allowing the business to keep a track of VAT received and VAT expenditure and giving a balance at the end of each VAT period

- payroll processing – calculating PAYE and National Insurance contributions

- invoicing – not only producing invoices but also customising their appearance and sending them by email

- the provision of management information and reports – enabling the system to produce data that can be analysed and acted upon

- credit control – highlighting customers that have exceeded their credit limits and provide the relevant documentation to chase payment.

Another important consideration is the accounts system in use by the business's accountant; it is helpful to choose the same one.

At present, the accounting software market is dominated by six accounting software brands. These represent around 82% of all accounts package sales to businesses. The creators are:

- Access

- Myob

- Pegasus

- Quicken

- Sage

- TAS.

Of these dominant providers, 45% of businesses with a turnover of less than £10m use Sage.

Many businesses choose software because it has been recommended, either by an accountant or by another business. When choosing accounting software, the four key criteria are:

- training and ongoing support

- software functions and applications

- price

- developer's stability and reputation.

Fig 8.7 Sage accounting software

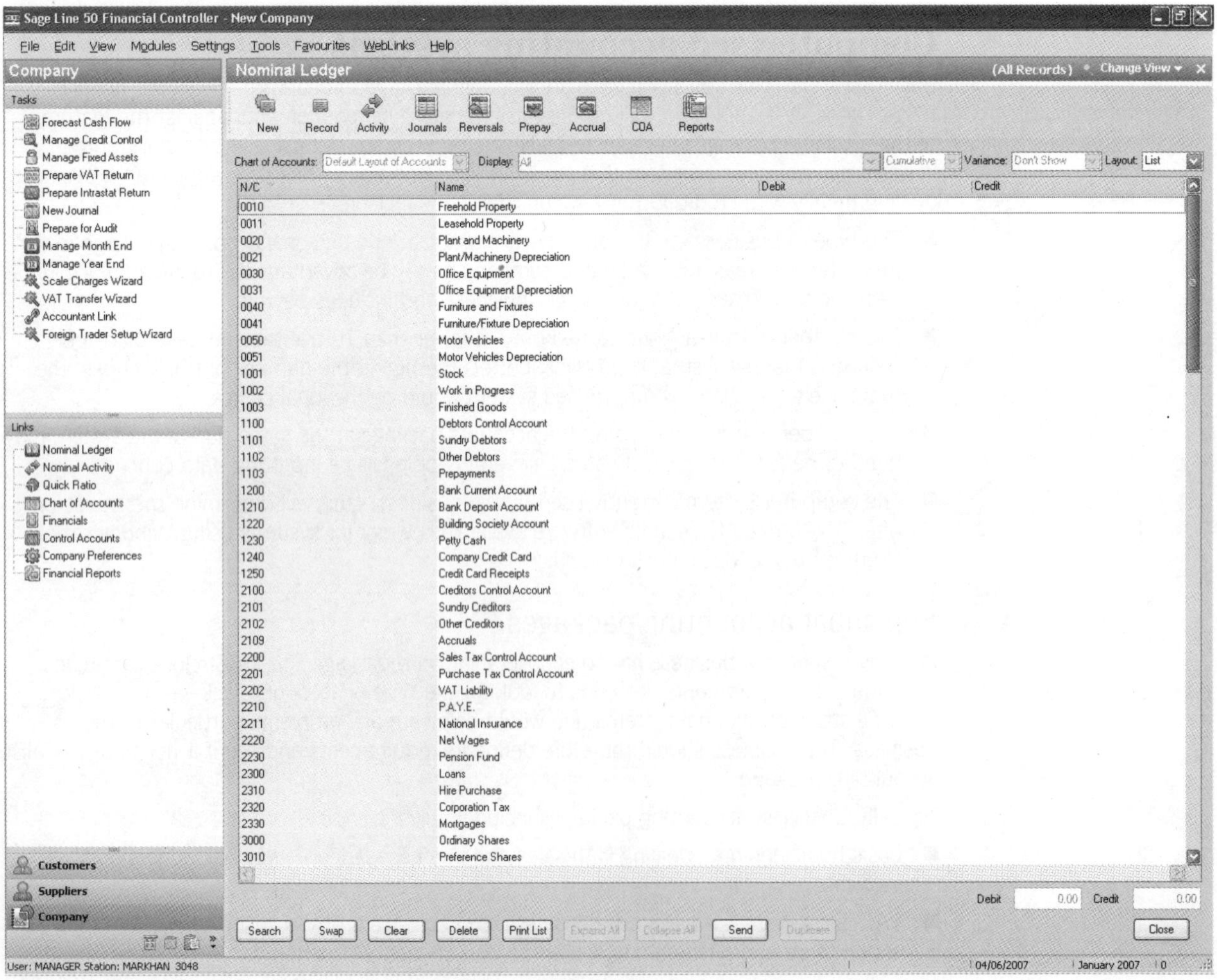

At the time of writing, Sage, Quicken and TAS all sold software for less than £500. The vast majority of users were satisfied with the functionality of the products. Very few businesses, even those with relatively high turnover, pay for custom-made accounting software, which can cost in excess of £10,000. Semi-customised products can cost anything from £3,000 to £10,000.

Spreadsheets

Many types of businesses routinely use spreadsheets, and smaller businesses may use software packages such as Excel. With their clear instructions and set-up, spreadsheets are capable of totalling figures and providing different forms of data output, such as charts and graphs. But spreadsheets do not necessarily provide the key features of specialised accounting packages, for example, invoices. However, it is possible to output stylised versions of statements of account.

Spreadsheets tend to be used for internal accounting calculations. Information derived from spreadsheets can be fed into compatible accounting packages.

Link See pages 374–379 in Unit 26 for more about Excel.

Software features

Each type of accounting package has a different set of features, and the range of features tends to depend on which of the following categories the software belongs to:

- Off the shelf – these are packages that can be bought with a set of basic and fixed applications; they are ideal for small businesses and tend to be the cheapest type of accounting software.

- Purpose-built – these are software systems that are designed to meet the specific needs of the business. The features have been determined by the business and created for it by software engineers. The cost ranges from £10,000 to £50,000.

- Add-on software – this is designed to be added on to existing software programs; it may include online invoice payments or PAYE calculations.

 For more information on accounting software, visit www.accountingsoftwarenews.com.

Benefits

A business may choose to use a computer-based accounts package to take advantage of the following benefits:

- It can save time because information needs only to be entered once.
- It is easy to keep track of the business's debtors and creditors.
- There is less of a delay between making a sale and generating an invoice.
- The packages will automatically calculate VAT.
- More accurate forecasting is possible.
- It is possible to add additional modules to the package to help calculate pay and to produce payslips.

There are, however, a number of disadvantages, including:

- The cost of the package
- The need to purchase maintenance and support
- Training and set-up may be required, usually provided by an accountant
- The packages are designed for most types of business but may not suit every type of business.

---

activity
INDIVIDUAL WORK
8.3

P3

1 Carry out research into the uses and features of computerised accounting, so that you can explain the benefits of using a computerised accounting system. Some research leads are shown in the information feature on page 105.

2 Produce a report based on the research. It should concentrate on how computerised accounting systems can be used to record financial transactions.

3 Make an individual or group presentation, highlighting the key areas of your research.

For an overview of options	InstantAdmin
www.startinbusiness.co.uk	www.instantadmin.co.uk
Sage	Access
www.dcmsoftware.co.uk	www.access-accounts.com
Quickbooks	Pegasus
www.intuitquickbooks.co.uk	www.Pegasus.co.uk
Mentec	Exchequer
www.mentec.com	www.business.iris.co.uk
Sunsystems	
www.sapphiresystems.co.uk	

activity
INDIVIDUAL WORK 8.4
M1

1 Continuing the work you did for P3, compare the benefits of using manual and computerised accounting systems to record business transactions.

2 Make an individual or group presentation, highlighting the key points of your investigations.

activity
INDIVIDUAL WORK 0.5
D1

1 In a group discussion or presentation, analyse the circumstances under which a business would adopt a computerised accounting system instead of a manual one.

The key factors to include in your talk or presentation are:

(a) How the choice of system may be dependent on the size of the organisation

(b) How the choice of system may be influenced by the complexity of the activities, operations and accounting needs of the organisation

(c) How the choice may be determined by the availability of trained employees, or may require the organisation to employ people with specific skills

(d) How the organisation will have to make sure that whatever system is used is appropriate for its particular requirements

(e) That choice may be determined by the availability of suitable hardware and software.

2 You will be expected to support your talk or presentation by presenting your key points in written form (probably as a short report).

The purpose of extracting a trial balance from the accounting records

Trial balance

The main purpose of a trial balance is to make sure that all of the entries that have been made in the ledger have been completed correctly. A trial balance is arranged in two columns, according to whether the balances are debit balances or credit balances. Debit balances on an account are entered into the debit column and credit balances on an account are entered into the credit column. In theory, the debit balances should be equal to the credit balances; so this means that in the ledger accounts every debit entry should have a corresponding credit entry. A trial balance is carried out as a check.

See page 39 in Unit 6 for more information on trial balances.

remember

A trial balance is only a list of balances. Accounts that do not have a balance are not entered.

remember

A trial balance is not an account, so it does not need to go in the ledger.

Once all the balances have been entered, the two columns are totalled. If the totals agree, this is a good indication that the ledger accounts are correct. It is not then necessary to check back through the ledger accounts to find any errors.

A trial balance is usually drawn up at the end of each month. It is useful for checking the mathematical accuracy of the bookkeeping: if there is a mistake, it can be identified as being the current month's error. If trial balances are not drawn up at the end of each month and there is an error, all of the ledger accounts for the entire year may have to be checked, and finding the error will be a much more onerous task.

It is worth bearing in mind that even if the trial balance is in agreement it does not necessarily mean that there are no errors in the ledger; some errors will not be revealed (we will consider this problem later).

Trial balances are always taken out on a specific date, and it is important to make sure that the date is written on the balance.

Let's have a look at a worked example.

Table 8.7 Bank account

			£				£
June	1	Capital	150,000	June	10	Trucks	49,500
June	4	Sales	1,250	June	14	Purchases	2,950
June	21	Sales	500	June	18	Drawings	1,000
				June	26	Insurance	1,750
				June	28	L Buchan	2,200
				June	29	Drawings	850
				June	30	Balance c/d	**93,500**
			151,750				151,750
July	1	Balance b/d	95,500				

Table 8.8 Capital account

			£				£
June	30	Blance c/d	150,000	June	1	Bank	150,000
				July	1	Balance b/d	150,000

Table 8.9 Purchases account

			£				£
June	3	L Buchan	2,700	June	30	Balance c/d	8,700
June	14	Bank	2,950				
June	22	T hall	3,050				
			8,700				8,700
July	1	Balance b/d	8,700				

Table 8.10 L Buchan account

			£				£
June	8	Returns outward	500	June	3	Purchases	2,700
June	28	Bank	2,200				
			2,700				**2,700**

Table 8.11   Sales account

			£				£
June	30	Balance c/d	3,950	June	4	Bank	1,250
				June	12	C Hunt	750
				June	21	Bank	500
				June	24	C Hunt	1,450
			3,950				3,950
				July	1	Balance b/d	3,950

Table 8.12   Returns outwards account

			£				£
June	30	Balance c/d	800	June	8	L Buchan	500
				June	27	T Hall	300
							800
			800				800
				July	1	Balance b/d	800

Table 8.13   Vehicles account

			£				£
June	10	Bank	49,500	June	30	Balance c/d	49,500
July	1	Balance b/d	49,500				

Table 8.14   C Hunt account

			£				£
June	12	Sales	750	June	30	Balance c/d	2,200
June	24	Sales	1,450				
			2,200				2,200
July	1	Balance b/d	2,200				

Table 8.15   Drawings account

			£				£
June	18	Bank	1,000	June	30	Balance c/d	1,850
June	29	Bank	850				
			1,850				1,850
July	1	Balance b/d	1,850				

Table 8.16   T Hall account

			£				£
June	27	Returns outwards	300	June	22	Purchases	3,050
June	30	Balance c/d	2,750				
			3,050				3,050
				July	1	Balance b/d	2,750

Table 8.17 Insurance account

			£				£
June	26	Bank	1,750	June	30	Balance c/d	1,750
July	1	Balance b/d	1,750				

It is now possible to draw up a trial balance by listing all of the balances in the ledger. It is important to make sure that nothing goes wrong at this stage. It is easy to put the balance in the wrong column or enter the figures incorrectly. Also double check that none of the entries has been missed out.

Definition, application and format

Before we create the trial balance from the accounts detailed above, we need to remember that the trial balance is meant to be a straightforward way of checking that all the entries in the ledger are correct. The hope is that, once we have identified the correct columns in which to put the figures, we will end up with a balance.

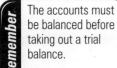

The debit balances should be equal to the credit balances.

When there is a debit balance on the account it goes into the debit column. When there is a credit balance on the account it goes into the credit column. The two column headers 'debit' and 'credit' are abbreviated as 'Dr.' (or 'DR') and Cr. (or 'CR'). Let's see what the trial balance for our business looks like as of 30 June.

Table 8.18 Trial balance as at 30 June

	Dr. £	Cr. £
Bank	93,500	
Capital		150,000
Purchases	8,700	
Sales		3,950
Returns outwards		800
Vehicles	49,500	
C Hunt	2,200	
Drawings	1,850	
T Hall		2,750
Insurance	1,750	
	157,500	157,500

When you open ledger accounts all transactions should be posted using double entries and correctly recorded.

The accounts must be balanced before taking out a trial balance.

The transactions must be in date order.

Always make sure that the date of your trial balance is clearly written in the heading.

When a trial balance is required, make sure that the accounts are balanced and that the balances are brought down. When balancing the accounts more lines are used, and this is important to make sure that the accounts are positioned several lines apart.

If you are given a list of balances in the form of a trial balance, the balances need to be entered into the appropriate accounts before any other recording takes place.

Transactions may also appear under several different headings, including purchases on credit and sales on credit. In order to deal with this, you should follow these guidelines:

1. First open an account for each of the balances.
2. Enter the date, the balance b/d and the amount, remembering that debit balances are on the debit side of the account and credit balances on the credit side of the account.
3. Now enter each of the transactions in their date order. You may need to open other accounts in order to do this, as they will need to be entered twice.
4. Once you have finished entering all the transactions, you must balance the accounts and remember to bring down the balances.
5. Extract your trial balance by listing all of the remaining balances.
6. Total the trial balance, but remember that accounts that do not have a balance are not included.

There are often some problems with the bookkeeping, and errors may have crept in. If there is a problem in getting the trial balance to agree, there is undoubtedly an error.

case study 8.3

Trial balance

In March the following transactions took place:

1 March – a cheque for £740 was received from B Smith

3 March – S Lloyd bought £1,070 of goods on credit

4 March – office equipment was purchased by cheque to the value of £560

5 March – K Dalgleish bought £930 of goods on credit

8 March – S Lloyd was paid £880 by cheque

11 March – K Dalgleish returned goods to the value of £37

14 March – B Smith bought £590 of goods on credit

17 March – A £500 cheque of drawings was written

20 March – £760 of goods on credit were bought from S Lloyd

22 March – K Dalgleish delivered a cheque for £1,100

26 March – K Dalgleish bought £710 of goods on credit

28 March – £98 of goods were returned to S Lloyd

31 March – Payment to salesman for salary of £480

activity

1 Open the ledger accounts at 1 March. (Remember that dates should appear as, for example, March 1, not 1 March.)

2 Record the transactions during March in the appropriate ledger account and open any other accounts that may be necessary.

3 Balance the accounts and extract a trial balance on 31 March.

Errors causing imbalance

If the trial balance does not agree, there are some quick-fix methods that you can use to identify precisely where errors may have originated:

■ First, check the addition of any totals. This will eliminate the possibility that there was an error in addition.

■ Now check the balances. One of the figures may have been entered into the wrong column.

■ Check to see whether any figure has been transposed: i.e. written or typed in with the numbers in the wrong order, such as £305 instead of £350.

■ Finally, check that you have calculated the balances on each of the accounts correctly.

Some errors are not revealed by a trial balance, as they do not necessarily affect the trial balance agreement.

Original error

The first major problem that could have occurred is known as an original error. This could occur, for example, if the document that was used to make the bookkeeping entries was wrong. Perhaps a total on a sales invoice was incorrect; as a consequence, the mistake was copied into the account. Or perhaps an invoice received from a supplier was for £350 but was entered into the supplier's account as £530 and into the purchases account as £530. The trial balance would still agree but the amount posted to the double-entry accounts was greater than the correct amount. The difference is £180. To correct the error, a debit entry of £180 has to be put into the supplier's account. A credit entry for £180 then needs to be put into the purchases account.

Error of omission

An error of omission occurs when a transaction has been completely left out of the accounts. Perhaps the document was lost; in this case neither a debit nor a credit entry has been made, so again the trial balance would agree. This error is one of the easiest to correct. When the error is discovered, it should be posted to the double-entry accounts, but remember that the entries should be dated correctly.

Errors of commission

Errors of commission occur when an incorrect action was taken. A frequent mistake is to put debit and credit entries into the wrong account. Typically, this happens when debtors or creditors have the same or similar names. Bearing in mind that the trial balance has agreed, it is important that, when the error is discovered, any debit entries are credited and any credit entries debited. Then the transaction should be put into the right accounts.

Errors of principle

Errors of principle occur when a transaction is entered into the wrong type of account. A common mistake is to treat purchasing assets as purchasing goods and to put them into the purchases account. This will have a drastic impact on the profits of the business. Once again, the trial balance will agree; the problem is that the assets figure will be too low and the purchases figure will be too high. To correct this, a debit entry needs to go into the asset account and a credit entry into the purchases account.

Compensating errors

Compensating errors occur when two mistakes cancel one another out. For example, two different errors for the same amount of money might have been made, with one affecting the credit column and the other affecting the debit column. The trial balance will agree, but the accounts will be incorrect. These errors may not be spotted because they cancel one another out. Details of any corrections need to be put into the double-entry accounts. For example, if £1,000 is put into the sales account's credit column in error and £1,000 has been put into the purchases account's debit column, the amount is cancelled out. To correct this, a debit entry is needed to reduce the sales account by £1,000 and a credit entry to reduce the purchases account by £1,000.

Complete reversal of entries

This type of error occurs when the entries for a transaction are reversed. The correct amounts have been entered into the correct accounts but have been put on the wrong side of each account. If, for example, a cheque for £500 was paid to a supplier and was entered onto the debit side of the bank account and the credit side of the supplier's account, the entries would have cancelled one another out and the trial balance would agree. These are the most difficult errors to correct, as double the amount of money is needed. If the original entries were cancelled out, there would be no entry for this transaction. In our example, to correct the error £1,000 needs to be put onto the debit entry in the supplier's account and £1,000 as a credit entry into the bank account.

Total debit balances equal to total credit balances

Until you have reached a point where the total debit balances are equal to the total credit balances, you cannot hope to move any further forward in the preparation of additional financial documents. Both the trading and profit and loss account and the balance sheet rely on the trial balance to provide the key financial figures, which will be required for the calculations and must, therefore, be correct.

See pages 4–5 in Unit 6 for information on profit and loss.

If total debit balances are not equal to total credit balances, there is no choice other than to work systematically back from the trial balance through each of the accounts until the errors are discovered. As we have seen, there can be many reasons why errors could have crept into the calculations. Bear in mind that, if an error has been made but has been balanced out by a similar error, it will not be revealed in the trial balance. But the error could have a drastic effect when the trading and profit and loss account and balance sheets are prepared.

See pages 24–28 in Unit 6 for information on balance sheets.

Period end and year end

Businesses need to prepare their financial records so that these are completed as of 31 March each year. This is effectively year end. In the first few years of their existence, some businesses may not necessarily conform precisely to this date. However, if the business is a limited company, it must have its accounts records and financial summaries prepared for 31 March. This is despite the fact that the financial records do not have to be submitted for inspection until a later date.

In preparation for the year end a business will routinely identify period ends. As we have seen, dividing the year into manageable pieces makes it easier to bring accounts up to date, balance them and extract a trial balance. It also makes it easier for the business to assess its performance at any point in the year. Although setting periods throughout the year makes bookkeeping more onerous, because preparation of the accounts and extraction of the trial balance are not quick tasks, it is time usefully spent. Completion of this work at period ends allows the business to identify more quickly any potential errors in the bookkeeping and focus in on the period during which the error could have occurred.

Typically, businesses identify weekly, fortnightly or monthly period ends. There may have to be some adjustment in the calculations at a later date, particularly if invoices, payments or other transactions were included for various reasons but did occur during that accounting period.

Extended trial balance

It is sometimes useful to prepare a rough trading and profit and loss account and a balance sheet, using the figures given in the trial balance. All we need is two additional columns in the trial balance; one for the trading and profit and loss account and the other for the balance sheet. This is known as an extended trial balance.

There are, however, some complications that might mean that we will need to make some adjustments to the figures. Let's look at an example of a trial balance prepared for 31 March.

Table 8.19 Trial balance as at 31 March

	Dr. £	Cr. £
Opening stock	100,000	
Sales		905,000
Purchases	510,000	
Wages	117,500	
Rates	15,000	
Electricity	19,000	
Insurances	22,000	
Motor expenses	47,500	
General expenses	51,500	
Premises	200,000	
Debtors	105,000	
Drawings	50,000	
Creditors		140,000
Motor vehicles	70,000	
Fixtures	45,000	
Capital		327,500
Bank	15,000	
Cash	5,000	
	1,372,500	**1,372,500**

To complicate matters, we are now going to add in some adjustments:

■ Stock, as of 31 March, was actually valued at £92,500.

■ Insurances were pre-paid to the amount of £5,000.

■ £21,500 of wages was owed.

■ Bad debts amounted to £5,000.

■ The motor vehicles should be depreciated at 20% on the cost.

The first part of making the extended trial balance is to deal with the adjustments, which will obviously give us different totals.

 See pages 36–38 in Unit 6 for more information on adjustments.

Table 8.20 Trial balance as at 31 March to include adjustments

	Dr. £	Cr. £	Adjustments Dr. £	Adjustments Cr. £
Opening stock	100,000		92,500	92,500
Sales		905,000		
Purchases	510,000			
Wages .	117,500		21,500	
Rates	15,000			
Electricity	19,000			
Insurances	22,000			5,000
Prepayments			5,000	
Motor expenses	47,500			
General expenses	51,500			
Premises	200,000			21,500
Debtors	105,000			5,000
Bad debts			5,000	
Drawings	50,000			
Creditors		140,000		
Motor vehicles	70,000		14,000	14,000
Fixtures	45,000			
Capital		327,500		
Bank	15,000			
Cash	5,000			
	<u>**1,372,500**</u>	<u>**1,372,500**</u>	<u>**138,000**</u>	<u>**138,000**</u>

In order to ensure that the trial balance balances after the adjustments, there are two entries: one in the debit and one in the credit columns of the adjustments. These ensure that the debit total and the credit total in the adjustments total are the same.

Expenses due are added to the relevant figures in the trial balance. These adjusted figures can then be transferred to the debit column of the profit and loss account. Drawings are shown on the debit side of the trial balance, but when the balance sheet is prepared the drawings need to be shown as a deduction from the capital and the net profit.

Table 8.21 Profit and loss account as at 31 March

	Dr. £	Cr. £	Dr. £	Cr. £
Opening stock	100,000	92,500		
Sales		905,000		
Purchases	510,000			
Gross profit	387,500			387,500
Wages			139,000	
Rates			15,000	
Electricity			19,000	
Insurances			17,000	
Motor expenses			47,500	
General expenses			51,500	
Premises				
Debtors				
Bad debts			5,000	
Drawings				
Creditors			14,000	
Motor vehicles				
Fixtures				
Capital				
Bank				
Cash				
Net profit			79,500	
	997,500	**997,500**	**387,500**	**387,500**

We can now transfer the information from the adjusted trial balance to create the balance sheet. Note that to complete the credit column of the balance sheet accruals will have to represent liabilities. Prepayments are dealt with in the same manner, but the entries are reversed. Prepayments are subtracted from the relevant trial balance figures and have been transferred to the debit side of the profit and loss account. However, since they represent assets they are on the debit side of the balance sheet.

Taking the gross profit figure and then deducting any further expenses carry out the calculation of net profit or loss. As we have seen on the balance sheet, the gross profit figure was £387,500 but, after taking out all of the necessary expenses in the profit and loss account, the net profit dropped to £79,500. Clearly, all of these additional expenses have to be taken into account, as they are expenses necessary to run the business. It is unavoidable that these costs are incurred.

Remember that gross profit is simply the sales revenue minus the cost of sales; net profit is taken from this gross profit figure but takes all of the other expenses of the business into account first. The business would pay tax on its net profit, rather than on its gross profit. If the expenses were more than the gross profit, the business would, of course, have had a net loss rather than a net profit. A net loss figure is traditionally shown on a profit and loss account by placing the relevant figure in brackets.

We have also seen that the adjustments that have been made to the trial balance have had an impact on the profit and loss account. Adjustments were made to stock, prepaid insurance, outstanding wages, depreciation and bad debt. All of these impacted on the figures that we transferred over from the trial balance to the profit and loss account after having made the adjustment to the figures.

Table 8.22 Worked example of balance sheet as at 31 March

	Dr. £	Cr. £
Opening stock	92,500	
Sales		
Purchases		
Wages		
Rates		
Electricity		
Insurances		21,500
Prepayments	5,000	
Motor expenses		
General expenses		
Premises	200,000	
Debtors	100,000	
Drawings	50,000	
Creditors		140,000
Motor vehicles	56,000	
Fixtures	45,000	
Capital		327,500
Bank	15,000	
Cash	5,000	
Net profit		79,500
	568,500	568,500

Accounting records

We have seen that many businesses split their accounts into four main ledgers:

- the purchases ledger
- the sales ledger
- the cashbook
- the private ledger.

We also saw that there is another ledger account, known as the general ledger or nominal ledger. We will now look at this and then at cash and bank accounts and see how these can also be useful accounting records.

A ledger's title is a clear indication of what should be put into it.

remember

General ledger accounts

All other accounts are kept in the general ledger, including the sales account, purchases account, returns inwards account and the returns outwards account.

However, instead of keeping a general ledger, businesses may choose to keep a nominal ledger. Most large businesses use a computerised bookkeeping system, which they call the nominal ledger. (Prior to computerised bookkeeping, the ledger was always known as the general ledger.) It is in this general or nominal ledger that all the key accounts are found.

Cash and bank accounts

All businesses have at least one bank account. Although the bank account may be classed as a business account, it works in exactly the same way as current accounts or deposit or savings accounts. A business uses its version of a current account for payments that have to be made – into and out of the account – on a regular basis. The business is given a paying-in book and has a cheque book from which cash can be drawn or payments can be made, provided that the cheques have been signed by authorised individuals.

Fig 8.8 Just like individuals, businesses also have bank accounts, including current accounts, deposit accounts and savings accounts

The key advantages of using a current account are:

■ The business does not have to hold significant amounts of cash on its premises.

■ Payments to its suppliers are both secure and convenient.

■ The cheque provides proof that payment has been made.

■ The business's customers may also wish to pay this way or transfer the money directly into the business's bank account.

Whilst a current account is useful in the management of the business's working capital, a deposit account may be the answer to keeping funds that are not likely to be required in the short term. The financial institution dealing with the deposit account will give interest to its customer as a reward for keeping money in the account. Usually money that has been placed in a deposit account cannot be taken out immediately; notice may have to be given to the bank that a withdrawal is required. Some deposit accounts allow only a certain number of transactions over a given period of time. Some attract particular rates of interest on the basis that the customer will ensure that the balance of the account does not fall below a specified minimum.

Periodically, usually monthly, the bank issues the customer with statements for their current and deposit accounts, showing monies paid into the account and money taken out. For bookkeeping purposes, the bank statements show precisely when and how much money has entered or left the account. There may be a difference between the money that a business believes that it has in an account and the sum shown on the bank statement. The difference in amounts may mean that another bookkeeping activity needs to be undertaken, called reconciliation.

In bank reconciliation the business looks at the closing balance in its cashbook and compares it with the balance on the bank statement. The two figures may be different for the following reasons:

■ The business enters cheques into the cashbook on the day that they are written. The bank only knows about the cheque when it is presented to it. Inevitably when a business writes a cheque and sends it to a supplier, there will be a time delay before that supplier presents the cheque to its bank. There will also be a delay whilst the supplier's bank uses the **bankers' clearing system** in order to draw money from the business's account, to put into its own account. Sometimes, cheques simply go astray or are not presented for several weeks.

■ If a business counts up its cheques and cash towards the end of the day and then deposits the money in its bank, this money would not be included if the bank issued the statement earlier in the day. It will appear on the next bank statement.

■ Sometimes, banks receive money on behalf of their customers, in the form of credit transfers, investments and other sources. The business will not know that this money has appeared in its account until it sees the next bank statement. Usually, the business enters this money into its cashbook when the bank statement arrives. It is important to remember that these amounts of money should always be entered on the debit side of the cashbook.

- Banks make direct debit payments and standing order payments on behalf of their customers. These items will appear on the bank statement and will have to be entered into the cashbook when the bank statement arrives. These items must be entered onto the credit side of the cashbook.

- Banks charge for some of their services, but it is not bank practice to send out bills. They take the money out of the account, perhaps charging interest on overdrafts or loans. When this happens, these amounts must be entered onto the credit side of the cashbook.

- Sometimes, cheques are not honoured and are therefore worthless. If this is the case when a customer's cheque is presented to the bank, the business will get the cheque back with the words 'refer to drawer' written on it. For some reason, the customer's bank has refused to accept the cheque, which is now a dishonoured cheque. Until the payment has actually been made, the debt needs to be restored.

case study 8.4 — Ledgers and cash books

P. Piggott Books

Table 8.23 Bank account

Dr.			£	2006			Cr. £
May	1	Capital	9,000	May	21	Machinery	1,710
May	30	N Alexander	600	May	29	P Stephens	1,100
				May	31	Balance c/d	6,790
			9,600				9,600
June	1	Balance b/d	6,790				

Table 8.24 Cash account

Dr.			£	2006			Cr. £
May	5	Sales	100	May	30	F Nole	170
May	12	Sales	210	May	31	Balance c/d	220
			390				390
June	1	Balance c/d	220				

Table 8.25 P Stephens account

Dr.			£	2006			Cr. £
May	6	Returns outwards	100	May	2	Purchases	1,200
May	29	Bank	1,100				
			1,200				1,290

Table 8.26 F Noble account

Dr.			£	2006			Cr. £
May	28	Returns outwards	80	May	3	Purchases	250
May	30	Cash	170	May	18	Purchases	190
May	31	Balance c/d	190				
			440				440
				June	1	Balance b/d	190

Table 8.27 N Alexander account

Dr.							Cr.
2006			£	2006			£
May	10	Sales	1190	May	23	Returns inwards	440
				May	30	Bank	660
				May	31	Balance c/d	150
			1190				1190
June	1	Balance c/d	150				

Table 8.28 K Farman account

Dr.							Cr.
2006			£	2006			£
May	22	Sales	220	May	24	Returns inwards	10
				May	31	Balance c/d	210
			220				220
June	1	Balance c/d	210				

Table 8.29 Precision Ltd account

Dr.							Cr.
2006			£	2006			£
				May	31	Balance c/d	2,700

Table 8.30 Capital account

Dr.							Cr.
2006			£	2006			£
				May	1	Bank	9,000

Table 8.31 Purchases account

Dr.							Cr.
2006			£	2006			£
May	2	P Stephens	1,200	May	31	Balance c/d	1,640
May	3	F Noble	250				
May	18	F Nole	190				
			1,640				1,640
June	1	Balance b/d	1,640				

Table 8.32 Sales account

Dr.							Cr.
2006			£	2006			£
May	31	Balance	1,800	May	5	Cash	180
				May	10	N Alexander	1,190
				May	12	Cash	210
				May	22	K Farman	220
			1,800				1,800
				June	1	Balance b/d	1,800

Table 8.33 Returns inwards account

Dr.							Cr.
2006			£	2006			£
May	23	N Alexander	440	May	31	Balance c/d	450
May	25	K Farman	10				
			450				450
June	1	Balance b/d	450				

Table 8.34 Returns outwards account

Dr.							Cr.
2006			£	2006			£
May	31	Balance c/d	180	May	6	P Stephens	100
				May	28	F Noble	80
			180				180
				June	1	Balance b/d	180

Table 8.35 Machinery account

Dr.							Cr.
2006			£	2006			£
May	21	Bank	1,710	May	31	Balance c/d	4,410
May	31	Precision Ltd	2,700				
			4,410				4,410
June	1	Balance b/d	4,410				

activity

Read carefully through the material presented in the case study and trace the connections between the entries in the ledgers.

activity

INDIVIDUAL WORK 8.6

P4

Using the information given in Case study 8.4 to help you, describe how a trial balance is extracted from a set of accounting records:

1 Prepare a plan showing where you will obtain the information needed to extract a trial balance from the set of accounting records.

2 Describe how account balances can be calculated and displayed on the accounts prior to being extracted into a trial balance.

Make sure that you obtain the necessary information from more than one source and that you place balances on the correct side of the trial balance.

Note that the work that you do here will help you enormously when you tackle P5, which asks you to prepare final accounts from your trial balance.

As an extension of the work that you carried out for P4, you are required to explain the purpose of a trial balance. You should:

1 Explain the importance of locating and correcting errors *before* you attempt to prepare final accounts.

2 List and describe the typical and different sorts of potential that could cause an imbalance. Make sure that you stress that any inaccuracies here will have serious implications.

(Remember that one of the main purposes of preparing a trial balance is to detect any errors in the bookkeeping. The normal course of events for businesses is to locate and correct errors before final accounts are prepared.)

Preparing a trading and profit and loss account and balance sheet

The next logical step for a business, as it puts together the documentation needed at the end of the financial year, is the creation of a trading and profit and loss account and a balance sheet.

The trading account will show the business's gross profit. The profit and loss account will reveal its net profit or net loss for the period. The balance sheet will show, in a logical manner, its assets and the financial position at the time that the balance sheet was created so that the stakeholders of the business can appreciate its liabilities.

Trading and profit and loss accounts and balance sheets need to be consistent and have to make sense to the individuals who will use them to form the basis of decisions. If these financial statements are not consistent, it will be impossible to compare one business's performance with that of another.

All limited companies must comply with rules and a qualified **auditor** has to check that the business has complied. The two key governing aspects are:

■ to follow the accounting treatments for each and every event or activity

■ to disclose the information using the correct formats or layouts for the trading and profit and loss account and the balance sheet.

Auditors must be satisfied that both financial documents give a true and fair view of the actual transactions. They will be inclined to check internal controls. This is done to safeguard the recording of the financial operations.

Sources

The sources of the financial data that will be used to create the two documents are the trial balances that have already been completed and the list of ledger balances.

Trial balance

As we have seen, the trial balance is a list of balances that have been extracted from the accounts in the ledger. The trial balance is usually created at the end of a financial period.

There are two main reasons why the trial balance is created. First, to check the mathematical calculations that have been performed in the ledger entries and, secondly, to make sure that the trial balance includes any necessary financial information that may be needed in the final accounts (specifically the trading and profit and loss account and the balance sheet).

When drawing up the trial balance, the business needs to list the name of each ledger that has produced either a debit or a credit balance. When the listed account has a debit or credit balance, the amounts are either placed in the Dr. or the Cr. column as appropriate. Credit balances go into the Cr. Column, and Dr. balances go into the debit column.

List of ledger balances

The relevant ledger account balances must be included in the trial balance. Above all, they should be balanced at points before the trial balance is completed because the business will want to know what money it has in hand.

case study 8.5

United Plastics Ltd

At the end of March 2008, United Plastics (Norfolk) Ltd extracted the following balances from its ledgers.

Table 8.36 Balances

Sales	£337,500
Purchases	£181,000
Premises	£252,000
Fixtures & fittings	£15,000
Stock	£35,000
Cash	£2,500
Debtors	£29,900
Creditors	£30,500
General expenses	£38,200
Capital (R Maitland)	£185,600

activity

1 How would you go about organising the data from the ledgers?
2 What is the trial balance?

Trading and profit and loss account

A trading and profit and loss account combines the features of a trading account and a profit and loss account. The trading account usually just shows the gross profit (or loss) that the business has made. The profit and loss account shows the net profit (or loss) made. They are often combined as one trading and profit and loss account so that both the gross and net profit can be shown in the same set of accounts.

The profit and loss account has several very useful purposes:

■ It can show how successful trading has been compared with the previous year's trading.

■ The profit calculated can be compared with expected profit.

■ It can be useful to the business if it wishes to obtain loans and financial backing from creditors and financial institutions.

■ It can help the owners and managers plan for the future.

The trading account shows how much revenue has been earned from the sales minus the cost of goods sold.

Sales

The sales total is equal to the turnover or the sales revenue of the business in the period in which the accounts are being prepared. Note that the turnover is just the income or the total receipts of the business and does not take into account any expenditure.

Cost of goods sold

The cost of goods sold refers to the ongoing costs of offering the products and services for sale to customers. The cost of goods sold includes the original purchase price of the goods if the business has purchased them for resale. The cost will also include any other costs that were incurred by the business in the process of buying, making, processing or selling the products. The cost of goods sold is often referred to as cost of sales.

Cost of goods sold is calculated by:

■ taking the opening stock (i.e. the value of the stock that exists at the beginning of the accounting period)

■ adding purchases of goods for resale made during the accounting period

Fig 8.9 A limited company's
final accounts

---

limited company final accounts
*** NAME OF COMPANY *** LIMITED
TRADING AND PROFIT AND LOSS ACCOUNT FOR THE YEAR PERIOD ENDED *** DATE ***

	£	£
Sales	x	(a)
Opening stock	x	
Purchases of production cost	x	
	x	
Less Closing stock	x	
Cost of Goods Sold		x (b)
Gross profits (a) – (b)		x (c)
Less expenses:		
e.g. Selling and distribution costs	x	
Administration costs	x	
Finance costs	x	
		x (d)
Net profit for year before taxation (c) – (d)		x (e)
Less corporation tax		x (f)
Profit for year after taxation (e) – (f)		x (g)
Less interim dividends paid		
ordinary shares	x	
preference shares	x	
final dividends proposed		
ordinary shares	x	
preference shares	x	
		x (h)
Forecasted profit for year (g) – (h)		x (i)
Add balance of invested profits at beginning of year		x x
Balance of invested profits at end of year (i) – (j)		x x

Notes:
- for a manufacturing business, production costs and the factory cost of manufacturing the products is shown instead of purchases
- depreciation of fixed assets is included in the costs for production, selling and distribution, and administration as appropriate
- directors' renumeration and debenture interest is included in the expenses

---

> **remember**
>
> Do not make the mistake of confusing purchases with stocks. Purchases of stocks are dealt with through the purchases account and not in the opening and closing stocks.

■ taking away the closing stock (i.e. the value of the stock that exists at the end of the accounting period). This means the value of the stock at the beginning of the year, less the items that have been sold during the year.

Gross profit

Gross profit is calculated by deducting the cost of sales (or cost of goods sold) from the sales. Gross profit is a measure of the difference between the turnover and the cost of either manufacturing or purchasing the products that have subsequently been sold. Gross profit is a measure of the profit that has been made on trading activities alone.

Gross profit is always calculated without taking into account other costs which are legitimate expenses, including:

■ expenses, such as administration and advertising

■ overheads, such as rent and rates.

Gross profit remains a useful measure of a business's performance. Typically, the level of gross profit will be compared with that of a competitor in a similar set of circumstances. If, for example, the level of gross profit is lower than the competitor's there must be a reason relating to the costs of goods sold. Perhaps the supplier is charging too much for the products that have been purchased.

Other income and profits

A business may have other income and profits from activities that are not directly related to the operations of the business. These incomes and profits may derive from investments that have been made by the business, perhaps in another business or a joint venture.

A business can make an investment just like a private investor, buying shares in another business and then taking a share of the profits of that business, either in the form of dividends or straight profits.

Businesses may also make more conservative investments, perhaps setting aside funds for investment in interest-bearing accounts. These would provide a small, but steady income, provided that the sum invested was sufficient, whilst protecting the sum invested.

> **remember**
>
> The income and profits from any investments would be included as a profit on the main business's profit and loss account.

Overheads

As we have seen, overheads are costs that are generated by a business but do not directly relate to the production process or the generation of sales. Many businesses refer to overheads as fixed costs or indirect costs. This is because they are costs relating to the ownership or the maintenance of property and support services, including heating, lighting and administrative costs.

Investors look at the amount of overheads a business is carrying as a proportion of its total expenditure and compare this figure with the business's total sales revenue (this is known as the overhead ratio).

Typically, the overhead ratio is calculated using the following equation:

Operating expenses/total net interest income + operating income

In this formula, a business's operating expenses are taken to include:

■ rent or lease payments

■ maintenance costs

■ depreciation.

> **remember**
>
> Overheads cannot be directly attributed to production of products or services or to their delivery.

Net profit

We know that sales less the cost of sales (costs of goods sold) gives us the gross profit figure. If we then take the expenses from the gross profit figure, we can calculate the net profit. In other words, net profit is equal to the gross profit minus the expenses. Net profit represents the surplus of sales made over the expenditure in the accounting period. If the expenditure were greater than the sales, there would be a net loss instead of a net profit.

Net or operating profit is a very useful measure of a business's performance. There are cases when a business makes a large gross profit but a relatively modest net profit. Possible reasons could be that the business has too big a wage and salary bill or is not distributing its products in the best way.

It is also worth remembering that investors in particular will be looking for the quality of the profit. This means that they will want to see whether the level of profit is unusual for the business or is expected to continue. A business, for example, might have sold off a major asset during the financial year for a price far greater than the original valuation. This would show up in the profit and loss account as a good profit. But, as the asset has already been sold and the business may not have a similar asset to sell in the next financial year, the actual profit quality is low.

Businesses calculate their profits or losses at intervals over the financial year. As we have seen, extracting a trial balance from various accounts and then creating either a trading and profit and loss account or a balance sheet, or both, can provide vital assistance to the business.

> **remember**
>
> Gross profit is simply the difference between the sales revenue and the cost of goods sold.

Trading and profit and loss account – worked example

When creating the trading account, the first action is to work out the correct figure for gross profit. All that is necessary to create the gross profit total is to deduct the cost of sales figure from the sales figure itself.

Table 8.37 Worked example 1

	£
Sales	20,000
Less cost of sales	(5,000)
Gross profit	15,000

The purpose of the line underneath the £5,000 is that it instructs you to make the calculation. The bracket around the £5,000 instructs you to deduct it from the £20,000 and not to add it.

Adding the opening stock and the purchases together and then deducting the closing stock gives us the cost of sales figure.

Table 8.38 Worked example 2

	£
Opening stock	2,000
Purchases	6,000
Less closing stock	(3,000)
Cost of sales	5,000

The total for the cost of sales is usually placed one column to the right, to allow us to deduct the £5,000 from the sales figure of £20,000 to give us a gross profit of £15,000 in the same column. It is important to begin doing this immediately; otherwise the situation becomes too complicated

Table 8.39 Worked example 3

	£	£
Sales		20,000
Less cost of sales		5,000
Gross profit		15,000

We'll turn now to the profit and loss account, the purpose of which is to create a net profit figure. Remember that this is achieved by taking the total expenses figure away from the gross profit:

Table 8.40 Worked example 4

	£	£
Gross profit		15,000
Rent and rates	500	
Wages and salaries	10,000	
Advertising	100	
Travel	250	
Light and heat	150	
Office expenses	100	
Miscellaneous	100	
Bank interest	200	
Depreciation	1,550	
Doubtful debts	40	
Bad debts	10	(13,000)
Net profit		2,000

The total of all of the expenses comes to £13,000. This is placed in the same column as the gross profit figure of £15,000. This allows us easily to deduct the total expenses from the gross profit to leave us with a net profit of £2,000.

Balance sheet

After the trading and profit and loss account has been completed, there will be some accounts that cannot be closed as they carry over into the next trading period. Any of the remaining balances are therefore:

- assets
- capital
- liabilities.

All the other balances will have been closed off when the trading and profit and loss account was completed. It is the balances that still remain that are parts of the balance sheet.

It is important to remember that the balance sheet is done at the end of a financial period and only shows a snapshot of the status of the business. It shows the financial position of the business on that day and that day alone. It does not take into account that something may be sold, purchased or disposed of the following day.

Technically speaking, balance sheets are not really a part of the double-entry system. However, as there are debits and credits, it can be considered part of the double-entry system in the broadest sense.

- The trial balance is to check that the balances are right and that the records are complete.
- The balance sheet is a list of balances that are arranged in a particular order according to whether they are assets, liabilities or capital.
- Each balance listed in the trial balance is only used once.

A balance sheet shows the following:

- fixed assets – what the business owns
- current assets – what the business is owed
- current liabilities – what the business owes and must repay in the short term
- long-term liabilities – including owner's (or owners') capital.

Fixed assets

> **remember**
>
> A fixed asset is usually kept by the business for at least a year.

Fixed assets are those that the business will be continuing to use; they may well be retained by the business for some time. The main examples of fixed assets are:

- land
- premises and buildings
- machinery
- fixtures and fittings
- office equipment
- cars, trucks and lorries.

On the balance sheet, these assets are traditionally arranged in order of permanence. This means that land would come first, and the least permanent items such as office equipment and vehicles would come last.

Fixed assets are allocated to the following categories:

- tangible assets – buildings, land, machinery, computers, fixtures and fittings – where relevant shown at their depreciated or resale value
- intangible assets – goodwill, intellectual property rights, patents, trademarks, website domain names, long-term investments.

Current assets

Current assets are items such as cash and anything that the business intends to sell in the short term. If the business has any credit bank balances, these count as current assets. A current asset is easily distinguished from a fixed asset; a current asset is one which the business must intend to sell or dispose of before the year is out. This means that the following fall into this category:

Fig 8.10 Balance sheet

*** NAME OF COMPANY *** LIMITED
BALANCE SHEET AS AT *** DATE ***

Fixed assets	Cost (a) £	Dep'n to date (b) £	Net (a) – (b) £
Intangible			
Goodwill	x	x	x
Tangible			
Freehold land and buildings	x	x	x
Machinery	x	x	x
Fixtures and fittings	x	x	x
etc.	x	x	x
	x	x	x (c)
Current assets			
Stock (closing)		x	
Debtors		x	
Bank		x	
Cash		x	
		x	(d)
Less Current Liabilities			
Creditors	x		
Bank overdraft	x		
Proposed dividends	x		
Corporation tax	x		
		x	(e)
Working capital (d) – (e)			x (f)
(c) – (f)			x (g)
Less Long-term liabilities			
Debentures			x (h)
NET ASSETS (g) – (h)			x (I)
FINANCED BY			
Authorised share capital			
x (number) preference shares of £x (nominal value) each			x
x (number) ordinary shares of £x (nominal value) each			x
			x
Issued share capital			
x (number) preference shares of £x (nominal value) each, fully/partly paid			x
x (number) ordinary shares of £x (nominal value) each, fully/partly paid			x
			x
Capital reserves			
Share premium account		x	
Revaluation reserve		x	x
Revenue reserves			
Profit and loss account		x	
General reserve		x	x
SHAREHOLDERS' FUNDS			x (j)

Note: balance sheet balance at point (I)

- stock (this is called the closing stock at the end of the trading period as it has been purchased in order to resell it)
- debtors (these are customers who owe the business money and should pay within the year)
- cash held on the premises of the business
- cash held by a bank or financial institution on behalf of the business.

Once again, the order on the balance sheet is by permanence. Current assets are listed in order of how easy it is to turn the asset into cash. Stock is always listed first as this is the hardest of the current assets to turn into immediate cash. The rest of the order is:

- debtors (as they will have promised to pay within a specified time period)
- cash held at the bank (as it has to be drawn out by the business)
- cash in hand in the business premises (as this can be readily accessible).

The full list of current assets includes the following:

- stock
- work in progress
- money owed by customers
- cash in hand or at the bank
- short-term investments
- pre-payments (e.g. advance rents).

Long-term liabilities

Long-term liabilities tend to be long-term loans that may be repayable by the business over a number of years. The loans are usually provided by:

- banks
- building societies
- private investors
- finance companies.

The business will have entered into a legal contract, which states:

- the amount of the loan
- the terms of the repayments
- the period over which the repayments will be made.

These types of loans do not have to be paid back by the business in the short term, so in terms of the balance sheet a loan will count as a long-term liability if it does not have to be paid back until at least a year after the date of the balance sheet.

Current liabilities

Current liabilities are those that will have to be paid back by the business in the short term. Current liabilities are usually amounts owed to suppliers for goods and services purchased on credit terms. They will have to be paid within 12 months of the balance sheet date and can include:

- trade creditors which are amounts owed to suppliers
- bank overdraft
- other creditors.

Working capital

Working capital is a measure of a business's ability to pay off its short-term liabilities. It is calculated by taking the current assets of the business and subtracting its current liabilities. Sometimes, a business refers to its working capital as operating capital. Usually, the more working capital a business has, the better the position it is in. However, too much working capital can be seen as wasteful as the cash could be turned in stock to sell or could be otherwise invested by the business. Many businesses do not have a great deal of working capital, despite the fact that they may have a considerable number of fixed assets. This situation can often occur if the business cannot turn its assets into cash.

Working capital is often expressed as either a positive or a negative figure. When a business has more debts than current assets, it has negative working capital. When current assets outweigh debts, a business has positive working capital. Changes in working capital will have an impact on the cash flow of the business.

Net assets

There are various interpretations of net assets. It is best to regard them as a measure of the money available to a business. At its simplest, net assets are equal to the business's assets less its current liabilities. Arguably, the long-term liabilities should be included in the calculation.

Another way of looking at net assets is to say that they are equal to the assets employed by the business. In other words, they are the fixed assets plus the net current assets (or working capital). This means that the calculations can either be:

- fixed assets plus net current assets
- fixed assets plus net current assets minus long term liabilities.

Capital

Capital is the owner's (or owners') original investment(s) in the business. In order to show how the capital was calculated, the complete details of the capital account are displayed on the balance sheet.

The capital is shown at the start of the trading period; then the net profit is added and the drawings are deducted so that the balance sheet shows the profits that have been earned in the trading period.

Profit

Profit is the balance between income and expenditure, i.e. the actual money made by the business over a period of time. The two key types of profit are:

- gross profit – the difference between the total sales revenue and the costs of goods sold
- net profit – the difference between the gross profit and the expenses of running a business.

Drawings

Drawings are cash sums (or other payments) taken out of the business by the owner(s). Drawings represent a withdrawal of funds from the business and are therefore considered to be assets that have been withdrawn from the business by the owner(s). Usually, the assets are cash, but any type of asset can be withdrawn. In company accounts, the assets are either:

- salaries – if the payments have been made for work carried out by the owner
- dividends – if the payments are a share of the profits.

Balance sheet – worked example

One of the first actions is to work out the value of the business's fixed assets. We do not put on the balance sheet the actual price that was paid for the fixed asset. Instead, we use the present value of the asset; this is known as the net book value. Assets tend to depreciate or lose value over time, particularly assets that are used, like plant and machinery, vehicles, fixtures and fittings.

A business that has £19,000 worth of fixed assets may find that even in the course of a year the actual value of those assets has decreased. If the business were to sell those assets it could not expect to receive anything like the purchase prices. This means that, when we are using fixed asset values on a balance sheet, we must always be aware of the net book value of the assets and not simply assume that a van purchased for £20,000 five years ago is still worth £20,000. It is more likely to be worth less than £5,000.

Current assets also need to be totalled because we need to know the value of net current assets. This is achieved by deducting the total current liabilities from the total current assets:

Table 8.41 Worked example 5

	£	£
Stock	3,000	
Debtors	3,040	
Provision for bad debt	(40)	
Prepayments	100	
Bank and cash	3,000	9,100

Note that in this example all of the figures in the left-hand column have been added with the exception of the provision for bad debt, which is in brackets. As it is in brackets it has been deducted from the total.

The total of £9,100 has been positioned in the column to the right, so that we can deduct the total of current liabilities from this figure to give us our net current asset figure:

Table 8.42 Worked example 6

	£	£
Current assets		
Stock	3,000	
Debtors	3,040	
Provision for bad debt	(40)	
Prepayments	100	
Bank and cash	3,000	9,100
Current liabilities		
Creditors	1,000	
Accruals	200	
Overdraft	2,800	4,000
Net current assets		5,100

We have already looked at current liabilities. These need to be totalled so that they can be deducted from the total for current assets to give us our net current assets.

Turning to the balance sheet totals, if we were to include figures for the business's fixed assets we could now arrive at a balance sheet total:

Table 8.43 Worked example 7

	£	£	£
Land and buildings			9,500
Plant and machinery			1,600
Fixtures and fittings			2,100
Motor vehicles			2,250
			15,450
Current assets			
Stock	3,000		
Debtors	3,040		
Provision for bad debt	(40)		
Prepayments	100		
Bank and cash	3,000	9,100	
Current liabilities			
Creditors	1,000		
Accruals	200		
Overdraft	2,800	4,000	
Net current assets			5,100
Long-term loan			(550)
Total			20,000

The bottom part of the balance sheet now needs to be calculated. Remember that it should match the top half of the balance sheet. Here is an example of how it could balance.

Table 8.44 Worked example 8

	£
Capital	15,000
Profits	12,000
Drawings	(7,000)
	20,000

This balances the balance sheet. Remember that the totals should always be the same; otherwise an error has been made, either on the balance sheet or at an earlier point in the process.

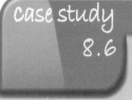

Trial balance

Bernice Jones started trading as a teddy bear and gift shop with an initial capital of £13,710 on 1 April 2008. She finished her first year of trading on 31 March 2009. She had achieved £49,530 in sales over the course of the year.

Bernice's cost of sales was £27,090. The stock in hand at the end of the period was £4,690. Her wage bill totalled £4,200 and she had drawn personal cash for herself of £11,000.

Rent and rates totalled £3,160. Electricity bills came to £1,130. Car expenses worked out at £1,690. Insurance was £690 and general expenses were £490.

Bernice had £270 in the safe in the shop. Her bank balance was £5,350 and she owed £6,570 to suppliers. Bernice's van was valued at £11,750. Bernice had invested £2,990 in shop fittings during the year.

Bernice has attempted to create a trial balance, but obviously something has gone wrong, as the two sides will not balance and she knows something is wrong, but she is not sure what or where:

Table 8.45 Trial balance for Bernice Jones

	Dr. £	Cr. £
Sales		49,530
Purchases	27,090	
Staff wages	4,200	
Drawings	11,000	
Rent and rates	3,160	
Electricity	1,130	
Motor expenses	1,690	
Insurance	690	
General expenses	490	
Cash in hand		270
Cash at bank		5,350
Creditors		6,570
Vehicle	11,750	
Fixtures and fittings	2,990	
Closing stock		4,690

activity

Identify the errors on the trial balance sheet.

activity
INDIVIDUAL WORK 8.8

P5

Use the information in Case study 8.6 to prepare a trading and profit and loss account and a balance sheet using the correct formats.

In view of the errors on the trial balance, it may be advisable to construct your own trial balance rather than relying on the version given in the case study. You should:

1. Prepare the trading and profit and loss account in the correct format.
2. Prepare a balance sheet in the correct format.
3. Ensure that you include the revenue income and the revenue expenditure.
4. Put the balance sheet items in the order of permanence (the most logical sequence).
5. Ensure that there are no errors or inaccuracies.

activity
INDIVIDUAL WORK 8.9

M3

D2

1. For M3, use the information in Case study 8.6 and explain why the extended trial balance is used to make adjustments to accounts. You should:

   (a) Explain how you would locate and detect errors in the trial balance.

   (b) Explain how the extended trial balance could be used to show the original account balances and subsequent adjustments. Remember that the adjustment columns are used to show those adjustments before the figures are extended into the columns of profit and loss or in the columns on the balance sheet.

   (c) Ensure that you have checked *all* the figures in case there are mathematical errors before you prepare your final accounts.

   (d) Ensure that the actual balance sheet does balance.

   (e) Give examples of potential errors that could affect the trial balance and explain how you would solve them.

   (f) Ensure that your teacher/tutor reviews any of your corrections.

2. For D2, evaluate the value of a set of final accounts to a business.

   (a) Comment on the value of the information that appears in your final accounts to the owners of the business and any other potential interested parties. (You are not expected to calculate performance indicators or ratios.)

   (b) Identify the benefits of obtaining some key figures that have resulted from the preparation of your final accounts.

Progress Check

1. What is the purpose of a goods received note?
2. What is VAT?
3. What can be found on a statement of account?
4. What is a business's most liquid asset?
5. Give four examples of daybooks.
6. What is another word used to describe a float?
7. Connect each word from (a) with one from (b) to make the right pairs:

   (a) Credit and debit

   (b) Receiver and giver

   Explain your answer.
8. What is a general ledger?
9. How is gross profit calculated?
10. Give five examples of tangible assets.

UNIT 10

An Introduction to Marketing Research

This unit covers:

- The main types of marketing research and how marketing research is used to make marketing decisions
- How to plan simple research
- How to carry out simple research
- How to interpret research findings

Marketing research is one of the prime means by which an organisation finds out about its customers and the environment in which it operates. Many businesses carry out continuous investigations into trends, opportunities and threats.

Each marketing research programme has its own objectives and set of constraints; it is important to work within these and choose the most appropriate means of answering the key questions posed by a business. This unit introduces the main methods of marketing research and looks at how a research project is planned. You will be asked to carry out your own research and interpret and evaluate the findings.

grading criteria

To achieve a **Pass** grade the evidence must show that the learner is able to:	To achieve a **Merit** grade the evidence must also show that the learner is able to:	To achieve a **Distinction** grade the evidence must also show that the learner is able to:
P1 describe the main types of marketing research and how they have been used to make a marketing decision in a given situation Pg 152	**M1** explain the context in which different marketing research methods are appropriate Pg 152	**D1** evaluate the application of a selected research method and plan, make and justify recommendations for improvement Pg 164
P2 select an appropriate method of data collection and plan research for a selected product/service Pg 158	**M2** explain the reasons for selecting the particular method of data collection for a selected product/service Pg 160	**D2** evaluate the findings from the research undertaken Pg 173
P3 conduct primary and secondary research, making use of an identifiable sampling method Pg 164	**M3** analyse own research and findings and make recommendations on how marketing strategies could be adapted Pg 173	
P4 interpret findings from the research and present them clearly in an appropriate format Pg 172		

The main types of marketing research and how it is used to make marketing decisions

Although the terms 'market research' and 'marketing research' are often confused and used interchangeably, in truth they are very different. Market research tends to be rather narrower in focus and is nearly always aimed at understanding consumer behaviour. Marketing research, on the other hand, is far broader; it encompasses any investigation into any element of the marketing mix, the environment in which the organisation operates or indeed any future impacts on the organisation. Marketing research is an information-gathering exercise; sometimes, it is a continual process that attempts to uncover data, views, concerns and responses to the organisation itself and its products or services or to the market in general or its customers.

Visit the website of the Marketing Research Society

www.mrs.org.uk

Broadly speaking, we can divide marketing research into two key types. The first is called primary research and involves the collection and collating of new information (i.e. information that has been collected solely for the purpose of the particular marketing research project). The other form of marketing research, which is called secondary research, utilises statistics and other information bought in from another source or reused from an existing source. In other words, secondary research involves the use of existing data that has already been collected by another organisation or was collected by the organisation undertaking the research but for another purpose.

Fig 10.1 Primary research now tends to be carried out by contacting respondents directly by telephone

Primary research

Primary research usually involves having to search out and collect information that is new. A business may **commission** a marketing research agency to do the work for it, or the business's employees may be assigned to the marketing project.

See Unit 3 in BTEC National Business Book 1 for information on the basics of primary research.

Primary data is usually collected by what is known as field research; this means that the individuals carrying out the research interact with the participants or **respondents** and collect the data or information directly from them.

Primary research is not a cheap option as it can be time consuming and very easy to get wrong. Once the key research objectives have been set, methods need to be developed or adopted in order to collect and collate the required information. Several ways in which this can be achieved are outlined in this section of the unit.

Observation

Observation, or observational field research, is a method borrowed from the social sciences that involves the researcher watching the behaviour of participants (the subjects of the research). One form of observation is known as non-participative (or non-participant) observation, as the researcher simply watches the participants' activities without influencing them in any way. In some studies, the participants may not be aware that they are being watched. For example, the researcher might be watching the shopping habits of customers in a department store or supermarket, using the CCTV.

The alternative is participatory (or participant) observation. In this type of observation, the participants are aware that the researcher is observing. Although the researcher simply tags along with them without seeking to influence what they do or say, the participants' behaviour is likely to be affected because they know that the observer is there.

It is easy to assess the reliability (consistency) of observational data by comparing the data from two researchers' observations of the same event. The validity of observational data is improved if participants are observed in a natural environment and also when participants are observed over a long period of time, as they become accustomed to being observed and are more likely to act normally.

See pages 354–355 in Unit 26 for more on validity.

Experimentation

In marketing research, an experiment is likely to involve participants chosen because they match the target group for testing out prototype versions of products and services. The research and development of new products and services is very costly and time consuming. As **prototypes** become available, they are routinely 'crash tested' by individuals who are representative of the types of customer who will later purchase them.

Experimentation allows the organisation to see how a product might be used, or abused, in a real-life situation. Clearly, it is important for many products to be durable, long lasting and not prone to breakage. Customers expect that products such as electrical goods, which will be used on a regular and routine basis, will not be prone to malfunctions that will make it necessary to replace them. Also, a business would not wish to launch a product that is unreliable, as this would not only have a financial impact but would also create the logistical problem of dealing with returns and repairs, not to mention having an adverse effect on the business's reputation.

Surveys

A survey is a research method used to collect data from a large number of participants. A range of methods are used by organisations (including the business itself or marketing research agencies working for a business), when collecting survey data concerning the responses and opinions of target groups.

Although behind the decision to carry out marketing research there may be reasons specific to an organisation, such research is generally done because the organisation wishes to collect information that will gain it an edge in the market and enable it to make better decisions. The focus of the research is often the business's customers; however, this group is not as clearly defined as you might think. It includes some or all of the following:

- current customers – those actively purchasing from the business
- prospective customers – those who have shown an interest in the business, its products or services but have not yet bought
- lost customers – customers who used to buy from the business but for some reason or other are not current customers
- community – the broadest group of individuals – those who may not have any connection with the business but can be current, prospective or lost customers

> **remember**
>
> The marketing research process is the systematic identification, collection and analysis of date for the purpose of assisting decision making in an organisation.

- employees (internal customers) – individuals who service the business in some way and whose actions have a bearing on how the organisation deals with its customers, past, present and prospective
- shareholders (internal customers) – those who have a financial stake in the organisation and can influence or control the way in which it operates and deals with its customers.

The groups listed above are very diverse, and an organisation that intends to carry out a survey would have to choose the method that best suits the target group. Otherwise the results of the research may not be worthwhile.

We will now consider some of the more popular ways of carrying out a survey.

Face to face

Face-to-face interviews can take place in a number of different locations, typically at the home of the respondent, their workplace, on the street or in a shopping centre or mall. When data is collected face to face, the interviewer can use stimulus material to prompt the respondent, for example advertisements, packaging, and lists of brands and show cards (which are prepared visual aids).

Face-to-face interviews can be longer than would be possible on the telephone, but this advantage must be balanced against the loss of goodwill from the respondent if the interview is overly long.

These types of interview do not tend to provide a random sample of the possible target market. For example, if the interviews are done in a shopping mall, only those prepared to stop and participate will be part of the sample; many others will refuse. Although the interviewer has chosen a respondent who appears to match the target group, there is no way of knowing whether that individual will take part in the interview.

See page 160–161 for information on random and non-random sampling.

Fig 10.2 Postal surveys have low response rates and often rely on incentives to encourage completion

Face-to-face interviewing increases the costs of carrying out the research, as interviewers need to be deployed in different locations; shopping malls often charge the research company, and the time taken for each interview is comparatively long. When the interviews are carried out in the respondents' homes, a definite time will have been arranged to cut down on wasted journeys. In the case of home and workplace visits, many of the respondents are recruited by telephone, and appointments are made.

Postal

Postal surveys, which are sometimes referred to as mail-out surveys, involve sending out a number of questionnaires to a target group of potential respondents. The questionnaires are designed by the organisation to be completed by the respondents in return for an **incentive**, such as a gift, voucher or entry into a competition. Usually, a business would choose some of its customers, or a mailing list can be purchased from a specialised marketing research company that provides names and addresses of people that match the **profile** of the target group. To a large extent, this form of marketing research is being overtaken by e-mail surveys.

The key advantages of a postal survey are that many questionnaires can be sent out and the costs are relatively low. Also, questionnaires can be useful for asking questions that it could be difficult to ask on the telephone.

The questionnaires must be well designed, and the questions need to be clear and unambiguous. Visual prompts or samples of new products can be included in the package sent to the respondents.

Visit the website of Ipsos **MORI**, a business that offers to carry out primary research for business and organisations

www.mori.com

The major disadvantage of postal surveys is the relatively low response rate; commonly less than 20% are completed and returned. The keys to improving the response rate are the inclusion of incentives, the ease of answering the questions, and whether the respondent is actually interested in completing the questionnaire in the first place.

The most significant problem with postal surveys is the likelihood that the poor response rate will adversely affect the representativeness of the data collected. As it is not possible to be sure who will answer and return the questionnaires, no amount of work on making sure that the initial number of respondents represents the target audience as a whole will have any bearing on what comes back to be analysed. Consistently, the organisation's most determined and loyal customers will be the ones who complete and return the questionnaires, which will bias the results of the survey.

Telephone

Unfortunately, telephone research has received extremely bad press and is viewed with suspicion by those who are called to take part in telephone-based marketing research. Many direct sales organisations often begin their conversation with a home owner by telling them that they are carrying out market research, when in fact they are making a sales call.

Dedicated telephone research, however, can bring important and, above all, rapid and cost-effective information and data to a business or to a specialised company undertaking the research on its behalf.

As with many different forms of marketing research, the basic success of telephone research depends upon the accuracy of the telephone list and the ability of those undertaking the research to match the people on the list with the characteristics of their target group.

In order to get the best results, market researchers need to be trained to work from a set of notes, often known as a script. This will ensure that the respondents actually answer the questions contained on the questionnaire. As there is no face-to-face contact with the respondent, the researcher can type the answers directly onto the screen so that the responses can immediately be added to the database, which can save time and effort.

Organisations such as **MORI**, which is a national opinion poll organisation, use state of the art telephone research facilities, which take full advantage of the advances in telecommunications, in order to speed up the data-gathering exercise.

Telephone research has become a very important aspect of marketing research, mainly because of the speed. One of the major problems, however, is the failure rate in telephone research. This is primarily related to unanswered calls, making calls at an inappropriate time or the wrong person answering the phone.

Fig 10.3 Ipsos MORI home page

(Source: www.mori.com)

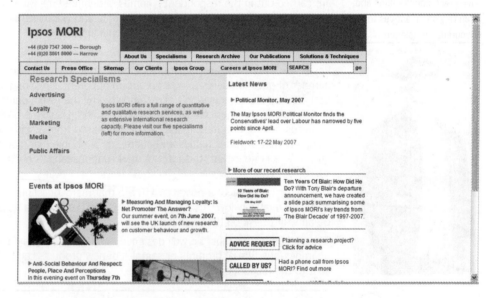

Email and e-marketing research

Broadly speaking, marketing research on the Internet falls into two categories:

- First, there is market research that is, effectively, secondary research into an organisation's online activities or an issue.

- Secondly, it can be used as a field research method for surveying opinions.

Email surveying enables an enormous number of people to be contacted quickly by bulk sending (or spamming). Although the response rate is likely to be very low, the sheer volume may mean that a large number of responses will be sent back.

E-Consultancy offers organisations and businesses ways in which they can improve their Internet marketing strategies

www.e-consultancy.com

The geographical location of the respondent is not a barrier (although questionnaires may have to be produced in languages other than English if the target groups are located in many different countries).

When email surveying was first used, response rates were relatively high compared with other methods. However, over time, potential respondents have become less likely to complete emailed questionnaires, as people receive thousands of spam emails. These days, people are likely to delete the email without answering it.

Compared with many methods of collecting survey data, the Internet is far cheaper, but an emailed questionnaire has to be created and programmed which could push costs up. The main advantage of the online questionnaire is that the data can be instantly exported to a database and be incorporated into the research findings for analysis.

The success or failure of online questionnaires depends largely on having sufficient time and budget to carry out the research, the questionnaire's complexity, and the sample profile (whether the respondents sampled are more or less likely to respond and/or have access to a computer).

The Internet can provide both qualitative and quantitative data. Exploratory research can be used to gain information on the following issues directly related to the online presence of the organisation:

- general website evaluation
- evaluation of online products or services
- competitor evaluation
- design/navigation/usability testing.

Focus groups

Putting together a focus group involves selecting a number of individuals who are representative of a larger target group. Typically, these individuals could be representative of a business's customers, distributors, or potential customers or they could simply be people who match a typical customer's age, gender or income level.

In effect, a focus group is a form of group interview. A moderator takes the role of group leader and leads the group, directing, encouraging and sparking off discussion so that group members' views and experiences of a product, service or topic can be collected. Focus group research can provide useful insights into people's shared understandings of various products etc.

It is part of the moderator's role to ensure that all individuals within the group have an opportunity to contribute. The more dominant members of the group can influence some of the others and it is, therefore, important that the moderator is not only a good leader but also has excellent interpersonal skills.

Focus groups are used to collect data about attitudes, beliefs, experiences, feelings and reactions. It is very difficult to obtain such data in other ways, although some information could be gleaned by observation or one-to-one interviews.

You can visit Tourism Victoria's website

www.visitvictoria.com

Panels

Panels are essentially a variety of focus groups made up of experts in a particular field. The experts are carefully chosen, so that they can bring with them ideas and opinions based on relevant experience. A business that deals with retailers, for example, would bring together a panel of retailers, rather than a focus group of consumers who purchase from the retailers. Having dealt with many different products and services over their business careers, the retailers can offer expert opinions and will be able to provide the researchers with valuable professional insights. This is information that could not be gathered direct from consumers.

Tourism Victoria – Part 1

Conducting focus groups will provide further insight into the behaviour and mindset of your target market. Focus groups are group discussion (usually six to eight people), comprising representatives of the target market, on a topic where an experienced moderator is briefed on the specific topics for discussion.

Tourism Victoria regularly conducts focus groups of key interstate markets. Focus groups have provided Tourism Victoria with an insight into its target markets and their current attitudes to Victoria.

Focus groups generally cost on average $2500 to $3000 per group.

Once you have established the target market for your marketing campaign it is useful to test how the target market will react to components of the campaign. Testing your target market's response to a marketing campaign is referred to as 'pre-testing'.

Pre-testing is particularly useful for components of your marketing campaign that cost large amounts of money. It allows you to reduce the risk of spending large amounts of money on marketing activities that do not achieve the desired objectives. A positive response to the test may be regarded as evidence of the potential positive effect of the campaign. A negative response to the pre-test gives you the chance to re-evaluate the campaign and make any changes deemed necessary prior to its implementation.

Research methods that can be used to pre-test components of a marketing campaign include conducting focus groups or interviews.

A core activity of Tourism Victoria's marketing campaigns is television advertising, which is a costly marketing activity. Tourism Victoria pre-tests its advertisements to measure effectiveness. Tourism Victoria usually hires a consultant to conduct interviews with representatives of its target market to explore their view of the advertisement.

It is also useful to 'post-test' an existing component of a marketing campaign. Post-test refers to testing the effectiveness of a component of a marketing campaign after it has been implemented.

(Adapted from www.tourismvictoria.com.au)

activity

1 Why are focus groups ideal for pre-testing research?
2 At what stage should you show a proposed marketing campaign to a focus group?

Field trials and piloting

Field trials take the testing of new products and services one stage further than experimentation. There are various ways in which a business could use field trials in order to gain valuable information about products and services before these are fully launched. The most basic form of field trial is essentially an extension of the work carried out by focus groups. In this variation, the product or service is offered to a representative sample of potential customers, or target groups, so that they can test the product or service under normal conditions in their own homes. Over a given period of time, the testers will note down their observations and experiences related to their use of the product. Periodically, at key stages of the research project, researchers will visit the testers and interview them, using prepared questionnaires.

A more extensive version of field trials involves the test launch of a product or service in a relatively restricted geographical area. A small area is chosen, which is, as far as research can reveal, representative of the larger target market. For example, an organisation could choose a city, such as Nottingham, a county, such as Norfolk, or even a region, such as East Anglia. The mini-launch of the product or service is supported by advertising and marketing, and the product or service is only available in the given area and for a relatively short period of time.

During this period, the organisation would monitor the response to the advertising and marketing and compare sales with costs, thereby allowing the organisation to judge the effectiveness of the marketing and the return on its investment. As the product or service is only being used by customers in a restricted area, the need for customer support, replacement, repair and other ongoing support functions will be limited.

Throughout the field trials the organisation would keep a close eye on customers' perceptions of the product, any problems that have arisen, repeat sales if appropriate and a host of other aspects. Knowing the potential demands will enable the business to prepare for a national or international launch of the product. In effect, the organisation has piloted or tested its product or service in a limited way, in preparation for the full launch.

Any research tool such a questionnaire should be piloted before it is used to collect the data that will be used for the research. Trying the questionnaire out on a small group of people who are similar to the target group will enable the researcher to see, for example, if the questions are easily understood, how long it takes to complete the questionnaire and how easily the data can be analysed.

Secondary research

Secondary research involves the collecting of existing data and manipulating it so that a summary of the findings of that data can be used for marketing purposes.

See Unit 3 in BTEC National Business Book 1 for information on the basics of secondary research.

Amongst the most common forms of secondary research are published statistics, including the **census**, and published texts, including books, magazines and newspapers.

The primary advantages of secondary research are that sources are cheap and relatively accessible. Secondary research is very useful for finding out large-scale trends.

For information on the latest census, visit

www.statistics.gov.uk

The major problem with secondary research is lack of consistency in how the data is collected. It is difficult to know if there is bias or inaccuracy. Many published statistics actually raise more questions than they answer. Also secondary data may not be collected for the particular purposes of the marketing research.

A business routinely uses both internal and external forms of secondary research. As we will see, an organisation has access to a wealth of information from within itself and beyond that it can purchase or acquire additional data from a number of different sources.

Internal sources

The term 'internal sources' refers to information or data that is routinely held by an organisation; this data is not necessarily used for marketing research. The different departments within a business collect and collate data related to their particular areas of interest, responsibility and expertise.

See Unit 3 in BTEC National Business Book 1 for information on internal sources for marketing research.

Departments may not routinely share this information with the rest of the organisation. Table 10.1 summarises the key sources of internal information:

Table 10.1 Internal sources of information

Internal source	Characteristics, benefits and drawbacks
Data records	Data records are basically customer records, containing information about the customer: e.g. name, address, purchasing habits, credit ratings. By matching the customers' purchasing habits and preferences with new products and services as they become available, the records can be used as the basis for targeted marketing and advertising. The key drawback is that customer records need to be entirely up to date and periodically checked; lapsed customers should be purged from the system, and updates made when customers' details change.
Loyalty schemes	Supermarkets, such as Tesco, run extensive loyalty schemes and programmes. Supermarkets are able to match customers' purchasing habits with targeted offers to encourage them to buy more of the same product or like products. Loyalty schemes encourage regular purchases, repeat purchases and volume sales. Increasingly, however, customers maintain several loyalty cards and switch from business to business, dependent upon the offers being made by the supermarkets. Loyalty schemes can also be seen as store cards, where customers are offered extended credit and special offers if they hold a charge card from that business. The key drawbacks are the increasing lack of loyalty of customers holding loyalty cards.
Electronic point of sale (EPOS)	EPOS was originally envisaged to make a link between the sale of a product and the stock control system. EPOS would enable the business to automatically generate a stock reorder once stock of a particular product had dropped to a minimum stock-holding level. Increasingly, however, EPOS is used in conjunction with loyalty cards to monitor customer purchases and to generate sales offers linked to popular brands. In its basic form, EPOS can indicate to a business which particular products are more or less likely to sell on a particular day or in a particular month. The business can then organise its sales displays or even its website to highlight popular sales items when these are most likely to be required by customers. The key drawback is that if it is used in its purest form EPOS simply tells the business what has been sold and when the sale was made. It does not indicate to the business the type of customer, particularly whether they are a regular customer or a casual buyer.
Website monitoring	Website monitoring is a form of observation. It involves monitoring the number of clicks made by customers on an organisation's website, noting how long they have been on the website and which pages they have visited. It is also possible to judge the activities on the website and the pages visited compared with the purchases made by the visitor. Businesses often encourage customers to register on the website and by doing this they can customise the way in which the page appears to match the preferences of that customer. Again, they can monitor the activity of that individual customer, noting purchases and favoured pages, so that on their next visit the customisation can be further refined. The main drawback with website monitoring is that there are many casual visitors to the website who happen on it by accident or chance, and their activities may or not be representative of real customers' behaviour.
E-transactions	E-transactions comprise all forms of monetary transaction on a website, including the use of credit cards, debit cards and electronic payments, such as PayPal. By linking up with specialised finance companies and banks, businesses, regardless of their size, can offer secure online payment systems. By monitoring e-transactions the business is able to ascertain the most popular form of payment, whether customers are hesitant about entering their credit card details, and which form of payment and customer provide the biggest share of sales and from which region of the world they come. The major problem with any form of online payment is security. Although many websites offer encrypted pages, there is still considerable reluctance on the part of many customers to risk typing in their credit card details; they fear that hackers will gain access to the details and steal from their accounts.
Accounting records	Accounting records can be differentiated from sales in as much as they detail when and how customers made actual payments. Customers do not always pay when they order products or services. They may pay in instalments, or they may pay on delivery or after the production of an invoice. By monitoring the accounting records a business is able to see how long, on average, it takes a customer to pay an invoice and which payment method they have chosen. Monitoring accounting records is only useful when a business is looking at changes in the payment methods used by regular customers. When accounting records include new customers or one-off customers, their payment method or payment habits may not be representative of the mainstream of customers.
Production information	Increasingly many manufacturers only have a relatively small buffer stock of products and do not overproduce and store huge levels of stock in anticipation of sales. Therefore production is very much reliant on accurate sales data or, at the least, accurate orders. Production figures can be viewed as a mirror of sales or orders. Some businesses produce products that then have to be sold, whilst other businesses take orders or make a sale, which is then fulfilled by their production department. In both cases overproduction or underproduction can have serious affects on the business's cash flow. If a business is unable to fulfil an order owing to underproduction, a sale may be lost. If the business fails to have products available for distribution to retailers then sales could again be lost. The primary drawback of production information is that it most closely resembles actual sales unless it is the business's intention to produce products and store them in anticipation of future sales.

Internal source	Characteristics, benefits and drawbacks
Sales figures	Sales figures should show the accurate level of sales, as well as peaks and troughs in demand. Theoretically, sales figures should be the most accurate way of showing when, where and how much each product was sold for over a given period of time. By looking at trends in the sales figures, businesses can more confidently predict the level of sales in a similar future period, assuming that the same conditions apply. A manufacturer of artificial Christmas trees could, for example, confidently expect to begin selling small volumes in October, rising to larger volume sales in December. By January, of course, the sales figures would have slumped to virtually nothing. The main drawback with sales figures is that they only tell the business what has happened, rather than what might happen. There are many unknowns in the future that could affect sales, in either a positive or a negative way.
Sales personnel	Many businesses recognise that professional sales personnel, whilst they have experience and knowledge of products and services, are not necessarily the best people to ask about future sales trends, product development or marketing. Many sales personnel are overly optimistic about new products and the impact of new advertising. Typically, a business would discover the opinions of its sales force by asking them to participate in focus groups or complete questionnaires. Some businesses compare such information with data from similar research carried out with consumers. In all probability, the midpoint between the two groups is closer to the truth than either of the extremes would be.

The Delphi Method

The Delphi Method, or Delphi Technique, is a means of collecting the opinions of groups of experts, with the purpose of producing accurate, unbiased estimates. The idea is for the experts to work within a structured environment, using their professional judgement to try to predict what might happen in the future.

Some businesses recruit experts from within their own business; however, this may be problematic as they may have prior knowledge of future developments or may be biased in favour of the area in which they work in the business. For these reasons, a business may prefer to recruit external experts, rather like it would have done for panels used in primary research.

Usually, research using the Delphi Technique is carried out by an independent organisation on behalf of a particular industry. Businesses can then buy into the information generated from the group and see whether it accords with their own primary research on the same subjects.

The experts are asked to consider a particular situation, perhaps a product, a brand or an entire industry. They have to discuss the product and estimate what might happen in the short, medium or long term. Each of the experts produces an independent estimate. These are then collated, and either the researcher creates an average estimate or the group is brought together again to discuss the results. In some cases, individual experts are asked to revise their estimates in the light of information provided by the other members of the group. Alternatively, the experts are asked to continue to repeat the process until all have reached a consensus of opinion.

External sources

There is a vast array of potential information and data outside the organisation. It is prepared in many different forms and for many different purposes. The business has to understand that, whatever the source was, the information was not collected for its benefit. A degree of caution has always to be applied when using external sources.

See Unit 3 in BTEC National Business Book 1 for information on external sources of information useful for marketing research.

As Table 10.2 shows, there is a variety of amateur, semi-professional, governmental and specialist information available. Sometimes this comes at a relatively high price.

remember

Data from internal sources has not been collected for marketing research purposes and may not cover the correct period of time, type of customer or product, etc.

Table 10.2 External sources of information

Internal source	Characteristics, benefits and drawbacks
Internet	The Internet is, of course, full of information. Much of it is incorrect; most of it is misleading, and some of it is an outright lie. It is very dangerous to rely on information that is often unaccredited and where the source not revealed. Many businesses use the Internet to trawl for information, reactions and opinions, either about themselves or about their competitors. That kind of information can be valuable, as can constant monitoring of competitors' websites, which can reveal information about future direction, strategy, tactics and advertising.
Government statistics	The government produces an enormous array of statistics from the census, the Department for Business, Enterprise and Regulatory Reform and a host of other sources. There is information about different industries, marketing initiatives and trade initiatives. Much of the data is well researched and has been collated from a wide range of sources. In addition to UK government statistics there is extensive European-wide information compiled by the European Union. This offers the opportunity for a business to look at similarities and differences in European member states. One of the major problems with statistics produced by governments is that the information is not sufficiently focused for a business to make positive use of it. Statistics may be able to reveal the number of homeowners in a particular area, but this cannot be crosschecked with purchasing habits.
Libraries	Businesses do not routinely make use of local libraries for information gathering, despite the fact that there may be access to online databases. Businesses tend to use dedicated business libraries, which compile data from industries by trawling magazines and newspapers, as well as the Internet, for clippings and references to specific businesses. These specialist libraries will provide an ongoing and regular supply of data in this form, as well as alerting the business to upcoming reports and releases. The main drawback of using business libraries is that, unless the library is given a clear brief as to the interests of the business, the business may be bombarded with irrelevant information that it has had to pay a relatively high price to obtain.
Universities	Research is a major part of universities' work. Individual university lecturers and departments have over time become centres of excellence with regard to particular business aspects. They will routinely carry out their own research and may well cooperate with businesses or industry to collect and collate data. However, the university may require payment for the information or distribution of the information may be restricted purely to preferred partners.
Company reports	The structure of a company report is determined by law; a business is required to outline its profit and loss, balance sheet and use of funds. The report is also a means by which the business highlights its key personnel, notes its major successes and failures and perhaps announces new initiatives. The primary drawback is that it is essentially a sales document and beyond the basic financial data a company report is designed to attract investors, so it will always be upbeat and optimistic.
Specialist agencies	A number of specialist agencies operate both nationally and internationally, routinely collecting data which they then compile into reports for sale to businesses. Examples include Mintel, Datastream, and Dun and Bradstreet. These organisations have extensive research and information-gathering potential and produce regular reports on particular industries, countries, markets and products. The main drawback is the cost of the reports. For smaller businesses, relevance and cost effectiveness may also be issues.
Trade journals	Nearly every industry, including the service industries, has its own dedicated trade journal. These are publications, like magazines or newspapers, which feature articles and information of interest to a readership that is restricted primarily to those in the industry. The journals also carry advertisements, information about special events and warnings about new legislation that may have an impact on the industry. Although useful, trade journals should not be seen as the sole source of secondary marketing research data.

Department for Business, Enterprise and Regulatory Reform (DBERR, formerly the Department for Trade and Industry)

www.dti.gov.uk

Mintel

www.mintel.com

Dun and Bradstreet

www.dbuk.dnb.com

Mintel

Mintel began over three decades ago, providing food and drink research in the UK. Now the brand spans all corners of the globe. Mintel's leading analysts are world-renowned experts in diverse areas such as leisure, consumer goods, retail, financial services, sales promotion and social trends. Traffic to the group website is a testament to Mintel's success, with hits exceeding 2.3 million every month. The US office, which opened in 1997, now rivals the UK office in terms of size and revenue. Mintel's reach also extends into continental Europe, Latin America, Australia, Israel, China and South Korea.

Mintel's ability to predict market developments has driven the company's strategic direction. Furthermore, the ability to analyse data and deliver it using the latest technology has allowed Mintel to stay one step ahead of its competitors. By identifying opportunities, the company has expanded accordingly, both in its product offering and the geographical areas of operation. Its portfolio has grown from supplying published research to offering a full-service research solution, giving clients the tools they need to surpass their business objectives.

Mintel's goal is to provide both insight and impact in everything it does. This aim is carried out not only through the research it provides, but also through the work that it carries out with clients to obtain the best possible results for their business. Mintel communicates this message through all media, the enhanced group website, the company's concise and educational marketing literature, informative client **webinars**, and continued presence at top industry trade shows.

Mintel's brand values have been condensed into one simple phrase: insight and impact. Mintel provides all its clients with insight into their markets, consumers and products, and creates a tangible impact by challenging established concepts and having a positive impact on profits. Internally, each person at Mintel aims to provide insights in everything they do, ensuring their output makes maximum impact on their clients' businesses.

(Adapted from www.mintel.com)

activity

1 What do you think is meant by 'full-service research solution'?

2 What is a webinar?

3 How might a client business use the information collected by an organisation such as Mintel?

Use of IT applications

When a business has spent considerable time and effort in collecting, collating and analysing marketing research data, it is important that this information is always accessible. Increasingly, information is stored using ICT. In some cases, it will be appropriate for the information to be contained in a database, or perhaps a spreadsheet, whilst reports and summaries will usually be found in simple documents.

IT can assist in the storage, the organisation and the retrieval of information. Provided that this information is kept up to date, it can be accessed and used to form the basis of a report.

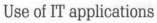

See Unit 26 for information about the management of business information.

Qualitative and quantitative research

Importance and use

The choice between volume and quality is at the heart of research, whether quantitative or qualitative.

Link See Unit 3 in BTEC National Business Book 1 for information on qualitative and quantitative research.

Qualitative research tends to be on a smaller scale with a great deal of in-depth information about, for example, opinions and ideas gathered from a relatively small sample of respondents or sources, it is the sheer detail of the information that is important rather than the scale of the information gathering.

Quantitative research, on the other hand, usually looks at far larger sets of data. In quantitative research, the data is in numerical form and can easily be analysed statistically.

The following table illustrates the features of qualitative and quantitative research and identifies the situations when they are appropriate:

Table 10.3 Research techniques

Method	Qualitative or quantitative	Characteristics, benefits and drawbacks
Postal survey	Quantitative	▪ Cost is low ▪ Response rate can be poor ▪ Answers may be incomplete ▪ Responses are coded and must be simple so people can understand them
Telephone survey	Quantitative	▪ It is a cost-effective method of achieving a robust sample ▪ Responses are coded ▪ Certain groups do not have access to the telephone, so may be excluded from the sample ▪ It is difficult to ask sensitive questions over the telephone ▪ Works well with employers
Face-to-face survey	Quantitative (can also be qualitative in part)	▪ Can include both open questions and coded questions ▪ Can achieve a robust sample ▪ Expensive and time consuming ▪ Ideal for gathering sensitive information or exploring complicated issues
In-depth interview	Qualitative	▪ Rich and detailed information can be gathered ▪ Interviewers are allowed more flexibility ▪ Answers to open questions can be difficult and time consuming to analyse ▪ Expensive and time consuming to administrate
Focus group	Qualitative	▪ A group discussion with around 8–12 people ▪ Usually lasts between 1 and 3 hours ▪ Capitalises on interaction between participants ▪ Participants are not representative of wider population which does not allow for generalisation ▪ Good for gathering sensitive data ▪ Data produced requires careful and unbiased analysis
Case study	Qualitative	▪ Researcher gains understanding of a specific person's experience through an in-depth interview ▪ Provides good quotations and rich data ▪ Can bring alive other research, such as survey data ▪ Findings cannot be generalised to a wider population

 Link See page 351 in Unit 26 for more on qualitative and quantitative information.

Triangulation

Regardless of the methods by which the marketing research data has been collected, it is important to ensure that the results are valid and accurate. When using multiple methods of data collection, results need to be triangulated. This means comparing the information from one source with information from another source and making sure that there are not any serious discrepancies.

In effect, triangulation integrates the different forms of research information, bringing them together so that they form a coherent set of results, rather than a series of different results that do not bear any relationship to one another.

Marketing strategies and activities

An organisation undertakes marketing research for a number of different purposes and at various different levels. A business may, for example, be interested in a broader view, in which case it will focus on strategic marketing research. Or the business may want a rapid assessment of customers' reactions to a particular product or service, in which case it will commission or carry out some ad hoc marketing research.

See page 144 for information about ad hoc research.

Strategic

Strategic marketing research, as the name implies, is designed to look at issues with implications for the longer term, such as where a particular organisation and its products or services fit into general trends and fashions or how it might be affected by the economic situation. The research will not be particularly focused on the organisation's own activities but will take a much broader perspective, looking at the environment in which the organisation operates.

Technical

Technical marketing research seeks to discover exactly how a particular product or service works. The researchers dismantle the product or service in question and look at its constituent parts. A product would literally be taken apart and each component examined for quality and source of manufacture and suitability for purpose. However, although a service is rather more difficult to look at in this way, the constituent parts can still be examined. For example, an insurance company's policy can be scrutinised to see what it covers, the small print, customer support, responsiveness and a host of other factors.

Data bank

It is important to a business to ensure that its records are up to date and that it has current information on its customers. A business will engage either a market research company or use its own sales and marketing functions to systematically contact each customer on its database and check that the customer's details are correct. This also provides an opportunity to try to make a sale.

Continuous research

Continuous research is also known as longitudinal research. It is carried out on a rolling basis, with no proposed end to the period in which the information will be collected. In effect, the organisation is monitoring a particular situation over the long term in order to pick out changes, trends, fashions or problems. Current results can be compared with those from previous points in the research; any changes can be immediately identified and any problems resolved without delay.

For example, a supermarket might carry out customer-flow research to note the busiest areas, most popular products and those areas of the store that do not receive the same level of interest. Based on data from the ongoing research, the retailer can change the position of products in the store, resolve possible blockages and hold-ups, and encourage customers to visit parts of the store that they do not routinely enter.

Fig 10.4 Supermarkets carry out continuous research, moving stock based on customer flow through the store

OK, that's 15,486 customers to the chocolate, alcohol and cake aisle and just 27 to the smelly cheese, bleach and cat litter aisle.

> **remember**
>
> It is often assumed that research will be carried out by members of the organisation itself, but those involved need to have both the capability and the time to do the research.

Ad hoc

Ad hoc research is research that has not been planned or organised in advance. Marketing research is carried out on the spur of the moment because a particular situation has arisen that needs investigation. If, for example, a store noted a considerable drop in the number of customers, it would carry out **immediate** research to discover the reason. If a previously popular brand suffers a slump in sales, any immediate research into the reason will be ad hoc because the slump in sales could not possibly have been predicted.

Although ad hoc research has to be done quickly, the organisation should ensure that it is valid and will answer the question that has been posed.

Purpose of research objectives

Many of the reasons why businesses commission research are standard. As we will discover in this section, the reasons relate largely to understanding customer behaviour, judging consumer awareness of the business's products and services, looking at the market and taking account of the activities of competitors.

Understanding customer behaviour

This is of vital importance to a business as it defines the way in which the business needs to operate and move. By matching its business strategy to its customers, the business can increase revenue and identify new opportunities.

Although many organisations collect a vast amount of data, few of them actually see the patterns in their customers' behaviour. Customer behaviour data can be identified from purchasing behaviour, returns and cancellations, complaints, frequency of verbal communication, web-browsing behaviours and a host of other sources.

Buying patterns, preferences and brand awareness

> **remember**
>
> Any investigation into customer behaviour and buying patterns will only give a business a snapshot of opinions. By the time that the data has been collected and analysed it may well be out of date.

One of the most basic types of marketing research is the Awareness, Attitude and Usage Study (AAU). This is used to assess the general state of the market for a particular brand, product, or service. Normally, the survey draws on the opinions of customers (both consumers and business customers).

Awareness is almost always tested first in this type of study; the respondent would have very little to say about the product or service if they were not aware of it. Awareness is tested in both unaided and aided forms. Unaided awareness consists of all the brands, companies, and product names that the respondent can recall. This is designed to be a quick and reactive measurement of awareness (sometimes called 'top of the mind' awareness). When testing aided awareness, the interviewer reads out a list of relevant brands and products and asks the respondent to state the ones that they have heard of. The sum total of unaided and aided awareness is known as 'total awareness'.

In this context, attitudes are the opinions of the respondents that are associated with the brands and products that are being tested. It is these attitudes that help highlight the brands' strengths and the weaknesses, so that action can be taken if appropriate.

Usage patterns are designed to reveal how the respondents interact with the brand. Comparative measurements can be made, such as whether the opinions of regular users of the brand differ from the opinions of occasional users. Demographics are also crosschecked, so levels of usage and opinion can be compared for different ages, income and gender. This can be helpful in identifying key potential customer groups.

case study 10.3

Poco Ropa children's clothes

Agency: Servon

Client: Poco Ropa

Project: Brand identity and marketing material design

Challenge
Poco Ropa, a family owned business importing babies' and children's clothes from small manufacturers in Spain required a distinctive brand identity to create and establish product recognition. The company marketed its clothing range at exhibitions throughout the country, but could not fully capitalise on the interest generated at the shows.

Process
We began by researching buying patterns in the market sector, and developing an understanding of the business. We designed a brand image that would be distinctive, memorable and closely linked to the company's products. The final design worked well on printed material, such as product swing tickets and marketing brochure, and also with digital media such as the company website. The website gave the company exposure on the web and gave clients basic information on the products available as well as contact details. After 12 months of successful trading, the website was expanded to include full product information and online purchasing facilities.

Result
Poco Ropa has a distinctive and memorable brand identity that is quickly gaining market recognition, allied with a web presence to retain customer interest and facilitate ongoing nationwide sales. The company no longer requires product brochures as the website is easily updated and provides a full listing of all available stock.

(Adapted from www.servon.co.uk)

activity

1 What do you think is meant by the term 'distinctive brand identity'?

2 How might the agency have tested whether customers or potential customers are aware of the brand identity?

3 Why might it be necessary for the business to hire the agency again in, say, five years to carry out marketing research for it? Suggest what it might need to know.

Poco Ropa
www.pocoropa.co.uk

Customer satisfaction

A major goal in marketing is to keep the current customer base satisfied and enthusiastic about the products and services offered by the business. Research can be used to test levels of satisfaction with an organisation's products and services relative to those of their major current competitors. In addition, gaps in satisfaction between what is currently available and the ideal or desired product or service can be identified. This may open up opportunities for new product development and enable the organisation to offer products and services that are recognisably different from those of its competitors.

After a basic customer satisfaction study is completed, it can be repeated on an ongoing basis. This process is adopted by many organisations in order to keep customer satisfaction at the fore-front of their attention and provide immediate feedback as to potential problems. Such studies can highlight problems that, if corrected, will result in the greatest net gain in satisfaction.

Advertising awareness

Advertising awareness or advertising tracking is used to measure the effectiveness of advertising campaigns and communications. When a business advertises its products or services, it is in its interests to measure the effectiveness of the communications and whether these have reached or had any impact on the target audiences.

Two different types of measurement are used. The first is an assessment of the advertising's performance. It begins with an awareness test given prior to the release of the advertising; this is used to measure the baseline awareness of the product or service, so that meaningful comparisons can be made after the advertisement has been launched. Similar research is carried out straight after the release of the advertising, and the results are compared with the baseline results. Changes in awareness and perception of the product or service can be picked up from the comparison and should indicate whether the advertising has had any effect.

The second type of advertising tracking looks at the longer-term effects of a marketing plan; this is referred to as a longitudinal study. Research is carried out over the period of a whole marketing exercise with the purpose of discovering whether in the long term the effects of repeated advertisements diminish. The research aims to see how long the life cycle of an advertisement is and whether it is an unnecessary or counterproductive exercise to continue running the advertisement. The impact of the advertisement is compared over this period with its highpoint of effect, and decisions can be made as to whether to continue the advertisement or scrap it and replace it. At some point, the advertising message will have to be revitalised, and this type of research aims to find out when that point has been reached.

case study 10.4 | Tourism Victoria – Part 2

An outcome of an effective marketing campaign may be a positive change in the knowledge, attitudes and aspirations of your target market, which in turn may lead to a change in behaviour, such as actual travel to a region or purchase of a product. It is difficult to correlate change in behaviour directly to your campaign, as a number of other factors will influence visitation levels such as the state of the economy. A series of indicators can be used to assess if your campaign has impacted on your target market's behaviour and on the market in general. Indicators of change in your target market's behaviour include:

■ Increased number of enquiries for your product/region as a result of the marketing campaign

■ Increased number of bookings for your product or purchase of your product

■ Increased number of 'hits' on your website

■ Increased number of visitors travelling to your region

■ Increased length of stay by visitors

■ Increase in visitor expenditure

■ Change in origin of visitors/users of your product

Operators can conduct their own research to measure the number of enquiries and bookings they have for a product resulting from their marketing campaign. One way is to ask a simple question at the time of enquiry or purchase: 'How did you find out about this product?' It is useful to keep records of all enquiries that are made for your product and then you can assess the conversion rate of enquiries to actual bookings or purchase. You could also add a question to a local visitor survey regarding the sources of information that influenced individuals to visit a region.

(Adapted from www.tourismvictoria.com.au)

activity

1   Tourism Victoria carried out an analysis of the marketing campaigns to promote its particular area of Australia. What key changes does it suggest looking for after an advertising campaign?

2   How would a business in the area measure, by market research, the impact of the marketing campaign that it might have run?

Product development success

Coming up with an idea that can actually be turned into a saleable product or service is always difficult. Only a handful of new products or services get beyond the concept stage. Many of the new products or services that reach the testing stage will, for various reasons, be dropped. Just a few will make it to the market, and even those will have undergone massive changes during the product development process.

At a very early stage, products and services are tested at concept level. This means testing the idea of the product or service, rather than its features. If the product or service passes this hurdle, it will be further developed and tested again at various key stages to see whether it still fits the purpose for which it was originally designed.

Once the business has a workable prototype this can then be tested, either in laboratory conditions or using individuals who are representative of the future target group. If, at any of these stages, there appear to be problems with the product or service, it may be scrapped, radically changed or merged with something similar.

New product development research tends to focus on three major aspects:

■   determining what the market actually needs and whether the product matches this

■   testing features and looking at design alternatives

■   measuring feedback related to possible sales and distribution.

New product opportunities

Customers tend to try new products based on the following:

■   how they are advertised

■   how they are packaged

■   what they are called

■   what kind of promotion is taking place

■   which stores carry the product.

These are the basic assumptions when looking for opportunities to develop new products. Each of the features in the list needs to match the target group. In other words, will they see the advertising? Will they respond well to the name and the packaging? Will they be attracted by a promotion, and do they shop in the stores likely to stock the products?

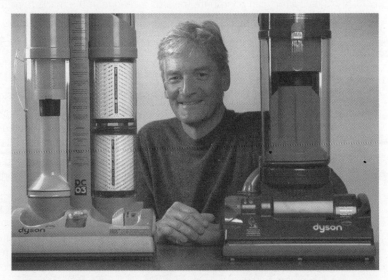

Fig 10.5 The Dyson cleaner was a revolutionary new product idea that has been much copied by competitors

Businesses look continually for new product development opportunities and routinely test different packaging, design, names, pricing, and product features. Above all, they will attempt to sell their products and services to a wider group, i.e. not just to their traditional customers.

Some businesses can be regarded as true innovators, for example Dyson or the ticketless airline EasyJet. Others can be considered followers; they recognise the success of a good, new idea and seek to emulate it with what is known as a 'me-too' product.

case study 10.5   EasyJet and Go Fly

EasyJet established itself as a no-frills, ticketless airline in 1995. Recognising EasyJet's success, British Airways established a company originally called Operation Blue Sky, but this was later renamed Go Fly. The new airline started operating in November 1997 and it competed directly with EasyJet, offering a no-frills transatlantic service.

The new business's advertising slogan, 'The Low Cost Airline from British Airways', angered EasyJet and its competitor Ryanair, which had established its operations from scratch, rather than being subsidised by British Airways.

For some time it was believed that British Airways was happy for Go Fly to run at a loss, pulling down prices and making it impossible for EasyJet and Ryanair to survive. As it transpired, Go Fly was actually profitable within two years and rather than helping British Airways it was attracting British Airways' own customers from more expensive scheduled flights. British Airways' priority was to its traditional business, and its existing managers in a management buyout bought Go Fly.

In May 2002, EasyJet bought Go Fly and the brand slowly disappeared. All of the flights formerly operated by Go Fly are now part of the EasyJet network.

activity

1   Why was EasyJet interested in buying Go Fly in May 2002?
2   Why might British Airways have been prepared to allow Go Fly to run at a loss? What would have been the purpose of this?

Easyjet
www.easyjet.com

Changes in the market and emergence of new markets

Many factors can contribute towards a change in the market, including any of the following:

- legal change (e.g. extended opening hours for pubs or Sunday shopping)
- economic change (e.g. lower interest rates leaving more disposable income for potential customers)
- social change (e.g. increased birth rates or ageing populations)
- technological change (e.g. new microprocessors for computers or miniaturised versions of existing products)
- environmental change (e.g. the need to produce only a limited amount of emissions from factories or the requirement to use cars that produce less pollution)
- political change (e.g. a change of government could mean a different approach to legislation, economics, the handling of social issues, support of technology, or environmental concerns).

In addition to the above, there are constant changes in trends, fashions, preferences and tastes. Products that were dominant market leaders in the past can become associated with a particular generation, and the next generation may not be as interested in that product or service. Businesses, products and services have to be frequently reinvented to appeal to new groups of potential customers and reflect changes in the marketplace.

It is possible for even the smallest business to operate worldwide; new markets are constantly emerging, as access to the Internet becomes more widespread around the world. New markets can also appear in countries in which a business may have been operating for many years. New uses for products and services, new groups of users and different patterns of purchase can emerge and produce a new market.

Through its continuing marketing research into the general environment in which it operates, a business will increase its awareness of changes in the market and the possibility of emerging markets. Once these trends or opportunities have presented themselves, the business will move quickly to adapt its products and services to take advantage of the situation, or at the very least to reduce the negative impacts that might otherwise occur.

PESTLE analysis

PESTLE analysis enables an organisation to look at the various external factors that can affect it. It is a management technique that aims to help the organisation understand the complexities of the external environment, and it may be used to keep a running observation.

The elements of the PESTLE analysis are:

- political – the current and future potential influences on the organisation from political sources (government, **pressure groups** and charities, etc.)
- economic – the way in which the local, national and world economies may impact on the organisation
- sociological (social) – how changes in society can affect the organisation; this also includes trends in attitudes and opinions of the population in general
- technological – how new and emerging technology does or could affect the organisation
- legal – the impact of existing and proposed laws and regulations on the organisation, from a local, national, European and world perspective
- environmental – how existing and potential environmental issues and concerns do or could have an impact on the organisation at local, regional, national and world level.

case study 10.6 — Hampshire County Council Best Value Pestle Analysis

The Government's Best Value initiative provided a catalyst for improving public services and managing local authority performance. Since its introduction in 1999 Hampshire County Council has broadened its approach into its Performance Management Framework. Part of the council's investigation into Best Value means looking at the external influences on the council and assessing their impact.

Table 10.4 PESTLE analysis by Hampshire County Council

External factors that influence the service	Opportunity	Threat
Political	Government initiatives Political change Beacon status	Government initiatives Political change
Economic	New government grants External funding sources Links with local industry/employers	Uncertainty over future funding levels Reduction in government grants Ability to recruit and retain staff in key areas
Social	Catchment area Housing developments	Catchment area
Technological	Development of ICT	Closure of old Hantsnet
Legal	New legislation	Change in legislation
Environmental	Public interest in environmental issues	Impact of global warming

(Adapted from www.hants.gov.uk)

1 What do you think is meant by Best Value?

2 How might the council deal with the opportunities and threats associated with the environmental considerations?

Competitor activities

It is common for an organisation to want to know more about its competitors. Marketing research can be used to discover not only the activities of the competition, but also customers' attitudes to the competitor and its products and services.

In fact, some form of competitor comparison is built into nearly all types of marketing research study. The process of comparing the competition in terms of brand awareness, awareness of advertising and other measures provides useful baseline information regarding the positioning and progress of the business.

There are two basic types of competitive analysis:

- Competitive intelligence – all hard data on a competitor, both published and unpublished, is gathered together for analysis. Published sources could include Internet searches, credit history and announcements about new product or service launches. Unpublished sources could include interviews with employees, distributors or the trade press to discover the direction in which the competitor is moving.

- Market perception studies – these are carried out in order to discover the strengths and weaknesses of a competitor; they focus particularly on the views of customers and how they perceive the organisation.

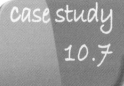

case study 10.7 — Marketing research and decisions for Bungay Safari Park

Bungay Safari Park was established in 1981. It is a fairly modest zoo, run by Brian and Kevin Williams and their extended family. It covers just over 200 acres of rolling countryside and is home to over 500 animals, from every continent in the world. The safari park employs over 150 people during the peak season, from March until late September each year. The zoo winds down through October and November, closing for all of December and through to the following March. It reopens each year in time for the first bank holiday of the year and remains fully open for the Easter break.

The safari park has not yet hit the top 100 tourist attractions in Great Britain. In fact it hovers at around the 200th place. Despite this the attendance figures have been gradually increasing, particularly over the last five years and now stand at 110,000 a year.

The safari park has compiled the following breakdown of attendance figures and average entrance price.

Table 10.5 Attendance figures

Category of visitor	2004	2005	2006	2007	2008
Total visitors	82,000	90,000	98,000	105,000	110,000
Singles	1100	1300	1400	1600	1500
Couples	3300	3500	3300	3200	2800
Families	35,600	44,200	55,300	45,200	46,700
Groups	42,000	41,000	38,000	55,000	49,000
Average entrance paid	£9.00	£9.20	£10.15	£9.45	£10.50

The safari park is based in East Anglia with several other key attractions as major competitors. The park is close to another zoo near Lowestoft, as well as to the seaside towns of Lowestoft and Great Yarmouth. There are also several other similar attractions that cater specifically for families and groups in the region. However, regionally the safari park is the fifth most popular tourist attraction (based on figures provided by the East of England tourist board).

Further research was carried out by the safari park to discover the travelling distances of visitors.

Table 10.6 Travelling distances

Distance travelled	2004 %	2005 %	2006 %	2007 %	2008 %
Under 20 miles	19	17	15	14	12
21–50 miles	32	35	31	32	33
51–75 miles	31	33	40	38	39
76–100 miles	15	11	10	11	10
100+ miles	3	4	4	5	6

In order to cater for families and groups, the safari park has competitions, animal adoption schemes, birthday parties, children's menus and junior members' clubs. For adults and for businesses it has tried to push its sponsorship schemes and offers the backdrop of the safari park as an ideal place for a business conference, or publicity event. It prints thousands of leaflets, which are distributed around the region and placed in motorway cafes, service stations and pubs. The safari park runs special ticket promotions during holiday periods to attract more families and groups. As a result of its research it has decided to concentrate the bulk of its newspaper and magazine advertising on regional newspapers and occasionally to run television-advertising campaigns on Anglia TV, which caters for most of East Anglia. The safari park also regularly runs radio-advertising campaigns on a number of local stations, which broadcast out to around 50 miles from the zoo.

The safari park uses specific key tabs on cash registers to record the category of each visitor at the entrance. The distance-travelled information is collected from prize questionnaires. The most recent market research that it carried out involved selecting 1000 typical customers or customer groups and requesting suggestions as to improvements to the park. The following table shows the key results.

Table 10.7 Results of market research

Suggestion	Percentage of sample making suggestion (from multiple answers, with free choice)
Elephants	78
Bigger children's section	31
Improved menus	19
Themed rides	12
More exotic animals	88
Cheaper entrance	68
More displays	31
Bigger enclosures	55
Educational packs	22
Reptile house	10

As a result of the findings the safari park has made a considerable investment in building four larger enclosures, acquiring five Indian elephants from another zoo, purchasing some captive-bred aardvarks and buying 18 goats and 68 rabbits for the children's section.

▶

1   Describe the main types of marketing research and how they have been used to make a marketing decision in a given situation. To meet the criterion for P1, you should:

(a)   Describe the main types of marketing research used by Bungay Safari Park.

(b)   Describe how the marketing research results helped the business make decisions about its future plans.

2   Explain the context in which different market research methods are appropriate. For M1, you should answer the following, explaining your answers:

(a)   Why do you think the safari park chose the marketing research methods that it used?

(b)   How did these research methods help it to rule out certain ideas and focus on others?

(c)   Were the marketing research methods used appropriate?

(d)   Do you think that the results were accurate?

(e)   Was the safari park able to make the right decisions under the circumstances?

Planning simple research

As we have seen, the purposes of marketing research are to forewarn the organisation of trends and opinions, to inform it about the environment in which it operates and to test new ideas, products and services on potential customers.

Without knowledge of the market, the customers, the competition and a host of potential opportunities and threats to the organisation, it is unlikely that the organisation will be in a position to make the correct decisions at the right time. Whereas if forewarned by marketing research of these opportunities and threats, the organisation can use its other marketing strategies to the best effect, refining its ideas and ways of delivering messages about its products and services.

Research stages

The marketing research process always begins with a brief outlining the purpose of the research. All the other stages of the research process build on that brief: the subject of the investigation is defined; the research objectives are set; and choices are made as to what kind of data will be collected, how and by whom. Marketing research has to be carried out within a given period of time, with milestones and cut-off points for when particular sets of data have to be collected.

Brief/proposal

All marketing research has a particular purpose: perhaps a problem has been identified or specific information is required. Identifying the purpose must always be the first step. Within the business or organisation, internal discussions will probably have taken place following identification of the problem. The problem now needs to be clearly defined and an unambiguous and concise brief developed to outline the purpose of the research.

Defining the issue

Usually marketing research starts with a question or series of questions. It is important to set questions that can be answered precisely, rather than in broad generalisations, and it has to be possible to collect evidence to support the answers. At this stage, it is useful to address how the questions will be answered (i.e. by what type of marketing research) and how the resulting information will be presented.

Setting and defining objectives

There are five key areas to consider when setting and defining objectives.

- The first is the project itself. Typical questions would include:
  - How difficult will it be to carry out the project?
  - How large will the sample be? (Large can be considered to be 500 or more respondents; small could be fewer than 200.)
  - What methodology will be used to collect the information?
  - How much data analysis will be required?
  - In what form will the results be presented? Is an in-depth and detailed report required or will a summary be sufficient?

- The second is the analysis of skills. Key questions include:
  - Can the business itself provide the skills required to meet the needs of the project?
  - Are these individuals available over the time period of the marketing research?
  - What parts of the marketing research may have to be handled by an outside agency?

- The third is budgetary; an important issue is who will pay for the marketing research. Key questions include the following:
  - Is the research focusing on a strategic or tactical issue?
  - Considering the cost of the project, what is the information actually worth to the business?
  - Will one or more parts of the organisation be prepared to make a contribution to the research?
  - Which part of the organisation is most likely to benefit from the research and are they therefore prepared to pay for it?
  - Over what timeframe will the budgets be available?

- The fourth is the general environment; this could affect the results of the marketing research project. Questions to consider include:
  - Does the overall economic environment have an impact on the data being collected?
  - Does the economic environment have an impact on the organisation's products and services?
  - What future legislation may or may not have a bearing on the data that is being collected?

- The fifth is the overall theory behind the marketing research as this frames how the marketing research is viewed and carried out. Questions to consider include:
  - What is the basic theory behind the marketing research? In other words, what is the belief about a particular issue before the research has taken place?
  - What does the research intend to show or disprove?
  - Regardless of the results of the research, will the organisation act on its findings?
  - Which parts of the organisation may be resistant to change if it is necessary as a result of the marketing research?

Planning data to be collected (methods of collection and timings)

Let's assume that, having considered how the data would best be collected, the researchers decided to use a questionnaire. The questionnaire has been designed and then field tested (piloted) before being finalised so that it is ready to be used in bulk for the marketing research. Target groups and subgroups have been selected.

Careful consideration must be given to timing at this stage because in most cases the data collection period takes up between 25% and 50% of the total time for the research project. Ways in which marketing research data can be collected quickly include:

- Computer assisted telephone interviewing (CATI) – some of these systems are digital and play recorded messages that prompt respondents to answer. Others are predictive diallers, calling several numbers at once and eliminating the time that is wasted in getting no answers, busy signals or disconnected messages.

- Internet surveys – these are distributed either by email or as pop-ups on websites.

- Interactive voice response – this allows respondents to call a freephone number and complete an automated survey by voice response and telephone keypad.

There are also:

- mailed surveys and questionnaires
- Internet and mail panels
- face-to-face interviews.

When choosing which type of data to collect and how, the researchers must consider:

- whether secondary information will be analysed
- whether there is a need to collect qualitative information
- how questions will be measured or scaled
- how the questionnaire will be designed
- the size of sample and the sampling method.

Link

See pages 161–3 for information about sampling methods.

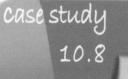

DTI Foresight programme: six hypothetical food products – Part 1

The Foresight programme aims to develop visions of the future, looking at possible future threats, needs and opportunities and making recommendations for what should be done now to make sure that all are ready for those challenges; building bridges between business, science and government, bringing together the knowledge and expertise of many people across all areas and activities in order to increase national wealth and quality of life.

The Food Chain & Crops for Industry Foresight Panel has been looking at ways of optimising the quality of discussions between scientists, government and the public on the subject of whether any given technology should be used in food products.

The task force worked with a group of scientists to generate a set of six hypothetical future food products that will be used as the subject of the debate mechanisms. The products are designed to illustrate the possible uses of a range of technologies that are at various early stages of development, including irradiation, 'next generation' bioscience, and sensor technologies.

(Adapted from www.foresight.gov.uk)

activity

1. What was the DTI and what is its new name?
2. Why might the DTI have been interested in people's reactions to food products that do not exist?
3. Suggest six future food products that could be tested in a research study like this.

Forecasting

Forecasting simply involves trying to predict the outcome of the research. The researchers may look at best- and worst-case scenarios, in which they either discover something that wholly accords with what they believed to be the case or is radically different from what they had expected. If the organisation is committed to following up the research, it has to recognise that the outcome may require changes to be made.

Types of data

We have already seen that there are a number of different types of primary and secondary research methods and sources. The most common sources of information tend to be internal and external secondary research.

remember

Secondary research information was collected for a different purpose but could be useful in the marketing research project.

case study 10.9

DTI Foresight programme: six hypothetical food products – Part 2

Foresight provided an initial draft of the self-completion postal questionnaire, along with short versions of the product descriptions. The final questionnaires were designed from the draft, in liaison with Foresight; researchers also selected participants; sent out the questionnaires with a Freepost return envelope; chased for responses until 100 responses were received in respect of each product; and upon receipt of the responses entered the data obtained on a database.

The group of participants was selected (from a large database of UK consumers) to provide a representative cross-section of the UK/GB population.

Each participant was asked to read a description of one of the six hypothetical food products and then complete a questionnaire designed to gauge their opinion of the product described. The questionnaire, which consisted of a combination of open and multiple-choice questions, was two or three pages long.

The hypothetical products were:

■ Scottish Banana

■ Anti-cancer Broccoli

■ Long-life Lasagne

■ Zero-calorie Cake

■ Smart Packaging

■ Chicken in a Bottle.

(Adapted from www.foresight.gov.uk)

activity

1 Why would the researchers have stopped chasing respondents after 100 responses had been received for each product?

2 What do you think is meant by the term 'self-completion postal questionnaire'?

The following are typical examples of internal secondary research data:

■ sales revenues

■ sales forecasts

■ **customer demographics**

■ purchasing patterns

■ other customer data.

This type of research is often known as data mining: the market researcher is exploring existing information to look for other trends and information that could be of value.

External secondary research data is easily available, particularly using the Internet. Again the data has been collected for another purpose and will need to be examined in order to see whether or not it reveals anything useful. The main sources of external secondary research data are:

■ newspapers and magazines

■ television

■ newsletters

■ industry reports

■ business directories

■ trade associations

■ government publications and websites

■ search engines.

Target population

The target population can only be chosen after the researchers have analysed existing customers, or potential customers, and identified their key characteristics. Usually, the characteristics include:

- age
- gender
- income
- home ownership
- marital status
- interests
- buying patterns
- educational background
- geographical location.

The researchers cannot hope to interview all members of the target population and have to choose a sample that is representative of the larger group. This is known as scaling. Questions to consider in relation to scaling include:

- Is the sample in proportion to the target groups?
- Are the selected respondents representative?
- Can results from these target groups be applied to the larger target population?
- Is the sample too small to be representative?
- Is it too large to be handled comfortably by the researchers?

Analysis and evaluation of data

The ways in which the data can be analysed and evaluated very much depend on how it was collected. For example, the more complex the questionnaire is, the more difficult it is to collate, analyse and evaluate the information. Straightforward questionnaires are far easier to handle.

Complex numerical data will need statistical analysis, and this will take time and will cost money to carry out. There are a large number of highly specialised statistical analyses: some look at factors within the information; others look for trends.

Key stages in the process of collating, analysing and evaluating questionnaire data are as follows:

1. The information is collated: in other words, the information is taken from each questionnaire and compiled into a single document.
2. Basic graphical representations of the responses to each question from the questionnaire are prepared, as this will aid the checking process.
3. Sample questionnaires are checked for errors.
4. The second collation process takes place after the crosschecking and is when an initial presentation of the data will be made.
5. The researchers look at links, trends and patterns, both within individual questionnaires, across questions and across the questionnaires.
6. The **raw data** is compared with existing data, perhaps from a previous marketing research project.
7. Significant shifts, changes or errors should now be highlighted.
8. Final presentation of the data in the preferred form can now be made.

Presentation of findings and making recommendations

As we will see in the last section of this unit, marketing research findings can be presented in many different ways. Generally, findings are presented either orally or in written reports, and the presentation may be formal or informal. Usually, the presentation is supported by visual aids.

Before the findings can be presented, however, the researchers must make recommendations arising out of the data collected. Hopefully, the researchers will have discovered patterns in the data, which can then be summarised. These patterns may suggest that the business should take some form of action. Questions will have been posed when detailing the brief and objectives of the research. The business will now want answers to these questions and will require suggestions as to how potential problems or opportunities can be handled. Thus within the framework of the original brief and objectives, recommendations can now be made.

Re-evaluation of marketing activities

A business may have decided to investigate customer behaviour, patterns, preferences or satisfaction. Alternatively, it may have looked at how aware the general population is about the business's brand or advertising. In some way, the business would have investigated one of its activities and compared its assessment to the perception of the target groups for which the activity was originally designed. Even large organisations make dreadful mistakes when it comes to making decisions about what they believe their customers want. A prime example is Coca Cola, which in the 1990s released a new formula of Coca Cola. This was very poorly received and, very quickly, the company was forced to re-release the original Coca Cola and gradually phase out the new formula. The company had underestimated its customers' brand awareness, tastes and purchasing habits.

case study 10.10

DTI Foresight programme: six hypothetical food products – Part 3

A total of 3530 questionnaires were mailed out (569 Scottish Banana, 569 Anti-cancer Broccoli, 569 Long-life Lasagne, 569 Zero-calorie Cake, 685 Smart Packaging [extra 116 mailed out], and 569 Chicken in a Bottle). 697 completed (valid) questionnaires were returned within the survey period, which represents an overall response rate of 20%. A more detailed breakdown of response rates is given in the table.

Table 10.8 Response rates

Product	Mailed out	Returned	Response rate
Scottish Banana	569	107	18%
Anti-cancer Broccoli	569	125	21%
Long-life Lasagne	569	110	19%
Zero-calorie Cake	569	136	23%
Smart Packaging	685	107	15%
Chicken in a Bottle	569	112	21%

Those with response rates above 20% were:

■ Chicken in a Bottle

■ Anti-cancer Broccoli

■ Zero-calorie Cake.

Those with response rates below 20% were:

■ Scottish Banana

■ Long-life Lasagne

■ Smart Packaging.

(Adapted from www.foresight.gov.uk)

activity

1 Suggest reasons why the response rate differed from product to product?

2 Do you think the subject of the research or the choice of respondents was more or less to blame for the poor response rate?

Fig 10.6 Evaluating market effectiveness

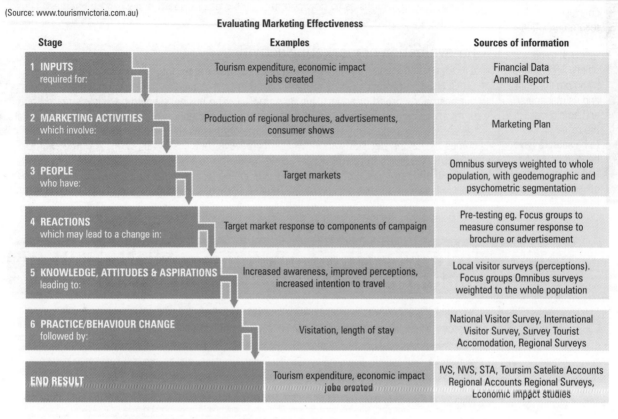

(Source: www.tourismvictoria.com.au)

Evaluating Marketing Effectiveness

Stage	Examples	Sources of information
1 INPUTS required for:	Tourism expenditure, economic impact jobs created	Financial Data Annual Report
2 MARKETING ACTIVITIES which involve:	Production of regional brochures, advertisements, consumer shows	Marketing Plan
3 PEOPLE who have:	Target markets	Omnibus surveys weighted to whole population, with geodemographic and psychometric segmentation
4 REACTIONS which may lead to a change in:	Target market response to components of campaign	Pre-testing eg. Focus groups to measure consumer response to brochure or advertisement
5 KNOWLEDGE, ATTITUDES & ASPIRATIONS leading to:	Increased awareness, improved perceptions, increased intention to travel	Local visitor surveys (perceptions). Focus groups Omnibus surveys weighted to the whole population
6 PRACTICE/BEHAVIOUR CHANGE followed by:	Visitation, length of stay	National Visitor Survey, International Visitor Survey, Survey Tourist Accomodation, Regional Surveys
END RESULT	Tourism expenditure, economic impact jobs created	IVS, NVS, STA, Toursim Satelite Accounts Regional Accounts Regional Surveys, Economic impact studies

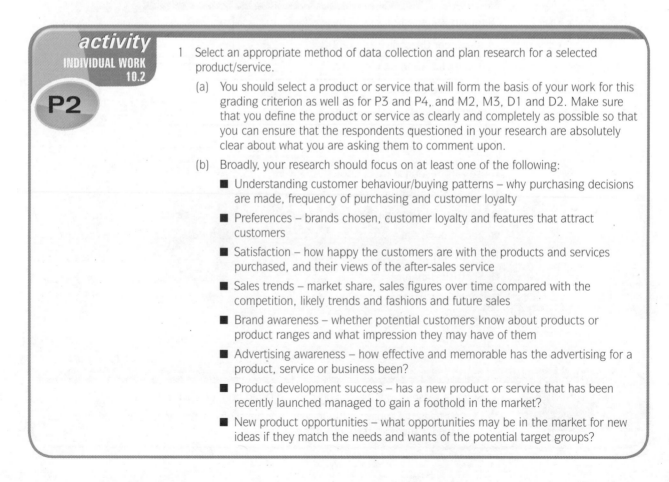

1 Select an appropriate method of data collection and plan research for a selected product/service.

(a) You should select a product or service that will form the basis of your work for this grading criterion as well as for P3 and P4, and M2, M3, D1 and D2. Make sure that you define the product or service as clearly and completely as possible so that you can ensure that the respondents questioned in your research are absolutely clear about what you are asking them to comment upon.

(b) Broadly, your research should focus on at least one of the following:

- Understanding customer behaviour/buying patterns – why purchasing decisions are made, frequency of purchasing and customer loyalty

- Preferences – brands chosen, customer loyalty and features that attract customers

- Satisfaction – how happy the customers are with the products and services purchased, and their views of the after-sales service

- Sales trends – market share, sales figures over time compared with the competition, likely trends and fashions and future sales

- Brand awareness – whether potential customers know about products or product ranges and what impression they may have of them

- Advertising awareness – how effective and memorable has the advertising for a product, service or business been?

- Product development success – has a new product or service that has been recently launched managed to gain a foothold in the market?

- New product opportunities – what opportunities may be in the market for new ideas if they match the needs and wants of the potential target groups?

■ Changes in the market – what significant changes have there been in the market, how has this affected sales and buyer behaviour and what might be the longer-term impacts?

■ Emergence of new markets – identification of the market, size, nature, features, problems, existing competitors, why the market has emerged

■ PESTLE (political, economic, social, technological, legal, environmental) – what are the key external impacts on a product, service or business and how can the business deal with them? What are the likely impacts in the near future and what can be done to prepare for them?

■ Competitor activities – what are the key activities of the competition? What are they doing right and what are they doing wrong? What lessons can be learnt from their activities and experience. What significant threats and opportunities are arising from their actions?

(c) Your primary research choices are:

■ observation – watching buyer behavior

■ experimentation – testing different features of a product or service or checking different responses to a product or service by different target groups

■ surveys – face-to-face, postal, email, telephone – using questionnaires to collect data on views and attitudes

■ e-marketing research – posting extensive questionnaires on to the Internet with a degree of interaction

■ focus groups – choosing a representative group from the target markets and collecting qualitative data on them

■ panels – similar to the above, but collecting data from experts in the market

■ field trials – giving representatives of the target market a chance to try out the product or service to gain their opinion of the features and benefits

■ piloting – test-releasing products or services in a limited area to test sales, attitudes and buyer behavior.

2 Specifically for P2 you must:

(a) Identify a product or service that you wish to investigate.

(b) State why the investigation will take place and the key objectives of the research.

(c) State what you hope to be the outcome of the research – what questions will be answered and how this will be useful.

(d) Say how you intend to collect the research data and why your choices are appropriate for the job

3 As far as the research plan itself is concerned, you must ensure that you provide a complete overview of your intentions, this must include (after agreement with your teacher/tutor):

■ proposal/brief – what you intend to research, why and how

■ definition of objectives – what the key objectives of the research are

■ planning – how you will ensure that your research plan will work

■ forecasting – what you expect to discover

■ collection of data – the methods chosen for data collection

■ analysis and evaluation of data – how you intend to deal with the data that you have collected

■ presentation of findings – how you will format or present the key points of your research findings to the intended audience

■ making recommendations – what the scope or implications of your findings might be in terms of the recommendations that you might be able to make

■ re-evaluation of marketing activities – the implications there may be for the business, product or service as a result of your recommendations.

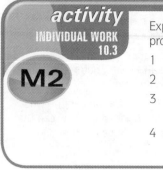

activity
INDIVIDUAL WORK 10.3
M2

Explain the reasons for selecting the particular method of data collection for a selected product/service. Carrying on from the work in P2, you should:

1   Give the reasons why you have chosen the specific research methods.

2   State why you feel they are appropriate and why you may have rejected other choices.

3   Say how your research choices might affect the overall results and the credibility of the research findings.

4   Identify any particular difficulties in gathering the data that you are likely to encounter as a result of your choices of research.

Carrying out simple research

It is usually impossible, even for the largest professional marketing organisations, to question every single person in a target group. Thankfully, it is also unnecessary. As we will see, it is perfectly acceptable, provided that the basis of choice is correct, to pick a sample of the target group and base your assumptions on those individuals.

Census versus sample

A census involves questioning every individual within a target group. Few organisations are geared up to do this. Every 10 years, the government carries out the only truly comprehensive census. Even then, the information provided is basic and focuses on age, gender, nationality and a handful of other considerations.

A sample can be chosen in a number of different ways, but the overriding requirement is for that sample to be an accurate representation of the target group. In many of the surveys that feature on TV, the sample interviewed numbers fewer than 1000 people, yet their views are portrayed as representative of all people in the UK with those characteristics.

Sample size and choosing the sample

There are no strict rules to follow in choosing a sample, but a degree of logic and judgement must always be applied. A small, carefully chosen sample must reflect or represent the views of the larger population. Ideally, each member of the population should have an equal chance of being selected as part of the sample; then the sample is truly random.

In terms of any research you might carry out for this course, a sample of no more than 100 is perfectly acceptable, provided that you can show that your sampling criteria have allowed you to select individuals that represent the larger target group.

Probability sampling

Sampling methods are always classified as either probability or non-probability methods. Probability samples mean that each member of the population has an equal chance of being chosen. These methods include random sampling, systematic sampling and stratified sampling. More information on these types of sampling can be seen in Table 10.9.

Table 10.9 Types of probability sampling

Sample method	Characteristics
Random	The purest form of probability sampling. Everyone has an equal chance of being selected. It is almost impossible to identify every member of the population, so there is a slight bias.
Systematic	A variation of random sampling, also known as the Nth-name selection technique. The required sample size is calculated and every nth record is chosen from a randomly selected sample. This is straightforward as long as there is no hidden order in the names.
Stratified	Probably the most commonly used probability method. Subsets of the population are created so that each subset has a common characteristic, such as gender. A number of participants from each subset are chosen by random sampling.
Multi-stage	This is a rolling form of sampling. An initial batch of individuals is chosen, using random sampling, and if these are non-responsive then a new replacement batch is selected. This way the research is staggered over a period of time.
Cluster	Cluster sampling involves choosing individuals from a relatively tight geographical region. First the region is chosen in relation to the population to see if it is representative. If it is, sets of respondents are chosen.

Non-probability sampling

Non-probability sampling means that members are selected from the population in some non-random manner, such as convenience sampling, judgement sampling, quota sampling, and by what is known as snowball sampling. More information on these types of sampling can be seen in Table 10.10.

Table 10.10 Types of non-probability sampling

Sample method	Characteristics
Quota	This is the non-probability version of stratified sampling. Subsets are chosen and then either convenience or judgement sampling is used to choose people from each subset.
Convenience	The respondents are chosen on the premise that choosing these will drive down the costs of the research project. Therefore, people local to the researchers are chosen as members of the sample.
Judgement	With this common non-probability method, a particular group of individuals, usually in a small geographical area, is chosen to be representative on the basis that the researchers feel that they are representative.
Snowball sampling	In this sampling technique, a few potential respondents are contacted and asked if they know any other people with the characteristics that the researcher is looking for. The initial contacts may have knowledge of not only individuals but also groups of other people.

Implications of different samples, cost and accuracy of information

Having chosen a particular sampling method, the researchers must be aware that their choice may affect the results of the survey. There is often a trade-off between cost and accuracy. Obviously, the more random the sampling method and the larger the sample, the higher the costs involved. This is both in actual time needed to complete the survey and in time required by the researchers to frame the project, collect the data and deal with the results.

Some research methods are chosen purely for their speed rather than their accuracy. They are designed to give an immediate snapshot of opinions and views and do not necessarily profess to be truly scientific.

Questionnaires

Questionnaires can be a simple and inexpensive way of collecting data. Above all, however, the questions in the survey must be able to fulfil the main task: in other words, enable data to be collected that will answer the research questions posed and provide information upon which additional research and refinement can be made.

The steps required to design and administer a questionnaire include:

1. Defining the objectives of the survey – be precise about what you actually want to ask and organise the questionnaire to ensure that you get the answers to the research questions posed.

2. Determining the sampling group – decide how many people will be included in the sample; it needs to be representative in terms of gender, age and other factors so as to accurately represent the whole of the target group or groups.

3. Writing the questionnaire – provide a mix of question types; you may want to include closed questions with a set of answers provided, or you may want to have some open questions with spaces left for the responses.

4. Administering the questionnaire – how is the questionnaire going to get to the respondents? Are you going to choose the respondent, then ask the questions, filling in the answers yourself; or are you going to send the questionnaire to the respondents (in which case, make sure that the questions are clear)?

5. Interpreting the results – how do you propose to sort out the information from the completed questionnaires? The more open questions there are, the harder it will be to interpret the results. If there are too many closed questions, you may not have the depth of answers that you need. Once you have sorted the information, you need to present it in an appropriate form and decide what the information has told you.

remember

It is important that the sample should be representative of the entire target group and that the way in which the sample was chosen can be justified.

Designing questionnaires

It is important that the questionnaire looks right. The questionnaire's appearance will have a direct impact on the number that will be completed. The better the quality, the higher the response rate and more data will be collected. Poorly designed questionnaires often appear too complicated, too long to complete, or boring.

Confusing layouts can also be a problem; this is particularly the case when the respondents are asked to complete the questionnaire themselves.

A number of key issues can affect response rate and ease of administration, and it is advantageous to consider the following:

- Use of booklet format – simply binding or stapling a questionnaire that has a number of pages makes it easier to handle; it is also easier for either the interviewer or the respondent to work through the questionnaire without getting lost or missing a page.

- Use of spaces and typeface – too many questionnaires are crammed into as few pages as possible to make the questionnaire compact and cheaper to produce. As a result, they are messy and difficult to read. Squeezing too much in is counter-productive as it makes the questionnaire look daunting and complicated. The use of blank spaces actually improves the response rate, as the pages are easier on the eye. A good choice of typeface is also important; it should be easy to read.

- The creative use of colour coding – clear coding will help enormously with the administration of the questionnaires. It is simple to colour code questionnaires by producing those for existing customers in one colour, those for potential customers in another colour, those for retailers or distributors in a third, and using other colours for other target groups of respondents.

- Interviewer instructions – if interviewers will be noting down the respondents' answers to the questions, it is a good idea to put instructions to the interviewers alongside the questions. This will help the interviewers to focus and will prompt them to probe for additional data if certain replies are made, thereby improving the overall quality of the data.

As a general rule of thumb, it is more practicable to opt for a questionnaire that is short. Once any questions that do not provide useful information have been ruled out, the resultant shorter questionnaire will reduce overall costs and interviewing time, making it less likely that the respondents will become bored. Even in the most ideal of circumstances the interviewer, or the respondent, should not be delayed by more than 20–30 minutes.

Types of questions

When designing a questionnaire, it is always important to consider whether questions are absolutely necessary. Each question should be evaluated and, in general, no question should be included unless it contributes to meeting the research objectives and provides data that is needed.

Fig 10.7 Questionnaires need to be well designed, uncomplicated and not too long to complete, in order to encourage respondents

However, redundant questions are sometimes useful or necessary. Even though it does not contribute directly to the research, an opening question might be inserted to capture the respondent's interest so that they continue with the questionnaire. Dummy questions are sometimes included so that the true purpose of the questionnaire is hidden from the respondent. For example, if a retailer of clothes wishes to hide the fact that most of the questions are on fashion, dummy questions relating to eating habits could be inserted.

Before we look at different types of question, it is important to consider sequencing. Normally, questionnaires begin with simple demographic questions, asking about age, gender, and location. Once these basic questions have been answered, more in-depth and specialised questions that are pertinent to the research itself can be asked.

Table 10.11 describes the main types of question used in questionnaires.

Table 10.11 Types of question

Sample method	Characteristics
Dichotomous	Dichotomous questions usually have two possible responses, such as 'yes' or 'no'; 'true' or 'false'; 'agree' or 'disagree'. These questions can often be used as filter questions, meaning that if the respondent answers yes or no to a basic question they can then be forwarded to a subset of questions related to that answer.
Multiple-choice	Multiple-choice questions offer the respondent a series of choices from which they may choose one or more options. A typical example would be 'Which of these daily newspapers have you read in the past month?' The respondent will be offered a full list of all daily newspapers and prompted to tick each one that they have read.
Scaled	Some scaled questions are called semantic differential questions, as the respondent is given two completely opposite pairs of words. For example, a respondent asked to rate a TV programme is given a scale with 'interesting' at one end and 'boring' at the other. Between the two is a set of five or more boxes, and the respondent puts a tick in one of the boxes between 'interesting' and 'boring' according to what they believe. There are other types of scale; some, for example, run from 'very much' to 'somewhat', 'neither', 'somewhat' to 'very much'; others run from 'strongly agree' through 'agree' and 'disagree' to 'strongly disagree'.
Open-ended	Open-ended questions ask a potentially complex question and leave sufficient space for the respondent to write in their own answer. These are the most difficult questions to analyse, as the answers may be very difficult to categorise. They are also the questions that respondents are the least likely to complete.

Length of questionnaire

Ideally, when you carry out your marketing research, your questionnaire should not be longer than two or three pages. Bear in mind that you should only ask questions to which you absolutely need to know the answers. Irrelevant questions will put respondents off and will provide you with information of no value. Ideally, 10 or 12 questions are the absolute maximum that you can assume respondents will be prepared to answer.

Bias, relevance and response

Researcher bias should not be a problem if you are not going to be present when the respondents complete the questionnaires. However, if you are asking the questions and completing the questionnaires on behalf of the respondents, there is always a chance that you may lead them to make the responses that you would prefer.

As we have already mentioned, questions should be relevant to the marketing research in question. If you do not need to know personal information, it is better not to ask for it as many respondents will be reluctant to complete those questions and may refuse to answer the questionnaire at all.

Response rates will differ, depending on your choice of target group, how well you have chosen your sample and the layout and design of the questionnaire. If you send out your questionnaires, it is highly probable that the response rate would be no more than 20%. Even when you ask respondents the questions yourself, the refusal rate is likely to be at least 50%. You should be prepared for this and have planned a multistage research data collection methodology in case it is necessary.

Piloting the questionnaire

It is always a good idea to test out your questionnaire before you launch into the research project itself. Piloting will highlight problems with your questionnaire, for example in the phrasing and sequencing of questions; it will also enable you to see any assumptions that may have crept in. Choose a small sample from your main sample and test the questionnaire out on at least 10 to 12 individuals. Ideally, they should complete the questionnaire without any prompting from you. Any problems at this stage can be rectified, and you will not have to deal with deficient questionnaires when you have dozens to analyse.

activity

INDIVIDUAL WORK
10.4

P3

Conduct primary and secondary research, making use of an identifiable sampling method.

Having written your research plan and had it agreed by your teacher/tutor, you must now carry out the research. Points to remember are:

- You should carry out both primary and secondary research.
- You must make sure that your research plan is achievable within the timeframe you have been given for this unit.
- Do not try to make your respondent samples too large, otherwise you will run into enormous difficulties when collating and analysing the data.
- If you use sampling, make sure that you state the sampling method and why it was appropriate for the purpose.

activity

INDIVIDUAL WORK
10.5

D1

Evaluate the application of a selected research method and plan, make and justify recommendations for improvement.

This activity should take place after the research has been carried out. You must specifically cover the following:

1   What were the main problems that you encountered during the research process?
2   Were your original ideas on how to carry out the research practical and achievable?
3   Did you have to amend your research plan in order to complete the research within the timeframe available?
4   How could the research process have been improved?
5   What would you do differently if you had to carry out the research again?

Interpreting research findings

Once you have collected all of your data, the next logical action is to collate the results. When dealing with a mass of data, you will need to employ various statistical methods to describe and analyse it. The aim is to produce figures that are easy to understand and interpret so that you can make well-founded recommendations.

Statistical procedures

Marketing researchers use a number of statistical procedures to assist in the interpretation of research findings. Many of these you will already have encountered in GCSE Mathematics. This section will focus on some of the statistical measures and procedures that are most common in marketing research.

Arithmetic mean

The arithmetic mean is the most frequently used type of average. It is calculated by adding up all the figures in a string of numbers and then dividing that total by the number of figures in the sum.

$$\text{arithmetic mean} = ? = \frac{a_1 + a_2 + a_3 + \ldots a_n}{n}$$

The arithmetic mean for 4 and 9 is therefore calculated in the following way.

$$\text{arithmetic mean} = \frac{4 + 9}{2} = 6.5$$

Median

The median is literally the middle number in a string of values. To find the median, first sort the numbers in ascending order. When the number of values is odd, the median is the middle number of the string. When there is an even number of values, the median is the average of the middle two and is usually calculated by working out the arithmetic mean of the two values. The median is a good way of finding the average as it takes into account the full distribution of values. Worked examples of the median can be seen in Fig 10.8.

Fig 10.8 Examples of the median

Examples:

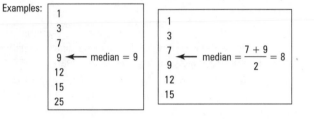

Mode

The mode is the simplest average to work out. It is the most frequently occurring number in the string. Again, sort the numbers in ascending order and pick out the most common number. In the following example, the most frequently occurring number is 6, and this is therefore the mode.

3, 3, 4, 4, 5, 5, 5, 6, 6, 6, 6, 7, 7, 8, 9, 9

Some sets of values have more than one mode.

Range

The range measures the spread of a set of scores; it is the difference between the lowest and highest values in that particular set. For example, if respondents were asked to state their ages in years, and the youngest was 16 and the oldest was 27, the range would be 11 years.

Inter-quartile range

The inter-quartile range equals the difference between the upper quartile and the lower quartile. The lower quartile is the point below which 25% of your results lie (i.e. the lowest 25% of values in your range of data). The upper quartile is the point below which 75% of your data can be found.

The inter-quartile range shows the spread of the middle 50% of your results (i.e. the range of values between the lower and the upper quartiles).

Scatter diagrams

Scatter diagrams are also called scattergrams. They are used to depict the correlation (relationship) between data collected for two different characteristics (variables), such as age and income. They can show you whether or not a relationship is likely to exist between the two sets of data and suggest how strong that relationship is.

A scatter diagram makes the relationship between the two sets of variables visually obvious. It can be used to highlight relationships that are not apparent from simply staring at the raw data.

Scatter diagrams are easy to construct:

1. Collect a large number of paired sets of data: paired meaning that there are two measurements for each person or entity (e.g. in a survey of factories, you might have data for each factory on the number of items produced and the number of employees on the production line).

remember

Correlation suggests that there is a relationship between two variables but it is important not to jump to the conclusion that changes in one variable cause changes in the other without trying to demonstrate it in another way.

Fig 10.9 Scatter diagram

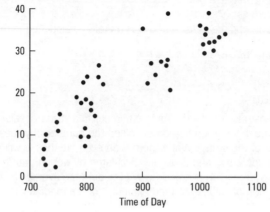

Elapsed Time (MInutes)

Time of Day

2. Draw two axes at right angles, with one variable (variable X) on the horizontal axis and the other variable (variable Y) on the vertical axis. Find the highest and lowest value of each variable in order to scale your axes, and then mark out the horizontal and vertical axis.

3. Plot the paired points on the diagram. If there is more than one set of pairs with the same value, mark that point on the diagram with a circle, adding another circle for each set of pairs that has the same values.

4. Finally, identify the patterns of association (relationship).

Fig 10.10 shows some examples of how the patterns of association can be classified.

Times series analysis

Times series analysis involves organising your data to show results over a period of time. When depicting time series data on a graph, two axes are set up as if for a scattergram, with time as the variable on the horizontal axis. The earliest set of results is the first to be plotted on a graph. You then plot the rest of the results in time order until you have completed the graph. You can choose a number of results to be displayed on the graph, say, for example, 100. Then when the 101st result becomes available it is placed at the end of the graph and your first ever result is removed from the graph. So your 101st result becomes your 100th, and your 2nd result becomes the 1st. In this way you can produce an up-to-date graph, which takes into account the time element in the collection of the data.

Fig 10.10 Interpreting scatter diagrams

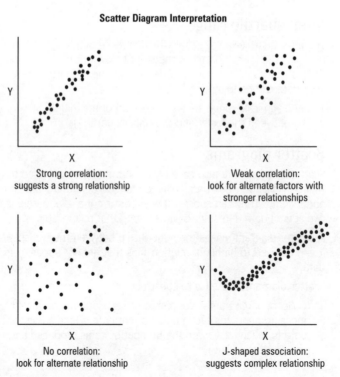

Scatter Diagram Interpretation

Strong correlation: suggests a strong relationship

Weak correlation: look for alternate factors with stronger relationships

No correlation: look for alternate relationship

J-shaped association: suggests complex relationship

Trends

If you want to increase your understanding of a time series graph, you will need to pick out the main features that are often described as the trend component. The trend is a long-term movement shown in a time series graph. You will notice that trends either go upwards or downwards, and the rate of change may be different.

For example, from looking at its sales over the year, a business may see that there are trends according to the seasons. From looking at data collected over several years, it will be able to see whether these trends are cyclical (recur each year).

Use of spreadsheets

Spreadsheets can cut down on the need to produce hand-drawn graphs. Once you have become proficient in the use of software such as Excel, it is easy to input data and produce a number of different graphs that enable statistical information to be displayed in a far more accessible form. In the next section, we will be looking at the use of computers for creating graphs, graphics and charts.

Link See pages 374–379 in Unit 26 for information on how to use Excel.

Presentation of findings

The presentation of your findings, whether in the form of an oral or written report, will probably benefit from some type of visual aid. Above all, you need to be aware of your audience who will expect you to produce clear conclusions and recommendations.

Oral reports

There are four basic steps when organising an oral report:

1. Decide your strategy for the particular audience. What will they be expecting you to produce? Ask yourself what your objectives are and how you will tailor your message to the audience.

2. Be flexible. By all means create a structure for your presentation but be prepared for interruption. Above all be logical, develop your argument and end with your conclusions and recommendations.

3. Prepare visual material that enhances but does not distract. It is important to remember that how you present is as important as what you present.

4. Be able to answer questions and challenges to what you have said. This will supplement your presentation.

Written reports

There are a number of different ways of presenting written reports, some of which would be considered formal, and others informal. A fully structured report should begin with an outline of the objectives of your research, followed by how you carried out the research. The main body of the report should deal with your findings. This should be followed by your conclusions, which is a summary of the findings. Finally, you should complete the report by adding recommendations.

A very formal report has a number of subsections within each of these parts, but a less formal report is probably what is required if you have opted for (or have been told to) produce a written report rather than an oral one.

Visual aids

Visual aids tend to fall into three categories:

- Computer graphics such as bar and pie charts, line graphs, and histograms – we will look at these in more detail a little later.

- Graphs – these can be hand drawn and can include some or all of those that can be made on a computer.

- Charts – these are useful for summarising data that is not easily turned into graphs.

remember

Visual aids for an oral presentation have to be large enough to be seen by the whole audience. An alternative is to produce hard copies to be handed out.

Presentation of conclusions and recommendations

Any conclusions or recommendations that you make during the presentation of your findings should be based on fact and not on assumptions. Your conclusions, which should be a summary of the information that you have collected, should be solidly rooted in your findings and include any particular concerns that the research has highlighted. Your recommendations should address these concerns by suggesting ways in which they can be handled. You must always try to justify your recommendations.

Audience

It is always difficult to assess the knowledge and understanding of an audience. It is important that the language you use is at the right level of complexity for your audience and that particular care is taken with the use of jargon and technical terms. You should try to assess your audience's previous knowledge of the subject and create your presentation to match this, neither under- nor overestimating what this might be.

Quality of information

The quality of the information in your presentation depends largely on how well you carried out the research process. If you selected an acceptable sample and were rigorous in the collection of data, the raw material on which you will base your interpretation should be sound. However, if you make mistakes at the analysis and interpretation stage, you could undermine the usefulness of the information collected. Check and double-check statistical procedures and make sure that any calculations are correct and meaningful and that your conclusions are supported by the data.

> **remember**
>
> When presenting research findings to decision makers, it is important that the report is professional and follows any guidelines or templates preferred by the organisation.

Diagrammatic analysis and presentation

Diagrammatic analysis and presentation should enhance your audience's understanding of what you are trying to explain. In this section, we look at some typical types of diagrams.

Pictograms

These have been used for at least 11,000 years. Our ancient ancestors used them on cave walls. A pictogram is a symbol that represents something.

Fig 10.11 A pictogram

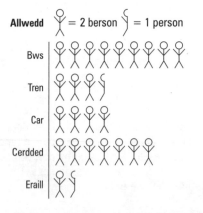

Allwedd = Key
Bws = bus
Tren = train
Cerdded = walking
Eraill = other

In this example, simple stick people have been used to represent individuals. Half a stick person represents one person.

Pie charts

A pie chart is used to represent data by assigning part of a 360° angle around the centre of a circle. So if you had 100 results, each result would be assigned 3.6°. Therefore 10 results would be represented by 36° and so on. Each segment of the pie can be colour coded to enhance the graphical representation of the data.

Bar charts

A bar chart is a simple means of displaying frequency data. It uses a conventional graph format and bars can be either horizontal or vertical. The bars represent each category

Fig 10.12 A pie chart

(Source: Defra/RAS/002.003
*Radioactive Wastes in the UK:
A Summary of the 2001 Inventory*)

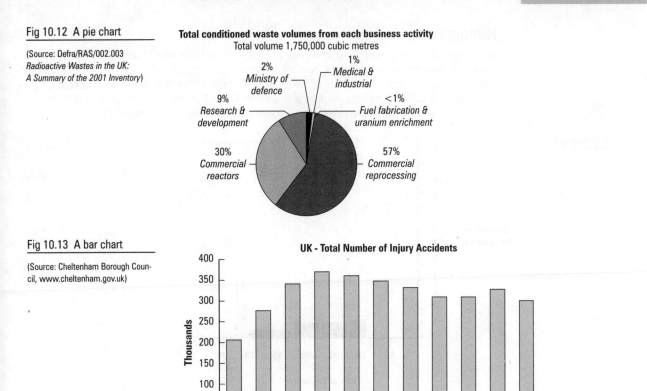

Total conditioned waste volumes from each business activity
Total volume 1,750,000 cubic metres

Fig 10.13 A bar chart

(Source: Cheltenham Borough Council, www.cheltenham.gov.uk)

of response; the frequency axis needs to be scaled so that the maximum frequency can comfortably be displayed and the other axis needs to be able to accommodate all the bars, which should be equally spaced. The bars can be colour coded.

Frequency curves

A frequency curve is a graphical representation of a continuous distribution of numerical data. The data is grouped into classes according to value, and the classes are marked along the horizontal axis; frequency is marked on the vertical axis. For each class, a cross is plotted at the point where the midpoint of the class is level with the point on the vertical axis that denotes its frequency. The crosses are then connected with a line, or curve.

A frequency curve is usually shown as a smooth curve. The curve of some frequency distributions is bell shaped, reaching a peak above the mean of the distribution and tailing off either side because in this type of distribution the frequencies in the lowest and highest classes are very small. Fig 10.14 shows another type of frequency curve; it illustrates cumulative percentages.

Fig 10.14 Cumulative percentage distribution

(Source: Department for Transport, www.dft.gov.uk)

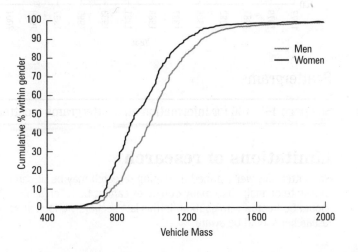

Histograms

A histogram is another way of summarising a continuous distribution of numerical data. The values are set into classes along the horizontal axis and each group is represented by a rectangle with base length equal to the range of values in that group. When the classes are not equal, the rectangles will have different widths and, as it is the area of the rectangle that represents frequency, the width has to be taken into account when plotting the heights of the rectangles.

Fig 10.15 A histogram

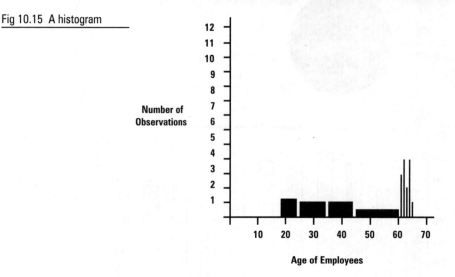

Number of Observations (vertical axis)

Age of Employees (horizontal axis)

Line graphs

Line graphs are the simplest form of graph. The axes measure two aspects of the data and a mark is made on the graph to correspond with the measurement on each axis. Each of the marks made on the graph is then joined up to create a line. The gradient of the line and the difference between lower and higher values are clearly seen.

Fig 10.16 A line graph

(Source: South West Water, south-westwater.co.uk)

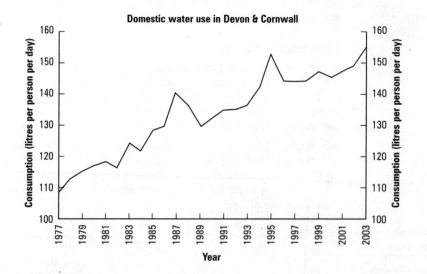

Domestic water use in Devon & Cornwall

Consumption (litres per person per day) vs Year

Scattergrams

See page 165–166 for information on scattergrams (scatter diagrams).

Limitations of research

No matter how well planned marketing research may be, it can only give a glimpse of the true state of affairs and many outcomes cannot be taken as fact. Therefore predictions should be treated with caution. In this last section, we look at various limitations of which a researcher should be aware.

Excess of information through customer databases

Customer databases contain a great deal of information, some of which may have direct relevance and are of use for marketing research. But much information does not provide any insight into customer preferences or future customer behaviour. Although a business may have extensive customer databases, simply trawling through the data, as a marketing research exercise may not reveal any illuminating factors of which the business is not yet aware.

E-business feedback overload

E-businesses asking for customer feedback may, like the traditional businesses, be overwhelmed with data that does not have any direct use. It is even more of a problem for e-businesses as the feedback may have been provided by individuals who have just visited the website and are not customers at all. The information needs therefore to be filtered so that only feedback from actual customers is included in the marketing research project.

Reliability of sample, accuracy, bias and subjectivity

As we have already seen, choosing the correct type of sample is imperative in order to provide meaningful sets of data, conclusions and recommendations. Businesses often run random checks to see whether individuals included in the sample are truly representative of their target group. Obviously, the smaller the sample, the less potentially accurate the results will be. There is also the problem of bias and subjectivity, particularly if employees of the business, rather than independent market research agencies, have carried out the research as individuals may seek to manipulate the data so that it more closely matches their view and preferred way forward for the organisation.

> **remember**
>
> An organisation's decision makers will neither have the time nor the inclination to read entire marketing research reports. They will expect to read the key findings on a single sheet and will draw their own conclusions regarding reliability, accuracy and bias.

Link

See pages 154, 155 and 157 to remind yourself about first three parts of the DTI Foresight programme case study.

---

case study

10.11

DTI Foresight programme: six hypothetical food products – Part 4

The respondents who did reply were asked what their major concerns were about the products. Table 10.12 summarises their points of view.

Table 10.12 Summary of respondents' concerns about six food products

Product/Major importance	Scottish Banana	Anti-cancer Broccoli	Long-life Lasagne	Zero-calorie Cake	Smart Packaging	Chicken in a Bottle
Food safety or consumer health are explored	85%	93%	89%	92%	86%	91%
The packaging of the food has clear labelling	67%	72%	74%	75%	73%	62%
Environmental impact is considered	63%	61%	68%	71%	60%	67%
The food itself looks good and appetising	41%	57%	55%	59%	56%	61%
Opinions from experts are obtained	61%	49%	39%	52%	45%	56%
Costs in the supermarket for food are considered	50%	54%	49%	47%	51%	49%
The needs of society in general are considered	44%	54%	48%	50%	40%	41%

Product/Major importance						
	Scottish Banana	Anti-cancer Broccoli	Long-life Lasagne	Zero-calorie Cake	Smart Packaging	Chicken in a Bottle
The ethics, morals and values of individuals are considered	37%	39%	37%	58%	44%	44%
Convenience for consumers increased	22%	29%	31%	33%	29%	28%
Costs are reduced for food producers	27%	34%	28%	25%	21%	27%
Science and technology is used to develop the food	12%	23%	14%	13%	18%	15%
Incomes are boosted for food producers	14%	20%	15%	11%	16%	9%
Pressure group opinion is taken on board	10%	11%	7%	16%	17%	10%
The food has a catchy name	1%	6%	3%	3%	5%	6%

(Adapted from www.foresight.gov.uk)

activity

1 Based on the information that you have already read regarding the sampling for this research project, how reliable are the results and the accuracy of the figures?

2 How would you choose to display these results for a presentation. Justify your choice of visual images or other methods.

activity

INDIVIDUAL WORK 10.6

P4

Interpret findings from the research and present them clearly in an appropriate format.

Now that you have collected your primary and secondary research data, you will need to collate and interpret the information. You will be expected to present the main points of the research findings either in the form of a written report or as an oral presentation supported by diagrams and handouts. You must:

1 Collate and present in diagrammatic form all of the key points of the research.

2 Comment on each of the individual findings (in relation to the questions posed – refer to your objectives for guidance).

3 Comment on the overall findings.

4 Present a series of conclusions from your findings.

5 Make sensible recommendations arising from your findings and conclusions.

6 Be prepared to answer supplementary questions arising out of your research methods, data collection and analysis and your conclusions and recommendations.

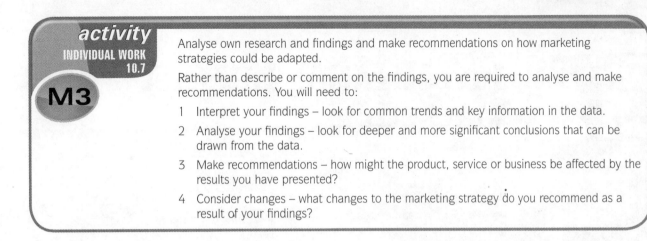

activity INDIVIDUAL WORK 10.7 M3

Analyse own research and findings and make recommendations on how marketing strategies could be adapted.

Rather than describe or comment on the findings, you are required to analyse and make recommendations. You will need to:

1   Interpret your findings – look for common trends and key information in the data.

2   Analyse your findings – look for deeper and more significant conclusions that can be drawn from the data.

3   Make recommendations – how might the product, service or business be affected by the results you have presented?

4   Consider changes – what changes to the marketing strategy do you recommend as a result of your findings?

---

activity
INDIVIDUAL WORK 10.8
D2

Evaluate the findings from the research undertaken.

Now that you have collected, interpreted and analysed your research and findings, you are ready to do the following:

1   Evaluate the process of creating the research plan.

2   Evaluate the research methodology used.

3   Evaluate the data collection and collation.

4   Evaluate the creation of your report or presentation.

5   Recommend improvement, as and where problems arose.

Progress Check

1. Give three examples of primary research.

2. How might a marketing research project take note of the movement of customers in a supermarket?

3. Give three examples of specialist agencies that provide market research data.

4. What are the six elements of PESTLE?

5. In terms of a professional marketing research project, how many respondents would be involved in a large sample?

6. If a research project got underway and was primarily concerned with the retention of customers, which parts of a retail organisation might be likely to contribute to its budget?

7. Briefly explain the difference between a census and a sample.

8. If a respondent was given a blank space after a question, what type of question would have been used on the questionnaire?

9. How do the arithmetic mean, mode and median differ from each other?

10. Explain the difference between a pictogram and a pie chart.

UNIT 12

Investigating Internet Marketing

This unit covers:

- The role Internet marketing has within a modern marketing context
- The benefits of Internet marketing to customers
- The opportunities offered to businesses by Internet marketing
- How to investigate the challenges faced by businesses using Internet marketing

Internet marketing has had to develop quickly in order to take advantage of the wide availability of computers and people's increasing use of the Internet. Internet marketing has also become more sophisticated in response to the growing demand from customers for a more personalised approach.

The unit begins by introducing the modern marketing context and looking at the contribution of Internet marketing. It then discusses the many benefits that customers receive from Internet marketing and the opportunities that it offers to businesses in terms of improved communications, product development and business efficiency. Finally, the unit examines the issues that businesses face when using Internet marketing and how these are investigated.

grading criteria

To achieve a **Pass** grade the evidence must show that the learner is able to:	To achieve a **Merit** grade the evidence must also show that the learner is able to:	To achieve a **Distinction** grade the evidence must also show that the learner is able to:
P1 describe the role Internet marketing has in a modern marketing context using selected organisations as examples Pg 194	**M1** analyse the benefits of Internet marketing to customers Pg 200	**D1** evaluate the effectiveness of Internet marketing in meeting customer needs for a selected business Pg 212
P2 describe the principal benefits to customers of Internet marketing Pg 200	**M2** analyse the marketing opportunities and challenges faced by a selected business when using Internet marketing within the marketing mix of a selected business Pg 211	
P3 describe the benefits and opportunities to the business of using Internet marketing within the marketing mix of a selected business Pg 207		
P4 describe the challenges facing a selected business when using the Internet as a marketing tool. Pg 211		

The role of Internet marketing within a modern marketing context

Internet marketing is assuming an ever-greater role in business. In the UK alone, Internet shopping continues its meteoric growth. In 2006, British consumer buyers made purchases on the Internet amounting to £1,000 per person (Office for National Statistics).

The competition faced by most businesses in high streets, shopping malls and out-of-town retail parks pales into insignificance compared with the number of businesses vying for those sales on the Internet. Internet marketing has therefore to be significantly more effective in order to combat strong opposition from businesses not only in Great Britain, but also in Europe and around the globe.

In Great Britain in 2005, the total UK consumer spend online was £6.7bn. This equates to €9.79bn. Germany was in second place with €9.71bn and France, a poor third, with €6.5bn. Before the expansion of the European Union in January 2006, online retail sales accounted for 65% of Europe's €40.2bn e-commerce market. This was a growth of 51% from the previous year (Mintel).

Office for National Statistics

www.statistics.gov.uk

Mintel

www.mintel.com

Fig 12.1 Amazon home page

Physical bricks and mortar shops are not sitting back and watching their business disappear. But nothing seems to stop the Internet from becoming not only the most competitive, but also the most popular means by which consumers can obtain products and services, without even leaving their own homes.

Modern marketing

Marketing is both a function of a business and a set of processes. It aims to:

- create value to customers
- communicate to customers
- deliver value to customers.

This is all within the context of providing benefits to the organisation and its **stakeholders**, in terms of turnover and profits.

Despite the fact that marketing has developed significantly in recent years, the two key primary goals of marketing still remain the same and are:

- to assess and identify the needs of consumers
- to satisfy those needs.

For marketing to have a chance of succeeding in any relationship between business and consumers, the latter have to have unmet needs and the business must have the desire and ability to satisfy those needs. The next stage is for the two parties to communicate. Only then can:

- the business exchange its products or services to satisfy the needs
- the consumer pay for them.

This is the heart of marketing and has been ever since products or services have been available for sale.

The first key objective of marketing is therefore always to discover the needs of the business's potential consumers. It is not always easy for consumers to identify and describe what it is that they need or want. A want is a felt need, and wants tend to cover the vast majority of products and services purchased by consumers. The basic needs are always shelter, food and clothing. Beyond these three, everything else could be considered to be a want.

The second key objective is to satisfy the needs of the targeted consumers. Even the largest business cannot possibly satisfy all consumer needs. It has therefore to focus on particular groups of potential customers (target markets) or become specialised in providing a specific want, which could be a niche market.

Having selected its approach, the business has to develop a way in which the wants of those potential consumers can be met. This naturally involves creating a unique marketing programme to reach them.

The integration and extension of the marketing mix

The marketing mix is a set of controllable variables, which are adjusted according to the particular target market, the products or services involved and the specific skills or expertise of the business itself. The marketing mix is one of the few aspects of marketing of which most people have any knowledge or awareness.

For many years the marketing mix was seen as a simple combination of four elements. The assumption was that, if these four elements were brought together in the correct balance, the business would be able to interact with its consumers and its potential consumers and enjoy a profitable relationship with them. Originally, the four elements or variables that were regarded as important were:

- product
- place
- price
- promotion.

These are known as the four Ps, and it will be useful to look at them before we examine why the marketing mix has been extended to incorporate other elements.

- Product – this is a definition of the characteristics of the product or service, so that it meets the needs of the consumer. The development of the product will be in line with the specific needs of the target market. This will extend to such elements as size, colour, reliability, design, packaging and a host of other product-specific factors.

- Place – another word for this would be distribution, or more specifically the distribution methods. It involves looking at the availability of the product or service and how the consumer can purchase it or find out about it with the minimum of effort. Obviously, there are huge differences in distribution and outlets through which the products or services can be purchased. Some products work better if they are available in multiple locations in almost every village, town or city. Others work when they are less commonly available. Of course, the Internet potentially makes any product immediately available, regardless of the location of the customer.

- Price – this is essentially a pricing strategy for the products or services that aims to identify the total cost to the consumer. The decision is based on many factors, including the desired profit level of the business, prices charged by competitors and the willingness of consumers to accept certain price levels.

- Promotion – this incorporates what many of us believe to be marketing. As such it comprises advertising, personal selling, sales promotions and public relations, all of which are business-to-consumer contact methods. They are ways in which the business attracts, encourages or actually sells the product to the consumer. Although advertising tends to be regarded as marketing, it is actually only an element of marketing.

We can see that the four Ps suggest a rather old-fashioned approach, as they do not include many elements of modern marketing. Initially, there were attempts to make the four Ps a little more modern, without adding additional elements. In the most common translation of the four Ps, they became the four Cs.

- Product became consumer needs and wants. This was a far more focused attempt to reinforce the fact that the design, characteristics and features of any product or service should match the precise needs and wants of consumers.

- Place became convenience. Making the product or service as freely available as possible and making it positively easy for the consumer to track it down became the driving force instead of looking at complex distribution methods.

- Price became cost to user. This far broader approach to prices and pricing strategies recognised that the product or service itself may well have ongoing costs to the user and that these would have to be taken into account in the overall strategy. A prime example would be a manufacturer of computer printers that sells its printers at low cost, whilst charging higher prices, relative to product cost, for its ink cartridges.

- Promotion became communication, thereby including any type of interaction between the business and the consumer. This allowed businesses to incorporate such activities as the sponsoring of television programmes and the use of banner advertising on the Internet combined with the facility for the consumer to click on the ad to be taken to their websites or ordering pages.

The new approach meant that, rather than businesses manipulating the situation to create a demand for products and services that they could offer, they had become more inclined to take the lead from their consumers. Businesses began to design products and services that precisely matched consumer needs and would be promoted at the correct price through a variety of distribution channels that matched the characteristics of the target markets.

Although transforming the four Ps into the four Cs was recognition of the ways in which marketing was changing, it was still necessary to incorporate other factors, in order fully to appreciate each aspect of marketing. This led to the identification of three additional Ps:

- people
- process
- physical evidence.

The first recognises the fact that unless the consumer is purchasing online, through a fully automated system, they will have some kind of contact with the employees or representatives of the business. Even with automated online sales it may be necessary for the consumer to call or email the business and interact with an employee. This makes the recruitment of employees and their training in how to deliver service to consumers important aspects of the overall marketing mix. Consumers make judgements about a business based on any interaction they have had with representatives of that business. Aspects such as interpersonal skills, attitudes and aptitudes, and service knowledge are all important.

Fig 12.2

In Britain, many businesses apply for **Investors in People** accreditation. This is seen as a measure of the value that the business places on its employees. It also indicates that they are trained to particular and exacting standards, which is not only a positive benefit for consumers but may attract them.

Process refers to the way in which the business actually delivers its services to its consumers. The focus is on efficient delivery of the original product or service and in the ongoing relationship with the consumers, at any level, including repair, complaints and general enquiries. The more efficient the service, the greater is the consumer's loyalty and confidence in the business.

Physical evidence relates to the environment in which the service or sale is being carried out. It provides consumers with an opportunity to make a judgement about the business; their perceptions will be influenced by what they see and what they experience. When consumers walk into a restaurant, they expect to see a clean and attractive environment. On an aircraft, they expect cleanliness and sufficient legroom. On the Internet, the physical evidence is the website itself: its design, features and, above all, its functionality. If the site is cluttered, complicated and difficult to use, the physical evidence being provided by the business is negative.

Relationship marketing

Relationship marketing grew from the direct response marketing of the 1960s. Direct response marketing sought to sell products and services direct to consumers via advertising on television and in magazines and newspapers. The advertisement incorporated a persuasive piece of sales literature, telling the consumer how their lives would be revolutionised and improved by purchasing the product or service. As well as the attempt to convince the consumer that they needed the product or service, the advertisement provided either a coupon to fill in and send back or a telephone number so that the potential consumer could make immediate contact.

By using direct response marketing, businesses hoped that they could cut out any businesses between them and the consumer and deal with the consumer direct. They hoped also to establish a long-term relationship with the consumer so that, armed with the consumer's details and facts about their preferences, they would be able to target them with other suitable products or services at a later date.

Relationship marketing seeks to develop the relationship: it aims to build a long-term connection between the business and the consumer, rather than dealing with them on a transaction-by-transaction basis. The relationship extends to understanding the changing needs of consumers, as they go through life. Take, for example, financial services: when consumers are fairly young, they may wish to obtain loans and mortgages; later they will think about pensions and savings and probably insurance. Later still, they will consider liquidating some of their assets, so that they can have more cash available to them. Theoretically, if a business maps the life cycle of its consumers, it can offer products and services at the right point in time, as long as the business has a broad range of products and services available.

Relationship marketing also grew out of business-to-business selling. Over a period of time, businesses tend to identify their preferred suppliers for key products and services. They will usually stick with these suppliers, provided that the level of service remains acceptable and the prices competitive. These long-term relationships rely on establishing and maintaining contact between supplier and customer.

A cynical view of relationship marketing might consider the whole process to be purely defensive. Businesses suffer from consumer turnover: whilst the business is continually attracting new customers, it is losing existing ones; consequently, the business has continually to try to attract new customers, not to grow but to maintain its position because it is losing customers. Relationship marketing provides a means by which the business can attempt to ensure customer loyalty whilst at the same time encouraging consumers to purchase more frequently. For those that view relationship marketing in this way, the whole focus is on reducing and managing the dissatisfaction of the business's customers. This is in stark contrast with most other marketing activities, which can be considered to be offensive because they focus on attracting other businesses' dissatisfied customers.

An essential part of relationship marketing is customer relationship management (CRM), the aim of which is to enable the business to acquire a full understanding of its customer base by looking at consumers' tastes, likes, dislikes, preferences and many other factors. By understanding these features and then making efforts to exploit them, the business can encourage customers to make repeat purchases.

New product development opportunities

Usually, consumer goods and goods sold to businesses can be categorised by their tangibility:

- Non-durable goods tend to be consumed after one or a few uses.
- Durable goods can be used over an extended period of time.
- Services are benefits, satisfactions or activities.

In relation to consumer goods, the following considerations are important:

- How involved the purchasing decision was – how long and how complex was the consumer's decision to purchase the goods?
- Marketing mix attributes – how complicated were the elements of the marketing mix in bringing the goods to the consumer?
- Frequency of purchase – how often do customers purchase the goods?

In fact, as far as consumer products are concerned, we can identify three main areas:

- Convenience goods – these are purchased on a regular basis with a minimum amount of thought involved in the purchasing process.
- Shopping goods – these usually require the consumer to compare alternatives based on their requirements.
- Speciality goods – consumers are usually happy to make an effort to find and to buy these.
- Unsought goods – these are goods that consumers do not know about or initially desire.

Business goods tend to be broken down into:

- Production goods – these are directly used during a manufacturing process and include components and raw materials.
- Support goods – these are any other supplies, services, equipment or installation that are used to run the business.

When defining a product or service as new it is important to remember that, to be truly new, one or more of the following must apply:

- It is functionally different from the business's existing products.
- It is a significant innovation or a revolutionary new product, which could be an extension of products already offered by the business.
- To use it requires a degree of learning on the consumer's part.

New products often fail for the following reasons:

- They are not significantly different.
- The product has not been properly defined before it has been developed.
- The potential target markets have not been properly identified.

remember

Products can be goods or services. They can also be a bundle of tangible and intangible attributes, aimed at satisfying consumers.

- The target market itself is not attracted to the product.
- There are critical errors in the product's quality.
- The product is priced at a level that does not make it sufficiently attractive to buyers.
- It has been brought out at the wrong time.
- The marketing mix is flawed.

Businesses seek constantly to develop new products in the hope that they can identify a saleable product or service and market it before their competitors identify the same opportunity and move to block their temporary advantage. Normally, businesses approach new product development in seven stages:

- defining the role of development within the business's overall objectives
- generating new ideas from a pool of different concepts, usually derived from research and development, competitors, employees and consumers
- screening and evaluating new product ideas, to eliminate those that are not workable, either from a production point of view or because they will not be sufficiently attractive to consumers
- analysing and defining the features of the new product and then developing a marketing strategy to introduce it, as well as forecasting future financial implications
- testing prototype products, within the business and then using consumers, to see if it meets the standards that have been set
- test marketing the product to prospective consumers, using realistic purchasing situations to see if they will buy the product
- full commercialised release of the product, incorporating its launch, full-scale production and a specific marketing programme.

Market development opportunities

Businesses look all the time for market development opportunities. Any new market development could potentially deliver business growth in three key areas:

- the marketing and sales of new products and services to existing customers
- the marketing and sales of existing products and services to new customers
- the marketing and sales of new products and services to new customers.

There is a reason for putting these three different market development opportunities in this order. Simply, the first is by far the easiest and the last is the most difficult.

Bearing in mind what has been said about relationship marketing, we can apply what is known as the **Pareto Principle** to these opportunities. The Pareto Principle states that 80% of sales can be achieved from the most loyal 20% of a business's customers. The remaining 20% of sales are achieved from the other 80% of customers. This is a guiding principle when businesses consider developments in markets. They know that having established

Fig 12.3 New product development opportunities

a relationship with their existing customers, there is a much greater likelihood that these customers will embrace new products. Strictly speaking, the existing customers are not a new market as such, but they have the potential to be if new products and services can match their requirements.

When a business is trying to develop new markets, the process is as follows:

1. The business will begin by trying to establish its market development aims and targets.

2. It will try to identify potential target markets and niches.

3. It will investigate how its marketing and sales currently work and whether these functions are capable of reaching this new target market and developing it.

4. The business will develop a clear profile of the type of customers in the market, possibly by creating a database to identify specific targets.

5. The business will try to establish many key advantages of its products, which can be conveyed to the target market. It will look at unique aspects of its products or services, how these compare with competitors' and their pricing levels compared with those of similar products, which might already be available to the market.

6. The business will design communication methods to engage with the target market, with the goal of generating enquiries.

7. It will organise its response and sales processes, so that these are ready to deal with the new potential demand from the target market.

8. Systems will be established to monitor progress and measure the effectiveness of activities.

9. At this point, the business is ready to try to exploit the new market as it emerges.

ICT strategies

The key tool used by businesses in their information and communication technology (ICT) strategy is customer relationship management. This does not, however, just comprise the application of the technology: it is a broader-based strategy that encompasses an understanding of customer needs and behaviours to enable the business to create a far stronger and longer-lasting relationship with its customers.

In this respect, CRM is not just a technical solution to the age-old problem of dealing with consumers in an efficient and effective manner. It is a broader business approach.

As we have seen, it is important for a business to retain its existing customers, otherwise expansion becomes almost impossible. It also costs a considerable amount of money, spent on marketing, advertising, promotions and public relations, to attract new customers to replace old ones. ICT has enabled businesses to use information in such a way as to produce many more opportunities for a customer to trade with the business. This has meant, as far as the Internet is concerned, offering direct sales and online sales.

It is necessary for a business to adapt in order to match its customers' needs in full. The better the relationship between the customer and the business, the easier it is for the business to generate income. It is, of course, important for the business to buy the right software. Generally speaking, as far as software is concerned, CRM solutions fall into one of the following four categories:

- Application service providers – this is an outsourced solution. Application service providers can offer online CRM solutions. Businesses would choose this option if they needed to implement the solution as quickly as possible. It is also a chosen route if the business does not have its own skills to begin the process from scratch. Usually, these solutions are geared to work hand in hand with online e-commerce.

- Off the shelf – there are several software applications that are designed to work with existing software packages. As a cost-saving option, a small business would be likely to use a version that has fewer functions. This approach tends to be the cheapest way of investing in CRM software. The main problem is that the software is not specifically designed for the business and may not do exactly what the business requires. As with most purchases, this solution is often a trade-off between, on the one hand, convenience and price, and, on the other, functionality.

- Bespoke software – there is a host of software engineers and consultants ready, willing and able to design a custom-made CRM system for any business. They will design it so that it is fully functional with existing software used by the business. However, this option is the most expensive and potentially the one with the longest timescale, as, although the design may be based on common elements, it will have to be personalised for the business.

■ Managed solutions – this can be seen as a mid-point between an outsourced and bespoke approach. The business rents a customised CRM application. Although this solution tends to be far more cost effective than bespoke software, the application may not be as fully functional.

Regardless of the type of software chosen, the business needs to build up its CRM information system. This involves collecting information about customers and then processing it in such a way as to improve both the business's marketing and the customer experience. There are six recognised stages:

1. Collection of information – this can usually be done by collecting information from the business's existing website or online customer service.

2. Storage of information in a relational database – this is a more flexible customer database that enables commonalities in customers to be quickly identified.

3. Access to information – this is an important stage as the business needs to ensure that useful information is made available to employees in an easy-to-use format.

4. Analysis of customer behaviour – this is known as 'data mining'. Patterns or relationships are analysed by looking at customer behaviour; this enables the business to profile customers and develop targeted marketing and sales strategies.

5. Improved marketing – taking the Pareto Principle into account, the use of customer relationship management gives the business a better understanding of its customers, so that the most valuable of them can be rewarded and targeted.

6. Customer experience – we know that a relatively small number of customers are the business's most profitable ones. We also know that a relatively small number of customers take up most of the business's time by lodging complaints and being generally more demanding. Identifying problems enables them to be quickly resolved.

Customer relationship management, however, does have some disadvantages, and even the application of the latest ICT strategies may not work if any of the following aspects are not addressed:

■ The application of CRM may mean a major cultural change within the business. In switching over to the use of ICT some existing relationships with customers may be damaged. This could be particularly true if there is a lack of commitment from employees. Everything must be looked at from a customer's perspective.

■ As a result of poor communications within the business, key employees may not be aware of what information is needed, or how to use it.

■ The business's owners must be fully behind the project and lead by example. They should make sure that everything is customer focused, and if it becomes apparent that current plans do not match the needs of customers then they should have the strength of will to cancel the project and rethink.

■ Looking at CRM as the Holy Grail, or ultimate answer to pushing the business forward is dangerous, as trying to implement it too quickly and too completely will lead to enormous problems and disruption to normal, everyday activities. A large amount of work has to be put into the project; systems have to be expanded and employees retrained. Above all, the customer must be fully in focus throughout the entire process and beyond.

■ The business must also cope with the necessity to comply with data protection legislation. Doing so may not have been a particular concern in the past, but, now that it is holding and using data regarding its customers, the business must rigidly apply the principles of the Data Protection Act 1998.

For more information about the Data Protection Act 1998

www.ico.gov.uk.

There are key questions that a business will have to ask of its CRM suppliers. Bearing in mind that the software or the solution can be an expensive and significant investment, making the right choice is vital. A business needs to be wary and to ask potential suppliers a series of questions:

■ How long has the supplier been in operation and what reputation does the supplier have?

■ What are the specific costs involved? (Costs may be a charge per user, renewable licenses or one-off purchases.)

- Can the supplier provide a version of the software so that it can be test-driven before commitment?
- What are the level and the cost of ongoing technical support?
- Does the supplier provide consultancy services and are these built into the price?
- Can the system be expanded as the business expands and, perhaps, include additional data in new fields and areas not presently considered vital?
- Can the supplier provide contact details of existing users so that their experience can be shared?
- Does the supplier provide training for employees and, if so, what are the costs?

case study 12.1 — Adding technology to the marketing mix

Developing the right blend of marketing and ICT is key to successfully promoting business. This was the message delivered by speakers at 'Technology Essentials: Communications & Marketing' on 22 November 2005 during ICT Forum Wales.

Michael Eaton, Director of Broadband Wales told delegates that 99% of Wales now had access to terrestrial broadband, compared with some 30% only two years before. Through a series of examples, Eaton demonstrated the potential that broadband can bring to business from simple websites to embedded media clips and 'virtual tourism'. He concluded by stressing the importance of accessibility and ensuring that any web presence is made available to the disabled.

Staying with the communications theme, Mathew Pickergill from Cisco explained some of the new developments in Internet communications including IP telephony and virtual working.

With the communications infrastructure covered, delegates then heard from marketing experts who integrate technology in the marketing mix. Stuart Williams is Publishing Director of Kerrang!, the UK's leading weekly music magazine, and he provided an informative and entertaining presentation into the evolution of the brand to its leading position.

While the marketing budgets of most SMEs would be incomparable with that of Kerrang!, Williams discussed many ideas used by his team which smaller companies could consider adopting. Williams described the need to understand consumer habits before developing the brand essence. Working with a mainly teenage audience, the first new product launched was the Kerrang! Website, and within a month the site had more unique users than the magazine had readers, and the strong community that developed on the site's message boards gave the team confidence to introduce further products including a radio station and TV channel.

Williams told delegates that technology has enabled the Kerrang! brand to connect with 5 million users in the UK, and that an integrated effort across all marketing and promotion was key.

In closing, Williams told delegates that in order to survive it was vital to develop brand clarity, brand consistency, and product flexibility. He finished with the statement, 'Don't be cool – be good!'

Paula Dauncey of Imaginet explained the process of acquiring, converting and retaining customers through strategic online marketing, and demonstrated the importance of achieving high search engine rankings. Some 81% of **web traffic** is driven by search engine results, and Dauncey stated that the only way to guarantee placement was through Pay-Per-Click search advertising.

Dauncey moved on to discuss websites, saying that creative design was vital to differentiate businesses from competitors, and asked delegates to consider what the purpose of their company website was – did they want customers to buy, interact or simply read a brochure? Once a company had customers, how should they develop the relationship to retain the customer? Options suggested included email marketing, personalisation and loyalty schemes.

(Source: ICT Forum Wales)

1   What is an SME?
2   What is meant by 'brand essence'?
3   What is meant by 'the only way to guarantee placement was through Pay-Per-Click search advertising'?

Targeting and segmentation

Targeting and segmentation always begin with data. A business needs to be very clear about the type of information that will be of most use. If it is asking online customers to complete forms or fill in questionnaires, any information requested on these virtual documents must be relevant. If a business asks too many questions, the process may seem too daunting and customers will not complete the process. Businesses should be able to identify key questions that will help them target and segment their customers.

One of the biggest mistakes that businesses make is to believe that their websites need to attract millions of visitors in order to be successful. The truth is that 5m people may visit a website, but only a handful will actually buy anything. A business should, therefore, focus on those visitors to the website who actually become paying customers.

In order to take full advantage of this smaller group of people, a business should target them through its marketing. So a business needs to know something about its customers before beginning any marketing campaign. Typically, it should ask itself the following questions:

- Who is interested in the products and services?
- How old are they?
- Where do they live?
- Are they male or female?
- Are they businesses or individuals?
- What price ranges can they afford?

The above represent a sample of the type of questions that can be asked. However, the following two-part question is the most important:

- How can I attract these customers to the site and then convince them to buy?

By targeting the right customers and only those customers – rather than trying to tell the whole world about its website and then trying to make the whole world buy from it – a business can save itself a lot of time and money.

Fig 12.4

Businesses should recognise that by narrowing down the field they are not reducing their ability to sell. The truth is completely the opposite: they are enhancing their chances to sell, as they are picking out the ideal customer and targeting their marketing to suit them.

Some potential customers will arrive at the website by using a search engine; others, surfing the Internet fairly randomly, will find the website by accident. These two groups are of value to a business, but it is the ones that are invited to the website that can prove to be the most valuable and profitable. They already have something in common with the business: an interest in the product or service. This type of customer is far more likely to purchase from the website. The questions are how do businesses identify this type of business or individual and where can they be found?

However good a business's marketing strategy may be, or its ability to identify particular target markets, it will undoubtedly fail unless it can use segmentation. Market segmentation is about understanding customers' needs. Identifying these needs enables a business to categorise its customers into groups, with each group sharing similar sets of values or criteria.

Having identified which of these groups it is best suited to serve; the business can target these knowing that the correct approach will bring greater levels of sales and a longer-term relationship. Market segmentation, therefore, involves dividing customers, or potential customers, into different groups or segments.

The most straightforward type of segmentation for consumers might be by:

- gender
- age
- income
- where they live
- how often they purchase.

For a business-to-business relationship, the approach can be slightly different, but notice that some of the characteristics are very broadly similar to the ones used for consumers. Segmentation of businesses may be by:

- turnover (income)
- size
- type of products or services produced
- location
- technology that the business uses.

Whichever type of segmentation or grouping is used, it is important that the following rules are applied:

- The business should be clear and specific about the segments that it has identified.
- The segments must be identified on the basis of hard facts.
- Customers will show a huge variety of different characteristics, but the business needs only to segment on the basis of characteristics that match its criteria for segmentation.
- The business should not overly segment: the more groups there are, the harder it is to reach them all.
- The business must be able to reach each segmented group and, for Internet marketing, this means that the groups chosen must have Internet access.
- The business must make sure that it is cost effective to reach each market segment and that the costs do not compromise profitability.
- The business must identify the most profitable group first and spend most of its time and effort on this group, with the remainder of its time focused on each group in profit order.

Although there are a large number of different ways in which customers can be segmented, the most common are **demographic**, **psychographic**, **economic** and **usage-based**.

Demographic segmentation incorporates age, gender, life cycle and family size, and type of house and its location. It is important to note that consumers' needs and wants change with their age. The marketing mix should therefore be adapted on the basis of age segments.

Some products and services are clearly aimed at particular age groups. Cosmetics are a prime example. The vast majority of Maybelline customers are in the age group 15–25. Products such as Calvin Klein are aimed at 15 to 24 year-old men. At the other end of the scale, anti-ageing products are targeted at women from their 40s onwards.

Gender is the second aspect of demographic segmentation. Certain car manufacturers have specifically targeted women (e.g. for the Ford Ka), although this is not a new trend as Toyota was targeting women in the 1960s. Other products, including cosmetics, clothing, magazines and interior design are all targeted at the female market.

The third aspect of demographic segmentation is what is known as the life cycle stage. Each part of a person's life cycle is designed to reflect the fact that there are changing needs and priorities for products and service, as can be seen in Table 12.1.

Table 12.1 Life cycle stages

Life cycle stages	
Bachelor stage	Young, single people not living at home
Newly married couples	Young, no children
Full nest I	Youngest child under six
Full nest II	Youngest child six or over
Full nest III	Older married couples with dependent children
Empty nest I	Older married couples, no children living with them
Empty nest II	Older married couples, retired, no children living at home
Solitary survivor I	In labour force
Solitary survivor II	Retired

The final aspect of demographic segmentation rests on the assumption that people can be divided into groups, based on the type of house and location of that house. It is seen as a relatively good way of predicting their purchasing behaviour and the types of products and services that they could buy. The system that tends to be used is known as ACORN. It utilises the 10-yearly population census, collected by the government. The last census took place in 2001. Table 12.2 shows a simplified version of ACORN, indicating the breakdown of the British population, according to housing type and area.

Table 12.2 ACORN

Acorn		
A.	Agricultural areas	3% of UK population
B.	Modern family housing, higher incomes	18% of UK population
C.	Older housing of intermediate status	17% of UK population
D.	Poor-quality older terraced housing	4% of UK population
E.	Better-off council estates	13% of UK population
F.	Less well-off council estates	9% of UK population
G.	Poorest council estates	7% of UK population
H.	Multi-racial areas	4% of UK population
I.	High-status non-family areas	4% of UK population
J.	Affluent suburban housing	16% of UK population
K.	Better-off retirement areas	4% of UK population
U.	Unclassified	1% of UK population

Psychographic segmentation aims to break down the market into social classes. It also takes account of personality characteristics and lifestyle. The assumption is that the individual's characteristics and patterns of living affect the types of products and brands purchased.

Division of the market into social classes has come under considerable criticism in recent years, as the instrument for doing this is not very precise. It is called a socio-economic scale and assigns individuals to a social grade. Table 12.3 shows the social grades.

Table 12.3 The socio-economic scale

Social grade	Description of occupation	Example
A	Higher managerial, administrative or professional	Company director
B	Intermediate managerial, administrative or professional	Middle manager
C1	Supervisory, clerical, junior administrative or professional	Bank clerk
C2	Skilled manual workers	Plumber
D	Semi- and unskilled manual workers	Labourer
E	State pensioners with no other income, widows, casual and lowest grade earners	Unemployed

For more information on how this social class system was created, visit the website of NRS Limited

www.nrs.co.uk.

Psychographic segmentation also looks at customers' lifestyles, examining a mixture of their interests, values, beliefs and opinions. There is no standardised model of lifestyle segmentation; one of the ones most commonly used was developed by the advertising agency Young and Rubican. It is known as the Cross Cultural Consumer Characterisation, or the four Cs. More information is given in Table 12.4.

Table 12.4 The four Cs

Consumer type	Characteristics
Resigned	Rigid, strict, authoritarian and chauvinist values, oriented to the past and to Resigned roles. Brand choice stresses safety, familiarity and economy. (Older)
Struggler	Alienated, Struggler, disorganised – with few resources apart from physical/mechanical skills (e.g. car repair). Heavy consumers of alcohol, junk food and lotteries, also trainers. Brand choice involves impact and sensation.
Mainstreamer	Domestic, conformist, conventional, sentimental, passive, habitual. Part of the mass, favouring big and well-known value-for-money 'family' brands. Almost invariably the largest 4Cs group.
Aspirer	Materialistic, acquisitive, affiliative, oriented to extrinsics, image, appearance, charisma, persona and fashion. Attractive packaging is more important than quality of contents. (Younger, clerical/sales type occupation)
Succeeder	Strong goal orientation, confidence, work ethic, organisation … support status quo, stability. Brand choice based on reward, prestige – the very best. Also attracted to 'caring' and protective brands … stress relief. (Top management)
Explorer	Energy – autonomy, experience, challenge, new frontiers. Brand choice highlights difference, sensation, adventure, indulgence and instant effect – the first to try new brands. (Younger – student)
Reformer	Freedom from restriction, personal growth, social awareness, value for time, independent judgement, tolerance of complexity, anti-materialistic but intolerant of bad taste. Curious and enquiring, support growth of new product categories. Selects brands for intrinsic quality, favouring natural simplicity; small is beautiful. (Higher education)

For more information about Young and Rubican's four Cs, visit

www.fourcs.yr.com.

Usage-based segmentation focuses more precisely on customer behaviour. Six elements relating to attitudes, uses, responses and knowledge about products and services are applied; these are:

- the number of occasions the individual purchases, uses or thinks about buying the product or service
- the specific benefits the individual is seeking from the product or service
- the actual usage rate of the product or service, which is identified as being light, medium or heavy
- the status of the individuals in terms of being non-users, potential users, first-time users, regular users or ex-users
- the loyalty level of the individuals, ranging from switchers, who will buy the brand that offers them the best price or benefits at the time, to hard-core loyal customers, who will purchase the product or service regardless.

An important part of usage segmentation is to look at how ready individuals are to purchase a product or service. This is used when trying to design and monitor marketing strategies that are intended to move consumers along the buyer-readiness scale so that they actually make a purchase. The buyer-readiness scale is outlined in Table 12.5.

Table 12.5 Buyer-readiness scale

Stage	Description
Awareness	At the launch of a new product, the target market may not even be aware that the product exists. Even established products seeking to enter new segments of the market may need to raise awareness of both the company and the product.
Knowledge	The audience may well be aware of a product or company but still have either very little knowledge of what the product or company does or, possibly worse, have the wrong impression of both the product and company.
Liking	Knowing about a company or product does not mean the audience will necessarily like either, they may well be ambivalent, have no feeling at all, or even dislike the product. An audience with knowledge of a product must therefore be moved to the stage of liking the product. Promotion must seek to develop a positive attitude towards the product, or, if market research identifies a poor product image in the market, promotion must seek to address these issues within its promotional campaign.
Preference	Given the level of competition in markets today, it is often the case that the potential customer will like several competing products on the market; promotion must now therefore seek to develop within the audience a preference for the product. Through research the business must establish the key features of the product in the eyes of the target market. These might include efficiency, performance, economy, value, and quality. Promotion will now therefore underline the advantages of the product in terms of these key features, which differentiate it from the competition.
Conviction	An audience that prefers a particular product may still not buy that product based on pure preference. In fact many customers will purchase a competitor's product, which they did not prefer, purely because they were convinced it was the right decision at that time. Promotion must now build confidence in the audience that their preference for the product is justified and convince them, through a range of promotion tools, including, for example, the use of positive press reviews and expert recommendations, that their product is the right one to buy.
Purchase	The last stage in buyer-readiness is purchase of the product. Unfortunately conviction to buy may still not result in actual purchase, and this may, for example, be due to the individual's current financial situation. Many customers will need further persuasion to make the purchase. Promotion may offer sales promotion discounts, or personal selling through sales representatives, in order to convert preference and conviction into a sale.

Business-to-business

According to eMarketer, the estimated expenditure on business-to-business (b2b) marketing communications in 2005 was £9.8bn in Great Britain. Around 176,000 people are directly involved in marketing to the b2b sector. It is a booming market, with budgets increasing year on year.

However, beyond websites and basic email marketing, the use of Internet marketing techniques is fairly limited. Around half of all businesses are investing in search marketing. This means paying to ensure that the business's website appears on the first page of a search engine's results when a search has been initiated by a user. Only 5% of British businesses use activities such as **podcasts**. Over 25% of businesses carry out their own b2b marketing themselves. The remainder use agencies.

The b2b Internet marketing carried out by businesses recognises that, as customers, businesses require far more complex information than normal consumers. To this end, the following types of Internet marketing are commonly used to reach buyers:

- comparison matrices
- webinars
- trials and demos
- downloads
- specification sheets
- white papers
- product brochures
- case studies
- newsletters.

As businesses recognise that up to 90% of all websites are underperforming, they are continually looking for means by which they can attract the right kind of visitor to their website. A huge number of b2b buyers use search engines during their buying process. Some 80% of all business on the Internet goes to the first three listings of the first page of a search engine's results page. Therefore, the design, content and programming of websites will influence the search rankings. Websites need to be designed so that buyers can find what they are looking for.

In order to create a website that fulfils these requirements, a business has to decide:

- precisely what the objective of the site is (Is it to generate leads, create sales, collect data or a combination of these?)
- which search words are likely to be used by target audiences.

eMarketer

www.emarketer.com

Business-to-consumer

Business-to-consumer (b2c) marketing has two elements: building traffic to the website and then maintaining customer loyalty. Online shoppers are notoriously price-sensitive. They demand high levels of customer service, and they can easily be lured away from the website, making it difficult for even the largest of brands to remain competitive.

The power of a brand such as Amazon is that for all of the thousands of key phrases that it uses to help it appear in a search engine's search results, the vast majority of its traffic comes from consumers typing the website's name directly into the browser. To some extent, the way in which Amazon has developed shows other businesses how it should be done. The company is accessible, visible and has a recognisable brand name. Many websites try to compete for the same money, and unfortunately the vast majority of these websites are invisible, never found and never visited by potential customers.

Sites that require log-ins put people off; other sites fail because visitors cannot find what they are looking for. Even more fail because high shipping costs are added late on in the transaction. Many online retailers do not have a clear vision of their website, so they never reach the full potential.

Fig 12.5

For any business seeking to become involved in b2c activities on the Internet, the important consideration is to develop an e-marketing plan. Although many of the basics of marketing remain the same, the difference is that there are other options available. Many businesses will continue to use advertising, public relations and direct mail as a means by which they can inform their target market of the existence of their website and online shopping facility.

The key benefits of e-marketing are:

- The business could achieve global reach.
- A properly planned e-marketing campaign can cost far less than traditional methods.
- If the business is using emails or banner advertising, the effectiveness of each of these can be measured.
- As the website is open all the time, any marketing effort could attract customers at any point of the day.
- Personalisation is possible, so that targeted offers can be made to particular types of customer.
- One-to-one marketing is possible by sending information directly to mobile phones or personal digital assistants (PDAs).
- The marketing campaigns can be more interesting, as music, graphics, videos and interactive features can be incorporated.
- Theoretically, there should be a better conversion rate. If a customer responds to an email, they can click on the link and be taken straight to the online shop.

The most common forms of e-marketing to consumers are:

- Emails – however, there is a high probability that unsolicited email will be sent directly to a bulk folder or will be stopped by a bulk mail or spam filter.
- Short messaging service – this allows short messages to be sent to a mobile phone.
- Banner advertising – this is a hugely flexible method, provided that the banner advertisements are placed on websites identified by customer profiling.

Consumer-to-consumer

Consumer-to-consumer (c2c) Internet marketing is designed to encourage and facilitate communication and transactions between customers. However, only 10% of all consumers seem to trust Internet advertising.

Again it revolves around creating a brand, such as eBay. In c2c marketing, the important consideration is that the business is only involved in the facilitating of the interactions and the transactions. It is not, strictly speaking, selling a product or service, but rather it is providing a platform through which the transactions can take place.

Businesses such as eBay receive funds in the form of a seller's premium. In eBay's case, each customer who places an item for auction or for immediate sale pays a listing fee and then a percentage of the sale price. eBay has also expanded into providing secure online payment transactions. It also levies a fee for money paid into PayPal accounts, rather like a bank would charge a handling fee for transactions.

What c2c marketing has done is to largely remove businesses from the transaction process. Having said this, many businesses use auction sites such as eBay and carry out b2c transactions. They do not use their own websites but rely on eBay shops or stores, in the knowledge that eBay will levy a percentage of their turnover.

Disintermediation and direct marketing communications

Disintermediation refers to the process of removing intermediate businesses from the supply chain that normally exists between the manufacturer, or provider of a product and service, and its end-user.

Traditional supply chains could involve several businesses, each taking a part in the movement of the product and service from the manufacturing location to the final retailing of the product to the user. Disintermediation means literally cutting out all of these middlemen and selling direct to the end-user.

The Internet has revolutionised this process. It is still a b2c activity, but instead of involving wholesalers and retailers between the manufacturer and the buyer, the manufacturer fulfils orders received from customers. There has been an immense impact on computer hardware and software sales, the use of travel agencies, and book and music sales. However, disintermediation has not worked in some areas, including furniture, groceries and pet supplies.

Dell provides the most striking example of disintermediation. The company receives computer components from its suppliers and interacts directly with its customers to create bespoke machines, completely bypassing the retail chains.

Fig 12.6 Dell home page

(Source: www.dell.co.uk)

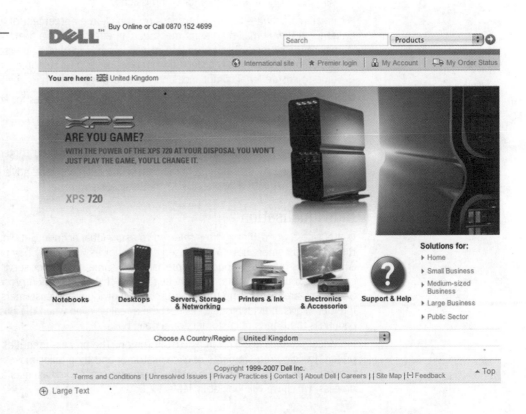

In order to offset disintermediation's negative impact on their sales, many traditional retail chains have responded by providing discounted online shopping to enhance their traditional store-based sales.

What has been particularly interesting is that many of the first businesses to move towards disintermediation have actually found that they have needed to revert back. This is known as reintermediation. Manufacturers underestimated the costs involved in dealing with a large number of small orders. They were also not geared up to provide customer service. In addition, they incurred the wrath of their retailers and former supply chain partners, all of whom were much less likely to cooperate.

In embracing disintermediation, the onus for marketing and selling fell on the manufacturers. In effect they had lost virtual and real shelf space: their products were not available in retail outlets and nor were they for sale on other businesses' websites. The jeans manufacturer Levi attempted disintermediation. It spent millions of pounds on its website and had to admit defeat, close the site down and return to its traditional use of wholesalers and retail outlets.

As already mentioned, by becoming involved in disintermediation the manufacturer has to take on the role of marketing. It can no longer rely on stockists to push its products, either through websites or in traditional retail outlets. The manufacturer has to have a direct dialogue with existing and potential customers. Businesses found that the only way to achieve this was to place direct response advertising in traditional media, such as magazines and newspapers. They found that they needed to place significant amounts of banner advertising and make use of email marketing communications.

Internet marketing

As far as most businesses are concerned, Internet marketing revolves around enhancing the power of search engines. The rules that produce results are not well understood, but search engine optimisation can enhance a business's position in search engine results. Search engine optimisation often requires adding unique content to a site and making sure that the content can be indexed by search engines. It may also require changes to the html source code of the site, as well as making the website design, content and menus search engine friendly.

There are many different approaches to Internet marketing, including:

- Affiliate programs – these involve getting a third party to sell the business's products or services online in exchange for commission.
- Email marketing – legally a business must have the agreement of all recipients before sending them email marketing messages. In effect, this is a form of permission marketing, where the recipient has opted into receiving email marketing messages. The database of potential recipients is collected from existing or past customers and then filtered each time to ensure legal compliance and the relevance of the message.
- Internet marketing strategy – this involves analysing websites for key words usage.
- Domain name selection – it is important to choose the right domain name after the business has identified all of its key words.
- Search engine optimisation – this enhances the chance of customers finding the website.
- Pay per click advertising – generally, these are search engine advertisements that connect the customer with a single click to the business's website.

Individualisation

In a business world that is often referred to as a global economy, it would be reasonable to think that customers have a decreased set of choices when they buy products and services. After all, it is possible to purchase precisely the same product or service in hundreds of countries around the world. Nonetheless, whilst this globalisation process is taking place, businesses are recognising the importance of individualising customers' experiences. The Internet allows individualisation to become a reality, even when the business is dealing with countless thousands of customers on a daily basis.

Individualisation is also known as customisation. The process identifies the key characteristics, preferences and requirements of each customer and then tailor-makes Internet marketing communications to match their profile. There are several key aspects to the individualisation process, which we will look at in Table 12.6.

Table 12.6 Individualisation

Individualisation criteria	Explanation
One-to-one relationships	One of the strong aspects of the Internet is that it gives businesses the opportunity to interact directly with their customers. This allows a close personal service, with the ability to create highly targeted personal relationships with customers. When the customer's preferences, shipping methods and other personal information are known, the marketing, fulfilment and customer service can be far more effective.
Mass customisation	Traditionally, before the Internet, the customisation of marketing communications came with a high price tag. Now customisation can be achieved through automated systems, allowing the business to specify the unique requirements of each customer.
Increased information	The question of information has two sides. First, by dealing with customers directly businesses are able to harvest a great deal of buyer behaviour preferences and personal information, which can then be used for targeted Internet marketing. Secondly, more information and detail can be provided by the business to the customer in a way in which allows the customer to see immediate benefits.
Cost-effective information gathering	When completing online questionnaires, forms and orders. customers reveal specific information beyond just the billing and delivery address. Businesses use databases to recognise specific trends and features of each customer, so that specific segmentation of customer types can be achieved. Rather than going out into the marketplace and collecting data in a traditional market research process, the information comes to the business while customers interact with it through its website.

Wider and more distant markets

As we have already seen, effective Internet marketing activities enable even the smallest business not only to reach a global marketplace but also parts of markets that were closed to it when doing business through traditional bricks and mortar retail outlets or using sales personnel.

Marketing no longer ends at the borders of a territory or a country. The Internet makes global initiatives possible. At the most basic level, a business's website can be mirrored in several different languages and customised to meet country-specific demands.

Businesses often enter into joint ventures with similar organisations in different parts of the world, collaborating in email campaigns and the placement of banner advertising. Businesses begin the process by learning about the likes and dislikes of business and consumer populations in each of their target countries. They will also need to understand local languages, legislation and regulations.

Such is the importance of global marketing that there are university degrees in the subject and many job titles stress global marketing responsibilities. The Internet is growing even in less-developed countries. This allows marketing communications to reach an ever-growing worldwide population. The number of computer owners is broadly doubling every three to five years. One of the major areas for growth has been Asia; just India and China alone account for a possible 2.1bn customers.

Product impact and enhancing marketing effectiveness

When products or services were offered in a traditional retail situation, the relationship between the business and its customers was not an important consideration until a new purchase was necessary; the exception was ongoing after-sales service. By using the Internet as the primary interface between business and customers, a business is able to make vast improvements not only in customer support but also in ongoing marketing and public relations efforts aimed at customers.

Computers, for example, can be registered online; this allows the business to capture data. In return, customers are given access to protected parts of the business's website, from which they can download additional files, programs and utilities. Maintaining a situation where customers are regular visitors to the business's website enables marketing to be far more effective, with routine offers of updates, further information and additional products and services.

Fig 12.7 Computer game sales are now rivalling music CDs and even cinema ticket sales in worldwide turnover

Even computer games, often considered to be a solitary leisure activity, are greatly enhanced by the ability to use servers to play against live opponents online. Traditional music stores, which primarily sold vinyl and CDs, now offer an alternative purchasing method, i.e. downloading MP3- or iPod-compatible tracks. Businesses are thus able to identify the music preferences of their customers and can then email them with new releases in similar music genres and by similar types of artist.

Borrowing DVDs from organisations such as Blockbuster has become less popular than borrowing DVDs from an online catalogue and having them delivered directly to the door. Payments for the loans of the DVDs are based on the number of nights that they are in the possession of the lender.

activity
INDIVIDUAL WORK 12.1

P1

Describe the role Internet marketing has in a modern marketing context using selected organisations as examples.

You will need to describe how the marketing activities of different businesses have been incorporated into Internet marketing. You must briefly explain the following, either in the form of a report or as a presentation:

1 Increased integration of marketing mix

2 Extended marketing mix

3 Relationship marketing

4 Importance of identification of new product opportunities

5 Development and market development opportunities

6 Modern information and communications technologies

7 Technology-enabled targeting and segmentation

8 Disintermediation and direct market communication by producers

9 Greater individualisation of market attention

10 Increased information and cost-effective information-gathering methods

11 Reaching wider and more distant markets

12 Product impact

13 Opportunities for enhancing marketing effectiveness

14 Understanding customers and targeting more effectively.

Understanding and targeting customers

As we have seen, by dealing directly with customers rather than using intermediaries, businesses are able to gain a better appreciation of their customers' requirements and preferences.

The more information that is captured with regard to customers' purchasing habits, the better understanding a business can have of its customers' interests. If the business understands customers' needs and their usage rates, as well as their preferred methods of purchasing and delivery, it is possible to target its marketing more effectively. The business needs also to note the frequency of customers' visits to the website and how many of those visits result in a sale, so that encouragement can be given to customers whose purchasing frequency is dropping.

remember

The key targeting and segmentation factors are important when profiling and then grouping different types of customer.

The benefits of Internet marketing to customers

As we will see in this section, although Internet marketing is primarily a tool which businesses can use to extend their visibility around the globe thereby generating more sales, there have been massive benefits to customers. For the first time, rather than having to visit dozens of shops in order to compare products in terms of features and price, it can now be done with a few clicks of the mouse. It also means that customers can demand lower prices on account of the fact that they will inevitably, after searching, discover the same product with the same availability at a lower price. Customers will also be aware of the latest developments and be able to take immediate advantage of business offers and sales, particularly in the field of airline ticketing.

Benefits to customers

Other primary benefits of Internet marketing to customers are the immediacy of online sales and customer service. Many businesses use digital complaints services, and businesses can respond to complaints and queries far faster than they could using traditional methods, such as post or call centres.

Comparing and selecting providers

There are many price comparison websites, which consumers can use not only to compare and select products and services but also to compare and select providers. When making comparisons, a customer is interested in:

- key features and description of the product or service offered
- how this compares with other similar products or services
- a price analysis
- delivery costs
- **ongoing cost analysis**
- a risk assessment (Has the customer heard of the business and does it have a good reputation?)

Businesses use a scoring mechanism when they choose suppliers. Such mechanisms measure many factors, some of which are included in the above list, which refers to normal consumer choices. Key aspects would, of course, include confidence, the safety of the product, its quality, price and, if relevant, ongoing support. Making supplier comparison decisions is said to bring down costs for businesses by between 7 and 8%. It can be a significantly larger margin for consumers.

Supplier comparison websites are very popular and cover almost every type of consumer product or service. In addition, there are price comparison sites for insurance, mortgages, financial services, travel and foreign currency exchange.

Table 12.7 contains a partial listing of British-based comparison sites.

Table 12.7 Examples of British-based comparison sites

Website	Products/services
Abcaz.co.uk	Compares high street shop prices in a large number of categories
Amazon.co.uk	Not often thought of as a comparison site but features prices from other retailers alongside its own prices
Ciao.co.uk	Comparisons and reviews across a wide range of categories
Find-dvd.co.uk	Compares DVD, CD and videogame over a number of sites
Foundem.com	A large number of categories
Froogle	UK Google's price comparison service, with ordering by price and breakdown by category
Jellydeal.co.uk	Comparisons over a large number of categories
Kelkoo.co.uk	A large number of categories including books, CDs, travel, computing and electronics categories (Kelkoo also run Shopgenie)
Lycos UK Shopping	A categorised and searchable database of products that can be ordered and filtered by price
MSN shopping UK	Gives comparison results taken from both Shopping.com UK and Pricerunner UK
Nextag UK	A wide variety of categories
Onlinepriceguide.co.uk	Only books, CDs and DVDs
Pricechecker.co.uk	Categories include music, games, and finance and computers
Price Clash	Only books, CDs and DVDs
Pricecomparison.co.uk	Comparisons of categories including digital cameras
Pricegrabber UK	Limited to PC goods and consumer electrical equipment
Priceguideuk.com	Categories include computers, consumer electronics, CDs, books and travel
Pricerunner UK	Many categories from books, through electrical appliances to travel insurance
Search-dvd	DVD and videogame comparisons
Shopping.com UK (also Dealtime and DoorOne)	A large number of categories, from appliances, through music to jewellery
Shopping.zdnet.co.uk	PC goods, digital cameras and camcorders
Shopzilla.co.uk	A wide range of categories, from clothing to video games and cosmetics
Zencudo.co.uk	A large number of categories
123PriceCheck	Comparisons of books, DVDs, CDs and videos

Bargaining power

As a result of increased choice and consumers' ability to compare and then select providers using their own unique set of criteria, consumers have growing power. Consumer bargaining power is a measure of their willingness to pay premium prices and their responsiveness to price drops for volume purchases or regular purchases.

Price is a paramount issue, and customers are acutely aware that businesses adopt a range of pricing strategies in their attempts to differentiate their brands from other 'value' products. In many cases, consumers do not fall for these attempts to differentiate items that are basically very similar but just have different branding. Consumers are able to use their purchasing power, enhanced by greater choice, to drive down the prices of branded goods.

Various businesses have tried to stop retailers from discounting their products in this way. The following case study is just one example.

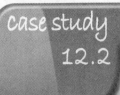

case study 12.2 Tesco v Levi Strauss

Just a few years ago, the supermarket giant Tesco and the clothes manufacturer Levi Strauss were in open conflict. Tesco had been selling Levi products at cut prices throughout its stores and online. Levi, considering itself to be a designer brand, was not keen on having its products sold at cut prices alongside cans of baked beans. Tesco was offering the jeans with a saving of between £20 and £30. Levi entered into a battle with Tesco over the fact that the supermarket had been buying genuine Levi jeans from outside the European Union at cut price. It was then bringing them into Great Britain and reselling them without Levi's permission.

A few years later, the two companies were talking to one another again, after Levi had won a court battle to stop Tesco selling its cut-price products. It had been a bad time for Levi, with 63 of its factories closing in the US alone. Now it was desperate to find a new market for its products at any price.

activity

1 Fashion has swung away from Levi's traditional style of jeans. Search the Internet and find Levi's website and identify its current attempts to win back customers.

2 Why was it important for Tesco to fight against Levi to sell discounted products through its stores?

Availability of comprehensive and up-to-date product information

With information directly available on businesses and manufacturers' websites, it is now possible for customers to make far more informed decisions about purchasing options. Businesses often use their websites as interactive forms of product brochures, enhancing the general information with video clips, photographs and user endorsements.

Up-to-date product information is vital so that businesses can focus potential buyers' attention on key features and product details. Many websites now enable buyers to compare product lines, so that they can more quickly and easily choose the specific product variant that suits their individual need.

Opportunities for lower costs via dynamic pricing

With dynamic pricing the pricing structure that operates between seller and buyer is fluid. This is at the other extreme of the scale from traditional fixed pricing methods.

There are many different types of dynamic pricing model, including:

- auctions
- reverse auctions – where the buyer sets the price they are willing to pay and suppliers then bid for their business
- trading exchanges
- price matching
- quantity pricing
- group pricing.

eBay and Priceline are perhaps the two most well-known e-commerce sites using dynamic pricing. Internet auction sites work rather like car boot sales. Sellers can offer one item at a time or offer multiple lots of the same type. Multiple items offered to customers are sometimes called Dutch auctions. This is a system where all buyers pay the price offered by the lowest successful bid.

More typically, the auctions are standard in that the highest bidder wins the lot. Sometimes sellers set reserve prices. If the bidding does not exceed the reserve price, the auction closes without the lot being sold. Auction sites such as eBay provide the forum in which the auctions take place, as well as systems by which potential buyers and sellers can communicate.

Internet auctions can either be b2b, b2c or c2c. The other key aspect of these auction sites is the streamlining of payment systems. Businesses offering products via websites such as eBay accept most forms of payment, including credit and debit cards.

Fig 12.8 Priceline Europe is a fast growing company, selling more than 5m room nights per year

(Source: www.priceline.co.uk)

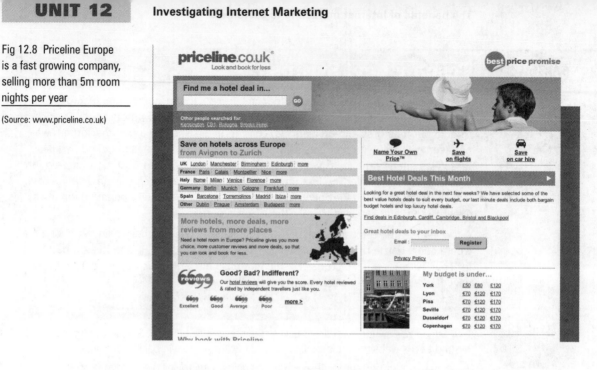

 Link See pages 87–88 in Unit 8 for information on debit and credit cards.

Convenience and responsive transaction facilities

It is essential in e-commerce to facilitate the completion of a transaction by allowing customers to pay immediately and receive confirmation by email of the transaction. Many businesses use a standard order form, which is filled in, in a secure environment in part of the website. The customer also provides their card details. This is not the most secure way of collecting card details. Secure order forms are far more effective.

In essence, **shopping cart technology** allows the customer to add products to an order and then proceed to a checkout. An offline, secure server encrypts the card details, which are processed by a bank providing a merchant account. There have been enormous problems with breaches in information security; hackers have broken into websites and stolen the details of customers' cards and other information. As customers are prompted to type in the three digits from the reverse of their card as a security measure, these are also available to the thieves.

A recent survey showed that around 40% of people have actually stopped carrying out a transaction online due to a security concern with the website. There is good reason for people to be concerned, as in 2005 alone more than 52m account records were stolen or misplaced.

i BBC Use the search facility to find the latest trends in online security.
www.bbc.co.uk

Immediate online sales and customer service

Despite some misgivings, instant online sales and ordering facilities are a huge benefit to customers, who can secure a product or a service, having established its availability. Customers of businesses, such as EasyJet, have to purchase their tickets with the airline online. This not only attracts immediate discounts compared with prices for conventional telephone sales but also allows the customer to view flight times and availability around their preferred travel times. The customer is thus able to choose according to their own requirements and preferred pricing. The secure ordering system takes the customer through the process and then sends an automated confirmation email, which the customer prints out for reference and to present at the booking-in desk at the airport.

Provided that the customer has confidence in the security of the system, they are able to make transactions without having to visit a traditional retail outlet. Even businesses that have always relied on their retail outlets, such as Argos, have turned to online sales as both an alternative and an addition to their overall sales offerings. It is now possible to:

- visit the retail store to check availability of products and then make the purchase
- use an automated reservation system on the telephone and then visit the retail outlet to make the purchase
- use the online reservation system and then visit the store to make the purchase
- use the online reservation system and complete the purchase online.

The only major disadvantage when buying products via the Internet is that buying from a remote location means that there are delivery costs to be incorporated into the price. Many businesses either make a small, standardised charge for delivery, regardless of the size of the order, or have built the delivery cost into the price of the product sold via the website. Many businesses now recognise that adding unreasonably high delivery costs at the online point of sale deters customers from completing the transaction. Rather than lose the sale, the pricing structure is reorganised to incorporate delivery charges. Businesses are able to do this as they are undoubtedly making a larger profit per unit sold, as they are dealing directly with the customer and not selling their products to wholesalers and retailers for resale. Of course, the issue of delivery costs does not apply when purchasing services online.

Pooling customer experiences

Another major benefit to customers is the use of customer experiences to grade or rate products, services or even suppliers; eBay, for example, encourages anyone involved in a transaction to rate their experience with either the buyer or the seller. Each buyer or seller has a number of points related to their name, reflecting the number of positive transactions that they have completed, either as a buyer or a seller.

Amazon uses a star rating: one to five stars are allocated to products available on its website and reviewed by customers. Travel operators, such as Thomson, have customer ratings for accommodation and resorts; these are either expressed as a mark out of 10 or as a percentage.

This kind of feedback from customer experience is regarded as having far more meaning than if the business simply said that everything available on its website is wonderful and great value. Whether positive or negative, these independent views help highlight key aspects of the product or service and offer the possibility of identifying any drawbacks.

case study 12.3 — The good and the bad

What makes a good e-commerce website? Site navigation, the checkout process and product descriptions are the three most important factors for making a decision to buy over the Internet.

According to the Office for National Statistics, the average British Internet user now spends 164 minutes online each day for personal use, the equivalent of over 41 days each year. This compares with 148 minutes spent watching television.

European consumers are now spending more time online than reading newspapers and magazines. Internet consumption has doubled from two to four hours per week in the last two years, but is not cannibalising print and TV. At the same time TV viewing rose from 10 hours per week to 12, while print consumption has remained static at three hours a week (according to Jupiter Research, October 2006).

So what's good in a website? A good e-commerce site:

- is easy to navigate and is user-friendly
- offers advantages over conventional buying in stores
- gives plenty of information about products
- offers a selection of payment options
- is quick to load
- offers goods that are suitable for selling online
- looks professional and trustworthy
- is widely promoted in search engines, on banner ads and by traditional methods
- is regularly evaluated to check that the products it offers are what customers want

- has a facility for customers to contact the seller for feedback and advice
- has options in different languages to broaden its appeal
- gives the customer an incentive to visit it regularly, perhaps through a general information section or regular special offers
- has a registration page to allow collection of customer details for marketing purposes.

And what's bad? Well. Anything that fails on two or more of these counts and many do.

activity

1. Giving reasons, identify two e-commerce websites that could be described as good according to the criteria.
2. Giving reasons, identify two e-commerce websites that could be described as bad according to the criteria.

activity
INDIVIDUAL WORK 12.2

P2

M1

1. Describe the principle benefits to customers of Internet marketing.

   For P2, use Case study 12.3 as the beginnings of your investigations and, ideally, refer in your answer to contrasting businesses. You should attempt to cover the following in relation to the benefits to customers of:

   (a) opportunities to compare and select providers

   (b) increased bargaining power

   (c) availability of more comprehensive and up-to-date product information

   (d) opportunities for lower costs via dynamic pricing

   (e) greater supply convenience through availability of responsive transaction facilities for immediate online sales and customer service without travel or unsatisfying sales experiences

   (f) availability of digital complaints services

   (g) opportunities to pool customer experiences collectively via chat rooms.

2. Analyse the benefits of Internet marketing to customers.

   Building on your work for P1 and P2, you should for M1:

   (a) Discuss the ways in which Internet marketing activities build on conventional off-line marketing principles.

   (b) Show your understanding of Internet marketing.

   (c) Explain how it can be more responsive to the needs of customers than traditional forms of marketing.

Opportunities offered to businesses by Internet marketing

There are three key areas in which businesses can benefit from Internet marketing:

- Clearly, one of the most important is increased and better targeted communications with their customers.
- The second is a highly valuable side benefit. Customers may make enquiries as to the reason why certain products or services are not offered or seek a certain mix of attributes in a product or service. This helps the business to identify opportunities for new product development and will, perhaps, facilitate a move into allied areas of business.
- Finally, Internet marketing acts as a catalyst for improving business efficiency.

We have already seen that features such as disintermediation simplify the supply chain. Electronic communications can be used to make immediate contact with customers, and monitoring and tracking customer behaviour can generate additional sales.

Communications

Any type of e-communication between a business and its customers can be considered a form of Internet marketing. As we have seen, businesses can slowly build up a profile of each customer in order to target them directly, and in a personalised manner, to encourage them to make additional purchases, take an interest in new products and services and remain loyal to the business.

Individualised communications, promotions, new services and purchase history

Just like a traditional business, businesses working online can use special sales promotions, including information about new product launches and special offers. One of the key aims of online promotions is to ensure that customers remember, or at least bookmark, the business's website, so that they can automatically visit the website as soon as they receive sales promotion information.

The most common form of Internet marketing communication for existing customers is, of course, emails. However, to attract new customers, pay per click advertising on relevant websites is the preferred system, along with paid-for submissions to search engines.

Businesses do not rely purely on repeat website visits for customers to discover, say, a new website design or an enhanced shopping cart, and many businesses believe that any form of communication with their customers is valuable. Nevertheless, it should be recognised that customers do not wish to be bombarded with unnecessary communications. The most important consideration prior to deciding to embark on an email marketing campaign is whether the business has genuinely new products or services to offer its customers.

Businesses take special heed of the purchasing history of their customers. When a user visits a website, a cookie is created. This cookie is a means by which the business can track the movement of that user through the website. The business can identify which pages were visited and which additional information links were clicked. Provided that the cookie is not purged from the user's computer, on the customer's next visit they will be offered a customised version of the website, highlighting that customer's particular preferences. This individualised approach is enhanced, of course, if the customer makes a purchase from the website. On subsequent visits, the website will be able to identify this individual as a unique visitor. The customer will be associated with the purchases that have already been made, and similar or allied products will be offered to the customer.

> **remember**
>
> To encourage the customer to visit the website, tailor-made email communications can be devised based on the customer's purchasing history.

Product development

It is rare to find a business developing a truly revolutionary product. However there are some exceptions, such as the Xbox and new television-enabled mobile phones.

Fig 12.9 These phones are capable of receiving, encoding and displaying digital broadcasts

New product development usually arises out of:

- the development of truly new production processes or services
- response to demands from customers.

Accurately responding to customer needs and wants

Increasingly sophisticated websites are enabling businesses to identify customers' precise needs and to do so more quickly. For example, it is now possible to use a travel operator's website to purchase:

- air flight and full package holidays
- air flight only
- full package plus insurance
- full package plus car hire
- accommodation only
- full package with in-flight meals
- full package without in-flight meals.

Whilst none of the products in the above list is necessarily new, the ability to mix and match specific sets of purchases is both a service and a product development.

Identifying product development opportunities

As already mentioned, new product development is very much related to supposed demand based on product enquiries made by existing customers. For example, a number of customers might enquire about the availability of flights from an airport that the tour operator does not currently use. Having established a base level of demand, the next steps would be for the business to define the new product development opportunity and then test it. Typically, an airline or tour operator would, in the first instance, offer a limited number of flights from a new airport. If sufficient demand were forthcoming then the business would step up the availability to match the increased demand.

Opportunities for immediate sales

Ultimately, the purpose of Internet marketing – and the reason for most websites – is to generate sales. Sales, as we have seen, can come either from existing customers who are frequent website visitors or from casual browsers who have found the website through a search engine.

The key purpose of the website is to transform the visit into a positive sale. As we have seen, improved and streamlined online transactions have gone a long way to encourage customers to part with their money, assuming that they can rely on the security of the website. The website will also feature key deals, special offers and discounts for immediate purchase. This approach extends across the range of businesses offering products and those offering services. Credit card companies offer lower interest rates for online applications. Discounts are available to customers who purchase online, rather than by using a call centre. Indeed some businesses have taken this to its logical end and charge an additional premium if the customer wishes to carry out the transaction via a call centre.

Possibility for substitute online forms of products

With the relative power and flexibility of the latest computers it is now possible to view streaming TV programmes, watch films and music videos, tune into worldwide radio stations and, of course, to download and listen to music. All of these are alternatives to traditional forms of delivery.

At first, music was only available through vinyl, then tapes and now CDs, which have gradually been replaced by digital downloads, a fact that has finally been recognised in the music charts as music downloads are now counted and given the same weight as the physical sales of CDs.

Films have passed through a similar process. The customer can now watch, download and then possibly burn a film onto a DVD, rather than purchasing a DVD from a store.

Most computers can access radio stations being broadcast from even the most remote location in the world. Clearly, there are additional opportunities here in terms of advertising and, of course, increased audience figures. If the computer has a TV tuner, there is software that allows the viewer to watch digital television, both from the UK and from further afield.

remember

The most difficult and expensive stage occurs when a new product is fully launched. The business has to be in a position to provide full support for the new product and deal with the additional volume of business.

The computer is expected to become the basis of most entertainment, either in its traditional computer form or as a dedicated box, like the products offered by Sky and the various freeview digital services.

Podcasts

We have already seen that businesses identify particular segments of their customer base which they target with specific marketing and promotions. Podcasts are a way of achieving this through the Internet. Podcasts are effectively radio-style programmes: they are audio in content and offer the facility to mix factual information with promotion and advertising. Podcasting allows businesses and individuals to distribute their own radio shows. There is an enormous network of podcasters.

The technical hardware has only been available since 2001, yet podcasting has already been embraced by businesses in the following ways:

- They use podcasts to distribute news about new products.
- They use them to distribute multimedia news to journalists and consumers.
- They broadcast audio content to drive traffic to their website.
- They use them as promotional vehicles for upcoming events.

Market development

Internet marketing can assist businesses to branch out into new markets and offer their existing products to new customers, either in the country in which they already operate or in new countries, which are experiencing growth in terms of Internet connection.

Some conversion in the way that the business operates, designs its products, offers its services or indeed markets them is likely to be necessary to take advantage of the cost savings that can come from using the Internet. For example, a comparison of Internet marketing with traditional forms of marketing, including the placement of advertisements, renting billboards and running sales promotions in specific marketplaces, shows that Internet marketing is far more cost effective.

When developing a new market, it is necessary first to understand that market and identify the opportunities that it offers. The business then needs to see if its existing products are suitable for the new market or if a new concept will be required. Next, the product has to be tested and a suitable price arrived at. Then the product is introduced into the market. The business will hope that over a period of time the new market will embrace either its existing products or the new product.

Low entry costs

Businesses have a number of choices with regard to website creation:

- A fully functional website designed by website specialists is likely to cost from £5,000 to £8,000.
- It is possible to purchase an off-the-peg website design with fully functional shopping carts. The design can be customised to incorporate the business's logo, designs, text, and product photographs.
- Website design software costs from as little as £50, although lower-cost software is often not as flexible as the more expensive and better-designed software options. It is perfectly possible with a minimum amount of experience for a business to create a basic website, albeit one with limited functionality. Adding secure shopping areas and the facility for online transactions makes the website significantly more expensive to develop.

Offering virtual services

A visit to the sites of most British estate agents and travel operators will reveal additional services that until only a few years ago were considered impossible. For example, potential buyers can now view properties via an estate agent's website. In addition to the traditional details, such as the dimension of rooms and general comments about the property, the viewer is given a virtual tour of the property. (The estate agent uses a hand-held video camera and overlays the visual information with verbal descriptions of each room.)

Similarly tour operators and owners of accommodation provide both moving panoramic views from the accommodation and videos featuring the rooms, reception, restaurants and other common areas.

To see the way in which tour operators use virtual tours to sell their holiday packages, visit the website of Thomson, where destination videos and accommodation videos are available

www.thomson.co.uk

Operating around the clock

In the not so recent past products and services were only available during a limited number of hours in a day and for a limited number of days in the year. Banks, for example, used to close at 3 p.m. There were no ATM machines, and neither businesses nor individual customers could interact with the bank in any way other than by visiting in person.

Banks now offer Internet banking, allowing businesses and individuals to access their bank accounts at any time of the day or night throughout the year. Statements can be ordered or printed off; transactions can be checked, and money transferred from one bank account to another. Obviously, the only thing missing from this raft of additional services is the ability to use your computer as a cash machine.

Whilst the owners and employees of British businesses sleep, orders can be placed with the business by customers in other parts of the world where it is still daylight. In the case of downloadable services, the customer can interact via the website, regardless of whether there is a live operator available to deal with customer queries. For the most part, customers can browse products and services on the website and then place an order, which can then be fulfilled by humans on their next working day.

Bricks and clicks and diversification

The terms 'clicks and mortar' and 'bricks and clicks' began to be used in the 1990s. Both mean pretty much the same thing. 'Bricks' and 'mortar' refer to traditional stores or retail outlets whilst 'clicks' refers to Internet trading of whatever type.

Businesses that are solely Internet based are clicks companies. They do not have a physical presence on any high street or in any shopping mall. However, a huge number of the businesses that we do see in these places also have an Internet presence. The adoption of Internet trading by such businesses was known as the 'rush to the middle'.

Fig 12.10 A bank's home page

(Source: www.hsbc.co.uk)

HSBC ⟨X⟩ The world's local bank   Site search: [   ] ▶Go

▶Personal
  ▶ Current accounts
  ▶ Savings and investments
  ▶ Credit cards
  ▶ Loans
  ▶ Mortgages
  ▶ Insurance
  ▶ International Services
  ▶ HSBC Premier

Personal Internet Banking
  ▶ Log on   ▶ Register

▶Business
  ▶ Business bank accounts
  ▶ International trade
  ▶ Finance and Borrowing
  ▶ View all products

Business Internet Banking
  ▶ Log on   ▶ Register

Your

HSBC World Match Play Championship
11th–14th Octo...

HSBC ⟨X⟩

HSBC World Match Play Championship. 11th–14th October 2007 – Wentworth Club, Surrey. Find out more. This link will open in a new browser window.

Find out more ▶

HSBC Bank Credit Card
0% interest on purchases for 12 months from account opening

4.9% p.a. interest on balance transfers until 31st January 2012, within 30 days of account opening.*

15.9% APR TYPICAL VARIABLE

*Conditions and a 2.5% balance transfer fee apply (minimum £5)

Find out more ▶

Bank Account Pl...
Includes worldwide family travel insurance

Currently £6.47 a month for the first six months*

*Normally £12.95 a month. Minimum 12 month contract applies.

Find out more ▶

...savings

6.25% AER (6.08% gross) variable.

Our best ever online savings rate. Open an account with as little as £1.

6.25%

Find out more ▶

Legal information | Accessibility | About HSBC | Site map | Contact us   Issued for UK use only | © HSBC Bank plc 2002 - 2007

Very few businesses are purely bricks or clicks; most are both (although some may be more brick than click or vice versa). For example, although Amazon does not have any retail outlets, it is actually a bricks and clicks business. It interacts with its customers and carries out transactions online but has warehousing to hold its stocks of products, and it is Amazon that organises the packaging and delivery of its products.

A true clicks company has neither a retail outlet presence nor necessarily any stock. It acts merely as a processing point between the orders received from customers and the fulfilment of those orders by suppliers.

A prime example of a business that combines bricks and clicks is the cosmetic company Lush. It has stores worldwide but still relies on Internet shopping for a considerable amount of its turnover, as well as on more conventional telephone and postal mail order catalogues.

Tesco is another significant business that has embraced bricks and clicks. It is also a prime example of **diversification**. Until relatively recently, Tesco was just another supermarket chain, selling a range of predominantly grocery products through high street and out-of-town stores. However, now:

- Everything that Tesco sells is available online and available for home delivery.

- Tesco does not restrict its product range to groceries; neither does it restrict its range of products to tangible goods, as it sells services, such as insurance, and has its own credit card.

Tesco has grown by incorporating these two key features into its long-term strategy. On the one hand, it retains its physical presence in the marketplace by building huge hypermarkets across the country. In the immediate area around each supermarket, Tesco also services the wider community by acting as a centre for home deliveries. This is the way that the business fulfils its Internet shopping orders.

Combined with this expansion, the business has also diversified and moved away from its traditional grocery roots. Alongside sprigs of broccoli and cans of baked beans, customers can purchase HD televisions, computers, clothing, DVDs and household and car insurance. In doing this, Tesco has relied on the loyalty of its customers and has embraced all of the possible opportunities that were outlined in this part of the unit, including:

- Individualised communications with customers – the customer loyalty card is used as the basis for capturing and using customer-specific information.

- Using communications to offer promotions and special offers – individualised special offers are created to match customers' buying habits.

- Offering new services to new and existing customers – these include new product ranges, services, Internet shopping and home delivery.

- Making maximum use of customers' purchasing histories – the customer loyalty card captures the purchases made by each customer and generates a customer-specific series of offers.

- Product development – in response to customer requests for particular ranges and services, Tesco has developed new ideas and tested them in selected stores and areas before launching them nationwide.

- Market development – the company has been able to expand into new markets in a cost-effective manner by basing much of its expansion on existing customer demand.

- Virtual services and around-the-clock operations – although the customers' experience in visiting a website such as Tesco's is not like visiting a regular supermarket, the business tries to organise its products and services in a familiar way. The website is always open and ready to accept orders. (Some of the stores are also open for 24 hours a day.)

Business efficiency

Like any business, an organisation involved in Internet marketing and sales seeks to become as efficient as possible. Use of the Internet could provide opportunities for better control of the supply chain, reducing the number of employees needed, increasing sales from existing customers, monitoring competitors, and an immediate increase in potential business.

Managing the supply chain

Having several organisations in a business's supply chain always creates coordination difficulties. A process known as supply chain management is used to integrate the supply and demand for products and services, and businesses use supply chain event management to look at the possible events or factors that could cause a disruption to the supply.

Having some form of direct contact with the end-users of their products enables businesses to shorten the supply chain and simplify coordination. Prime examples of supply chain management can be found in organisations such as Hewlett Packard and Dell.

Electronic communications to reduce staff costs

The automation of any function reduces a business's need for staff and, consequently, its staffing costs. There is, however, a point beyond which these cost reductions can become counterproductive: when an automated email response is not sufficient to resolve a customer's query, human interaction is required.

Increasing sales from existing customers

As we have seen, 80% of most companies' sales and profits come from the most loyal 20% of their customers. Running an Internet business does not mean that the organisation can ignore this. Through a series of processes from identifying the key segments of customers through to individualisation, the timely offering of product or service, and gradual expansion and diversification, businesses hope to continue to increase sales from existing customers. In order to do so, however, businesses will gradually need to change some of their customers' characteristics; certainly, customers need to purchase more regularly and increase their usage rates.

Monitoring competitor activity

Limited companies are obliged by law to post financial documents to Companies House; it is also usual for the documents to be incorporated into a section of the business's website. This is one way in which a business can monitor its competitors and analyse their financial results.

Although it is more difficult if the business does not have a legal obligation to divulge its financial figures, monitoring can still take place. Daily or periodic checks of competitors' websites can reveal new trends in their marketing and also warn the business of price changes, special offers and incentives being offered to visitors to those websites.

Internet business opportunities

Some features of Internet marketing are not available to conventional marketing media. For the most part, traditional marketing is a passive experience for those who either view the advertisement or are offered a particular sales promotion. It requires them to read and digest the information and then to respond. The Internet, on the other hand, is more instant, more interactive and, of course, fully connected.

Businesses routinely purchase pay per click banner advertising on websites. A website that attracts customers with the same segmentation profile would be an ideal target for the purchase of paid-for promotions, whether conventional banner advertising or special offers. These special offers allow a clickable link that sends the user to a holding page on the business's website. From there, they can input a special offer code to acquire a discount when making a purchase.

Search engines provide two ways in which the website can appear in a prominent position. One option is to purchase paid-for links on the first page of search results associated in any remote way with the business, its products and services. Alternatively, the business can submit its website to the search engine, making sure that it incorporates the maximum number of key words that could be used in a search by a user.

Web portals are another means by which some degree of customisation or personalisation can be achieved, thereby drawing the user towards particular websites. Hosted websites attract individuals interested in a particular industry, business, leisure activity or other features. There they will find targeted search engines, which will direct them towards businesses offering specific services or products to match their requirements.

Links are probably one of the most common and straightforward means of attracting web traffic. Businesses often enter into mutual link exchange. This means that both businesses will feature the other's link on their own website. This is usually the case when the businesses are in partnership in some way, perhaps in a supply chain or in the fulfilment of products and allied services.

activity
INDIVIDUAL WORK
12.3

P3

Describe the benefits and opportunities to the business of using Internet marketing within the marketing mix of a selected business.

You will need to select at least two different e-commerce websites. For a website that offers independent reviews of e-commerce sites use www.truste-marketing.co.uk. All of the sites are graded and updated in real time, and there is a chart of the most highly rated sites by actual users. Choose at least two websites, and then:

1   Outline the key benefits of the sites to users.

2   Briefly describe the features and the scope of each of the sites.

Make sure that you give references to the actual sites and to any other sites that you might use in your investigations.

Investigating the challenges faced by businesses using Internet marketing

When an organisation is involved in b2b, the following factors tend to define its marketing strategy:

- Its name and probably its reputation will be unknown to potential customers.
- The challenge is to create an online visibility.
- It must deliver information in a fast and simple manner.
- Its online effectiveness can be measured using logs and statistics.

In comparison, an organisation involved in b2c works within the following set of criteria:

- The business will be known to its existing customers but not necessarily to its potential customers.
- Online visibility is usually achieved through traditional promotional methods, such as advertising and the use of billboards.
- Presentation is often more important than content.
- Online effectiveness is monitored by measuring sales.

Competition through global website visibility

Around 45% of worldwide Internet sales take place in the United States, which is still the biggest economy in the world.

Whilst a business may be able to attract new customers in a variety of different markets around the world, it also faces an increased level of competition from other businesses that would not remotely have been considered competitors in the past. Not only will a business acquire new competitors in each new country that it deals with but it will also have a host of new competitors among those hoping to take advantage of the Internet.

eMarketer
www.emarketer.com
Forrester Research
www.forrester.com

Channel conflict and disintermediation

Retailers and manufacturers seek to serve their empowered consumers, but moving online has left many businesses, particularly manufacturers, with what is known as channel conflict. The electronic marketplace depends on the nature of the industry and of the individual businesses. By moving online and dealing with customers directly, businesses that do not own or closely control their traditional distribution channels risk damaging, or even destroying, decades of relationships with customers.

The problems facing a business in this situation revolve around what is termed cannibalisation: the business is actually taking away sales from its existing partners in the supply chain. This is even more serious if the number of direct sales combined with those achieved through normal distribution is no better than it was before the online presence was established. In other words, the business may be making the direct sales but at the expense of losing the same sales via its distribution partners. Obviously, a time arrives when the members of the supply channel no longer wish to deal with the business, as handling its products or services no longer provides them with sufficient revenue and profit.

case study 12.4 — HMV and Next

In 2006 HMV's website sales were up by 150%. However, sales in its stores dropped by 5.4%. This was an improvement as it was thought that sales had dropped by as much as 17%. At the same time, Next saw its overall profits rise. Its sales through the Next Directory catalogue and the Internet rose by 15.3%. Sales through the stores fell by 7.5%.

This seems to be a growing trend. Even Domino's Pizza, Britain's largest home delivery pizza chain has seen a 57.6% rise in sales as a result of the Internet and interactive television. The business runs 7000 stores in 50 countries.

Overall Internet sales are growing strongly but at the cost of traditional sales through stores.

(Sources: www.hmvgroup.com; www.next.co.uk; www.dominos.co.uk)

activity

1   Using the Internet, try to find another traditional bricks business that is seeing the same trend as HMV and Next.

2   What could be the major problem with Domino's Pizza and why is it likely that its overall level of sales is unlikely to increase without it opening new premises?

Customers and payment security

Recent research has shown that, as a result of fraud, a business loses £1 out of every £1,000 of transactions. There have been frequent and well-publicised problems with online payment security. Businesses often claim that their websites are completely secure and that hackers or fraudsters can access none of the credit card details. Nonetheless, credit-holder-not-present fraud is now the biggest fraud type and is increasing at a rate of 6% per year. With around 10% of all spending via credit cards taking place online, this is a significant issue.

Whilst customers are warned to use antivirus software, firewalls and only to shop at secure websites, some still fear that their financial details will be stolen and used for fraudulent purposes.

Coping with high reliability expectations and market feedback overload

High reliability can refer both to the business itself and to its ability to cope with increased traffic, queries, orders, deliveries and potential complaints. Or it can refer directly to the functionality of the website. Having attracted potential customers to its website, a business must assume that these visitors have no prior knowledge of the tools, navigation or layout of the site. There should be absolutely no learning curve involved; everything should be straightforward.

Since the vast majority of people arrive at the website via search engines, they are looking for specific information to be presented to them immediately and are not interested in flashy features. Businesses should recognise that visitors do not come to the website to view the business's content. They are looking for their own content: in other words, content that interests them.

Certain pitfalls are inevitable. If its website looks amateurish, the business may not be perceived as professional. Functionality should always allow visitors to find and use the information they want as quickly as possible. Each day around 400m searches are made, many of which are searches for products or services. If the website is accessible worldwide, the business should expect it to attract a huge number of visitors if Internet marketing has been successful.

Another major problem is feedback overload caused when customers provide too much information. When a business first enters a new market it will experience a surge in feedback, as new customers interact with the business for the very first time. Whilst the business should encourage customers to feedback their experiences of dealing with the business, there is a point at which the level of feedback becomes so huge that it is impossible either to read it or to incorporate it into any future planning.

Keeping pace with change and revising marketing goals

Many businesses recognise that they invest thousands in state-of-the-art infrastructure and software, which is obsolete within months. Technology is moving so fast that new solutions or upgrades are offered on a monthly basis. Nevertheless, at some point, businesses have to jump on this moving conveyor belt of change and make the necessary investments.

Technological change is often driven by real change; however, the need to adopt new technology is largely driven by the marketing activities of the manufacturers of the technology. Businesses try to look at technology before they adopt it, including software related to the website and the capture of information. Decisions about what to adopt are crucial, and businesses recognise that there is an upgrade cycle, with infrastructure and software having to be routinely and regularly updated. In many instances, it is not simply a case of adding on hardware or software: the entire system has to be scrapped and replaced with a new blend of technology and software.

In addition, there are changes to the market, which are often beyond the control of the business. Specifically, the following could occur:

■ There may be new economic conditions in the marketplace affecting sales and demand.

■ New businesses may have entered the market, either traditional ones or new online businesses.

■ The business may have recognised that a particular market is not cost effective and may choose to pull out of the market and leave it unsupported.

The ability to adapt marketing goals is essential to any marketing planning process. A marketing planning process requires a business to take the following steps:

1. Situation analysis – the business begins by looking at its current position, the features of the markets in which it operates, along with the activities of competitors and the likelihood that regulations and legislation might impact on its operations.

2. Setting objectives – these are broad marketing objectives, which are designed to be measurable and achievable within a specified time frame. The business would seek to increase its visibility in terms of customer awareness or simply to use marketing as a driver to create greater sales revenue. The objectives will usually be stated in either time or financial terms.

3. Formulating strategy – having arrived at a set of objectives, the business will begin to break down the objectives into achievable sets of activities. Each set of activities will be designed to achieve each of the objectives.

4. Developing action programmes – these are the nuts and bolts of each of the strategies that will be used by the business. This stage may involve identifying specific newspapers or magazines, within which to place advertising, or devising a particular public relations exercise and special promotions.

5. Implementation – having reviewed all of the previous steps, the business will begin putting its action programmes into effect. Over the course of several days, weeks or months, the action programmes will begin to frame the strategies aimed at achieving the objectives.

6. Control – during the whole process and particularly throughout the implementation stage, the business will seek to control its activities so that necessary actions are taken when required and adjustments can be made if certain programmes are not working.

7. Review – periodically both during implementation and after the whole campaign, activities will be reviewed in terms of their cost and effectiveness. The business wants to know how much benefit came to it as a result of particular costs and, by reviewing the whole process, the business can identify key areas of success and failure.

8. Evaluation – the final part of the process is to evaluate all of the steps in preparation for a new marketing plan. This is particularly important if marketing goals have been adapted in the light of changes in products and services, the market, competition or legislation.

Ensuring maximum access

When discussing maximum access, the correct term to use is **bandwidth**. This is the capacity of the communication channel between the business's website and the individual visiting the website.

Bandwidth is a measure of the amount of data that can be carried at a particular time. The amount of traffic is determined by the bandwidth. Most businesses have dedicated bandwidth, but there will probably be a limit to the amount of data that can be transferred to and from multiple connections.

One byte can store approximately one character. Therefore, the more complex the website, the more bandwidth will be taken up when an image of that website is transferred along the network to the user's computer. There is no ideal amount of bandwidth. It depends on such factors as:

- the average number of visitors per day
- the average number of page views
- the average size of each page
- the average file downloads
- the average size of those downloadable files
- the fudge factor – this indeterminate factor refers to trying to ensure that the actual bandwidth calculation is at least one and a half to three times the business's estimated minimum requirement for bandwidth.

Ensuring site security

A website's security is designed to protect sensitive data. The levels of security used range from 0 to 128bit. Encryption is the most effective means of protecting information; the data is scrambled so that only the intended recipient can unscramble it and read the contents.

As the Internet is a publicly accessible network, viruses and hackers can access the website and try to break into it at any time of the day or night. Businesses constantly monitor for potential threats.

Access to sensitive areas of the website should be restricted to key personnel only. Many businesses require individuals to have user accounts with passwords. These work just like cash point pin numbers.

Before a business even posts up a website the following should be considered:

- Choice of web hosting company – this choice must be made with care. The business needs to know about the company's privacy and security policies, the measures it has taken against attacks at server level, and the quality of its firewall and virus scanners. Another issue is the types of site that are running on the server and whether any has already been exploited. Misuse of one site could affect all websites using the same server.

- Website design – this should incorporate a way in which sensitive data and administration areas can be protected. Usually, this is achieved by using cookies or sessions to track legitimate administrators. Password protection directories are often used at server level. Databases can have encrypted passwords, and all data submitted by forms on the website should be scanned and checked for malicious entries, particularly those that allow file uploads.

Linguistic and cultural sensitivity

A business has to recognise the diversity of its customers' backgrounds. Any translation of a website should be both accurate and culturally appropriate for unique consumer groups. Therefore, more is required than a simple word-for-word translation. Sometimes, literal translations create misunderstanding and cause difficulties. A poor translation that shows a lack of cultural sensitivity could alienate the customer, resulting in the loss of an immediate sale, and the business could acquire a reputation for insensitivity.

When designing a website, it is, therefore, essential that the information takes into account the cultural and linguistic sensitivities of the target audience. This is in addition to ensuring that the basic messages remain the same, so that the visitor to the website is as likely to purchase from the business as they would be if the website were written for the home market.

Additional legal complexities

Even though e-commerce is essentially marketing and selling products and services via the Internet, legally there are some differences between e-commerce and dealing with customers face to face. Much of the legislation related to e-commerce focuses on forming and enforcing legal contracts between the buyer and the seller. It is important to remember that a business would be responsible for ensuring that it complies with the regulations in force in the countries in which it does business with its customers.

In Britain, the E-Commerce Regulations, which came into force in 2002, are part of a European-wide drive to ensure that electronic contracts are legally binding and enforceable. It is important as far as Internet marketing is concerned that there are limits to the type of communications that can be sent from businesses to potential customers. With regard to advertising, email and mobile phone messages, commercial communications, as they are classed, have to be clearly recognisable and identify which business has sent the marketing communication.

Spam email or unsolicited commercial communications must be identifiable from the subject line of the email, so that, if the user wishes, they do not need to read it.

The other important consideration for e-commerce is the Distance Selling Regulations 2000, according to which consumers have the right to:

- have details in writing about the supplier and the terms of the transaction
- a written confirmation of their order
- any relevant further information, including cancellation rights, after-sales service, guarantees and complaints
- delivery within 30 days unless otherwise agreed.

Clearly, this deals with the sales process rather than with the marketing process, but these regulations are the minimum set of standards to which all businesses should adhere in order to ensure that they have continued and improved financial relationships with their customers.

For more information on the Distance Selling Regulations, visit the website of the Office of Fair Trading

www.oft.gov.uk

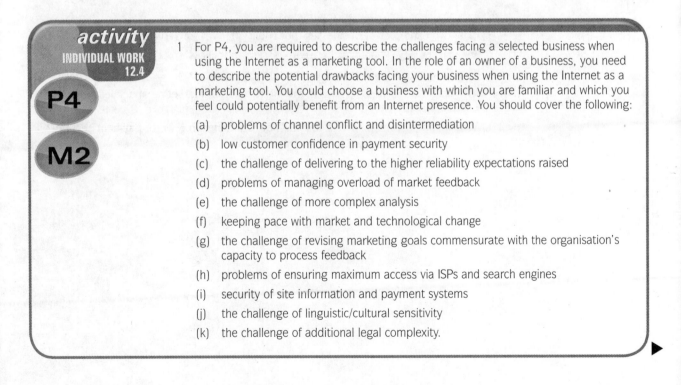

activity

INDIVIDUAL WORK 12.4

P4

M2

1 For P4, you are required to describe the challenges facing a selected business when using the Internet as a marketing tool. In the role of an owner of a business, you need to describe the potential drawbacks facing your business when using the Internet as a marketing tool. You could choose a business with which you are familiar and which you feel could potentially benefit from an Internet presence. You should cover the following:

(a) problems of channel conflict and disintermediation

(b) low customer confidence in payment security

(c) the challenge of delivering to the higher reliability expectations raised

(d) problems of managing overload of market feedback

(e) the challenge of more complex analysis

(f) keeping pace with market and technological change

(g) the challenge of revising marketing goals commensurate with the organisation's capacity to process feedback

(h) problems of ensuring maximum access via ISPs and search engines

(i) security of site information and payment systems

(j) the challenge of linguistic/cultural sensitivity

(k) the challenge of additional legal complexity.

2 For M2, you are required to analyse the marketing opportunities and challenges faced by a selected business when using Internet marketing within the marketing mix of a selected business.

This brings together P3 and P4 and asks you to go one stage further. You should:

(a) Analyse the ways in which Internet marketing can create new business opportunities.

(b) Analyse the ways in which Internet marketing presents new challenges.

(c) Look at contrasting businesses in order to achieve this.

---

activity
INDIVIDUAL WORK 12.5

D1

Evaluate the effectiveness of Internet marketing in meeting customer needs for a selected business.

Building on the work that you have carried out so far, you should:

1 Evaluate how integrating Internet marketing into its overall marketing strategies can enhance the performance of a selected business.

2 State how this could happen despite the fact that problems could be encountered.

3 Cover the principles, benefits, opportunities and challenges of Internet marketing.

4 Try to apply weight to sets of considerations before presenting a final view.

Progress Check

1. Identify the seven Ps.

2. Distinguish between b2b and c2c.

3. Describe what is meant by 'disintermediation' and say what the reverse of this is called.

4. Explain what is meant by 'mass customisation'.

5. Explain what 'dynamic pricing' means.

6. Give two examples of businesses that could offer virtual services.

7. Explain the key differences between 'bricks' and 'clicks'.

8. Explain what you understand by the term 'diversification'.

9. Why might a business relying on the Internet for its marketing and sales have a less complex supply chain?

10. Why might customers have a low level of confidence in website payment security?

Investigating Recruitment and Selection

UNIT 13

This unit covers:

- The processes involved in recruitment planning
- The documentation involved in the recruitment process
- How to participate in a selection interview
- The implications of the regulatory framework on the process of recruitment and selection

When looking for new employees, all organisations wish to recruit the most appropriate individuals. It is therefore necessary to put in place a series of processes and procedures that will ensure that successful candidates are able to meet the requirements of the organisation and the challenges of the post.

The unit starts by examining why vacancies arise and the means by which new staff are recruited before looking at the documentation that is prepared by the organisation for sending to applicants and for use in the recruitment and interview process. The third section of the unit introduces the three stages of the interview process and looks at how organisations conduct interviews in order to ensure that they are fair. The final section covers the legal and ethical framework with which organisations must comply when recruiting and selecting staff.

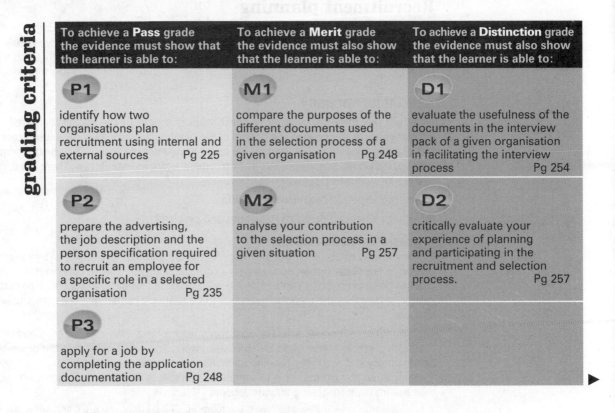

grading criteria

To achieve a **Pass** grade the evidence must show that the learner is able to:	To achieve a **Merit** grade the evidence must also show that the learner is able to:	To achieve a **Distinction** grade the evidence must also show that the learner is able to:
P1 identify how two organisations plan recruitment using internal and external sources Pg 225	**M1** compare the purposes of the different documents used in the selection process of a given organisation Pg 248	**D1** evaluate the usefulness of the documents in the interview pack of a given organisation in facilitating the interview process Pg 254
P2 prepare the advertising, the job description and the person specification required to recruit an employee for a specific role in a selected organisation Pg 235	**M2** analyse your contribution to the selection process in a given situation Pg 257	**D2** critically evaluate your experience of planning and participating in the recruitment and selection process. Pg 257
P3 apply for a job by completing the application documentation Pg 248		

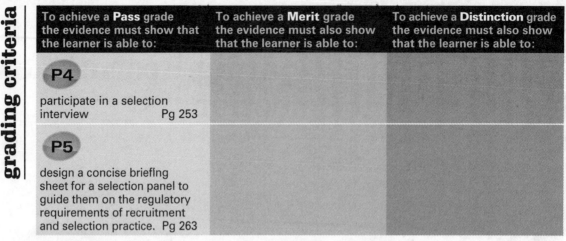

grading criteria	To achieve a **Pass** grade the evidence must show that the learner is able to:	To achieve a **Merit** grade the evidence must also show that the learner is able to:	To achieve a **Distinction** grade the evidence must also show that the learner is able to:
	P4 participate in a selection interview Pg 253		
	P5 design a concise briefing sheet for a selection panel to guide them on the regulatory requirements of recruitment and selection practice. Pg 263		

The processes involved in recruitment planning

In countries such as Great Britain, with a relatively low unemployment rate, it has become increasingly difficult for businesses and organisations to attract and retain good, competent members of staff. Experienced and well-motivated managers and other key employees are vital to the short and the long-term success of the business or organisation. This means that **human resources management**, as personnel departments are now known, is at the centre of an organisation's planning for the future. It is important for the organisation to be able to project an attractive image, not only to its customers but also to individuals who could become its key employees.

Recruitment planning

The process of recruiting new employees may of course be triggered by a number of different factors. The requirement to recruit usually begins with a vacancy. Increasingly, however, human resources management has to predict when additional staffing is likely to be needed. Failure to do so could cause severe disruption and pressure within the organisation.

Reason for vacancy

As we will see, some vacancies are a direct result of actions by the organisation itself. Others, however, are beyond the control of the organisation and, to some extent, cannot be predicted. Human resources must therefore have a flexible approach to recruitment, with systems in place and contacts in employment agencies established. There are two key reasons for vacancies:

- internal expansion and **diversification**
- employee-related decisions, situations and problems.

Organisation-related reasons

The first relates to decisions actually made by the organisation. If a business is increasing its volume of business, it may find that it no longer has sufficient staff to cope with the work. In order to be assured that it can sustain the additional staff required to cope with the increased volume of business, the organisation needs to be relatively certain that the higher volume will continue.

The alternative, of course, is to use what many refer to as a 'sticking plaster' method, to cope with perceived short periods of increased work. This could mean that the business takes on temporary staff who may have no particular attachment or motivation to do the work. The only other real alternative is to suggest to employees that they work increased hours and then reward them for their additional labours.

A business that is in the process of diversifying into new areas of work will need to employ specialists with experience in these new areas and may find that existing employees cannot readily transfer across; perhaps very few of the existing employees or managers have a working knowledge of the new processes or procedures required.

Fig 13.1

Employee-related reasons

When vacancies arise due to employee-related issues, such as maternity leave or long-term sickness, decisions have to be made as to how the vacancy will be handled in the short or long term, and human resources management will become involved. Maternity cover may mean having to take on an employee on a short, **fixed-term contract** for perhaps as long as six months. Providing cover for those on long-term sick leave is more problematic as there can be no accurate prediction as to when the ill employee will return to work, if at all.

The need for short-term vacancy planning also arises when employees take a year out to study, travel the world, or, perhaps, be seconded elsewhere to receive training and experience. To a large extent, of course, these events can be planned for, as can maternity cover.

One of the most difficult recruitment situations is the replacement of an experienced employee who has chosen for some reason to leave the organisation. Depending on the length of their service and contract conditions, the employee will have to give the organisation a period of notice. This means that they will continue to work for a period of time, after they have made it clear to the organisation that they are leaving. Theoretically, this will give the organisation time to recruit or promote an individual who can then work alongside the existing employee as part of an **induction** process.

Retirement also causes a particular problem for any organisation, as the person leaving the job will usually be a highly experienced and well-placed member of staff. Their knowledge of the principles of the organisation and its processes will be difficult to replace, no matter how good the candidates for the vacant position.

Decision to recruit

As we have seen, the organisation may have created a situation where it has to recruit additional employees. Equally, it may have been forced into a situation where it needs either to replace or provide temporary cover for existing employees.

Many organisations are slow in reaching the decision to recruit even when aware that a situation exists where additional or replacement employees would be desirable. Organisations know that the recruitment process is potentially a long and costly one and will avoid having to go through this unless the situation is critical. All too often organisations wait, deferring the decision and thereby placing enormous pressure on remaining employees, which could in turn cause them to leave or take time off due to sickness.

The decision to recruit usually comes from the direct line manager, who must argue the case either for additional staff or for replacement staff. The manager must show good reason for a recruitment drive and illustrate that additional staff are necessary or that existing staff cannot cover the work of an employee who has left or is on long-term leave.

Ultimately, in larger organisations, the recruitment process will be turned over to the human resources department. The department will work in concert with the line manager, framing the requirements that candidates will have to meet and identifying the key responsibilities and duties relating to an identified vacancy.

Kent County Council: improving recruitment practices – Part 1

Kent County Council (KCC) is one of the largest authorities in England. It covers a mix of rural and urban areas in the southeast of England, with no single large metropolitan area. Kent CC has 34,000 staff, with 700+ services delivered to 1.5m people with an annual budget of £1.3bn.

Background – staff care package

In 1998, in response to recruitment and retention difficulties, Kent Social Services introduced a staff care package, which would bring incremental long-term benefits to the service rather than provide a quick-fix solution.

The staff care package brings together a number of initiatives designed to tackle low morale, publicise success, and encourage managers and staff to articulate and be proud of the work they do. Since its inception, vacancy rates have dropped from 27 to 6% in social services.

Streamlining recruitment processes

Building on the success of the staff care package, in 2001, Kent's HR and Social Service managers carried out a review of recruitment processes to consider how they could be made more efficient and quality assured. E-recruitment and response handling/advertising methods were covered as part of the review.

To carry forward the recommendations of the review, a recruitment group was set up including HR and service managers. The groups met on a monthly basis and provided progress reports to the People and Development strategy board to achieve buy-in and resource support for intended recruitment initiatives.

Response handling/advertising

One of the first tasks of the group was to look at advertising spend and how recruitment was handled within social services. There was a general consensus that current practice was too disparate and uncoordinated. The situation was such that a social services manager with a vacancy would hold a budget for advertising and place an advert independently, with no consultation with others. It became apparent that there was no consistency in the process. In addition, social services had no overall branding or identity to which potential recruits could relate.

To deliver improvement in this area, an approach was developed whereby a centralised process for quality assuring adverts was set up in the HR unit, which would help to coordinate the recruitment process. The plan was to manage the process with a programme of regular countywide adverts rather than placing weekly 'spot' adverts. In addition, the business support side of personnel would advise managers on job descriptions, timings and location of advertisements.

(Adapted from www.kent.gov.uk)

activity
INDIVIDUAL WORK

1   What do you think is meant by 'retention difficulties'?
2   To whom did the recruitment group report and why?
3   Explain the problems when managers placed their own advertisements for vacancies.

Internal recruitment

Internal recruitment refers to the filling of vacancies from within the business or organisation. Existing employees are either encouraged to apply or are selected for a vacancy that has arisen for whatever reason.

The business may choose to recruit internally if it believes that it already has employees with the right skills for the job. These employees will have adopted the ways in which the business operates and may have undergone training and development programmes.

Internal recruitment is achieved in a number of different ways:

- The vacancy may be advertised on a staff notice board.
- Details of the vacancy may be placed on the organisation's Intranet.
- The details may be included in the organisation's in-house magazine or newsletter.
- The vacancy may be announced at a staff meeting.

There are a number of key advantages to using internal recruitment:

It gives existing employees opportunities to advance their careers and gain promotion and additional skills and experience.

Restricting the vacancy to internal candidates can also help retain employees who may otherwise have left the organisation.

The employer knows much more about the aptitudes and abilities of the internal candidates, thus reducing the chance of selecting an inappropriate candidate for the post.

Internal recruitment tends to be a far more rapid process than external recruitment and is, of course, far cheaper.

The principle disadvantages of internal recruitment are that:

- The number of potential candidates for the post is limited to those from within the organisation.
- There may be far better external candidates; they may have more experience and better qualifications.
- If an internal candidate is selected to fill a vacancy, a new vacancy instantly arises.
- Some employees, whether competent or not, may feel that they have an automatic right to be given a more senior post.
- The business may become stagnant, as no new ideas, attitudes and perspectives are brought into the organisation.

External sources of recruitment

External recruitment is probably the most common method of recruitment. With external recruitment, job vacancies are filled by individuals from outside the organisation. An organisation may choose to do the recruitment itself, by advertising a vacancy in order to attract the widest possible audience of suitable candidates and then carrying out the selection process, or it may outsource recruitment to a specialist organisation.

Depending on the nature of the vacancy, the recruiting organisation or consultancies, agencies and Jobcentres working on its behalf will advertise the vacancy in specialist magazines, local, regional or national newspapers, or on the Internet.

Most businesses tend to use external recruitment agencies on a regular basis. As a great many organisations have a high staff turnover, a large proportion of their employees are constantly leaving for opportunities elsewhere. Therefore, to take the strain from the organisation's human resources function, external agencies are used as a constant, rolling source of new employees.

A number of different types of organisation will undertake the recruitment and selection process on behalf of a client organisation.

Employment/ recruitment agencies

These are perhaps the most common source of external recruitment. The agencies are highly specialised organisations, used to dealing with specific human resources requirements; many specialise in specific sectors, such as finance, administration or travel. Individuals register with the agency; when a vacancy arises, the agency scans its list of registered candidates and comes up with a shortlist of suitable individuals who match the specification of the vacancy. Invariably, agencies have a ready supply of potential candidates. Agencies can provide both permanent employees and temporary staff and can significantly reduce the administrative burden on the recruiting organisation.

In most cases, employment or recruitment agencies charge up to 30% of the first year's wage to the recruiting organisation. So, for a vacancy attracting a salary of £20,000 the recruiting organisation would pay the agency £6,000.

Fig 13.2 'But I've only
applied for the part-time
clerical assistant's post.'

Headhunters and recruitment consultants

For more specialist and senior posts, organisations can turn to **headhunters** or recruitment
consultants. They too have lists of registered applicants (some of whom have not made it
clear to their existing employers that they wish to move jobs). The recruitment consultants
systematically match their registered applicants against the requirements of the vacancy. They
use sophisticated filtering methods to produce a precise shortlist of potential candidates. The
cost of using headhunters or recruitment consultants is considerably higher than the cost of
using a recruitment agency.

Jobcentres

For the majority of posts that become available in organisations, the government-run
agency known as the Jobcentre is an ideal starting point for identifying local candidates,
particularly for clerical, manual and semi-skilled posts. Jobcentres provide a free service to
employers. Candidates register with the Jobcentre, and it is the centre's role to match the
skills and experience of registered applicants with jobs that are placed with them by recruiting
organisations. Candidates using the Job Centre are not always unemployed.

case study 13.2 — On-line Recruitment Kent County Council: improving recruitment practices – Part 2

Website development

E-recruitment functionality was also developed as part of the wider efficiency drive.
There is now a separate social services recruitment page on KCC's website where
candidates can search for jobs and apply online. The pages also deliver information
on living and working in Kent with details on the staff care package. All social services
vacancies now go on the website, although for some posts it is necessary to use the
national press to reach a targeted audience. Regular reviews are carried out to monitor
recruitment activity and expenditure.

Outcome measures

By promoting better co-ordination of recruitment activity, the council has identified
cost savings in recruitment advertising and reductions of spend on agency staff in
social care. Printing and posting costs have also dramatically reduced as most social
services jobs are now advertised on the website.

Kent CC is committed to e-recruitment and is currently considering how on-line
applications can be made more user friendly and less bureaucratic. One option under
review is to activate or deactivate certain sections of the application forms depending
on the type/level of job being advertised. By doing so, the application process is made
more efficient for the user by reducing the burden of form administration.

In addition to revitalising internal recruitment processes, the council is also dedicated to localised recruitment drives and regularly attends schools and colleges, and invests in stands/presentations. The council reaps the benefits of attending such events and sees it as a major factor in helping to raise the profile of the authority and improve recruitment and retention levels.

(Adapted from www.kent.gov.uk)

1   What do you think is meant by 'e-recruitment functionality'?

2   Kent County Council used its website to advertise jobs, but why did it also use the national press for some vacancies?

3   What do you think is meant by 'making online applications less bureaucratic'?

Cost and time considerations of external sourcing

remember

As employment is high, there are fewer potential candidates, making it harder to find suitable candidates.

Recent research by the CBI (2006) has shown that recruitment can take up to 20% of a manager's day. The manager will have to write advertisements and organise for them to be placed in newspapers. Once the potential applicants start getting in touch with the organisation, hours could be spent on the telephone and in the preparation of information packs and application forms. Then the actual applicants have to be screened, checked, short-listed and interviewed. Even at the end of this process, the organisation may not have found a suitable candidate.

Placing an advertisement in a national newspaper can cost as much as £6,000. It is not unknown for agencies or consultants to charge between 20 and 40% of the advertised salary. Both options, therefore, involve time and cost considerations.

Fig 13.3 The ideal stages in the external recruitment process

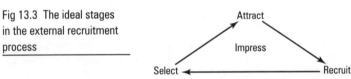

Recruitment advertising

As we saw in the previous section, there are two different types of recruitment: internal and external. Clearly, less is involved when advertising vacancies internally, i.e. within an organisation, than when advertising vacancies to the wider general public, in the hope of attracting suitable candidates.

Internal advertising

Fairness and equal opportunities must be watchwords in internal recruitment, just as they are when external candidates are offered the opportunity to apply. Normally, an organisation will take steps to ensure that all existing members of staff are made aware of vacancies, either before or at the same time as the vacancy is advertised externally to other candidates.

If there is an internal candidate who is suitable for the vacancy, the recruitment process will be cheaper and simpler. If the candidate would be leaving a more junior position to fill a more senior role, it may be easier to find someone to fill the junior position than to attempt to recruit someone from outside to the more senior post.

Internal vacancies can be advertised on bulletin boards, in memoranda, newsletters and in-house magazines and be announced at staff meetings. Usually, existing employees are allowed a period of time in which to apply before any external advertising takes place. This gives potential internal candidates the opportunity to make informal or formal approaches to the part of the organisation with the vacancy; they have a chance to talk to employees with whom they may work, seek the advice of managers and then, if they wish, express a firm interest in the post through the human resources department.

In many larger organisations, internal candidates are allowed up to 21 days to respond to advertising for vacant posts. If at the end of this period suitable candidates have not come forward, the business will advertise externally or engage a specialist agency to find suitable candidates.

External advertising

External advertising for vacant posts normally takes place when the organisation has exhausted its search for a suitable internal candidate. Whilst many organisations will themselves undertake the writing and placement of advertisements in the media, others will be more inclined to use agencies to carry out this function for them.

Choice of media, type of advertisement, acceptable costs and whether or not external agencies are used depend very much upon the nature of the post in question.

Organisations are aware that there is a great deal of competition for good candidates; increasingly, it is the candidates rather than the potential employers who can pick and choose. Organisations are also discovering that the proportion of jobs being filled (whether by internal or external recruitment) is falling and that recruitment consultancies are particularly important for filling senior posts.

According to a survey carried out for *Personnel Today*, external advertising fills 47% of vacancies. This is a drop of 9% since the last survey in 2005. Internal recruitment accounts for some 27% (a drop of 4%). In 26% of all vacancy cases, recruitment consultancies were used. This is up 13% on the last year.

Many people believe that higher recruitment costs are making it difficult for businesses trying to find suitable staff in the most cost-effective manner possible. The growing cost of advertising in newspapers and magazines has caused the beginnings of a shift over to online recruitment. Increasingly, organisations will look to use online employment sites and special pages on their own websites as the means by which they can attract potential candidates.

Recruitment advertisements in local or regional newspapers tend to be relatively straightforward, simply featuring the job title, a brief description, closing date for application and necessary contact details. Whilst these small 'display' advertisements may be suitable for recruiting relatively unskilled workers, something more sophisticated is required to draw the attention of more experienced and potentially key members of staff.

The advertisement needs not only to attract but also to maintain the interest of a suitable candidate who should be intrigued or challenged by the prospect of working for the business. For this purpose, larger advertisements in national newspapers are often required, with an indication as to salary ranges and future prospects and an eye-catching image or slogan.

It has become more difficult for a single organisation's job advertisement to stand out in the more traditional media, where the recruitment pages are overloaded. On a particularly busy day a national newspaper, running job advertisements for specific sectors, can have upwards of 100 pages of recruitment advertising. This has brought almost £2m in advertising revenue to the newspaper, but the volume means that only the largest, most prominent adverts stand out.

Legislation

As we will see in the last part of this unit, several pieces of British law, as well as European Union legislation and regulations, apply to the process of recruitment and selection. One of the most important is the Sex Discrimination Act, which we look at here in some detail in relation to the recruitment and selection process.

The Sex Discrimination Act (SDA) makes it unlawful for an employer to discriminate because of a person's sex or marital status when appointing to a post. There should be no discrimination:

- in the arrangements made for deciding who should be offered the job
- in relation to any terms offered, such as pay, holidays, or working conditions
- by rejecting an applicant or by deliberately avoiding consideration of an applicant.

The 'arrangements' for deciding who should be offered a job include:

- the job description
- the person specification, which is an assessment of the essential skills, experience and qualifications required to carry out the job
- the advertisement (this includes any advertisement of the post)
- the application form

- short-listing
- the interview
- final selection.

See pages 257–258 for more information on the Sex Discrimination Act. See also page 279 in Unit 14.

The Race Relations Act (1992) must also be adhered to, as it expressly forbids discrimination on the grounds of race, colour or creed.

The Equal Pay Act (1970) focuses on the concept of equal pay for like work. This means that members of one gender cannot be offered less pay or worse conditions simply on the grounds of their gender.

The Disability Discrimination Act 1995 focuses on offering equal opportunities and employment protection to those with a wide range of disabilities, both physical and mental. Increasingly, British employment law has become influenced by a number of regulations and directives from the European Union. The Working Time Directive, for example, covers reasonable working hours and the effects of shift work or split working on employees. Over the decades, British employment law has gradually developed. One of the most recent, the Employment Act 2002, brings together many of the features of older laws and brings them up to date. As a result of European Union regulations, national minimum wages have now been introduced for employees (these are related to age).

Finally, as we will see at the end of this unit, the Data Protection Act 1998 is applicable to recruitment and selection. Candidates will be revealing personal details about themselves, both in the application and in the interview processes. The potential employer needs to ensure that this information is used only for the recruitment and selection process and that any data collected is kept secure and not circulated beyond those involved in the decision making.

For more information on the Race Relations Act, Equal Pay Act, Disability Discrimination Act, national minimum wage, and the Employment Act, see pages 259–263 and pages 281–282 in Unit 14.

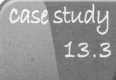

case study 13.3 **Ageism**

A quarter of companies could face legal action if they do not take steps to review their recruitment policies ahead of new age laws that came into effect in October 2006.

To coincide with Age Positive Week, which is being spearheaded by the government to help employers prepare for the new age legislation, consultancy Water for Fish conducted an audit of 75 recruitment ads in a national Sunday newspaper.

It found that 27% would be potentially open to legal action when the new legislation comes into force.

Bonita Bryan, consultant at Water for Fish, said: 'Although the age legislation does not come into force until later this year, it is worrying that a quarter of companies are disregarding the new requirements in their recruitment drive.

'Companies need to review their whole recruitment selection process now if they want to ensure that they are going to comply.' Some common pitfalls include:

- Asking for an applicant's date of birth or other date-bound information which may reveal age
- Requesting a specific number of years' experience for a position which may adversely disadvantage younger applicants
- Using particular words or phrases in adverts, which might betray the intention to discriminate, such as 'mature' or 'energetic'

'Recruiters need to stay clear of using terminology that directly discriminates on the basis of age, or that may give the connotation that they intend to discriminate. Words such as "energetic, mature, dynamic, fresh, young, old, X years of experience, youthful, new graduate" may fall foul of the regulations,' Bryan said.

(Adapted from www.waterforfish.com)

1   What do you think is meant by 'might betray the intention to discriminate'?

2   What do you think would happen to the 27% of recruitment advertisements in a Sunday newspaper if they were repeated today?

3   Suggest five other words or phrases that could betray the intention to discriminate.

Methods of application

Businesses and organisations differ in how they prefer to organise recruitment. Typically, they could use any of the following application methodologies:

■   The candidates are required to contact the organisation to receive an information pack and application form. When the completed application form is sent back, a simple covering letter is all that is needed.

■   The candidates are asked to write a letter of application and to enclose an up-to-date curriculum vitae (CV).

■   The candidates are asked to call a specific manager or the human resources department (in some cases the recruitment agency); this is an initial phase in the short-listing process.

■   The candidates are asked to complete an online application or to download an application form, which can then be printed out, completed and posted to the potential employer.

■   Open days are announced and potential employees, usually for bulk recruitment, are invited to attend screening sessions, which will direct them into a more formal recruitment and selection process.

Fig 13.4 A CV

CURRICULUM VITAE

WILLIAM JAMAL

75c Graceland Road, Salisbury, Wiltshire WS23 7RL

Tel: 0722 0030

Date of Birth: 25.5.80

Qualifications:

June 1988	GNVQ Advanced in Business (Merit)		
June 1996	GCSE	English Language	B
		English Literature	C
		Mathematics	C
		Music	D
		History	B
		French	C

Education:
Sept 96 – June 98   Greenwood College of Further Education, Eastfield
Sept 91 – June 96   Wallace Road Secondary School, Eastfield
Sept 85 – June 91   Clifton Street School, Little Parva

Employment:
Aug 98 – present   Administrative Officer, Department of Social Security
I have been in this post for just over two years during which I have worked in a range of jobs within the department. These have included visiting the premises of employers with the inspector as well as the work within the section.

My current responsibilities involve dealing with queries relating to National Insurance contributions, assessing liability for payments and interviewing members of the public. This demands knowledge, flexibility and tact. In the course of my employment I have gained experience of both manual and computerised office systems. As well as meeting the public I am in frequent contact with other offices within the UK.

Leisure interests: I enjoy most sports although I am particularly keen on swimming and cricket and I represented my school at both. I still swim regularly and have kept wicket for the town second XI for the last two seasons.

See pages 232–234 for information about writing application documents.

Many organisations encourage applicants to complete documents, using word processing or their own handwriting. This tests applicants' use of English, grammar and understanding of questions and acts as a filtering mechanism; candidates who are insufficiently literate are likely to be weeded out.

case study 13.4 — Poor spelling

More than three-quarters of employers would be put off a job candidate by poor spelling or grammar, a survey has found.

A study by Hertfordshire University in 2005 of 515 companies found bad English alienated 77% firms surveyed.

The biggest draw for potential employers was relevant work experience, mentioned by 46%, followed by a 'good work ethic' (43%).

Just a quarter (24%) of employers said they were interested in a candidate's class of degree and 14% in the reputation of the university they had attended.

Research from the CBI indicated that 42% are unhappy with the basic skills of those applying for jobs. Even graduates are writing illiterate memos and are in need of constant supervision, employers report.

(Source: www.herts.ac.uk)

activity — INDIVIDUAL WORK

1 What is meant by the term 'good work ethic'?

2 What is the CBI and whom does it represent?

3 Why is it of vital importance to check everything that you have written before sending it to a potential employer?

case study 13.5 — Recruitment procedures

1 University of Nottingham recruitment procedures

The recruitment process begins when you know you need someone new in the School or Department, either because an existing staff member has left, or because there is new work to be done. It doesn't finish until after the appointment has been made and you have reflected on any changes that you would make in future recruitments.

The main stages are identified in the table.

Table 13.1 The main stages in recruitment

Recruitment activities	Good practice
Identify vacancy	Review existing job specification or prepare a new one; prepare background information about the workplace and notes for the applicant.
Prepare job description and person specification	Speak to all those involved with the post to establish tasks required. Ensure that all those involved with the post agree with the role. Describe accurately the requirements and duties of the job. Avoid any wording that implies that members of one sex are more likely to be able to do the job. Avoid wording such as 'fit and able-bodied' – concentrate on the tasks required to fulfil the post. Produce a specification of the essential/desirable attributes and characteristics of the person required to carry out the job satisfactorily. Assess each individual against set standards.
Advertise	Post should be advertised in appropriate areas, e.g. correct publications and journals. Consideration should be given to advertising in publications targeted at minority groups, such as the *Caribbean Times*. Draft advertisement to reflect job description. Give closing date of a minimum of two weeks after the advertisement appears. Inform job centres, private employment agencies and management consultants that you are keen to interview minority groups.

Recruitment activities	Good practice
Managing the response	Send out the application form or invite CVs to be sent in. Ensure that candidates are sent information about the post including the job description and person specifications. Log applications received. Acknowledge receipt of applications.
Short-listing	Use the objective set standards of the person specification as the basis for short-listing. Arrange for people to be part of a short-listing panel. Make sure they are available for interview. Make sure all short-listing panel members understand the selection criteria. Send papers in advance. Read applications. Short-list and record decisions. Process men's and women's applications in exactly the same way. Write to unsuccessful candidates.
Visits	Arrange where appropriate. Avoid unless this is an opportunity that every candidate is able to take advantage of.
References	Send a copy of the job description and allow time for return before interview date.
Arrange interviews	Send papers to interviewers in advance. Write to candidates with details of the interview, including any tests, which might be used. Book an appropriate room – check if candidates have any specific requirements, e.g. access might require a ground-floor room.
Conduct the interview	Assess candidates against selection criteria. Relate the questions to the requirements of the job. Where it is necessary to assess whether personal circumstances will affect performance of the job, discuss this objectively without detailed questions based on assumptions about marital status, children and domestic obligations. Base assessments, wherever possible on factual evidence of past performance, behaviour and achievements. Arrange for candidates to be assessed by a panel rather than by one person alone. Record decisions on individual interview sheet.
Decision making	Decisions on all candidates [are to be] made at the end of the interview. Base judgments on facts rather than impressions. Match the profile of all job requirements against the complete profile of the individual. Pause and question whether sex or racial bias has influenced the proposal to reject a candidate. Allow each assessor to form an independent view. Allow junior members of the panel to express their opinions first (to avoid influence). Final decision is summarised and recorded.
Convey the decision	Candidates are written to with the decision. Appropriate feedback is given. All interview documents are kept.
Appointment action	Agree starting date. Make any necessary pre-employment checks. Issue appointment letter.

During the process as a whole be objective and seek to identify the candidates' abilities. Judge on individual merits and set the same standards for all.

(Adapted from www.nottingham.ac.uk)

2 Walsall Council recruitment procedures

The eight Steps to Walsall Council's recruitment process are:

■ A vacancy arises. Sometimes this is due to the creation of a new job; on other occasions it may be because an existing member of staff has been promoted or is retiring.

■ The job description is updated and an employee specification is written. The job description lists the duties of the job whilst the employee specification gives details of the experience, skills and abilities needed to carry out the job.

■ A vacancy advertisement is written and is circulated via Walsall Council's weekly bulletin, *Job Shop Weekly*. Other media can be used including newspapers, Internet recruitment sites, specialist publications and the Employment Service.

- Application forms are sent out along with copies of the job description and employee specification and must be returned on or before the closing date that has been set. See our applying for jobs page for further information.

- A shortlist is compiled of applicants who are going to be invited to attend for interview. This is done by the recruitment panel who compare each application form with the requirements of the employee specification. Feedback can be provided (upon request) to those not short-listed and applicants have the right to complain if they feel they have been unfairly treated.

- Interviews are held. The panel will use the same set of questions with each interviewee. The interview may include a selection test. Feedback can be provided (upon request) and unsuccessful applicants have the right to complain if they feel they have been unfairly treated. See our interviews page for further information.

- References will be requested. The successful applicant for jobs working in certain areas, including working with children or vulnerable adults, will be asked to apply for a criminal disclosure check through the Criminal Records Bureau.

- Appoint the successful candidate and arrange induction training.

(Adapted from www.walsall.gov.uk)

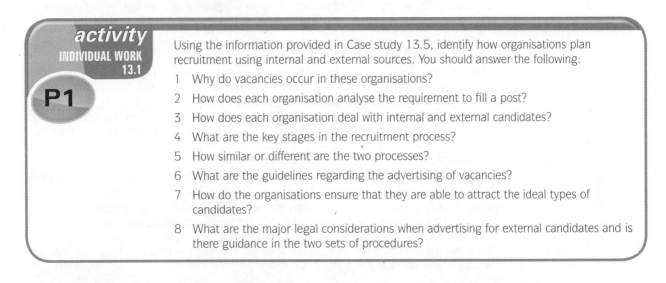

activity

INDIVIDUAL WORK 13.1

P1

Using the information provided in Case study 13.5, identify how organisations plan recruitment using internal and external sources. You should answer the following:

1 Why do vacancies occur in these organisations?

2 How does each organisation analyse the requirement to fill a post?

3 How does each organisation deal with internal and external candidates?

4 What are the key stages in the recruitment process?

5 How similar or different are the two processes?

6 What are the guidelines regarding the advertising of vacancies?

7 How do the organisations ensure that they are able to attract the ideal types of candidates?

8 What are the major legal considerations when advertising for external candidates and is there guidance in the two sets of procedures?

The documentation involved in the recruitment process

Two key documents appear very early on in the recruitment process. Collectively, they frame the exact nature of a vacancy and are a blueprint for the type of individual who would be a perfect match for the requirements of the job. The two documents in question are job descriptions and person specifications. For any post, the job description must work with and mirror the person specification.

In both cases, there is certain material that it is necessary to include, but the format can differ from organisation to organisation and there is no standardised form. The level of detail will depend not only on the job but also on the requirements of those who compiled and approved the documents.

Job description

The job description is designed to detail the exact nature of the job. Only once this has been done can a person specification be created. The writer of the job description aims therefore to identify all the key duties and responsibilities; in turn these will suggest the necessary attributes, skills and experience to be included in the person specification.

The job description is usually created in two different ways:

■ a literal description of an existing job, probably compiled by the individual who undertakes the job, their manager or someone who works in a similar role in the organisation

■ a new job design, which seeks to identify the duties and responsibilities of a new post that had not existed prior to the creation of this new job.

Purpose and standard formats

The main purpose of the job description is to state clearly the job title, its functions, duties, and responsibilities and say to whom that individual would report.

Beyond these basic purposes, standard formats are not common and job descriptions come in a wide variety of formats. The one chosen will very much depend on the time and resources allocated to the creation of job descriptions. Ideally, job descriptions should be readily available in the organisation as all existing employees should have a copy of a job description relating to their post.

Title of job

The first key decision concerns the job title; the title should indicate the nature of the work involved in the vacant post, as well as the postholder's status in the organisation. Typically, descriptive phrases such as 'finance', 'administrative', 'customer', 'retail' and 'support' indicate the area within an organisation, perhaps a department or section, in which the individual will work. Terms such as 'assistant', 'supervisor' or 'manager' can be added. The combination, for example, of 'retail' and 'manager' to give 'retail manager' would indicate that the person will work in a shop environment and will have some sort of supervisory role.

Department and location of post

Whilst to some extent this may be indicated in the job title, the job description will specifically state the precise position of the post within the organisation. Obviously, organisations are structured in many different ways. Not all have a clear-cut structure comprising departments, divisions or sections. In every organisation, however, there will be a line of management and it should be possible to give a clear indication of the duties and responsibilities of the various parts of the organisation. This will allow the job post to be placed within a section of the organisation, perhaps in sales, marketing, administration or finance.

Increasingly, organisations operate on multiple sites. There may be a headquarters or head office where staff are involved in overseeing the running of the organisation. The headquarters may be administrative only. The rest of the organisation may be split into stores or branches located across the country. When there are multiple sites, the job description should state precisely where, geographically, the position is based. For example, if an organisation has branches throughout the country, it should state that the post is in, say, Glasgow, indicating that, although the organisation operates nationally, this is where the job is located.

Broad terms of job

No job description, however detailed, could possibly hope to include a description of every single duty and responsibility that the postholder may from time to time be required to carry out. In this respect, 'broad terms' means statements such as 'assisting in the preparation of final accounts', or 'handle day-to-day customer queries'.

Within these broad terms are many implied responsibilities and duties. The broad terms of the job indicate the key specific job tasks and duties. There is often an additional line that states 'or any other duties deemed reasonable'; this is to cover anything that has been missed off the basic list.

Responsible to whom

This brief section of the job description simply states the direct line manager or supervisor for the post. It indicates where the job fits into the overall structure of the organisation. Junior members of staff are responsible to team supervisors; more senior staff may be directly responsible to departmental managers, and departmental managers may be responsible to directors.

Usually in order to ensure the longevity of the job description, the job title of the direct line manager or supervisor is given, rather than an individual's name.

Responsibilities

In many respects these can be seen as extensions of the broad terms, tasks and duties that have already been identified in the job description. The specific responsibilities are clarified in a precise statement of what is required of the person holding the post. An IT technician, for example, might be expected 'to regularly backup all data'.

Fig 13.5 An IT technician at work

Scope of post

This covers the range of responsibilities and duties that will have to be carried out by the postholder. Just like the responsibilities, this should be kept to a minimum so that it is clear and easily understood. After all, job descriptions that contain responsibilities extending to 20 or 30 points are more like operating manuals than job descriptions.

Education and qualifications

This section indicates the minimum qualifications required for the post. These are usually stated in the broadest terms, such as 'four GCSEs or equivalent', or perhaps 'an HND in a relevant qualification'. From this can be inferred the basic level of education and understanding for the job. The higher the qualifications, the more demanding the employer believes the post to be; it may perhaps be seen as beyond the immediate ability of someone less qualified or educated.

Compiler, approver and date of issue

The individual who has put together the job description is often named at the end of the document. In many cases, job descriptions are the product of involved conversations between postholders, supervisors and managers. Ultimately, a blueprint of the job has to be created, and in many cases one individual will be left to identify the key duties and responsibilities before passing the job description on to a more senior member of staff for approval.

In order to ensure that the most up-to-date version of a job description is used, the documents are often dated or given code numbers so that they can be traced back to a particular review period or to the last time the job description was reviewed. Periodically, the nature of the job will change, perhaps with the inclusion of additional responsibilities and duties or because technology has taken over manual procedures.

Functions

Overall, job descriptions are designed to clarify the employer's expectations of the employee. They can be useful in setting the key measurements for job performance. As far as potential candidates are concerned, they provide a baseline description of the job.

Job descriptions also have a number of other key functions, including:

- a framework to help the postholder to understand the structure of all jobs and how their activities, duties and responsibilities fit into the organisation
- a way of ensuring continuity if there is a **high turnover of staff**
- the basis for grading and pay scales
- a reference tool for **disciplinary procedures** and for disputes
- a reference point for training and development
- a way in which sets of skills and behaviour can be identified.

---

case study
13.6

Administrative assistant – typical job description duties

An administrative assistant's job description varies according to the role and organisation.

- Type and word-process various documents and electronic information.
- Create financial and statistical tools and reports using spreadsheets.
- Manage, organise, and update relevant data using database applications.
- Communicate and provide information by relevant methods internally and externally to assist and enable organisational operations and effective service to connecting groups.
- Analyse and interpret financial statistics and other data and produce relevant reports.
- Interpret instructions and issues arising, and then implement actions according to administrative policies and procedures.
- Research and investigate information to enable strategic decision making by others.
- Arrange and participate in meetings, conferences, and project team activities.
- Approve decisions, requests, expenditure and recommendations on behalf of senior people in their absence, according to agreed guidelines and policies.
- Adhere to stated policies and procedures relating to health and safety, and quality management.
- Adhere to procedures relating to the proper use and care of equipment and materials for which the role has responsibility.

(Adapted from www.businessballs.com)

activity

Use this outline as the basis for a job description that is relevant to your own situation.

Person specification

A person specification identifies the attributes, characteristics, attainment, experience, intelligence, aptitude and personality of the ideal candidate for a job post. The person specification is designed to make it easier to identify the individual who is best able to fulfil the tasks and requirements of the post. Candidates are matched against the specified criteria.

Purpose and standard formats

Person specifications can be organised in many different ways. Generally, however, the following are included as an absolute minimum:

- physical makeup – this may include specific physical requirements, such as good eyesight, particular height or level of fitness
- current attainments – the individual's qualifications, whether or not they have a driving licence and, if applicable, any previous experience

■ a measure of the intelligence of the individual – particular qualifications or the ability to pass entrance tests

■ aptitudes – which could include social skills, listening and communication skills, the ability to touch-type or to write legibly

■ interests – whether there are any relevant sports or leisure activities relating to the job role

■ disposition – whether the individual is able to cope with a variety of problem situations; whether they are tactful and diplomatic when dealing with people

■ individual circumstances – which may include their domestic situation, personal relationships and their ability to work unsocial hours.

case study 13.7 — West Midlands Police

Do you have the skills we look for? If so, demonstrate them in the form to make your application form count. The application form must show us that you have or can develop the qualities needed to become a police officer. In particular, we look for people who are able to show us that they have the following skills:

a. Effective communication – Communicates all needs, instructions and decisions clearly. Adapts the style of communication to meet the needs of the audience.

b. Community and customer focus – Sees things from the customer's point of view and encourages others to do the same. Builds a good understanding and relationship with the community that is served.

c. Personal responsibility – Takes responsibility for own actions and for sorting out issues or problems that arise.

d. Resilience – Remains calm and confident, and responds logically and decisively in difficult situations.

e. Problem solving – Gathers information from a range of sources to understand situations, making sure it is reliable and accurate. Identifies risks and considers alternative courses of action to make good decisions.

f. Respect for diversity – Understands other people's views and takes them into account. Treats people with dignity and respect at all times no matter what their background, status, circumstances or appearance.

g. Team working – Works effectively as a team member and helps build relationships within it.

(Source: www.west-midlands.police.uk)

activity

1 How many of the seven skills do you have?

2 How could you seek to gain these skills or develop them if you wished to apply to become a police officer?

Typically a person specification identifies the following in relation to the job description:

■ physical attributes required or desired

■ proficiencies required or desired

■ manual skills required or desired

■ knowledge skills required or desired

■ personality traits required or desired

■ social skills required or desired.

remember

The job description and person specification should complement each other.

Job title, reference number and location in management line

The job title will mirror the name given to the job role in the job description. A reference number may be used so that the person specification can quickly be matched to the job description.

The job description will already have identified the status or importance of the job role and therefore given a clear indication as to the job's place in the management line.

Essential and desirable attributes

The employer will have tried to identify qualities that are either essential or desirable. Essential attributes are those that the potential candidate must have in order to carry out the job. For example, someone expected to deliver goods to a customer would have to be able to drive.

Desirable attributes are qualities that in an ideal situation the individual would also be able to display. For example, it would be advantageous if a delivery driver had strong social skills and was able to work under pressure.

Many organisations use what is known as a seven-point plan to help identify the essential and desirable attributes. The seven categories are:

- the physical makeup of the candidate
- their attainments
- their general intelligence
- special aptitudes relevant to the job role
- their interests
- their disposition
- their personal circumstances.

Physical characteristics

Although physical makeup is not relevant to some job roles, many jobs do require certain minimum physical requirements. These could include:

- minimum height (e.g. for the police force)
- maximum weight – which could be measured in body mass index
- hearing – which is important for a telesales operator
- eyesight (e.g. for the fire brigade)
- looks – where body image is important
- grooming – to present a professional approach and look
- dress – to look smart and presentable
- voice – so that the individual can be understood.

Attainments and qualifications

In addition to paper qualifications, which give an idea of a candidate's level of understanding, employers are interested in a candidate's ability to display certain skills as evidence of their aptitude for the job. Person specifications tend to focus on three key aspects:

- general education
- work experience
- on- or off-the-job training.

Previous experience

If the person specification demands that an individual has worked in a similar environment for a number of years, this suggests that the organisation is looking for someone who has considerable relevant work experience and skills and will transfer readily into the new job role.

For some junior positions, however, no previous experience is necessary, giving individuals the opportunity to enter that field of work. Usually, full training will be provided so that new postholders learn the organisation's policies and preferred procedures.

General intelligence

Employers are becoming increasingly dismayed by the standard of candidates' numeracy, writing and communication skills (even in the case of candidates with degrees). Some larger organisations require potential candidates to undertake tests during the recruitment and selection process. (These are like entrance tests: the aim is to gauge the candidate's reasoning skills and intellectual ability.) Other organisations specify GCSEs or equivalent, A levels or equivalent, or a degree or equivalent as an indicator of the baseline intelligence required for the post.

Special aptitudes

Particular skills or aptitudes are essential for some job roles. Some jobs require manual skills whilst others require the postholder to work with words and/or figures. Examples of special aptitudes include:

- mechanical skills – such as the ability to service cars
- dexterity skills – such as the ability to handle machinery
- word skills – either written or oral
- figure skills – the ability to work with numbers
- artistic skills – for design and art work.

Temperament and personality

Temperament and personality are often known as disposition. A problem with including these in the person specification is that assessment of dispositional attributes tends to be subjective. Aspects of temperament and personality of interest to an employer include:

- acceptability – is the individual easy to get along with?
- leadership – has the candidate shown any signs of being able to control individuals or teams?
- stability – both in mental and domestic terms
- motivation – does the person have self-starter skills and are they motivated and driven?

Hobbies and interests

Hobbies and interests can give the employer an insight into the candidate's intelligence and aptitudes and how they use their leisure time. A candidate's hobbies and interests may reveal:

- their intellectual interests
- their practical interests
- their physical or sports interests
- their social interests.

Fig 13.6 A candidate's leisure activities can give an employer vital clues during selection

Personal circumstances

It is illegal for an organisation to discriminate against individuals on the basis of their personal circumstances. Therefore, organisations have to be very careful when looking at a potential candidate's personal circumstances, including:

- the candidate's age
- their marital status
- whether they have dependants
- their geographical mobility or willingness to move location
- where the candidate lives
- their financial circumstances.

remember

Collect as much information about a specific role in an organisation as you can. Then use this later to prepare your advertisement, job description and person specification.

Application documentation

The purpose of application documentation is to provide information in as standard a format as possible so that meaningful comparisons can be made between applicants. The documents can also be used to identify whether the applicant has the essential and desirable skills and attributes set out in the person specification.

Depending on the organisation's requirements, an applicant for a job may have to do any or all of the following:

- write and send in a letter of application
- send in a curriculum vitae (CV)
- complete and send in a form.

Letters of application are, perhaps, the hardest of the above. After all, an application form has boxes to complete and instructions for what to write, and a CV has commonly-used headings.

Letter of application

The basic rules for writing a letter of application are:

- State clearly in the first paragraph the particular post that you are applying.
- State in the first paragraph where you saw the information about the vacancy.
- Indicate any enclosures, such as an application form or curriculum vitae.
- Use the letter of application to summarise your major strengths (as detailed in your application form, if applicable).
- Stress your suitability for the post.
- Be enthusiastic.
- Try to restrict your letter of application to no more than one side of A4.
- If the organisation asks you to provide a handwritten letter of application do so (a handwriting analyst may be asked to look at applicants' letters).
- Use the correct tone.
- Make sure that your letter has the correct layout for a business letter.
- Be formal and use correct salutations and complementary closes.
- State that you are available for interview.
- State that you are able to start the job.
- Take a photocopy or print out a second copy.
- Make sure that any certificates required have been photocopied and attached.

Curriculum vitae

This is normally sent to an organisation when full details have been requested. Curriculum vitae means 'course of life', and you should use the document to provide a summary of your personal details and past experience. CVs should always be clear and concise, should only include relevant facts and figures and should be in note format. The key criteria for a CV are:

- It should always be word processed or typed.
- It should be no longer than two sides of A4.

- It should be a summary (not an essay).
- Check for spelling, spacing, punctuation and layout.
- The tone should be positive and optimistic.

Your CV should include the sections detailed in Table 13.2.

Table 13.2 Curriculum vitae

Section	Explanation
Name	Surname first in capitals then forenames. Indicate the title desired, such as Mr, Mrs or Ms.
Date of birth	Present this as a simple numeric date of birth, e.g. 24.4.88 or, in full, 24 April 1988. Make sure you follow this format with all dates you include in your CV.
Address	The address should be in full, including home number, street, town, county, and full postcode.
Telephone number	For a landline put the prefix first, followed by a space or dash and then the rest of the number. If necessary, in brackets, put the times at which you will be available on this number. If you have a mobile phone, put this number in as well but not instead of your land line.
Employment history	Always work backwards in time. Your latest or last employer should be first in the list then work backwards. Give the employer's name in full along with the address. If possible, state tasks, job roles and duties carried out. Give accurate dates; explain why there is a gap in your employment record if this is the case. Be truthful; include salary details and state reason for leaving each job.
Education and training	Put your most recent education or training first and work backwards in time. Give names and addresses of institutions you have attended but do not put your qualifications in here as these are covered in the following section.
Qualifications	Make sure you put your grades and state the examining board. If you have not received results for particular qualifications put 'pending'. Put down your qualifications in reverse chronological order and include the year you achieved them.
Other relevant achievements	Put down any duties, responsibilities, special awards or any time you have appeared in the press, such as in connection with the Duke of Edinburgh Award Scheme, but don't put that you have a 25m swimming certificate unless you are applying for a job as a lifeguard.
Interests	Do not put in interests such as going out drinking with mates. Be careful not to say that you enjoy doing things that you don't do, as the chances are the employer may ask you about it in the interview.
References	Always include your present or last employer, your school's head teacher or college principal. You cannot use direct family members. In most cases you'll be asked for two referees, sometimes three. Make sure that anyone whose name you give is prepared to give you a reference. You will need to put in their name and contact details.

Application form

An application form may appear to be daunting, but you can follow a number of key steps to make sure that your form is filled in correctly and appears neat and tidy:

- Always take a photocopy of the original application form and fill in the photocopied version in rough first.
- Spend time thinking about the questions and sections of the form.
- Make sure that you have spelled everything correctly and used the correct grammar.
- Make sure everything is legible.

- If you are asked if you have any specific skills, focus on the ones that you think are useful for the job.

- When you mention your achievements, identify things that show your personal development and initiative.

- Make sure that you know the examining boards and the dates of all examinations.

- Be especially carefully when answering open-ended questions, such as 'Why have you applied for this post?' Refer back to the person specification if you have it, or the job description, to identify the skills and competences the employer is looking for.

- Before you enter anything onto the original application form make sure that you have answered all the questions.

- Check that you are being positive.

- Ask yourself if you have been absolutely honest and can back up everything you have said.

- Check if you need to attach a photograph or proof of qualifications. If yes, do so.

- Take a photocopy of the completed application form and study it before interview.

Link

See page 236 for information about application packs.

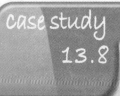

case study 13.8

Help, I need somebody!

Jamiesons, the national supermarket chain is desperate to recruit a trainee buyer for the Produce Trading department.

The trainee will need to demonstrate good negotiation and influencing skills have a professional manner with the drive to succeed and the ability to work under pressure and to deadlines.

The trainee will also have to learn and fully understand the trading operating systems, which control the sourcing, availability and profitability of the company product ranges.

The business offers an excellent benefits package, including competitive salary, pension scheme*, free life assurance*, annual profit share*, subsidised canteen and staff discount (*after qualifying period).

The department is responsible for the purchase and consistent supply of all fresh produce, which ranges from fruit and vegetables to salad goods to fresh flowers and plants.

Ideally, the candidates should be interested in facing a new challenge and have the skills to strengthen our team further; if so then the company wants to hear from you.

To apply, candidates need to contact ned.bulter@jamiesons.net

Candidates should have a good eye for detail, and excellent communication skills are also key qualities for the role.

As a Trainee, the person will be provided with training and support to become proficient in the company approach to the buying and selling of products whilst ensuring that all aspects including packaging, merchandising and efficient selling are fully considered.

If you are interested in facing a new challenge and have the skills to strengthen our team further, then Jamiesons wants to hear from you.

The trainee will be working as part of the buying team; we are looking for a self-motivated individual to take on an exciting opportunity to join the team as a Trainee Buyer.

If you have working knowledge of the produce market place within your current or previous roles and/or experience in food retail background then this would certainly be advantageous.

You can also fill in an application form online at www.jamiesons.net from the Job Application section of the site. You will also need to complete a health questionnaire.

activity

You will be using the case study as the basis for creating the necessary documents for filling a vacancy. All the information that you need is included in the case study, but it is deliberately jumbled and confused. Read the case study through again and identify the information that you will need.

activity

INDIVIDUAL WORK 13.2

P2

Prepare the advertising, the job description and the person specification required to recruit an employee for a specific role in a selected organisation.

1   Use Case study 13.8 as the basis for creating the necessary documents.

2   Try to find similar jobs on the Internet; ideal places to look are shown below. Look for the recruitment or job vacancies sections. You will often find links to these through the corporate part of the website.

www.morrisons.co.uk

www.tesco.com

www.waitrose.com

www.somerfield.com

www.sainsburys.co.uk

www.asda.co.uk

3   To fulfil the requirements of the grading criterion, you must:

(a)   Create a job description.

(b)   Create a person specification.

(c)   Create a job advertisement.

(d)   Ensure that the documents are checked and presented in a professional manner.

(e)   Ensure that you identify the possible newspapers, magazines or other media that will be used to advertise the post.

(f)   Ensure that you have laid out the job advertisement in a typical format used by businesses for vacancies.

Participating in a selection interview

As a major part of your assessment for this unit you will be expected to take part in a selection interview. In the normal course of events you would be looking for a suitable job to match your qualifications, skills and interests. Usually the job will have been advertised in the media, or you will have become aware of it through a recruitment consultant, agency or job centre.

Participation in the selection process presumes that you have maintained an interest in applying for the job. When applying for work with an organisation it is useful to think about answers to the following questions:

■   Am I in a position to apply for this post? – Do I have the skills required?

■   What do I already know about, or what can I find out about, the organisation?

■   Does the organisation have a good reputation?

■   How does it treat its staff?

■   Are there opportunities for personal development and promotion?

■   Is it clear to whom I will have to apply?

■   Will I need to send a letter of application?

■   Is the job really for me?

■   Will I discover that the job is actually unsuitable?

■   How will I react if I do not get the job or if I turn down the job having been offered it?

Pre-interview

The pre-interview process seeks to eliminate unsuitable candidates before considerable amounts of time and effort have been spent interviewing the short-listed applicants. When an applicant is required to complete forms or a prepare letter and curriculum vitae (CV), the intention is not only to provide the organisation with basic information but also to dissuade time wasters.

Application packs and information

Organisations have their own preferences regarding what to put in application packs and the supporting information to be sent to each individual who has expressed an interest in the post. The application pack usually includes the following:

- an application form
- a full job description
- a person specification
- notes on completing the application form and other relevant application-related information.

In terms of supporting information, the organisation may well send an up-to-date copy of its annual report, press clippings, newsletters, brochures and other relevant printed information. It may also direct the applicants to its website.

The purpose of the application and information packs is to provide the applicants with necessary background information so that they are aware of the nature of the organisation's work; in many cases, questions will be asked at interview stage to see if the applicant has read the information.

Selcotion criteria for short-listing

Once the closing date for receiving applications has passed, the employer will use the person specification to help with short-listing the applicants and will judge from the application documentation how well candidates meet the essential and desirable criteria. See Table 13.3. It is important for the employer to be uniform and objective when dealing with all of the applications. Some organisations insist that a panel undertakes the short-listing.

All the criteria are looked at in an objective manner, and any applicant who lacks essential criteria is left off the short list. Ideally, anyone who meets the criteria should be invited to the interview.

Inevitably some of the applicants will score highly in some factors and lower on others. Some organisations treat short-listing as a purely numerical exercise, adding up candidates' points, whilst others make a judgement as to whether or not the applicant is suitable for the short list.

The aim is to reduce the long list of possible interviewees down to a manageable number. Usually, organisations opt for around five or six potential interviewees, although this number would be extended if it is difficult to differentiate between candidates at this stage.

References

The point at which an organisation chooses to take up references varies considerably. Most employers argue that it is advisable to do so before interview; some prefer to wait until after interview.

With regard to timing, there are four options:

- Taking up references at application stage – this is an onerous task as all applicants' references have to be obtained; another drawback is that some applicants may have asked for them not to be taken up before interview stage.
- Taking up references at short-listing stage – this is probably the ideal time to take up references, as the candidates who most closely match the essential and desired criteria will have been chosen (on the basis of their application documents), and a provisional shortlist drawn up. As there are now fewer references to obtain, less administrative time and effort is required; and the references might help to reduce the shortlist, saving time and expense at the interview stage.

Table 13.3 Candidate short-listing form

CANDIDATE SHORTLISTING FORM

Post Title:

Post Reference:

Date of Shortlisting:

Record your scores on each of the applications received here:

1 = Fully Meets Criteria   2 = Partially Meets Criteria   3 = Fails to Meet Criteria

Criteria	Candidate Number: (as listed in Person Specification)												
Specific Skills													
Experience/ Knowledge													
Interpersonal Attributes													
Qualifications/ Training													
Capacity for Career Development													
Others													
TOTALS													

■ Taking up references after interview – references are requested as a backup measure to check statements made by the applicants before the final decision is taken as to which applicant will be offered the post. The problem with taking up references at this stage is that there will be a delay between the interviews and offering the post to the successful candidate.

■ Taking up references after appointment (i.e. when the successful interviewee has been offered the job, subject to satisfactory references, and the unsuccessful candidates have been informed) – the organisation has only one individual to seek references for but if the references throw doubt on the successful candidate's fitness for the post, the entire process may have to be repeated.

Types of interview

There are two major categories of recruitment and selection interviews:

Fig 13.7 Formal 'across a table' interviews can be daunting to the candidate

■ the screening interview, which is used before the actual selection interview to identify whether a candidate meets the basic requirements of the job

■ the hiring or selection interview, which is usually quick, efficient and low cost and looks at the short-listed candidates.

Organisations use a number of different interview types. Face-to-face interviews are popular with many organisations, as these give interested people in the organisation a chance to meet qualified candidates and the candidates get a taste of the organisation. Many people believe that face-to-face interviews are rather like beauty contests: if the applicant likes the organisation and the organisation likes the candidate then a successful 'marriage' can be achieved. Interviewers can be seen as the organisation's gatekeepers: they are there to ensure that the candidates have the kind of attitudes, experience and characteristics that the organisation feels comfortable with.

 Link

See pages 248–252 where face-to face interviews are discussed in more detail.

Telephone interviews are often used for initial screening as they are a fast and cost-efficient way of reducing a long list of applicants. They can help the interviewer and candidate decide if the application is worth pursuing.

Computer interviews are becoming more common. The applicant is asked to answer a series of multiple-choice questions or is required to fill in a brief résumé (CV), online.

Organisations also use assessment websites, particularly if they are looking for individuals with keyboard and mouse skills. Responses can be timed and an assessment can be made as to the candidate's computer proficiency.

Videophone and videoconferencing interviews are becoming more popular. These are convenient because they reduce the need to have key personnel available in a single location for the interview process. Video interviews can take place as long as there is compatible software, a camera and a microphone, which means that potential applicants could be interviewed in their own homes.

Face-to-face selection interviews are the most traditional way of assessing potential candidates. There are various types of face-to-face interviews, including one-to-one, serial, sequential, panel and group interviews. Table 13.4 describes the various types.

Table 13.4 Types of interview

Face-to-face interview type	How it works
One-to-one	A single, senior individual in the organisation personally interviews every candidate, giving each a unique interview. It gives the employer a much better understanding of whether the candidate will fit into the organisation.
Serial	The candidates are passed from one interviewer to another interviewer throughout the course of the day. Specialist interviewers examine different aspects of the candidates' experience, personality and attributes. Gradually, the field of candidates is cut down until a final interview takes place at the end of the day.

Face-to-face interview type	How it works
Sequential	The candidates meet a number of times with one or more interviewers on a one-to-one basis. This process can happen over the course of several days or weeks. Each time, the interview is designed to enable candidates to learn more details about the position and move them progressively closer to the offer of a job.
Panel	A committee or panel of interviewers is assembled and candidates are evaluated on interpersonal skills, qualifications and their ability to think on their feet. This can be one of the most intimidating of all interview types.
Group	Several candidates are interviewed at the same time. The idea is to find out about a candidate's leadership potential and style, and the strength of their argument and persuasion skills. Candidates may also be required to solve problems together and will be observed doing so.

Tasks and tests

Organisations assess applicants in many ways: application forms, letters of application, interviews and group discussions, written tests and practical tasks. Psychometric testing is becoming increasingly popular. Psychometric tests are designed to measure mental characteristics; they enable attributes to be assessed in a reliable way. Scoring is standardised, which allows the organisation to compare applicants' performance. Many tests can be administered by computer.

Aptitude, ability and intelligence tests tend to have similar characteristics:

■ The tests are administered under timed examination conditions.

■ Test items often take the form of multiple-choice questions, where the testee has to select the right answer from the options given.

■ Test items tend to become increasingly difficult as the test progresses.

■ Applicants are not necessarily required to complete the entire test. An applicant's score relates to their performance compared with that of individuals with the same levels of aptitude, ability and intelligence.

■ The score can be used in a number of different ways. Some tests have a pass mark and, if that mark is achieved, the candidate is automatically offered a job. Alternatively, individuals with marks in certain bands are offered interviews.

Aptitude tests and intelligence tests measure an individual's aptitude for learning and ability to think logically. Some items are in the form of multiple-choice questions; others are simple maths or word puzzles, and others are designed primarily to test language skills. Many of the items designed to test logical reasoning use images or numbers rather than words.

Some psychometric tests assess personality; personality questionnaires are designed to see how the candidate responds to others and how they might react in stressful situations. Questions do not have right or wrong answers; there are, however, trick questions, or repeated questions, put in to identify whether the applicant is lying. The results are usually presented in the form of a personality profile.

Go to the BBC website and find the science section; there is a personality and individuality test, which will assign one of 16 possible personality types to you
www.bbc.co.uk

Some organisations use occupational preference tests to examine work interests, motivation and personality. The tests are designed to be integrated career developers; careers advisors in schools or colleges usually offer students the opportunity to complete one. The test assesses the individual's primary work interests, other interests and facets of their personality and matches these with job types that would suit them.

Specialists in the interview

During the interview, the applicant should be questioned in such a way as to reveal additional information to aid the selection process. The composition of the interview panel is therefore of prime importance. Normally, an organisation chooses a representative from the department or area in which the potential candidate would work, perhaps a peer or manager. A representative of the management and one from human resources usually make up the remainder of the interviewing panel.

It is particularly important in cases where a degree of technical knowledge or skills is required that a practising specialist is asked to take part in the interviewing process. The specialist will be able to ask specific questions, the scope of which may be beyond the other interviewers, to reveal the depth of the applicants' knowledge and understanding and will be able to make an informed judgement as to their abilities and skills.

It is normal practice for the interviewers to have equal status on the interviewing panel. Different panel members handle particular lines of questioning. The representative from the human resources department is there to answer specific questions about contracts and pay scales, for example, whilst specialist individuals can ask and answer questions regarding procedures.

Interview questions

The interview is essentially an information-gathering exercise for both the panel and the applicant. The applicant will be expected to provide full answers and express opinions if required.

There are four major categories of question:

- Trust questions – these will show the interviewer if the candidate has faith in their own abilities and enable the interviewer to check if that confidence is justified.
- Clarifying questions – the interviewer asks a subsidiary question on something that the applicant has given only a basic answer to so far.
- Empathising questions – these are designed to deal with any possible problems or concerns.
- Open questions – these do not necessarily have a right or wrong answer and are used to give the applicant the opportunity to reflect and answer in depth.

There are four other types of question that are slightly more difficult for the interviewee to cope with:

- Criticisms – the interviewer expresses some doubt as to the applicant's experience or ability to do the job. The applicant's response will be judged on how well it shows that the criticism is unfounded.
- Testing – the interviewer will try to discover whether the interviewee is capable of making a right or wrong decision in a certain situation. It is difficult for the interviewee to guess what the correct answer may be, but a clear response is always a good one, regardless of whether the answer given is right or wrong.
- Leading – this type of question attempts to get the applicant to respond in a manner that the interviewer expects. It might, for example, be framed as 'You do agree with this don't you?' The applicant has to decide if the interviewer is trying to trap them.
- Closed – these will elicit simple, quick responses. Answers are most likely to be yes and no, but dates, times or other straightforward responses may be required. There is no room for elaboration.

Informing candidates

Deciding exactly when to tell interviewees whether or not they have been successful can be a problem. Timing also depends on whether the interviews were for a single post or for multiple positions.

Certainly, the interview panel should not tell an applicant that they have or have not been successful until after all the applicants have been interviewed. Sometimes all applicants are asked to wait until all of the interviews have taken place and are then informed there and then before they return home. Other organisations prefer to allow the applicant to leave with

remember

Neither very short, vague answers nor long, rambling ones are likely to create a good impression.

Fig 13.8 For an employer it is always advisable to ensure that the successful candidate is happy to take the job before informing unsuccessful candidates

the promise of a telephone call either later in the day or on the following day. Organisations may also opt not to contact any of the interviewees by telephone, but to inform them by post or email.

A major difficulty arises when a successful candidate is offered the job and declines it. If the unsuccessful candidates have already been contacted, there is no going back and the recruitment and selection process will have to start again from scratch.

Normally, the organisation will have identified their ideal candidate and, perhaps, have a backup candidate in mind. First, the organisation will make sure that their preferred candidate still wants the job. If they answer positively and start dates are discussed, the unsuccessful candidates can be informed. If the preferred candidate is unsure or turns down the post, the next-best choice can be contacted.

case study 13.9 | Working for Morrisons

It was in 1899 that egg and butter merchant William Morrison, the father of the current Chairman, Sir Ken Morrison, began work to create the company we know today. From a stall in a Bradford market came the inspiration to innovate and lead the way in supermarket retailing.

There are currently more than 360 Morrisons stores across the country, welcoming around 10 million shoppers each week. The company currently employs more than 130,000 members of staff in stores, factories, and distribution centres and head office administrative functions.

The company has a vacancy for a POS (point of sale) Trainee based at Hilmore House, Gain Lane, Bradford, as can be seen in the following advertisement.

(Adapted from www.morrisons.co.uk)

Fig 13.9 Morrisons job advert

(Source: www.morrisons.co.uk)

Marketing
Opportunities...

POS Trainee
Hilmore House, Gain Lane

Based within the Marketing department, the Point Of Sale (POS) team is now recruiting for a Trainee to provide support to the team. If you love process, can juggle multiple tasks and have a "hands on" approach then this is the role for you. Reporting to the Seasonal and Themed POS Manager, your main responsibility will be to support the team and help with the specifying, ordering and delivery of signage to stores.

Your day to day duties will include contact with internal departments and external suppliers to ensure the order process remains on track, specifying store POS requirements for revamps and placing orders. You will also handle store queries and one off POS requests and assist with competitor reviews and information gathering for new initiatives as required.

Attention to detail, accuracy and IT literacy is also essential as you will be using an in-house system to gather information. Previous retail experience is desirable, though not essential.

Experience gained within this role will result in an opportunity to develop your skills further and evolve within the team. Full training will be provided but to succeed you will need excellent communication skills and an organised, methodical approach in order to prioritise and complete your work to meet tight deadlines.

Working hours are 8.15am-6pm, Monday to Friday and you will be asked to visit our stores as part of this role. If you are ambitious, keen to develop and have a proactive approach to your work, and you're now ready for a new challenge, then we want to hear from you.

We offer an excellent benefits package, including competitive salary, pension scheme*, free life assurance*, annual profit share*, subsidised canteen and staff discount (*after qualifying period).

If you are interested in facing a new challenge and have the skills to strengthen our team further, then we want to hear from you. To apply please email your details to jobs@morrisonsplc.co.uk or download and complete our Application Form and Health Questionnaire quoting the following reference: JAM-POSP.

More reasons to work at

Fig 13.10 Morrisons job application form

(Source: www.morrisons.co.uk)

Thank you for applying to us for employment.

The information you are asked to provide will be used to assess your suitability for the position for which you are applying. All information will be treated in the strictest confidence.

Please ensure that you complete all sections of the application form in full, if you need any help completing the form, or you require the form in an alternative format, please contact the Personnel Department at the store/site of interest.

Personal Details

Title (Mr, Mrs, Miss etc.)	Address
First Name(s)	
Surname/Family Name	
Tel No. (incl. std code)	Post Code
Mobile No.	Email address

Are you over 18? Y N   If no, provide date of birth D D M M Y Y Y Y   Have you completed this form yourself? Y N

Emergency Contact Details

Contact Name	Address
Relationship to you	
Tel No. (incl. std code)	
Mobile No.	Post Code

Vacancy Details

Position applied for:

If you are not applying for a specific vacancy, what type of work are you looking for?

Where did you find out about the vacancy? e.g. in store, newspaper advert, job centre, other (please state)

Which location/store is of interest?

Are there any other locations you would consider?

Would you be willing to relocate? (Management only)   Yes ☐ No ☐

If yes, please give details:

Do you hold a valid full clean driving licence? Yes ☐ No ☐   OR   No driving licence ☐

If no state endorsements and dates _____

Education

Please detail any qualifications relevant to the position you have applied for or that you would like us to be aware of:

Qualification(s)	School/College/University

Additional Qualifications/Memberships/Licences

Please detail any qualifications or memberships to professional organisations/bodies relevant to the position you have applied for e.g. LGV C+E, First Aid, Fork Lift Truck, British Pharmaceutical Society. Pharmacy/Medical Professionals please provide registration number.

Qualification/Membership/Reg. No.	Organisation	Date Awarded

Current/Most Recent Employment Details

Full name and address of employer	Outline the nature of your job and your responsibilities

Job Title	Date from to	Notice period required
Annual Salary/Hourly Rate	Additional Benefits:	

Reason for leaving:

Previous Employment

Full name and address of employer	Outline the nature of your job and your responsibilities

Job Title	Date from to
Annual Salary/Hourly Rate	Reason for leaving:

Full name and address of employer	Outline the nature of your job and your responsibilities

Job Title	Date from to
Annual Salary/Hourly Rate	Reason for leaving:

Full name and address of employer	Outline the nature of your job and your responsibilities

Job Title	Date from to
Annual Salary/Hourly Rate	Reason for leaving:

Please provide dates and reasons of any periods of absence (excluding holidays) from your employment in the last two years lasting longer than two weeks: (if necessary attach additional sheet)

Asylum & Immigration Act 1996

Under the Asylum and Immigration Act 1996, you are required to provide evidence of your right to work in the UK, if called for an interview you will be advised of the documents you will need to provide which will then be checked to ensure the company complies with current legislation

If you have a National Insurance number please write it here:

Rehabilitation of Offenders

Have you been convicted of a criminal offence which is not spent under the Rehabilitation of Offenders Act 1974.

Please tick   Yes ☐   No ☐

If yes, please provide details:

Equal Opportunity Monitoring

As an equal opportunities employer the following information is for monitoring purposes only, and is not part of the selection criteria. Ethnic origin questions are about colour and broad ethnic groups. Regardless of your nationality, place of birth or citizenship, you can belong to any of the groups indicated. Describe your race or cultural origin by **CHOOSING ONE SECTION FROM A TO E,** then tick the appropriate box to indicate your cultural background.

WHITE: A1 White British ☐   A5 White Irish ☐

A0 Any other White background, please state:

MIXED: B1 Mixed White & Black Caribbean ☐   B2 Mixed White & Black African ☐

             B3 Mixed White & Asian ☐

B0 Any other Mixed background, please state:

ASIAN: C1 Asian Indian ☐   C2 Asian Pakistani ☐

             C3 Asian Bangladeshi ☐

C0 Any other Asian background, please state:

BLACK: D1 Black Caribbean ☐   D2 Black African ☐

D0 Any other Black background, please state:

CHINESE or OTHER: E1 Chinese ☐

E0 Any other background, please state:

As a ⚫ symbol user we guarantee to interview all disabled applicants who meet the minimum criteria

Please tick if you are disabled   ☐

We're supporting
AGE POSI+IVE

Data Protection

Upon receipt of your application form, Morrisons will be the Data Controller of your personal data. Morrisons will hold all the information you have given on this application form for legal requirements and for the purposes of personnel administration and statistical analysis.

Your information will be held on a manual file and will also be entered in its current or altered format onto the company's computerised database. No information may be passed onto a third party unless contracted to Morrisons for specific employment services without your express agreement unless required by law.

Your signature below indicates your agreement to the above.

Declaration

I declare that the information given on this application form is, to my knowledge, true. I understand that if it is subsequently discovered that any statement is false or misleading, my offer of employment may be withdrawn or I may be dismissed from my employment by the company without notice. I also agree to a medical examination if required.

If I take up employment I understand it may be necessary for security purposes for Morrisons to carry out a credit reference check on Senior and Duty Management, all Cash Office employees, Warehouse, Petrol and Pharmacy Management, Checkout Manager and Security and Central Salaried Personnel

Please tick here if you have any objection to such a check being undertaken. ☐

It must be understood that for certain jobs, a refusal may preclude an offer of employment being made

At any time after employment has commenced the Company may require the provision of a Subject Access Report for certain positions. Failure to provide this document or if the Subject Access Report is deemed to be unacceptable we reserve the right to terminate your employment. It is the Company's sole right to determine if the information provided is unacceptable.

Please tick here ☐ if you have any objections about obtaining this report.

Signed:

Date: D D   M M   Y Y Y Y

Location issued:

Return to: Closing Date:

References

Please note that **EMPLOYMENT REFERENCES** will be sought from your last employer, and after acceptance of employment also from your current employer. Where there are no relevant employment referees, you must provide **two personal referees**. These should not be relatives, but could be a school/college tutor or other professional person.

Name	Name
Address	Address
Post Code	Post Code
Profession	Profession
How long have you known this person?	How long have you known this person?

The company retains the right to withdraw the offer of employment or terminate the contract of employment should unacceptable references be received. Completion of this application form will be taken as your consent to apply for references.

Availability

Please indicate what type of employment you would prefer (please tick appropriate boxes):

Management ☐   Permanent ☐   Temporary ☐   Full time ☐   Part time ☐

For part time only, what is the minimum and maximum number of hours you are willing to work per week?   Min ☐   Max ☐

Please indicate any day/times you are unable to attend an interview:
Please give the dates of any holidays or appointments booked in the next 6 months:
Please tell us of any specific details regarding your availability to work:

Applying for a position in a store

Full time appointments (39 hours or more) are fully flexible positions and include working evenings and weekends. For part time positions only (8-30 hours) please indicate in the applicable boxes the times you are available to work.

	MON	TUES	WEDS	THURS	FRI	SAT	SUN
EARLY MORNINGS (e.g. starting from 6am)	☐	☐	☐	☐	☐	☐	☐
MORNINGS (e.g. after 8am)	☐	☐	☐	☐	☐	☐	☐
AFTERNOONS (e.g. from midday to 4pm)	☐	☐	☐	☐	☐	☐	☐
EVENINGS (e.g. from 4pm to 10pm)	☐	☐	☐	☐	☐	☐	☐
NIGHTS (e.g. from 10pm to 7am)	☐	☐	☐	☐	☐	☐	☐

Offer Details (Internal use only)   **Checks: References** ☐ **M Check** ☐   **Administrator Name:** _____ Date _____

Position: _____   **Induction Location:** _____

Department: _____   **Start Date/Time:** _____

Location: _____   **Salary/Rate of Pay:** _____

Contract Hours: _____

Status F/T: P/T: Temporary

Part Time positions indicate weekly schedule:

☐ Mon   ☐ Tues   ☐ Wed   ☐ Thurs   ☐ Fri   ☐ Sat   ☐ Sun

Wm Morrison Supermarkets Plc
Hilmore House
Gain Lane
Bradford BD37DL

More reasons to work at   (M) MORRISONS
www.morrisons.co.uk

activity

1   Read the case study and job application form.

2   Check that you have available the factual information that you will need to complete the application form.

---

activity

INDIVIDUAL WORK
13.3

P3

Using Case study 13.9 as a guide, you must now follow through the application process for the vacancy.

You can fill in (or download) a copy of the application form via the Morrisons website or take a photocopy of the one included in this activity.

1   Complete the application form with your real details.

2   Complete a full curriculum vitae to accompany the application form.

3   Submit a typed covering letter to accompany the two other documents.

(You must complete all of the forms, even if this means duplication, so make sure that you have an application form, a curriculum vitae and a covering letter.)

---

activity

INDIVIDUAL WORK
13.4

M1

As a follow up activity to P3, you will now compare the purposes of the different documents used in the selection process of a given organisation.

1   Identify all of the key documents that are used by businesses and candidates in the recruitment process (letter of application, application form and curriculum vitae).

2   Explain the purposes of these documents.

3   Explain how interviewers might use these documents.

Interview

In this section of the unit, we will look at the specifics of an interview. The organisation will almost certainly have allowed those on the interview panel to meet beforehand to frame the nature of the interviews. There will be a set of agreed questions, and each interviewer will probably be given a checklist. Each member of the interview panel is likely to be assigned a specific line of questioning so that they can find out more about particular attributes and behaviours and clarify the information in the application documents. Many interview panels have a chairperson to control the direction of the interview and to make sure that it does not overrun the allotted time.

Interview protocol

There are usually three main sections to an interview:

- activities carried out by the interview panel prior to the interview
- behaviour, processes and procedures during the interview
- procedures and processes after the interview.

Prior to the interview, the panel will usually have carried out the following:

- They will have identified each interviewee and made note of essential background information on each of them.
- Arising out of this they will have designed a set of interview questions tailored to the interviewees and the post.
- They will have confirmed the date and time of the interview.

During the interview, they will ask the identified questions, take notes and ensure that they are clear about the candidate's abilities and qualities and have no unanswered questions.

After the interview, the panel will meet, exchange notes, possibly compare the candidates with the essential and desired checklist and finally reach mutual agreement as to the best candidate. Then the successful interviewee will be contacted to arrange a start date and induction.

Confidentiality

In line with the requirements of the Data Protection Act 1998, potential employers must ensure that any personal information to which the organisation has access is used only for the specific purpose for which it was collected.

Unless otherwise agreed by applicants, any unsuccessful candidates' information should be destroyed or returned to them.

Not only will the interview panel have access to addresses and telephone numbers, but they will also be aware of private personal circumstances, as well as pay and salary details. Private information to which the interview panel has access is not for general circulation within the organisation.

Fairness

In order to ensure fairness and equality of opportunity, some organisations make sure that their interviews follow exactly the same format. This means that the following steps are taken:

- Applicants are given the opportunity to state when they are available for interview.
- Applicants have their expenses paid.
- Applicants are given the same amount of interview time and are interviewed by the same panel of interviewers.
- Applicants are asked exactly the same questions and are given an opportunity to ask questions themselves.
- The full process is transparent and open to the applicants, and they are assured that decisions will not be made without due regard to their skills, aptitudes and experience.

Interview environment

In many cases, selection interviews can appear confrontational. One or more interviewers sit behind a desk with prepared papers and control the situation. The interviewee sits on a chair in front of the panel and expects to have questions thrown at them.

Some organisations prefer to maintain this kind of interview environment, as it puts the applicants under pressure and gives the interviewers an opportunity to see how the applicant behaves in a stressful situation. Whether this gives a true reflection of the applicant's attitude and behaviour is questionable.

Other organisations try to put applicants at their ease so that both the panel and the interviewee can get the most out of the situation and have a fairer opportunity to put their views across.

The way in which the interview environment is set up will very much depend upon the way in which the interview process has been arranged. Formal interviews require rooms to be set up in advance, whereas informal interviews can take place in offices. If group interviews are to be undertaken, larger rooms will have to be prepared.

Agreed questions

The panel will have established precisely what they wish to discover about the applicants. Typically, applicants will be asked why they have applied for the job, what interests them in this line of work and how the job fits with their career aspirations.

The panel will want to investigate any aspects of the applicant's documentation that are unclear or contradictory. Their main focus will be on ascertaining whether the applicant has all of the essential skills and attributes for the post.

Checking personal information

Ideally, much of this will have been done before the interview. If there are discrepancies in the curriculum vitae or application form then the applicant will have been contacted or previous employers and/or schools and colleges will have been checked to confirm what has been written.

If there are any remaining uncertainties about the personal information, the interview will be the panel's last opportunity to clarify matters.

Interview checklist

The interview checklist is likely to be extensive; it is usually split into several different sections, the first of which is the preparation for the interview itself:

■ setting up a strategy with the panel members for how the interviews are to be conducted

■ preparing questions and tasks

■ assessing how long it takes for a candidate to answer questions

■ creating a core selection of identical questions for each candidate

■ minimising the number of questions so that some can be used for deeper discussions.

During the interview, the following should be taken into account:

■ putting the candidates at ease with appropriate seating, lighting and refreshment arrangements

■ asking questions to confirm the panel's impression of the candidate

■ allowing silences to see what the candidate has to say

■ using waiting time as an opportunity to check the candidates' literacy

■ using waiting time to ask candidates to make some simple calculations to check numeracy.

Typical interview questions would include the following:

■ Why did you choose this job/company?

■ Why would you like to work here?

■ What have you learned about the organisation?

■ Why did you leave (or why are you considering leaving) your current position?

■ Will you be prepared to carry out flexible work if necessary?

■ Have you worked in a diverse environment before?

■ What challenges do you expect this job role to offer?

■ What are your attitudes to job training, appraisal and evaluation?

■ What are your career goals and ambitions?

Once the interview is over, the panel will have to decide if any of the applicants are suitable. Key considerations will include:

■ how the candidates presented themselves

■ their manner, openness and tone

■ how they handled the stress of the interview situation

■ whether their verbal answers matched their application form

■ how well they match the requirements of the job and person specification

■ whether the panel is happy with the references or other factual information.

Control of interview

Usually, in the case of panels, one of the interviewers is given the role of chairperson. It is that person's responsibility to ensure that the applicants are all treated in the same manner and are given an equal opportunity to answer questions and impress the panel.

When a number of interviews are undertaken during the day, strict timing is essential to ensure that candidates later in the interviewing schedule do not have to wait for their interview longer than is reasonable. Any delay would be likely to increase the stress they feel.

Normally, an interview takes the form of brief introductions to the panel, followed by a series of questions, including those from specialists. Towards the end of the interview, assuming that there is sufficient time, the applicant is given an opportunity to ask questions. The type of questions asked by the candidate can be as revealing as their answers to the questions posed by the panel.

Decision criteria and documentation

The interview panel will have been working on the assumption that all of the applicants match, to a greater or lesser extent, the person specification. However, candidates will not perform equally well at interview, even if they are of similar age and background. Some will come across even better in person than on paper, whilst others who appeared good on paper will be hesitating and halting in interview.

Normally, key criteria, such as abilities, aptitude and experience, will be noted on an interview checklist, and an on-the-spot assessment will be made by each of the panel members. The panel members will also make notes as to the suitability of candidates as they see them throughout the day, and each will have their own views as to the suitability of the candidates.

Discussion as to how well the candidates match the essential and desirable abilities and aptitudes required for the job will be informed by the panel members' impressions of how well each candidate performed in the interview room. The aim is to reach a majority decision as to the most ideal candidate.

Communicating to candidates

The application pack may have contained information as to when the decision to appoint is likely to be made. If this was not the case, the interview panel will tell each applicant when to expect the decision.

As we have already seen, once the best candidate has been selected, that individual should be contacted promptly and asked about their impressions of the interview and the job on offer. It is possible that they may have changed their mind about the job and, having experienced a taste of the organisation through the interview process, they may no longer wish to work for it. It is likely that many of the candidates have also applied for other jobs, so in order for a particular organisation to get the best candidate it must make a positive decision at the earliest possible point.

In many cases, unsuccessful candidates will ask for feedback and may wish to know what part of their application, qualifications, experience or performance at interview ruled them out of consideration for the vacancy. The organisation should respond to such a request from candidates who were interviewed but is not expected to do so if the request comes from an applicant who did not reach the shortlist.

Communication and listening skills

It is important that the candidates understand any instructions or communication from the interviewers. Interviewers must always appear professional and must be clear and concise in what they say; they must also listen carefully. The panel will have a list of questions to cover during the interview but should not simply gallop through all of the areas of investigation with each applicant. A strong measure of the applicant's abilities will be found in their responses to questions. It is therefore important for the interview panel to have good listening skills. They should also be able to cut tactfully through any candidates' responses that are long-winded and do not address the point.

Body language

The interview panel will be looking to use and read candidates' body language. However, not only is the applicant's non-verbal communication revealing but body language can also give much away about the interview panel. At all times, the interview panel should:

■ not fidget or appear bored
■ not exhibit distracting mannerisms or inappropriate gestures
■ use appropriate facial expressions.

Fig 13.11 Body language can reveal aspects of a candidate's personality they would rather not have portrayed

The reading of body language requires a great deal of experience. Candidates cannot always be expected to understand non-verbal messages put out by the interview panel.

In general, the following basic principles are useful:

- Always try to read body language in the light of what the speaker is actually saying, as what the speaker is actually saying and doing can give clues.
- When an individual avoids eye contact, they may not actually mean what they are saying or be saying it with any conviction.
- Complex, multiple or groups of body language signs may be very difficult to interpret.

Questioning techniques

Some golden rules when asking questions during the interview are:

- Ask open questions that require the applicant to give more than a simple yes or no response. Open questions will reveal much more about the applicant.
- Use silence as a means of getting more out of the applicant. They will seek to fill the silence.
- Do not speak for more than 30% of the interview time.
- Be flexible; even if the interviewers have a set of prepared questions, they should not stick to them if circumstances suggest otherwise.
- Take notes but do not be so interested in getting things down on paper that it is at the expense of listening to the applicant.
- Make sure that if the candidate were offered the job they would accept it.
- Ask the candidate to give some feedback on the whole of the recruitment and selection process.

> **remember**
>
> It is important to ensure that the candidate is comfortable and has understood what has been asked of them.

Barriers to communication

It is important to remember that any interview is a stressful experience for the interviewee. They will be nervous, keen to impress and may make mistakes. The interview process is not designed to humiliate candidates, but rather to draw out information from them and assist them to display the skills and aptitudes that the interview panel is looking for. A bombardment of questions may well be one of the greatest barriers to communication in an interview, as it places undue pressure on the interviewee.

Jargon, complex terms, and unfounded expectations about the candidates' familiarity with specific organisational policies and procedures are all possible barriers. Interviewers should always be prepared to re-state a question in a different way if the candidate is struggling to understand.

Analysing and summarising

Throughout the course of the interview, the interviewers will examine specific aspects that they deem important, particularly if there are discrepancies between what an applicant claims and the level of understanding that they display in the interview. Follow-up questions give applicants an opportunity to flesh out answers and assist analysis.

Summarising can either bring to an end a particular aspect of the interview or the interview itself. The chairperson makes a summation of the interview conversation, giving the candidate an opportunity to respond to a précis version of events or comments and correct any misunderstandings.

> **remember**
>
> If it is possible, try to be both an interviewer and an interviewee in mock selection interviews. This will give you the most experience and the chance to collect together the maximum amount of documentation.

case study 13.10   Interviews

The structure of interviews should be decided in advance. The chair of the panel will agree and record with the appointments panel a format for the interview. This format should include:

- a welcome by the chairperson
- an introduction to the panel members
- a brief explanation of the interview format

■ a questioning session with reference to the person specification for the post

■ a section where candidates are offered the opportunity to ask any questions.

The questioning areas to be explored by each panel member should be decided by reference to the person specification for the post. The same areas of questioning should be covered with all candidates and assumptions should not be made regarding the expertise or abilities of candidates because of their employment history. Interview questions should be phrased so that they do not favour any one candidate. Supplementary questions should be used to probe for further information or clarification where answers are incomplete or ambiguous. Care must be taken to avoid questions that could be construed as discriminatory, for example questions about personal circumstances that are unrelated to the job. It is, for example, legitimate to ask for confirmation of whether individuals can comply with the working patterns of the post but not to ask details of their domestic or child care arrangements, etc. It is the responsibility of the chair of the panel to ensure that such questions are not asked.

Where a candidate being interviewed has a disability for which adjustments may need to be considered, the candidate's requirements should be discussed with him/her once the planned questioning is complete. The outcome of these discussions must not influence the consideration of the candidate's application.

Appointments panels act for the business in making selection decisions and are accountable for them. Interview notes must be taken to help the panel to make an informed decision based on the content of the interview. Such notes must relate to how candidates demonstrate their education knowledge, skills and experience in relation to the person specification. The Data Protection Act allows applicants to request disclosure of such notes in the event of a complaint and an employment tribunal would expect the business to have notes of every selection decision. The lack of such notes would seriously impede the business's ability to contest such a complaint. Any inappropriate or personally derogatory comments contained within the notes could be considered discriminatory and are unacceptable.

It is good practice to offer internal candidates feedback after interviews. Feedback should be specific, relating to the person specification, and honest.

(Adapted from www.iop.kcl.ac.uk)

activity

1 Imagine that you are an interviewer; using the information in this case study, make a list of items that you will need to prepare for the interview.

2 Imagine that you are an interviewee, make a list of items that you will need to prepare for the interview.

activity

INDIVIDUAL WORK
13.5

P4

You will be assigned the role of either an interviewer or an interviewee and will participate in a mock selection interview for the post of Point of Sales Trainee. Use Case study 13.10 for guidance on either dealing with or running an interview panel. You should also use the work that you carried out for P3 as the basis for the mock interview.

As interviewer or interviewee you must demonstrate that you have:

1 Prepared for the interview

2 Completed any required documents

3 Read any subsidiary information (in the form of the two case studies and any other additional information)

4 Taken part in the interview process, either as an interviewer or an interviewee, taking appropriate notes and contributing fully to the situation. (You may be required to undertake both roles at different times.)

You should expect the evidence for P4 to be generated by a recording of your performance supported by observational records compiled by other students and witness statements completed by your teacher/tutor.

activity

INDIVIDUAL WORK
13.6

D1

Evaluate the usefulness of the documents that you have either prepared or had submitted to you during the interview process. (This is a follow-up exercise to the interview role-play.) You should answer the following:

1   What was the benefit of having the information presented in a standardised format?

2   Did the process enable you to make objective decisions based on a combination of the documented information and the performance of the candidates?

Post interview

There are a number of timing issues to consider in relation to the post-interview period. As we have already seen, the organisation will have informed candidates of the possible timescale for notifying them of the decision.

The post-interview period is really the last chance that the representatives of the organisation have to decide if they have selected the right candidate for the job. Once the panel members begin contacting candidates, there is no going back.

Informing candidates

The exact point at which the candidates are informed of the interviewer's (or panel's) decision will depend upon when in the recruitment and selection process references have been obtained. References may have been taken up at the short-listing stage; however, many candidates are reluctant for potential employers to contact their existing employers, as they do not wish them to know that they are seeking alternative employment. This may mean that a decision has to be made to offer one of the candidates the job subject to acceptable references.

Each of the candidates will have been informed that this is the case and that the references will be dealt with post-interview. It is probable that the organisation will seek references for both their ideal candidate and a backup candidate. Assuming that the references are acceptable then the next stage would normally be to make a job offer to the ideal candidate.

Making job offers and contents of job offer

Essentially there are two ways in which an organisation can make a job offer: verbally or non-verbally. Verbal job offers include face-to-face offers and offers made over the telephone. Non-verbal offers tend to be in the form of letters, emails or faxes. Very often a verbal job offer is followed by written confirmation.

The contents of the job offer should include the following:

■ Start date – this is a date, mutually agreed by the organisation and the successful candidate, that takes into account any notice period the candidate may have to work for their existing employer or the end of an educational course.

■ Wage or salary rate – this is negotiable between the candidate and the organisation, based on the candidate's educational ability and previous experience.

■ Hours of work – these will probably be standardised, but the candidate may be required to work unsocial hours or to accept shift work or overtime should the circumstances arise.

■ Holiday entitlements – the organisation will usually have a formula by which it works out an individual's holiday entitlements, i.e. the number of paid days off each year. Holiday entitlement will usually increase each year that the employee works for the organisation. To begin with, it may be a statutory minimum plus bank holidays.

Other conditions and considerations

We have already looked at the question of taking up references at this late stage of the recruitment and selection process. If the references obtained are poor, the entire selection process may be derailed.

Some organisations ask candidate to complete an initial recruitment test.

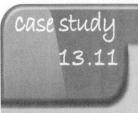

case study 13.11

Police Initial Recruitment (PIR) Test

Numerical test

Will last 12 minutes

There is a total of 25 numerical questions to answer

You will have five answers to choose from

Calculators are not allowed

Fig 13.12

Verbal logical reasoning test

Will last 25minutes

There is a total of 31 questions to answer

You will be given a situation and some facts about it

You will then be given some statements relating to it and you must decide if they are true, false or impossible to say given the information provided

You should only go by the information given in the passage, not any additional knowledge you may have about the situation

Four interactive role plays

Four interactive role play exercises

Lasting 10 minutes each

Five minutes to prepare

Five minutes to role play

Full instructions will be given before completing the exercise

Two written exercises

Lasting 20 minutes each

Full instruction will be given before completing the exercise

(Source: www.west-midlands.police.uk)

activity

1   Explain the purpose of the numerical test.
2   Why would verbal logical reasoning be important for jobs such as this?
3   Suggest a topic for one of the interactive role-play exercises.

Some organisations require new employees to undergo medical tests or have particular forms completed by their general practitioner. In some cases, a poor medical history can mean rejection at this stage.

In addition to medical checks, some organisations and professions require successful candidates to undergo police checks. For example, the police check that new teachers have not committed certain offences. If a candidate fails the check, the organisation is perfectly within its rights to reject the application, even at this late stage.

Some job offers may be contingent upon the candidate passing specific examinations with specific grades. (This is certainly the case for school and college leavers.) In other words, the organisation makes a conditional offer of employment. Once the results of examinations have been released either in the summer or in the spring of each year, a firm offer will be made.

Post interview is also the time for the organisation to accept and pay candidates' expense claims. Most organisations have specific forms for this purpose to which can be attached travel tickets or petrol receipts. These should be dealt with promptly and payment should be made at the earliest opportunity.

Many organisations feel that it is important to gauge the candidates' impressions of the recruitment and selection process. Unforeseen problems could have arisen which the organisation could take steps to prevent in future interviews.

case study 13.12

Fit for the police

If you get through to the final stage of becoming a police officer – all that remains to be done, is a test to see if you are fit enough!

There is no reason to fear the fitness test. From the date you requested your application form, you will have approximately 12 months before being called for a fitness test. So, if you feel you are not fit enough, you can do something about it now.

There are two parts to the fitness test:

Circuit

One lap of the circuit contains 8 activities

You must complete three laps of the circuit

You have 3 minutes and 45 seconds to complete the course

You must perform each activity safely

Push pull machine

Simulates struggling with an assailant

This test lasts 20 seconds

(Source: www.west-midlands.police.uk)

activity

1   If you were applying for the police force, what training would be required in order to pass this fitness test?

2   Why is the simulation of a struggle with an assailant included in this fitness test?

3   Explain why the police force or the armed forces would be exempt from having to consider disabled applicants.

Rejection of candidates

Even though unsuccessful candidates have been rejected as potential employees, they are still entitled to be shown common courtesy by the organisation. Many organisations do not respond to applications made by potential candidates who are not selected for interview. They do, however, tend to contact unsuccessful candidates who have been interviewed. But, unfortunately, many organisations simply send out duplicated rejection letters and ignore candidates' verbal requests at interview for feedback.

Although unsuccessful candidates may not have impressed the interviewers on this occasion, they could prove to be valuable to the organisation in the future. It is therefore advisable to couch rejection letters carefully, saying for example, 'On this occasion you have been unsuccessful', rather than send a blunter rejection. It is useful, both to the failed candidate and ultimately to the organisation, to identify why that applicant was not chosen. Therefore, feedback is valuable to both parties.

---

activity

INDIVIDUAL WORK 13.7

M2

Analyse your contribution to the selection process in a given situation. This is a follow-up activity that can be tackled along with D1 and P4. It relates to the work that you carried out when preparing for and performing during the mock interviews. You are required to:

1 Prepare an application pack for all the students who will take the role of interviewees during the role-play activity.

2 Prepare the documentation and completed application forms, curriculum vitae and covering letters so that they can be reviewed and used by the interview panel.

3 Prepare any forms, documents or other materials that the interview panel may need during the role-play.

4 During the interviews, demonstrate that you are well organised.

5 During the interviews, conduct yourself in a professional manner.

Observers will be looking for evidence of your preparation. A witness statement will support your evidence.

---

activity

INDIVIDUAL WORK 13.8

D2

Critically evaluate your experience of planning and participating in the recruitment and selection process by commenting on your performance in the role-play sessions. You should:

1 Evaluate your own experiences of the mock interviews.

2 Evaluate your contribution to the planning of the mock interviews.

3 Evaluate your own participation in general during the whole process.

The implications of the regulatory framework on the process of recruitment and selection

In this section of the unit we will look at the key regulations that relate directly to recruitment and selection.

 Link

See pages 272–283 in Unit 14 for a more complete explanation of the laws and of employer responsibilities.

Current UK and EU legislation

Organisations must adhere to a number of laws passed by the British parliament, the names of which tend to end in the word 'Act'. Other regulations and guidelines are derived from the European Union and are usually called directives. Businesses must treat legislation equally seriously, whether it emanated from Westminster or from Brussels.

Sex Discrimination Act 1995/97

The law covers a broad range of workers including contract workers. It applies regardless of length of service in employment or the numbers of hours worked. It allows for employees to take a case to an employment tribunal. If the case is successful, they will receive compensation for any financial loss they have suffered; an award for injury to feelings can also be made.

In terms of recruitment and selection, an organisation should not:

- appoint on the basis of gender
- appoint on the basis of marital status
- offer less favourable terms and conditions on the basis of gender
- appoint on the basis of sexual orientation.

There are what is known as genuine occupational qualifications, or GOQs. These can be applied by organisations when specific requirements can be proved to be necessary; circumstances in which GOQs apply include:

- physiology (e.g. using a male model to model men's clothes)
- privacy and decency (e.g. when clients of a particular gender need to be cared for by care assistants of that gender)
- where there is single-sex accommodation (e.g. for the crew of a submarine).

Fig 13.13 Legislation does not require employers under certain circumstances to have to offer the job to both genders

 Link   See page 279 in Unit 14 for details on the Sex Discrimination Act 1975.

Fig 13.14 Despite the Sex Discrimination Act and the Equal Opportunities Commission, some occupations are still considered to be 'women's jobs'

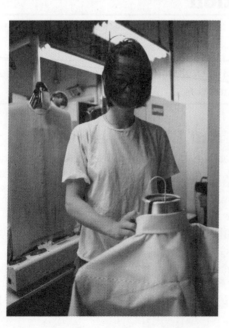

Visit the website of the Equal Opportunities Commission and check under 'relevant legislation' to find information about the Sex Discrimination Act

www.eoc.org.uk

Race Relations Act 1992

It is unlawful for a person, in relation to their employment at an establishment in Great Britain, to discriminate against another in any of the following ways:

■ in the arrangements they make for the purpose of determining who should be offered that employment

■ in the terms on which they offer the individual that employment

■ by refusing or deliberately omitting to offer the individual that employment.

Under this law, 'racial discrimination' means treating a person less favourably than others on racial grounds (i.e. race, colour, nationality or ethnic or national origins). The Act protects individuals against people's actions, not their opinions or beliefs.

Link

See page 281 in Unit 14 for more details on the Race Relations Act 1992.

case study 13.13

Veil row

A Muslim classroom assistant suspended by a school for wearing a veil in lessons lost her claim of religious discrimination at an employment tribunal in October 2006.

Aishah Azmi was asked to take off the veil after the Church of England school in Dewsbury, West Yorkshire, said pupils found it hard to understand her. The tribunal dismissed her claims of religious discrimination and harassment on religious grounds. Aishah Azmi was awarded £1,100 for victimisation.

The government's race minister, Phil Woolas, demanded that she should be sacked, accusing her of 'denying the right of children to a full education'.

Aishah Azmi said in response: 'Muslim women who wear the veils are not aliens, and politicians need to recognise that what they say can have a very dangerous impact on the lives of the minorities they treat as outcasts. I will continue to uphold my religious beliefs and urge Muslims to engage in dialogue with the wider community, despite the attacks that are being made upon them.'

Kirklees Council said the decision to suspend the teaching assistant was taken after a monitoring period in which the impact of wearing the veil on the teaching and learning was studied.

The council said: 'In this case the school and local authority had to balance the rights of the children to receive the best quality education possible and Mrs Azmi's desire to express her cultural beliefs by wearing a veil in class. The education of the children is of paramount importance and it is disappointing that the school was unable to reach a compromise with Mrs Azmi in this case.'

(Adapted from www.bbc.co.uk)

activity

1 In your opinion, which is more important; the religious beliefs of an employee or the rights of customers, clients or pupils?

2 Why do you think the classroom assistant lost her claim for religious discrimination?

Visit the website of the Equal Opportunities Commission and check under 'relevant legislation' to find information about the Race Relations Act

www.eoc.org.uk

Equal Pay Act 1970

Under this Act, every employment contract should include an 'equality clause' which guarantees both sexes the same money for doing the same or broadly similar work, or work rated as equivalent by a **job-evaluation** study.

The clause operates unless an employer can prove that pay variation between the sexes is reasonable and genuinely due to a material difference between their cases.

In 1983, the Equal Pay (Amendment) Regulations came into force. These give a person a right to claim equal pay for work of 'equal value' to that of a person of the other gender in the same employment, where there is no existing job-evaluation scheme, and where there is no person of the opposite sex engaged on 'like work'.

In terms of recruitment and selection, it is therefore illegal for an organisation to offer a job at a lower rate of pay to one gender when compared with a similar offer to a member of the other gender.

Visit the website of the Equal Opportunities Commission and check under 'relevant legislation' to find information about the Equal Pay Act

www.eoc.org.uk

See page 279 in Unit 14 for more information about the Equal Pay Act 1970.

Disability Discrimination Act 1995

The Disability Discrimination Act binds all employers during the recruitment and selection process. Many have demonstrated that they have a positive policy towards employing disabled people. Employers who encourage disabled applicants have a 'two ticks' disability symbol placed on their advertisements in Jobcentres. This means that the organisation has a commitment to employing disabled people and will guarantee them a job interview, provided that they meet the basic criteria of the person specification.

There are good reasons for an individual to declare their disability: under the Act employers are required to make reasonable adjustments to working conditions to enable disabled people to work for them. It is advisable for applicants to state their disability at the earliest possible stage, rather than wait for a medical questionnaire to be completed.

The Directgov website has a large amount of information regarding disabled people and work; type 'disability' into the search engine

www.directgov.co.uk.

See page 282 in Unit 14 for more information about the Disability Discrimination Act 1995.

European Working Time Directive

The aim of the European Working Time Directive is to prevent organisations from forcing their employees to work:

- excessively long hours
- without adequate rest
- disrupted work patterns.

When recruiting new members of staff, an organisation must comply with the directive. The application pack should make it clear that no potential employee is expected to:

- work longer than a 48-hour week
- work without a daily rest period in an 11-hour day
- work without half an hour's break if they work for 6 hours in one day.

In addition, it should be clear that employees:

- have a minimum one day of rest in a week
- are entitled to a minimum annual paid holiday of 4 weeks
- do not have to work at night for longer than 8 hours.

See pages 289–291 in Unit 14 for more information about the Employment Working Time Directive.

Employment Act 2002

This Act actually came into force in April 2003. It was designed to tidy up several other previous Employment Acts. In terms of recruitment and selection, the following areas were addressed in this Act:

- Maternity leave was increased from 18 to 26 weeks.
- Paternity rights were added, allowing a father to have 13 unpaid weeks of parental leave.
- Adoption leave was introduced up to 26 weeks.
- Employers would have to have a compulsory grievance and disciplinary procedure.
- A new, flexible working provision for individuals with care responsibilities was brought into force.

These changes mean that employers must take into account care responsibilities and freely offer leave where it is required. In addition, the flexible working provisions, which come into force after an employee has worked for an organisation for six months, are designed to help those with care responsibilities. Organisations can interpret flexible working as:

- a mutual change in working hours
- favourable consideration of requests to work at home
- favourable consideration of requests for staggered working hours
- favourable consideration of requests for flexitime
- accepting requests for time off in lieu
- organising job shares
- favourable consideration of shift work or shift swapping
- contracting the working year into term times.

The full Act can be found on the website of the Office of Public Sector Information; look for 'Acts' and the year '2002'

www.opsi.gov.uk

See page 278 in Unit 14 for more information about the Employment Act 2002.

National Minimum Wage Act 1998

The minimum wage is a legal right that covers nearly all employees above compulsory school leaving age. It sets the absolute minimum hourly rates for groups of employees in different age bands. As of October 2006, a 16–17 year old is to be paid a minimum of £3.30 an hour and employees over the age of 22 are to be paid £5.35 an hour.

In terms of recruitment and selection this means that employers would not be able to advertise vacancies attracting hourly rates of less than the minimum wage.

To find out more about the national minimum wage visit the website of HM Revenue and Customs

www.hmrc.gov.uk

See pages 282–283 in Unit 14 for more information about the national minimum wage.

Data Protection Act 1998

The basic principle behind the Data Protection Act 1998 is that anyone has the right to have access to information that is held about them by an organisation. The Act also governs exactly what type of personal information an organisation can hold, including how it acquires, stores, shares and disposes of it.

The Data Protection Act is relevant to recruitment and selection in the following ways:

- When a candidate makes an application for a job, they will be revealing personal information in their curriculum vitae, application form, letter of application and other documents. The organisation needs to be clear how this information will be used and who will see it.

- When an organisation makes checks on an applicant, it will acquire information from a third party. (Examples are personal information from referees, security or police checks and medical reports from doctors.)

- Decisions may be made as to the suitability of a candidate based on data acquired or held by the organisation.

- Certain health, education and social work records are exempt if the applicant wishes to see what an organisation holds on them.

- The organisation must ensure that the data held on an individual is accurate. Any incorrect data should be destroyed or erased; if, as a result of such data, a negative decision were to be made about an applicant, they could seek damages.

Any individual can write to the data controller at the organisation holding information on them. The organisation has 40 days to answer a request and can only turn down the request to see the information on two grounds, which are:

- In letting the individual see the information the organisation would be revealing information about someone else, or the source of that confidential information.

- Disclosing the information would stop the prevention or detection of a crime.

There is an enormous amount of information about the Data Protection Act on the website of the Information Commissioner's Office

www.ico.gov.uk

Ethical issues

Ethical issues in relation to recruitment and selection can really be reduced to a single word – objectivity. In this respect, all candidates should be given an equal opportunity to prove themselves as potential employees. In other words, having a baseline for questions and policies for dealing with potential employees can mean that ethically the organisation has done everything to ensure equality.

Asking candidates the same questions

Assuming that the interview panel has had the opportunity to prepare for the interviews, they will have been able to establish a series of basic questions that they intend to ask of all candidates. Provided that each of the candidates is interviewed for the same amount of time, the use of identical questions can not only help towards maintaining equality but can also enable useful comparisons between candidates to be made.

It is not always possible for the interview panel to control the situation entirely: candidates may give longer or shorter answers to questions; or certain aspects of an individual candidate's application may need specific examination.

Relationship to candidates

If there is a blood relationship or a close friendship between one of the interviewers and a candidate, this should be admitted at the earliest possible opportunity. The panel member in question could either be replaced or would not take an active role in the decision-making process when the successful candidate is chosen.

In many cases application forms have a section that asks the candidate to state whether they know someone who works for the organisation. Having knowledge of any such relationship at this early stage of the selection process makes it less likely that a member of the interview panel will have to be replaced.

Gender and ethnic balance on panels

As far as is practicable the interview panel should reflect the gender and ethnic balance of the organisation. In general, interview panels should not be single gender (i.e. all male or all female), and the panel should not ask about:

- marital status or intentions to marry
- childcare arrangements or the intention to have children
- religion, political affiliation or trade union membership
- sexual orientation or disability.

Most potential problems can be avoided if the chairperson of the panel has undergone training in how to conduct selection interviews and has a thorough understanding of responsibilities in terms of equal opportunity matters. The panel as a whole has a collective responsibility to ensure best practice.

---

activity

INDIVIDUAL WORK 13.9

P5

You should prepare a document, brochure or leaflet that could be distributed to the members of a selection or interview panel to help them follow the key regulatory requirements related to the process of selection. It is important that the material be as brief as possible, that it only contains the key points and is easy to refer to and to understand. You must include the following:

- Sex Discrimination Act 1995/97
- Race Relations Act 1992
- Equal Pay Act 1970
- Disability Discrimination Acts 1995 and 2005
- European Working Time Directive
- Employment Act 2002
- National minimum wage
- Data Protection Act 1998 (and any future amendments)
- Ethical issues
- Asking candidates the same questions
- Interviewers not related to candidates
- Gender and ethnic balance on panels.

Make sure that the regulatory requirements you include relate to recruitment and selection. Key words and phrases are more valuable than long paragraphs.

Progress Check

1. What do you understand by the term 'human resources management'?
2. Which type of recruitment is enjoying a large increase in popularity with organisations?
3. Give six key functions of a job description.
4. In a person specification what might the term 'aptitudes' mean?
5. Give an example of a job where minimum height can be legally stipulated.
6. What are the three application documents that a candidate might use when applying for a job?
7. At what point in the recruitment and selection process would it be advisable to take up an applicant's references? Explain your answer.
8. Give two examples of tests that could be presented to candidates whilst they wait for their job interview.
9. Racial discrimination means treating a person less favourably than others on racial grounds. Name four other bases for discrimination.
10. Give three examples of how employees could be adversely affected if the European Working Time Directive is not followed.

UNIT 14

Understanding Aspects of Employment Law

This unit covers:

- The different types of employment contract and the impact of employment legislation
- How to explain the rights and responsibilities of employees and employers
- The various perspectives in employee relations
- How contracts of employment may be terminated

It is vital for an organisation's success that good working relationships are maintained between employer and employees; to a large extent, that relationship is controlled by ever-changing legislation.

This unit introduces you to different types of employment contract and examines the obligations of employer and employee and their rights and responsibilities. The unit then looks at how employer–employee relationships are developed and maintained. When contracts are terminated, set procedures must be followed: these are addressed in the unit's final section, which covers dismissal and redundancy.

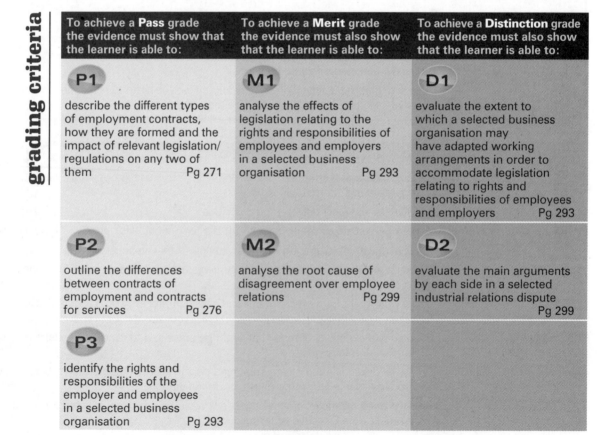

To achieve a **Pass** grade the evidence must show that the learner is able to:	To achieve a **Merit** grade the evidence must also show that the learner is able to:	To achieve a **Distinction** grade the evidence must also show that the learner is able to:
P1 describe the different types of employment contracts, how they are formed and the impact of relevant legislation/ regulations on any two of them Pg 271	**M1** analyse the effects of legislation relating to the rights and responsibilities of employees and employers in a selected business organisation Pg 293	**D1** evaluate the extent to which a selected business organisation may have adapted working arrangements in order to accommodate legislation relating to rights and responsibilities of employees and employers Pg 293
P2 outline the differences between contracts of employment and contracts for services Pg 276	**M2** analyse the root cause of disagreement over employee relations Pg 299	**D2** evaluate the main arguments by each side in a selected industrial relations dispute Pg 299
P3 identify the rights and responsibilities of the employer and employees in a selected business organisation Pg 293		

grading criteria

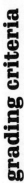

grading criteria

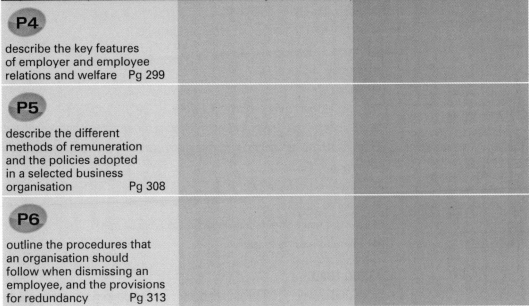

To achieve a **Pass** grade the evidence must show that the learner is able to:	To achieve a **Merit** grade the evidence must also show that the learner is able to:	To achieve a **Distinction** grade the evidence must also show that the learner is able to:
P4 describe the key features of employer and employee relations and welfare Pg 299		
P5 describe the different methods of remuneration and the policies adopted in a selected business organisation Pg 308		
P6 outline the procedures that an organisation should follow when dismissing an employee, and the provisions for redundancy Pg 313		

The different types of employment contract and the impact of employment legislation

Types of employment contract

According to the Office for National Statistics (2006), at the beginning of 2005, some 28.5 million people were employed in Great Britain. This is the largest number of employed people since records began. At the same time, there were some 1.4 million people unemployed (this is 4.7% of the potential workforce of the country).

Traditionally, most employed people were in full-time, permanent employment, and this was reflected in the type of contract that they were given. However, there are other more flexible types of employment contract, including:

- annual hours
- casual workers
- fixed-term
- home-workers
- job sharing
- flexi-time
- part-time
- term-time working.

And, of course, some people are self-employed.

Permanent

Permanent employment contracts assume a long-term commitment by both the employee and the employer. A permanent contract does not necessarily mean that the individual is a full-time worker; it is possible to have a permanent contract for a part-time job. The important fact is that the post is a permanent one and not temporary.

Part-time

The number of part-time workers in the UK has grown by 7% since part-time workers won equal treatment rights in 2002 (Office for National Statistics, 2006). As a result of that ruling, part-time workers enjoy **pro-rata** terms and conditions compared with full-time employees. By law they are entitled to equal pro rata:

- rates of pay
- rates of overtime pay
- entitlement to pension schemes and benefits
- access to training and development
- holidays
- career breaks
- sick pay, maternity and parental leave
- treatment when the employer is selecting for promotion and for redundancy.

Employers have recognised that employing part-time workers brings the following benefits:

- improved flexibility
- increased productivity
- reduced absenteeism
- a wider range of potential employees to choose from
- ability to hold on to staff.

remember

With the additional protection for part-time workers there have been slight reductions in the number of jobs, as employees have more responsibilities.

Fixed term

Since 2002 when equal treatment rights were introduced for employees on fixed-term contracts, the number the agency workers has fallen by 14% whilst the number of staff on fixed-term contracts has only fallen by 8% (**Trade Union Congress**, 2004).

Fixed-term contracts can be for relatively short periods of employment or they can be for as long as a year. Many organisations use these types of contracts to cover temporary shortfalls in staffing levels: for example, during periods of extended sickness or for maternity cover.

Fixed-term contracts provide the employer with the opportunity to cover fluctuations in workload, as well as to bring in individuals to carry out particular projects or tasks. Fixed term contracts allow an employer to reduce its long-term commitments in terms of its wage bill.

Temporary

In Great Britain, temporary agency workers are usually the most vulnerable employees. Typically, they are to be found in low-skilled jobs (e.g. in catering, the care sector and call centres).

Fig 14.1 Recruitment agency's home page

(Source: www.newappointmentsgroup.co.uk)

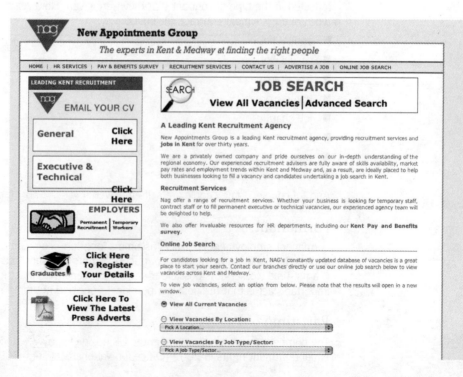

Temporary workers tend to be younger, and they lose out on many of the benefits that other workers receive, including:

- pay
- holidays
- entitlements such as paternity and maternity rights
- training and career development.

Since peaking in 1998 (7.9%), and despite strong employment growth, all forms of temporary work have fallen, in absolute terms and as a share of the workforce, to 6.5% in 2002 and 6% in 2004 (Trade Union Congress, 2004).

Home working and teleworking

Home working enables an employee to work from home for short or long periods of time and can be permanent. Apart from the location, an employee who is home working works in exactly the same way as if they had travelled to the employer's place of work.

Home working is not necessarily suitable for all jobs, and each job is tested on its suitability for remote work. It does, however, have many advantages, primarily:

- flexible working – being able to fit work round the individual's personal and domestic responsibilities
- the reduction or elimination of travelling time
- a comfortable and quieter working environment.

Teleworking is slightly different from home working in as much as the employee is, by definition, working on a computer or using telecommunications technology. In effect, teleworking means transferring all of the technology available to that employee to their home so that they work on a remote computer station or an extension of their employer's telecommunications network.

> **remember**
> The Trade Union Congress is the organisation to which most British trade unions belong.

Agency

According to the Trade Union Congress (2004), 28% of agency workers positively choose agency work over a permanent job and around 40% are temping because they could not find a permanent job.

As we saw in Unit 13, agencies can be brought in to act as 'middle men' between the employee and the employer. Agencies do not just operate as finders of permanent members of staff. An agency registers potential workers and places them on an as-and-when-needed basis with a pool of employers. The agency can, at very short notice, provide additional staff for busier working periods and to fill in gaps that have arisen due to staff absences.

The classic temping relationship is as follows. The employee registers with the agency, which notes the employee's skills, abilities and experience and availability for work. The agency either places the employee immediately with an employer or contacts the employee when a vacancy arises. When in work, the temp is paid on an hourly basis by the agency. Obviously, the agency pays the temp considerably less per hour than the employer is paying the agency for the services of the temp. The agency usually takes responsibility for the temp's tax and National Insurance.

See pages 217–218 in Unit 13 for more information on agencies.

Job share

In job sharing, two or more people share the responsibilities, pay and benefits of a single full-time job. They share the pay and benefits in proportion to the number of hours they contribute towards the full-time job. Typically, job sharers work split days, weeks or alternate weeks and, in many cases, some of their hours overlap.

Job sharing is beneficial for employees because it enables them to manage their domestic and other responsibilities outside of work. Employers have also recognised the advantages of job sharing, including:

- greater flexibility when there is a high workload
- continuity of work, regardless of sickness or holidays
- a wider range of skills, experiences, ideas and views

remember

Job shares are still relatively uncommon; however, they favour employers as at least two fresh employees are sharing the same role.

- increased employee commitment and loyalty
- being able to hold on to valuable members of staff.

However, there are disadvantages to job sharing as far as the employer is concerned. These include:

- additional induction, training and administration costs
- the fact that some job sharers are not as productive as others
- communication problems between job sharers
- difficulty in recruiting a job sharer if one leaves
- lack of clarity as to which job sharer has responsibility.

Link

See Table 14.1 on page 291 for more on job sharing.

Flexible working

Flexible working practices are beneficial both to employers and to employees and can be achieved in a number of different ways.

Flexi-time

The most common form is flexi-time, which allows employees to manage their own working week within limitations. For example, an employee who is expected to work 35 hours per week normally works seven hours a day, five days a week. That employee would probably begin work at 9.00 a.m. and, having taken one hour off for lunch, would complete their work at 5.00 p.m. Flexi-time would allow an employee to begin work at 7.00 a.m. and work through until 3.00 p.m. Provided that the employee does the total number of working hours expected of them in a working week, they can, in this way, manage their time throughout the week. Usually, the employer insists that all employees are available during core times, which are usually 10.00 a.m. to 3.00 p.m.

Compressed working time

Compressed working time is a variation on flexi-time and is also quite common. An individual required to work 35 hours per week can work the required number of hours over three or perhaps four days. If the employee were to work three nine-hour days and one eight-hour day, the complete working week would have been completed by Thursday afternoon.

Annualised hours

With annualised hours, the employee works out their working arrangements on a yearly calendar. Scheduling the hours to be worked is an onerous task: an individual working for 37 hours a week would be expected to work 1,929.29 hours per year minus their annual and statutory leave. Working days and time off are identified; in addition, reserve days are specified, i.e. days when the employee may be needed to come into work at short notice. Usually, the employer states the minimum and maximum number of hours that can be worked in a particular week. In consultation with the employee, the future working year can then be organised so that the employee can balance their working life and other domestic responsibilities whilst covering their job to the employer's satisfaction.

Link

See Table 14.1 on page 291 for more on flexible working.

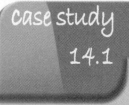

Examples of structured and unstructured flexibility

Structured, permanent: e.g. fixed part-time, where hours are organised to meet peaks and troughs in demand and cover a finite period at the same time each day and a constant number of hours per week.

Structured, temporary: e.g. a fixed-term contract with finite start and end dates, often covering a particular task or position where the permanent member of staff is absent for a fixed period, such as maternity leave.

Unstructured permanent: e.g. annualised working hours where employees are allocated a fixed total of hours over the year and the exact distribution of these hours is determined by different factors, such as the volume of work or the non-work commitments of the employee.

Unstructured temporary: e.g. casual employment where staff may work intermittently for the same employer for several years (as is the case in many hotels), but the employer has ultimately no commitment to offer them work nor has the employee any obligation to accept work offered. Thus the nature of the employment relationship remains highly tenuous and is limited only to the period of time for which the employee actually works. However, the introduction of the Working Hours Directive now forces employers to recognise that they have wider responsibilities towards such employees – notably, the requirement to provide, pro rata, holiday pay related to the hours they have worked for the organisation.

(Source: Institute for Employment Research (2007) – work carried out for the Joseph Rowntree Foundation)

activity

1   What do you think is meant by 'structured and unstructured' in this sense?

2   Give another term used to describe 'unstructured temporary work'.

To find out about the Institute for Employment Research, visit the University of Warwick's website

www.warwick.ac.uk

Impact of legislation and regulations

After decades of problems between employers and employees, particularly in the 1970s and the 1980s, new legislation and regulations have begun to help employers and employees achieve the most from their relationship. On the one hand, as we will see later in this unit, employers can make reasonable demands on their employees in exchange for pay and benefits; on the other, employees are more protected now than they have ever been.

Whereas employees in full-time, permanent positions have a long-term relationship with, and commitment to, their employers, for those in temporary positions the relationship is much briefer. However, successive waves of legislation and regulations have meant that, regardless of the type of employment contract they have, employees have approaching equal status. The law now states that temporary employees must be treated as if they were permanent.

Fig 14.2 John Hutton, Secretary of State for Business, Enterprise and Regulatory Reform

Laws have gradually allowed and encouraged individuals to seek work around their other commitments without losing rights and benefits. Obviously, in the long-term, it is in the interests of all in Great Britain for the maximum number of people to be in employment. By equalising rights and responsibilities, regardless of the employment contract, many more people have been encouraged to seek and to keep work, rather than rely on benefits to live.

case study 14.2 — Haddiscoe Engineering

Until recently, Haddiscoe Engineering had been one of the biggest manufacturers of industrial chain saws in Europe. It had exported all over the world and at the peak employed nearly 7500 people. The business operated from six factories, four in Great Britain, one in France, and another in Germany.

Three years ago, the business decided to diversify into hedge trimmers and mechanical diggers; this would mean a radical reorganisation of the business. The two overseas factories were adapted to make all three different product lines. Two of the four British factories retained their chain saw production lines. One of the four was adapted to produce hedge trimmers only and the other mechanical diggers.

This was a major decision made by the Human Resources (HR) department based at the London headquarters and showroom of the business. From this point on, each of the factories was expected to run at a profit and make its own decisions based on fairly detailed requirements provided by HR. Each HR manager in each factory could make their own operational decisions in consultation with the production line managers. The idea was for each factory to create its own solutions to the requirements of production and to the demand to make a profit.

This morning, the HR manager at one of the British factories still making chain saws received an email from head office HR; it contained the following points:

■ We have noted a large decrease in the sales of chain saws in overseas markets.

■ It had been decided that the factory will have three months to switch over to the production of hedge trimmers and diggers.

■ It has further been decided that the current workforce will be cut by 25%.

■ From this date, all operational HR decisions will be made by head office HR.

■ You are to begin a process of replacing all employees' permanent contracts of employment with annually renewable contracts.

■ Each contract of employment will be reviewed on an individual basis at the end of each year.

■ You are to terminate shift work patterns and to replace them with a day work shift; any necessary evening or night work will be carried out by casual workers (temporary and paid hourly).

■ Fixed salaries will be replaced under the new annual contracts with a piece rate pay scale and a scale of bonus if production and profit targets are met.

■ You are no longer to authorise the payment of sick or maternity pay without reference to head office.

■ You may either close the canteen or begin charging full cost price (plus a contribution towards staff costs) as the canteen will no longer be subsidised.

■ Employees may no longer purchase any of the company's products in excess of the standard customer discount scales.

■ You will cease any ongoing discussions or negotiations on pay and conditions with individual employees or representatives of employees. All such matters are now to be referred to head office.

■ You are to post this email in full on all notice boards by 12.00 today.

The email came as an enormous shock both to the management of the factory and to the employees. It was clear that changes had to be made. Within hours of posting up the notice as ordered by head office, employees, managers and trade union officials besieged the factory's HR office.

Many of the employees are over 50 years old and have worked for the business for many years. Many of them are concerned that they do not have the skills for new production lines. The trade unions believe that the demands are unreasonable and want a more gradual switch over, but the factory's HR office cannot negotiate.

activity
INDIVIDUAL WORK 14.1

P1

Use Case study 14.2 as the basis for your investigation into different types of employment contract, how they are formed and the impact of current legislation and regulations. You should:

1   Describe the different types of employment contract mentioned in the case study.

2   Describe the impact of current legislation and regulations on at least two of them (e.g. minimum wage, flexible working or disability provisions).

> **remember**
>
> Someone with a contract of employment has direct employment rights, whereas an individual who has a contract for services is effectively working for the organisation but not as part of it.

Contracts of employment and contracts for services

The simplest difference between someone with a contract of employment and a person with a contract for services is that the former is directly employed by the organisation, whereas the other is effectively self-employed.

It is very common for organisations to call workers 'casual workers' or 'trainees' and class them as being self-employed. This avoids not only a great deal of unnecessary paperwork but also having to give them employment rights.

Differences between the contracts

It is sometimes difficult to determine whether an individual is an employee or is providing services under contract. More often than not the individual is an employee if the following apply:

- The employer tells the employee what work needs to be done and how to do it.
- The employer pays the employee a regular amount of pay at regular intervals.
- The employer provides the main tools and machinery required to do the job.

On the other hand, if someone is self-employed and therefore providing a contract for services the following are usual:

- The individual goes out and finds their own work.
- The individual has to find someone else to do the work if they are unable to do it.
- The individual supplies their own tools and machinery.

> **remember**
>
> In some industries, self-employed contract workers are referred to as freelancers or consultants.

Status

There is always a contract between an employer and an employee. Although it may not necessarily be in writing, a contract still exists. The basic principles are that the employee undertakes to do work for the employer and in return the employer pays the employee for their time and labour. This means that the employee and the employer have certain rights and obligations; these can be stated in one of the following ways:

- **Express terms** – these are explicitly agreed in the contract between the employer and the employee.
- Implied terms – these are not necessarily written down in the employment contract but are agreements that can be found in most contracts of employment.

Link   See page 273 in this unit and pages 337–8 in Unit 21 for more about expressed and implied terms.

As far as an individual supplying services under contract to an organisation is concerned, there is not necessarily any particular complex contract involved. Usually the contract will state that a certain fee will be paid if the contract is terminated. Alternatively, it will simply state that the individual will be paid for all work carried out to the point when the contract was terminated.

The individual supplying the services is not an employee; they are responsible for their own insurance, tax and National Insurance, and do not receive pay if they are off work due to illness or holiday.

case study 14.3   Louise's zero contract

Louise used to work a 35-hour week; one of the days was a Saturday, but she always took Monday off in lieu. She did not mind. Saturday was busy and the time went quickly. But everything changed three months ago.

Another company bought the shop, and it seemed to Louise that they had bought the staff as well. A few days after they took over the shop, Louise was given a new contract of employment. It was sold to her as being really good and flexible, a zero contract. It does not say in the contract how many hours she has to work each week and, as things are in September and October, there are hardly any customers about, so she has hardly been in the shop and she's hardly earned a penny. She is at her wits' end and does not know how the next lot of bills is going to be paid.

activity

1   Explain to Louise what is meant by a 'zero contract'.

2   She could have signed a key time contract, where she was guaranteed some work but not regular hours. Her other choice would have been to have stayed on her old contract. Which should Louise have done?

> **remember**
>
> **Statutory rights** are not always included in contracts of employment as it is accepted by all parties that they will apply to every case.

Employment protection

Later in this unit we look at the principal employment protection rights. However, these rights depend on an individual's employment status. An employee, someone who has a contract of employment, will have full protection. The self-employed or casual staff will only have limited protection. A prime example is that an employee would be protected against unfair dismissal, but a self-employed or casual worker would not.

Sometimes it is very difficult to determine an individual's employment status, but this is essential in order to establish their employment protection rights.

Terms and conditions of service

An employee should be issued with a written set of terms and conditions of employment at the earliest opportunity. These written details are often referred to as a **statement of particulars**. Usually this statement is included in a contract of employment.

The details in the statements are specified under the Employment Rights Act 1996. The law sets minimum terms of employment, which are automatically incorporated even if the employer fails to include them. The employer can, of course, offer more generous terms than those set out by law.

The Employment Rights Act 1996 was amended by the Employment Act 2002, which we deal with in some detail in the next section of this unit. The original Act set out the primary protection rights, as well the minimum terms and conditions of service.

In the contract of employment, the primary rights and duties of both employers and the employees are included. These fall into two categories:

- express terms – including pay, hours and holidays, details of which should be put in writing and handed to the employee within eight weeks of beginning work
- implied terms – which are not expressly stated but are fairly obvious to both the employer and the employee (e.g. statutory rights, including equal pay, and a duty of care).

Legislation and regulation

Key aspects of the contract of employment that are supported by legislation and regulations are:

- the payment of wages and the rights of employees to receive at least the minimum wage
- the ability to determine the hours of work and negotiate flexible working
- the protection of an employee's personal data under the Data Protection Act 1998
- the employee's and the employer's duties of trust and confidence (i.e. neither should behave in a way that is likely to destroy or seriously damage trust and confidence)
- other obligations, including:
  - the employee's obligation to disclose previous convictions when applying for a job in those professions where a disclosure is necessary (however, there is no onus on the employee to do so when applying for jobs in other professions)
  - the employer's obligation to provide the employee with work
  - the employer's obligation to provide a fair and accurate reference should they agree to act as a referee (however, an employer is not obliged to provide a reference).

In addition, employees have a legal right to take time off without pay for public duties. The employer must not suspend or lay off an employee without pay and without agreement.

Fig 14.3 Jury service is one public duty that employees have a legal right to take off without pay to fulfil

See pages 276–292 for more on legislation and regulations.

case study 14.4   **Contracts**

Fig 14.4 shows an example of a standard contract of employment.

Fig 14.4

(Adapted from www.sunshinenannies.co.uk © Sunshine Nannies 2003)

Statement of Conditions of Employment

Date of Issue:
Name and address of employer:
Name and address of employee:
Date of commencement of employment:
Previous services counting towards continuous employment (if any):
Job Title:
Place of work:
Names of children and ages:

Duties: Sole responsibility for the children of the family including preparing meals and feeding the children a healthy diet, their laundry, taking them to suitable social activities, groups, their physical and intellectual development and pre-school and school education, keeping their rooms and play areas tidy, organising and undertaking any visits to doctors, dentists, child health clinics and other such duties as a nanny would undertake.

The employee is entitled to:
☐ Meals (please specify):
☐ Use of car:
☐ To use own car:
☐ Petrol costs (per mile):
☐ Mileage to and from work:
☐ Other benefits:

Renumeration
The employee's salary is   Net per week payable weekly/monthly in arrears by standing order/cheque on the 1st of each month. The employer will pay all tax and National Insurance contributions.

Hours of work
The employer will work from   a.m. to   p.m.   days per week. The employee will remain with the children of the family if the employer cannot return before   p.m. The employer will use reasonable endeavours to return before   p.m. These hours of work may only be changed by mutual agreement.

The employee will be allowed   week's paid holiday each year. In the first or last years of employment the employee will be entitled to holiday on a pro-rata basis. Paid compensation is not normally given for holidays not actually taken. Holidays may only be carried into next year with the express permission of the employer. The employee will be free on all Bank Holidays or will receive a day off in lieu, by agreement.

Holidays will (unless otherwise agreed) be taken when the employer is on holiday. The employee should give at least one month's notice for blocks of holiday exceeding three days and as much notice as possible otherwise and holidays may only be taken at times that are agreed by the employer.

Confidentiality
It is a condition of employment that now and at all times in the future that, save as may be lawfully required the employee shall keep the affairs and concerns of the employer and the household and her and its transactions and business confidential.

Pensions
The employer does not operate a pension scheme.

Sickess
The employer will pay statutory sick pay as stipulated by the Government at the rates stipulated by legislation. Any additional sickness payment will be made at the discretion of the employer. The employee will notify the employer as soon as possible of any illness preventing the employee employee coming to work and no later than 7.00 a.m. on the day in question.

Discipline
Reasons which might give rise to the need for discipline measures include the following:
☐ Causing a disruptive influence in the household
☐ Job incompetence
☐ Unsatisfactory standard of dress or appearance
☐ Conduct during or outside working hours prejudicial to the interest or reputation of the employer
☐ Failure to comply with instructions and procedures, for example being unable to drive due to a driving ban
☐ Breach of condidentiality clause

In the event of the need to take disciplinary action, the procedure will be: Firstly – oral warning; secondly – written warning; thirdly – dismissal.

Reasons, which might give rise to summary dismissal, include the following: theft, drunkeness, illegal drug abuse, and child abuse, acting unsafely with children.

Termination

In the first four weeks of employment, one week's notice is required in either side. After four week's continuous service either the employee or the employer may terminate this contract by giving four weeks' notice and after six weeks' continuous service either the employee or the employer may terminate this contract by giving six week's notice.

Additional items:

☐ Smoking is not permitted in the house or near the children of the family.

☐ The employee may use the telephone for reasonable local calls and, in an emergency, for national calls. Calls should not exceed,   per quarter.

☐ The employer may in consultation with the employee arrange with another family and their Nanny (The Other Nanny) that in the event of either the employee or the Other Nanny being absent due to illness or holiday either the employee or the Other Nanny (as the case may be) will care for the children of both families.

☐ During working hours the employee will not look after any children other than the children of the family without the consent of the employer.

☐ In addition to the children of the family, the employee will look after such other children (but not more than two) during working hours as the employer may reasonably request.

Signed by the employer .... Date ....

Signed by the employee .... Date ....

Fig 14.5 shows an example of a contract for services.

Fig 14.5 Consultant's agreement

(Adapted from an agreement used by the National Council for Voluntary Organisations)

Consultant's Agreement

1. Introduction and Definitions:

This Agreement is between _____ (organisation's name and address) (herein after called _____) and (_____) herein after called 'the Consultant').

The Agreement will be in accordance with the following Terms and Conditions unless and until an alternative is specifically agreed between the Parties.

2. Purpose of the Agreement:

The purpose of the Agreement is:

Further details of the Agreement are set out in the attached Schedule.

3. Commencement date and duration of the Agreement:

This Agreement will commence on (_____) and is to be carried out in accordance with the following conditions:

It may be terminated by either party giving one month's notice in writing. _____ may terminate the agreement immediately in the event that the Consultant commits any material breach of the terms of this Agreement, or is guilty of gross misconduct.

4. Fees and expenses:

Fees for the Agreement will be as follows:

Where necessary, VAT will be added at the appropriate rate.

Where appropriate, travel, subsistence and other expenses will be paid at cost and in accordance with arrangements specifically agreed, in advance, with the Consultant.

5. Invoices and payment:

Unless specifically agreed otherwise, invoices will be submitted monthly by the Consultant and payment made within 30 days.

6. Taxation:

The Consultant is a self-employed person responsible for taxation and National Insurance or similar liabilities or contributions in respect of the fees and the Consultant will indemnify [organisation] against all liability for the same and any costs, claims or expenses including interest and penalties.

7. Confidentiality:

The Consultant will not divulge to third parties matters confidential to (_____) (whether or not covered by this Agreement) without (_____) explicit permission. Except where specifically agreed otherwise, all material, data, information et cetera collected during the course of hte Agreement will remain in the possession of (_____) and not used without their permission.

8. Publication of material:

Where the Agreement provides for the publication of material, the following specific conditions shall apply:

(a) _____ will retain the right to edit the final draft prior to publication subject, in the case of joint publications, to amendments proposed being agreed with the author(s).

(b) prior to publication, the Consultant and/or others associated with the publication shall not disclose any material obtained or produced for the purposes of the project to any other party unless _____ have given prior approval in writing.

(c) the Consultant will provide to _____ copies of all material, data et cetera colected specifically for the project and indicate the source of other material used.

(d) _____ will, except where specifically agreed otherwise, hold copyright to the publication.

Other matters relating to the use of the material shall be covered as an Appendix to this Agreement. Where other uses are agreed, all material and publications based on the project shall acknowledge _____ .

9. Restrictions:

The Consultant shall not whilst this Agreement is in force be engaged or concerned directly or indirectly in the provision of services to any other party in the same or similar field of business or activity to _____ without the prior written consent of _____ .

10. Other conditions:

Any other conditions, including variations to the terms set out above, shall be included as an Appendix to this agreement.

For _____ (Organisation)

Signed: _____

Date: _____

Name: _____

For the Consultant

Signed: _____

Date: _____

Name: _____

Designation: _____

activity

P2

Outline the differences between contracts of employment and contracts for services. Referring to the two sample contracts given in Case study 14.3,

1   Compare the two different types of contract.

2   Explain the key differences between the contracts.

3   Explain the consequences of the differences as far as the employee is concerned.

4   Explain the consequences of the differences as far as the employer is concerned.

The rights and responsibilities of employees and employers

Law governs the very basic rights and responsibilities of employers and employees. The employer must, for example:

- provide a safe place of work
- ensure safe working methods
- provide appropriate training
- provide safe equipment.

Broadly speaking, the rights of employees and employers are specific entities that are mentioned in law. On the other hand, responsibilities can be governed by law but are inferred by the relationship between the two groups.

Employer rights and employee obligations

When the employer and the employee enter into a contract, in this case a contract of employment, certain rights and obligations are either expressly stated or implied within the contract itself. Employers can rightly expect their employees to work diligently for them and to work the number of hours required in the contract. In all cases the employee will be acting on behalf of the employer: sometimes as the public face of the employer. Therefore, the employer has a right to expect these individuals to project the business or organisation in a good light.

By signing and accepting the terms of the contract of employment the employee acquires a number of obligations. To a great extent the employee must comply with the wishes or orders of their employer. They must take note of instructions given to them and take heed of training.

In this section we will look at specific rights and obligations, focusing on the work itself, the organisation's aims, health and safety, and the use of resources.

Working to contract

The contract of employment is a legally binding document between the employer and the employee; it states a number of express and implied terms. It is not possible to provide the employee with a contract that covers all aspects of the relationship, and, in any case, legislation and organisational policy will change from time to time. Normally, the contract of employment refers to several subsidiary documents, which are often bound together in an employee handbook. Having these additional documents enables changes to be made without the need to re-write and re-sign the contracts of employment.

The contract of employment sets out the precise nature of the employee's job responsibilities and obligations, including:

- the total number of hours to be worked per week
- the starting and finishing times
- the number of paid days off
- details of sick leave, maternity and paternity leave
- rights in respect of pension schemes
- grievance procedures

- periods of notice to be worked
- details concerning resignation and termination.

The employer will also inform the employee about some or all of the following:

- company rules and regulations
- codes of behaviour
- dress codes.

Supporting the aims of the employer

Many organisations ensure that their employees are aware of the organisation's objectives. This helps to strengthen the relationship between employer and employees as they are working for the same purpose.

It is in the interests of employer and employees to identify the primary aims and objectives of the organisation. Employees need to be aware how their part of the organisation's work contributes to the attainment of its objectives. Many business objectives are wide and imprecise and can often only be found as a reference in the company's documentation, such as its **mission statement**.

Objectives will change over time, and employers know that the spread of misinformation within the organisation can be damaging. Therefore, steps are usually taken to ensure that employees are made aware of current objectives.

Supporting health and safety

There are many health and safety requirements in the workplace. Specifically, the employer is required to:

- provide a safe working environment
- provide adequate welfare facilities
- ensure that entrances and exits are safe and clear
- ensure that equipment and systems are safe and serviced on a regular basis
- take steps to ensure that the safe handling of heavy objects and the safe storage of dangerous items are priorities
- provide instruction, training or supervision as required
- ensure that all accidents are rigorously investigated and the causes of the accidents are eliminated.

remember
If you read that employers have a 'duty of care' towards their employees, this is referring to the employers' health and safety responsibilities in the workplace.

Fig 14.6 Where thefts are common an employer may routinely search employees as they leave work

Use of resources

The reasonable use of the employer's resources is usually an implied term in the contract of employment. Sometimes, it is expressly stated. Employers do not have the right to search employees when they leave the premises; however, in some organisations, where thefts from the premises have been identified in the past, this is a longstanding custom and practice.

Theft or misuse of resources actually goes far further than removing a box of staples from the stationery cupboard. Increasingly, employees have access to the Internet at their desk. A supervisor or manager does not always directly overlook them. Theoretically, the employee could spend the day surfing the Internet and emailing friends. In practice, many employers with computer networks have taken steps to limit access to the Internet and only allow employees to access approved sites. Search engines are often out of bounds and specific key words, if typed in, fail to produce any search findings.

Employer responsibilities

The relationship between employers and employees has become increasingly legislated. In the past employers could confidently expect to be left to their own devices with regard to working conditions, treatment of employees and pay. Many of the employer's basic responsibilities are contained, at least as references, in the contract of employment, but an employer's responsibilities go beyond those.

Observance of employment legislation

Employment legislation is probably the fastest moving aspect of human resources management. New legislation is always in the pipeline, and adoption of European regulations, which have an impact on existing British law, is an added complication, so mistakes and misunderstandings are more than possible.

Employment Act 2002

The Employment Act 2002 was an incredibly important piece of legislation. It brought about major changes to the dispute resolution process, improved the rights of working parents and put in place a process to ensure more equality in pay between men and women who performed similar work.

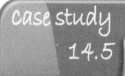

case study 14.5

Flexible working and the Employment Act

"Flexible Working improves recruitment and retention, reduces absenteeism and increases motivation and performance," said John Blackwell, Managing Director of JBA Ltd. "Unfortunately, many companies remain unprepared for the changes this new legislation will bring. Britons already work the longest hours in Europe with an average of 43 hours a week, compared with 40 hours in other countries. Forty per cent of UK managers work in excess of 51 hours per week, and one in six work in excess of 60 hours per week. Research has shown that more than eighty per cent of us have felt under pressure to stay longer at work, even when the workday has finished. In addition to the immediate changes in the short term, we believe the Employment Act signals the beginning of pivotal changes in the workplace, attitudes to work, and the traditional infrastructure supporting it."

According to the Office of National Statistics, just seven per cent of the UK workforce or 1.8 million people presently work from home. By 2020, this figure is expected to be 25 per cent. The UK workforce will increase over next 10 years by 1.5 million. Eighty five percent of them will be women. With the ongoing pressure to find balance between work and home, Flexible Working will become a de-facto part of everyday working, rather than an exception to the norm.

"Twenty five percent of managers today are female and seventy eight percent of UK women with children work," added Blackwell. "Although legislation is behind the enforcement of Flexible Working, we believe socio-economic insecurities will also force a new set of workplace dynamics that more accurately reflect the lifestyles, demographics and needs of the changing workforce. We also believe it signifies the death of the 'job for life' as it will become more common place for people to have 'portfolio careers' with shorter assignments and multiple employers."

(Source: www.onrec.com)

activity

1   What do you think is meant by the term 'traditional infrastructure'?
2   Why is it likely that more women will enter the workforce over the next 10 years?
3   Why might employers be unprepared for the increased demand for flexible working patterns?

Equal Pay Act 1970

When men and women are doing the same or very similar work, but are being paid or treated in different ways, this is discrimination. The Equal Pay Act 1970 made it unlawful for employers to discriminate between men and women in terms of their pay and conditions.

When the Equal Pay Act was first introduced in 1970, the pay gap between men and women stood at 37%. Five years later it had closed to 30%. Under the Equal Pay Act there must also be equality in the contract of employment: i.e. in pay, conditions, bonuses, holidays and sick leave. The Act has been extended, and employers are also required to give equal pay in redundancy, travel, pension contributions and pension benefits.

The key principle of the Equal Pay Act is comparable work. If a person believes that they are being treated or paid less well than an individual of the other gender, they need to find a comparator. This must be a person who does a similar job and has similar status in the business. The person can, of course, compare themselves to their predecessor who held their job before they joined the company. If it can be proved that another individual or the previous post holder has or had better working conditions and better pay, the person has a right to claim that the business has broken the Equal Pay Act.

When making the complaint, the individual's first step is to use an Equal Pay questionnaire; if the employer does not accept the claim, the claimant would then refer the case to an employment tribunal.

Sex Discrimination Act 1975

The Sex Discrimination Act can be seen as a partner to the Equal Pay Act, as it also covers discrimination on the grounds of gender. The Act makes it unlawful for an employer to discriminate on the grounds of gender in training, education, facilities, services and premises.

There are two different types of sex discrimination: direct and indirect. Direct discrimination takes place when an individual is or would be treated less favourably than someone else on the grounds of gender. To prove direct discrimination the following has to be shown:

- that the treatment was less favourable than the treatment that would have been given to a person of the opposite gender
- that the treatment given was less favourable because of the gender of the person involved.

In October 2001, a European directive broadened the definition of indirect discrimination. It now means that indirect discrimination can be proven when:

- A practice puts or would put one gender at a particular disadvantage compared with the other gender.
- A practice puts an individual at a disadvantage.
- The employer cannot show that the practice is for a sound and legitimate reason.

The Sex Discrimination Act also covers harassment and sexual harassment. Harassment is described as unwanted conduct that takes place on the grounds of an individual's gender. To count as harassment, the behaviour has to have the effect of violating a person's dignity, intimidating them or degrading them.

Sexual harassment is any form of verbal, non-verbal or physical conduct of a sexual nature. Again it must be proven that the harassment intended to violate someone's dignity, intimidate them or humiliate them.

To find out more about the Sex Discrimination Act, visit the website of the Equal Opportunities Commission

www.eoc.org.uk

See pages 281–282, 290 for more on discrimination.

Health and Safety at Work Act 1974

Prior to 1974, employees did not have a legal right to safety protection in the workplace. The Act was brought in to provide a legal framework to promote, stimulate and encourage the highest possible standards of health and safety in the workplace.

Everyone has a responsibility to comply with the Act, which applies to:

- employers
- employees
- trainees
- the self-employed
- manufacturers
- suppliers
- designers
- importers of equipment that will be used in the workplace.

Employers have a general duty to 'ensure so far as is reasonably practicable the health, safety and welfare at work of all their employees'. This means that employers are required to:

- provide and maintain safety equipment and safe systems of working
- make sure that materials used are properly stored, handled, used and transported
- provide training, information, instruction and supervision
- ensure that employees are aware of any instructions that have been provided by manufacturers and suppliers
- provide a safe working environment
- provide a safe place of employment
- provide a written safety policy
- provide a written risk assessment
- ensure the safety of others, including the public
- have continued conversations with safety representatives.

In addition, employers cannot ask employees to carry out tasks that could prove to be hazardous to them, particularly if they lack the necessary safety equipment to carry out the job.

Employees must:

- be aware of their own health and safety and that of others
- be aware that their actions may be liable to charges
- cooperate with employers
- not interfere with equipment or anything that has been provided in the interests of health and safety.

In order to ensure that employers comply with the Health and Safety at Work Act, local authorities employ environmental health officers. A representative of the **Health and Safety Executive** may visit large manufacturing, construction sites and other industrial sites. When carrying out inspections, environmental health officers and representatives of the Health and Safety Executive have the following powers:

- They can enter the premises without appointments at reasonable times.
- They can investigate and examine the premises and equipment.
- They can take equipment apart and take samples of substances and equipment.

- They can see any documents and take photocopies of them if necessary.
- If they are barred from entry, they can ask the police to ensure that they gain access.
- They can ask employers and employees questions under caution.
- They can seize any equipment or substances if they feel that there is an immediate danger from them.

Employers who continue to avoid following the requirements of the Act face enforcement action. Two things may happen:

- They will be issued a legal notice, which will either require them to improve the situation within a set period of time or will prohibit them from using equipment or unsafe practices immediately and until the situation is resolved.
- They could be prosecuted (as could employees), facing a maximum fine of £5,000 in a magistrates' court or an unlimited fine and a prison term in a Crown Court.

> **remember**
>
> Employers are legally bound to cooperate with and follow the instructions of inspectors. They risk closure if they fail to comply.

Visit the site of the Health and Safety Executive

www.hse.gov.uk

See page 300 for more information on health and safety.

Race Relations Act 1976

The Race Relations Act was amended in 2000, after the Stephen Lawrence enquiry, and now extends to all public authorities, including the police.

Fig 14.7 In April 1993 Stephen Lawrence was murdered because of the colour of his skin. A later enquiry showed that the police force made a number of mistakes during the investigation

In this context, discrimination is treating an individual less favourably because of their race, colour, culture or ethnic origin. The Act, which not only covers employment but also education, housing and the purchasing of goods, facilities and services, makes it unlawful to discriminate against an individual, either directly or indirectly, on racial grounds. Direct discrimination takes place when an individual is treated less favourably because of their racial background, compared with someone else of a different race in similar circumstances. Indirect discrimination takes place when employment conditions would mean that a smaller proportion of people from a particular racial group would be accepted for a job vacancy.

For more information on the Race Relations Act, visit the website of the Commission for Racial Equality

www.cre.gov.uk

Disability Discrimination Act 1995

The Disability Discrimination (Amendment) Act 1995 Regulations came into force on 1 October 2004. The amendments were introduced as a result of the European Directive on Equal Treatment in Employment and Occupation. The directive prohibits direct and indirect harassment on the grounds of:

- religion or belief
- disability
- age
- sexual orientation.

This applies to the fields of employment, self-employment, occupation and vocational training. The main reason for the changes to the existing Act was to expand the discrimination protection to:

- employees
- contract workers
- police officers
- job applicants.

The law prohibits harassment against disabled people and removes the old threshold. This threshold had meant that employers with fewer than 15 employees were excluded from disability discrimination laws.

Age discrimination

In October 2006 the Employment Equality (Age) Regulations came into force. These new Regulations apply to both employment and training, outlawing, for the first time, both direct and indirect age discrimination. They also tackle harassment or victimisation on the grounds of age. The Regulations have had an impact on retirement and also:

- remove the upper age limit for unfair dismissal and redundancy rights
- allow pay and non-pay benefits to continue when these are related to the length of service an employee has had with an organisation
- remove the age limits for statutory sick pay, maternity pay, adoption pay and paternity pay
- remove the upper and lower age limits for redundancy schemes.

Some employers had set mandatory retirement ages, and this new legislation allows employees to continue working beyond these, should they so wish.

There is no fixed state retirement age in Great Britain. It is the government's intention to raise the age at which state pensions are paid to 65 for both men and women; the plan is to introduce this by 2020.

Remuneration

Under the terms of the contract of employment, the employer undertakes to pay the employee in return for their labour. The contract states the payment terms; typically, these are either an annual salary split into 12 payments or an hourly pay rate based on the number of hours worked each week.

In addition to establishing the amount of pay, the employer indicates when and how that pay will be given to the employee, for example:

- a monthly salary paid directly into the employee's bank account
- cash without deductions, paid to self-employed or casual workers responsible for their own tax and National Insurance
- weekly pay cheques or cash, minus tax and National Insurance.

Minimum wage

It is now illegal for any employer to pay less than the minimum wage. The National Minimum Wage Act 1998 became law in April 1999, and since then the minimum wage has been increased.

New minimum wage levels were set by law at the beginning of October 2006, since when the minimum wage for employees aged 22 years or older has been £5.35 per hour. A lower hourly rate of £3.30 per hour was the minimum wage set for employees under the age of 19 but over the age of 16. There are exceptions, including what is known as a development rate, which applies to employees aged between 18 and 21 years and was set at £4.45 per hour. In effect, the development rate acknowledges that the individual is still learning their trade or job. However, it does not apply to apprentices. Apprentices under the age of 19 do not qualify for the national minimum wage. Apprentices over 19, in their first year of apprenticeship, also do not qualify for the national minimum wage.

Liability insurance

An organisation, or an employer, has a legal responsibility towards employees, customers and the public, and can be held legally liable and may risk being sued if an employee or a member of the public is injured. If injury occurs, the organisation or employer is considered to be negligent and in breach of duty. In the vast majority of cases, the employer will need to take out insurance against such a risk.

Liability to employees

Employer's Liability Compulsory Insurance (ELCI) requires employers to insure their liability to their employees for disease or bodily injury that may occur in the course of the employees' work. It is intended to provide financial security for the employer, who might possibly be faced with crippling costs, and to ensure that employees are fully protected in terms of compensation should the worst happen. The employee may need financial support for many years, and the ELCI will continue to protect them even if the employer goes out of business.

Several factors will be considered when the cost of the insurance (the premium) is being worked out. The premium depends on the book rating, which is calculated using a base rate set by the insurer. The base rate depends on the type of business in which the employees work; some are considered more dangerous and others less so. In effect, the insurer works out the level of risk in the particular industry. An industry with a high occurrence of accidents, for example, would be more expensive than one that is not associated with a great deal of risk to employees. In addition, the insurer will look at the claims history of the employer. If there have been a number of claims arising out of accidents, the premium will be higher or it may be difficult for the employer to find an insurer willing to take on the risk. The insurer may also look at the claims of other businesses in the same industry. If there are one or two particularly bad employers with a string of accidents, the premiums for all of the other businesses in the industry could be affected.

By law, an employer must have ELCI and be insured for at least £5m. It is common practice for insurers to automatically provide cover for at least £10m. By law, the employer must display a copy of the certificate of insurance where employees can easily read it. Employers must also keep copies for at least 40 years, or they risk an automatic fine of up to £1,000.

Public liability

In the case of public liability, the risk is based on the turnover of the business and whether the business operates outside its own premises. If members of the public or customers visit the premises of the business, or representatives of the business visit the customer's premises, it is a good idea for the business to have public liability insurance.

The insurance is designed to cover the costs of any awards given to a member of the public because of injury to them or damage to their property caused by the business. It also covers any legal fees, other costs and expenses.

This is not a compulsory insurance, but there are some businesses, such as horse riding schools, that need to take out the insurance. Increasingly, customers are asking to see copies of the insurance certificate before they will allow the business to carry out work for them.

Rights of employees

An employee's rights at work depend on:

■ their statutory rights
■ their contract of employment.

An employee's contract of employment cannot take away legal rights. For example, the law states that all employees are entitled to four weeks' paid holiday per year, so if an employee's contract that states that they are only entitled to two weeks' paid holiday per year, this part of the contract is void (cancelled) and does not apply to the employee.

If an employee's contract gives them greater rights than they have under law, such as if the contract were to state that the employee is entitled to six weeks' holiday each year, then the contract applies and not the statutory minimum.

Terms and conditions of service

Fig 14.8 A full time
employee should enjoy at
least four weeks paid holiday
a year

Almost every employee, regardless of the number of hours per week they work, has certain legal rights. Some workers are, however, not entitled to certain statutory rights. In some circumstances, an employee will only gain their statutory rights after they have worked for an employer for a certain length of time. When this time has passed, they are then, like most employees, entitled to the following:

■ a written statement of terms of employment within two months of starting work

■ an itemised pay slip from the very first day of work

■ to be paid at least the national minimum wage from the first day at work

■ not to have illegal deductions made from pay

■ at least four weeks' paid holiday per year

■ time off for trade union duties and activities (The time off does not have to be paid. If an employee takes part in official industrial action and is dismissed as a result, this will be unfair dismissal.)

■ the right to be accompanied by a trade union representative to a disciplinary or grievance hearing

■ paid time off to look for work if being made redundant (This only applies to employees who have worked for the employer for at least two years.)

■ time off to study or train (applies to 16–17-year-olds)

■ paid time off for antenatal care

■ paid maternity leave of 26 weeks and the right to return to work after this maternity leave (If the employee has worked for the organisation for 10 months, they are entitled to more maternity leave.)

■ paid paternity leave

■ paid adoption leave

■ to ask for flexible working

■ to take unpaid parental leave (both men and women), provided that the employee has worked for the organisation for 12 months

■ to take off a reasonable amount of time to look after dependents in times of an emergency

■ to work no longer than a maximum 48-hour working week

■ weekly and daily rest breaks (There are special rules for those who work at night.)

■ to be protected against discrimination on grounds of sex, race, disability, sexual orientation, age, religion or belief

- to work until the employee is at least 65
- to have a notice of dismissal provided that the employee has worked for the employer for a month
- to be given written reasons for dismissal from the employer provided that the employee has worked for the organisation for a year (Pregnant women on maternity leave are entitled to written reasons for dismissal without having to have worked for any particular length of time.)
- claim compensation if unfairly dismissed (This usually means that the employee must have worked for the organisation for at least a year.)
- claim redundancy pay if made redundant, assuming that the employee has worked for the organisation for two years
- not to be victimised or dismissed for 'blowing the whistle' on a matter of public concern (malpractice) at the workplace.

Part-time workers have the same pro-rata contractual rights as full-time workers. Fixed-term employees have the same contractual rights as comparable permanent employees. Employees may have additional contractual rights, which can usually be found in the contract of employment.

Maternity

Following new legislation that came into effect in April 2003, a woman, regardless of how long she has worked for an organisation or whether she works part time, has basic rights in respect of pregnancy. These include:

- paid time off for antenatal leave (This can include parent craft classes and relaxation classes.)
- suspension from work on full pay if there is an unavoidable health risk at work and the employer cannot find suitable alternative work
- 26 weeks of ordinary maternity leave, during which time all aspects of the contract of employment apply, apart from the salary
- a right not to suffer unfair treatment, including being dismissed or selected for redundancy because of the pregnancy or maternity leave
- the right to return to work after the maternity leave ends.

Once an employer receives a written note that a woman is pregnant they are required to carry out a health and safety risk assessment, as the pregnant woman must avoid certain hazards including:

- certain chemicals
- lifting heavy objects
- standing for long periods of time
- excessive travel.

If such risks cannot be avoided, the employer must try to find alternative work for the pregnant woman. If this is impossible, the employer can suspend the pregnant woman from work on full pay for the duration of her pregnancy. If a woman works nights and this could affect the health of the baby then again the employer must shift the work pattern to day working or suspend her.

If a woman has a pregnancy-related illness during the last four weeks of pregnancy, her maternity leave starts immediately. At other times, absence owing to pregnancy-related illness is classed as sick leave.

There are two different types of maternity leave. Ordinary maternity leave, which is 26 weeks, can be taken from 11 weeks before the expected week of childbirth or the 29th week of pregnancy. The woman has to notify her employer by the 15th week of pregnancy of her intentions with regard to taking maternity leave. The employee and the employer will then discuss when the woman will return to work after the maternity leave. When she returns to work she must be given the same job on the same terms and enjoy any improvements in terms of pay or benefits that may have been introduced whilst she has been away.

If a woman has worked for an employer for 26 weeks or more, she can take additional maternity leave (AML). This is another 26 weeks of unpaid leave. In other words, a woman can take up to a year after the birth of the child, with six months being paid leave and six months unpaid.

During AML the employee's contract still continues to be in force, but only with regard to notice periods, redundancy, grievance and disciplinary processes.

A woman is entitled to statutory maternity pay during the ordinary maternity leave period. For the first six weeks the employer pays 90% of the average earnings, but for the remaining 20 weeks £100 per week is paid.

Paternity

If an employee is a working father, he is entitled to one or two weeks' paternity leave when he and his partner have a child. An employee can also qualify for paternity leave when he adopts a child. Most fathers will be entitled to statutory paternity pay for their paternity leave. Statutory paternity pay is paid at the same rate as statutory maternity pay.

In order to qualify for paternity leave for a birth, the employee must:

■ be employed and have worked for his employer for 41 weeks by the time the baby is due

■ be the biological father of the child or be married to or be the partner of the baby's mother (this includes same-sex partners, whether or not they are registered civil partners)

■ have some responsibility for the child's upbringing

■ have given his employer the correct notice to take paternity leave.

In order to qualify for paternity leave for an adoption, the employee must:

■ be employed for at least 26 weeks by the time he is matched with his child for adoption

■ not be taking adoption leave

■ have some responsibility for the child's upbringing

■ have given his employer the correct notice to take paternity leave.

Paternity leave can start on the day that the baby is born or on a date agreed with the employer in advance. The paternity leave cannot start before the baby is born and it must be completed within 56 days of the birth of the child.

Fig 14.9 Paternity leave gives fathers valuable time with their newborn children

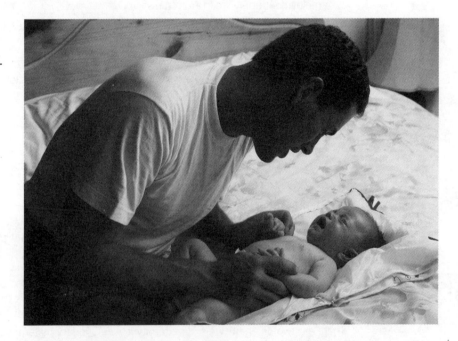

An employee must be able to show that he is entitled to paternity leave and must provide the following information to the employer:

■ his name

■ the due date of the baby (or the date that an adopted child will be placed with him)

■ the date that he would like the paternity leave to begin

■ whether he is taking one or two weeks' leave.

The employee must give the employer notice that he wishes to take paternity leave; the notice should be in writing. Ideally, the notice should be given 15 weeks before the baby is due or as soon as is practicable. For adoption, the notice should be given within seven days of being matched for adoption.

Sickness and pay

Every year, sick leave costs the British economy £13bn. On average, employees are off sick for 10 days each year. Employers are becoming wary of persistent sick leave, and some have introduced formal procedures for those who are considered to be taking too much time off.

The rules for sick leave are:

■ If the individual takes more than four consecutive days off, they may be asked to complete a self-certification form, giving details of the illness.

■ After eight or more consecutive days, a doctor's note is needed.

■ By law, the employer must pay the minimum weekly rate of statutory sick pay for the first 28 days.

---

case study 14.6

Investigating sickness

Many organisations now use a return-to-work interview. A manager discusses the reasons for the time off with an employee on their return, as a key monitoring strategy. The interviews should extend to all employees and should be carried out even when an employee has only taken one day off.

'If all staff are aware that each time they are off sick they will be asked why, it will help them realise they are important to the team and their absence is noted,' said Margaret McMahon, senior policy adviser at ACAS the government-backed employment-relations body.

Maintaining records of when and why employees have missed work can also be useful for revealing patterns in absences. 'If you discover a member of staff is taking every other Monday or Friday off sick, you may want to talk over concerns about whether they were really ill,' said Amanda Galashan, director of employment law advice company EmployEase.

Management should never be afraid to ask about the specifics of an illness instead of accepting that someone was 'generally run down'.

'Rather than greeting an employee with "Hi, how are you?" when they return, it can be useful to find out more,' added McMahon.

One way of doing this is to get employees to fill in a self-certification form – particularly if the period of absence is less than seven days, the amount of time required before a doctor's note can be issued. This can also be important when tracking the amount of times employees have had similar illnesses and looking at what can be done about it.

(Source: www.bcentral.co.uk)

activity

1 Do you think employers have a right to investigate reasons for sickness when the reasons may be delicate?

2 Suggest how an employer could take action to reduce the number of days lost to sickness each year.

Time off for public duties

Employees have the right to take time off for certain public duties and services. Their rights depend on what job they do and what duty or service is involved. Under the law an employee is entitled to take off time for any of the following:

■ serving as a magistrate

■ being a member of a local authority, police or local education authority, an educational governing body, a health authority or a primary care trust

- being a member of a **statutory tribunal**, an environmental agency or on the board of prison visitors

- jury service – if an employee is selected for jury service, the employer must give them time off.

Visit the site of the Department for Business, Enterprise and Regulatory Reform (DBERR, formerly the Department for Trade and Industry) for a complete list of public duties that qualify

www.dti.gov.uk

Some employees are not entitled to take time off for public duties; they include:

- agency workers
- police officers
- members of the armed forces
- those employed on gas or oil rigs at sea
- merchant seamen
- fishermen on fishing vessels
- civil servants whose public duties are connected to political activities.

In order to qualify, the time off must be classified as being reasonable. This will depend on what the duties are, how long the employee will be off work and the impact on the employer's business. Another consideration is the number of times the employee has taken time off for public duties in recent months.

Trade union representation

Provided that an employee is an official of a trade union recognised by the employer, they can take paid time off to carry out some union duties. Such duties include:

- negotiating terms and conditions of employment
- helping with disciplinary or grievance procedures on behalf of union members
- negotiating matters about union membership
- discussing issues that could affect union members
- being trained by the union.

In addition to paid time off, unpaid leave can be taken for:

- going to workplace meetings to discuss and vote on negotiations
- meeting with full-time union officials to discuss issues that affect the workplace
- voting in union elections.

If an individual is not given the time off, they can take the matter to an employment tribunal. If they are sacked as a result of carrying out union activities, they can go to an employment tribunal and claim unfair dismissal.

> **remember**
>
> A trade union official is entitled to these rights only if the employer recognises the union (accepts that the union will negotiate on the employee's behalf).

Discrimination

It is unlawful to discriminate against a person at work on the grounds of:

- sex
- race
- disability
- colour
- nationality
- ethnic or national origin
- religion or belief
- sexual orientation
- age.

As we have seen, discrimination can be classed either as direct or indirect. Direct discrimination happens when a person is treated less favourably at work because of their sex, race, religion, age, sexual orientation or disability: for example, a man is not selected for promotion because he is male. Indirect discrimination happens when a particular employee cannot meet a requirement that is not supportable in terms of being necessary for the work and they are disadvantaged as a result. For example, if an employer only gives training before 8 00 a.m., this would discriminate against people with young children. The requirement to attend training at that time is not supportable as training could be arranged for another time.

Harassment is another form of discrimination. Harassment can include:

- verbal abuse
- suggestive remarks
- unwanted physical contact.

An employee can also be discriminated against if they are victimised because they have tried to take action about discrimination.

It is unlawful for an employer to discriminate against an employee on the grounds of their sexual orientation. This means that they cannot be discriminated against or harassed in the workplace because they are gay, lesbian, bisexual or heterosexual. All employees are protected whatever their sexual orientation.

It is unlawful for an employer to discriminate against employees on the grounds of their religion or belief. Religion generally means any religion, religious belief or similar philosophical belief. It does not include political beliefs. Employees are protected from discrimination whatever their employer's religion or belief, and whether they are already working for the employer or are applying for a job.

You can also find more information on the website of the Advisory, Conciliation and Arbitration Service (ACAS)

www.acas.org.uk

remember It is also unlawful discrimination when an employee is paid less than an employee of the opposite sex for doing the same or similar work.

If an employee has been discriminated against because of their religion or belief, they should get help from an experienced adviser as there is a strict three-month time limit for taking legal action on these grounds.

Working time rights

Working time rights are complicated and some do not apply to everyone. Usually employers and employees agree on working time rights. Important points are that:

- On average an employee should not work for more than 48 hours per week.
- This average is calculated in different ways for different jobs.
- Some individuals and groups of employees are not included, such as:
  - transport workers
  - offshore workers
  - junior doctors
  - members of the armed forces
  - the police
  - domestic staff in a private house.

In order for working time to count, an employee has to be at their workplace, carrying out working duties under the direction of their employer; such duties include:

- training at the workplace provided by the employer
- travel time to visit clients
- working lunches.

The following are not included:

- travelling to work
- time when the employee is on call but not working
- training at college
- time taken to travel to occasional meetings away from the normal workplace.

Sometimes individuals – or groups of employees – may choose to opt out of the 48-hour limit.

The limits also apply to people who work at night. Night officially begins at 11.00 p.m. and ends at 6.00 a.m. the following day. An employee working an evening shift that finishes at 2.00 a.m. is a night worker. Those who work at night should not do more than an average of 8 hours' work in each 24 hours. Working out the averages for night workers is particularly difficult. A night worker might work 9 hours per night over 5 nights per week. On paper this would break the 8 hours per 24 hours maximum, but in order to make the calculation a sixth night is added. So this reduces it to 7.5 hours, which is not over the limit.

See page 299 for more on Working Time Regulations.

Holidays and pay

Nearly all employees are entitled by law to four weeks' paid annual leave per leave year. But, in some cases, employees are not entitled to paid holiday.

Unless an employee's contract of employment gives them the bank holidays in addition to their four weeks' statutory paid holiday, bank holidays are included when calculating the four weeks' holiday. Therefore, an employee who is entitled only to the four weeks' statutory paid holiday and takes five days off in a year for bank holidays would only have another three weeks' holiday left to take.

Sunday working

Shop-workers who are employed in large shops (over 280 square feet) have certain rights if they are asked to work on Sundays. Those who work in betting shops count as shop-workers, but employees in the catering business do not and are not protected from having to work on Sundays. The catering business covers pubs, restaurants and cafes.

Shop workers have the same rights to limits on hours of work and entitlements to rest breaks as other employees in other industries.

If an employee is a shop-worker, and they started working for their employer before 26 August 1994 (4 December 1997 in Northern Ireland) they are called 'protected shop-workers'. If they do not wish to work on Sundays they do not have to, and, if their employer tries to dismiss them because they refuse to work on Sundays, they can automatically claim unfair dismissal at an employment tribunal (industrial tribunal in Northern Ireland). This applies regardless of:

- how long they have worked for their employer
- whether they work full time or part time
- how old they are.

Fig 14.10 Shop opening times

General Stores
Opening Times

Monday: 07.00 – 23.00
Tuesday: 07.00 – 23.00
Wednesday: 07.00 – 23.00
Thursday: 07.00 – 23.00
Friday: 07.00 – 23.00
Saturday: 08.00 – 23.00
Sunday: 10.00 –16.00

If an employee is a protected shop-worker, their employer must not treat them unfairly just because they do not wish to work on a Sunday.

Flexible working

The term 'flexible working' refers to flexibility in terms of time and location. There are several different types of flexible working as can be seen in Table 14.1.

Table 14.1 Flexible working

Flexible working practice	Description
Part-time working	Employees are contracted to work less than the standard or full-time hours.
Flexi-time	Employees have the freedom to work in the way they choose, outside a set core of hours determined by their employer.
Staggered hours	Employees have different start, finish and break times, allowing an organisation to operate longer hours.
Compressed working hours	Employees can cover their total number of hours in fewer working days, by working for longer hours on 2–4 days.
Job sharing	One full-time job is split between two employees who agree the hours between them and with the employer.
Shift swapping	Employees arrange shifts amongst themselves, provided that all shifts are covered to the employer's satisfaction.
Self-rostering	Employees nominate the shifts they would prefer to work, leaving the employer to compile shift patterns matching their individual preferences while covering all required shifts.
Time off in lieu (TOIL)	Employees take time off to compensate for extra hours worked.
Term-time working	An employee remains on a permanent contract but can take paid/unpaid leave during school holidays.
Annual hours	An employee's contracted hours are calculated over a year. The employer allocates the shifts and the remaining hours are kept in reserve so that employees can be called in at short notice as required.
V-time working	Employees agree to reduce their hours for a fixed period with a guarantee of full-time work when this period ends.
Zero-hours contracts	Employees work only the hours they are needed.
Home working/ teleworking	Employees spend all or some of their week working from home or somewhere else away from the employer's premises.
Sabbatical/career break	Employees are allowed to take an extended period of time off, either paid or unpaid.

Unfair dismissal

Unfair dismissal occurs when an employee is dismissed from their job and the employer does not have a valid reason for sacking them or has not acted in a reasonable way. Dismissal effectively ends the period of employment.

Dismissal can take place either verbally or in writing. Employers need to be careful when dismissing employees, as a claim for unfair dismissal could follow, with the case being referred to an employment tribunal. It is up to the employee to show that they have been dismissed unfairly and for the employer to show that they had a valid reason to dismiss the employee and that they acted reasonably.

Some reasons for unfair dismissal include:

- the employee using a statutory employment right, such as taking parental leave
- the employee becoming pregnant
- the employee being either a member of a trade union or refusing to join a trade union.

Other reasons could possibly be considered to be unfair but are harder to prove; these relate to:

- the employee's conduct
- the employee's ability to do the job
- the employee being chosen for redundancy
- the employee being forced to retire
- the employee being prevented from doing their job for a legal reason, such as losing their driving licence
- any other substantial reason.

See page 310–311 for more on other substantial reasons.

When dismissing the employee, the employer must give at least the notice stated in the contract of employment. The exception is dismissal due to gross misconduct. Gross misconduct means that the employee has committed an act that is serious enough to warrant their being instantly sacked. Examples of such misconduct are theft, fraud, and violence.

An employee who has been unfairly dismissed should first appeal under their employer's dismissal or disciplinary procedures. Sometimes, ACAS becomes involved in this. If things cannot be sorted out directly with the employer, the case may have to go to an employment tribunal. If the employee wins the case, they are entitled to get their job back or to receive compensation.

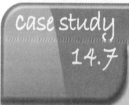

case study 14.7 — National Children's Home

Whether you're interested in working with children, a job in fundraising or another type of charity career, NCH is an employer of choice for jobs in the voluntary and social care field.

We work in England, Scotland, Wales and Northern Ireland to help vulnerable and disadvantaged children achieve their full potential. As a leading provider of children's services, we offer a really diverse range of career opportunities.

NCH's values

Our values and beliefs, together with employment legislation, form the basis of all our employment policies. We state these policies clearly; so all our employees know what they can expect from us.

At NCH we are committed to equality and diversity, for our workforce as well as the young people we support. We actively try to recruit people from a wide variety of backgrounds and with different life experiences.

We aim to make sure that everyone who works for us is treated fairly and consistently. We recognise that race, gender, disability, religion and other differences can affect our employees' rights and needs, and we address these wherever possible through working practices that are inclusive, anti-discriminatory and respectful of difference.

What it's like working for us

NCH is committed to helping people achieve their full potential, and that includes our employees. We understand that investing in our people is part of what makes us grow and move forward.

We aim to give all employees the opportunity to learn and develop their skills; through high-quality training that will help them do their job even more effectively. And we provide ongoing support, for instance through regular appraisals.

NCH aims to provide family-friendly working conditions, and our employment policies include provisions for maternity, paternity and adoption leave, and flexible working. We are also able to offer part-time career opportunities.

(Adapted from www.nch.org.uk)

Department for Business, Enterprise and Regulatory Reform (DBERR, formerly the Department for Trade and Industry)

www.dti.gov.uk

---

activity

INDIVIDUAL WORK 14.3

P3

M1

1 For P3, using Case study 14.7 as the basis for your investigation into polices, terms and conditions of contract, you will be expected to:

   (a) Identify the rights and responsibilities of employees and employers in a selected business organisation.

   (b) Research the organisation's policies and terms and conditions of contracts.

   (c) Apply current legislation and regulations to an organisation (in particular implied terms in contracts of employment).

2 For M1, which extends the work that you carried out for P3, you should:

   (a) Analyse the key effects of legislation on employees in the organisation.

   (b) Analyse the key effects of legislation on the employers in the organisation.

---

activity

INDIVIDUAL WORK 14.4

D1

Evaluate the extent to which a selected business organisation may have adapted working arrangements in order to accommodate legislation relating to rights and responsibilities of employees and employers. Building on the work for P3 and M1, you are required to:

1 Evaluate the extent to which a selected business organisation may have adapted working arrangements in order to accommodate legislation relating to the rights and responsibilities of employees.

Make sure that you do not just provide a description or analysis of the legislation but show awareness of the response prompted from employers.

Fig 14.11 UNISON's home page UNISON is Britain's biggest trade union, representing people who work in public services, the voluntary and private sectors

(Source: www.unison.org.uk)

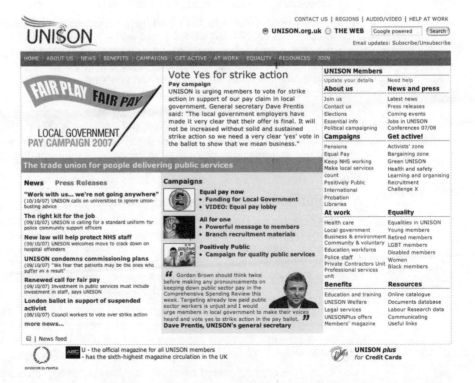

The various perspectives in employee relations

Organisations have begun to appreciate that good employee relations are not only desirable but could mean the difference between success and failure. Good employee relations with management can:

- reduce absenteeism
- avoid disputes
- encourage goodwill
- improve productivity
- encourage employees to be more committed and effective.

Increasingly, organisations are taking a number of steps to help establish and improve employee relations.

Establishing employee relations

The four cornerstones to effective employee relations are:

- Development – when employers are willing to encourage employees to improve their skills, this not only enables the employees to make a greater contribution to the business's performance but it also enhances their perception of the organisation and their self-esteem.

- Cooperation – many successful businesses focus on cooperation between management and other members of staff. They concentrate on establishing an ethos in which successes and failures are perceived as joint responsibilities and achievements.

- Communication – it is important that employers communicate effectively with their employees: messages must always be coherent, concise and clear.

- Leadership – this should be shown in the setting of objectives that will provide a sense of purpose for the organisation, by indicating to employees the long-term strategies and targets of the organisation, in which all can share and contribute to success.

> **remember**
>
> Increasingly, employees are being kept up to date about company matters by newsletters, meetings and email.

Types of contract

As we saw earlier in this unit, there are a number of variations in contracts of employment, with a wide variety of different working conditions, patterns and practices becoming increasingly common in nearly all types of work.

The key word is flexibility, both from the perspective of the employer and the employee. Much has been said and written about work–life balance. Flexible contracts move towards this goal, where an employee's existence is not dominated by set periods in which they must work for their employer. By acknowledging that employees have responsibilities and duties outside the workplace, an employer can generate conditions that enable the employee to be fully focused on their work during work time.

By recognising that employees increasingly desire non-standard contracts of employment, certainly in terms of working patterns, the employer is showing flexibility. For their part, the employees recognise that the employer is taking a flexible approach to their employment and see that the employer values their contribution to the extent that the employer is prepared to be flexible about working hours and practices.

Joint decision making and problem solving

For generations, decision making has been the responsibility of management. However, many organisations now see the benefit of including their employees in the decision-making process, rather than leaving all decisions in the hands of senior management. One reason is that, through working at the sharp end of an organisation's operations, employees are often more acutely aware than a senior manager of relationships with customers, suppliers and members of the public. Another is that joint decision making encourages mutual trust.

Bringing employees into the decision-making process provides management with new ideas, helping the organisation to innovate and streamline and improve the way in which it operates. A business may find that some employees are able to provide valuable insights into the organisation's policies and practices; this should be encouraged.

Employees are empowered when they are involved in key decisions and given the chance to participate in joint problem solving. With joint problem solving, employees have the opportunity to identify practical, as well as cost-efficient, ways of sorting out difficulties within the organisation. (They may often have struggled with outdated, irrelevant or unnecessarily complicated procedures that had been set up by managers in the past.) In some organisations, employees can join groups, often referred to as quality circles, where they are encouraged to contribute ideas to improve productivity, reduce waste, avoid accidents and injuries and, ultimately, increase profitability. It is important that the organisation makes it clear that, if, as a result of adopting employees' proposals for improvement, more profit is made, a proportion will be passed on to the employees.

Appraisals and performance management

Appraisals

Performance appraisals are designed to help manage and evaluate employees. They are also used to help develop individual employees, as well as for improving organisational performance. Many organisations use formal performance appraisals annually for all employees in the organisation. It is usual for employees to be appraised by their immediate line manager. The managing director, who in turn could be appraised by the chairperson or the owners of the business, can appraise directors.

The purposes of the annual appraisals are:

- to assist management
- to monitor standards
- to agree expectations and objectives
- to delegate responsibilities and tasks.

Usually performance appraisals are designed to review an employee's performance against specific objectives and standards. These would have been agreed at the previous appraisal meeting. Many organisations view performance appraisals as essential for:

- improving staff motivation
- improving attitudes and behaviours
- communicating the organisation's aims
- encouraging positive relationships between management and the rest of the staff.

Performance appraisals provide a formal and recorded regular review of performance, and the outcome is a basis for planning the employee's future development. In performance appraisals, employees identify their individual training needs, allowing managers to plan the overall training needs of the organisation.

It is important that appraisals do not discriminate on the grounds of sexual orientation, race, religion, gender, and disability or age. Organisations recognise that managers need guidance, training and encouragement in order to conduct appraisals properly and effectively. A well-prepared and well-conducted appraisal can provide a unique opportunity to help employees and, as a result, the organisation itself.

There are several different types of performance appraisal, some of which are carried out monthly, quarterly, bi-annually or annually; these include:

- formal annual performance appraisals
- probationary reviews
- informal one-to-one reviews
- counselling meetings
- on-the-job observation
- job- or skill-related tests
- assessment centres
- surveys to gather the opinions of those who deal with the employee
- **behavioural assessments**
- **handwriting analysis**.

In order to carry out an ideal performance appraisal, the manager should:

- ensure that everything is prepared in advance, including any documents required
- inform the appraisee in advance, so that they can assemble documents and gather their thoughts
- ensure that the venue is private and free from interruptions

- ensure that the layout of the room is informal and that the appraiser is not sitting behind a desk
- introduce the appraisal in a way that relaxes the appraisee, probably by starting with a positive statement about them
- ensure that the appraiser and the appraisee cooperate to review and measure what they have done in the period running up to the appraisal
- ensure that an overall action plan is agreed
- help the appraisee to identify specific objectives to be achieved before the next appraisal
- ensure that any necessary support for the appraisee is offered and provided
- give the appraisee the chance to make other points and ask questions
- ensure that the appraisal finishes positively
- record the main points, agreed action and follow-up and pass these on to the human resources department and the manager's/appraiser's line manager.

Performance management

Performance management is designed to encourage individual employees to contribute effectively to the organisation's performance. Therefore, managers must try to establish with their employees a shared understanding about what needs to be achieved.

Performance management involves three key areas:

- performance improvement – for individual employees, for teams of employees and for the organisation itself
- development – of individual employees and teams in order to ensure that performance improves
- management of behaviour – to encourage individuals to behave in ways that bring about better working relationships

All this places a considerable weight on the manager. In order to achieve performance management, a manager needs to be able to manage effectively, which means:

- ensuring that employees understand what is expected of them
- taking steps to ensure that employees have the skills and abilities to do what is expected of them
- ensuring that employees are given feedback on their performance
- discussing and contributing to individual employee and team aims and objectives.

When managing performance, regular appraisal is needed in order to identify:

- whether employees are aware of what is required of them
- whether they have the necessary skills and abilities to carry out their work or need to develop new ones.

Regular appraisal also gives the manager the opportunity to give employees feedback on their performance. As a consequence, the organisation is committing itself to the learning and development of its employees. In many cases, this is achieved by drawing up a personal development plan for each employee.

Other useful methods of improving an employee's performance include:

- coaching – putting an experienced employee alongside a less experienced one

Fig 14.12 Coaching

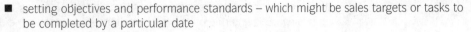

■ setting objectives and performance standards – which might be sales targets or tasks to be completed by a particular date

■ identifying competences – what people need to be able to do to perform a job

■ measurement – knowledge of current performance and how it compares with desired performance levels

■ pay – some organisations introduce performance-related pay; employees are paid in relation to the level of performance that they sustain, or meeting objectives and improving performance standards are directly linked to pay.

Social responsibility and employee welfare

In the next few years there may well be government legislation to encourage corporate social responsibility by ensuring that businesses and organisations take social responsibility seriously and are punished in cases where they have ignored it. Corporate social responsibility draws an organisation's attention to:

■ community involvement

■ producing socially responsible products, using socially responsible processes

■ having socially responsible employee relations.

In the context of employee relations, corporate social responsibility means that an organisation should:

■ encourage diversity within its workforce

■ ensure that there is equal opportunity in the organisation

■ have a strong commitment to training and development

■ take health and safety issues seriously

■ ensure that as far as is practicable employees are part of the decision-making and problem-solving processes.

For further information on businesses' social responsibilities, visit the website of Corporate Social Responsibility

www.csr.gov.uk

In many organisations where there is an employee welfare panel or discussion group, the panel, or group, focuses on the organisation's policies relating to health, safety or welfare. But other organisations take a broader view of employee welfare.

See pages 299–305, where employee welfare is looked at in detail.

Dispute resolution

The Employment Act 2002 outlined the main ways in which disputes between employers and employees should be settled. Disputes at work can be stressful, disruptive and expensive, but in many cases can be solved by discussion.

The Employment Act set out to:

■ encourage employers and employees to discuss disputes and look at ways to resolve them

■ ensure that the employment tribunal system is effective.

At the very least, employers and employees have to follow a three-stage process:

1. Write a letter explaining the issue.

2. Have a meeting to discuss the issue.

3. Hold an appeal meeting if necessary.

Other organisations will become involved in dispute resolution if this is required.

Trade unions are independent organisations representing employees. They can provide specialist representatives from within the organisation where the employee works or bring in experts from the trade union to help resolve a dispute.

Employment tribunals are independent bodies that are set up to listen to the views of the opposing sides and rule on the right way forward to resolve the dispute. Both the employer and the employee will undertake to abide by the tribunal's decision.

ACAS (Advisory, Conciliation and Arbitration Service) is an independent organisation that seeks to provide best-practice advice for both employers and employees. It has various codes of practice for dealing with different types of dispute. If ACAS becomes involved in a dispute, both parties will agree to abide by its ruling on the situation.

Staff associations are set up as an alternative to trade unions and are usually funded by the employer. Staff associations and trade unions have access to similar information, and, like a trade union, a staff association can provide individuals with assistance in resolving a dispute without involving an external organisation.

remember

Staff associations are not independent organisations. They are run and funded by the business and usually do not negotiate on behalf of employees.

Visit the website of ACAS

www.acas.org.uk

---

case study
14.8

ACAS gets busier

In the period 2005–6 ACAS received over 900,000 calls for assistance in employment issues. Over the same period it dealt with 952 large-scale disputes. The ACAS website received 1.7m visits and over the same period there were over 109,000 applications to employment tribunals, of which nearly 36,000 related to unfair dismissal.

ACAS tries to advise on ways of managing conflict and disputes by acting as a neutral third party. Its services are voluntary and confidential. The organisation was founded in 1975 and now has over 30 years' experience. Around 750 staff work for the organisation in 11 regional centres throughout England, Scotland and Wales.

(Adapted from www.acas.org.uk)

activity

1 Why do you think ACAS is experiencing an increasing number of requests for assistance?

2 Why do you think unfair dismissal is a common cause for complaint?

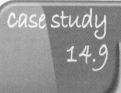

case study
14.9

Trouble with chain saws

The Haddiscoe Engineering factory in Salford is in chaos. The same could be said for all of the factories. The Salford factory is on strike and the other factories are refusing to cooperate with management and head office.

Head office has given the striking workers 48 hours to give in, otherwise they intend to sack every one of them and close the factory. The trade unions are convinced that this was the plan all along. The trade union representative has said: 'After years of devoted labour by our members, the company is content to cast them aside in the name of cost cutting. The company's employees deserve better than this: to have unreasonable new working conditions imposed on them on a take-it-or-leave-it basis. We'll dig in for the long term and seek help in the courts.'

Harold Haddiscoe, now 89 and the founder of the business replied: 'This is my business! I mean that! I will not pussyfoot around with these people. I'm the boss, they do as they are told or they get out. I don't give a damn about them, never have, and never will!'

His grandson Harold Haddiscoe Jnr added: 'Grandad is a bit old-fashioned. But I'm equally convinced that we make the decisions, not the workforce. I want to come to terms with them, but not on their terms, mine.'

Two days later, trucks started arriving at the factory to remove machinery and a 'for sale' sign was posted at the factory gate. There were clashes that day between the employees, the police and the truck drivers and it was the lead story on the TV news that night.

---

activity
INDIVIDUAL WORK 14.5

P4

M2

1 For P4, using the information presented in Case study 14.9, the continued story of Haddiscoe Engineering (Case study 14.2). You should:

(a) Explain the key features of the relationships between the employer and the employees in the dispute.

(b) Explain the welfare implications of the dispute.

2 For M2, using the case studies based on Haddiscoe Engineering. You should:

(a) Analyse the main causes of the disagreements.

(b) Ensure that you analyse the previous set of working conditions and agreements compared with the new situation.

(c) Identify which party has caused the dispute.

(d) Suggest how it could be resolved.

(e) Give examples of similar disputes in Great Britain and in the European Union.

---

activity
INDIVIDUAL WORK 14.6

D2

Following on from the work for P4 and M2 and using the case studies about Haddiscoe Engineering, you are required to:

1 Outline the main arguments presented by both sides in the dispute.

2 Assess and weigh up their claims and requirements.

3 Evaluate each side's case.

4 Make a judgement about the rights and wrongs and which side is correct.

Employee welfare

It is in the interests of employers to ensure that staff are cared for whilst at work. This care often goes beyond the hours spent at the workplace and extends to their health, retirement, personal issues, family responsibilities and stress levels.

Working Time Regulations

For many years Great Britain had the longest working week for employees. By the time that the Working Time Regulations came into force in 1998 (amended in 2003), many countries in Europe had already passed laws limiting the number of working hours.

It is in the interests of both employers and employees that employees are not overly tired when at work. Lack of sleep and too-short periods between shifts can not only cause accidents at work but also health problems.

Now employees must not work an average of more than 48 hours per week. They must also not work more than 8 hours in each 24. Alongside these restrictions the Working Time Regulations set out:

■ an employee's right to 11 hours' rest a day

■ the right to a day off each week

■ the right to have an in-work rest period if the working day is more than six hours

■ a right to four weeks' paid leave each year.

Medical schemes

Many different types of private medical insurance are offered in Great Britain. Organisations often opt for comprehensive medical insurance for their employees, as this shields the organisation from the financial impact of large medical bills. Also, once the organisation has paid for the insurance, it is the insurance company's responsibility to handle administration and obtain private medical treatment for the employees. Another very practical reason for running a medical scheme is that the organisation's employees can benefit from health screening or health checks.

Usually, core provisions in private medical insurance include:

- cover for short-term, acute medical conditions
- surgery
- hospital accommodation and nursing
- in-patient tests.

Each insured employee is required to complete a medical history declaration, which will reveal existing medical conditions. Any existing medical conditions are usually excluded from the insurance cover.

Although some employees may have their own private medical insurance, it is always better to become part of a company medical insurance scheme for the following reasons:

- As the organisation is buying a bulk amount of medical insurance, it can obtain a better price.
- The insurance automatically covers the employee's partner and children.

Health and safety

It is the responsibility of employers to ensure that their employees know what hazards and risks they may face in the workplace and how to deal with them. For this reason, employers arrange health and safety training during working hours. The employer should make sure that all employees receive appropriate training. Some employees may have particular training needs, for example:

- new employees
- employees changing jobs or taking on extra responsibilities
- younger employees (they are statistically more likely to have an accident).

The Health and Safety at Work Act 1974 states that:

- Employees must be trained and clearly instructed in their duties.
- Employers and host companies must ensure that any contractors are properly trained and can work safely and competently.

Occupational health screening

Some health screening is driven entirely by health and safety at work considerations. For example, employees working in a factory environment may have to have regular hearing tests. Even before an employee starts work candidates may have an employment screening to test their fitness for the job.

The main purpose of occupational health screening is to:

- establish and maintain a healthy working environment
- ensure the best physical and mental health in relation to work
- adapt work to the capabilities of employees in relation to their physical and mental health.

At its very basic level, occupational health screening is used to confirm an employee's fitness to continue work. Key occupational health issues include:

- smoking, and drug and alcohol abuse
- stress
- **repetitive strain injury** and back pain
- control of hazardous substances
- disease prevention and control
- violence, bullying and harassment
- work–life balance.

case study
14.10

Occupational health issues

Over the years, occupational health screening has highlighted particular problems in different industries. A lorry driver, for example, spends a number of hours at the wheel each day, so their bones and their muscles need to be checked. In agriculture, chemicals and pesticides can be a problem. In offices, seating, desks, lighting and noise levels can all cause health problems. In food and catering, some employees may have allergies or infections if they are in contact with certain substances. In a warehouse, an employee may be exposed to sudden changes in temperature; they may need to life heavy objects, and often there is poor lighting.

In order to combat the basic occupational health problems, employers must provide clean toilets with water, soap and a towel or drier. Drinking water should also be provided. Employees should work in clean areas, with waste material removed on a regular basis. They need to have adequate space to work in, and there should be a comfortable working temperature.

activity

1   What is the term used to describe office equipment that has been designed to give maximum comfort and support?

2   How might a kitchen worker, allergic to cleaning materials, be protected?

Redundancy counselling

The organisation making the employee redundant has a responsibility to help them obtain work. This extends to assisting them to look for work and attend interviews and selection processes. Redundancy counselling includes identification of the employee's marketable skills, knowledge and experience. Assistance can also be given in how to create a CV, write effective covering letters and complete application forms. Training in interview skills may also be provided.

See pages 235–257 in Unit 13 for more information on interviews.

Sometimes, the organisation that the employee is leaving will be in a position to carry out the redundancy counselling; alternatively, an outside agency can be brought in to assist the employees. This is likely to be the case if the organisation doesn't have sufficient resources or expertise or is closing down.

The key aims of redundancy counselling include:

■   helping employees through a traumatic situation

■   providing them with best-practice advice

■   providing them with ways to develop new career ideas

■   assisting them in practical and urgent job searches

■   providing a caring environment for staff that have been retained

■   softening the blow of redundancy by providing assistance

■   helping the families of employees that are under stress

■   providing positive help in a negative situation

■   demonstrating the organisation's integrity.

See pages 311–312 for more about redundancy.

Retirement preparation and pensions

The average employee may spend 20 years getting to a position where they know what kind of job they would like to do and 40 years at work. During this time, they may give little consideration to what will happen when they retire.

There are many issues for employees to consider, such as what they will do with their time, how they will stay fit and healthy, and how much money they will have. A typical British household's income falls by 60% at retirement. Assuming an average annual income of nearly £23,000, retired people will have to live on less than the minimum wage each week.

Retirement preparation programmes usually cover:

- adjusting to a new lifestyle – re-orientating the importance of work and establishing new goals and routines
- health issues – how to improve health, exercise and nutrition
- home and environment – whether the home will serve the person as they get older and whether they should realise any of their assets
- leisure interests – encouraging and increasing interests, such as hobbies and activities
- retirement career options – whether the employee wants to carry on working in some capacity and what their options might be
- family and relationship issues – how these may be affected by retirement.

Fig 14.13 Adapting to retirement can be problematic and may also lead to money concerns

It very much depends on the individual's personal circumstances as to what type of pension they will receive when they finish work. In the majority of cases, individuals will be entitled to a state pension paid by the Pension Service, which is part of the Department for Work and Pensions. Some of those individuals will also have occupational pensions, which have been set up by their employers to provide them with income in retirement. There are different types of pension scheme:

- With a final salary scheme the employee receives a percentage of the total available pension for each year they have worked for the organisation.
- With a money purchase scheme, the amount of money paid into the scheme and how that has been invested has a bearing on how much the ex-employee receives during retirement.
- Personal and stakeholder pensions are investment policies for retirement; these are often referred to as personal pension plans. The individual contributes to the plan; the money is invested and the fund builds up. When retirement occurs the individual can take up to 25% of the value of the fund, and the remainder becomes the fund from which their pension is paid. Minimum standards for personal and stakeholder pensions are laid down by law.
- Specialist pension arrangements include employer-financed retirement benefit schemes. These are usually designed to provide additional benefits for high-level/highly paid executives.

remember

Final salary schemes are in danger, as pension funds have insufficient cash to support them. This has meant reductions in payouts and requests from employers for employees to postpone retirement.

Loans

Employers may choose to make loans available to employees, to buy for example:

- a season ticket
- a computer
- a bicycle.

The repayments are nearly always made through the payroll system in the form of deductions from the employee's salary or wages. The employer will:

- make deductions of the amount specified by the loan agreement
- keep records of the deductions that have been made
- ensure that the deductions reduce the loan balance.

An employee's eligibility for an interest-free or low-interest loan is likely to depend on their having worked for the organisation for a minimum number of months or on successful completion of their probationary period of employment.

Benevolent funds

Occupational benevolent funds provide assistance for employees, past and present, as and when the need arises. The funds, which are charities, provide a range of support services to individuals with a connection to a particular organisation, industry, trade or profession. Some funds were set up in the nineteenth century. Recipients of help include:

- children with difficulties
- single parents
- people with physical or other support needs.

There are benevolent funds related to the army, the Royal Air Force, the civil service veterinary surgeons and actors.

Visit the websites of the civil service benevolent fund or the actors' benevolent fund

www.csbf.org.uk

www.actorsbenevolentfund.co.uk

Assistance with housing costs and travel

In certain parts of the country, housing costs are so high that organisations find it very difficult to attract recruits. If high housing costs make it difficult for an employee to live close to the organisation, the alternative is to travel considerable distances to and from work. This can be a considerable drain on the employee and put them off applying for a job or staying with an organisation.

Organisations recognise that unnecessary financial pressure is placed on employees who find it difficult to afford suitable accommodation and may be forced to live further afield. To offset some of these difficulties, organisations have begun to consider subsidising housing and travel costs.

Usually, most employees can only receive money spent on travel if the travel is related to their work. Organisations may consider some or all of the following:

- subsidised season tickets
- company cars
- encouragement of car sharing.

The real solution to high housing and travel costs is for the employer to encourage – and provide the infrastructure for – employees to work away from the main site. This requires considerable reappraisal of their employee–employer relations, control processes and management style.

Personal problems

An employee may experience personal problems due to:

- work pressure
- long hours

- management style
- problems at home
- inability to relax
- promotion to a position where they cannot cope.

Such problems create stress for the employee (and sometimes their families too). According to the findings of the Health and Safety Executive, on any given day around 0.25 million people in Britain are off work due to stress. It is believed that stress is responsible for around 40% of all absences from work. It can also reduce an employee's performance by 70%. Work- or home-related stress costs British organisations nearly £4bn each year (Health and Safety Executive, 2005).

Before an employee can be assisted with personal problems, it is first necessary for someone in the organisation to notice that there is a problem. Secondly, the employee has to be aware that someone within the organisation is prepared to discuss problems brought to their attention.

To fend off the possibility of additional health problems and depression, some organisations offer stress management courses or deal with each issue on a one-to-one basis with stress counselling. In this way, employees feel supported by their workplace, and most stress-related problems can be resolved after 6 to 10 sessions with a counsellor.

Créches and nursery schemes

In order to attract and retain working parents, employers have recognised the need to provide subsidised créche and nursery schemes, and some do so as part of their overall employee welfare package. (Créches are designed for the very young; nurseries are set up to provide a bridge between the créche and school.)

Inevitably, demand outstrips places. It is important for the organisation to ensure that there is no bias in the allocation of spaces and that each employee has an equal chance for their children to attend.

Fig 14.14 A créche

Job share and flexible working

As we have already seen, job shares require the blessing of the organisation, along with the cooperation of other employees who will share the full time post. Job sharing has become increasingly popular as it combines many of the advantages of a full-time job with the flexibility offered by only working part of a week. Employers have recognised the value of job shares, realising that having two or more individuals responsible for covering a single post can be more beneficial than having just one employee. This is despite some occasions when the work may be disjointed because the job sharers are swapping over.

Job shares are just one example of a flexible working practice; as we saw earlier in this unit, there are a number and they are becoming increasingly popular. Flexible working has advantages for employer and employee. It enables both parties to compromise on working arrangements to take account of the demands of the work itself; it may come about with the support of the employees, or be requested by employees and supported by the employer.

Finally, flexible working can be viewed as an integral part of employee welfare because it takes into account the demands of employees' responsibilities outside the workplace, particularly their responsibilities as carers.

Remuneration

The term remuneration refers to salaries and wages received by employees. Pay has a major effect on relationships at work; organisations have become aware that pay and benefits affect not only the efficiency of the organisation but also the productivity and morale of the employees.

Salary and wages

When setting up its employee remuneration packages, the organisation's first major choice is whether payment will be made as a salary or as a wage. Both systems are designed to reward individuals for their contribution. Ideally, the payment system would be simple and straightforward, so that everyone can see exactly how they are paid and why they are paid that amount.

Salaries refer to a stated yearly amount of money that will be paid to the employee before tax and other deductions. Normally, this total amount is split into 12 equal payments to be made at some point in each month (usually the same day). Salaries are usually paid directly into employees' bank accounts.

Wages, on the other hand, simply refer either to an agreed weekly payment or to payment based on an hourly rate. Again, for the most part, tax and other deductions will already have been taken out before the employer passes on the payment to the employee. Payment may be made in cash or by cheque. It is difficult for the employer to pay weekly by bank transfer without knowing in advance just how much the pay will be for that week. This can be alleviated by paying wage-based employees a week in arrears.

Time rate systems

With time rate systems, remuneration is made on the basis of the number of hours worked by each employee over a given period of time. The system may be used because the number of hours is uncertain each week or the employees are not on full-time contracts. In either case, an agreed payment per hour is established, up to a certain number of hours per week. Beyond that an overtime rate, higher than the usual rate, will be paid. Normally, time rate employees are paid wages rather than salaries.

See pages 315–348 in Unit 21 for more information on contracts.

Payment by results

With this system there is a direct link between pay and output: the harder the employee works, the more they will earn. Although payment by results is one of the strongest incentives, there is a major difficulty with the system. An employee's earnings may fall due to a drop in output for which they are not responsible and over which they had no control. It may be that managers did not allocate work appropriately or properly control output, or the targets may not have been reasonable. It could be that shortages or delays affected production.

Incentive schemes

Incentive schemes are usually overlaid on top of basic pay. The intention is to reward employees for having achieved or exceeded certain targets or objectives over a period of time. The reward may take the form of bonuses or additional payments related to the profitability of the organisation.

Skills-based payments

These schemes, which are sometimes known as competency-based payment systems, have increased in popularity over recent years. The employer must first identify the competences needed and how to assess them accurately. Reward then depends on how good an employee is in carrying out the job: in other words, how they apply their knowledge, skills and behaviour to perform the job to the best of their ability. The system relies on the employees' gaining new and improved skills and encourages multi-skilling and flexibility.

High day rate and measured day work

A day-rate system sets the basic pay to be received for a particular shift. Low day-rate systems are a problem as there is no incentive for the employee to be productive. High day-rate systems, however, rely on the honesty and integrity of employees to put in a productive day's work for the relatively high daily rate.

Measured day work is a hybrid system that falls somewhere between payment by results and a basic wage-rate system. The pay is fixed and performance standards are set. Employees are kept motivated by good supervision, monitoring and goal setting. This payment system is now relatively rare as it only suits organisations where a high, steady and predictable level of performance is required.

Salary and wage structures

The salary and wage structure within an organisation is a reflection of the value that the organisation places on employees at different levels in terms of responsibility and experience.

Clearly, any salary and wage structure will favour the following:

- employees with specific and/or rare skills and experience
- employees who have stayed with the organisation for a considerable period of time
- employees who have taken advantage of training opportunities and have followed a clear career path.

The salary and wage structure will also reflect an individual's level of education, certainly when they are first matched to a job role within the organisation.

The payment structure usually mirrors the organisational structure. Individuals in relatively unskilled posts, and perhaps with a varied level of work, are more likely to be paid wages rather than salaries. It is usual for office-based staff to be paid salaries, even in relatively unskilled administrative jobs.

When developing any kind of payment structure, an organisation should begin by gathering information: some comparisons need to be made with like organisations or competitors. Sources of data include:

- local and national salary surveys
- pay rates in similar organisations
- recruitment pages in the local and national press
- local authority pay scales.

See pages 357–358 in Unit 26 for more on external sources of data.

Reward systems

An integral part of motivating staff is to recognise their achievements and reward them by putting them higher up the pay scale or increasing their benefits.

The three categories of reward systems are:

- monetary rewards (e.g. bonuses, commission, lump sums for excellence, annual bonuses and profit sharing)
- monetary equivalent rewards (e.g. cars, telephones, insurance, tuition fees, holidays, club subscriptions, company discounts, low-interest loans, gifts and gift vouchers, and other benefits, such as clothing or accommodation)
- non-monetary rewards (e.g. additional status, plaques, certificates, bigger offices and promotion).

Fig 14.15 A system of rewards can be used as an incentive

Additions to basic pay

There are three major types of addition to basic pay:

- Overtime is an enhanced hourly rate of pay, which is applied to hours worked over and above the normal working week.
- Bonuses are paid either on an individual, group or organisation-wide basis; they relate to employees' contributions to the organisation's success and profitability. In effect, the employees are given a small share of the additional profit.
- Special allowances: for example, the organisation pays for medical insurance, provides loans or subsidises travel and housing costs.

Income tax, National Insurance contributions and other stoppages

Normally, the organisation deals with stoppages or deductions from an employee's pay. Each employee is allocated a personal allowance or tax code. This specifies the amount of pay that they can earn in a year before they must pay tax. The percentage of income tax paid is dependent upon the taxable income of the employee. For the most part, individuals pay 22%. If the taxable income is over £33,000, they pay 40% tax.

Tax is not the only government-required deduction from earnings. National Insurance contributions are levied at a rate of 11% on any earnings above £97 per week.

The organisation may make other stoppages, including:

- the employee's contribution to a pension scheme
- the employee's payment to a trade union
- repayment of a loan made by the organisation
- payment in response to a court judgment requiring collection of money due as a fine
- payment to a savings clubs
- payment to the Child Support Agency.

Major influences on pay

As in many situations where one group of individuals has something to offer that another group wishes to buy, pay is very much a question of supply and demand. If there is low unemployment in an area then an organisation must, in order to attract employees, offer pay and benefits at a better rate than other businesses in the region.

In the past, trade unions had a very strong impact on the rates of salaries and wages. In some types of work, nearly all employees were members of trade unions and employers had to negotiate with the trade unions on pay, benefits and conditions. Trade unions are no longer as strong as they were, and many organisations deal directly with individual employees to agree pay and conditions.

Employers have recognised the value of having 'transparent' or clear pay structures to offset problems and to offer opportunities for progression.

As we have seen in this unit, organisations are aware of the fact that employees respond positively when additional payments are made to reward their productivity. However, the system of performance-related pay only works well if the organisation has established reasonable levels of productivity as the benchmarks for reward.

As a member of the European Union, Great Britain is obliged to follow its regulations, including those relating to national minimum wage and working time. These have a direct impact on pay.

Traditional customs and practices can also have a direct bearing on pay. Sometimes, there is a long-established way of paying employees that neither the employees nor the employer wishes to change. These customs and practices include paying more to employees with specific skills or experience or longer service.

As we have seen, with relatively low unemployment in Great Britain, there is fierce competition for the best potential employees. As many employees are prepared to travel considerable distances to work and competition for the better candidates is fierce, pay is one of the main ways in which they can be attracted.

On the one hand the government wants to reduce unemployment and on the other it wants to improve the working conditions of employees, but it recognises that pay, benefits and conditions have to be affordable to employers. So the balance between better conditions for employees and workable procedures for employers is always important.

Policies for wages and pay

Wages and pay policies need, above all, to appear to be transparent and fair. As we will see in this section, some of these policies are directly related to the shortage of suitable employees; others focus on the balancing of costs, and others put in to practice the requirements of the law.

Key purposes of policies

When setting their wages and pay policies, organisations usually have one or more of the following purposes in mind:

- to attract suitable staff
- to retain and reward existing employees
- to recognise and reward key employees
- to make a link in fortunes between the employee and the organisation
- to ensure that one or more parts of the organisation do not have a heavy wage or pay burden
- to ensure that the minimum legal requirements are applied
- to ensure that employees remain motivated by the promise of rewards.

remember

Lack of suitable candidates does not just apply to the local area. Employers have to cast their net far wider than ever before, even looking abroad, within the European Union, to find potential employees.

---

activity

INDIVIDUAL WORK 14.7

P5

Describe the different methods of remuneration and the policies adopted in a selected business organisation.

For this task, you will need to select an organisation that has a wide range of different pay schemes in operation. Ideally, you should choose one that has both permanent and temporary staff, full and part time, and uses casual or hourly paid workers. You should:

1　Investigate the organisation's policies on remuneration.
2　Describe the policies on pay.
3　Explain how the payments are made.

How contracts of employment may be terminated

As we have seen, there have been a number of changes to employment law and regulations. In theory, employment can still be terminated at any time. However, unless the dismissal is fair, the employer can be found guilty of unfair dismissal at an employment tribunal.

In the second part of this section we will look at redundancy, which is a slightly different set of circumstances but also ends with the termination of the contract of employment.

See pages 315–348 in Unit 21 for more information on contracts.

Dismissal procedures

There are three basic steps in what is known as the dismissal and disciplinary procedure. These are governed by the Dispute Resolution Regulations 2004 and apply to all types of dismissal, including:

- dismissal on grounds of conduct
- dismissal on grounds of capability
- redundancy
- retirement
- expiry of a fixed-term contract
- unsuccessful probationary period.

The standard three-step dismissal and disciplinary procedure is:

1. The employer sets out in writing why the dismissal or disciplinary action against the employee is being considered.
2. A meeting takes place to discuss the matter.
3. An appeal procedure is then established.

Disciplinary procedures

The first step in a disciplinary procedure is a written statement by the employer, setting out why the disciplinary action is being taken. The employer may choose to suspend the employee at this stage, but suspension is not a punishment and it must be made on full pay. The employer will then investigate the situation and copies of the resulting documents will be given to the employee.

After the initial statement has been made by the employer, meetings are usually organised. Employees have a right to be accompanied to the meeting, possibly by a trade union representative. Either at the end of the meeting or shortly after, the employer will make a decision regarding the action to be taken; this could be:

- no further action
- a verbal warning
- a written warning
- a final warning
- demotion
- dismissal.

As we will see later, the employee has a right to appeal and to take their case to an employment tribunal.

Grievance procedures

Grievance procedures involve an employee making a complaint about the employer. Typical problems leading to grievance procedures relate to:

- terms of employment
- pay and working conditions
- disagreements with other employees
- discrimination
- breach of statutory employment rights.

There is a straightforward three-step procedure, which begins with the employee setting out the grievance in writing. After this, a meeting should be held to discuss the problem and the employer will then undertake to remedy the situation and arrive at a decision as to how it should be dealt with. If the employee is not satisfied with the decision, there is a right to appeal. The appeal is first made to the employer and, if the situation is not remedied, the case can be referred to an employment tribunal. The matter needs to be referred to the tribunal within three months.

Unfair dismissal

Unfair dismissal occurs when an employer does not have a valid reason for dismissing an employee, or their actions were unreasonable. Dismissal can occur with or without notice and can be carried out verbally or in writing.

Some reasons are automatically unfair; these include:

■ the employee taking or attempting to take a statutory employment right, such as parental leave

■ the employee falling pregnant

■ the employee either deciding to join or not to join a trade union.

Reasons for potentially unfair dismissal can include:

■ conduct

■ ability to do the job

■ redundancy

■ retirement

■ another substantial reason.

The individual should first appeal directly to the employer. If this appeal fails, ACAS can be used or an employment tribunal. If the tribunal finds in favour of the employee, the employee is entitled either to get their job back or to be paid compensation.

Grounds for dismissal

Employers must have a good reason for dismissing an employee from a job. The reason needs to be justified and genuine.

Reasons relating to conduct include:

■ continually failing to turn up to work

■ poor discipline

■ drug or alcohol abuse

■ theft or dishonesty.

Reasons for dismissing an individual on the grounds of their capability include:

■ not keeping up with technological changes

■ not being able to get along with other employees

■ long-term or persistent illness, making it impossible for them to do their job (if the employee has a disability then the employer has a legal duty to find a way around this problem).

Redundancy is another reason for dismissal, as we will see in the next section. Finally, there is a category of grounds known as 'other substantial reasons'; these include

■ imprisonment

■ an irresolvable personality clash with another employee

■ if the business moves to another location and it is not possible for the employee to move

■ unreasonably refusing to accept reorganisation that may change the terms of employment.

Appeals and employment tribunals

This is effectively the third step of the statutory procedure. All employees have a right to appeal against the decision made by their employer. An appeal can be made for the following reasons:

■ The employee thinks the decision is wrong.

■ Unfair procedures were used.

■ The punishment is too harsh.

■ New evidence has come to light.

In certain cases the employee can go to an employment tribunal, but not if they have just received a warning. Usually the employment tribunal will listen to the case if:

- There was unlawful discrimination in the procedure.
- The employee was punished in breach of their statutory rights (such as for joining a trade union).
- There was constructive dismissal (the employee felt they had to resign after the decision had been made).
- The dismissal was unfair.

Employment tribunals are less formal than other courts. Applications must be made within three months, and the tribunal will check to see whether the employee has a reasonable claim. Usually, once employers are aware that an employment tribunal will become involved, they seek to sort out the matter beforehand.

Redundancy

Redundancy means that there is no longer enough work for a particular employee to do. This situation can occur if:

- The employer closes or restructures.
- The employer relocates.
- The employer needs fewer workers.

Basic provisions

The first major problem is for the employer to decide who will be made redundant. The choice will, of course, depend on the circumstances, but the most commonly used procedures are:

- **last in first out**
- asking for volunteers
- looking at disciplinary records
- selection on the basis of appraisals, skills, qualifications and experience.

Employers may not unfairly select individuals for redundancy. Unfair reasons include:

- membership or non-membership of a trade union
- an employee exercising their statutory rights
- **whistle blowing**
- lawful industrial action
- taking action on health and safety grounds
- doing jury service.

Legislation

The laws relating to redundancy can be found in the Employment Rights Act 1996, as amended, and in the Trade Union and Labour Relations (Consolidation) Act 1992. These laws set down the basic provisions and describe what counts as fair and unfair dismissal as a result of redundancy. When the reason for redundancies is given as reduction of the workforce, the employer must prove that fewer employees are needed. If closure is cited as the reason for redundancies, there must be a genuine reason for closure.

For more information about the Employment Rights Act 1996, visit the website of the Office of Public Sector Information (look for Acts passed in 1996)

www.opsi.gov.uk

Procedures, policies and provision

Having established that there is a real need for redundancies, and regardless of the methods of selection, the employer is encouraged to consult with the employees. This can be done either collectively, by talking to the whole group (or subgroups) of those who will be made redundant, or on an individual basis.

An elected employee representative or trade union representative needs to take part in the discussions. The consultation usually covers ways in which redundancy could be avoided, with the plan being to minimise the number of dismissals. The employer should talk directly to each employee about why they have been selected and investigate alternatives to redundancy, such as retraining the employee for another job within the organisation.

Calculation of payments

As well as a redundancy payment, the employer should give the employee proper notice of termination of employment or pay in lieu of notice. The employer must give at least the statutory minimum redundancy payment. When calculating the redundancy payment, the following are taken into account:

- how long the employee has been continuously employed
- the employee's age
- their weekly pay, up to the current legal limit of £290.

The employee will receive half a week's pay for each complete year of service below the age of 21. They will receive a full week's pay for each year between the ages of 22 to 40 and a week and a half's pay for each complete year above the age of 41.

The first £30,000 of any termination payment, which includes redundancy pay or notice pay, is tax free. All employees have a right to a redundancy payment as long as they have worked continuously for that employer for at least two years.

---

case study 14.11   Dismissal

At all stages the employee will have the right to be accompanied by a Trade Union official, or any other person.

Informal Stage – Informal Warning

The line manager, in discussion with the employee concerned, shall normally have raised the matter of concern informally. It is part of day-to-day activities that line managers offer professional advice and guidance to staff and that any concerns relating to standards of performance or conduct are dealt with initially in this way. Advice and instruction should be clear and explicit relating to the nature of the concern and confirmed to the employee in writing.

A mutually agreed, adequate and specified time shall be given for the employee to respond to the advice/instruction given. If the matter of concern relates to the employee's physical or mental health the procedure relating to incapacity should be followed (see section 15).

Formal Stage – Disciplinary Procedure

If the employee does not respond in the specified time to the advice/instruction given, or if, following investigation of allegations of misconduct, a manager decides that the disciplinary procedure should be implemented, then a formal interview will take place.

The employee will be advised that the formal procedure is being invoked and will be given details of the allegation/concern and arrangements in writing. The interview will be carried out by the employee's line manager or by another manager more senior than the employee who has not been directly involved in the investigation. A member of the staff of Human Resources will be present to provide advice and guidance to the manager and keep a formal record of the meeting. Other persons may be present for all or part of the interview as determined by the manager conducting the interview.

The Director of Human Resources will notify the arrangements for a formal interview in writing to the employee. Five working days' notice will be given and the interview will normally take place no later than ten working days following the date of the notification. The employee will be made aware of his/her right to be accompanied by a Trade Union representative, or any other person.

The stages of the interview hearing are as follows:

■ The line manager will present the matters of concern relating to the employee and any oral or written statements by witnesses or examples of professional work giving concern. The employee and/or the accompanying person will have the opportunity to ask questions.

■ The employee and/or the accompanying person will be given an opportunity to respond and produce any oral or written statements by witnesses to support their case.

■ Both parties may ask questions/clarify points arising from statements made.

■ Both parties will be allowed to sum up.

■ Adjournment will take place to enable consideration of all the facts by the manager hearing the case so that a decision can be made as to what, if any, sanction or other action needs to be taken.

■ The employee and the accompanying person will be informed of the decision made, and the reason for the decision orally. The Director of Human Resources will confirm all of this information in writing.

(Adapted from www.uclan.ac.uk)

---

activity
**INDIVIDUAL WORK
14.8**

P6

Outline the procedures that an organisation should follow when dismissing an employee, and the provisions for redundancy. You should:

1 Explain the procedures used by the organisation to deal with dismissals.

2 Explain the likely procedures that it would adopt in cases of redundancy.

Progress Check

1. What term is used to describe work found via an employment agency?

2. What is the difference between structured and unstructured flexibility?

3. What do you understand by the term 'statutory rights'?

4. In which year was the Health and Safety at Work Act passed?

5. Whose tragic murder triggered changes in the Race Relations Act in 2000?

6. Give three examples of employees who are not entitled to take time off for public duties.

7. What does the term ACAS mean and what does ACAS do?

8. Give four purposes of an annual appraisal.

9. Under the Working Time Regulations, what is the maximum average number of hours that can be worked in a week?

10. What is a benevolent fund?

Aspects of Contract and Business Law

This unit covers:

- How to apply the requirements for a valid contract
- The impact of statutory consumer protection on the parties to a contract
- The meaning and effect of terms in a standard form contract
- How to apply the remedies available to the parties to a contract

Contracts are at the heart of a business's relationship with other businesses and with its customers. However, these contracts are not always in written form: the simple act of selling products or services to another business or to an individual implies a contract.

The unit starts by looking at types of contacts and their legal status before examining ways in which contracts can be invalidated. Each contract comprises a number of terms, which have to be agreed by both parties or are upheld by law. Having discussed types of term, the unit goes on to look at the statutory legislation that enforces them and protects the weaker party should a contract be unfair. The final section covers the remedies available to parties when contractual terms are broken.

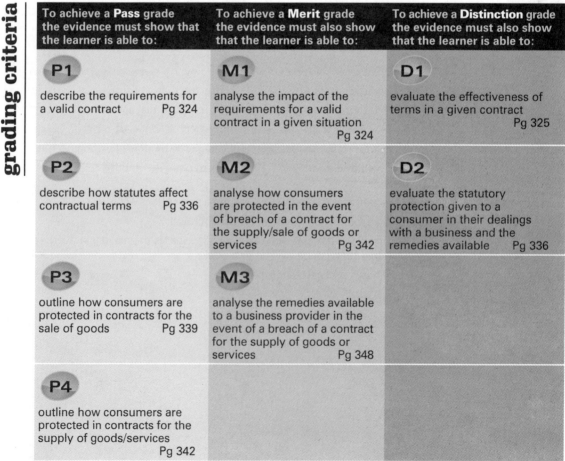

grading criteria

To achieve a **Pass** grade the evidence must show that the learner is able to:	To achieve a **Merit** grade the evidence must also show that the learner is able to:	To achieve a **Distinction** grade the evidence must also show that the learner is able to:
P1 describe the requirements for a valid contract Pg 324	**M1** analyse the impact of the requirements for a valid contract in a given situation Pg 324	**D1** evaluate the effectiveness of terms in a given contract Pg 325
P2 describe how statutes affect contractual terms Pg 336	**M2** analyse how consumers are protected in the event of breach of a contract for the supply/sale of goods or services Pg 342	**D2** evaluate the statutory protection given to a consumer in their dealings with a business and the remedies available Pg 336
P3 outline how consumers are protected in contracts for the sale of goods Pg 339	**M3** analyse the remedies available to a business provider in the event of a breach of a contract for the supply of goods or services Pg 348	
P4 outline how consumers are protected in contracts for the supply of goods/services Pg 342		

To achieve a **Pass** grade the evidence must show that the learner is able to:	To achieve a **Merit** grade the evidence must also show that the learner is able to:	To achieve a **Distinction** grade the evidence must also show that the learner is able to:
P5 describe the remedies available for breach of contract Pg 348		

Applying the requirements for a valid contract

A contract is effectively a promise or a set of promises that the law will enforce. Businesses enter into dozens, hundreds or thousands of contracts every day. The term 'contract' is used very broadly and covers any of the following:

- a series of promises or acts which, in themselves, make a contract
- a document or series of documents that create a contract, or evidence that a series of promises have been made
- the legal relations resulting from those series of promises.

As we will see, a contract is often defined as a legally binding agreement. It is this agreement that creates any rights or obligations that could later be enforced in court.

Link

See page 347 for information about enforcement.

Contracts – definition and types

There are two different ways of classifying contracts. The first divides them into two broad categories:

- Contracts by deed – a deed is a formal legal document, which is signed and witnessed; deeds can be used to transfer property or create a legal obligation or contract.
- A simple contract – these are informal and may be made in any way, either in writing or verbally, or they may just be implied.

The second way of classifying contracts is by whether they are bilateral or unilateral:

- In a **bilateral contract**, one of the parties makes a promise in exchange for a promise from the other. The fact that the two parties have exchanged promises is enough to make the contract enforceable. We enter into bilateral contracts every time we purchase anything from a shop: as one party to the contract, we agree to pay the price; and the other party, the retailer, promises to deliver the goods. When we make a bilateral contract with a business that does not ultimately deliver the goods, we have a case that we could take to court because the contract has been broken.
- In a **unilateral contract**, one party promises to do something in return for an act carried out by the other party, as opposed to a promise to act. If you lost your school or college bag and posted up a notice offering a reward, you would have made a unilateral contract with the person who finds your bag and returns it to you. The contract has stated that someone who searches for the bag and finds it is entitled to the reward that you have offered – when they return the bag to you.

Fig 21.1 Lost

Lost

My green and black school bag.

Was last seen by the lockers near the science block on Tuesday morning.

A **£10** reward is on offer for its safe return. If you have any information please call Ravi on:
07779 123456

Verbal and written contracts

In order to form a contract the two parties simply need to agree what each party will do under the terms of the contract. They must have the intention to form contractual relations and there must be consideration.

Link

See page 318–319 for information about consideration.

It therefore does not matter whether the contract is verbal, partially verbal and partially written, or written. As it is often commonsense for there to be a recording of the agreement, a written contract will, where possible, be created. This will be of particular use if there is a future dispute.

Both verbal and written contracts are legally binding. An agreement is reached when one party makes an offer, which is clearly accepted by the other party.

There is no legal reason why the parties cannot enter into a contract based on verbal statements. However, in such cases the binding terms of the contract are far more difficult to establish. A court, for example, would look into the history of the statements that have been made by the parties, in order to determine what was actually agreed. Often it is clear that one party has not performed their part of the bargain. The court usually steps in when things are more uncertain. Draft contracts, letters, order forms or emails can support verbal contracts. When there is no written contract, the court's ruling is usually based on agreements reached in similar situations.

> **remember**
>
> A contract does not have to be written down and signed, although if it is both parties clearly understand their obligations.

Standard form

A standard form contract can cover most situations because it embodies a way of working and a set of agreements that are general across similar situations.

A standard form contract is one that has not been individually negotiated with the customer. Examples are the printed conditions on a delivery note or an airline ticket. Very few people ever read these and, if they did, they would probably not understand them. In addition, they would probably not know what to do if they objected to any of the conditions. In most cases, they would be told to take it or leave it.

Many standard form contracts appear to be one-sided and to contain many unfair terms. The government, in particular, and the Financial Services Authority are two major critics of standard form contracts.

The problems of standard form contracts have been brought into focus in recent years by the following:

- common law decisions – which have been made in court regarding their validity
- the need for **equity** – so that they match common law
- international commercial law – which is demanding the introduction of conventions and codes
- European law – which is pushing forward common principles, EU directives and concepts such as good faith
- human rights legislation – which is putting restrictions on legislation and common law.

See page 332 and 336–342 for more on standard form contracts.

Offers and invitations to treat

An offer is an expression of willingness to make a contract with the intention that it shall become binding on the party that offers it, as soon as the person to whom it is offered accepts. It is important to make the distinction here between a genuine offer and what is known as an invitation to treat.

With an invitation to treat, a party is simply inviting offers that they are then free to accept or reject. The following are examples of invitations to treat:

> **remember**
>
> *Name* v *Name* [date] refers to a specific legal case.

- At an auction the auctioneer's request for bids is an invitation to treat, or a request for offers. The bids that are made by people who are bidding can be accepted or rejected by the auctioneer. At the same time, a bidder can retract their bid before it is accepted (*Payne* v *Cave* [1789]).

- Displaying goods in a shop window or even on a supermarket shelf with a price ticket on them is not an offer to sell but an invitation for customers to make an offer to buy (*Fisher* v *Bell* [1960]; *PSGB* v *Boots the Chemist* [1953]).

- Advertisements for goods or services are invitations to treat (*Partridge* v *Crittenden* [1968]). However, advertisements that have offers for rewards are not invitations to treat but true offers (*Carlill* v *Carbolic Smoke Ball Co.* [1893]).

- A statement of the minimum price that someone is willing to sell does not amount to an offer (*Harvey* v *Facey* [1893]; *Gibson* v *Manchester City Council* [1979]).

- Tenders are not offers but invitations to treat. They are classed as requests by the owners of the goods for offers to purchase them (*Harvela Investments* v *Royal Trust Co. of Canada* [1985]; *Blackpool Aero Club* v *Blackpool Borough Council* [1990]).

Counter-offers and communication of offers

If, in a reply to an offer, the **offeree** introduces a new term or varies the term of the offer then the reply does not count as acceptance of the original offer. Instead the reply is a counter-offer. The original **offeror** is free to accept or reject the counter-offer.

In effect the counter-offer is a rejection of the original offer, which cannot usually then be accepted (*Hyde* v *Wrench* [1840]).

As we will see shortly, if A makes an offer on a standard document and B accepts on a standard document containing conflicting standard terms, a contract will be made on B's terms, if A acts upon B's communication. This is called the battle of the forms (*Butler Machine Tool* v *Excell-O-Corp* [1979]).

Acceptance

Once an offer has been accepted a binding contract is made and the offer ends. The general rule is that acceptance must be communicated to the offeror. Unless acceptance is communicated the contract does not come into existence.

The offeree or someone who has been authorised by the offeree can communicate the acceptance. In cases where someone accepts on behalf of the offeree but does not have authorisation to do so, this is not classed as acceptance. The offeror is not allowed to impose a contract on the offeree against their wishes, and by the offeree not accepting in as many words it can be assumed that it has not been accepted.

There are some exceptions to the communication rule:

- In a unilateral contract the normal rule for communication of acceptance does not apply. It is considered that carrying out the task is enough to constitute an acceptance.

- The offeror may waive the need for the communication of acceptance, such as in examples when goods are despatched in response to an offer to buy.

- Where acceptance by post has been requested or where there is an appropriate way of communication between the parties. Acceptance is completed once the letter of acceptance is posted. This means that, even if the letter is late in arriving, or is destroyed or lost, the acceptance has still been made.

Battle of the forms

Businesses often get into difficult situations where purchase orders and conditions of sale are sent backwards and forwards. As a general rule the last set of conditions incorporated before the contract was formed apply. This is regardless of whether they may radically change previous conditions. Let's look at an example.

A business sends a purchase order containing its own terms and conditions to a supplier and the supplier sends back an order acknowledgement with its own conditions of sale. Which set of conditions apply? In law the business that sent the purchase order has made an offer. The supplier has made a counter-offer. When the purchasing company accepts the goods, the contract is formed. This means that the supplier's conditions apply and overrule any of the customer's conditions.

In another example, a customer rings up a software company's order line to order software described, with the prices, in an advertisement in a magazine. Over the telephone, the supplier confirms the price and when it will be despatched. The supplier then sends the software, along with an invoice which has its own terms and conditions. Which set of conditions applies? If we assume that the supplier did not say on the telephone that its

remember

The battle of the forms refers to the question of offers and counter-offers. The last party to write will usually be the winner in any subsequent disputes.

standard terms and conditions were to apply, the contract was formed on the telephone. The conditions on the back of the invoice or delivery note are irrelevant because these came into the equation after the contract was formed.

To see how the battle of the forms is dealt with by the Department for Business, Enterprise and Regulatory Reform (DBERR, formerly the Department for Trade and Industry), find the 'procurement' section on its website www.dti.gov.uk.

case study 21.1

Whose conditions?

A business sends a purchase order, which includes its conditions, to a supplier. The supplier then sends its own conditions of sale back to the customer. The customer then resubmits its purchase order. The supplier goes ahead and supplies the goods.

activity

1 Whose conditions apply?
2 Explain your answer.

Consideration

In law, consideration is an act or a promise to do something in return for value. All that the law requires is valuable consideration. Provided that there has been an offer and acceptance then, no matter the value, the purchaser can sue the supplier.

Both parties must provide consideration if they wish to sue on the contract. For example, if a business promises to carry out a service for another business then the promise can only be enforceable if the customer has a contract and has provided consideration. The customer would normally make a payment of money, but payment could consist of some other service that the other party agrees to accept in return.

The promise of money or a service in the future is enough to be classed as a consideration. There are two types of consideration:

■　Executory consideration – this is an exchange of promises to perform acts in the future. If a business promises to deliver goods to a supplier at a future date and the customer promises to pay when they are delivered, a bilateral contract has been created. If the supplier then does not deliver them, this is a breach of contract and the customer can sue. If the supplier had delivered the goods this was its consideration and it can then sue if the customer refuses to pay.

■　Executed consideration – this is when one party makes a promise in exchange for the completion of an act by another party. A prime example would be a unilateral contract when an individual offers a reward of £100 for the return of their lost dog. If someone then finds the dog and returns it, the person who has returned it has a consideration and should receive the £100.

Rules in relation to consideration are as follows:

■　The consideration must not be past. If one party voluntarily performs an act and the other party makes a promise, the consideration for the promise is said to be in the past. In other words, past consideration is not a consideration. It is not valid. For example, if a business offers to deliver another business's products on its own truck and the other business promises to make a contribution towards the fuel costs after the delivery has been made, the business that owns the truck cannot enforce this promise, as the delivery is past. There are some exceptions to this. If the two businesses have a history of workable acts and promises, these will be legally binding and applied to the next situation. In business situations if it is clearly understood by both sides that payment will be involved then past consideration is valid.

■　Consideration must be sufficient but need not be adequate. Assuming the consideration has some value, courts do not look at its adequacy. Where the consideration has some value it is either described as a real or sufficient consideration. It is not the place of the court to see whether parties receive equal value in a contract.

- Consideration must move from the promise. When a business wants to enforce a contract they must show that they have provided consideration. It is not sufficient to show that another party has provided consideration. The business that made the promise must show that they provided consideration. This means that there are some difficulties when three parties are involved in a contract.

- Forbearance to sue – if a business has a valid claim but promises not to enforce it, this is a valid consideration if the other party has promised to settle the claim.

- Existing public duty or contractual duty – if an individual under public duty to do something agrees to do that task, there is not sufficient consideration for a contract. But it could be argued that it is if they exceed their public duty. The same basic approach applies to existing contracts. If a business promises to do something that it is already bound to do under another contract, this is not a valid consideration.

remember

These five rules are generally accepted and may not necessarily appear in a contract.

The Contracts (Rights of Third Parties) Act 1999

The Contracts (Rights of Third Parties) Act 1999 received Royal Assent on 11 November 1999. It reforms the rule of 'privity of contract' under which a person can only enforce a contract if he or she is a party to it.

This rule means that, even if a contract is made with the purpose of conferring a benefit on someone who is not a party to it, that person (a 'third party') has no right to sue for breach of contract.

Section 1 of the Act states the circumstances in which a third party is to have a right to enforce a term of the contract. The situations in which such term may be varied or rescinded are set out in section 2, and the defences available to the promisor when the third party seeks to enforce the term are set out in section 3.

The Act makes it clear that section 1 does not affect the promisee's rights or any rights that the third party may have which are independent of the Act (sections 4 and 7(1)). The Act does not apply to certain contracts (whether wholly or partially) (section 6).

The provisions of the Act do not apply to any contract entered into before the Act came into effect. The Act applies to all contracts, except those detailed in section 6.

The purpose of the Act is to give the right to a third party to enforce a term of a contract to which that third party is not a party.

A third party may only enforce a term of a contract if:

- The contract expressly provides that the third party may do so.
- The term of the contract purports to confer a benefit on that third party.

The second provision does not apply if on a proper construction of the contract it appears that the parties did not intend the term to be enforceable by the third party.

The third party must be expressly identified in the contract either by:

- name.
- as a member of a class
- as answering a particular description.

A third party is only given the right to enforce a term of a contract subject to and in accordance with any other relevant terms of the contract. It is open to the parties to the contract to limit or place conditions on the third party's right.

When a third party enforces a right, they can be awarded any remedy that would have been available to them in an action for breach of contract if they had been a party to the contract. This means that the rules relating to damages, injunctions, **specific performance** and any other relief shall all apply accordingly. Such rules act to place the burden in respect of causation and remoteness on the third party as well as imposing a duty upon them to mitigate their loss. This fact alone has led many legal organisations to offer their services to claim and recover damages for those injured at work or by council negligence or when a business offers an endowment mortgage that does not subsequently perform to promised levels. The Act also enables a third party to enforce a 'positive' right and to take advantage of an exclusion or limitation clause in the contract.

The Act, for example, allows a term of a contract that excludes or limits the promisee's liability to the promisor for the **tort** of negligence and expressly states that the exclusion or limitation is for the benefit of the promisee's 'agents or servants or sub-contractors' and is to be enforceable by these groups.

In cases when the third party has a right to enforce a term of a contract, the contracting parties may not, by agreement, rescind or vary the contract in a way that affects the third party's right without the third party's consent in the following circumstances:

(a) the third party has communicated his or her assent to the term to the promisor

(b) the promisor is aware that the third party has relied on the term or

(c) the promisor can reasonably be expected to have foreseen that the third party would rely on the term and the third party has in fact relied on it.

Note that the use of the term 'variation' in the Act is strictly in its legal sense to mean a variation of the terms of an agreement by further agreement between the parties to the original agreement.

This restriction does not affect the terms of a construction contract, which allow one of the parties to that contract unilaterally to alter, or 'vary', the details of the work to be carried out. Such a 'variation' is made 'under' the contract, not 'to' the contract.

The assent referred to in (a) above may be by words or conduct, and, if sent to the promisor by post or other means, shall not be regarded as communicated to the promisor until received by him.

The Act allows the contracting parties to rescind or vary an agreement where the agreement contains an express term permitting them to do so without the consent of the third party.

Alternatively, the agreement may contain terms which specify the circumstances in which the consent of the third party is required before the agreement can be either rescinded or varied.

The Act provides certain powers to the court or tribunal to dispense with any consent that may be required under certain circumstances. In such an event the payment of compensation to the third party may be ordered if the tribunal thinks it fit.

The Act enables the promisor, in a claim by the third party, to rely on any defence or set-off arising out of the contract and relevant to the term being enforced, which would have been available to him or her, had the claim been by the promisee. The promisor may also rely on any defence or set-off, or make any counterclaim, where this would have been possible had the third party been a party to the contract.

The rights of the third party do not affect any right of the promisee to enforce any term of the contract. Where the promisee has recovered damages (or an agreed sum) from the promisor in respect of either the third party's loss or the promisee's expense in making good that loss, the court or arbitral tribunal shall reduce any award to the third party enforcing a term in accordance with the Act to take account of the sum already recovered.

The Act does exclude the rights of third parties in respect of several matters including:

- a contract on a bill of exchange, promissory note or other negotiable instrument
- a contract binding on a company and its members under section 14 of the Companies Act 1985
- any term of a contract of employment against an employee
- any term of a worker's contract against a worker (including a home worker)
- any term of a relevant contract against an agency worker
- a contract for the carriage of goods by sea
- a contract for the carriage of goods by rail or road, or for the carriage of cargo by air, which is subject to the rules of the appropriate international transport convention.

The Act does not affect any existing right or remedy of the third party and allows for the judicial development of third-party rights.

The Act prevents a third party from invoking section 2(2) of the Unfair Contracts Terms Act 1977 to contest the validity of a term excluding or limiting the promisor's liability under the Act to the third party for negligently caused loss or damage (other than personal injury or death).

The Act applies the standard limitation periods for actions for breach of contract by third parties. The Act makes it clear that the third party shall not be considered as a party to the contract for the purposes of any other Act.

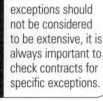

remember These seven exceptions should not be considered to be extensive, it is always important to check contracts for specific exceptions.

To see the full text version of this Act, visit the website of the Office of Public Sector Information

www.opsi.gov.uk.

See pages 271–275 in Unit 14 for more information on employment contracts.

Capacity

It is the general rule that a person is competent to bind him or herself to a contract provided that the contract is not illegal or void for other reasons. There are exceptions to this rule in the case of businesses. Other exceptions relate to children, married women, intoxicated people and those who are considered mentally incompetent.

For our purposes we need to focus on the first, which covers corporations. Until quite recently a business incorporated under the Companies Act was only allowed to make contracts that were in the scope of its Memorandum of Association. Anything beyond that was considered to be **ultra vires**, which means beyond the power and void. The most important case in this area was heard in 1875; it was *Ashbury Railway Carriage and Iron Co. Ltd* v *Riche*. The business's Memorandum stated that it was:

> 'to make and sell, or lend on hire, railway carriages and wagons, and all kinds of railway plant, fittings, machinery and rolling stock; to carry on the business of mechanical engineers and general contractors; to purchase, lease, work and sell mines, minerals, land and buildings; to purchase and sell as merchants, timber, coal, metals, or other materials, and to buy any such materials on commission or as agents.'

The directors of the company bought a concession to build railways in Belgium. They then entered into a contract with Riche to construct the line. The operation was out of the area of work as laid out in the Memorandum and the contract was void. This would have been the case even if each shareholder of the business had approved.

In this case the directors committed a breach of duty by creating the contract. The directors had no power to make the contract in the first place.

Some changes were made by the Companies Act 1989, making it the duty of directors to ensure that they did not exceed their powers derived from the business's Memorandum.

 For more information about the Companies Act 1989, visit the website of the Office of Public Sector Information

www.opsi.gov.uk

An individual entering into a contract with a business, but unaware of the fact that the contract is beyond the powers of that business, is deemed to be operating in good faith, as they will not know that they have entered into a void contract.

Application of requirements

When business agreements are made, the law assumes that both parties intend to make a contract. The contractual intention can be ignored if there was evidence that the agreement was a goodwill agreement, without the intention of creating legal relations.

Although it may appear in the following situations that the parties have entered into an agreement, contracts have not been created:

- Mere puffs – these are ways in which businesses make vague or exaggerated claims to attract customers. The term 'mere puff' means a statement of opinion, and mere puffs

Fig 21.2

These requirements are often applied to unreasonable or seemingly fantastic advertising in order to prevent outrageous claims by advertisers.

are not intended to form the basis of a contract. However, if a business promises that its prices are the lowest and it says that, if the customer can find a lower price from a different supplier, the business will pay the difference, then this could be a binding contract.

- Letters of comfort – if a third party sends a communication to a creditor, saying that they are concerned to ensure that the debtor meets its obligations then, depending on the wording, the communication may either be a binding contract or just an assurance based on goodwill.

- Letters of intent – if a customer contacts a business and says that they might place a contract with the business but are not yet ready to enter into it then this is a letter of intent.

Factors which invalidate or vitiate

Contracts can be set aside. A contract can be made voidable, void or unenforceable. The following terms are used in this context.

- 'Voidness' means that the contract never actually came into existence.

- 'Voidability' means that both parties have a right to declare that the contract is ineffective.

- 'Unenforceability' means that neither party can have the right to apply to the court for a remedy.

- 'Rescission' means 'taking a contract back'.

- 'Vitiate' comes from the Latin word meaning fault. It applies in a situation that renders a contract ineffective, such as fraud.

See pages 342–7 for more about rescission.

As we will see, there are several reasons why a contract could be considered ineffective or invalid.

Misrepresentation

Misrepresentation is a false statement that has been made by one party to the other. The statement does not necessarily have to be part of the contract, but it has helped or convinced the other party to enter into the contract.

The net effect is that if misrepresentation is proved then the contract can be made voidable. This gives the innocent party the right to cancel the contract and, perhaps, claim damages.

In order for misrepresentation to be actionable it must be a false statement of fact; this rules out opinion or future intention. There five ways of categorising misrepresentations:

- Statements of opinion – these are not misrepresentations of the facts. However, if it could be proved that when giving the statement the person knew the true facts and could not reasonably have held the view given, the opinion is counted as a statement of fact.

- Statements as to the future – a false statement about what the individual will do in the future is not misrepresentation and is not binding unless that statement becomes part of the contract. However, if the person making the statement knows that they will not carry out the act in the future and that in making the promise they have convinced the other party to enter into the contract then they are liable.

- Statements of the law – a false statement about the law is not actionable because everyone is presumed to know the law.

- Silence – silence is not misrepresentation because the other party has no duty to disclose problems. There are three exceptions to this rule:

  - Half-truths – when somebody is only telling part of the truth, the statement does not represent the whole truth and is regarded as misrepresentation.

  - Making statements that become false – the statements were true when they were made but due to changes in circumstances become false by the time they are acted upon.

  - Contracts **uberrimae fidei** – this means contracts of the utmost good faith. These impose a duty to disclose all important facts because one party is in a stronger position to know the truth. A prime example of this would be in insurance, where the person applying for insurance cover has a duty to disclose to the insurer.

- Other representations – it is important that the term statement is not interpreted too literally. There were two cases, one in 1986 and one in 1994. In the first, *Gordon* v *Selico Ltd*, it was held that painting over dry rot just before a property was sold was fraudulent misrepresentation. In *St Marylebone Property* v *Payne* the use of a photograph taken from the air, with misleading arrows showing land boundaries, was actionable misrepresentation because the arrows were presented as statements of fact.

The most important aspect of misrepresentation is that it must have induced one of the parties to enter into the contract. There are two main areas, materiality and reliance:

- Materiality – the misrepresentation must be material, so that it induced a reasonable person to enter into the contract.

- Reliance – the person who made the statement must have relied on the misrepresentation in order to induce the other person to enter the contract.

Once misrepresentation has been identified, it is necessary to determine if it is fraudulent, negligent or wholly innocent:

- Fraudulent misrepresentation is a false statement made knowingly and probably without belief in its truth, which is reckless or careless and without regard to its truth. If somebody makes a statement that they believe to be true, this is not fraudulent. It is difficult to prove fraud, and the onus is on the person who believes that fraud was involved to prove it.

- Negligent misrepresentation is a false statement that has been made by someone who did not have reasonable grounds to believe that the statement was true.

- Wholly innocent misrepresentation is a false statement made by someone who believed that what they were saying was true, even though it was not.

For more information on fraudulent misrepresentation, look at the 1969 case, *Doyle* v *Olby*.

For more information on negligent misrepresentation, look at the 1976 case, Esso *Petroleum* v *Mardon*, or the 1991 case, *Royscott Trust Ltd* v *Rogerson*.

For more information on wholly innocent misrepresentation, see the 1996 case, *Thomas Witter* v *TBP Industries*.

Mistakes

For a mistake to impact on a contract it must be an operative mistake. In other words, a mistake that operates to make the contract void.

Common mistakes are probably the most obvious. A common mistake occurs when both parties make the same mistake about a fundamental fact. There are three categories of common mistake:

- *Res extincta* – a contract will be void if the subject matter of the agreement is non-existent. This has been supported by section 6 of the Sale of Goods Act 1979, which states, 'where there is a contract for the sale of specific goods, and the goods without the knowledge of the sellers have perished at the time when the contract was made, the contract is void'.

- *Res sua* – a person makes a contract to purchase something that in fact already belongs to them.

- Mistake as to quality – this is a mistake as to the quality of the subject matter of a contract. The ruling was originally outlined in *Bell* v *Lever Bros. Ltd* [1931].

When there has been an identical mistake, the court can:

- refuse specific performance

- cancel the contract document between the parties

- impose a deal between the parties, so that neither side loses.

Mistakes that occur when only one party is involved can be categorised in two ways:

- A mistake as to the terms of the contract – one party is mistaken about the nature of the contract and the other party is aware of the mistake. In such cases, the contract is void.

- A mistake as to identity – one party enters into a contract with another party, believing them to be a third party. In such cases, this mistake usually makes the contract void.

Several other types of mistake can be made. For example, both parties may have made a mutual mistake because they have not understood one another. They have misunderstood one another's intentions and are working at cross-purposes. In most cases the contract will be cancelled; however, when cancelling the contract would cause hardship it is held to be valid.

Mistakes can be made relating to documentation. The basic rule is that if someone signs a contract then, regardless of whether they have understood it or even read it, they are bound by it.

Originally, rulings were based on protecting illiterate people who had been tricked into signing documents. The plea was *non est factum*, which means 'it is not my deed'. In modern times, the following have to be established in order to make a successful plea on these grounds:

- The person who signed the document was not careless in signing it.
- There was a significant difference between the actual document that was signed and the document that the person thought they were signing.

Duress

The general rule is that, other factors apart, a contract is valid if both parties have entered into it freely. Duress refers to situations when one party was forced into the contract, either by violence or by threat of violence.

Originally, duress could not be applied to duress of goods, in as much as it meant that if a person unlawfully took or threatened to take someone else's goods then this was not duress. Later, however, it was considered to be duress.

More recently, the concept of duress has been expanded to recognise that businesses can come under economic duress. The law seeks to avoid businesses being put under pressure to enter into contracts that are not in their best interests: for example, one business might be intimidated into entering a contract when it would not otherwise have done so. The effect of duress is to make the contract voidable but not void.

Undue influence

Someone who has entered into a contract by the undue influence of another person is entitled to make that contract voidable. Undue influence was described in the nineteenth century as, 'some unfair and improper conduct, some coercion from outside, some overreaching, some form of cheating and generally, though not always, some personal advantage gained' (*Allcard* v *Skinner* [1887]).

There are two classes of undue influence:

- Class 1 is actual undue influence: the wrongdoer has exerted undue influence to make the other enter into a transaction that is impugned (questionable).
- Class 2 is presumed undue influence: the individual who complains is only required to show that a trusting relationship existed and that the wrongdoer abused that relationship to enter into a questionable transaction.

---

activity

INDIVIDUAL WORK 21.1

P1

M1

1 For P1, you are required to describe the requirements for a valid contract.

You should explain when and how a contract would come into existence. Your teacher/ tutor will give you a sample copy of a mobile phone contract; you should keep this, as you will be able to use the contract for further activities for this unit. You must:

(a) Analyse the law relating to invitations to treat.

(b) Explain and identify which party makes the offer.

(c) Identify and explain:

    (i) when any counter offers are made

    (ii) how acceptance of a contract occurs

    (iii) how the law is applied to contracts.

2 To achieve M1, you need to analyse the law as it is applied. Your teacher/tutor will expect you to:

(a) Translate the given contract in clear English.

(b) Explain what is meant by a typical offer and acceptance.

(c) Investigate and come up with a solution for a typical problem with the contract.

(d) Explain clearly how the law is applied to contracts.

activity

INDIVIDUAL WORK 21.2

D1

For D1, you need to give justified conclusions and evaluations from the point of view of both parties to the contract. You should therefore:

1 Give careful consideration to the chosen contract.

2 Consider the effectiveness of the terms from the point of view of both parties. (In other words, the business would seek to protect itself from losses through non-payment or claims for incomplete performance. Consumers, on the other hand, would look for protection regarding defective goods, poor service or late delivery).

The impact of statutory consumer protection on the parties to a contract

Although there have always been laws to determine the validity of contracts and courts have made hundreds of rulings, the current comprehensive raft of statutory consumer protection is relatively recent. Successive governments and the European Union have recognised that businesses routinely enter into thousands if not millions of contracts each day. It is also the case that not only are many customers unaware of the terms of the contract that they are entering into but also businesses do not take it upon themselves to inform them about the contractual terms.

Unsurprisingly, the thousands of consumers who have found themselves at serious disadvantage, after having entered into contracts with businesses, have found little recourse to law. Many of the contracts were biased in favour of the business and left no room for manoeuvre or fairness. As a result, there has been a move to identify key areas where there are contractual problems and bridge the gaps in existing law in order to deal with them, so that consumers have recourse to law.

Fig 21.3 The flag of the EU
Increasingly British law is being adapted to incorporate European Union directives

Some of the statutes that have become law in Great Britain emanate not necessarily from our own parliament but from either the translation of a European Union directive or simply by applying a directive. This is part of a process within the European Union to **harmonise** all aspects of business relations, so that businesses can enter into contracts across the continent in the knowledge that similar contractual terms will apply.

Types of term

When a contract is stated in express terms, the terms are spelled out or expressed by the parties. An alternative is statement in implied terms; these are terms that are read into the contract by the court or by statute or custom.

Express terms

The express terms of a contract are those that have been written into the contract or said by either party when the contract was made. Obviously, in order to discover terms in oral contracts it is necessary to find out what the parties said at the time.

Normally, if the contract is in writing then additional oral evidence will not be allowed if it alters or contradicts what has been put in writing. This means that if there is evidence that something was added while the contract was being made the addition cannot be counted. This is called the parol evidence rule.

Express terms usually include the following:

- the commitment of particular individuals, according to the contract
- the specification of any services or products to be provided
- standard operating procedures
- performance criteria
- fees, payment terms and reimbursement of expenses
- ownership of any intellectual property or materials and when they pass from the ownership of the business to the customer
- any reporting obligations
- restrictions on contact with competitors during or after the contract
- both parties' obligations if the contract is terminated
- any liabilities in the event of loss or damage resulting from the contract.

Implied terms

Implied terms are read into the contract from another source. Although not actually part of the written contract, they are an integral part of the contract because the court or a statute has made them such by default.

Implied terms come into effect in the following ways:

By statute – particular types of contract will always have the same terms put into them by an act of parliament. The most common examples are sections 12 to 15 of the Sale of Goods Act 1979, which are a list of promises that are made by the seller of goods to the buyer about goods that are being sold.

By custom – although these are unusual, these are customary implied terms; in other words, ways in which contracts have always been interpreted.

By the courts or common law – the court may read terms into certain types of contracts because court cases in the past have established the terms in this particular type of contract. The other way courts can read terms into a contract is to give business efficacy. This means that the courts will decide if the parties' agreement made sense only if a clause was added and that the parties must have meant to put that clause in.

remember

The courts will be directed to apply a similar remedy to the case, provided that the situation is broadly similar, otherwise the court may look for another fair judgment.

Link

See pages 337–339 for more on the Sale of Goods Act.

Differences between express and implied terms

The main differences between express and implied terms of a contract are, as we have seen, that express terms are actually written into the contract. Express terms need to be as clear and unambiguous as possible; they exist so that they can be referred to easily and enforced if the need arises.

Implied terms are not included in the contract, but tribunals or courts insert them in order to cover certain sets of circumstances that may not have been foreseen. Implied terms could therefore be inserted during proceedings when a court believes that the terms would have been inserted if both parties had foreseen certain events.

Thus, practically speaking, there is little difference between express and implied terms. The key difference between the two is that express terms depend on what the parties to the contract actually agree, whereas implied terms do not depend upon agreement but on other circumstances, including the conduct of the parties. The most striking example is fitness for purpose. If the supplier knows that the buyer is relying on the supplier's judgement in respect of the goods, there is an implied term that the goods are fit for purpose if the supplier does not say anything. When the supplier does say that they are fit for the buyer's purpose, the goods' fitness for the buyer's purpose is an express term.

Impact of contractual terms

As we will see, contracts are rarely read in minute detail. They are more often scanned to highlight the key, specific terms of the agreement or transaction. For the most part, contractual terms are standardised. This is particularly the case in large organisations that enter routinely into hundreds or thousands of contracts each day.

Searching for the precise contractual terms is an onerous and almost thankless task. Nonetheless, the contractual terms inserted into terms and conditions are often a fallback position for businesses when there is some dispute about the transaction. Businesses insert limits and exclusions and lay down the precise rules under which the contract can be challenged or goods and services rejected. They also cover reservation of title, which is important as ownership and possession of goods do not necessarily mean the same thing. Ownership is only vested in a business or an individual once full payment and conditions have been met. The buyer may possess the goods but until payment and conditions have been met they do not own the goods.

 See page 331 for more on reservation of title.

Time for performance

Contracts specify a series of promises relating to both the buyer and the seller. The buyer, for example, makes a series of promises, perhaps for delivery of goods or services, in exchange for actual payment or the buyer's promise of payment. The contract incorporates a reasonable period within which the business has to provide what they have promised to the buyer. In many cases this is a fallback position, which is often at the discretion of the seller and also to the seller's advantage. Although promises may have been made at point of sale by the business, once the customer signs the contract or terms and conditions they will have been seen to have accepted the business's interpretation of the time in which they should act.

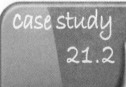

case study 21.2 Timing

This is a sample set of delivery conditions.

Delivery

(a) Every effort will be made to adhere to the delivery date quoted but the Company accepts no liability to the Customer or to any other person if for any reason delivery is delayed beyond the quoted delivery date. Failure to make delivery shall not vitiate this agreement.

(b) The Company will make the arrangements for the delivery of goods to the premises of the Customer, unless otherwise informed in writing. If a delivery is postponed at the discretion of the Company, the invoice date will become the date quoted by the Company as the dispatch date. Costs associated with packing and carriage may be charged to the Customer at the discretion of the Company, and as determined by the terms of delivery agreed with the Customer.

(c) The risk in the goods shall be deemed to pass to the Customer in accordance with the rules of delivery as defined by ICC Incoterms 1990 unless otherwise agreed in writing with the Customer.

(d) Any discrepancy between goods ordered and goods delivered must be notified in writing by facsimile and by post to the Company within 10 days of delivery failing which the goods delivered shall be deemed to comply in all respects with the order of the Customer.

(e) Any order accepted by the Company may at the sole discretion of the Company be delivered in instalments, the Company may then request payment for those goods delivered to the Customer.

---

activity

1 Find out what is meant by ICC Incoterms 1990.

2 Identify any conditions that are unfavourable to customers.

Rejection of goods

As we will see when we investigate some of the laws relating to the sale of goods and the supply of goods and services, minimum periods within which to reject goods or services provided by a business have been established. Nonetheless, businesses specifically state particular exclusion clauses or limits, particularly in relation to time for the rejection of goods and services by customers.

In cases where the business's terms and conditions are not as favourable as legislation, the legislation always applies. In many cases businesses go above and beyond the minimum requirements by legislation, stating that they will accept the return of rejected goods and services over a longer period than is legally necessary.

The key aspects relating to the rejection of goods are their suitability, their intended use and the possibility that substitute goods supplied are not of the same or sufficiently similar specification to the goods that the customer expected to receive.

In entering a contract with the customer the business will have undertaken to provide goods that fall within the Trade Descriptions Act and adhere to both the Sale of Goods Act and the Supply of Goods and Services Act. If the goods do not match the description or the purpose intended, the customer has a legal right to reject those goods and demand that the contract is cancelled.

---

case study

21.3

Rejection of goods

The following is the London Borough of Camden's policy on the rejection of goods.

REJECTION OF GOODS

9.1

The Authority shall not be deemed to have accepted the Goods or any part of the Goods until after the Authority has actually inspected the Goods and ascertained that they are in accordance with the Contract. The Authority's representative's signature on any delivery note or other documentation in Connection with delivery of Goods is evidence only of the number of packages received. In particular, it is not evidence that the correct quantity or number of Goods has been delivered or that the Goods delivered are in good condition or of the correct quality.

9.2

The Authority may by notice to the Contractor reject any of the Goods, which are not in accordance with the Contract. Furthermore, if by the nature of the Goods any defects therein or any failure thereof to conform as aforesaid does not or would not become apparent (despite carrying out of any examination or test) until after use, the Authority may reject the same even after a reasonable period of use. The Contractor acknowledges that in the case of Goods, the Authority may exercise the aforesaid rights of rejection notwithstanding any provision contained in section 11 or section 35 of the Sale of Goods Act 1979 as amended by the Sale and Supply of Goods Act 1994.

9.3

Goods so rejected shall be removed and (unless otherwise specified by the Supervising Officer) replaced by the Contractor at its own expense. The Contractor shall replace the rejected Goods with Goods of the right quality and which comply in all respects with the Specification, within 24 hours of such rejection or as otherwise agreed by the Authority.

9.4

The Contractor shall pay to the Authority on demand, or by way of setoff against any sums due or becoming due to him under the Contract, any additional costs, fees or expenses incurred by the Authority by reason of any delay in removal and/or replacement of such rejected Goods.

9.5

The Council shall be entitled to a refund from the Contractor in the case of Goods not replaced.

(Source: London Borough of Camden, www.camden.gov.uk)

activity

1   Rewrite the councils' five conditions in shorter statements.
2   Has the council covered every possible eventuality? Explain your answer.

Price variation

There are two ways in which price variation can be interpreted:

- price variation between sellers
- price variation between signing the contract and delivery of the goods owing to increased cost of raw materials.

These have radically different impacts on contracts.

Price variation between sellers

In an increasingly competitive marketplace, businesses are acutely aware of the fact that their pricing policies need to be in line with those of their closest competitors. As part of a potential contract with customers, a series of promises are often made by retail businesses. The two examples shown in Fig 21.4 are typical.

Fig 21.4 Promises

> If within 30 days of your purchase from us you find a local competitor offering a lower price on an available product of same brand and model, we will refund the difference plus another 10% of difference.

> If you have seen a lower advertised price from a local store with the same item in stock, we'll gladly beat their price by 10% of the difference. Even after your purchase, if you see a lower advertised price within 30 days, we'll refund 110% of the difference. Our guarantee means you don't have to wait for a sale to know you're getting the best price.

There has been considerable debate about price matching and whether this is **anti-competitive**. In fact, many people suggest that major businesses collude to keep higher prices.

Price variation between signing the contract and delivery of the goods

Clauses can be inserted into contracts to take account of the fact that the cost of raw materials, components or some other item may vary between the contracts being signed and the product or service being delivered. The net impact of these clauses allows the selling business to adjust the selling price if the price of a key material changes.

In many areas of sales, this type of price variation is either impracticable or unacceptable. The mechanism used to deal with this is to produce a price list and then apply price adjustments to it.

Payment terms

Most businesses will give a degree of credit to their customers. Problems arise when customers do not make their payments on time. Businesses explain their terms and conditions, sending out written confirmation of their payment terms with the goods.

There are several different payment terms, which are explicitly mentioned in a contract or in terms and conditions. These are outlined in Table 21.1.

Table 21.1 Payment terms

Payment Term	Description
Net monthly account	Payment due on last day of the month following the one in which the invoice is dated
Net 7	Payment seven days after invoice
Net 10	Payment 10 days after invoice
Net 30	Payment 30 days after invoice
Net 60	Payment 60 days after invoice
Net 90	Payment 90 days after invoice
EOM	End of month
21 MFI	21st of the month following invoice
1 per cent 10 Net 30	1 per cent discount if payment received within 10 days otherwise payment 30 days after invoice
COD	Cash on delivery
Cash account	Account conducted on a cash basis, no credit
Letter of credit	A documentary credit confirmed by a bank, often used for export
Bill of exchange	A promise to pay at a later date, usually supported by a bank
CND	Cash next delivery
CBS	Cash before shipment
CIA	Cash in advance
CWO	Cash with order
1MD	Monthly credit payment of a full month's supply
2MD	As above plus an extra calendar month
Contra	Payment from the customer offset against the value of supplies purchased from the customer
Stage payment	Payment of agreed amounts at stages

(Adapted from Business Link)

For more information on Business Link, visit
www.businesslink.gov.uk

Quality and quantity of goods delivered

The quality and quantity of goods delivered are governed by the initial agreement that was made between the buyer and the seller. In order to fulfil the contract, the supplier needs to make sure that the goods correspond to the specification and in every other respect (such as the number of items ordered and colour required), otherwise they risk the buyer rejecting the goods.

Usually, businesses supply or display samples of the products or give an explanation of the services to be provided. It is on the basis of what the customer has seen and what they have been promised that the original contract is signed. This means that deliveries need to be supervised by both the sender and the receiver. The receiving business would prepare a copy order and only sign off the delivery when it is satisfied with the quality and the quantity of the goods that have been delivered. Factors checked include sell-by dates, in the case of foodstuffs; the condition of the goods, i.e. whether they are undamaged and intact; and that the quantities received correspond with those ordered. It is reasonable for a customer to complain if the quality or quantities of goods delivered do not match the agreed contractual specification or if the goods are not in a fit state to be used.

A business that supplies bricks and building materials might set out the following terms relating to quality and quantity:

> The customer shall be solely responsible for checking the quantity of goods delivered. In the event of a shortage being discovered the company shall have no liability therefore unless such shortage is communicated both by endorsement on the appropriate delivery ticket upon delivery, and by letter to the company within seven days of delivery.

Reservation of title

This is a contractual term; reservation of title means that ownership of goods sold does not pass to the customer until the supplier has been paid. Sometimes, the term Romalpa is used; this is derived from an important case heard at the Court of Appeal in 1975 (Aluminium *Industrie Vaassen BV* v *Romalpa Aluminium Limited*).

Here is an example of a set of clauses in terms and conditions that deal specifically with reservation of title:

Reservation of title

6.1 The Company shall retain title to the Goods until it has received payment in full of all sums due in connection with the supply of the Goods to the Customer or in connection with any other transaction. For these purposes the Company has only received a payment when the amount of that payment is irrevocably credited to its bank account.

6.2 If any of the Goods owned by the Company is attached to or incorporated into other goods not owned by the Company and is not identifiable or separable from the resulting composite or mixed goods, title to the resulting composite or mixed goods shall vest in the Company and be retained by the Company for as long as and on the same terms as those on which it would have retained title to the Goods in question.

6.3 If the Customer fails to make payment to the Company when due, enters in bankruptcy, liquidation or a composition with its creditors, has a receiver, manager or administrator appointed over all or part of its assets, or becomes insolvent, or if the Company has reasonable cause to believe that any of these events is likely to occur, the Company shall have the right without prejudice to any other remedies.

6.3.1 To enter without prior notice to any premises where the Goods owned by it may be, and to repossess and dispose of any such Goods owned by it so as to discharge any sums owed to it by the Customer.

6.3.2 To require the Customer not to re-sell or part with possession of the Goods owned by it until the Customer has paid in full all sums owed by it to the Company.

6.4 The Goods shall once the risk has passed to the Customer in accordance with Clause 4.3 or otherwise be and remain at the Customer's risk at all times unless and until the Company has retaken possession of such Goods.

Exclusion clauses

Exclusion clauses can be inserted into a contract in order either to exclude or to limit the liabilities of one party if the contract is breached or there is negligence. There are, however, limits to the scope of exclusion clauses:

- if the party in question relies on such a clause if it has been incorporated into the contract
- if it relies on such a clause as a matter of interpretation
- if it relies on such a clause its validity might be tested under the Unfair Contract Terms Act 1977 and the Unfair Terms in Consumer Contracts Regulations 1999.

If a party wishes to rely on an exclusion clause, it needs to show that it formed part of the contract. Exclusion clauses can be added into a contract by notice, by a course of dealing or by signature.

remember

It is not illegal to insert exclusion clauses, but they must be legal in themselves and the limits must be clear.

If a party signs a document containing an exclusion clause, the party is bound by its terms and the exclusion clause is part of the contract. This is regardless of the fact that the party may not have read or understood the document. The exception to this is when one party has made a misrepresentation as to the effect of the exclusion clause.

Exclusion clauses can also be included in unsigned documents, such as a ticket. The existence of the clause has to be brought to the notice of the other party when the contract is entered into. Sufficient notice of the clause needs to be given. However, if it is a reasonable exclusion clause then no notice is required.

Exclusion clauses can be put into contracts when there has been a series of contracts between the parties using the same terms. This often means a considerable number of transactions. If there is no long-term relationship between the two parties, the exclusion clause could become part of the contract through custom or general usage.

Even when there are exclusion clauses the battle of the forms applies. If one business sends a form stating that a contract is to be made on particular terms, but the other party accepts by sending a form with its own terms on it then the contract is on the second party's terms. As we have seen, the contract is nearly always made on the last set of terms that were sent.

> **remember**
>
> The battle of the forms applies to exclusion clauses.

Standard form contracts

The standard form contract is sometimes referred to as an adhesion or boilerplate contract. This means that the contract does not leave any room for negotiation. This type of contract is often entered into between two parties when one has unequal bargaining powers. The other party, usually a customer, is not in a position to negotiate away from the standard terms of the contract and the salesperson does not have the authority to make any amendments.

The advantage of standard form contracts is that they substantially reduce the transaction costs each time a sale is made; this is because the contract does not have to be negotiated in detail each time. On the other hand, the contracts may in themselves be unfair or unjust because the seller does not have to renegotiate or modify any terms of the contract.

Standard form contracts are in widespread use. Key points to note are:

■ They are lengthy and they are rarely read. They are often referred to as 'small print' and written in legalise, which does not appear to be relevant. The customer would not necessarily derive anything useful from reading the information. Even if they did, the customer is not in a position to bargain because the business is offering the contract on a take-it-or-leave-it basis. As the customer will not be able to take any action if they read the contract, the business has a high expectation that none will bother to do so.

■ Often the full terms of the contract are not presented to the customer and the document that they sign is not the full contract. The customer will be told that the rest of the terms are elsewhere, such as in the terms and conditions for electrical goods. Collectively, the retailer's terms and the manufacturer's additional terms make up the contract signed by the customer. For example, included in the customer's contract with the retailer who is selling them a television are additional terms laid down by the manufacturer of the television.

■ Some of the terms relate to situations that have a very low probability of happening. Additional terms are added into the contract, referring to statutes and other legislation that are unlikely to have an impact on the transaction. Their presence simply extends the terms and conditions, making it even less likely that they will be read.

■ Customers may be put under pressure to sign the contract without reading it: it is implied that it is unreasonable for them to read or question any of the terms. The salesperson may tell the customer that the terms are simply something required by law.

■ Standard form contracts often exploit the unequal balance of power between the buyer and the seller. If the buyer really needs to purchase something and there is no other alternative, the seller is in a position to take advantage of the situation and force the buyer to accept the terms.

Impact of statutes on common contractual terms

Over the years, the framing and application of contracts between businesses and between businesses and consumers have become increasingly subject to regulation. The legislation, which relates largely to consumer protection, has been instigated either by the British government or by the European Union in the form of EU directives. In this section of the unit, we will look at the implications that this increasing raft of legislation has had for contracts.

Unfair Contract Terms Act 1977

The main purpose of the Unfair Contract Terms Act (UCTA) was to restrict the extent to which liability in a contract could be excluded for breach of contract or negligence. The Act does not apply to the sale of land, the contracts relating to companies, shares or insurance. It does, however, deal directly with business liability, which it defines as the liability of a person whilst carrying out work as a business or in a job with a business.

The Act gives the greatest protection to customers. It makes an important distinction between a consumer and a business: a consumer is anyone who does not contract as a business.

The Act places some restrictions on contractual terms. It lays down the rules for selling businesses and how they can use exclusion clauses:

- Excluding liability for death or injury is not permitted.
- Excluding liability for losses caused by negligence is only acceptable if it is reasonable.
- The same applies in respect of defective or poor quality goods.

Table 12.2 outlines the effect of the Act.

Table 21.2 Liability

Source of liability	Definition of liability (where relevant)	Effect on consumer	Effect on non-member
Negligence leading to death or injury		Void s.2(1) UCTA	Void s.2(1) UCTA
Negligence leading to loss or damage		Acceptable if reasonable s.2(1) UCTA	Acceptable if reasonable s.2(1) UCTA
Sale of goods with defective title	s.12 Sale of Goods Act 1979	Void (UCTA s.6(1))	Void (UCTA s.6(1))
Sale of goods that do not match their description	s.13 Sale of Goods Act 1979	Void (UCTA s.6(2)a)	Acceptable if reasonable (UCTA s.6(3))
Sale of goods that do not match their sample	s.14 Sale of Goods Act 1979	Void (UCTA s.6(2)a)	Acceptable if reasonable (UCTA s.6(3))
Sale of goods that are of unsatisfactory quality	s.15 Sale of Goods Act 1979	Void (UCTA s.6(2)a)	Acceptable if reasonable (UCTA s.6(3))
Any other passage of goods where the goods are of unsatisfactory quality or do not match their sample or description		Void (UCTA s.7(2))	Acceptable if reasonable (UCTA s.7(2))
Breach of standard-form contract		Acceptable if reasonable (UCTA s.3)	Not affected
Misrepresentation	s.3 Misrepresentation Act 1967	Acceptable if reasonable (UCTA s.8(1))	Acceptable if reasonable (UCTA s.8(1))

It is important to test what is meant by reasonable; the court will take the following into account:

- what information was available to both parties when the contract was written
- whether the contract was a standard form or negotiated
- whether the buyer had the bargaining power to negotiate better terms.

Unfair Terms in Consumer Contract Regulations 1994

This set of regulations is designed to protect consumers against unfair standard terms in contracts. The regulations begin with a test to see whether a term is fair. It is unfair if:

> 'contrary to the requirement of good faith it causes a significant imbalance in the parties' rights and obligations under the contract, to the detriment of consumers'.

In this respect, good faith means dealing fairly and openly with consumers. It is acceptable for standard terms to be created, but they must be limited to protecting legitimate commercial interests, whilst taking into account the interests and rights of consumers. The standard term must be intelligible and in plain English. It could be challenged if the consumer is not clear about its meaning. If there is any doubt about what the term means, the term is always given the most favourable meaning as far as the consumer is concerned. The vast majority of standard terms are covered by these regulations.

The following table provides a comparison of the Unfair Contract Terms Act and the Unfair Terms in Consumer Contract Regulations (UTCCR):

Table 21.3 UCTA/UTCCR

	UCTA 1977	UTCCR 1999
Who can benefit?	Anyone, but consumers get greater protection	Only consumers
Definition of 'consumer'	A person who 'neither makes the contract in the course of a business nor holds himself out as doing so; and the other party does make the contract in the course of a business'	'Any natural person who, in contracts covered by these Regulations, is acting for purposes which are outside his trade, business or profession'
Scope of contractual terms affected	Exclusion and limitation clauses only	All terms that are not negotiated
Identification of affected terms	Certain terms are entirely void. Others must satisfy a test of 'reasonableness'. Reasonableness is not defined, but there are guidelines	All 'unfair' terms. Terms are unfair if they significantly imbalance rights and responsibilities against the consumer
Effect on draughting	None	Impose an obligation to write standard form contracts in terms intelligible to the consumer
Introduce an element of 'good faith' in contractual statements	No	Yes (see r.5(1))

The Consumer Protection (Distance Selling) Regulations 2000 (as amended)

The Distance Selling Regulations apply to businesses that sell products or services to customers via the following media:

- the Internet
- digital television
- mail order
- catalogue shopping
- telephone
- fax.

The purpose of the legislation is to:

- give consumers confidence to purchase products or services in situations where they do not have face-to-face contact with the supplier
- make sure that all businesses selling at a distance meet basic criteria.

The regulations state that the business must give customers information, so that they can make an informed choice, and provide a cancellation period. The regulations do not apply to the sale of land, construction, financial services, conditional sales or hire purchase, vending machines, business-to-business deals or auction sales.

Before entering into a contract, the business must give the following information to the consumer:

- the business's identity
- the main characteristics of the products or services offered
- prices, including taxes
- delivery costs
- payment options
- arrangements for delivery or performance of the service
- the consumer's right to cancel
- the cost of the telephone call if the consumer has to use a premium rate telephone number
- how long the price or offer will remain valid
- the minimum duration of the contract
- the fact that the business will pay the cost to the consumer of returning any products supplied as substitutes because the original ones were not available.

An example of how these regulations have been applied to distance selling enterprises can be seen from the following extract from a newspaper's photography archive.

Fig 21.5 Extract from *The Independent*

(NewsPrint Ltd)

1.0   Confirmation

The regulations state that 'after making a purchase the consumer must be sent confirmation'.

If you fill in the e-mail field when you make an order, you will receive a confirmation by e-mail. This should be immediate. If you do not fill in the e-mail field, or send in an order by post, you will be sent a confirmation by post. As our order fulfilment system works automatically as soon as the order is received, it is quite possible that you will receive your prints before the confirmation, which requires more human intervention.

1.1 Cooling-off period

The regulations state that 'consumers must have the right of cancellation of an order within a 'cooling-off' period of 7 working days'.
In this instance the NewsPrints Ltd system is an exception and customers do not have the right to cancel because 'the supply of goods has been made to the consumer's personal specification', i.e. image number, print size, etc.

1.2 Cancellation period

The regulations require 'the supplier to inform the consumer prior to the conclusion of a contract that he will not be able to cancel, once performance of the service has begun'.

In this instance the placing of an order, using the NewsPrints Ltd system, will be deemed as your agreement for us to begin the service and therefore you willl not have the right to cancel of this regulation.

1.3 Information

The regulations require 'the supplier to provide the customer with certain information'. This information is provided within the NewsPrints Ltd site in the 'Checkout', 'Customer Service and 'Consumer Protection (Distance Selling) Regulations 2000' pages.

In order that you have this information in a durable medium, please print out these pages at the time of making your order and keep them safe until your order has been satisfactorily fulfilled.

There is a useful guide to distance selling on the Office of Fair Trading's website
www.oft.gov.uk

The Electronic Commerce (EC Directive) Regulations 2002

This set of regulations applies to businesses if they:

- sell goods or services to businesses or consumers via the Internet or by email
- advertise on the Internet or by email
- provide electronic content for customers or provide access to a communication network.

The main purpose of the regulations is to establish the law as it applies to online selling and advertising. Customers using an online service must be given clear information about the business and how to complete online transactions.

If a business does not comply with the regulations, customers have the right to:

■ cancel their order

■ seek a court order

■ sue for damages.

There are useful guidelines to e-commerce regulations on the website of the Department for Business, Enterprise and Regulatory Reform (DBERR, formerly the Department for Trade and Industry); look under 'Electronic Commerce Directive' in its 'Business sectors – international ICT policy' section

www.dti.gov.uk

For the full text of each of these British Acts and EU regulations, visit the website of the Office of Public Sector Information

www.opsi.gov.uk.

The EU regulations can also be found on the Office of Fair Trading's website

www.oft.gov.uk

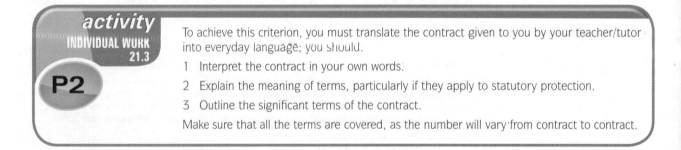

activity
INDIVIDUAL WORK
21.3

P2

To achieve this criterion, you must translate the contract given to you by your teacher/tutor into everyday language; you should.

1   Interpret the contract in your own words.

2   Explain the meaning of terms, particularly if they apply to statutory protection.

3   Outline the significant terms of the contract.

Make sure that all the terms are covered, as the number will vary from contract to contract.

activity
INDIVIDUAL WORK
21.4

D2

This activity follows on from D1; you should:

1   Evaluate the effectiveness of the statutory protection for consumers.

2   Make a comparison with the protection that is afforded to businesses and consumer purchasers from another business. Ensure that you mention that this will often relate to the validity of the contract terms.

3   Consider the effectiveness of the remedies.

4   Make sure that you cover the potential difficulties of enforcement. (You do not need to consider the underlying problems of the limits of equitable remedies.)

The meaning and effect of terms in a standard form contract

Standard form contracts are now required to conform to three key Acts, which were designed to improve the confidence of consumers when purchasing products or services from businesses. The three key Acts cover the definition of what will be sold or supplied and the main implied terms and remedies that can be applied if a business is found in breach of the implied terms of the standard form contract.

Sale of goods

The Sale of Goods Act deals specifically with situations when purchases go wrong for some reason. It is therefore in the interests of businesses to understand the implications of the Act and their responsibilities under it. The Act states that whatever is sold must:

- fit its description
- be fit for its purpose
- be of satisfactory quality.

If one or more of these minimum requirements are not met, it is the obligation of the supplier to sort out the problem.

The difference between goods and services

In order to determine the consumer's legal rights, it is important to know whether they have been provided with goods or services. Examples of goods are:

- clothes
- furniture
- groceries
- household appliances.

Examples of services are:

- hairdressing
- dry cleaning
- home improvements.

Sometimes, however, there is a blurring between the two, and aspects of the contract involve both goods and services. For example, if you were to take your car to a garage and, as part of the work that needed to be carried out, the engine were to be replaced, the engine would be the goods and the labour to fit it would be a service.

> **remember**
>
> There are many other situations where the customer is purchasing goods and services as part of a package. This complicates the legal rights.

Fig 21.6 Having a car engine replaced by a car mechanic means a contract involving both goods and services

Implied terms

Implied terms about title

Section 12 of the Sale of Goods Act provides:

> (1) In a contract of sale ... there is an implied term on the part of the seller that in the case of a sale he has a right to sell the goods, and in the case of an agreement to sell he will have such a right at the time when the property is to pass.

(2)   In a contract of sale ... there is also an implied term that –

(a)   the goods are free, and will remain free until the time when the property is to pass, from any charge or encumbrance not disclosed or known to the buyer before the contract is made, and

(b)   the buyer will enjoy quiet possession of the goods except so far as it may be disturbed by the owner of or other person entitled to the benefit of any charge or encumbrance so disclosed or known.

The term implied by s12(1) is a condition and the term implied by s12(2) is a warranty: s12(5A).

Sale by description
Section 13 provides:

(1)   Where there is a contract for the sale of goods by description, there is an implied term that the goods will correspond with the description.

(1A)   ... the term implied by subsection (1) above is a condition.

(2)   If the sale is by sample as well as by description it is not sufficient that the bulk of the goods corresponds with the sample if the goods do not also correspond with the description.

Implied terms about quality or fitness
Section 14 provides:

(2)   Where the seller sells goods in the course of a business, there is an implied term that the goods supplied under the contract are of satisfactory quality.

(2A)   ... goods are of satisfactory quality if they meet the standard that a reasonable person would regard as satisfactory, taking account of any description of the goods, the price (if relevant) and all other relevant circumstances.

(2B)   ... the quality of goods includes their state and condition and the following (among others) are in appropriate cases aspects of the quality of goods -

(a)   fitness for the purposes for which goods of the kind in question are commonly supplied,

(b)   appearance and finish,

(c)   freedom from minor defects,

(d)   safety, and

(e)   durability.

(2C)   The term implied by subsection (2) above does not extend to any matter making the quality of goods unsatisfactory -

(a)   which is specifically drawn to the buyer's attention before the contract is made,

(b)   where the buyer examines the goods before the contract is made, which that examination ought to reveal, or

(c)   in the case of a contract for sale by sample, which would have been apparent on a reasonable examination of the sample.

(3)   Where the seller sells goods in the course of a business and the buyer, expressly or by implication, makes known –

(a)   to the seller ...

any particular purpose for which the goods are being bought, there is an implied term that the goods supplied under the contract are reasonably fit for that purpose, whether or not that is a purpose for which such goods are commonly supplied, except where the circumstances show that the buyer does not rely, or that it is unreasonable for him to rely, on the skill or judgment of the seller ...

The terms implied by sections 14(2) and (3) are conditions: s14(6)

Sale by sample
Section 15 provides:

(2)   In the case of a contract for sale by sample there is an implied term –

(a)   that the bulk will correspond with the sample in quality;

(b)   that the transferee will have a reasonable opportunity of comparing the bulk with the sample

(c) that the goods will be free from any defect, making their quality unsatisfactory, which would not be apparent on reasonable examination of the sample.

The term implied by s15(2) is a condition: s15(3).

Modification of remedies for breach of condition in non-consumer cases

Section 15A provides:

(1) Where in the case of a contract of sale –

   (a) the buyer would, apart from this subsection, have the right to reject goods by reason of a breach on the part of the seller of a term implied by sections 13, 14 or 15 above, but

   (b) the breach is so slight that it would be unreasonable for him to reject them,

      then, if the buyer does not deal as a consumer, the breach is not to be treated as a breach of condition but may be treated as a breach of warranty.

(2) This section applies unless a contrary intention appears in, or is to be implied from, the contract.

(3) It is for the seller to show that a breach fell within subsection (1)(b) above.

---

activity

INDIVIDUAL WORK 21.5

P3

This activity asks you to look at the Sale of Goods Act. You are required to:

1 Give an outline description of the effect of legislation regarding contracts for the sale of goods.

2 Cover only the Sale of Goods Act 1979, implied terms, which can be found in Sections 12 to 15.

3 Explain any technical terms that are used, including 'satisfactory quality'.

Supply of goods and services

Under the terms of the Supply of Goods and Services Act 1982, which was amended by the Sale and Supply of Goods Act 1994 and the Sale and Supply of Goods to Consumers Regulations of 2002, additional contracts for services, including holidays, double-glazing and repair work, have all been brought into line.

The law itself requires that any work carried out be done with reasonable care. It must also be done in reasonable time and for a reasonable price.

Implied terms

A sample section from the Act deals with the following areas:

Implied term about care and skill

Section 13 provides:

In a contract for the supply of a service where the supplier is acting in the course of a business, there is an implied term that the supplier will carry out the service with reasonable care and skill.

Implied term about time for performance

Section 14 provides:

(1) Where, under a contract for the supply of a service by a supplier acting in the course of a business, the time for the service to be carried out is not fixed by the contract, left to be fixed in a manner agreed by the contract or determined by the course of dealing between the parties, there is an implied term that the supplier will carry out the service within a reasonable time.

(2) What is reasonable time is a question of fact.

Implied term about consideration

Section 15 provides:

(1) Where, under a contract for the supply of a service, the consideration for the service is not determined by the contract, left to be determined in a manner agreed by the

contract or determined by the course of dealing between the parties, there is an implied term that the party contracting with the supplier will pay a reasonable charge.

(2)   What is a reasonable charge is a question of fact.

Work and materials

Under the Supply of Goods and Services Act 1982 any work carried out by a business should be done with the following guidelines:

- with reasonable care and skill
- in a reasonable time
- for a reasonable price.

In addition to this, the goods or materials that are used to carry out the work should be:

- of satisfactory quality
- fit for their purpose
- as described.

The Act covers most problems with quality of work, including home improvements and repairs. A repairer is obliged to put things right if they:

- use faulty parts for a repair
- fit parts incorrectly
- damage the property whilst doing a job.

Implied terms for hire of goods under the Supply of Goods and Services Act 1982

As far as the Act is concerned, when there is a contract that involves the hire of goods one party agrees to bail goods to another by way of hire. This does not include hire purchase agreements or goods that are bailed in exchange for trading stamps.

In a contract for the hire of goods there is an implied condition that the party hiring the goods has the right to transfer possession of the goods by way of hire. There is also an implied warranty that the person who is hiring the goods will be able to do so for an agreed period, but this does not affect the right of the party hiring the goods to repossess them if necessary.

There is also an implied condition that the goods will correspond with the description. In other words they will do what the party hiring the goods claims they can do.

False trade descriptions

Trade Descriptions Act 1968

The Trade Descriptions Act 1968 aims to protect consumers, as well as businesses. Every business has a responsibility to ensure that it is not knowingly misleading the public. The Act covers suppliers, services, manufacturers, accommodation providers and facilities. It is vital that a business is honest about the products or services it offers, otherwise a business may find itself falling outside the legalities as laid down in the Act.

Trade description

The trade description can apply to any aspect of a product, including:

- the size, quantity or gauge of goods
- claiming they were handmade when they were machine processed
- claiming they were made from one material when they were in fact made from another
- claims about strength, performance or accuracy, such as stating that something is unbreakable
- falsely claiming that goods have characteristics that they do not have
- stating that the goods or services have been tested or approved by an individual or organisation when they have not
- making false claims about the country or origin
- making false claims about when they were made
- claiming they were made by one individual or a factory when they were not.

> **remember**
>
> Even if a person who incorrectly describes goods for sale does so innocently they will be considered guilty and there is no defence, even if they offer some form of disclaimer.

In order to be an offence, the indication must be false to a reasonable degree. Traders will not be charged if they have made a tiny inaccuracy.

It is a defence for those accused of false trade description to tell the court that the mistake was made as a result of reliance on information supplied by others. If the trader can show that all due diligence was applied, they may not be held responsible for the false trade description.

Normally, complaints about false descriptions are dealt with by Trading Standards Officers. However, the police will automatically become involved when offences are more serious.

There are three offences in relation to false trade description.

Applying a false trade description

Under the Act, it is a criminal offence for a business or an individual to apply a false trade description to goods or services in the course of business.

Supplying goods with a false trade description

The second offence is supplying or offering to supply goods or services to which a false description has been applied. In many respects this piece of law is intended to deal with careless traders – particularly in the second-hand, antiques and art markets – who may have bought something falsely described and are now selling it on. It does not matter whether or not the trader is aware that the item has a false description.

A prime example would be reducing the mileage on a used car. A car trader selling cars that have been 'clocked' could be charged with supplying goods to which a false trade description has been applied. If the car trader was involved in clocking the cars before offering them for sale, they would be charged with applying a false trade description and supplying goods with a false trade description.

In both cases, i.e. selling or supplying goods with false trade descriptions, the courts are not actually interested in whether the buyer has received good value for money. The important consideration is how the trade description has been applied or used.

Falsely describing a service

The third offence is falsely describing a service. The Act also covers the provision of services, accommodation or facilities. In this respect, the business must describe precisely what the service will be and to make this description as accurate as possible.

Effect and link to misrepresentation

Misrepresentation occurs when one party makes a false statement of fact to another. Whilst it may not actually be part of the contract, the false statement induces the other party to enter the contract. If proved, misrepresentation renders a contract voidable: it gives the innocent party the right to cancel the contract and to claim damages.

In order to be classed as misrepresentation, a statement must be an unambiguous assertion of existing fact.

Puffs, opinions and intentions do not constitute representation:

- Puffs are not representations, as established in *Dimmock* v *Hallett* in 1866. Statements of opinion are not representations, as established in *Bisset* v *Wilkinson* in 1927.
- Statements of intention, if they are honestly held, cannot be misrepresentation; but, if such a statement is dishonestly represented then it is, as established in *Edgington* v *Fitzmaurice* in 1885.

To be misrepresentation, the statement needs to be addressed in such a way as to mislead the other party. The statement must also induce the contract. The test will fail, however, when the person making the representation is not aware that they are misrepresenting.

There are three main types of misrepresentation:

- Fraudulent misrepresentation – the representation is made with the intent to deceive and the party making the misrepresentation knows it is untrue.
- Negligent misrepresentation – the representation has been made in a careless way, whilst the party has no reasonable reason for believing it to be true.
- Innocent misrepresentation – the party making the representation had reasonable grounds for believing that the false statement was true.

The key remedies are either rescission or damages. Rescission is a remedy that wipes out the existing contract and restores the parties to the situation, prior to entering the contract.

In most cases, this means cancelling the contract and any money paid by one party to another is returned. Rescission can take place either as a result of fraudulent or innocent representation, as well as for a number of other reasons, such as mutual mistakes.

Under the terms of the Misrepresentation Act 1967, a court would have discretion as to whether or not damages are awarded to the innocent party. In the case of fraudulent misrepresentation, damages are often awarded to the innocent party. Sometimes damages are calculated under the guidelines of the Misrepresentation Act. In some cases, courts have even awarded damages for losses of profit, as the situation caused the innocent party to lose other investment opportunities.

For more information about the Misrepresentation Act 1967, visit the website of the Office of Fair Trading

www.oft.gov.uk

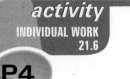

activity

INDIVIDUAL WORK 21.6

P4

This needs a very similar approach to the one you used for P3, but this time you should look at goods and services. You will need to look at the Supply of Goods and Services Act 1982 and any relevant associated legislation and cases. You should:

1   Give an outline of the legislation in your own words.

2   Explain any technical or jargon terms.

3   Explain the implications of any implied terms.

activity

INDIVIDUAL WORK 21.7

M2

Analyse how consumers are protected in the event of breach of a contract for the supply/sale of goods or services.

Your teacher/tutor will now give you a situation where the terms of the contract you have already been using have been breached. You must make sure that you look into the breach carefully and:

1   Cover any relevant terms in the contract that relate to the breach.

2   Examine the exclusion clauses and see if they are relevant.

3   Outline and comment on any relevant legislation that applies to the validity of those clauses and terms.

4   Suggest a likely outcome to the breach of contract.

The remedies available to the parties to a contract

Signing the correct kind of contract in the first place is always the best way of avoiding possible breaches. However, no contract is good enough to prevent a breach of contract by the other party. As we will see in this final section, several remedies are available to the party that has suffered as a result of a breach of contract by the other party.

Most commonly, breaches of contract occur because either one party refuses to perform their obligations under the contract or they do perform their obligations but their performance is defective.

Remedies

If the other party breaches a condition of the contract, it is possible for the innocent party to **repudiate** the contract. This means that the contract will be terminated and the innocent party can attempt to claim damages for their loss. They could also seek to **affirm** the contract and claim damages.

Damages

The two main types of remedy for breaches of contract are money damages and equitable remedies. Where money damages are concerned there are several ways in which the damages can be calculated.

Damages are designed to compensate the innocent party. However in order to establish an entitlement to damages the injured party must establish the following:

- that the actual loss was caused by the breach
- that the type of loss is recognised as giving entitlement to compensation
- that the loss is not too remote (see below)
- the quantification of damages to the required level of proof.

In cases where there has been a breach of contract but there has been no actual loss, the injured party will be entitled to nominal damages.

In the vast majority of cases the burden of proof rests with the claimant. They are asserting the breach and loss so they must prove it. Claims can be documented using appropriate records kept at the time. Amounts that have been arrived at by theoretical calculations can be acceptable.

The claim for costs usually means putting the claimant back into the position where they would have been had it not been for the breach of contract. The claims are not designed to turn a loss into a profit.

The law only allows losses that are not too remote. The law states:

> 'such losses as may fairly and reasonably be considered as either arising naturally according to the usual course of things from the breach of contract or such as may reasonably be supposed to be in the contemplation of both parties at the time they made the contract, as the probable result of breach of it'.

There are three possible measures of a loss:

- the loss of bargain
- wasted expenditure or reliance loss
- claim in restitution.

We will look at these in more detail.

- Contracts involve the making of bargains and create expectations from both parties. The expectations are fulfilled by the performance of the contract obligations. The measure of damages is there to protect the expectations of the parties. Loss of market value is also a measure of damages, as defective work or breach of contract could lead to a loss in the market value of any products or services involved. Loss of profit is also an area for damages. When the contract is breached, the injured party is unable to complete a further contract with another business or individual.

- Reliance loss is related to wasted expenditure. One party will have had expenses, which have been rendered futile by the breach of the contract.

- Finally, restitution requires two measures of damages; loss of bargain and wasted expenditure. The injured party can make a claim in restitution if the other party has been overpaid and failed to complete, or has not performed but has been paid.

Liquidated and unliquidated

In 1829, it was decided that the parties to a contract could agree a sum of money that would be paid to the injured party in the event of a breach of contract. This is known as a liquidated damages clause and is enforceable. The clauses are referred to as liquidated damages clauses because a court is not required to quantify the losses sustained by a party. There are limits to the clauses and they must not be overly punitive.

In the 1915 case, *Dunlop Pneumatic Tyre Co Ltd* v *New Garage Co Ltd*, the court decided that a liquidated damages clause would be considered a penalty and unenforceable where the sum to be paid by the party that made the breach of contract was 'extravagant and unconscionable in amount in comparison with the greatest loss that could conceivably be provided to have followed from the breach'.

The court will take the following into consideration:

- whether the contract refers to the clause as a liquidated damages clause or a penalty
- where the estimate of loss is imprecise, whether the sum is a genuine estimate of the losses that would be sustained or whether it was disproportionate to the actual losses sustained
- a stipulated sum is not disproportionate simply because it is notably greater than the actual loss sustained
- whether such an imbalance of bargaining power existed between the parties at the time of the contract, that one party effectively dictated the terms of the contract.

For the most part courts do not interfere with these clauses. However, they will look at the sums involved to see if they are disproportionate.

There is little reason why a liquidated damages clause cannot be calculated as an estimate linked to a formula or a time period. The principle is that the clauses are enforceable when they apply equally to both parties. Liquidated damages are often shown as a penalty: a simple form of the clause could be, 'if in the event the goods are delayed the supplier shall pay the customer the sum of £100 per day until delivery up to a maximum of £1,000'.

If a party is unable to enforce a liquidated damages clause, they may have to resort to having to prove unliquidated damages. This means that the party will try to claim for the actual loss they have suffered as a result of breach in the contract by the other party.

Whether or not a party can do this depends on the liquidated damages clause and on whether liquidated damages are the only remedy. In a lot of contracts this is the case, but ultimately if liquidated damages are not deemed enforceable the only recourse is for the damaged party to claim unliquidated damages.

Mitigation of loss

It is the duty of the injured party to mitigate their losses. This means not to increase the amount of damage done. The three rules are:

- The injured party cannot recover for loss that they could have avoided if they had taken reasonable steps.
- The injured party cannot recover any losses that they have actually avoided, even though they took more steps than were necessary to avoid the losses.
- The injured party can recover losses incurred in taking reasonable steps to mitigate their losses, even if they did not succeed in avoiding those losses.

Failure to take reasonable steps means that they cannot recover anything in respect of the extra loss. However, they are not expected to take risks in order to mitigate the losses. If the injured party obtains any benefits as the result of their mitigation then these must be taken into account.

Rejection

Rejection is a buyer's remedy in a case of breach of contract. Rejection means that the buyer can get their money back and return the goods. They can also claim damages for material breaches. In the case of consumer contracts, any breach of the implied terms is taken to be material. Rejection is not allowable when the buyer has actually accepted the goods.

Damages can be claimed irrespective of whether or not the goods are rejected. The damages are usually calculated as the estimated loss that has flowed directly and naturally in the course of events from the seller's breach.

Lien

With lien one party is allowed to retain the other party's property in their possession until payment has been made under the terms of the contract. A prime example of this is known as repairer's lien. In cases when items are being repaired the repairer does not have to give up possession of the repaired item until the payment for the repair has been received from the customer.

A lien can be either general or particular:

- A general lien gives the person holding the lien the right to retain possession of all property that he holds belonging to the person who owes him the debt until that debt has been paid, whether or not that property relates to the debt in question. A general lien may be difficult to establish.

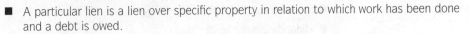

- A particular lien is a lien over specific property in relation to which work has been done and a debt is owed.

The following conditions must all be met if a right of particular lien is to exist:

- The goods retained must be the property of the party who owes the money and not of a third party, no matter how closely connected.
- The goods must have come into the possession of the owner by proper means.

Resale

The passing of property or the transfer of ownership is an important aspect in contract law. There are two different situations:

- where the seller is the actual owner of the goods
- where the seller is not the owner of the goods.

The general rule is that ownership of the goods is passed from the seller to the buyer when both parties intend that ownership to pass. However, determining when ownership passes is important for the following reasons:

- The buyer or the seller may go bankrupt.
- There is a risk of damage or destruction of the goods because the passing of the risk follows the passing of the ownership.

There is a general rule that 'no one gives what he does not have'. This applies to situations where the seller is not the owner of the goods. There are four exceptions:

- the owner is not allowed by their conduct to deny the seller's authority to sell
- sales under voidable title
- the resale by the seller in possession to a third party, in good faith and for value
- resale by the buyer in possession to a third party, in good faith and for value.

The following terms are implied in contracts that involve the sale of goods:

- that the seller has the right to sell the goods
- where the sale is by description that the goods correspond to that description
- where the seller sells the goods in the course of business that the goods supplied are of a satisfactory quality.

Reservation or retention of title

Retention of title (ROT) clauses relate to the seller's entitlement to be paid for goods they have supplied.

The need for retention of title clauses can be seen from the ruling related to a case in 1993, *Compaq Computer* v *Abercorn Group*:

> 'The broad purpose of an agreement that a seller retains title to goods pending payment of the purchase price and other moneys owing to him is to protect the seller from the insolvency of the buyer in circumstances where the price and other moneys remain unpaid. The seller's aim in insisting on a retention of title clause is to prevent the goods and the proceeds of sale of the goods from becoming part of the assets of an insolvent buyer, available to satisfy the claims of the general body of creditors.'

When sales are made on credit term, there is also the problem of insolvency, as the 1981 case *Borden* v *Scottish Timber Mills* illustrates. The problem is that **unsecured creditors** rank fairly low down in the list of creditors and are unlikely to receive their goods back or any sort of payment. The payment order is usually:

- **fixed charge holders**
- expenses of the winding up
- **preferential creditors**
- **floating charge holder**
- unsecured creditors
- members of the company.

When there is retention of title, the supplier of the goods is at the head of the list of distribution:

- fixed charge holders and reservation of title holders
- expenses of the winding up

- preferential creditors
- floating charge holder
- unsecured creditors
- members of the company.

A retention of title clause could be written in the following manner:

'The ownership of the goods supplied to the buyer shall remain with the seller until payment in full for all the goods shall have been received by the seller in accordance with the terms of this contract or until such time as the buyer sells the goods to its customers by way of bona fide sale at full market value. If such payment is overdue in whole or in part the seller may (withoùt prejudice to any of his rights) recover or re-sell the goods or any part of it and may enter upon the buyer's premises for that purpose. Such payment shall become due immediately upon the commencement of any act or proceeding in which the buyer's solvency is involved.'

The supplier is unable to rely on the retention of title clause in the following cases:

- Title is not actually reserved.
- The clause is not incorporated into the contract (*Butler Machine Tools* v *Ex-Cell-O Corporation* [1979] and *John Snow* v *DBG Woodcroft* [1985]).
- The goods supplied under the clause have been sold (*AIV.* v *Romalpa Aluminium* [1976] and *Armour* v *Thyssen Edelstahlwerke AG* [1991]).
- The goods sold under the ROT clause have been mixed with other goods or they have been altered or used in manufacture (*Chaigley Farms Limited* v *Crawford, Kaye and Grayshire* [1996]).

Injunctions

A court may be in a position to stop one of the parties from committing a breach of contract by applying an injunction. There are three different types of injunction:

- interlocutory injunctions – which are designed to regulate the parties before a hearing
- prohibition injunctions – which order the **defendant** not to carry out an act that is in breach of contract
- mandatory injunctions – which require the defendant to reverse the consequences of an existing breach.

The court can exercise its discretion as far as prohibitive injunctions are concerned. However, with a mandatory injunction the court will refuse relief if the hardship caused to the defendant by complying with the order outweighs the advantages that will be afforded to the **plaintiff**.

Generally injunctions will not be granted if the effect is to directly or indirectly make the defendant carry out acts for which the plaintiff could not have specific performance.

Specific performance

Sometimes damages will be insufficient compensation to the victim of a broken contract. The court can compel the defendant to fulfil the terms of the contract they have broken. The major difference between this type of judgment and an injunction is that specific performance requires a positive set of actions from the defendant, whereas an injunction usually applies negative stipulations on the defendant.

Certain considerations must apply in order for the court to grant a claim for specific performance:

- The plaintiff has to show that damages would be inadequate. This might mean that the plaintiff could not get a satisfactory substitute (such as a specific plot of land or a piece of artwork, both of which may be unique).
- The court considers granting specific performance as it is equitable to do so. This means that if it is impossible for the defendant to comply with the order then specific performance will not be granted.
- The final consideration is the type of contract. Specific performance is not granted when the contract involves personal services or building contracts. A court will not demand that an employee do any work by ordering specific performance of a contract of employment and likewise an employer cannot be forced to employ someone against that person's wishes. In cases relating to building, courts do not generally order specific performance

because it is a far simpler task for the plaintiff to engage the services of another builder to complete the work.

Application of remedies

Ultimately, if the two parties that have entered into a contract cannot agree between themselves a remedy for the breach of contract then the courts may become involved. As we have seen, there are clear lines drawn with regard to the breach of contract, fault and remedies.

The courts tend to apply remedies that fall in line with previous judgments in similar cases. Looking at previous judgments allows the court to identify the particular breach and the possible claims for damages made by the injured party.

Courts and time limits

Litigation involves the arguing of the case from the two perspectives, usually by legal professionals on behalf of the two parties.

Normally, the injured party would apply for a court order to compel the other party to perform their obligations under the contract. This is known as specific implement.

Alternatively, the individual who has suffered from the breach of contract may attempt to enforce a negative obligation. This is known as interdiction: the injured party attempts to forbid the other from taking action in breach of contract.

As we have seen, damages must attempt to put the injured party in the same position, as they would have been if the other party had acted according to the contract. The burden of proof is on the injured party in the following respects:

- They must prove that they have suffered a loss.
- They must show that the losses suffered were as a direct result of the breach of contract.
- They must show that the loss was reasonably foreseeable as a result of the breach.

As already mentioned, the injured party has to take reasonable steps to mitigate their losses. The court will look at the damages and how they can be retrieved on behalf of the injured party. The court may find that frustration was the cause for the breach of contract. If circumstances outside the control of either party made the performance of the contract impossible or made the situation radically different from what was originally anticipated, the contract may be considered frustrated. In these cases, both parties are released from their contractual obligations. Here, the two key aspects are that:

- The event that caused the frustration could not have been foreseen.
- Neither party was at fault.

The precise time limits on bringing breach of contract cases to court may depend on the exact nature of the contract itself. In the case of a mortgage or financial agreement, the time limit for bringing a breach of contract is three years. In most employment cases, proceedings have to be initiated within six months. However, the case will not necessarily appear before a court within the stipulated time limit, although the court will attempt to open proceedings; if nothing else it will wish to encourage both parties to begin negotiations to solve the situation without requiring the court to impose a judgment.

> **remember**
> Taking the other party to court over a breach of contract can potentially result in high litigation costs.

case study 21.4 — The Central London County Court mediation scheme

Established as a pilot project in 1996, the Central London County Court (CLCC) mediation scheme has since become a permanent part of that court. It offers low-cost mediation in cases with a claim value above £5,000 (the small claims limit). It was the first court mediation scheme of its kind in the UK.

The CLCC mediation scheme is available for parties who have themselves decided they would like to mediate or have been advised to consider mediation by a judge. The CLCC scheme has been entirely voluntary, and no party has been forced to use mediation.

Any case with a claim value of £5,000 or higher is eligible for mediation in the scheme. This applies to cases which start at the Central London County Court as well as to cases which are transferred to it from other courts, as it is the main civil trial centre in London.

Almost any type of case is eligible for mediation, including breach of contract.

Some cases are not suitable for mediation, for example where an urgent injunction is being sought.

(Source: www.justice.gov.uk)

activity

1   Find out about similar mediation schemes in your area.

2   How does their handling of breaches of contract compare with conventional court proceedings?

activity
INDIVIDUAL WORK 21.8

P5

M3

1   Describe the remedies available for breach of contract.

For the criterion for P5, you will need to look at the question of damages. You should:

(a)   List and explain the different types of damages that could be awarded.

(b)   Explain what is meant by damages as compensation for loss.

(c)   Identify which losses can be claimed and which are too remote.

(d)   Briefly mention equitable remedies, including injunctions.

(e)   Explain real remedies, such as refusing further performance and re-sale.

(f)   Show that you understand that there is a difference between the terms ownership and possession.

2   Analyse the remedies available to a business provider in the event of breach of a contract for the supply of goods or services.

The work for M3 is a continuation of the work you carried out for M2. You are required to:

(a) Analyse the law, as you did for P5.

(b) Make sure that you take into account the availability of a remedy and the most appropriate remedy.

Progress Check

1.   Distinguish between bilateral and unilateral contracts.

2.   What is an invitation to treat?

3.   What is the general ruling in the battle of the forms?

4.   What is meant by undue influence?

5.   What are the three sources of implied terms?

6.   What is reservation of title?

7.   What is an exclusion clause?

8.   Outline the Consumer Protection (Distance Selling) Regulations.

9.   Describe section 13 of the Sale of Goods Act.

10.   What is lien?

UNIT 26

Managing Business Information

This unit covers:

- Understand the importance of information to organisations
- Know how organisations use business information
- Be able to maintain an information system
- Be able to produce information to support decision making in organisations.

It is essential for an organisation to keep track not only of information that it generates but also information that it gleans from the general environment. To be useful, business information has to be up to date, accurate and valid and presented in a readily digestible format that can help the business to make decisions.

The unit begins by looking at the types of information that businesses routinely collect and at the various sources of that information before examining the purposes to which information is put and the legal and ethical issues governing its use.

The second half of the unit introduces methods of inputting and manipulating data using spreadsheets and databases and ways of presenting information to support decision making.

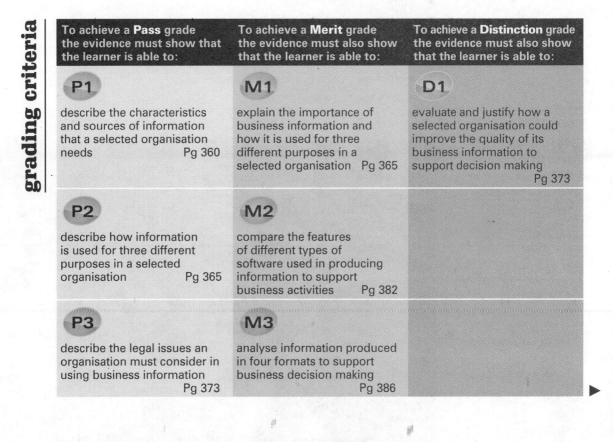

grading criteria

To achieve a **Pass** grade the evidence must show that the learner is able to:	To achieve a **Merit** grade the evidence must also show that the learner is able to:	To achieve a **Distinction** grade the evidence must also show that the learner is able to:
P1 describe the characteristics and sources of information that a selected organisation needs Pg 360	**M1** explain the importance of business information and how it is used for three different purposes in a selected organisation Pg 365	**D1** evaluate and justify how a selected organisation could improve the quality of its business information to support decision making Pg 373
P2 describe how information is used for three different purposes in a selected organisation Pg 365	**M2** compare the features of different types of software used in producing information to support business activities Pg 382	
P3 describe the legal issues an organisation must consider in using business information Pg 373	**M3** analyse information produced in four formats to support business decision making Pg 386	

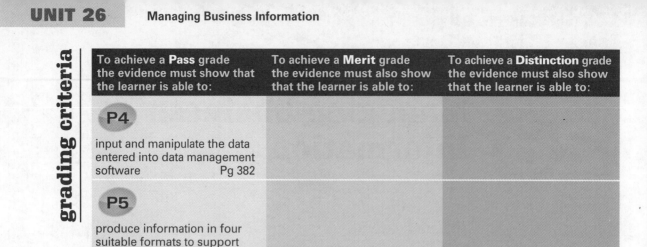

The importance of information to organisations

Before we even look at the importance of information in the business context we need to make one very clear distinction. Although the words 'data' and 'information' are often used interchangeably, they do not really have the same meaning. Raw data requires processing in order to become information.

Data can, of course, come in many different forms, most commonly numbers, words and symbols. Data represent facts, transactions and events. However, taken on its own, a simple list of numbers is not that useful, even if the numbers refer to the transactions carried out by a retail store on a specific day. If you were to purchase a product from a retail store the following data would be captured:

- the time, date and year of the transaction
- the value of the transaction
- details of the products or services bought and how many were bought
- how you paid for the products or services
- which employee in the store processed the transaction
- whether any discounts were given to you
- whether you had a loyalty card.

Fig 26.1 Computerised till systems are vital to stock control, re-ordering and for capturing customer data

Businesses that sell products and services to customers find this one of the simplest sets of data to collect. It is, of course, taken at the point of sale. The vast majority of businesses have computerised till systems linked to a stock control system and a reordering database. From this raw data the store would be able to:

- obtain the total value of sales for a given day
- identify the busiest period of the day
- identify which employee processed the most sales
- identify the most popular products sold
- identify the most common form of payment.

Characteristics

The data's source largely determines the data's characteristics, i.e. whether it is in the form of numbers, words or symbols or is a mixture. Initially, data is often generated in the form of an enormous disorganised list that has no apparent value until it has been processed. Importantly, the data collected should eventually provide the business with useful and actionable information. It would therefore be of no use to a business that sells stationery items to collect data about whether or not people wear spectacles. As we will see, the data has to have a translatable value and it has to have relevance to the business that collects it. It may not be possible for the business to collect the data itself, in which case it may commission another company to collect the data on its behalf or it may purchase data from an external source.

Qualitative and quantitative information

The simple way of distinguishing between qualitative and quantitative information is to consider the difference between detail and bulk. Generally speaking, qualitative information is highly detailed and descriptive and because of the amount of detail there is neither the time nor the resources to collect huge amounts of it. Quantitative information is numerical and does not contain a great deal of detail, but there is lots of it. Here is an example:

> A business has a limited budget to collect some research information about its customers. The basic choice is whether to collect qualitative or quantitative data. If the business opts for qualitative then it can afford to carry out 50 in-depth interviews with customers to find out about their backgrounds and buying habits. This should provide some valuable information. However, the problem is whether the 50 customers chosen will be representative of all the business's customers. The alternative is to opt for quantitative research. The business could, over a period of a month, log the number of customers going into and out of a retail store and compare it with the number of individual sales made. This could show how many visitors to the store actually buy products. The problem here is whether this research would tell the business very much about its customers' buying habits.

In this situation, the business has to define precisely what it wants to find out and then select an affordable research method that would, hopefully, collect that information. In the example, quantitative data collection would provide very limited information about many customers. The business may wish more data had been collected on a wider variety of aspects. Qualitative data would provide detailed information about a relatively small number of individuals. To be cost effective the additional information should bring new ideas to the business. If qualitative research could provide the answers, there are sampling techniques that can be used to ensure that the customers chosen for interview are as representative as possible of the wider customer base. However, the comparatively small sample size will have to be taken into account when the results are evaluated.

See pages 160–1 for information about types sampling techniques.

Primary and secondary information

In the example used to illustrate qualitative and quantitative data, the business was collecting the data that it needed directly from its customers in order to answer a specific question. It was doing primary research. In primary research, data is collected for the sole purpose of the research task. Whether a business does its own data collection or employs a consultancy to collect data from consumers on its behalf, this is primary research.

When collecting primary data, a business hopes to be able to frame the questions and design the research to provide it with the answers that it is seeking. Starting from scratch like this is, of course, complicated and expensive. The business may know what it wants to find out, but it may not know how to find that data. It also needs to be assured that any data collection

remember

Data only becomes information when it has been processed. In other words, it has to be given meaning.

remember

An organisation is likely to use a mixture of qualitative and quantitative data. It may begin with the raw figures (quantitative) then collect qualitative data for more detail.

exercise is efficient, relevant and will provide accurate information that can be acted upon.

The alternative is to use secondary data, which, as the term implies, is second-hand. Somebody else has collected it for another purpose. Typical examples are government statistics and **marketing intelligence** reports collated by marketing agencies. The government or the marketing agency will have collected or collated its own primary data, which it will have processed and turned into information that it needs or that it perceives will be of value to others. However, there are problems with secondary data:

- Because the data has not been collected specifically to meet the business's needs, it may not necessarily answer all its questions.

- The data may have been collected several months previously. In some cases, the data may have been collected years ago, and it may have taken a long time to process the data before presenting it in its current format.

- It may not be clear what research methods were used.

- The sample from which the data was collected may not have been representative.

- The researchers may be making assumptions based on very little original data.

Provided that businesses can afford to carry out primary research and are confident that the primary research will provide the data that is needed, they tend to opt for this in preference to secondary research. Secondary data, however, can be useful for providing clues or suggesting trends and fashions that a business can use as a base for its own research.

Quality of information

Not all information would be useful to a business. It may be out of date, too complicated or may have cost far too much to collect. Ideally, the data should match the business's specific requirements: it needs to answer the questions that the business has posed.

A business may ask itself why, according to its sales figures, sales have gradually fallen away over the past six months. What it needs to do next is find a way of collecting data that will help explain why this trend is happening. The business also needs to find out what it can do to reverse the trend. The data has therefore to be accurate, collected quickly and relevant; it must also be cost effective, and, when processed, it needs to produce clear messages that the business can act upon with the minimum of delay. To be useful, data and the information that it produces once it has been processed need to possess certain key qualities. Table 26.1 outlines these.

Table 26.1 Quality criteria

Quality criteria	Explanation
Valid	The validity of data underpins everything in the research process. A questionnaire or any other measuring tool is valid if it actually measures what it claims to be measuring. A business needs data that are directly useful and relevant, particularly in terms of the research questions that the business asks. What this means is that the research has to collect enough data from appropriate sources to make sure that the results are actually a true reflection of the situation.
Complete	Given that it is impossible for any business or government agency to collect every single piece of possibly relevant information from every single possible source, the term 'complete' is not a particularly good one to use. The information collected must, at the very least, answer the basic questions posed by the business. If it can do this then at a very basic level the research is complete. Businesses will always wish to extend their understanding of a situation beyond what is absolutely necessary at the time. They may wish to ask more questions and delve deeper into situations. However, as far as answering key questions in a research project is concerned, the data needs to be complete only in so far as it does what it set out to do and nothing beyond that. Obviously, the more information that is collected, the longer it will take to process and probably the more complicated and confusing the results will be.
Accurate	Accuracy is a prime consideration when collecting data. There can be many sources of errors, which will lead to the feeling that the data is not as accurate as it could have been. At a very basic level, figures need to add up and all data that has been collected should be included in the sets of data processed and commented upon. It should be made clear where estimates or assumptions have been made. There should be spot checks of the data to make sure that there have been no data processing errors. A research project is rarely likely to produce absolutely perfect information; therefore the business needs to balance perfectly accurate information against the need to process the data as quickly as possible and provide the necessary information for the business to act upon.

Quality criteria	Explanation
Timely	Complex and long-winded research projects may produce perfectly accurate information. The major problem is, however, that by the time the data has been collected, processed, presented and discussed, it will be out of date. In order for a business to obtain any value from the time and resources put into the data collection and processing, it needs to turn that data around as quickly as possible so that it can have maximum value from it.
Fit for purpose	This means that the data collection exercise and the information it finally produces should meet the needs of the business or the users of that information. On a regular basis, retail stores produce enormous printouts of their sales figures. These may be of direct interest to the accounts department of a business, but the managing director will have neither the time nor the inclination to trawl through them. What the managing director needs is a summary of the sales.
Accessible	As with any presentation of data, the information produced by research should be easily understood and simple to use, as far as the users of that data are concerned. It needs to be presented in a clear manner, probably using charts and summaries. The research material itself is of no interest to the users; they are interested in the results of the research. More importantly, they want to see the information in a format that they can understand and can use. Many businesses use research templates so that users become used to seeing research findings presented in the same manner. Usually these are shown at presentations or distributed in printed reports or email attachments.
Cost effective	Data is expensive and time consuming to collect. But that is only part of the job. Data has to be processed and analysed, and someone has to sit down and create a report, outlining the key aspects of the research project's findings. Even after the report has been printed the users need to sit and read it and understand the key points. The true value of the money spent on research is apparent at this stage. The users will see the information that has been collected, collated and analysed and will be able to make a judgement as to whether or not the money and time were well spent. Factors they will consider are accuracy, meeting the needs of the user and whether or not the information is up to date.
Intelligible	Users with access to the information provided by a research project need immediately to recognise that they can use it and that it will help in their decision making. Therefore, the information should be presented in a format that can be readily used and will become an immediate part of any decision-making or problem-solving process. The usefulness of the information is the ultimate test of any data collection exercise. If the users understand the information's relevance and can immediately put it to use, the exercise has been a valuable one.

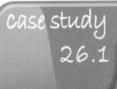

case study 26.1 — Market Research – Graphisoft UK

Graphisoft is a developer of architectural Computer Aided Design applications. It was actively searching for a partnership in the building services market.

Graphisoft hoped that this would help it provide a coordinated service to large companies in need of both architectural design and building services solutions. Cymap, one of the leading UK building services software providers, emerged as a possible partner. Graphisoft wanted to measure the image and awareness of Cymap and its products with a view to a possible business alliance and approached Business Advantage with a request for a market survey.

In total, 100 interviews were carried out to determine levels of prompted and unprompted awareness of these products and those of their closest rivals. Eighty companies were interviewed in the heating, ventilation and air conditioning (HVAC) sector. A smaller sample of actual users of the product was interviewed to gain an indication of satisfaction levels amongst customers. Acting on estimates of the proportion of companies aware of the company and its product and rival products, Graphisoft came to the conclusion that Cymap was an ideal partner to integrate building services solutions with its Virtual Building technology. After this, Graphisoft announced the acquisition of Cymap into the Graphisoft Group.

'The market survey of Business Advantage confirmed our view that Cymap represents leading-edge building services technology which we have been seeking for a long time. The B2B research helped us greatly with our decision-making process,' commented Andras Haidekker, Managing Director of Graphisoft UK.

(Adapted from www.business-advantage.com)

activity

1 What were Graphisoft's research needs?

2 What do you think is meant by 'prompted and unprompted awareness'?

3 What is meant by 'acquisition'?

remember

To be a truly successful organisation, a business has to use its available data sensibly and consider not only that it is paying for data to be collected and analysed but also that the data could be useful to other parts of the organisation.

Sources of information

Before a business embarks on any research-gathering exercise it will have to decide what kind of information it needs. Many businesses begin by looking at information that has already been published. This secondary research material includes market reports, official statistics and trade publications. Some of the information is free, but information from some sources has to be paid for.

Next the business will have to decide whether the information is already to hand or if it will have to hunt for the data that it needs. The first place to begin looking is inside the business itself. A business routinely collects an enormous amount of data but may not use it for any other purpose than its primary one: for example, sales figures may be routinely passed to the accounts department for analysis but may not be seen elsewhere in the organisation.

Whether the business is going to use internal sources of information or external ones, there are five key considerations for any type of data.

Fig 26.2 Checklist

Data checklist

Trustworthiness – is the data credible, reliable and can it be confirmed?	4
Validity – can comparing it to the data from another source check the validity of the data?	4
Dependability – Will the users be prepared to depend upon the data, assuming that they trust its source?	4
Transferability – can the data that has been collected for one purpose be used for another with the minimum of effort?	4
Confirmability – is there access to the raw data and is it clear how the data was analysed? If spot checks can be made on this then more users will trust the data.	4

Internal

The term 'internal data' refers to all types of information that has been collected by the various parts of an organisation. Usually, the data is routinely collected by a particular department or division for its own specific purpose. For various reasons, the data may not be circulated around the whole organisation; some users within the organisation will, however, have access to the data when making decisions and solving problems. Access to these sources of information is often limited to key decision makers, as some of the information may be sensitive (e.g. personnel records) or of great commercial value to competitors (e.g. data concerning new products and services in development). The key sources of internal information are outlined in Table 26.2.

Table 26.2 Internal sources

Internal sources	Explanation
Financial	The accounts records of an organisation are prime sources of internal information. They have potential value for other parts of the business. They routinely detail the transactions made by the business, which can be used as the basis for future planning. The primary aim of the accounts department is to record precisely what happens to the financial resources of the business. Its records show where money came from and what it was spent on. The records will also detail what assets a business has, what profits or losses it has made and how particular activities have affected these two figures. Financial information is not just restricted to figures. From financial data, trends in sales can be interpreted, as can dealings with particular suppliers or customers. A great deal of internal information is directly linked to the accounting systems but may not necessarily be part of them. Whilst the accounts detail the total amount spent on salaries and wages, the breakdown of that spending is dealt with the human resources department.
Human resources	The human resources department deals with the employees of an organisation. The department works hand in hand with the particular departments in an organisation and relies on the accounts department to deal with payments to employees, as well as other expenditure. The human resources department holds records on all employees in the organisation. Routinely, it keeps personal details, details of salaries and wages paid, training records and information on individuals' skills and experience. A business could use the data held by a human resources department for a number of different purposes. If, for example, before introducing a new computer system, it wished to identify the general skills level of employees, an accurate assessment of computer skills could be provided. A business would also be able to assess the value of each employee in terms of costs and productivity.
Marketing	In many organisations the role of marketing is integral to sales. However, marketing provides a very valuable service to the whole organisation and can shape the way in which it develops. Marketing has two key roles. The first is to publicise and popularise the products and services offered by a business. It does this by placing advertisements, carrying out public relations exercises and a host of other activities. The second role is to collect two key types of data on behalf of the business: first, data on the business's competitors; secondly, data on the business's customers. Marketing can therefore be a primary source of information. The impact of marketing activities is routinely assessed and regular updates are provided as to the activities of competitors, as well as the trends, feelings and opinions of customers.
Purchasing	The role of purchasing within a business organisation is to obtain raw materials, finished goods and consumables of the highest possible quality at the lowest possible cost. Many businesses have preferred suppliers with whom they have had a longstanding business relationship. Other businesses may have overarching strategies in their purchasing, which commit them to fair trade with developing countries or to the development of suppliers in different areas of the world. The purchasing department can provide useful data on the costs of business processes. It tracks the costs of raw materials, machinery, finished goods and consumables, comparing them month on month and year by year. The purchasing department may also be able to predict whether costs will increase or decrease in the near future: this can alert the organisation to possible price increases that may need to be applied; it can also allow a business to purchase additional stocks so that it can avoid the impact of increased prices.
Sales	It is often said that sales departments tend either to be incredibly optimistic about future sales or so pessimistic that they are convinced that sales will be poor and that little can be done about it. Sales figures, if interpreted correctly, can provide useful insights into trends and help the business to predict possible sales levels in the future. It is important to remember that sales figures may not incorporate any particular interpretation or explanation as to why the sales figures were at that level at that time. As many factors can affect sales, sales figures should be viewed in the context of the larger market, the activities of competitors and the buying patterns of customers. Once these factors have been included and applied to the figures, sales data can possibly provide the most accurate prediction available to a business.
Manufacturing	Manufacturing can provide a wide variety of different types of information. At a basic level it can provide information on the reliability of the machines that it uses. In addition, it can state whether the machines are working at full capacity and how often they need to be repaired. Manufacturing can also provide useful data that can be used by the sales and marketing departments. A good example would be an estimate of how long it would take to produce a particular order for a customer. Manufacturing must work closely with sales and marketing because customers will expect to be given fairly accurate delivery times for their orders. Sales may promise a particular delivery date, but manufacturing actually make the products and they will be able to give the more accurate date. Manufacturing also work closely with purchasing. They will require purchasing to acquire additional machinery and equipment, and they will also be interested in knowing how much particular raw materials cost, so that manufacturing costs can be added on to the product's cost. This is of vital importance because the final sale price of a product should incorporate the cost of all of its components, as well as the cost to the business of processing those components. There should therefore be a continual interchange of information between purchasing, manufacturing, marketing and sales.

A single transaction can provide each part of an organisation with useful information.

Fig 26.3 If a business's
advertising works, the
sales department should be
geared up to start expecting
customer calls

Fig 26.3 If a business's advertising works, the sales department should be geared up to start expecting customer calls

The following example explains how this might work:

■ A customer calls the sales department.

■ The customer has called as the result of seeing an advertisement placed in a magazine by the marketing department.

■ The sales department asks the customer to quote a reference number.

■ The reference number has been put on the advert by the marketing department so that they can assess how many responses they have received from each advert they have placed.

■ The customer orders a product, which is made to order.

■ The sales department checks with the manufacturing department to see how long it will take for the product to be processed.

■ The manufacturing department checks with the purchasing department to make sure that the necessary components to make the product are in stock.

■ All being well, the sales department can now confirm that the customer will receive the product in a certain number of days or weeks, based on the information provided by the purchasing and manufacturing departments.

■ The customer makes the order.

■ The sales department passes a hard copy of the order to the accounts department, which issues an invoice to the customer.

All parts of the organisation are dependent upon one another. Of course, in this example we did not mention human resources, but that department would be directly involved with every single individual in the organisation. The human resources department helped during the recruitment process and is involved in the ongoing training of employees.

> *remember*
>
> Not all organisations routinely use their internal data to help them make decisions. Some lack the systems necessary to allow access to data collected by one or more parts of the organisation.

External

Whereas internal sources tend to produce primary information, external sources of information tend to provide secondary data. Although this information has been collected by another organisation, probably for a different purpose, this does not mean that it is not useful to the business; it may provide a valuable lead or stimulate research.

Why might a business wish to use external sources? Why don't businesses collect the information themselves? The answer to both questions is usually that the amount and scope of the information that is needed are simply too great. Typically, businesses try to collect information about the following from external sources:

- general economic and market trends
- new products being developed by competitors
- competitors' plans
- forthcoming legislation that could affect the business or market
- information about advertising and sales promotions.

There are, of course, many external sources of information and in recent years supplying information to businesses has become a massive business. Market research organisations provide regular analysis of market trends. Such information can be purchased by businesses on subscription, or individual reports can be purchased on publication.

To be useful, externally sourced data needs to be trustworthy. However, trustworthiness is far more difficult to assess in the case of generalised information about a market or a range of products. It may not be abundantly clear how the data was collected, and it may not be clear whether the information is up to date. Relying purely on external sources of information can be dangerous, and a business will usually back up the information that it has obtained from external sources by comparing it with data from additional research that it has carried out itself. Typical external sources of information are outlined in Table 26.3.

Table 26.3 External sources

External sources	Explanation
Government	The Office of National Statistics is the primary source of government statistics. It combines data on the economy, population and society at both local and national levels. All the summaries of its data are published free of charge. More extensive information can be purchased directly from the Office of National Statistics. In addition, information is collected by local government and by specific government departments. Data on the environment, for example, would be collected by both the Department for Environment and Rural Affairs (DEFRA) and by the Office of National Statistics.
Trade groupings	There are tens of trade associations in the UK. They are designed to provide a forum and a source of information and support for businesses involved in particular types of activity. For example, organisations involved in offshore oil and gas would be members of the Association of British Offshore Industries. Travel agents and tour operators would be members of The Association of British Travel Agents. Most trade associations have websites with shared information, usually only accessible by members.
Commercially provided	There is a bewildering array of commercially provided sources of information. These range from regular market reports on specific industries through to detailed analysis of particular business organisations. The UK 15,000 service, for example, provides information on all UK businesses with over 100 employees and £10m or more of sales each year. Several online subscription services provide up-to-date analysis and study of particular types of industry. One example is E-Consultancy, which has over 10,000 reports available at any one time. As with all sources of information, particularly if it has to be purchased, it is important for the business to analyse the probable value of the information before buying. It needs to be good quality: i.e. valid, accurate, cost effective and fit for the purpose.
Databases	Many commercial, European Union, government and trade associations have accessible databases with market information that is regularly collected and collated and is accessible, usually by subscription. In order to obtain full value from the data provided, a business has to be sure that it will make use of these commercially produced sources of information.

External sources	Explanation
Research	Many universities and other educational establishments carry out ongoing research as part of their academic activities. In its raw form, much of the information can be of value to businesses. Some universities are associated with particular types of research information. A prime example is the Sir Norman Chester Centre for Football Research at the University of Leicester. Now called the Centre for the Sociology of Sport, it has an enormous amount of information on football and other sports, including fan surveys. Information about fans would be of interest, for example, to football clubs or to organisations that target football fans to sell products, such as football shirts, calendars and signed photographs, and a host of services.

For a full listing of the majority of British trade associations, visit the website of the Trade Association Forum and select 'directory' from the top menu bar; this gives an A–Z listing

www.taforum.org

The UK 15,000 service

www.uk15000.co.uk

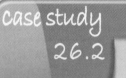

case study 26.2 — Using external agencies for market research

A large international company in the flash data storage industry had already established its presence in China and had a local sales team. Revenues, however, did not meet expectations. The company's managers were looking to understand the unique characteristics of the market in China and to adjust their market strategy accordingly.

Asia Direct was hired to conduct comprehensive market research, which covered market overview, consumer behaviour, competitive analysis, distribution channels and potential partnerships with other players in the industry. Asia Direct and the client then developed strategic solutions for the business.

Asia Direct's team of researchers conducted preliminary research and reviewed market information to help our client grasp the market conditions, value, trends and major players in their industry.

Additionally, Asia Direct conducted in-depth primary interviews throughout all levels of the industry to further flesh out consumer behaviour; distribution networks dynamics and real price margins and distribution quantities.

Additional primary interviews were conducted with major manufacturers of flash storage data products, as well as with manufacturers of PCs, distributors and wholesalers. This research explored potential partnership avenues and new distribution strategies, and was the basis of our competitive analysis of this industry in China.

(Adapted from www.adhitech.com)

activity

1   What was the problem that the business wished to solve?
2   How was the data collected?
3   What did the business want Asia Direct to find out?

Information can come from routine business transactions. If the information comes from an external source, that external source needs to be found and verified as being reliable.

Supermarkets routinely collect information about the shopping habits of their customers. Customers exchange this for the use of a customer loyalty card. The information gathered includes:

- the date and time of purchases
- the checkout number

- the method of payment
- the products purchased
- any promotional coupons used.

This will provide the supermarket with a very detailed picture of the transactions and buying habits of the customer. Additional information about typical customers can be bought in from external sources; such information includes:

- disposable income
- lifestyle
- regulatory concerns
- activities of competitors.

case study 26.3

Customer loyalty cards – ups and downs

Every business loses customers. What is not generally appreciated is that, even if you can win more new ones than you lose, you are still missing out on a major growth opportunity. Bain, an American consulting group, has demonstrated that by hanging on to an extra 5% of your customers each year you can double profits. As on average companies lose and find half their customers every five years, there is plenty of scope for improvement. The reasons that 'loyalty' improves profitability are:

- retaining customers costs less than finding and capturing new ones
- loyal customers tend to place larger orders
- loyal customers don't always place price first, while new ones do.

To see if implementing a customer promotion or reward scheme would work for you first calculate the proportion of customers who desert you each year. Then work out the cost versus potential value of setting up the reward system of your choice. Complete the task by identifying other methods to improve your loyalty ratio.

A customer reward scheme can be carried out in any number of ways to try and retain customer loyalty. However, nothing beats the basic creeds of business – knowing your customer and serving their needs. Without the customer service element no 'reward' schemes will help any business. Calculate the proportion of customers who desert you each year.

Some people believe that loyalty cards have never really lived up to their promise. When they were launched, retailers made big claims as to how they would be gathering tons of invaluable data about customers. But mostly they have been left with huge virtual warehouses of information that hasn't been used. Database mining, or analysing the buying habits of millions of shoppers as their cards are swiped at the till, can be prohibitively expensive and few companies have used much of the data gathered to make their customers feel special and hence want to stay loyal.

This is not to say that loyalty cards are without merit. Used effectively, these cards can make customers feel their loyalty is being recognised and rewarded by companies. For example, by earning points every time they spend money on your products and services, your customers will feel they are getting added value. These points may then be redeemed for other products or prizes.

If you do implement a loyalty card scheme, you can ask members whether they would like to receive information from you on occasion. This is an opportunity to promote your business through using newsletters, magazines, letters about incentives or special offers, or you could even send a questionnaire to find out more about your loyal customers. But remember not to overwhelm and risk driving away your customer base.

(Adapted from www. bestforbusiness.com)

▶

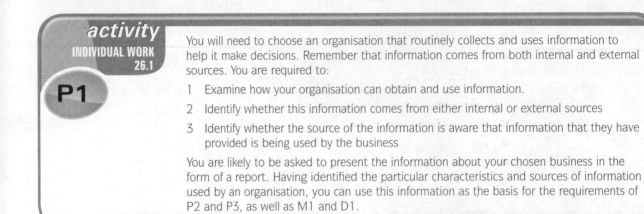

You will need to choose an organisation that routinely collects and uses information to help it make decisions. Remember that information comes from both internal and external sources. You are required to:

1   Examine how your organisation can obtain and use information.

2   Identify whether this information comes from either internal or external sources

3   Identify whether the source of the information is aware that information that they have provided is being used by the business

You are likely to be asked to present the information about your chosen business in the form of a report. Having identified the particular characteristics and sources of information used by an organisation, you can use this information as the basis for the requirements of P2 and P3, as well as M1 and D1.

How organisations use business information

A business is legally required to collect, collate and keep certain information, particularly with regard to its transactions, as such information is required for tax purposes. This aspect of data collection and organisation is the responsibility of the accounts department. However, a business collects information for other reasons too:

■   To know on a day-by-day basis how the business is doing – this is achieved by monitoring transactions and other activities.

■   To plan for the future – information can provide useful indicators as to patterns and trends. The business will use these to try to predict its level of activity at various points in the future.

Data collection requires a balance to be struck between quantity and usefulness. There is a limit to the value of raw data, but sufficient raw data has to be collected to be transformed into useful, actionable information. Some raw data is of little value to a business at all, beyond helping it restock after a sale.

Thought needs to be given to sharing information. Information that is collected by one part of an organisation to help it become more efficient and to assist in decision making might, in summarised form, be useful to other parts of the organisation. As we will see later in this section, when collecting data and using and sharing information the business must make sure that at all times it complies with legal requirements and behaves ethically.

Purposes

Unless a business is a sole trader or a small partnership, it is almost impossible for any one individual to have access to and an awareness of everything that is going on. The larger the business, the more complex are the activities and, of course, the greater the number of activities going on at any given time.

A business is organised in such a way that individuals (e.g. managers and directors) can monitor, control and coordinate its activities. These individuals therefore need access to the information they require to fulfil their responsibilities and report on their activities to senior managers.

Working through its managers and directors, it is possible for the organisation to record, monitor, control and coordinate all its activities. Once the business has a clear view of what is happening it can make plans for the future, analysing activities and attempting to make accurate predictions of the requirements that the business might face.

Recording transactions and activity

Every time an invoice is created or a sale is made through a cash till in a store, a record of that transaction is produced. The transaction is one of many transactions and activities taking place in an organisation in a given day, hour or minute.

The recording of transactions begins when invoices are raised for a business to pay for the products, raw materials or components that it purchases from suppliers. Once the items have been received by the business they can be processed. Processing may involve using

Fig 26.4

electricity, gas, coal, water, petrol and a host of other resources; wages and salaries have to be paid. These are all transactions relating to expenditure.

But once the items are ready for resale to customers or other businesses the organisation can begin to make transactions that will provide it with income. Each time a sale is made, a record of that transaction is kept. At the end of a financial period the business will be able to compare its expenditure with its income to discover whether it has made a profit or loss. However, a business does not wait until the end of a financial period to find this out. Ideally, it needs constant access to the latest financial data and to be aware of the current situation with regard to its income expenditure. It falls to the accounts department to keep track of income and expenditure and at any point, on any day, be able to report on the state of the business's finances.

Monitoring, controlling and coordinating activity

Many employees working for organisations are not directly involved in the selling process. They may not even be involved in the making, storing or distribution of products. They may purely be in a supporting or administrative role. Therefore, not all activities within an organisation are directly related to the production of income. However, any activity undertaken by an employee or a manager requires expenditure, as wages and salaries have to be paid.

A business needs to know exactly where, when and why money is being spent. It also needs to know how, where and how often money is being made. In this way it can make judgements about supporting particularly successful areas of the business and choose to discontinue activities that are not beneficial. This decision is unlikely to be made purely for financial reasons; it may be based, for example, on efficiency. As we have seen, not all employees or areas of a business are in a position to make sales and generate income.

Access to accurate and up-to-date information in the form of summarised records of transactions and activities is essential. By constantly monitoring what the business does, senior managers are able to control the activities. If, for example, a business is experiencing a higher rate of demand, senior management can allocate additional funds to enable extra staff to be employed to take the strain. They can also make decisions if products or services are not selling and instruct the marketing department to place additional advertising or the sales department to offer discounts.

It is the role of senior management to coordinate all the efforts or activities of the business, so that it runs as efficiently as possible, and to assist each manager and supervisor all the way down the organisational chain to monitor and control those activities for which they are responsible and make accurate and timely decisions.

Planning activity

By having access to information, whether it focuses on transactions or activities, senior management will be in a better position to plan future activities. No business can be truly efficient and ready at all times, but senior management will try to organise the business so that it can cope with almost anything that might be thrown at it. It is difficult to predict what might happen in the future, even with business information at your fingertips, but it is impossible to plan for the future if this information is not available or is incomplete.

As senior managers are not involved in the business's day-to-day activities, they can only react when they receive summaries of the events that have taken place. With increasingly sophisticated software it is possible for senior management to keep a closer eye on activities as they occur, but they are still reliant upon departmental managers, other directors, managers and supervisors to pass information back up the organisational chain, so that a clearer picture of what is happening is presented to them.

Typical concerns when planning include:

- Cash flow management – the business should keep a constant check on its income and expenditure and try to make sure that its income is in excess of its expenditure. The alternative is that the business would run out of money.

- Over-trading – although it might seem to be to a business's advantage to be selling vast amounts of products and services, over-trading can lead to problems. At its most basic, over-trading occurs when a business takes on more work than it has the capacity to do. If the business cannot meet the demand for products and services, these will run out. The business will not have enough direct cash to buy new products quickly enough to be able to sell them on. It can be fatal for a business.

- Managing suppliers – having a good relationship with suppliers is vital, not only to negotiate the best prices but also to negotiate collaboration and mutual reliance. Many businesses use their suppliers as an additional warehouse, knowing that they can supply products at very short notice. It means that the business can avoid paying for the products until they are absolutely sure they are needed.

- Seasonal business – a major problem for some businesses is the seasonal nature of the products or services they offer. A business that makes winter clothing will need to find something to do and a way to earn money when its products are not required. The same can be said for businesses in the travel and tourism sector; many of these have found alternative tourist destinations to provide them with an income during the winter months.

Analysis and predictions

Once data is collected and processed into intelligible information, the business has to analyse so that it can see any patterns and trends. Analysis may provide the business with clues as to why sales figures are at the current level, why customers may not be buying as much as they were this time last year, or even why more products are being returned as faulty.

Trend analysis looks for patterns in sets of figures or information over a period of years or months. The more significant particular patterns and trends are, the more likely it is that they will recur. However, when identifying trends it is important to distinguish between what might be probable and what might be possible. If, for example, a business noticed over the past five years a significant surge in sales in November and December, it would be probable that a similar surge in sales might occur in the November and December of the next year. If, however, the same business noticed a surge in sales in two of the five previous years then it is only possible that it would see a surge in sales in the forthcoming November and December. The same note of caution would apply if a pattern of poor sales has been identified in previous years.

Recognising trends and patterns in sets of data enables a business to prepare itself and create solutions to deal with expected changes. Techniques that a business can use to predict what might happen in the future include extrapolation and the use of 'what if?' scenarios; these are outlined in Table 26.4.

remember

A business that analyses trend data correctly is ready to cope with probable problems or opportunities.

Table 26.4 Prediction method

Production method	Explanation
Extrapolation	Extrapolation means constructing new sets of data at the end of a series of known data. In effect, a business will extend a graph or chart to take into account the patterns that it has recognised in the existing data that has been collected. What the business may do is to plot a graph of the data and draw a line (the line of best fit) that passes through the centre of the data. The line can then be extended. This will take into account the general trends in the existing data, but it will not take into account any unknown factors that may affect the data in the future. Generally speaking, extrapolation is not a very reliable way to predict the future. In order for extrapolation to be reliable the original data has to be very consistent and without significant variation. It needs to follow a fairly regular and predictable pattern.
'What if?' scenarios	'What if?' scenarios are used to work out the probable impact on data if certain things happen in the future. A business will have collected existing data and will have identified any patterns or trends in it. The business will then extend the data, but not as it would in extrapolation. The first thing the business might do is to see what might happen if it were to increase the prices of its products or services. Or it might see the impact on its sales if a new major competitor entered the market. The process is designed to find out what would be the most likely outcome if there were a certain change in the future, which would impact on the business's activity.

Fig 26.5 Line of best fit

(Source NHS)

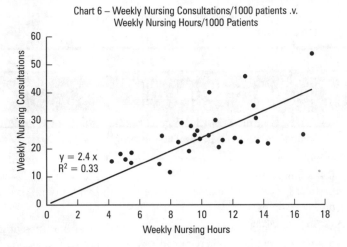

Chart 6 – Weekly Nursing Consultations/1000 patients .v. Weekly Nursing Hours/1000 Patients

$y = 2.4x$
$R^2 = 0.33$

Planning and using a 'what if?' scenario

'What if?' scenarios are not only used to predict what might happen in the future but also to prepare a business to deal with that situation should it happen. The business evaluates the various strategies that it could use and has the best strategy to hand should the situation actually happen.

To do this, the business needs to follow a series of steps:

1. Define what might happen in the future within a certain period of time. This allows the business to get a feel for the fact that the future is uncertain.

2. Identify the major **stakeholders** in the business. How might their roles, interests and power change in the near future?

3. Identify the current trends. These will affect the future in some way and can be helpful in seeing how significant a major change in the future might be if these trends are still valid.

4. Identify the key uncertainties, in other words what cannot be predicted, certainly in respect of variables over which the business has no control.

5. Construct one positive scenario and one negative scenario, identifying respectively the best case in the future and the worst. These are extreme situations and any future change is likely to fall between the two.

6. Identify whether either of these two extreme scenarios could actually happen. If one or either cannot then new ones have to be constructed that could occur.

remember

'What if?' scenarios are vital planning activities: they help the business prepare for a set of circumstances that might occur in the future, allowing the business to respond quicker as it has a plan in place.

7. Eliminate combinations that are impossible. The business may have identified the worst-case scenario and then have piled on other major problems. By looking at those that could not happen, the business can begin to refine its reaction to what could occur.

8. Revise the scenarios and identify how the stakeholders would behave.

9. Make sure that all possibilities have been identified and that the business has a clear list of what could occur and how it could deal with the situation.

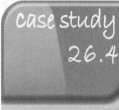

case study 26.4 — Extrapolation

Sarah has three children, Jenny, Angela and Mary. On 1 January 2006 Jenny was 1.2 m tall; Angela was 1.1 m tall, and Mary was 0.8 m tall. A year later on 1 January 2007, Jenny was 1.4 m tall; Angela was 1.2 m tall, and Mary was 1 m tall. Sarah wants to work out by extrapolation how tall her three girls will be on 1 January 2008.

activity

1 Using extrapolation, what will be the heights of the three girls on 1 January 2008?

2 If Jenny does grow at the rate suggested by extrapolation, how tall will she be on 1 January 2010?

3 Why might extrapolation be completely useless in working out the girls' heights using the available data?

---

case study 26.5 — The Tesco Clubcard

Tesco now controls 30% of the grocery market in the UK. In 2007, the supermarket chain announced over £2.5 billion in profits.

Dunnhumby specialises in consumer data, Tesco owns most of the company. Dunnhumby was hired by Tesco 12 years ago to help with its customer loyalty card, Clubcard. Every four weeks, two-thirds of British households shop at Tesco. It takes nearly £1 in every £7 spent in Britain's shops.

Martin Hayward, director of consumer strategy and futures at Dunnhumby said: 'We use your purchasing behaviour to create a picture of the kind of person you are.'

Using Clubcard data, Dunnhumby can tell that customers have a new baby, or that their children have left home. It can judge your social class and knows whether you are a good cook. It also gives Tesco clues about what products or service it could sell more of and to which customers. Dunnhumby turns the information from the 13m Clubcards into five billion pieces of data. Each separate product bought has its own set of attributes. The information is stored in a vast search engine that can be used by suppliers trying to launch products.

Dunnhumby makes about £30m a year selling Tesco data to more than 200 companies, such as Coca-Cola, Procter & Gamble and Unilever. As soon as a product is launched and in stock at Tesco, the brand managers can track who is buying their products or responding to their promotions.

Hayward explained: 'If you understand who is buying and how they are buying, you can make better decisions. Because Tesco is so representative of the country it is the best source of insight a supplier can get.' Using census data, **market intelligence** companies help make decisions on where to open a shop. Hayward explained: 'The argument was that if you live in a street full of flats, you are one sort of person; if you live in leafy suburbs, you are another sort of person.'

In 1993, a trial programme was run to see if it was worth Tesco introducing a loyalty card. Months were spent collecting shoppers' data at tills in a handful of trial stores, then sending reward vouchers to customers' homes. It became obvious that loyalty cards were effective both at getting customer data and encouraging shoppers back into stores. The trials continued throughout 1994 using 14 stores. The impact saw sales increase by upwards of 12%. The Tesco board were amazed and decided to adopt the Clubcard concept.

Hayward said: 'Clubcard has brought about a step-change in the size of the company. We started off being able to understand the departments that people shopped in and the frequency at which they shopped, and we worked with those two variables.'

At the basic level, Tesco divides its customers into 'convenience' shoppers (sub-divided into 'time-poor, food-rich' and 'can't cook, won't cook') and 'price-sensitive' ones ('stretching the budget' and 'cheapest I can find'). There is also 29% who are more discerning and opt for 'finer foods' (whether 'natural chefs' or 'cooking from scratch'). The 'mainstream' customers (who buy lots of 'kids' stuff', or 'commonplace brands') are the mid-market group. 'Less affluent' shoppers make up 27% of Tesco's customers; there are also sub-categories – 'traditional' and 'price sensitive'.

Tesco can use the Clubcard data to make informed strategic decisions. Two examples were the launch of the Internet shopping website and the smaller Tesco Express convenience stores. The data has also helped Tesco develop pet insurance, its Finest range and mobile phones.

Over 33% of Britons have a Clubcard. Joining is easy. Tesco asks for your name, address, telephone number and basic details about your household. It also asks if you are diabetic, teetotal or a vegetarian.

In return, Tesco gives customers one point for every £1 they spend in its shops, petrol forecourts and on its Internet site. There are extra bonus points to be gained for mobile phones, broadband and credit cards. When enough points have been earned, Tesco gives its customers money off from future purchases. Tesco sends out money off vouchers four times a year along with targeted special offers. Last year, it gave £250m in discounts.

Tesco is very protective about the Clubcard information. Through Dunnhumby, it does sell data to some companies, charging up to £50,000 for access to the data. Dairy Crest is one such client; the chief executive said: 'We are sharing common, real-time data with Tesco. We use it to make sure we have the right ranges in store and the right shelf space, and we use it in discussion with Tesco themselves. You can target customers. Without getting too detailed, you can do a cross-correlation of who is most likely to be using your brand in Tesco.'

(Adapted from www.ft.com)

activity
INDIVIDUAL WORK 26.2

P2

M1

1 Describe how information is used for three different purposes in a selected organisation. For P2, you need to use the information in Case study 26.5 and:

(a) Describe how the information is gathered.

(b) Describe what it is used for (monitoring, controlling, coordinating or planning).

(c) Describe how it is used to make decisions.

Your answers will form the first part of your report for this unit.

2 Explain the importance of business information and how it is used for three different purposes in a selected organisation. This work for M1 extends the work carried out for P2. You should:

(a) Explain why the business information is important to the success of the organisation.

(b) Explain three different uses of the information (purposes that the information is put to) by the organisation.

Information use

Increasingly, the management and use of information is becoming known as information resources management. Its two key areas are:

- the use of IT-related information systems
- the techniques used in information-based libraries.

An information audit is the first step in helping a business use information more effectively. The audit seeks to identify and pull together all the various sources and types of information available. Typically, the following will happen:

1. The business will look for gaps in its information and for duplicated information.

2. Individuals who own and use information will have their roles and responsibilities clearly defined.

3. Some kind of centralised system will be brought in to obtain and handle the information, reducing duplication.

4. Each type of information source will be looked at in terms of its costs and its benefits.

5. Finally, the organisation will seek to find ways in which the information can be used directly to support the decision-making process.

Operational support

Employees in various parts of the business need immediate access to data so that they can carry out their work. At a very basic level, the employee needs to know how to carry out a task. In the course of their work they will need to pass on information and report on the progress of projects and tasks; they may also have to make decisions on the basis of the information that they have available.

Most businesses have a centralised computer system, often set up as a network, allowing all employees access to files and information. Employees have to input their password in order to gain access to the information. Some of the information is locked so that unauthorised individuals cannot amend it. Routinely, employees are responsible for updating the data held on the network, particularly in the case of stock levels, prices, delivery dates and financial information.

It is now possible for networks to be accessed remotely by employees who are working away from the workplace. This is achieved via personal digital assistants and laptop computers, connected to the business's information systems either via a telephone network or wirelessly using mobile telephone technology. Again, passwords give authorised staff access to parts of the business's network or website.

Decision making

Provided that they are up to date, accurate and relevant, information and knowledge can be even more important than the physical assets owned by a business. If a business has organised itself in a disciplined manner in order to exploit the information assets that it owns then inevitably it can make better and more well-informed decisions.

If information is to be used in decision making, it must be accessible; and the decision maker must be aware of its existence, be allowed access to it and understand it. Decisions are made at various levels within an organisation, and it is important that the correct information is available to the appropriate employee, or manager, as and when it is needed. We can identify three key levels of decision making within an organisation, each of which has its own particular informational requirements:

Table 26.5 Decision points

Decision points	Explanation
Operational	The operational level in an organisation is the day-to-day, routine work carried out, often by the lowest grade employees in the organisation. Operational work, therefore, would be done by a sales assistant in a retail store or a customer service advisor in a call centre, or indeed a bus driver on a transport network. Their information needs may be limited, but they will require specific information in order to work efficiently and make decisions. A sales assistant needs to know if products are in stock, when products might be delivered and current pricing levels. A customer service advisor needs to know the policies and procedures of the organisation and whether refunds, discounts or other incentives can be offered to the customer. A bus driver needs to make decisions regarding the speed of the vehicle and when coping with traffic delays and other situations that could affect the timing of the service.

Decision points	Explanation
Tactical	This is the next stage up in decision making. Typically, the employees involved at this level will be supervisors and relatively junior managers. A store manager makes tactical decisions, as does a customer service supervisor and, perhaps, a bus inspector. These individuals all have authority over the employees carrying out operational work and therefore need to make decisions as to how to best deploy their subordinates. They are also the point of contact for decisions that cannot or will not be made by their subordinates, and they, therefore, require sufficient information to make informed decisions.
Strategic	At this level would be the sales director of a retail chain, a customer service manager and, perhaps, a director for a privatised bus service. These individuals have to make decisions based on information passed to them from other areas of the business, as well as on information passed up to them from employees working at operational or tactical levels. They do not, of course, usually have a hands-on interest in the day-to-day running of the business, but it is their decisions that frame the work of all those who work below them in the organisation. Their decisions tend to focus on achieving key business aims. They search for strategies in order to achieve aims, such as increased profitability, increased numbers of customers, reduced wastage and increased production.

Administration

As we have seen, employees need information that has been collected, collated and formatted by other parts of the business.

All information coming into an organisation has to be processed and a decision made as to its value; some of the information has to be stored for future reference. Therefore, the organisation has to set up systems to cope with the inflow of information, its storage (in a logical manner) and its extraction should the information be needed at some point in the future.

Traditionally, this has been a paper-based exercise, involving filing cabinets, folders, and index systems. Systems for extraction of information have tended to be rigid, requiring anyone who removes information from the system to sign it out, so that anyone else needing it can trace it. Clearly, some of the paperwork that is stored is required for ongoing work. The accounts department would routinely store financial documentation that may be needed at a later date for **auditing** or if tax inspectors choose to check the accounts of the business.

Fig 26.6 Paper-based filing is still a tried and tested means of storing vital documents

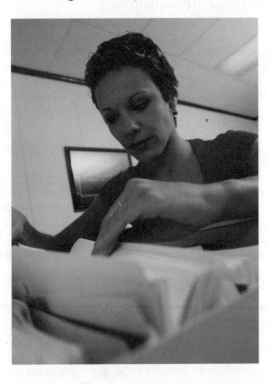

remember

Auditing is a requirement for all limited companies. HM Revenue and Customs requires it and it is a safeguard for investors.

Some organisations have a discrete administration department, responsible for handling the collection, storage and retrieval of all paper-based documentation. Many smaller businesses will have made the shift to digital filing systems, although even in the smallest of businesses some documentation has still to remain paper-based.

Promoting efficiency

All organisations are awash with information, and, unfortunately, managers and employees may be completely unaware of the existence of information that could enable them to perform their jobs far more easily and efficiently. We have already seen that an information audit can help organise, categorise and facilitate access to information. To be truly efficient means avoiding unnecessary duplication of work and not making decisions based on incomplete information. To promote efficiency, it is imperative that information is accessible to all who would potentially find it useful. Therefore, businesses should:

- ensure that information is accessible when needed
- ensure that there is an interface or way of searching information sources
- ensure that there are multiple databases, which are not just copies of one another but are information-category specific
- ensure that retrieval of information is a simple task
- ensure that all individuals have been trained in how to search, access and retrieve information.

Within the organisation, each type of information should be the responsibility of named departments or individuals; otherwise that information could be lost or simply stored and never used. Other key considerations in improving efficiency are:

- sorting out exactly what information needs particular users may have
- ensuring that they can acquire that information
- ensuring that they or someone manages that information.

Information has a definite lifecycle. When information is fresh and put to immediate use, it is probably far more valuable. As information ages, its relevance begins to decline and it becomes gradually less useful; decisions made on the basis of out-dated information are less likely to be correct. If a business can use information when it is fresh, it will have a high leverage with that information. In other words, the information may have some intrinsic value, but using the information enables a far better decision to be made, making the information all the more valuable.

Developing competitive advantage

Putting relevant information in front of key decision makers at the appropriate time is the primary way in which a business can develop a competitive advantage and possibly increase its market share. A competitive advantage gives an organisation, even if only for a short period of time, an opportunity to out-compete its major competitors. It may know something that they do not know or have not acted upon. For example, if a major supplier is running out of stock of an essential component for a product and will not be re-supplied for some time, a business that is aware of the situation could purchase all existing stock, leaving its competitors unable to restock.

Increasing market share

Each product type or geographical area is said to be a market; a market has a total value. For example, a market could be described as being worth a certain amount of money, representing the total sales of all of the businesses offering that product or service.

Each business selling that product or service sells a percentage of the total value to the market. This is its market share. For example, if the market was worth £100m and a particular business sold £5m of products, it would have a 5% market share.

Of the following two ways in which market share can increase, the first is straightforward and the second less so:

- taking sales away from a competitor – so that it sells fewer products into that market and you sell more
- increasing market share as a result of the size of the market increasing. Sometimes an increase in sales may not, strictly speaking, represent an increase in market share. If the market increased from £100m to £110m and the business still continued to sell £5m then it would have lost market share. If it had sold £5.5m it would have retained its market share. Only if it had sold more than £5.5m would it have increased its market share.

Information and its timely use can give a business an opportunity to take sales away from its competitors. Although there will always be a percentage of a competitor's sales that can never be taken because it has loyal customers, many buyers of products and services search for better-quality products or lower prices, and a well-timed marketing scheme might convince them to make the switch.

Legal issues

A business not only has to consider how to collect, collate, format, use, store, retrieve and reuse information but it also has to be acutely aware of several legal issues regarding the use of information or data. Many of the new rules relating to the handling of information have come into force over the past 20 years, driven largely by businesses' increased use of computer information systems. Computer storage enables businesses to keep far more information than is feasible with paper-based systems. It is relatively easy to set up a database on a computer, and it takes far less space than paper records. Not only is the number of separate data entries that can be held significantly greater but also the scope and detail of each entry.

The three cornerstones of data management and protection are the Data Protection Act 1998, the Freedom of Information Act 2000 and the Computer Misuse Act 1990. These key laws relating to the use of business information are subject to regular revisions to ensure that, regardless of the technology used, all uses of data are incorporated into the legal framework.

Data Protection Act 1998

The Data Protection Act was brought into force just as computers were becoming more powerful and far easier to use. As a result, much more information was being stored about individuals. Businesses found that data stored on computers could be far more easily accessed and was flexible as different types of searches could be made. People were becoming concerned that the information held on individuals could be misused or passed on to unscrupulous individuals.

The Act covers all information or data related to living people that might be stored on a computer or in a paper filing system and sets up the rules that businesses have to follow. The rules are enforced by the Information Commissioner.

Under the Data Protection Act, eight principles must be applied by any business that processes personal information:

- The information must be fairly and lawfully processed.
- It must be processed for limited purposes.
- The information held must be adequate, relevant and not excessive.
- It should be accurate and up to date.
- It should not be kept for longer than is necessary.
- It should be processed in line with individuals' rights.
- It should be secure.
- It should not be transferred to other countries without adequate protection.

Any organisation that wishes to store personal data has to register with the Information Commissioner. The business has to state what type of data will be stored and how it will be used. The register entry will contain the following information:

- the data controller's name and address
- a description of the information that will be stored
- what the information is going to be used for
- whether the data controller will pass the information on to other individuals or businesses
- whether any of the data will be passed on to countries outside the UK
- how the data controller intends to keep the data safe and secure.

> **remember**
> The eight principles of the Data Protection Act 1998 apply to computer-based records and to paper records.

> **remember**
> The data controller is a named individual in a business that collects and keeps data about individuals; the data subject is a living person who has data stored about them, which is not under their control.

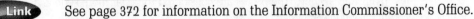

Link See page 372 for information on the Information Commissioner's Office.

case study 26.6

Personal and sensitive data

Some data that is stored on individuals must be kept confidential. This means that only they should have access to it, other than the business or organisation that has collected it. Prime examples of personal data that should remain confidential are pay, bank details and name, address and medical details. The Data Protection Act strictly controls unauthorised access to this personal data. But there are even more sensitive types of data, such as an individual's religion or whether they belong to a trade union. Understandably, there are more safeguards for sensitive data than for ordinary personal data. It is usually the case that if sensitive data is going to be stored the individual in question has to give their permission.

activity

1   Suggest other areas of sensitive personal data that could be stored on an individual.

2   Why might a business wish to store sensitive personal data?

The Information Commissioner's Office is responsible for enforcing the Data Protection Act

www.ico.gov.uk

Freedom of Information Act 2000

The Freedom of Information Act gives any person the legal right to ask for and be given any information that is held by a public authority. The Ministry of Justice is the government department with responsibility for freedom of information and data protection policies.

The Freedom of Information Act applies only to public authorities or businesses that are wholly owned by public authorities. The organisations in question have to respond to requests for information. However, if the cost of finding the information is too prohibitive, they do not have to provide the information.

The Ministry of Justice

www.justice.gov.uk

Computer Misuse Act 1990

The Computer Misuse Act 1990 created three new criminal offences:

■   It is illegal to access a computer system unless an individual is authorised to do so. This was designed to deal with hacking. Hacking refers to gaining illegal access to a computer system by using another individual's ID or password and then outputting data or a program, altering it, deleting it, copying it or moving it. It is irrelevant whether the hacker is actually at the place of business or in a remote location.

■   It is also illegal to make unauthorised access to a computer system with the intent to do something to that system in the future. For example, an individual could gain unauthorised access to a computer system using someone else's ID and then transfer funds from one bank account to another, which would be theft or fraud. In other words, the unauthorised access was one offence and the additional activity was a second offence.

■   It is illegal to modify computer programs and data. This is designed to cover the introduction of viruses, which deliberately delete or corrupt programs.

In practice, only the unauthorised access to computer systems would be handled in a magistrates' court. The others are considered to be far more serious and could attract large fines and jail sentences.

A business should be very careful about its use of personal IDs and passwords. It should encourage users to ensure that these remain secret and that on a regular basis IDs and passwords are changed.

For more information about the Computer Misuse Act, visit the website of the Office of Public Sector Information

www.opsi.gov.uk

Ethical issues

The storage of data and information brings with it certain responsibilities, including **ethical** use of the data. Data should only be used in a reasonable manner and not to the detriment of the individuals whose data is held.

There are many ethical considerations in the use and storage of data. Table 26.6 addresses some of the following questions:

- Who should have access to the data?
- Who owns the data?
- Who is responsible for maintaining its accuracy and security?
- Is there a responsibility to monitor the use of the data?
- Should its use be analysed to prevent risks to data subjects?
- What information is necessary and relevant for making decisions?
- Should certain data follow individuals throughout their lives?

Table 26.6 Ethical issues

Ethical issue	Explanation
Privacy and access	Personal data needs to remain confidential and only authorised individuals should have access to it. However, computer support technicians have automatic access to everything held on a database by virtue of their job role. Normally levels of security controls, involving personal ID and passwords, will protect data. Some systems can be deliberately designed so that only data and information for general use can be accessed via the main network.
Organisational IT protocols	Businesses have different views as to how the data they hold can be used. They deliberately encrypt and password-protect data so that unauthorised individuals cannot gain access to it. In the past, confidential data that was held on paper was locked in secure rooms. Today an enormous amount of data can be held on a relatively small computer system. Users are required to follow the IT protocols of the organisation; these usually include the use of ID and passwords, not taking copies, even electronic ones, away from the building, and simple steps such as setting up screensavers in public areas so that information on screens cannot be read by visitors to the business or organisation.
Codes of practice	Businesses will have their own codes of practice, but the two most dominant codes are actually derived from the Information Commissioner's Office and the British Computer Society. These seek to institute minimum standards of behaviour when dealing with information. They require organisations to operate beyond the strict legal requirements. They recognise the value of information to organisations but seek to impose the ethical use of that information by restricting access, ensuring that confidential information remains so and ensuring that organisations bring in IT protocols and train staff accordingly.

See page 372–373 for information on the British Computer Society.

case study 26.7 Not very charitable

In October 2005 Daniel Cuthbert, a computer consultant, was fined £400 and ordered to pay £600 costs in a magistrates' court. On New Years Eve 2004 Cuthbert had clicked on a banner advertisement, with the intention of donating £30 to the Disaster Emergency Committee, which was collecting money for the Indian Ocean Tsunami disaster. He made the donation but did not get a confirmation email to thank him for it. He feared that he had been conned by a fake banner advert and had unwittingly given his credit card details to criminals. He decided to test the Disaster Emergency Committee website to see if it was for real. It immediately triggered off the website protection system and the police were called in. The so-called attack on the site was traced to Cuthbert. The judge said, 'Unauthorised access, however praiseworthy the motives, is an offence.'

(Adapted from www.theregister.co.uk)

activity

1   What was Cuthbert legally guilty of?

2   How might the Disaster Emergency Committee know who had tried to break into its website?

Information Commissioner's Office

All public and private organisations are legally obliged to protect any personal information they keep. Public authorities must also provide public access to official information.

The Information Commissioner's Office (ICO) is a public body set up to promote access to official information. It also aims to protect personal information by promoting good practice. It makes rulings on eligible complaints, provides information to individuals and organisations, and takes appropriate action when the law is broken.

The ICO deals with four main areas:

■   data protection

■   privacy and electronic communications

■   freedom of information

■   environmental information regulations.

For more information on the work of the ICO, visit its website

www.ico.gov.uk

British Computer Society (BCS)

The British Computer Society (BCS) is a charity; it was formed in 1957 and is the leading body for those who work in information technology. It has a worldwide membership of some 50,000 members in around 100 countries. The society's main purpose is to promote the study and the practice of computing and to advance knowledge and education in the field of information technology.

Fig 26.7 British Computer Society's home page

(Source: www.bcs.org)

All members agree to abide by the BCS's code of conduct and observe the code of good practice:

- The BCS's code of conduct sets out the professional standards required by BCS as a condition of membership. It applies to members of all grades, including students, and affiliates, and also non-members who offer their expertise as part of the BCS's Professional Advice Register.

- The BCS code of good practice describes standards of practice relating to the contemporary demands found in IT.

To find out more about the BCS and the codes of conduct and practice
www.bcs.org

---

activity

INDIVIDUAL WORK 26.3

P3

Organisations cannot hold certain data on customers and must be clear about how data is kept and the purposes of keeping it. For the second part of the report you must:

1 Describe the constraints on data use under the Data Protection Act 1998.

2 Describe the constraints on data use under the Freedom of Information Act 2000.

3 Describe the constraints on data use under the Computer Misuse Act 1990.

4 Describe ethical issues in the collection and use of data (privacy, access, organisational IT protocols).

5 Describe the codes of practice from the Information Commissioner's Office (ICO) and the British Computer Society (BCS).

---

activity

INDIVIDUAL WORK 26.4

D1

This is a follow-on activity that requires you to make some justified conclusions about the quality of information produced by an organisation. You should refer to the information in Case study 26.5 about Tesco Clubcard and should:

1 Give justified conclusions about how an organisation could improve the quality of the business information that it produces.

2 Make judgements about the value of different ways of presenting information to users.

3 State how improving the quality of information will actually improve the business itself.

4 Suggest the most appropriate format in which information should be presented to different users.

5 Explain why the same information needs to be formatted in different ways for different users.

Maintaining an information system

For most businesses using computer-based information systems, a spreadsheet program and a database are adequate for data management. However, specific parts of a business may choose to use specialised computer programs that are designed to cope with their particular needs. For example, an accounts department's payment systems may use Sage software. There are also stock control software systems, applications designed to store personnel records and a host of other department- or function-specific applications.

Although for this unit you will not need to design and build a database yourself, you will need to know how to input and manipulate data in a database or spreadsheet system. A precise understanding of the parameters of any database or spreadsheet will help you to understand not only what types of data can be inputted into the system but also what can be extracted from it.

Businesses design databases or spreadsheets to suit particular purposes. A customer database, for example, is likely to contain basic personal details, particularly contact details. The database is also likely to hold information about the types of products and services purchased by the customer, how they pay and whether they are entitled to discounts. There may also be the facility to record comments that are relevant to the business's relationship with the customer.

A database, such as Microsoft's Access, is a fairly flexible system that can be designed to hold a variety of different types of data; usually this is in alpha form (words, such as names and addresses) or numeric (e.g. credit limits or prices). Each of the data types or areas of information inputted into the system is known as a **field**. The user has to know how to input and amend the data, as well as how to manipulate the data to create lists and extract information.

Spreadsheets, such as Microsoft's Excel, are also flexible. Even though spreadsheets are more closely associated with numerical data, they offer a very handy way of listing customer details. Spreadsheets are easy to search, lines can be added, and they can cope very well with text as well as numbers. Above all, they can be the basis of visual images, lists, and contact sheets.

We will look at both spreadsheets and databases in this section. They have been treated separately to avoid confusion.

Inputting and manipulating data in spreadsheets

Inputting data

As we have seen, there are two basic types of data:

- alpha data – letters, such as a person's name
- numeric data – figures or strings of figures.

You can also have alphanumeric data, which incorporates both words and numbers, for example an address.

In Excel, you can enter:

- text
- numbers
- **formulae**.

These go into what is called a cell. A cell is just one square of a spreadsheet. There can be hundreds or thousands of cells in a spreadsheet. The spreadsheet is made up of columns (headed A, B, C, D, etc.) and rows (numbered 1, 2, 3, 4, etc.). When you open a new spreadsheet the cursor will be in the top left-hand cell – A1.

Excel allows users to make calculations and save data so that it can be amended at a later date.

A business might use spreadsheet software, such as Microsoft Excel, for:

- keeping a list of sales
- calculating costs
- calculating profit
- working out employees' pay.

Spreadsheets are very flexible tools. They can:

- allow numbers, text or a formula to be entered into a cell
- use formulae to make calculations (such as adding up all the numbers in a column or a row)
- copy formulae into other groups of cells
- save time because once a word or phrase has been entered into the spreadsheet, the software will predict it and offer the opportunity of pasting it in the next and subsequent times.

When you want to put data into a spreadsheet, it is useful to have all the information to hand; and you should ask yourself a few questions before you begin:

- How should the information be laid out?
- Do I have all the data needed or are there gaps?

remember

It is vital to maintain and upgrade information systems, as users will constantly be placing new demands on the systems. Many organisations employ external contractors to maintain and update their systems.

- What do I want the spreadsheet to do for me?
- How do I want the spreadsheet to present the information to me once the data has been inputted?

One great bonus with Excel is that many of the icons along the top of the screen are exactly the same as those in Word.

case study 26.8 — Katy's spreadsheet – Part 1

Katy is just getting to grips with her new job as an assistant manager in a shop. One of her weekly tasks is to send a spreadsheet, attached to an email, to head office. The spreadsheet needs to tell the accounts department how many hours the staff worked that week. Katy has to send the spreadsheet on a Monday, covering the previous seven days (i.e. up to Sunday).

Table 26.7 Katy's spreadsheet

Name	Mon	Tue	Wed	Thur	Fri	Sat	Sun	Total
Carol	7	7	0	7	7	7	0	
Ted	0	7	0	8	6	7	9	
Paul	8	0	8	5	8	8	0	
Sylivia	7	7	7	7	0	7	0	
Naomi	8	8	8	0	0	8	8	
Katy	8	8	8	0	0	8	8	

The first thing Katy needs to do is work out how many hours people have worked in the week and put that figure in the total column.

Katy's been told that all she has to do is go to the first cell in the Total column and press AutoSum then she'll see a formula. This will add up cells B2 through to H2. Then she needs to copy the formula and paste it into each of the other Total cells. The spreadsheet will automatically make a slight change to the formula so that it will add up all of the figures in that row.

activity

1 Create a new spreadsheet and key in the data from the table.
2 Follow the instructions that Katy was given and total the work hours for each employee.
3 Save your work as 'Katy spreadsheet'.

Sometimes the labels for columns or rows and the text and numbers that need to be put into cells just won't fit. The easiest thing to do is to resize the cells. This is achieved in the following way:

- Your cursor appears on a spreadsheet as a fat, white cross.
- Move the cursor to the grey column or row headings – it changes into a thin, black cross.
- Click on the line between the columns or rows and move your cursor to the left or right. This increases or decreases the size.

Keep an eye on the dotted line on the right-hand side because this shows you how much of the spreadsheet can be printed on one page of A4 paper.

Inserting and deleting data and amending a spreadsheet

Sometimes a spreadsheet has to be amended to record additional information or changes to information. Extra rows or columns may be needed to accommodate additional information.

When making some changes to data, the user will have to click on each cell and manually change the values. Additional formulae may have to be added.

Inserting rows and columns

To insert a row, highlight the row above where you want to insert the new one by clicking on the row number, then click on the 'Insert' menu and choose the 'Row' option.

To insert a column, click a cell in the column immediately to the right of where you want to insert the new column and then click on 'Insert', selecting the 'Column' option. For example, to insert a new column to the left of column C, click a cell in column C.

If a column or row does not have a title, it is relatively straightforward to add one.

Deleting rows and columns

To remove a whole row or column, highlight the row or column in question by clicking on the row number or column letter, then select 'Edit' and choose 'Delete' from the drop-down menu.

Amending and adding, subtracting, multiplying and dividing data

Amending a label is achieved by highlighting the cell and typing to replace the existing label, or by double-clicking on the cell. You can then change the label in the same way as you would change text in word processing. If you just want to remove the label, highlight the text in that cell and hit the space bar.

Adding new values or numbers on a spreadsheet may first mean adding new rows or columns. Sometimes you may need to add numbers to a spreadsheet and put them into cells that were blank. Any empty cell can be typed straight into by simply clicking on it. But you must remember that if you do this in a full cell the existing number will be removed as you type the new one in. To avoid this when amending numbers you should double-click on the cell and change the values just as you would in Word. When you type a number into a cell it will automatically be **right aligned**. When you type in text it will automatically be **left aligned**.

A formula always starts with the = sign.

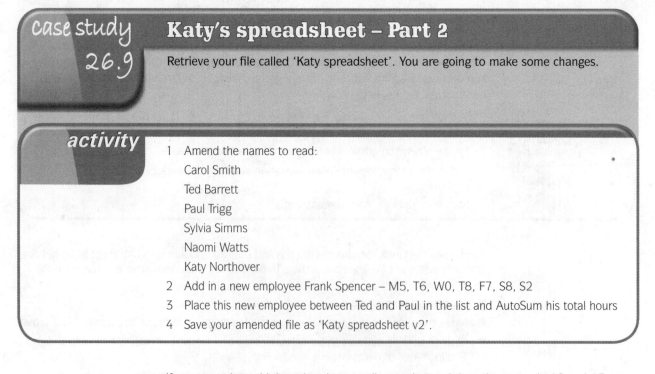

case study 26.9   **Katy's spreadsheet – Part 2**

Retrieve your file called 'Katy spreadsheet'. You are going to make some changes.

activity

1   Amend the names to read:

Carol Smith

Ted Barrett

Paul Trigg

Sylvia Simms

Naomi Watts

Katy Northover

2   Add in a new employee Frank Spencer – M5, T6, W0, T8, F7, S8, S2

3   Place this new employee between Ted and Paul in the list and AutoSum his total hours

4   Save your amended file as 'Katy spreadsheet v2'.

If you wanted to add the values in two cells together and the values were in A2 and A3 you would click on A4 and type in =A2+A3. Other formulae are just as easy: - would subtract the second figure from the first (=A2–A3); * would multiply the two figures (=A2*A3); / would divide the two figures (=A2/A3); and if you wanted to find out the percentage of a figure you would just type in, for example, 20/100*A2. This would give you 20% of the number in cell A2.

When amending a formula it is usually better to start from scratch. Simply go to the cell, hit the space bar and re-type the formula, so that it takes into account any additional rows or columns you may have added. Obviously, if you were just deleting the formula you would click on the cell and hit the space bar.

Changing a cell's format

As we have seen, the format of a cell depends on whether you are typing in numbers or text. You can change the way the cell looks. It would be laborious to change each cell one at a time. So the best way of formatting cells is to highlight all of the cells that you wish to change.

There are many things you can do to format the cell to fit the purpose of the job. Sometimes it is simply a case of making the spreadsheet look clearer when it is printed out. All options appear by clicking on 'Format' and selecting 'Cells'. Options include:

- Number – by scrolling down the list you can tell the spreadsheet whether you are inputting dates, currencies, ordinary numbers or numbers with decimal points.

- Alignment – you can click on left align, right align, centre or justified. You can also set the text to appear at the top or the bottom of the cell and, particularly importantly for text, you can click on 'Wrap around'. This automatically creates a text column rather than just a line.

- Font – just like with Word you can change the font in a cell, all cells or some cells. You can also change the size of the font.

- Borders, patterns and shading – these can be used to highlight or draw attention to some or all of the spreadsheet.

Fig 26.8 Format cells box

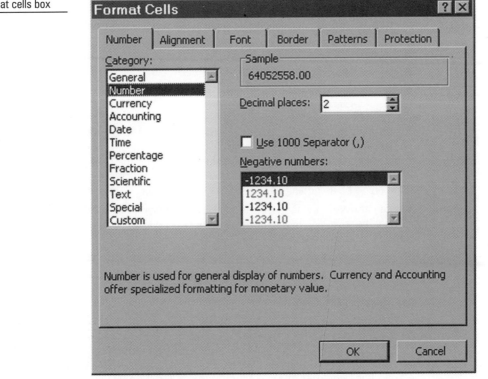

Showing formulae

Sometimes when you print out an Excel spreadsheet it would be useful to see the formulae used, so that these can be checked. Normally, when a spreadsheet is printed it shows the results of the calculations and not the formulae.

When we set up Katy's spreadsheet, we entered data and used the AutoSum button on the toolbar to give us a total of hours worked. In order to see the AutoSum formula all we need to do is to click on 'Tools' scroll down to 'Options' and a box will appear. From the tabs at the top of the box select 'View' and click to tick the 'Formulas' box.

The formula cells on Katy's spreadsheet will look like this when we have selected this option:

Table 26.8 Formulae

Total	Standard week	Overtime
=SUM(B2:H2)	30	=(I2-J2)
=SUM(B3:H3)	30	=(I3-J3)
=SUM(B4:H4)	30	=(I4-J4)
=SUM(B5:H5)	30	=(I5-J5)
=SUM(B6:H6)	30	=(I6-J6)
=SUM(B7:H7)	30	=(I7-J7)
=SUM(B8:H8)	30	=(I8-J8)

If you wish to print the spreadsheet with the formulae visible, remember that the length of the calculation in any of the columns or rows may have changed the width or length of your spreadsheet. It may not now fit on an A4 sheet. You may have to change the widths of the columns or rows or reduce the point size of the font that you have used. The other alternative is to change the page layout from **portrait** to **landscape**.

If you wish to check whether a formula is correct, click on the cell it is contained in and look at the formula bar. This is the long, thin bar at the top of the spreadsheet.

Sorting

Depending on the type of information included on a spreadsheet, it may be valuable to sort the rows of data or information into a particular order. Perhaps information has been added to the spreadsheet as and when it was discovered rather than as it occurred, so there is no logical order to the data in the spreadsheet. There are three basic options:

- numerical ordering
- alphabetical ordering
- **chronological** ordering.

To sort rows in numerical order, you need to highlight the column that you wish to sort into numerical order. Having highlighted the column, you should click on 'Data' then select 'Sort'. A box will then tell you that you can either just reorder the column or expand the sort to include all of the data. At this point, you will be given a choice as to whether you want the numbers to be ascending (smallest first) or descending (largest first).

You can also sort alphabetically; you can choose whether to sort beginning with the letter 'A' or from the letter 'Z'. Highlight the cells involved then click on the A–Z icon at the top of the screen to sort the data in ascending order. If you want to sort in descending order choose the Z–A icon.

Sometimes you might want to sort chronologically. For a column containing dates, use the same principles as those for numerical or alphabetical sorting, and sort either from the earliest date to the latest date or in reverse.

> **remember**
>
> Always use 'Print Preview' in the 'File' menu to check the width and height of the spreadsheet – or part of the spreadsheet – that you wish to print out and choose the most appropriate paper orientation to fit.

> **remember**
>
> If you do not choose the 'expand' option, only the figures in the column that you have selected will be sorted, leaving the rest of the spreadsheet unchanged. This would not be very useful.

case study 26.10   **Harold's accounts**

Harold has been checking the sales figures in his shop. He would really love to know the total sales of each different type of product. He would also like to know the total sales per month. The problem is that his information is badly organised.

In August he sold £450 of paint, £100 of brushes, £500 of power tools, £350 of cement and plaster and £250 of nails and screws.

In September, October and November he sold £120 of brushes. In the same three months he sold £350, £400 and £550, respectively, of paint. He only sold £100 of cement and plaster in September, but he sold £600 in the other two months. As for nails and screws, it was £420 in November, £325 in September and £400 in October.

Then in October Harold started selling hammers and chisels. He only sold £60 the first month but doubled it the month after. Harold stopped selling power tools at the end of August.

Fig 26.9

activity

1 Construct a spreadsheet showing the information in the case study.
2 Calculate the overall best-selling and worst-selling lines of products.

Records and files

Each line or column of a spreadsheet is considered to be a record (strictly speaking a record is all of the data associated with a single data subject).

A business saves spreadsheets as separate files (with a name, time and date); this ensures that the business can refer to the most up-to-date version of the data.

Securing data

Under the terms of the Data Protection Act, it is imperative that the business restricts access to the data held on data subjects; data should be available only to those with authorised access. It is possible to password protect individual spreadsheets for this purpose. It is also important for the business to save and backup copies of the data in case of a major accident or computer error.

Combining, extracting and linking in spreadsheets

Table 26.9 shows how you can use the features in Excel to manipulate data.

Table 26.9 Data manipulation

Data manipulation	How to do it
Creating a hyperlink to a new file	Right-click the text or graphic you want to represent the hyperlink, and then click 'Hyperlink' on the shortcut menu. Under 'Link to', click 'Create new document'. Type a name for the new file in the 'Name of new document' box.
Combining text and numbers	To combine multiple strings of text or text and numbers, use the concatenation operator, which is the ampersand (&). (This joins several text strings into one text string.)

Data manipulation	How to do it
Extracting data	This usually means exporting the data as a table and inserting it into a Word document. This is achieved by highlighting the table area, right clicking and choosing 'Copy', then switch to the Word document, select the position in the document and then right click 'Insert'. Note that you may have to resize the table or change the orientation of the page to make it fit. Extraction can also mean creating a chart with the data in the spreadsheet and inserting that into a Word document.

Inputting and manipulating data in databases

The old-fashioned way of keeping records was to put them into some kind of paper-based filing system. For centuries this has worked fairly well and it still does. However, with the development of databases as software applications, people have realised that there is an alternative. Instead of searching through a card-based index, then finding the right filing cabinet and hoping that the file is there, computerised files are taking over. Nonetheless, many businesses still cling on to the old ways of doing things.

Microsoft Access

This is the leading software application used by businesses around the world. It has some powerful features, including:

- the ability to store data in the form of records, relating to individuals or items
- the creation of a specific database with types of information called fields, so the user actually defines what the database holds in terms of information
- the ability to enter information onto the database and sort it in a variety of different ways
- the ability to take information from the database as individual records, lists or groups of records
- the ability to combine the data into a report so that it can be included in other documents.

Because Access can be used to collect and sort enormous amounts of information, it could be used for the following:

- details about customers
- information about stock in a warehouse
- membership details of a club or society
- patient details at a dentist or a surgery
- student or pupil records at a college or school
- job vacancies at an employment agency
- lists of the suppliers used by a business
- properties for sale or rent by an estate agent
- a collection of books in a library.

When you look at a telephone directory, you see the following information:

- a person's name
- a person's address
- their dialling code
- their telephone number.

If we were putting this information into Access, each of the four pieces of information would be called a field. This would allow us to search the database by name, by address, by area from the dialling code and by telephone number.

A data capture sheet is any type of form, like a **warranty card** or a **guarantee**, an application form or a questionnaire, which is designed to collect information about an individual or their opinions.

Businesses routinely collect data about their customers and their suppliers. They also hold data on their employees. A local library holds records on everyone who borrows its books.

When you join a library, you are asked to complete a form, giving your name, address and telephone number, and you will probably have to provide proof of these details. Once you are a member, the records are extended to include a note of every loaned book, CD or DVD. The database has to be clever enough to tell the library if what you have borrowed is overdue and to allow the library to note that you have returned an item.

Data types

In theory, a database can take any type of information. But in practice the following categories are most common:

- text only, including simple entries, such as yes or no, and longer entries, such as the person's name
- alphanumeric – a combination of letters and numbers (e.g. a postcode)
- numbers only – such as an individual's age
- dates – the ideal date format is --/--/--; this can be useful for searching for diary entries or for birthdays
- time – you can also insert times using a 24-hour clock, so an employee starting work at 8.00 a.m. would have a data record of 0800.

Inserting, editing and deleting records

You can add new records to your database simply by typing into the blank row at the bottom of the database records. This row is marked with an asterisk (*). The database will automatically create a new blank row as soon as you have finished inserting data into the existing blank row. This works in exactly the same way as in Excel, creating a new row ready for new data.

The easiest way to edit records is to move around the datasheet using the cursor keys (in this case the arrow keys). You can move from section to section using the arrow keys until you locate the data record in a particular field that you wish to amend. You can also use the icons at the bottom left-hand corner of the datasheet. These will allow you to:

- move to the first record in the datasheet
- move to the next record in the datasheet
- move to the last record in the datasheet
- check the total number of records in the datasheet
- show you where the cursor is currently placed in the set of records, such as 4 of 10.

You can delete records on a datasheet by placing the cursor in any field of the record row and then selecting 'Edit' then 'Delete Record' from the menu bar. Deletion can also be achieved by clicking the 'Delete Record' button on the datasheet toolbar. Note that this will delete the entire record.

It is better to add and delete columns in 'Design View', as this offers you more options. You can add them quickly in 'Datasheet View'. This is achieved by highlighting a column by clicking its label at the top of the datasheet. The new column will appear to the left of the column you have selected. If you are happy with its position then select.'Insert' then 'Column' from the menu bar.

In the same way you can delete an entire column. Click on the column and then select 'Edit' then 'Delete column' from the menu bar. This will remove the entire column or data field, along with all the records contained in that field.

> **remember**
>
> If you have made any changes to your database, make sure that you save the new version each time.

Sorting records

One of the most useful features of Access enables you to reorder your records, so that you can view only the records in the table that match what you are looking for. The most common way of reordering records is sorting. You can sort records by date, number or alphabetical order.

To sort you need to be in 'Table View'. Place the cursor on the column that you want to sort by. You then need to select 'Records', then select 'Sort' and then choose 'Sort Ascending' or 'Sort Descending'. These are exactly the same kind of options that you had in Excel, but with buttons to click on instead of using the menus.

Another neat thing is that you can sort by more than one column. You can highlight more than one column by clicking and dragging the cursor over the field labels. You can then select the kind of sort method that suits you. This is an ideal way to sort records alphabetically or by date.

There are other ways to select and sort data, which we will be looking at in the next part and in the activity.

Selecting particular records

In order to select particular records we need to pick the field that we want to **filter** them by. To do this we click on 'Filter by Selection' on the toolbar, or we could select 'Records' then 'Filter' then 'Filter by Selection' from the menu.

The other thing to do is to create a query. This means searching for common features of several records. This is the procedure:

■ Go to Design View.

■ Select the queries icon on the left of the box.

■ Click on new query.

■ Click on query in Design View.

■ You'll see your table in the box – this will be highlighted.

■ Click on 'Add' to select that table as being the one you wish to make a query then close the box.

■ You'll see the field names from your table in a small box on the left-hand side of the screen.

■ Double-click on each one to make the fields appear at the top of each of the query columns.

■ Now close that small box.

■ Enter your query in the criterion field.

---

activity
INDIVIDUAL WORK 26.5

P4

This is the first of a series of practical tasks. You will use a system that already has records and has been set up by your teacher/tutor. You must:

1 Show that you could add, delete, update and amend records within the system.

2 Show that you can record transactions of different types.

3 Show that you can manipulate data and produce new information.

4 Use features to create and extract information.

5 Show that you can amend records with new valuations and descriptions.

6 Show that you can send information from one application to another.

---

activity
INDIVIDUAL WORK 26.6

M2

Your teacher/tutor will have chosen an appropriate software package for you to perform the tasks for P4. In order to achieve the M2 requirements, you should:

1 Compare the facilities in different types of software used to produce business information.

2 Identify how one of the applications might be better than another in different circumstances. (When compiling a report, a word processing package would be more useful than a database or a spreadsheet, whereas a spreadsheet would be better than a database for manipulating figures).

Producing information to support decision making in organisations

The last part of this unit deals with producing information in a suitable format to aid decision making. You will have been given data in an existing information system. You will have inserted additional data, deleted some data, amended data and then have manipulated it to extract information. You now need to be able to produce the data in a format that will allow it to be used to its maximum efficiency.

Information format

There are several different ways in which you can present information. The choice will depend on the audience and the requirements of the users. There is never a hard-and-fast rule about how information should be formatted, although, in some businesses or organisations, there are preferred ways in which information is presented. The answers to the following questions would affect the choice of format:

- Will the data have to be easily understood by a wide audience?
- Will the data have to be circulated to a number of users in different locations within the business?
- Will the users have to manipulate the data further for their own purposes?
- Will the users have to store, retrieve and regularly use the information?
- Is the business reliant on paper-based distribution of information or on computer-based distribution of information?

Choice of format may also depend on the size and complexity of the information being presented. Some formats are more suitable for short, self-contained pieces of information, whilst more complex information may require an altogether different approach.

Written

Reports and memoranda are probably the two key written formats for information. Reports are used for more complex information that is handled in greater detail. Memoranda are often used for information updates that can be given in a shorter form. These can be printed, paper documents or could be attached to emails. Some businesses set up email templates that have the same format as memoranda so that they are instantly recognised as such by the recipient of the communication.

Tabular

> **remember**
>
> Graphs, charts and tables are far easier for users to read and understand than pages of text with the key figures hidden amongst the words.

When information is produced in tabular form, the compiler of the information has presented it in the form of a table or chart. These make information easily accessible – there is no need to go delving for the information within a written report – and easier to understand. Tables and charts are very useful for summarising information; the content can be presented in words or as figures.

Graphical

Graphical formats include:

- pie charts
- graphs
- bar charts
- line graphs.

These are often designed to illustrate trends in sets of figures and may be accompanied by the data in tabular form. It is far easier to understand and appreciate the importance of particular data if it is presented in a visual format.

See pages 168–170 in Unit 10 for information about types of graphical representation.

Images

There are a number of ways in which a visual image of data can be produced. Instead of using a bar chart or line graph, graphs can be created using scaled images to represent relative sizes or importance of data. Images can be used to reinforce key points; they enable those being presented with the data to associate certain key facts with particular images.

Paper-based

As we have seen, many organisations have a predominantly paper-based information system. They may extend this to the formatting of data for decision-making purposes. Paper-based information can be in various different formats, including reports, memoranda, newsletters, circulars, information updates, tables, charts, computer printouts, graphical images and hard copies of presentation slides.

Creating and circulating multiple copies of information in a suitable format gives all users the opportunity to read and understand the information, perhaps before meetings or before major decisions have to be made.

Many organisations that rely on computer-based information systems actually prefer to create hard copies of key documents and information.

Fig 26.10 Keeping hard copies of notes and comments of a meeting or decisions made can be vital in the preparation of professional documents

Presentation

The industry-standard presentation software application is Microsoft PowerPoint. This comes complete with a series of templates, which are designed for the user to input text, figures, charts, tables and images.

One of the major advantages of using systems such as PowerPoint is that information can be passed on to many employees in a single event. Using a laptop computer attached to a projector it is possible to present a series of PowerPoint slides, visible to all in the room. Particular issues relating to each slide can be discussed. Another key advantage is that hard copies of the slides can be printed out; there is also an optional print format that allows each user to take notes alongside each slide.

Presentations have to be well planned; it is inadvisable to put too much information on a slide. Not only does an excess of information create a poor visual image but also each key point should be given a discrete slide of its own so that its importance can be enhanced.

Electronic or screen-based

Many businesses recognise that it is unnecessary and wasteful to transform electronic information into paper-based documents. It is a relatively easy task to distribute information to all users using electronic systems.

Typically, electronically stored data can be held on a network, where all users can gain access to it. However, important information can be circulated and presented in a short format, with attachments, using email. For individual users, Microsoft Outlook offers a powerful solution for both diary and calendar-based information. Some of the key features of emails, electronic diaries and calendars are covered in Table 26.9.

Table 26.10 Screen-based formats

Screen based	Explanation
Email	All employees with access to a computer at work will be issued with an email address. Providers of information will gradually set up a circulation list of employees who require access to particular types of information. It is a very easy task to create a standard email and possibly add attachments and then send multiple emails to all relevant individuals. The email will be a short introduction and explanation of any attached documents or images. In this way, the sender can attach reports, tables, spreadsheets, images and even presentation slides.
Diary	Microsoft Outlook is another industry-standard software application. For many people the use of Microsoft Outlook does not go beyond sending and receiving emails. However, in its full form, Microsoft Outlook is a useful system by which individuals can schedule their work, organise their contacts and tasks and record their own activities.
Calendar	This is also a useful extension of Microsoft Outlook. The user can block in and mark particular days when meetings will be held or when they will be out of the office. Those with access to this calendar system are able to check the individual's availability on a given day.

Communication channels

Broadly speaking, the term 'communication channels' refers to the ways in which information and instructions are passed up and down an organisation and across it. At each organisational level, individuals rely on information in order to carry out their work. Therefore they need access to appropriate channels and the information channelled to them should be as up to date and accurate as possible. When sending email and other forms of communication, the circulation list is an important consideration.

Audience needs and communication protocols

When deciding on the correct format for information, it is vital to consider the actual needs of the users or audience for that information. Some users require the information so that they can be kept up to date with the current situation. Others may have to use the information as the basis for immediate decisions. Others may have to manipulate the data to fit their own particular needs.

As far as communication protocols are concerned, a business may decide that it is important to have standardised formats for particular data. It may also expect information updates to be sent to those on the circulation list at particular intervals, per day, week or month. Information is often circulated beyond those individuals who will take decisions based upon it. For example, a business's communication protocol may require that all individuals of a certain rank in the organisation are routinely informed of events, regardless of whether or not they will need to become involved in decisions or action.

Decision making

We have already seen that decision making occurs at various levels within a business organisation and that decisions cover everything from day-to-day operations to major strategy. In some respects, the way in which information is formatted will depend upon the level of detail required to make a particular type of decision.

> **remember**
> The individuals who have to make decisions can only do so if they have been given sufficient information in a suitable format.

Operational level

At operational level, the individual may be interested in the precise details of an interaction with a customer so that they can deal with a particular situation. Normally, this kind of information would be passed on verbally; however, a memorandum or email would serve a similar purpose and there would be a hard copy.

Tactical level

At tactical level, the individual (e.g. a supervisor or manager directly controlling day-to-day operations) is still involved in hands-on decision making and is close to the basic work of the organisation. Here too, verbal communication of information is probably the most efficient. However, an email or memorandum could remind the individual about certain decisions that need to be taken and the information related to them.

Strategic level

At strategic level, the individuals involved are not necessarily interested in the minute details of operational or tactical work. They need to take more of an overview in order to guide and control the work of the organisation as a whole. Strategic decision makers rely on supervisors and managers at tactical level to keep them apprised of general trends and information. At the same time the information that they work from, possibly compiled by the accounts, sales or marketing departments, will have to be translated into information that can be actioned at tactical and operational level. Although it is possibly far more relevant to present information to those at strategic level in a formal format, they will always require a summary sheet so that they can quickly see the main points.

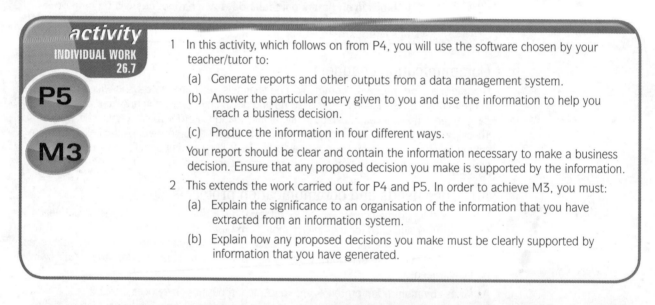

activity
INDIVIDUAL WORK 26.7

P5

M3

1   In this activity, which follows on from P4, you will use the software chosen by your teacher/tutor to:

(a)   Generate reports and other outputs from a data management system.

(b)   Answer the particular query given to you and use the information to help you reach a business decision.

(c)   Produce the information in four different ways.

Your report should be clear and contain the information necessary to make a business decision. Ensure that any proposed decision you make is supported by the information.

2   This extends the work carried out for P4 and P5. In order to achieve M3, you must:

(a)   Explain the significance to an organisation of the information that you have extracted from an information system.

(b)   Explain how any proposed decisions you make must be clearly supported by information that you have generated.

Progress Check

1. Distinguish between qualitative and quantitative information.

2. Suggest eight ways in which the quality of information could be assessed.

3. Suggest at least five different types of information that might be collected and collated by a human resources department.

4. Briefly explain extrapolation.

5. How might the use of information give a business a competitive advantage?

6. Briefly explain the code of practice of the British Computer Society.

7. Give one example of an accounting software package.

8. What are the two most common data types that you can input into Microsoft Access?

9. Which Microsoft product incorporates emails, a diary system and a calendar system?

10. Briefly distinguish between decision making made at tactical and strategic levels.

Glossary

Affirm
Uphold or insist that the contract is legally binding

Annual report
By law public limited companies that offer shares on the Stock Exchange must publish an annual report, including their profit and loss account and balance sheet; it also includes information about the key management of the organisation and the organisation's progress since the last report was written

Antenatal
The period of pregnancy before the birth

Anti-competitive
Actions which are seen to be contrary to fair competition and therefore not in the interests of consumers

Auditing
This is carried out by an independent specialist, who makes spot checks on the accounting systems of a business, in order to identify and eliminate errors and discrepancies

Auditor
A professional and independent individual who systematically checks a business's accounts to ensure their correctness and that they comply with legislation

Bandwidth
The maximum capacity of the channel, usually related to the amount of data or information that can be transmitted using certain media or devices

Bankers' clearing system
A scheme operated by the banking profession whereby cheques paid into a bank are processed and the account of the writer of the cheque is debited, after which the account of the receiver of the cheque is credited

Bank reconciliation statement
An attempt by the accounts department to check any discrepancies between the business's bank statements and the cashbooks

Behavioural assessments
Formal tests to review and measure performance at work with a view to revising and improving performance

Bilateral contract
A contract in which both parties make promises

Biological assets
Living animals or plants and agricultural produce, including wool, logs and grapes; the term is normally used in relation to businesses involved in agriculture

Business rate
A tax on all businesses and non-domestic properties, collected by local councils

Capital
The money that can be invested by a business, usually in the form of cash or assets that can be turned into cash in the short term

Capital equipment
Also known as an asset, in this case machinery

Capital maintenance
The accounting principle is that it is possible to determine the value of capital in order to calculate profit after the initial value of the capital of the business has been restored

Cash flow forecast
Usually a table detailing expected income and expenditure over a period of time

Census
A population and housing survey covering the whole of Great Britain, carried out every 10 years; the next census will be in 2011

Chronological
In date order

Clock card
A way of recording hours worked; a clock card requires the employee to insert the card into a clock machine, which stamps the card with the current time and date

Glossary

Commission
In the context of marketing research, appoint or hire an independent company to carry out the research

Components
Manufactured or ready parts, either manufactured by a business or provided by a supplier

Consumer Price Index
An official measure calculated each month by taking a sample of products and services typically purchased by an ordinary household

Corporate reporting and governance
The checks and balances that are in place to ensure that the correct principles and performance measures are used by a business, both in the way it prepares and presents its financial statements and in the way that the business is run

Corporation tax
A government levied tax on profits, after the profits have been adjusted for depreciation, allowances and provision; it is currently 30%

Course of dealing
This is how the two parties to a contract have always operated in their dealings with one another and reflects the understanding that they have between them

Credit
Purchasing products or services for which the supplier expects payment some time after delivery

Credit control
The process of managing debtors

Current assets
The assets owned by a business that are expected to be used – by being sold or consumed – within a year

Current liabilities
The debts owed by a business that must be settled within a year

Customer demographics
Basic information on the customer, including age, gender, address and income

Defendant
The party who is required to answer a complaint made by an injured party in court

Demographic
Segmentation based on age, gender and other population-based factors

Depreciation
A gradual loss in the value of an asset due to its use and its age

Disciplinary procedures
Processes and procedures set in motion should an employee break the rules of the organisation, as outlined in the contract of employment

Disclaimer
A statement that seeks to absolve the business of any responsibility related to the product or service; generally, disclaimers are meaningless

Discount
A reduction to the basic price of a product or service

Diversification
This occurs when a business spreads its investments into different areas of activity and other markets to lessen risk or moves into new areas of business

Double-entry bookkeeping
A standard accounting practice for recording financial transactions; all transactions are entered twice onto the accounts system

Economic
Segmentation based on an individual or household's income and expenditure

Economic Statistics Division
The data collection and analysis department of the Scottish Executive

Equity
(a) The value of an asset compared with any charges or loans secured against it; (b) fairness or similarity

Ethical
Relating to the set of moral values or responsibilities followed by an organisation in the use of any data that it collects, particularly from customers

Express terms
Terms mentioned specifically in the contract, rather than being implied

Extended credit
An agreement made between a supplier and a customer, which in effect allows the customer to borrow, usually on an interest-free basis, and not pay for the products or services until the extended credit agreement elapses

Field
In Access, a category of information, such as first name, last name, address or postcode

Filter
In Access, this eliminates records that are not relevant to the selection criteria

Finished products
Products that have passed through manufacturing or production and are now ready for resale to customers

Fixed charge holders
A party with a secured claim over the assets of a business

Fixed-term contract
A signed employment contract that specifically states the maximum period of time that the individual will be working for the organisation

Floating charge holder
A party that holds a general charge on the assets of a business

Formula
(pl. formulae) A sum: it may be a simple addition (+), multiplication (*), subtraction (–) or division (/); the formula will affect all the cells to which it is applied and the figures in them

Glossary

Guarantee
Many products come with a standard one- to three-year guarantee from the manufacturer, stating that it will repair or replace the product within reason over that period

Handwriting analysis
Also known as graphology; it is believed by some people that this reveals compatibility, hidden talents, problems and other factors

Harmonise
An attempt to bring legislation into line, making it broadly similar in all EU countries

Headhunters
Specialist recruiters who seek actively to lure key employees away from one organisation to place them in another organisation

Health and Safety Executive
A government agency with responsibility for enforcing health and safety law and regulations

High turnover of staff
A measure of the number of employees joining and leaving the organisation over a period of time

Human resource management
The increasingly scientific management of employees in the work situation

Incentive
A gift or reward for completing a questionnaire

Induction
Initial training given by the organisation; it is used to introduce the new employee to policy, procedures and working practices

Interest rates
The cost of borrowing; the rate is set independently by the Bank of England

Investors in People
An organisation concerned with the development of employee relations and the improvement of working life

Jargon
Sometimes called 'technospeak', this refers to words, phrases or shortened versions of terms that only mean something to those directly involved with a particular field of work or organisation

Job evaluation
An independent look at a particular job role to determine exactly what duties and responsibilities are involved

Joint venture
Either a jointly owned company, set up by two other businesses, or a strategic alliance, where two businesses share in the ownership of a business activity, sharing the profits, losses and control

Landscape
An alternative page layout, which switches the long side of a sheet of A4 to the top

Last in first out
The understanding that the most recently appointed employee will be the first to be selected for redundancy

Leasing
A contract that transfers the right to possess a particular property; it is a way of purchasing equipment, materials, machinery or other assets without having to pay the full amount; the business leasing pays a monthly fee for use and, perhaps, ultimate ownership

Left aligned
On the left-hand edge of the cell

Market intelligence
Information relevant to a company's markets, gathered and analysed specifically for the purpose of accurate and confident decision making in determining market opportunity, marketing strategy, and new market development

Materials purchase budget
Part of a production budget, which details the forecast amount of money that will need to be spent on the purchasing of raw materials

Minority interests
The rights of external shareholders of subsidiary businesses

Mission statement
A concise and clear phrase, or short sentences, summing up the basic intentions and purpose of the organisation

MORI
Market and Opinion Research International, the largest independent market research company in Great Britain

Offeree
The party to whom the offer is made

Offeror
The party who makes the offer

Ongoing cost analysis
A means by which continual expenses are monitored and controlled

Operating costs
The day-to-day expenses of a business, related to sales and administration, for example, rather than production

Pareto Principle
Named after the French Italian sociologist and economist, but actually created by business management thinker Joseph Juran in the 1940s

Performance appraisal
A formal meeting (usually every 6 or 12 months) between employee and line manager; at the meeting performance targets are compared with actual performance in order to work out progress, training needs and pay awards

Glossary

Petty cash
A small amount of money held in cash by a business for occasional or incidental expenses

Plaintiff
The party who initiates a complaint in court and is the injured party; usually a claim or a complaint is made against a defendant

Podcast
A digital media file, which is hosted on a website and can be accessed and either listened to or downloaded by a user

Portrait
The standard way of printing, with the short side of A4 to the top

Preferential creditors
Usually HM Revenue and Customs; these creditors have a claim on assets ahead of unsecured creditors

Pressure groups
Sometimes called interest groups, these are formal or informal organisations concerned with a particular issue or cause, for example Greenpeace

Price elasticity of demand
The concept that demand is responsive to a change in price; elastic products whose prices fall are more likely to stimulate extra demand

Profile
A set of descriptions or characteristics that define a type of person

Pro rata
A proportion: if a full-time employee is entitled to six weeks' holiday then someone working 50% of a job share would be entitled to three weeks

Prototype
An early version of a product or service

Psychographic
Segmentation based on personality, characteristics, lifestyle and social class

Raw data
The initial data collected during marketing research, without any comment or particular ordering

Raw materials
Unfinished products, such as sheet metal, which would be transformed by the business as part of the manufacturing process

Repetitive strain injury
(RSI) This is damage done to the body as a result of repeated actions during work, such as clicking a mouse button or using a poorly sited monitor

Repudiate
Reject the contract and effectively cancel it

Respondent
An individual who is the subject of a marketing research project

Retail Price Index
(RPI) A general-purpose domestic measure of inflation used since 1947; it includes housing costs

Right aligned
On the right-hand edge of the cell

Scottish Executive
The devolved government for Scotland, which is accountable to the Scottish Parliament

Share capital
The capital created from the sale of shares; the individuals forming a company decide on the amount of capital to be raised by the sale of shares

Shopping cart technology
A system usually provided by a third party, enabling users to select, review and then pay for products and services online; it is an essential e-commerce tool

Specific performance
This is a discretionary remedy that a court may impose on a party to compel them to perform their obligations according to the terms of an agreement or contract that the party has made; it is usually applied when monetary compensation would not be a sufficient remedy

Stakeholders
Individuals or groups who have an interest or an influence on a business or organisation and are directly or indirectly affected by its activities

Statement of particulars
A term used to describe a contract of employment

Statutory rights
Legal rights based on laws passed by Parliament

Statutory tribunal
A group that performs a legal duty on behalf of the public

Stock
Finished goods or other goods held by the company, ready for immediate sale

Subsidised
The employer pays a proportion of the cost to lessen the financial effect on the employee

Timesheet
A timesheet is a record of hours worked by an employee, completed by the employee and authorised by a supervisor or manager

Tort
A term that is used to describe a legal wrong; this is usually a civil wrong, but it can be a criminal wrong

Trade Union Congress
An organisation to which trade unions belong; it acts as a major pressure group on their behalf

Transaction
A financial transaction involves a change in the status of the finances of two or more businesses or individuals

Uberrimae fidei
Utmost good faith

Ultra vires
Beyond the power of the company and void

Unilateral contract
A contract in which one party makes a promise in return for an act by the other

Unit price of product
The price for each individual product

Unsecured creditor
A party that does not have the benefit of any security interests over the assets of the business

Usage based
Segmentation based on buyer behaviour, with particular reference to buying patterns

VAT
Value Added Tax, a tax levied on most products and services at a rate of 17.5%

Videophone and videoconferencing
Remote conversation tools that allow individuals in different parts of the country or the world to talk in real time with pictures

Warranty card
This comes with certain products; the customer has to complete the card and send it back to the manufacturer to ensure that the product is registered for repair or replacement if necessary

Webinar
A type of web conference, usually conducted using either a forum or a message board

Web traffic
The amount of data sent and received by visitors to a particular website, usually determined by the number of unique users or the number of pages that they have viewed

Whistle blowing
Informing the police or another independent party about illegal activities taking place within an organisation

Index

Index